FEAR IN NORTH CAROLINA

FEAR IN NORTH CAROLINA
THE CIVIL WAR
JOURNALS AND LETTERS
OF THE HENRY FAMILY

REMINISCING
BOOKS

Compiled and edited by
Karen L. Clinard and Richard Russell

Published by Reminiscing Books
Asheville, North Carolina
Library of Congress Control Number 2008923981
ISBN-13: 978-0-9793961-3-7
ISBN-10: 0-9793961-3-1

Printed in The United States of America by
Edwards Brothers, Incorporated

Direct all correspondence to:
Reminiscing Books
1070-1 Tunnel Rd
Suite 10, Box 326
Asheville, NC 28805

info@reminiscingbooks.com
ReminiscingBooks.Com

On the cover:
Marriage photograph of William Lewis Henry
and Cornelia Catherine Smith

Table of Contents

Dedicated to Cornelia Henry,
for without her commitment to her journals,
the experiences and hardships the Henry family endured
would never have been known by those who followed.

The journals and letters of the Henry Family were compiled and
reproduced from the Henry Collection, courtesy of
Pack Memorial Public Library, Asheville, North Carolina.
Journals originally donated in 1980 by William Vance Henry.

Special thanks to Elizabeth Henry Laisy for unlimited and extensive use
of additional Henry family documents and photographs
and for her enthusiastic support.

Thank you to:
Ann Wright, Zoe Rhine and Laura Gaskin at Pack Memorial Public Library,
Karen Loughmiller at West Asheville Public Library,
Charles Haller, Ray Elingburg, Nancy Manning, Sandy Samz and Nancy
Dockery at Old Buncombe County Genealogical Society,
Kim Cumber at North Carolina State Archives, Raleigh NC

Thank you also to Debbie Russell, Terrell Garren, Don Taylor,
Jim Holbrook, Joey Woolridge, Leon Kirk, Larry Clinard,
Martha Barnhill Horner, Jan Lawrence, Tammy Walsh
Charles C. Clinard, June Clinard, Avalene N. Lewis

Introduction

The Cornelia Henry journals have been described by Pack Memorial Public Library in Asheville, North Carolina as "one of the best local sources for daily information in Western North Carolina during and immediately following the Civil War." The journals, donated in 1980 by William Vance Henry, grandson of William L. and Cornelia C. Henry, provide an intimate view into the lives of a Confederate family prior to, during and following the Civil War. Although often quoted, the writings of Cornelia Henry have remained relatively unknown to the general public.

In view of their historical value, and to bring the words of Cornelia into the present day, the decision was made to compile all the journals, letters and additional family documents and photos into a single, easy to read volume, including an extensive index.

Cornelia Henry's original journals total three volumes and span a time period from January 1, 1860 through October 18, 1868, the first being dated January 1, 1860 through January 19, 1862. A second book begins January 20, 1862 and ends September 25, 1864. The third, and last known volume begins September 26, 1864 and concludes October 18, 1868. The final volume also includes a few entries penned by Cornelia's husband William L. Henry, dated January 13, 1861 through February 9, 1861, which we have placed at the appropriate point in time.

Cornelia's innermost thoughts and feelings are documented from her hopes for southern independence, through the defeat and surrender of the Confederacy. "Oh! 'tis so sad to think we are subjugated," she would lament.

Cornelia describes events at home after the war, the actions of sympathetic and "Tory" neighbors, and the attitudes of the now free slaves. Particularly poignant are letters to and from husband William while he was away with the Confederate forces, and when fleeing from Federal troops bent on killing him after Asheville's occupation.

The story of the Henry family in Buncombe County, North Carolina begins with the arrival of Robert Henry in the early years of the nineteenth century. The son of Thomas Henry and Martha Shield Henry, Robert wrote that he was born January 9, 1767 in Mecklenburg County, now Lincoln County. On May 31, 1814, at age fifty-three, he married Dorcas Bell Love, the seventeen year old daughter of Robert Love, founder of Waynesville, North Carolina. They were divorced thirty years later in 1844.

Robert seemed to have a knack for witnessing and making history. As a young boy he witnessed the signing of the Mecklenburg Declaration of Independence. He was injured by a bayonet at the Battle of King's Mountain and participated in the fight at Cowan's Ford. Later he joined with David Vance, father of future North

Carolina Governor Zebulon B. Vance, to survey the line between Tennessee and North Carolina and on his return worked to become Buncombe County's first teacher, first lawyer and first doctor.

In 1815, Robert acquired 770 acres on Hominy Creek in what is now West Asheville for $1200. On this land he "discovered the sulphur springs the last of February 1827." The springs were so named because of the slight rotten egg odor of the water. It has been written that he was accompanied by his slave Sam, or even that Sam was the discoverer of the springs.

About 1831, Robert and his new son-in-law Reuben Deaver, "neither of whom were acquainted with making and keeping a boarding house,"[1] decided to move their families into Robert Henry's home and start taking in boarders. Reuben opened a store and stocked it with merchandise and goods in order to attract new visitors. A sawmill was added on the banks of Hominy Creek about 100 feet below the present day Old Bear Creek Road bridge.

When their experiment proved successful, a wooden hotel was built on the hill about 400 yards above the springs by Deaver, and was open for business by 1834. In addition, the springs had been improved by adding a granite basin to control water flow. The resort was promoted to the public as Deaver's Sulphur Springs.

Spring water was directed to a cistern where a wire and pulley system filled buckets and moved them up the hill to the hotel, where a waterman was on duty at all times. The waters became famous for their medicinal and healing properties, said to be excellent for dyspepsia and increasing the appetite, and the hotel drew a good number of prominent visitors.

It was noted "The position of these Springs make them a delightful summer resort. There is always a pleasant, cool breeze stirring. The view, from almost any point of the grounds, is fine, presenting, in front, the Blue Ridge and its spurs; in the west, Mount Pisgah, and the Haywood Mountains."[2]

The "House is built on a high hill between two branches about 200 yards from each ... in the form of an L, one side about 150 feet long the other 120, two story with piazzas running all around out-side to each story, upstairs is divided into 29 or 30 lodging rooms."[3]

John Preston Arthur grandson of Robert Henry, describes other amenities; "there were cabins on the grounds. There were bowling alleys, billiard tables, shuffle-boards and other games. A large ball-room and a string band, composed of free negroes from Charleston and Columbia, provided the music for dancing.[4]"

Today the only remaining visible evidence of the once popular springs is a single overgrown concrete structure, built in later years, located just off School Road in the Malvern Hills subdivision of West Asheville.

A portion of the original 770 acres located above the springs was set aside by Robert Henry for use as a cemetery. Originally nine acres, it is now a small section

---

[1] Testimony from Reuben Deaver vs. Robert Henry and Dorcas B. Henry, 1851
[2] "Mountain Scenery" by Henry E. Colton, 1859
[3] Letter dated July 4, 1837 from John Harrington to Rev. W. M. Reid
[4] From "Western North Carolina: A History 1730-1913"

surrounded by the property of Asheville School and still in use today. According to Robert Henry, the first person buried there was John Kitt in 1836. Several members of the Henry family, including Dorcas Bell Henry and William L. Henry are entombed in the cemetery, as well as members of the Deaver family.

The cemetery includes a slave section with grave sites identified with unmarked field stones. Several slave burials are mentioned by Cornelia Henry in her journal entries, remarking at one point that slaves "sicken and die and nobody cares."

Disaster struck the well known hotel in March of 1861. Cornelia tells us, "Uncle Andy woke us in the night by hollering 'what a fire.' Yes, the hotel was burned this night & set afire." The origin of the blaze remains unknown, although Cornelia did have her suspicions. The hotel lay in ruins until 1887 when a larger brick hotel was built in the same location by Edwin Carrier and renamed Carrier's Springs. Later called the Belmont, in 1892 it too was destroyed by fire.

William L Henry, son of Robert Henry, was born November 24, 1823. On April 5, 1855 he married Cornelia Catherine Smith of South Carolina, born August 19, 1836. Over the years they had nine boys and three girls, eight of whom survived to adulthood.

William became owner of the Henry estate in 1859 when he purchased the "Sulphur Springs Place" from his father for $10,000. Having leased the hotel operation to C. C. Terry, Mr. Henry and his family planned to move into the hotel on the expiration of Terry's term in January, 1860. When Mr. Terry did not want to leave, a court battle and arbitration ensued. Unfortunately for the Henry family, by the time Terry was to vacate the property, the hotel had burned, a total loss. The Henry's had been living in the "lower house," where they then continued to operate a boarding house for many years.

In addition to his many farm duties at home, William Henry served as postmaster for Sulphur Springs in the mid to late 1850's, and for a time during the Civil War for the CSA. He served for a time in the Confederate military and was Captain of the local Home Guard, often hunting and capturing deserters. He was a miller, participated in laying out roads and collecting tolls, and often served in Asheville Court.

The majority of William's time was spent overseeing the operations of the Henry farm and mill. With the help of his slaves and other hired help, the family grew wheat, corn, flax and oats and maintained apple and peach tree orchards. They raised chickens, cattle, sheep, goats, and hogs. The crops and livestock provided food for the family, slaves and boarders. Excess was sold or traded in the community, while lumber and grain processed in the mills augmented income.

During the War, Mr. Henry participated in several local skirmishes. In January, 1863 he went to the troubled Shelton Laurel area in Madison County. In October, 1863 he was wounded while with an advance party from Woodfin's Battalion at Warm Springs. Major John Woodfin was killed there by George W. Kirk's men. William was present at the Battle of Asheville in April of 1865, and he related, "we repulsed them handsomely."

Struggling with the loss of slave labor after years of war, the time finally came when William could no longer pay his existing and mounting debts. After a series of long, drawn-out lawsuits he eventually lost most of his property through a Sheriff's sale. He was able to hold on to a parcel of 530 acres which he sold to his wife Cornelia in 1879 for $85.00.

———————

Throughout the journals Cornelia gives us an understanding of her routine daily activities; tending to her children, making clothes for her family and the slaves, cleaning the boarding house, and boarding visitors. Mrs. Henry was an avid reader of the newspaper, magazines, books and especially the Bible, which she had read at least three times. She describes the state of Asheville during and after the Civil War. Her entries and letters written during those years reveal her deepest hopes and fears.

Cornelia seldom referred to her servants as "slaves," instead using the term "negroes." Several of her slaves had served the Henry family for years, but ultimately all were regarded as property. Property to be disciplined, hired out or sold. Cornelia hated to see slaves mistreated, and many were loved as family members. Often the whites and slaves attended the same local church together. However, Mrs. Henry became dismayed and expressed anger after the war regarding the loss of her slaves, and as they began to insist on pay for work or refused work, Cornelia had to learn and perform duties she had never done before, such as the laundry, cooking and hauling firewood.

Cornelia suffered from severe headaches, some lasting for days. Often depressed, feeling trapped at home, she longed to visit her family in South Carolina, and at times expressed this was a "cold, unfeeling world." Despite the headaches and other "burthens" she carried, she lived to be eighty-one years of age.

———————

To facilitate ease of reading, the editors made the following adjustments to the text: Paragraph and sentence breaks were added, as Cornelia rarely started or stopped a sentence with punctuation or capitalization. Selected original spelling was corrected. Letters, documents, newspaper advertisements, and photos were inserted chronologically between journal entries for continuity.

North Carolina Historical Marker located on US Highway 19/23 (Haywood Road) in West Asheville

Top: 1920's photo of Sulphur Springs Park
Note pool with stairs on the right
(William A. Barnhill Collection, Pack Memorial Public Library, Asheville, North Carolina)
Bottom: Remains of Sulphur Springs structure in 2008

View of Asheville from Beaucatcher Mountain, 1851
(North Carolina Collection, Pack Memorial Public Library, Asheville, NC)

1860-1861

"...I fear we will have a bloody war yet..."

January 1860

Began on Sunday Jan 1, 1860 - Snow six inches deep fell yesterday, weather very cold. Mr. George Jones, Sr. was to have been preached today but disappointed on account of the cold. Mr. Henry[5] returned in the evening from a meeting of the Jones Gap Turnpike company. The meeting was held yesterday at Wm. Johnston's in Henderson. The officers of the road are Messers L. T. Gash, Col. Orr, Col. Hamilton & W. L. Henry Esq. The road extends from Sulphur Springs to Jones Gap on the Blue Ridge in the direction of Greenville So. Ca..

Our family consists of two children, Pinck & Arizona, Cora[6] having died Sept. 10th, 1858, 25 minutes of 9 o'clock Friday in the fore noon. She was born 10 minutes after three o'clock on Tuesday, November 17th 1857 in the evening. Pinck was born on Sunday five minutes of 12 o'clock (day) July 20th, 1856. Arizona was born Monday, March 21st, 1859, 25 minutes after 9 o'clock in the morning.

Mr. Henry has employed for this year A. Fullbright & a mulatto boy Frank Ellison to attend the stills. George Jones, Carse Wells, Bill Parker on the farm. George attends the mill, France Corn to repair the hotel.

January Monday 2nd - Very cold & disagreeable but fair wind from the south.

Tuesday 3rd - A little more moderate than yes'day. Fair winds variable.

Wednesday 4th - Nothing of consequence occurred today. A great deal of ice.

Thursday 5th - More pleasant. Began some embroidery for a band.

Friday 6th - Cloudy. Wind from East. Thawed all day. Worked some on band.

Saturday 7th - Raining at daylight. Warm. Snow & ice nearly all gone. Rained till twelve o'clock. Pinck got his hands burned yesterday at the mill. Robt. Patton came for some flour & borrowed Bellows' lecture sermon & Bellows' letters & got 986 lbs. flour at 8 cts. per lb. Worked some on my band but did not finish, got lazy in the evening.

Sunday 8th - Warm bright day. No snow in sight, only on Pisgah & Cold Mountain. Mr. Henry & I went to the stillhouse, no one there. We went up the meadow & by Daniel Ledford's & came back by Quin's but did not call. We came to the hotel and called. Eat some apples. Pinck & I came together & Mr. Henry & George Summers who came for some beef that they shot for, one Mr. Henry sold.

---

[5] Cornelia Henry refers to her husband, William L. Henry, as "Mr. Henry"
[6] Robert Pinckney, Cora Aletha and Mary Arizona Henry

I wrote a letter to Sister Jane & Lou[7] & thought of writing to Patsey Peake but have not. Mr. Henry has a beautiful lot of shoats at Stillhouse. 60 cost 107.16. My ever kind husband is nursing Ara our youngest to sleep, sitting here grinning at his Dinah[8].

I forgot to mention in the proper place that old Mr. Henry[9] was living with us, also Martha Tidwell.[10] That C. C. Terry rented the hotel in 1859 & his time was out 1st Jan 1860. We are living at the lower house. Susie Sutton is here tonight. Both children are asleep. As I feel wearied, I shall soon retire.

First of Henry family to settle Buncombe County,
Robert Henry in his 94th year
(Photo courtesy Don Taylor)

---

[7] Sarah Jane, sister of Cornelia Henry, and Lucy (Lou) Smith. Lou is not referred as Cornelia's "Sister" in the journals. Census records indicate she may have been the second wife of Cornelia's father, William Smith

[8] William L. Henry sometimes refers to his wife as "Dinah"

[9] Robert Henry, father of William L. Henry

[10] Martha A. (Matt) Tidwell, daughter of Elizabeth Henry (sister of William Henry) and William B. Tidwell

2

SULPHUR SPRINGS, BUNCOMBE COUNTY, N.C.

William L. Henry having become sole proprietor of this well-known watering place,
takes this method of announcing to the public,
that the House will be open for the reception of
visitors the 1st day of June next. Having fitted
up the house and furnished with new and elegant
furniture, and having provided himself with polite
and accommodating servants, he hopes by strict
attention to the wants and wishes of his guests to
give general satisfaction   His table shall be furnished with the very best the country affords.—
While his stables are large and commodious, will
be supplied with grain and provender and attended by faithful and attentive Ostlers. A first rate
band of music will be in attendance all the time. In
short no pains or expense will be spared to render a
sojourn at the springs pleasant and agreeable, and
the proprietor hopes by unremitting attention to
the comfort of his guests to secure a continuation
of the patronage heretofore so liberally bestowed
on the springs; assuring all who may visit the
Springs for health or pleasure that they will find
the accommodations at least equal to what it has
heretofore been.

He deems it unnecessary to say anything in re-
gard to the Medicinal qualities of the Sulphur
Springs, as they have been so long and so favor-
ably known, and their healing virtues tested by
hundreds and thousands who have visited them
in years past.

A comfortable hack with safe horses and an
experienced driver, will run daily between the
Springs and Asheville, affording those who may
arrive at Asheville by stage a certain means of
going and returning from the Spring at pleasure.

WILLIAM L. HENRY.

June 1, 1854.   1m.

Early advertisement for the Sulphur Springs Resort
The Asheville News, July 6, 1854

Monday 9th - Very pleasant, almost like Spring. Little frost in morning. Work on mill dam.

Tuesday 10th - Tuesday till Sunday very mild. Court in Asheville this week. I worked on Mr. Henry's coat with Mrs. Terry Monday, Tuesday & finished Wednesday.

Wednesday 11th - Mr. H. Went to Asheville Court, came back at night. Col. Jones of Turkey Creek staid all night. Very mild.

Thursday 12th - Mr. Henry went to Asheville & staid all night. Cloudy. Terry's people gave a candy stew. We are invited but did not go. W. B. Tidwell who is here went. He came Tuesday night. They had a time dancing.

Friday 13th - All are well. Very wet. The grounds dreadful muddy. Mr. Henry came home after dark. Very dark being cloudy. I was sick all day with headache.

Saturday 14th - Rained a good deal in the morning but cleared off about ten o'clock. Mr. Henry went to stillhouse, staid all day & brought Pinck some ginger cakes from Alf Wells. Mrs. Terry started over to Greenville today.

Sunday 15th - A beautiful day, very pleasant. The ground very muddy. Old Mr. Henry is suffering a good deal from cold. He has a dreadful cough, seems quite weak. Ara, our babe, was very restless last night. I suppose it was her teeth. She has five. Has not stood alone yet. Pinck is trying to learn his A. B. C.

Sunday 22nd to Sunday 29 - Very pleasant for the time of year. Seems like spring thaw.

Sunday 29th - Sun for some two weeks & turned a good deal colder Thursday night last. Old Mr. Henry wrote his will Last Wednesday.[11] Mr. Henry, Pinck & I went to Sandy Bottom & on Tuesday 24th were on the mountain & had a good view of the surrounding country. We eat dinner at L. Case's. I suffered a good deal with headache that night.

Sunday 29th - A beautiful morning. Mr. Henry & I went to the bird traps in the pinto field below the big walnut tree. It had 9 pigeons in it (wild). One got away. Mr. Henry did not mash its cranium sufficiently. We went to one on the other side of the creek but nothing in it. Mr. Henry has some hands at work on the mill dam & some at the hotel fences around the house. Joe Green moved Thursday & Friday.

Monday 30th Jany 1860 - Mail passed and failed to call at the Post office.

Tuesday 31st - (W. H.)[12] Turned cold in the night and snowed. The ground frozen on top. None of my hired men worked this day except Mr. Parker, who took the waggon to the shop having the day previous broke the axel. Let Wilie Knight work the oxen for putting in the axel. Fair and cold.

---

[11] See Appendix A for complete text

[12] (W. H.) indicates entries made by William L. Henry in other areas of the journal. These have been moved and included at the appropriate dates for continuity

4

February 1860

Feby 1st - (W. H.) Fair. George Jones & Tim Foster cut coal wood in the old field, on the Jarret land, the field in which Father first settled.

2nd - (W. H.) Fair and cold. Mrs. Terry and my Lady went to the village to see Mrs. Brittain. Hands worked cutting wood at Hominy.

3rd - (W. H.) My wife & I went to a place I own known as the Tom Cook place. Nothing uncommon happening in the country.

5th Sunday at 5 o'clock - No snow, warm and cloudy. At daylight commenced snowing & at 10 o'clock a.m. the earth heavily covered and now at this writing 5 o'clock p.m. the snow mostly all gone. Mrs. Singleton's child, an infant, died last night at the Hotel. Mary Taylor[13] came to my house having to leave home for want of necessarys of life.

6th - Fair and warm. All are well.

7th - Fair until noon then cloudy and at 9 p.m. commenced snowing and snowed on until morning when the snow lay about 4 inches deep. Soon melted & fair & warm.

March 1860

March 4 Sunday 1860 - Very warm for the time of year, the grass beginning to peek out. Mr. Henry started to So. Ca. yesday morn to attend to the rail road affair. Old Mr. Tidwell, Martha's father, arrived Friday & is an old man. Martha & him have gone to see Mary today. Mr. Henry has been working at sawmill, nearly ready to put up Branton the workman. No gardening done yet but the weather fine. Pinck has not been well with chicken pocks. The baby has not taken it yet. I have been sick with chills, had one Monday, Tuesday & Wednesday last week but am up again. Old Mrs. Terry spent the day here Thursday. I wrote to Lou this morning. Pinck has gone to Hotel. Very windy today & last night. All are well.

April 1860

April 8 1860 Sunday - Today has been very warm and unpleasantly so & very dry. Mr. Henry was gone a little over two weeks to So. Ca., was down at home. They were all well. I had a letter from Sister Jane on Monday last. They were all well. She spoke of coming this summer. I will be very glad for it seems so long since I saw any of them & don't know when I shall unless they come to see me for I've no way of getting there. Martha, her father & Bob Tidwell started on the 4th April for home. Matt did not want to go. I helped her sew nearly two weeks before she left. I went to the hotel with her. It sprinkled rain that morning a little but not enough to do much good, 'tis very dry. The peach trees are shedding their bloom & the apple trees begin to look green.

Old Mr. Henry starts for Cherokee in the morning. I never expect to see him again. A man named Harbert staid here last night from Cherokee. Court in Ashe-

---

[13] Possibly Mary Belle Tidwell, niece of William and Cornelia Henry, who married Newton Taylor

ville this week. Mr. Henry & I went to the mill this evening. Part of the fobay timber is in for the sawmill. They are ploughing the field below the stables. Mr. Henry intends it for corn & grass.

My little children are very well. Arizona cannot walk yet alone but tries to talk. Fannie & old Andie[14] were married Saturday night 20th of March & Pinck Jones & J. Ballew 13 of March 1860.

April Monday 9th – Dealt with toothache. Very dry & warm. Old Mr. Henry started to Cherokee this morning. Very frail to go so far. I had a letter from Lou today.

Tuesday 10th - Mr. Henry went to Asheville. I went to Col. Moore's, took Ara & Jinnie[15] & spent the day. Her babe is four weeks old. Lou Candler was there. I spent the day pleasantly; very warm.

Wednesday 11th - Began to clean the house, got old Mr. Henry's room cleaned. Mr. Henry off to Asheville.

Thursday 12th - Continued to clean up. I moved into the work hands room. No one at work on sawmill. Branton drunk. Mr. Henry went to Asheville.

Friday 13th - Mr. Henry did not go to Asheville, quite unwell with a cold, confined to the house. Finished cleaning house.

Saturday 14th - Mr. Henry went to Asheville. I went to hotel in the evening. I met him there on his way from Asheville. Bob Henry[16] started his books to Franklin today. All are well. Very dry. Some of the hands plowing. Jones & Charlie, Bill Sutton & Bill Parker hauling manure. Atheline, Tena, Sarah & Sam raking it up in stable. George[17] at the mill gets a good deal of custom F. Corn in the shop. Branton & Ham Canon at sawmill.

Sunday 15th - Preaching at the Academy today, Proffit the minister. He & Patty are on the circuit this year. We had some frost yesterday morning. The peach trees have shedded their blossoms. The apple trees in full bloom also pears & plums. Mr. Henry has gone to salt the sheep at Stradley place. Stanerford Jones rented it this year. Anderson Towe & Frank Patton live on the Murrey lands.

May 1860 – June 1860

May 21st - I started home on Monday 21st May & got there on Saturday. Mr. George Peake went with me. I got home Saturday night between 8 & 9 o'clock. Mr. Peake came up home with me.

June 23rd - We got home Saturday.

December 1860

Dec. 30th 1860 Sunday - A very disagreeable day, been sleeting, snowing & raining alternately all day. Mr. Henry's miller began last Monday 24th Dec. A

---

[14] Fanny and Andy were Henry family slaves
[15] Henry Family slave, sister of Tena
[16] Robert M. Henry, brother of William L. Henry
[17] Atheline, Tena, Sarah, Sam and George were Henry Family slaves. Atheline was the daughter of Sam and Tena

Scotchman by the name of Lindsay, has a wife & two children. Are staying at the hotel now, but will live down here when we go to the hotel which we will before long. Terry is still there, does not want to leave. Mrs. Britten gone to Asheville to live. I took dinner at the hotel on Saturday before Christmas. (On Tuesday) Mrs. Terry had some company & sent for me as Mr. Henry was there. Zonnie has been sick with cold but is well again. Pinck is a fine hale healthy great big boy. Zona is beginning to talk a little, not much yet. Mrs. A. B. Jones & Tilda spent Christmas day with me. Mr. Henry went to Asheville Monday & brought some Christmas tricks for the children, Zonnie a doll & Pinck some marbles besides candies. By the way, Santa Claus filled my stocking with chestnuts Christmas Eve. The sore throat is raging a good deal at present. Jinnie has a slight attack, also Zonnie. Mrs. Byrd died with sore throat on Thursday Dec. 27th leaving four or five little children. Byrd is our circuit preacher rider this year. Her youngest child is some two years old. Another strange incident happened on Sunday 23rd Dec. There was an infant found in a box in a culvert on the new Haywood street in Asheville. It had been dead three or four days apparently. Supposed to have been put there soon after its birth. They could not tell whether it was white or mixed blooded. The guilty mother has not yet been found.

We have preaching at the Academy this year on Saturday. I think Byrd will have a small congregation. Pinck Allen & Rachel Murry are to marry today. She had a bastard sometime in November. Mr. Henry was to marry them but he had to go to Henderson on business about the new turnpike road. He went on Friday & is to be back tonight, but the day has been so unpleasant I don't expect him. He started very early as there was a hog driver refused to pay toll at the gate at Sandy Bottom & knocked the gate down. Mr. Henry went to Asheville Thursday night to get a writ for him.

Joe Green lives at Sandy Bottom. W. Snelson lives in the Joe Green house. F. M. Corn in the cabin at the hotel. Henry Cook is attending the stills & lives up there. W. Pettitt lives in the Branton house. Stanford Jones at the Stradley place. D. Ledford near the stillhouse. Patton & Towe on the Muse place. Old Mr. Fulbright left the day after Christmas. His old woman came after him, so he has gone to stay. Mr. Henry has but few regular hands now. Old R. Boyd has been fixing the sawmill & is still working here off and on. I don't know who will work with him next year but I hope he may get better hands than he has had this. Old Pettit has been attending the stills for three or four months but he does not please Mr. Henry. Mr. Henry came home late in the evening. A very bad day for riding.

December 31st 1860 Monday - Snow fell last night over shoe mouth deep. A pleasant day over head. The snow melted a good deal. Mr. Henry married P. Allen & R. Murry this evening.

January 1861

1st Tuesday - A very disagreeable day. Cold. The snow melted slowly.

Wednesday & Thursday 2 & 3 - Cloudy also Thursday. I have been doing some little sewing for the last few days. Miss Julia Morris died Monday night with sore throat, was buried Wednesday at Sardis. Sprinkled rain all day.

Friday 4th - Mr. Henry went up on Bent Creek to locate a road. The roads are very muddy. Snow melting slowly.

Saturday 5th - Mr. Henry sold the Sandy Bottom today to E. Glen for 2500$.

Sunday Jan. 6th 1861 - Mr. Henry & I went to church at the Academy today. Rev. John Renolds preached, not a large congregation. He the negroe's minister this year & last also. He preached a very good sermon. Mr. Byrd was there also, he looks badly. I sympathise with him, his children are about among the neighbors.

The snow is not all gone yet, the roads are very muddy. This has been a very pleasant day, the sun shines warm. Mr. Henry has gone now over in the widening field to look at the wheat & I am alone with Pinck & Zonnie, the last setting on my lap whilst I write. Pinck has learned nearly all the alphabet, does not like his letters much, is very fond of a book but only to see the pictures. Zonnie is beginning to talk a little. Our family are all well at this time. Not much sickness in the country at present.

Mr. Henry went to Asheville on Wednesday & brought me a beautiful New Years gift, "Sovenous Gallery."

Jan. Monday 7th - A pretty day. Atheline & I tacked a comfort & began another. Mr. Henry went to Asheville being court week there. He staid all night, something unusual. He was anxious to hear from Charleston as there is considerable excitements going on now in politics on account of a Black Republican being elected president. South Carolina has already seceded & the other cotton states will follow. I had two letters from home, from Dora & Matt.[18] Sister Jane & Dora sent Pinck & Zonnie some little Christmas presents. Mr. George Peake came in just at night & staid till morning then off to Asheville.

Tuesday 8th - Mr. Peake went to Asheville. I cut out Mr. Henry a black jeans[19] coat, did some little on it & baked some Washington cake after dinner. It was late when Mr. Henry & Mr. Peake came home between 7 & 8 o'clock. Pinck & I were at supper when they came. Mr. Henry got his coat & vest today from the tailor, an overcoat. A pleasant, bright day. Some snow yet.

Wednesday 9th - Mr. Henry & Mr. Peake off to Asheville again. I have been sewing on Mr. Henry's coat today. Atheline got out the comfort this evening. Got the corn all up in the crib at last. Mr. Henry hired some negroes from James Love Sr. They came this morning. We have had a warm day, cloudy, some snow on north hill sides yet.

Thursday 10th - Mr. Henry & Peake off to Asheville. A very windy day, turned cold in the evening. Atheline & Fannie tacking comforts. I have been sewing on Mr. Henry's coat. W. B. Tidwell came to the hotel last night.

Friday 11th - Been sewing on the coat, finished it this evening. Pinck was vomiting today since dinner but is well again. I guess it was something he eat. Mr. Henry & Mr. G. W. Peake went to Asheville this morning, not returned yet, nearly dark. The children very playful at this writing. Mr. Henry bought them some candy yesterday. The negroes splitting wood to burn.

---

[18] Madora (Dora) and Martha (Matt) Smith, sisters of Cornelia Henry
[19] Spelling began in journals as "janes", then "jaens", and later "jeans"

Saturday 12th - Fair & windy from the south. G. W. Peake left for home. Mr. Henry went to Asheville.

Sunday 13th January - We had a good deal of company today. Stanaphas Jones & his wife spent the day here then were several other men here besides & staid until late this evening. All are well, the children lively. Pinck has a great idea of writing, has been trying tonight. It was quite cool this morning, a heavy frost.

Sunday 13 January 1861 - (W. H.) Was cold and windy day. Wind from S. E., cloudy all day. Last week was court week in Asheville. Mr. G. W. Peake was here several days of last week and left on Saturday for Tryon (mtn.). Dr. Peak's family were all well when he left home a week ago. Mr. Tidwell is in from Tusquitte where my aged Father now lives and says that my Father & family are all well. My Father was borned on the 10 Jany 1767. Consequently he is now 94 years old.

The war commenced in the part of Charleston South Carolina by the forces of South Carolina firing on the Federal Government vessel Star in the West. The Government holds Fort Sumter in the Port of Charleston and was sending reinforcements to that Fort. The Fort is commanded by Magr. Robert Anderson and has force of sixty or seventy men, no demonstration against the Fort so far as heard from, the firing on the vessel was from Morris Island.

14th Monday - Last night a little rain fell covering the earth with ice about 1/4 inch thick. Drizzling rain all day, cold and unpleasent. I made Pinck a coat today. Got the pattern from Mrs. Dr. Hilliard some time ago.

15th Tuesday - (W. H.) Cloudy and warm at sundown, the rain commenced and is now raining a regular summ shower. Roads are very muddy. My family are all well and no sickness in this section of country. Messrs. Tomas Murray & Jessie Jarret start to move to Georgia this day. The news from Washington City is very unfavorable, and the pollicy of the present administration is now fully develloped, and we may now consider war inevitable and may prepare for the worst. Jany 1861 on the ninth of this month the State of Mississippi passed her ordinance of Secession, and thus became one of the nations of the world. South Carolina having passed her ordinance on the twentieth day of December 1860 and taking the lead in this matter of self Protection. God protect the right.

Tuesday 15th - Cloudy & warm. At sundown began to rain & rained a regular summer shower. The roads are very muddy. I've been sewing on some little gowns. Pinck & Zona very well & lovely little creatures.

Wednesday 16th - A pretty day. We have had a good deal of rain, consequently the streams are up. French Broad hardly fordable at the lower end of Sandy Bottom.

Hack on the French Broad River, traversing high water on a side ford
(North Carolina Collection, Pack Memorial Public Library, Asheville, NC)

16th January 1861 - (W. H.) Was as pretty and clear a day as ever comes in the winter. The rain raised the water considerably, the rivers being out in the road at the lower end of the Sandy Bottom and was bearly fordable along the road.

17th - (W. H.) Tolerable warm & cloudy all day with occasionally a little sun shine. Hauled corn from L. Case's on the mountain. I acted as magestrate in the marriage of Jack Kerkindol to Sarah J. Case, of Bent Creek. Got home at night.

Thursday 17th - Tolerable warm with clouds & sunshine all day. Mr. Henry acted as magistrate in the marriage of Sarah Jane Case & Jack Kirkendol, got home between 7 & 8 o'clock at night.

Friday 18th - Snowing in the morning, cleared off by noon. Warm. Atheline put in the last comfort today.

18th - (W. H.) Raining in the morning, cleared off by noon. Warm. Worked at manure & sawmill. The several states of South Carolina, Florida, Alabama, & Mississippi have Seceded from the union. Red at sunset.

Saturday 19th - Mr. Henry went to Asheville, staid all day. Bought Pinck two little primers of which he is very proud. My little children are all the company I have in day time. Mr. Henry is out all day long. The front door fell down yesterday & nearly frightened me to death. I thought it had fallen on Zonna. It knocked Pinck down but did not hurt him. God bless & protect my little ones I pray. Pinck knows his A. B. C. I poured a candle stand this evening, a large one.

19th - (W. H.) Cloudy and tolerable cold but not freezing. I went to Asheville and stayed all day talking of the State of the country. Strong Secession feelings existing through all the country. Sawed timber for head Block. Red at Sunset.

Sunday 20th - A very pleasant day. Mr. Henry & I at home all day. In the evening we walked down to the mill but as my teeth were aching we did not stay out long. Our little ones went to the hotel after dinner. Oh! how I doat on my children. How thankful I am that they enjoy such good health & spirits. 'Tis true they are very noisy sometimes but I love to see them joyous & happy. I too was once a child & had no care.

20th - (W. H.) Sunday fair & warm. Stayed all day with my family in the House.

Monday 21st January - Disagreeable day. Cold & cloudy all day. I have been working on some little flannels today. Nothing of interest going on in the country. Generally healthy. J. Snelson began to work with Mr. Henry today for a year. I don't think he will stay that long.

21st - (W. H.) Disagreable. Mr. Tidwell went to Asheville & stayed all night at the hotel.

Tuesday 22nd – I have got up very early this morning, not yet five o'clock. I did not sleep well, was restless. I had a letter from Sister Jane yesterday. Also one from Lou. All well with both.

I went to bed & took a good long nap. It has been a very cold day all day. Mrs. Jamison & daughter Betsey spent the day here. William Tidwell left today for Cherokee. Mr. Henry told Terry's people to leave today which made them very angry.

22nd - (W. H.) Came home and started to Cherekee county, payed him $919.75, on my land debt.[20]

Wednesday 23rd - (W. H.) It began to snow this morning before day & snowed & sleeting. All day long a heavy snow. Began to thaw about dark & has thawed all night. Finished the flannels today & began to work a little pink gingham dress.

23rd - (W. H.) Snowing in the morning and snowed all day. Snow about 4 inches deep at sun down. The snow commenced melting and melted all night.

Thursday 24th - Cloudy & rain all night.

24th - (W. H.) Cloudy and warm all day. Joe Parker went to Asheville for the newspapers, the Government is now idle, not disturbing the States that are Seceeding or withdrawing from the federal compact of states. Thawing all day.

25th - (W. H.) Mail broat no news more than stated in yesterday's journal. Cloudy with occasional sunshine thawing all day, snow getting off the road and

---

[20] William bought the "Sulphur Springs Place" and 770 acres from his father, Robert Henry, December 6, 1859 for $10,000

South sides. Mr. G. W. Candler was at my house hunting the news, declairs he & his three Sons will meet the enemy at the threshhold. We will see what we will see.

26th - (W. H.) Rained a good part of the last night, at five o'clock the snow pretty well all gone but a new supply commenced falling and continued to fall as fast as it ever falls, I reckon until about 9 o'clock, when it stopped. I started and went to James Smith sixpence sale. He is selling off his household goods and will now be driven about like a stray dog.

27th - (W. H.) Sunday cold in the morning. Fair and warm and as pretty as ever shown. Snow melting and now mostly gone on the South sides of the hill, the snow not broken on the mountains. My family are all well. Oscer Willis spent part of the day here.

28th Jany Monday - (W. H.) Fair & warm, snow melting. All are well.

29th - (W. H.) Mr. Corn worked in sheep for Terry. Set fire in brick kiln. Went to Asheville, fair & warm. Road almost impassable.

30th - (W. H.) Went to Sandy Bottom & found all well. Fair wind from N. is a little cold.

Thursday 31st - Mr. Henry, Pinck & I went to the brick yard. Got back at dinner.

31st - (W. H.) Was at Brick Kiln with my wife & son Pinckney. Fair & warm.

February 1861

Feb 1 Friday – Killed 6 hogs. Rained all day. The creek pretty high.

Febry 1st - (W. H.) Mail came, no news of any importance. Cloudy wind from E. Commenced raining at 10 o'clock and rains on regular. Snow pretty well all off the earth on all the South sides, plenty of snow in the mountain. Quit the Brick. Killed 6 hogs & let Lindsay have half of one. Mr. Morgan called today. R. Pinck Allen has worked five days up to 1 Feby 1861.

2nd Saturday – The creek very full. Mr. Henry & I went to see the dam. So much back water can't grind.

2nd - (W. H.) Creek up two feet higher than when the dam broke, rained until noon.

Sunday 3rd – Mr. Henry & I went to the Academy to church. Rev. John Reynolds delivered a very good sermon. He is preacher for the negroes this year. He took dinner with us.

3rd Sunday - (W. H.) Creek falling a little. Rev'nd Reynolds preached in Sulpher Springs Academy. Cloudy & warm. Reynolds took dinner with my family.

Monday 4th – Sam and John Commons (a negro) began to cover the kitchen. I began some little dresses and have been sewing on little things all this week.

4th - (W. H.) The water up so as to prevent grinding until noon. I went to Asheville to a union meeting. Mr. Montraville Patton was nominated for the union candidate in a State convention on Federal Relation.

5th - (W. H.) I went to Asheville and got writs for C. C. Terry who is now in my Sulpher Springs Hotel. Fair & warm.

Portion of a ledger page kept by William L. Henry
showing charges owed by C. C. Terry for the year 1860
(North Carolina Collection, Pack Memorial Public Library, Asheville, NC)

6th - (W. H.) Went to Stephen Jones' & G. W. Jones'. Came by Thos. Morris. Gave Terry written notice to leave my house & property. Fair & warm.

Thursday 7th – The wind high all day. Mr. Henry & I went to stillhouse after dinner. Zonnie lost the smoke house & pantry keys & we can't find them anywhere. She is getting so she can say nearly any word. Pinck has began to spell a little. He learns very fast for the attention he gets.

7th - (W. H.) Waited until noon for C. Moore to come to see me according to his appointment. Windy & fair.

Feb 8th Friday 1861 – All are well. Mr. Henry been at the stillhouse all day fixing something about the furnice of stills. I have been making some little aprons. Not done the kitchen yet. We have had a beautiful day, almost like spring.

8th - (W. H.) Visit the large still. Fair & warm. No news from Government of any consequence.

Saturday 9th - Sam & John finished covering the kitchen but not the inside. Atheline & I made some napkins of table linens (old). I heeled Pinck's socks in the evening. Mr. Henry went to Asheville, staid all day. Wm. Morgan & a Mr. Sluder came home with him & staid all night. A pleasant day, rather cloudy.

9th Saturday - (W. H.) Went to Asheville. A meeting of States Rights men nominated N. W. Woodfin to Represent Buncombe in a State Convention. Mr. James W. Patton looks feeble. Mr. Chapman made one of the most effective speaches ever I heard on the Northern aggression.

Feby 9th 1861 - (W. H.) R. P. Allen lost 1/2 day.

10th Sunday - (W. H.) Rained in morning. Mr. Morgan & F. Sluder staid all night with me. Wrote to Harry Deaver[21], to R. B. Prather, Woodfin & Henry & Mark Erwin.

Sunday 10th - Mr. Henry & I at home all day. We have been laying before the fire a good part the day. I have not felt well all day but eat a harty dinner of opossum. Drisley rain all day, rather a dull day. Uncle Sam fixed the pantry yesterday so we could get in. The keys not yet found.

Nicholas W. Woodfin
(North Carolina Collection, Pack Memorial Public Library, Asheville, NC)

Sunday 17th - Rainy all day. Cloudy a little, snow on the ground. We have had a pleasant week up to yesterday. Mr. Henry & Terry are trying to arbitrate their business. Mrs. George Jones came here Wednesday evening as a witness between Mr. Henry & Terry. She left on Friday evening. It rained very hard on Thursday nearly all day. Mrs. Jamison came here & staid a short time, got a sley from us. Monday it rained nearly all day. Mrs. Ely Glenn came here after dinner to see about moving to Sandy Bottom, also Charles Moore & R. L. Jones. The two last on business with Mr. Henry. I have been making some britches for these hired negroes. Atheline & Mrs. Jones to help. I have been crocheting some & made some fringe to trim the tidies with on Friday & some Saturday. Pinck fell down Monday & cut his hand, a big gash, on a piece of plate at the back door. Sam & Jim[22] finished the kitchen chimney this week & have been fixing up the garden fence. Mr. Henry sent George to Wm. McDowell's in Asheville on Swannanoa to get a ram goat. It is a pretty

---

[21] William Harrison Deaver, son of Reuben Deaver and Mary Louise Henry
[22] Henry Family slave

animal, cashmers stock. Mr. Henry went to Asheville on Saturday & staid till late. Tom Hendrix came home with him, staid till after supper. John Branton & a young Love are here tonight. It had been reported that Branton was dead. Old Aunt Tena has been quite unwell for several days, cold I guess. Mr. Henry is going to Asheville on Tuesday to try & settle his arbitration with Terry. I very much fear they are a bad set to deal with. B. Boyd had Frank here this week to help him on something they are making. Head block for sawmill I think. He has began a wheel to run something with. Pinck is asleep & Mr. Henry is getting Zona to sleep. He is so kind to take her off my hands, especially now.

Monday 18th - Mr. Henry had a letter from Davenport today saying Lou had lost her babe. I am really sorry as she is very fond of children. I selected for my scrap book also Mr. Henry's. Ely Glenn was here in the evening. Mr. Henry has been out all day to Sandy Bottom, he & E. Glenn.

Tuesday 19th - Mr. Henry went to Asheville today, something concerning his & Terry's affair. Brought me some Magnesia & the children some candy. The apples are all gone & have been for a week. I continued to select for our scrap books.

Wednesday 20th - Pasted in & finished the scrap books. Read & knit some in the evening. Reread "Ralph Runnion or the Outlaw's Doom." Mr. Henry went to Haywood today, to be gone two or three days to see J. Russell & Abram Fulbright concerning his & Terry's affair. Branton & the young man Love started this morning. Branton drinking all the time he was here. Atheline staid down here tonight. I read in that novel till bedtime & knit on Pinck's socks footing some for him.

Thursday 21st - Cut pieces for Atheline to begin her a quilt. I fixed a swiss night cap. Aunt Tena has got nearly well, has a cough yet. I finished my stockings tonight, also reading Ralph Runnion. Pinck went to sleep on the floor on Atheline's bed. Pea staid down with him tonight. Old Mrs. Parker was here this evening & borrowed our quilting frames & got 2 lbs. cotton which I owe Abbe for work last summer. We have had high winds nearly all week. Ely Glenn & John have been hauling today to build Joe Green a house as he will not leave Sandy Bottom unless they hire him. And ingratitude you are a poor pay master. Mr. Henry has done so much for that man & knows he forgets it all but the time may come when Green may again need help & then I hope Mr. Henry will not assist, but he is too generous to all. Glenn staid all night.

Friday 22nd - I got up very soon this morning & felt badly all day. From it, did not do much of anything. Began to crochet a tidy for the rocking chair. I fear it will be very ugly, it is intended for a bird. The day has been very pleasant. The children out at play all day. Zonnie can say nearly any word, tries to sing "Mama hear the baby cry" & is a very fond lovely child. Pinck is a good boy but very noisy. His hand is nearly well but I fear will leave an ugly scar. E. Glenn & John still hauling. Glenn staid all night again.

Saturday 23rd - Crocheted on tidy till dinner & baked some ginger, also in the evening. All are well. Yesterday a very pleasant day. Today raining & sunshine alternately. Mr. Henry not home yet. It rained a hard shower at dark. The children staid out in the kitchen till after nine o'clock & one of those hired negroes play on the fiddle. Old Mr. Boyd & his two boys, George & Frank, staid all night. They were all drinking. The old man the most. I sit in my room reading till the little ones came in. Pea staid down here with Atheline tonight. She finished her quilt or at least the squares today. Zonnie did not go to sleep till after ten o'clock. She was in such a glee from hearing the fiddle & dancing as the children all took a hand at it. I looked for Mr. Henry tonight but he has not come. I guess something has detained him for I think he loves his home & family. He is so kind to the children, yes & too kind to all for his own good. Glenn & John still hauling. Glenn went home tonight.

Sunday 24th - A good deal cooler this morning & cloudy, looks like snow. I slept well last night, did not wake till 6 this morning. Breakfast late as usual on Sunday. Mr. Henry not come yet. If he comes today it will be ugly riding for the wind blows considerably. The Boyd's left after breakfast. John came in a little while ago & asked me to write a letter for him. I guess he will be in soon for me to do it. I want to write to Sister Ell today, also Lou & perhaps Lena.[23]

I wrote John's letter today also one to Lou. Mr. Henry came in the evening also Joe Russell as a witness. It was a very unpleasant day all day. I staid in the house with Pinck all day. Zonnie out with Atheline.

Monday 25th - A more pleasant day but still cold. Aunt Patsey Jimerson spent Thursday here. Mr. Henry about the farm all day. We had two letters from Sister Jane. In one she sent me some little trimming, in the other she said she could come if he would meet her in Spartenberg if he would come after her. I am so very glad she is coming. Cut out three night caps for myself & mended one.

Tuesday 26th February 1861 - Mr. Henry went to Asheville today, also Russell. I made another cap & began the third one. All are well. A pretty day.

Wednesday 27th - I finished caps and began a gown to put the trimming on Sister Jane sent over. She is a good sister to me, so kind of her to come and stay with me through my confinement in which time lags so on my hands. It was so kind in my dear husband to write asking her to come but he is ever mindful of my comfort. Mr. Henry went to Asheville today & he & Terry had a finish of their arbitration. Terry gets the house this year for $500 and allows Mr. Henry nothing for last year. Oh! he is a vile old wretch as ever went unhung. At night Jim Nicholds & a man named Cole came down about 11 o'clock (two patrols) saying George[24] was at the stillhouse playing the fiddle for them to dance, which so provoked Mr. Henry as he had given him a pass to his wife's house telling him not to stop at the stillhouse, but the men deceived him & had the negro to come & play for them, so Mr. Henry & Terrys (the old man & two boys) picked a fuss with Mr. Henry and they had a general row. No one hurt much. Old Terry got the worst end of the row & Bill Terry I guess hurt him as he did all the shouting but thanks to a Divine Providence, Mr. Henry & negro George come out with no bones broken, 'tho George got a lick on the neck which will disable him several days. Old Terry got a hole through one ear besides other scratches & so ended that row. I fear they will have more of it yet.

---

[23] Elmira Ann (Sister Ell) and Celena Emeline Smith (Lena), sisters of Cornelia Henry
[24] Henry Family slave

16

Thursday 28th - Mr. Henry went to election at Bent Creek and got a warrent for Terry & his boys. Came back in the evening & he & Tom Hendrix & Hendrix had another warrent put out for them as they threaten his life so they were both sent that night to J. Rich by D. Ledford. Hendrix staid all night, Russell left his morning. We are having some pretty weather, spring like. The frogs been hollering some time. The birds singing like spring & lastly the ducks are laying. Finished my gown. Atheline finished her quilt. Paid Mrs. Jones for some onion buttons in a bunch of thread.

March-April 1861

Friday March 1, 1861 - Made some paper boxes for Sunday purposes & crocheted some on cover for chair. Mr. Henry about the mill all day. A very pretty day. Fannie took up the cabbage to crout as they are growing.

Saturday 2nd - Sam & Fannie made crout today. John gone to Haywood for wheat, to be back sometime tonight as he started yesterday. The Terry boys left out this morning when they thought J. Rich would be after them. Old Sack Singleton swore out a peace warrent today for Mr. Henry. Old whore. She did it for meanness & nothing else. Mrs. Jimison spent the day here today. Mr. Henry here about the mill till dinner time & then went over to old dam to kill some otters that were seen. He could not find them. Mrs. Jimison got a pair of shoes here today. Mr. Henry wrote to Sister Jane to meet him in Spartanburg on the 8th of this month. John Snelson here ploughing in garden today. The weather still good. Old Jones & others had a trial here this evening. Finished on lid & tonight pasted paper on my boxes, fancy pictures. Aunt Tena ironed and among the things were some wee clothes which she washed this week. Ham Cannon's son Watson is laying very low with typhoid fever at this time. Jinnie & Atheline have cleaned the hen house and began to clean under Fannie's this week. Sam did not get both stands of crout to press.

Sunday 3rd - A beautiful morning. Mr. Henry & I went over to mill dam to see if we could find the otters, also Pinck, but saw nothing of them. We came back by some land he has been exchanging with A. B. Jones. He & Tom Hendrix started to church soon after we came back. Old Mr. Reynolds preaches at the Academy today. Mr. W. D. Miller came soon after they left wanting to see Mr. Henry & has gone up there. Atheline has taken Zonnie to church. Pinck is here with me playing about. Mrs. Miller & children are all well. The negroes gone to church mostly & somewhere else. This is indeed a beautiful day, so warm & bright. Mr. Henry will start for Sister Jane on Tuesday or Wednesday & will be back in five or six days. He is the kindest & best of husbands & so kind in Sister Jane to come. I am indeed blessed in a loving husband & fond little children & the best of sisters but 'tis so seldom we appreciate our blessings 'till they take their flight. W. D. Miller staid all night. Mont Stradly came in the morning, he staid also.

Monday 4th - Today old Abe Lincoln takes his seat as president. Mr. Henry & Mr. Hendrix went to Asheville, another Terry (?). Terry said he would give possession of house & hotel in two weeks. Mr. Henry got some cups & saucers, the children some candy, me a pair shoes & some cloth for sacks for wheat & other bolt for flour. I made sacks for wheat at night & mended some old coffee sacks. John got back from Haywood Saturday night with the waggon. Cleaned the yard all day Sunday. I began to work a skirt today. Sister Jane gave me one ready pointed so I layd off another like it. Atheline stewed some fruit & I made the pies after dinner.

Tuesday March 5th 1861 - Mr. Henry went to Bent Creek today, staid till late in the evening. I worked some on embroidry before dinner, made cake and ginger bread. In the morning it turned a good deal colder yesterday & a very unpleasant day, today snowing occasionally. Mr. Henry's Aunt Ann Gudger died on last Friday. Aunt Patsy Jimison moved to her son Wilburn's today. I had not heard of her going till she was gone.

Wednesday 6th - Old Terry sent the negroes out the garden today saying he was not done with it yet. He is a scamp. Mr. Henry sent Charlie[25] to Asheville today after a set of buggy harness & a whip, intended to start this evening to Spartanburg but had to go to Night's shop after buggy tongue so did not get off. He is going to work John Smith & the Well's horse Jim. They do finely together, make a good match. I worked some quilt pieces in evening for Atheline to piece me a rag quilt. More pleasant than yesterday.

Thursday 7th 1861 March - Mr. Henry left for Spartanburg this morning. Sister Jane is to be there tomorrow if she got the letter. Fannie & Atheline scoured upstairs & the hall room & front piazza & scalded the beds, took them down & downstairs. I worked some on embroidry. Mr. Henry sent the hands back in garden at hotel this morning. Terry said nothing of note. I have been knitting & reading tonight. J. Snellson is staying all night. He works here but does not stay every night. I asked him to stay till Mr. Henry gets back. Pinck is asleep. Zonnie is out in the kitchen to hear the fiddle with Atheline. George stays here now at night & he keeps the old fiddle agoing. It is now near nine o'clock. A pleasant day today after the frost got off. Jinnie has been cleaning the yards. John is to start to Haywood in the morning after more wheat. I wonder where Mr. Henry is tonight. I hope he got along well. He is the kindest & best of men to his family & indeed too kind to all. I miss him so much when he is away. Jessy Jarrett started all to Georgia to live today.

Thursday 7th 1861 March till April 7th - Uncle Andy woke us in the night by hollering "what a fire!" Yes, the hotel was burned this night & set afire. I shall never forget my feelings as long as I live. God grant I may never have such again. Nothing saved. I sent J. Foulson after Mr. Henry. There was a great deal of company here on Friday. Till Jones came & staid till Sunday & Sunday evening Dora & Mr. Henry came. I was so glad to see them. They were all well at home. I feel so sorry for Mr. Henry. He regrets the loss so much. It is estimated at $12,000. It will be a long time if ever we get over the loss. I hope the guilty persons will yet be found & suffer the penalty. If justice never over takes them in the world it will certainly in the next. I was confined with a son on Monday 11th March, a fine large son weighing 9 1/2 lbs.[26] Every thing went off well. Old Mrs. Parker & Abbe were here. Dr. Hilliard the granna. Mr. Henry has not slept well since he heard about the

---

[25] Henry Family slave, son of Sam and Tena
[26] William Smith (Willie) Henry

house. It has made him prematurely an old man. Oh! how I would love to see one woman hung but I must bear in mind that "Vengeance is mine I will repay" said the Lord.

Hotel Burnt – The hotel at the Sulphur Springs, near Asheville, N. C., a popular summer resort, was burnt on the 13th inst. It was owned by Wm. L. Henry, and the loss is estimated at $12,000.
- Richmond Daily Dispatch, March 20, 1861

April 1861

April Sunday 7th 1861 - This is a disagreeable day, rather cold & rainy. I have got along very well in my confinement, had a little cold once. Dora has been so kind to me & my little ones. The babe seems to grow finely but is rather fretful at night. Dora & I get up with it some nights and Atheline some. It was born March 11th at 15 minutes after 6 o'clock in the evening on Monday 1861. Pinck and Zona love it a great deal especially Zona. I have got as stout as usual. Dora & I went to the mill the other day. She weighs 142 lbs., I weigh 139, Pinck 45 & Zonnie 28. I am very fleshy indeed.

Mr. Henry thinks of building again. I hope he may find it a profitable investment this time for if the house does not make money right away we will be bound to break. It is an establishment that will pay provided it is rightly managed but I much fear he will be as he ever has been, too lenient. I must stop writing as my eyes are weak & I fear I may injure them. Dora is asleep in the large arm chair. Mr. Henry has gone out somewhere. The widow Singleton keeps wanting to see Mr. Henry. I hope he will not let her see him.

Sunday April 21st 1861 - Many things have happened since I last wrote. Mr. Henry attended court till Thursday the 11th of April & he & Dora started to South Carolina as Dora had a letter from Sister Jane requesting her to come home immediately. They got there on Saturday & Sister Jane was married on Tuesday 16th at 10 o'clock & took the train at 2 for Spartanburg. The horses ran away down the mountain but fortunately no bones were broken. The tongue of the carriage broke was the cause of it. They staid at Dr. Neilson's all day Friday or at least got there to dinner & came over here Saturday the 20th, Sister Jane & Dora. Neilson did not come, was having his carriage fixed up again. Sister Jane & Dora staid all night. Neilson came this morning & took Sister Jane to Asheville to go to church. She did not care to go much. They start from Asheville this morning. There is a quarterly meeting going on in Asheville now. Sister Jane brought me some mighty nice cake from the wedding. Oh! I pray that her marriage life may be as happy as heart could wish. May she never pine for the loved ones at home. 'Tis my earnest prayer.

Mr. Henry will be here tomorrow with Matt, he went to Columbia. Dora & I have had a lovely day of it. I have felt so sad so I can't write much more. The babe is doing very well, the children all well. We have had high winds. The peaches all killed. Frost for several nights of late.

Monday 22nd - A pleasant day. Mr. Henry & Matt came home in the evening & Mr. Henry & I went to the mill. He is much pleased with the new sawmill, it goes well. I cut out some shirts, began one. Fort Sumter was surrendered on the 14th April. The fight began the 11th. There has been a fight or two in Maryland. Oh I so much fear my dear husband will be called out to help defend his country. God protect the right is my humble prayer.

Tuesday 23 - Mr. Henry went to Haywood today. I sewed some on a shirt. Dora & Matt doing some work for themselves. The babe is doing finely. Zona & Pinck are getting on very well. It has been cloudy today & a little rain.

Wednesday 24 - Mr. Henry got home at night. It rained a little. All are well.

Thursday 1861 April 25th - Nothing of importance going on. Some volunteers start on the 29th of April from Asheville. Oh I fear Mr. Henry will have to go. My family are very well. Atheline has been sick this week but is well again.

Friday 26th - The mail came this morning, brought no news of any importance. All are well. A very pretty day. Dora & Matt went to the mill this evening & took Zona. I went after I gave out supper.

Saturday 27th - Mr. Henry & Matt got ready to go to Asheville this morning but it rained so they went in the evening & took Pinck. He was delighted with the trip. It rained some in the evening but they did not get wet. Matt is coming back tomorrow.

Sunday 28th - We got up late this morning. It rained last night & this morning. The wind is from the South & cold. Mr. Henry is going to Asheville today to see them muster as they start tomorrow. Dora had a letter from Sister Jane yesterday. She is not at all satisfied. I fear never will be. She spoke a little of coming back to the examination. Mr. Henry bought the children some shoes yesterday. Mr. Henry, Dora & I took a long walk this morning & got a good many wild flowers. We went down the creek & up through the widening field. He did not go to Asheville this evening as we got back from walk at 1 o'clock & they paraded at 3. Late in the evening Mr. Henry, Dora & I went to the Sulphur Springs & came back by the old hotel place. The place looks lonely.

Monday 29th - Mr. Henry went to Asheville, staid all day. Capt. McDowell's company left today. Mr. Henry & Matt came home in the evening. We were all sad. I at the thought of my dear husband being called off. It really seems more than I could bear, to see the only one on whom I can lean for support torn from me by war. I would not expect to see him again till we met in God's blest abode. It makes me so sad to think of it.

Tuesday 30th - Mr. Henry got his sewing machine home today. Dora and I worked nearly all day trying to get it to going right. Did but little sewing. Hemmed some sheets. Mr. Henry started to Hendersonville today to sell some flour, to be gone a day or two. Everything is in a whirl of excitement about the war. 5,000 troops have already been called to Richmond Va. I do trust & hope we may not have war.

May 1861

May 1st 1861 Wednesday - Nothing of importance going on. Hon. Z. B. Vance's company leave on Friday for Raleigh & then to Va. The weather has been rather cool for the time of year. The peaches all killed & a good many apples too. Dora & Matt dressed in boys clothes or rather in Mr. Henry's a'right, we enjoyed it finely. Mr. Henry not come home yet. I am mistaken, he only started this day after dinner, to be back Friday.

More Troops for the War!

I AM AUTHORIZED BY THE SECRETARY of War to raise a

LEGION FOR THE WAR.

I want an ADDITIONAL REGIMENT OF IN-FANTRY, two Companies of CAVALRY, and one Company of ARTILLERY. A BOUNTY of

One Hundred Dollars

Will be paid to each soldier upon his enlistment. Cavalry are required to furnish their own horses, for which the government will pay them forty cents per day, and their full value if killed in battle. The best arms and equipments to be had in the Confederacy will be furnished. Recruits will be received singly or by companies. Turn out, and let's make short work with Abe. ☞ Address me for the present at Kinston, N. C.   Z. B. VANCE,
Col. Com'g 26th Reg.
N. C. T.

May 1, 1861.   4t

Zebulon B. Vance   The Asheville News May 1, 1861
(North Carolina Collection, Pack Memorial
Public Library, Asheville, NC)

Thursday 2nd - Nothing going on of note. All are well.

Friday 3rd - Mail came this morning, no letters for me. I reckon Lou has forgotten me. John that took the flour to Henderson, came this evening & Mr. Henry at night. Warm today in the middle of day. Sewing machine doing finely.

Saturday 4th - Mr. Henry went to Asheville and New Found today. Came back before night & we went up to the spring & round by the old hotel place. I am so affraid my dear husband will go to the seat of war. If he has to go, God protect him I pray & bring him back safe to his family is my every wish. Warm this evening & cloudy. Dora & Matt here working on machine today. All are well. Began to plant corn in the apple orchard today.

Sunday 5th - Drisley rain this morning. Mr. Reynolds preaches today at the Academy. There are several men here this morning to hear the news. I think they are not doing much at the seat of war. I will stop soon & take the babe. Zona can talk nearly anything she tries. Pinck is a large healthy boy.

June 1861

June 9th 1861 - Well journal I have neglected you a good while but will try in future to write at least once a week. Nothing of interest has transpired in the last month. The examination came off the first of May in Asheville. Dora & Matt attended & started to Sister Jane's the Thursday after. I have had one letter from Dora since. They speak of coming back here in July.

The sewing machine is doing finely. I made three pair pants for the volunteers, one pair being for J. L. Henry. I made one pair britches yesterday for Uncle Sam & 16 sacks for the mill on machine besides attending to babe. He is a very good child, bothers me but little. Pinck nurses him when he gets tired of laying. Pinck is a good boy. Zona crys a good deal.

The wheat crop looks well, the corn is doing well. We need rain now & have had little showers along.

The United States Government is still in an uproar, things seem to be going on badly. How I wish there could be a peaceful separation of the states. N. C. is out of the Union. Tennessee will soon be too. There has been two or three little spells of fights, not much. The Lincolnites are in possession of Alexandria Va. Killed Jackson, the proprietor of a hotel there & took some 40 southern prisoners. I fear we will have a bloody war yet. Thursday 13th of June is set apart as a day of thanksgiving & pray by President Davis of the Southern confederacy. We of the South ought to at least offer up our humble prayer for war to cease as it all lies in the hands of our great Creator.

There was preaching at the Academy on Friday. Mr. Wexler from Asheville. Mr. Henry was in Asheville yesterday, got me a hoop & Zona & I a scoop. I will trim them tomorrow. I have made up part of the negro clothes & part is still in the loom. The lapped briches in yet. The thread is here for the woman's dresses but done nothing with yet. The loom in the back Piazza.

Atheline does the cooking now. She fixed a box and some dirt at one end of the piazza & part of one side yesterday evening & day before. I went to preaching last Sunday 2nd of June at the Academy. Mr. Renolds minister. He preaches the first Sabbath in every month to the negroes but the whites go too.

Strawberries are ripe now. I don't think I shall get any for preserves. Cherries will soon be on. Our garden at hotel looks well, most of our vegetables are there. Cabbage planted down here & very small yet. This is a lovely day, not too warm & so bright.

There is still one company of volunteers in Asheville, the company Mr. Henry is in. I hope it may never have to leave for it seems to me I could not stand it to part with my dear husband. With the prospects of war upon us, what would become of me & my poor little ones. God only knows but he has promised to be a father to the fatherless. There will be many a sad heart in homes where the protector has been called away. May God protect the right is my humble prayer.

Men gathering to enlist at Pack Square, Asheville, NC
(North Carolina Collection, Pack Memorial Public Library, Asheville, NC)

June 10th Monday - I made Jinnie a copperas dress. Mrs. J. H. Green spent the day here. I sewed up her sack on the machine & sewed some on Hanes'[27] pants. A warm day. Mr. Henry off to Asheville.

Tuesday 11th - Finished Hanes' pants & made Pea's, also an apron for Tena. Very warm & dry.

Wednesday 12th - Trimmed mine & Zona's scoops. Jim Welch eat dinner here. He is a volunteer, was unwell & going home from Raleigh on a furlough of a month. Mr. Henry loaned him the buggy. A warm day needing rain badly. The wheat has some rust on the leaves.

Thursday 13th June Thanksgiving Day - Mrs. Henry Cook & Cordelia Cook came here this morning on Thursday to church, we all went. Mr. Henry, Pinck & I heard a good serman from Dr. Cummings. Mr. Renolds was there too. We did not keep past day. I had a dreadful headache that night, went to bed before supper. Atheline had to leave her supper & attend to the baby. A very warm day. All are well. Zona is very fretful, I think she has worms.

Friday 14th - I got up free of headache & went to Asheville to do some shopping, left the baby. Got back about 1 o'clock. Very warm. Mr. Henry & I went over in the wheat, took a long walk, came out through the new ground. Saw the Haywood volunteers going on, they are marching in very good order. Made but few purchases in Asheville. Had the headache very bad all night, went to bed before supper.

Saturday 15th - Got up with a headache this morning which lasted all day. Zona was vomiting this morning, threw up a worm, is rather fretful. Jinnie is in the house yesterday & today. Muster at the Hotel place. Mr. Henry up there. A very warm day, needing rain badly.

Sunday morning 16th 1861 - A very warm morning. We dressed this morning without fire, the first morning this summer. Zona very fretful. The others all well.

---

[27] Henry Family slave, son of Sam and Tena

Willie is growing finely. Mr. Henry gone off somewhere on the farm. The children are all at play whilst I write.

There has been some fighting between the North & South, not a great deal of damage on either side. Oh! how many hearts are sent asunder at the thoughts of loved ones in the battle field. I feel as if my life would be a burthen if my dear husband should go. What would become of me & my little ones God only knows.

Monday 17th - Fannie scalded & scoured today & I helping a little. Atheline & I put up the beds & fixed the room. Began giving Zona some worm medicine.

Tuesday 18th - We fixed upstairs in the evening. I had the toothache, front teeth, at night. They hurt me considerable but slept very well. My lip began to swell & by morning was puffed considerably. Very warm weather & dry, gardens doing no good. Mr. Henry went to Asheville, brought me a letter from Frank. All are well down there. Jane Jenning is dead. She has been an invalid a good long time.

Wednesday 19th 1861 June - My teeth pained me a good deal all day. I did not work much. All are well. Mr. Henry got a top for fly catchers yesterday, it does not do very well.

Thursday 20th - Nothing new going on. There has been some battles of late. The Buncombe Rifleman[28] have been in two little fights. Children all well. Very warm & dry.

William Wallace McDowell, Captain
Company E, 1st Regiment,
N. C. Volunteers, in full
"Buncombe Rifles" uniform
(Courtesy Smith-McDowell House Collection,
Asheville, North Carolina)

---

[28] On April 18th, 1861 the Buncombe Riflemen left Asheville for Raleigh and became one of the first two companies from western North Carolina to enter the war. A flag made by young women of the town was presented to them on their departure, was adopted as the regimental flag of the 1st Regiment, and dedicated at Big Bethel, the first battle of the war. (Sources: "The Heart of Confederate Appalachia, Western North Carolina in the Civil War," by John C. Inscoe & Gordon B. McKinney, p 64, and "History of the McDowells and Connections," by John Hugh McDowell, p 262)

BETHEL FLAG

Made for the First Company Leaving Asheville Commanded by Capt. W. W. McDowell. ✎ ✎

This Flag was made by the Misses Woodfin(Annie and Lily), Kate Smith, (the late Mrs. Marcus Erwin), and Mary Patton. It was made out of their ball dresses.

This Flag was adopted as the Regimental Flag by the First Regiment, commanded by Gen. D. H. Hill, and was dedicated at Big Bethel Church battle, June 10th, 1861.

9 x 6 cardboard commemorating the flag of the 1st Regiment
(North Carolina Collection, Pack Memorial Public Library, Asheville, NC)

Friday 21st - Mail came but brought nothing new. Mr. Henry started to Henderson with a load of flour, to come back tomorrow. Atheline & I put up a bed in the side room this evening. It was very warm & a great deal of trouble.

Saturday 22nd - Tom Cook & T. Knight corded the bed this morning. They are making a fish trap, will put it in this evening. I fixed the side room & put away all the winter clothes & so on. Very warm & dry.

Sunday 23rd - One year today since I came home from So. Ca. Many changes have taken place since then. Sister Jane is married & gone. I hope she may never repent it. I have not heard from Dora in some time. I will write to Sister Jane today. I wrote to Frank, Lena & Ell last Sunday. The babe has been unwell all day. I got frightened about it at dinner. It cried so I was affraid of its going into a convulsion. Mr. Henry sent over Dr. Hilliard. He came in the evening, gave it some powders & on Monday it seemed well enough.

Monday 24th - We had a little rain, not much. One company of volunteers came on this evening from Cherokee. Capt. Hays company of cavalry. We baked bread for them. It was an undertaking indeed. Some of the men staid all night here, the others camped at the old hotel place & slept in the old store house. William Tidwell is along. It makes me sad to see so many of our brave men led up to be shot at but such is the fate of war.

Tuesday 25th - Mollie Henry[29] & her sister Hattie Alexander spent the day here. Mollie's babe looks badly. Is not well at all, can't walk yet, was a year old the 15th of May. Volunteers left this morning, left two ovens & lids. They had some wash-

---

[29] Wife of James L. Henry

25

ing done & paid Fannie & Jinnie for it. I have been sewing on the negroes clothes. Will get the pants all done this week by Thursday.

Wednesday June 26th 1861 - Had a very good rain this evening. All are well. Zona not very well, very fretful. Worms I think. She is a dear child, often comes to me & says "tap a lap mama," wanting to get in my lap & after says "both tap a lap mama." I should miss my dear little ones a great deal if I had none. Pinck is a good boy.

Thursday 27th - I finished the coarse sewing this evening. Had the sick headache dreadful bad. Eat some green apples & cherries which made it worse.

Friday 28th - Mail came this morning. My head well. Nothing new of importance. A. B. Jones came over for the news. He takes a paper from Richmond. Mrs. Parker here this evening. We all went up to the hotel garden. I eat a good many currents & had the headache all night. Mr. Henry & Pinck went to the fish trap & got four little ones. It was getting dark when we got back.

Another company are to be along from Cherokee on Sunday or Monday, going on to Asheville. There are eight companies in Asheville now. The cavalry consists of J. W. Woodfin's company, "The Buncombe Rangers", one from Watauga, Capt. Folk. Meclenburg Cavalry, Capt. I forgot who now. Juna Luska Guard, Capt. Hays of Cherokee, these of Cavalry & some of infantry. Grey volunteers Capt. Roberts of Buncombe. A second company from Haywood, Capt. Sam Bryson. Second company from Henderson Co. Gen. B. M. Edney. A Cavalry company from Macon Capt. Siler. Bob Henry has gone on. He belongs to the Jeff Davis Guards from Macon. All of Papa Henry's sons belong to the state for her defense & three grand sons. Poor old man, he is growing old very fast.

Saturday 29th - I had the headache very badly till dinner & then it eased off. I had it all night Friday night. I did nothing of any consequence. I trimmed Atheline's scoop yesterday. Zona getting better, has not been sick much. We had a good season today. Set out a good many cabbage plants this evening, also tobacco & potatoe slips. Mr. Henry's hands have been cutting wheat this week. Not done yet by a good deal, will keep on till he gets done.

Sunday 30th - Late breakfast this morning as usual on Sunday. We are having a nice time eating fish & mutton. Mr. Henry & I went up to the old Hotel place this morning. Got some June apples & today we have our first apple dumplings. Willie is laying in the large arm chair before me. He is a dear good child. He lays in it nearly all day. Very warm this morning. I think we will have rain by evening. I will stop as I must write to Sister Jane today. I had a letter from Dora on Friday. I did not write last Sunday for Willie was sick a day.

Second Sulphur Springs Hotel, built in 1887 by E. G. Carrier on the site where the Henry's first hotel was destroyed by fire in 1861
(North Carolina Collection, Pack Memorial Public Library, Asheville, NC)

Roster of the Turkey Creek and Sulphur Springs Home Guard
(North Carolina Collection, Pack Memorial Public Library, Asheville, NC)

44

Names   Ayes   Noes

K. A. Cosado
Alexander McCourty
John Liotfora

James Meadows
Manning Warlick
Henry Paris
Reuben Paris
James C. Plemons   80
William James   81
Ambrose Snelson   82
Andrew J. Block   83
Warren James
Reuben Coffey
Waren James
Jacob Martin

Turkey Creek Sulphur Spring home gards
June 29th 1861
                    I certify that O. K.
Helmet Benjamin Hawkins D. A. Blackwell
James Hughes and James Block was Elected
delegates to represent this Company in a
Convention proposed to Be held in Asheville
On the 4th day of July next
                            D Block Capt

July 1861

Monday July 1st - A very warm day. Stanaphor Jones' wife & Mrs. Plemons spent the day here. Mrs. Plemons' husband has gone to the war. I made Fannie & Jinnie an apron apiece, some that was left by of the britches. Needing more rain. Another company of volunteers camped at the hotel place Sunday night. The negroes cooked their bread for them.

Tuesday 2nd - I finished Zona's tatten for her chimise & sewed it on in the evening. Cut out some drawers for myself, two pair & a skirt for Zona. Going to put the trimming on that. Matt gave her some rose tatting. Went down to the mill with Mr. Henry, took Willie & Zona.

Wednesday 3rd - Sewed on my things, the machine did not do well. I got it to work at dinner time & I stitched one pantlet on it & went to Henry Cook's in the evening who has a sick child. Pinck & Mr. Henry went. Also we went to the fish trap but nothing in it. We have had several small fish. Nothing of any importance going on in the country. I went to sleep before supper as I had a bad headache.

Thursday 4th - Northern Congress sets today. I fear we will have some bloody battles soon. I finished one pair drawers today with rose tatting, eight tucks. The others have five & I am going to point them. Col. Moore's babe died this morning with flux,[30] several children have it about here. Mary Knight's babe is very low now. Began to rain at dark, rain slowly all night.

Friday 5th - Mail came, brought but little news. I got a letter from Pa[31] today, all well down there. Pa will be up in August or Sept. Rube (Aunt Annie's) is dead & Bets has her leg broke from a cow running over her. Mr. Henry, Pinck & I went to Mary Moore's & went with the corpse to the Capt. Moore's grave yard. It rained on us a little just before we got home. Not much. It made my cold worse and Willie has a cold too. I left him longer today than I ever have. He did not cry. They fed him. Atheline attended to him. I sewed some on my pantlets, pointed & tucked one. Also made Fannie a gingham bonnett. After dinner made some ginger cakes for my little ones. Some one took some wheat out of the wagon last night. George got in from Haywood with a load of wheat late at night & today they found it. George & Andy had taken it themselves. George is a mean negro as ever went unhung.

Sunday 7th - Mr. Henry has gone to Sandy Bottom today to see Ely Glenn on business. He was here yesterday. I went to the Academy to preaching. Mr. Renolds preached a good sermon. I forgot where the tent was. A large congregation. Byrd preached at Sardis this morning & at the Academy this evening at 3 o'clock. The negroes have all gone but Charlie & he has a sore foot. Zona & Willie are with one daughter washing her hands in a tub of rain water at the door & I am now rocking Willie to get him to sleep. Yes he is asleep. Tom Night & Hendrix eat dinner here today. Mr. Henry not come yet. Aunt Patsy Jimison was at church today. I have not

---

[30] A form of dysentery
[31] William Smith, Sr.

seen her before since Feb. She has moved up to her sons. There is another company of volunteers to come on in the morning from Cherokee.

Monday July 8th - Finished my pantlets, pointed ones, & warm all day.

Tuesday 9th - I have forgotten what I did. Oh! now I remember. Aunt Patsy came and spent the day. Warped the piece for the negroes dresses & hemmed it in the evening. It began to rain about three o'clock & rained a hard shower & continued to rain all evening. Aunt Patsy staid all night. Mr. Henry went to Asheville as it is court week. All are very well.

Wednesday 10th - I arose early this morning. Cool enough for fire. I fixed my things for going to Cousin Sam Gudger's. Mr. Henry went with me to Col. Moore's as Cousin Mary & I went in our buggy. Took Willie, left Zona & Pinck at home. Got there about 10 o'clock & enjoyed the day & night finely. Took a walk in the evening. Carried Hanes along to help with Willie.

Thursday 11th July - A company of volunteers went on this morning from Athens, Geo., Grady's company I think. We left Cousin Betsey Gudger's after the soldiers had past about 10 o'clock. Spent the day very pleasantly at Cousin Lou Candler's. Had a nice dinner, beans the first I have eat this season. Went over to Candler's office in the evening & started home about 4 o'clock. Met Mr. Henry & Pinck at Night's shop waiting for me. Mr. Henry is very kind to me. I am blessed with good children & the kindest of husbands & well I appreciate them too. Found all well at home. Everything gone on well. I think Hanes was more rejoiced to get home than any one else.

Friday 12th - Mail came, nothing new. I did not get a letter. I looked one from Lou as it has been so long since I heard, not since Feb. I look for Dora & them soon. I handed some threads to Aunt Tena. She got her cloth ready to go to weaving on Monday as she will iron tomorrow. Mr. Henry has got a thrashing machine, started to run by water, it goes very fast so they say. Mr. Henry got half a box of tobacco this evening.

Saturday 13th - I got up with headache this morning, not very severe. I sewed a little on Zona's skirt, finished putting on the tatting (rose) & basted one tuck. I lay down just before dinner & eat none but eat a bunch of radishes & apple pie. Pie left last night at supper. I felt very unwell but threw up about 4 o'clock & got well enough to bake some apple pies & molasses custard. Took Willie in kitchen. Mr. Henry & all the children took a nap in side room. I lay down with Willie but did not sleep though he did.

Sunday 14th - Got up late, breakfast late as usual. The mutton chops badly cooked. Fannie is a good cook but wears my patience out doing so badly. After I got things straightened out at the house, I went with Mr. Henry, Pinck & Zona over the creek towards Snelson's to gather black berries for a pie for dinner. Mr. Henry turned some hogs in the wheat field pasture, the old saw house field. Old Linsey's house not done yet, the chimney about half done. I must stop writing & go make my pies as 'tis nearly 12 o'clock. Joe Green here for dinner. Nothing new. Lincoln has called for 400,000 troops & 4 million dollars more to subjugate the south. He will find that hard to do. We have got 4 very pretty little goats by old cashmere Billie. We have eat the other billies, one of the little ones a very pretty thing. Pinck is here saying I must go & make the pie as Fannie is waiting.

Sunday 28th - Two weeks have gone by since I wrote. A great many things have happened since then. There was a bloody battle fought last Sunday 21st July near Manassas Junction. A good many killed on both sides. Report says Willie Hardy was killed. He was aid to Col. Kershaw of So. Ca. I have heard of no others that I know. I expect Aunt Rosa is in a sea of trouble for I think Thomas Taylor was in the fight though I have not yet heard.

On July the 27 Saturday, there was a barbacue up at the hotel place, a good many there. Tilda Jones came here in the morning & her, Mrs. Joe Green & I went up and took dinner. Mary J. Lusk & husband staid here all night that night. They made up a few volunteers. Lusk & N. W. Woodfin spoke on the occasion. I had the headache very badly that night. Tilda & Tom Morris left a little before sun down. Sunday, Mary J. Lusk & old man staid till evening. Mr. Henry & I went to the fish trap, nothing in it. Took a good long walk, came back by the Sulphur Springs. Jim Ledford was with us, he staid all night & went after Pinck Allen to go to the election of Capt. for a company raised called the Pisgah Guards. Mr. Henry went also, the election at the Baptist church this side of Sam Gudger's. Elected G. Howell Capt. Are to march into Asheville tomorrow Tuesday. Mr. Henry bought me some nice apples from Candler's. Pinck went with his Papa.

Tuesday 23rd I went to Asheville with Mr. Henry, also Pinck & Zona. Staid at J. L. Henrys. The Pisgah Guards met the infantry in front of Jim's house. Gen. Edney made a short welcome speech. I have been very busy this week fixing to go to see old Mr. Henry & we start on Tuesday the 30th. I had a letter from Dora on Friday 26, they will be here the last of July so she said. I have had a letter from Lou too since I wrote before. She has not been at all well. Mr. Henry & I have been to Locust Knob today to preaching, came back for dinner. Morgan preached, not many went. I went with Mr. Henry to A. B. Jones' on Friday 26th, spent the evening. Tilda came home with us, staid all night & went with Mr. Henry to the (?) at Sam Gudger's meeting house. Pinck also. I staid at home & trimmed Till's bonnet. I think 'tis a bridle one for 'tis trimmed in white ribbon & flowers. She also bought a white swiss to make. She went home yesterday evening or rather Mr. Henry went by her house & took her. I have been making Willie some aprons trimmed with pink & yellow.

September 1861

September 1st Sunday - A month has gone by since I wrote. It seems a short one. Mr. Henry & I & the children started to Cherokee on Friday the 2nd of August about 12 o'clock & got to Hayesville at dusk. I was very sick with headache. We staid there till Monday. I went to church with Mr. Henry & Aunt Welch, heard a very good sermon from Mr. Moody a baptist minister. On Monday we went to Uncle John Love's, got there for dinner, staid all night. On Tuesday went to Uncle Dillard Love's, got there about 4 o'clock & staid till morning & Wednesday went to Mr. Henry's father's. We traveled over some awful roads on Tusquitte Mountain. The scenery is grand on Nantahala, truley sublime. I enjoyed it finely. It was dark when we got to Papa's. We staid till Monday. Sunday the 11th we took dinner with Mrs. Garrison a renter of Papa's. I enjoyed the trip finely. Monday 12th we started for home, rained nearly all day on us. Branton came with us over the Tusquitte Mountain to keep the hack from turning over as the road was so washed. We came to Uncle Dillard's that night & spent Tuesday there. One of our horses took sick in the evening & died that night, old Jim's horse. Mr. Henry went to Franklin Tuesday evening. Wednesday we came to Uncle John Love's, got there late in the evening. Thursday started early. Mallie McBee came on with us going to Asheville. Got to Hayesville in the evening, sundown. We heavy loaded as the man whose horse we got to bring us home is along & Mallie so we have a load. Heard at Hayesville that Sister Jane had come. Friday started for home, got here nearly sundown. Found all well. Sister Jane & them in Asheville. Saturday Mr. Henry went after them. I had the toothache badly, it came after dinner & Mallie & I & Pinck went up as far as Parker's, the old Murray place to meet them. It rained a little on us coming back. Sister Jane staid till Wednesday & started back as she is anxious to hear from Neilson who has gone to Kentucky to buy horses. Mallie & Matt went to Asheville Tuesday. Matt came back Monday in Sister Jane's carriage. Sister Jane was not well whilst here, complained a good deal. On Sunday after she left, Dora, Matt & I went to camp meeting at Ashbury campground but few attended. We took our dinner & went in the worst old hack imaginable, an old thing that has been standing in the lot a year or so. We enjoyed the day finely. Tilday Jones & Tom Morris were married on last Thursday.

Aug 28th - Pa & Berry Hogan[32] came this evening at night. Pa looks well. We heard Friday 30th that Mr. Neilson was a prisoner in Kentucky. Sister Jane wrote Pa & co. started on Saturday. Quin is along too. I have been quite idle since Dora & Matt came. I had the headache very bad on Friday last. Willie has two teeth through, found them Friday 30th. He is not six months old till the 11th of Sept. He is a dear good child. Mr. Henry says Zona will be an old maid because she is so nice about everything. Pinck is growing finely, a good boy. The Cavalry have left Asheville, all but Hays company from Cherokee. There is a Regiment of infantry there. Clingman Vol. & five other companies besides. I fear we will have an awful time of it yet right here, for there are so many union men in East Tennessee all about where Sister Jane lives. Pa was telling us Caroline Lawson was dead, died at Aunt Sallie's. The army made sad havick with about three acres of Mr. Henry's corn. It was at the worst about the middle of August & then rain set in so they have done no harm since.

Sept. 1st - Staid at home all day. Preaching at Academy but some of the whites went. Mr. Renolds preached, not many out so the negroes said.

Monday 2nd - Tilda Jones came here today. We heard Mrs. Green's babe was dead & learned that is two children she has lost lately with sore throat. Jim Night brought us a bag of peaches, very nice. Tilda Morris left before dinner as she heard the Regiment was ordered from Asheville & her old man was in it. Cassius Gudger

[32] Married Margaret Frances "Sister Frank" Smith, sister of Cornelia Henry

was married to Mary Willis last Tuesday. I think they had better stay single till peace is made anyhow, let it be long or short.

Tuesday 3rd - A pretty day, nothing new going on. Mr. Henry is busy at the mill, began to plough in the field where the old Alford house stood. Dora, Matt & I started to old Quinn's to get grapes. We found Mr. Henry up there & went where they were ploughing & then went on & got some excellent grapes. Not quite ripe. Quinn bought us a jug of cider this evening. All are well.

Wednesday 4th - I moulded some candles today, sewed some on shirts for Jim & John, not much. Had a peach pie yesterday & today. All are well. Dora & Matt are reading "Jane Eyre" out to me, though I have read it. Grinding at the mill every night nearly. Went to walk up on the hill towards stable in the pasture field.

Thursday 5th - Moulded candles & sewed some on negro's shirts. Fair & pleasant. Matt, Dora & I went to the Murry place with Mr. Henry & rode back on Josiah Jones' waggon, he coming from Asheville. We saw a great many people going & coming from Asheville. The Col. Clingman Regiment (the 25th) leave Asheville on Monday 9th Sept.

Friday 6th - Mail came, no news. All quiet at the seat of war. We went to the hotel gardens this evening, got some grapes & apples & got some watermellons out of our garden down here. Dora & Matt wanted to go to Asheville this evening to see the soldiers in dress parade but it rained & the buggy was not at home.

Brig. Gen. Thomas L. Clingman
(Courtesy of the North Carolina Office of Archives and History, Raleigh, NC)

Saturday 7th - All well. We saw in the Asheville News the other day of the release of Mr. Neilson. Glad of it. Hope he may never be in another such scrape. Pa not back yet. Moulded up all the tallow today. Dora, Matt & Mr. Henry got ready to go to Asheville but it rained all the evening so they could not go. I patched some today. Nothing new going on. Alfred Webb has both his children with sore throat. Also Sam Green one & the orphan child that lived with old granna (Creasman?) is dead. I hope it may not get among my little ones. If it does I will do the best I can & if it please God to remove them from me I will give them up as well as I can but none knows how hard a trial it would be.

Sunday 8th - A dull day, cloudy & gloomy. The coffee this morning had a chicken feather in it. I do think we have the dirtiest cooks ever was in the world. I often wish there was not a negro in the world. These fret my life away nearly. I sometimes think it would be a relief to lie down in the quiet grave where trouble never comes & then another & better thought rises within & says live for your children for you know what it is to have a step mother. Oh! God spare me to raise my children. Give me wisdom to raise them in fear & admonition of Thee & when it seemeth good in Thy sight remove me from this world of care & trouble. Pa &

Berry came this evening. Had two matches, two mules & a mare he had purchased in Ten. All well at Neilsons.

Monday 9th - Dora & I made Sam a pair of pants Sister Jane gave him. She finished them by dinner. We all went to Asheville this evening to see them in camps & I did a little shopping, got a calico dress & some other little things. Dora got some candy for Zona & a little engine for Pinck. Matt went down to Dr. Neilson's after some hankerchiefs they left there but Mrs. Neilson was not at home. We went back to the encampment & seen them on dress parade. It was sundown before we left Asheville. The moon shone bright before we got home. Berry did not go. We went in Pa's carriage, Zona & Pinck too. Mr. Henry got Matt & Dora some books for birthday presents today.

Tuesday 10th - Dora lined Berry's sheep skin. Matt sick all day with headache. We are having some right nice mellons, small but sweet. All are well & I am glad of it. Mr. Henry gone to Bent Creek. I fear they will have trouble up there with old Jim Case. He don't want Newton Taylor to live there. I fear 'twill be a fuss. Mr. Henry came back at night, nobody hurt. Dora & Berry went to the grave yard this evening & rode the new matches very gentle. Matt & I went to the hotel orchard & came back with Berry & Dora as they came around the road from grave yard.

Wednesday 11th - Pa & them started this morning. Zona & Pinck want to go. I hated to see them leave. Zona cried to go with Aunt Doda as she calls her. Soon as they left Mr. Henry & I took Pinck & Zona up to the hotel place to hunt Matt's breast pin as she could not find it this morning. Atheline found it under the little round table in hall room. I did but little work today, I feel so lonely. Atheline begun to pick wool for to send to carding factory. Mr. Henry is going to have it carded this year.

Thursday 12th - Cloudy this morning. The air feels like fall, cool nights. I have a bad cold & feel badly generally. Aunt Tena & Atheline picking wool. Mary Rollins came about 11 o'clock & helped all day. Got along slowly. I am fixing an under body.

Friday 13th - Mail came, no news of importance. I did but little work, picked wool after dinner. Ham Rollins came by in the evening & Mary went home. Mr. Henry went to Asheville after dinner & staid after supper. Col. Bill Jones staid all night here. All are well. Having pretty weather at present.

Saturday 14th - I slept late this morning & felt dull all day. Aunt Tena not well. Atheline ironing. I made 27 sacks for flour & attended Willie. He weighs 22 lbs., Zona 28 lbs. & Pinck 45 lbs. I, 120 lbs. I ironed some too. After dinner Mr. Henry & I went up to Sulphur Spgs., saw a good many volunteers going home. It was very warm walking, about 4 o'clock when I got back.

Sunday Sept. 15th 1861 - I woke early this morning. Willie is a very early riser. Breakfast late as usual. Aunt Tena has moved in her house. Seems to be comfortable enough. I was up there this morning for the first time since she moved. Nothing new going on. Old Mr. George & old man & volunteer from Cherokee & another man are here, going to start after dinner for Cherokee. Going in Mr. Henry's buggy. Stan Jones going too. He (Jones) finds the horse. These men say there is a great deal of discontent in the camps on account of the officers. Some of them being from another state. Chinkapins are beginning to open. I must stop as I want to write to Lou & Sister Jane today & perhaps Dora & Matt. Did not write any letters at all. Mr. Henry went off after dinner, did not get back till night. I spent a long lonely evening by myself.

Monday 16th - I made or rather fixed up Willie & Zona an old doll apron, did but little. Put on Willie a stocking striped black & white.

Tuesday 17th - Cut out Willie some linnin aprons, sewed but little as I attended to him. Tena, Atheline & the children picking wool. Looks like they will not get done soon. Jinnie get dinner and helps all she can. Mr. Boyd put up the loom that came from Stines this morning, will try to get it work next week. All are well. The days warm with cool mornings.

Wednesday 18th - Mr. Henry & I went to Asheville today as the 25th Regiment of volunteers left there. Was a good many people in Asheville. I saw Rachel Miller there. Her husband is in the 6th Regiment. We went horse back. Came back to dinner. I had the headache all the evening badly. Took a nap but found no relief. Mr. Henry took a nap also, bought the children some toys. Two little dogs & an indian rubber ball.

Thursday 19th - I sewed till about ten o'clock then Mr. Henry & I went to old Quinn's to get some grapes. I eat a great many & had headache again this evening. We brought a good many home with us. Cool mornings & nights.

Friday 20th - Mail came, no news. Zona had a fever last night & a breaking out. I fear she will have sore throat. Finished Willie an apron today making some out of the old carriage cushion covers. Pinck very stout & well.

Saturday 21st - Mr. Henry went up the creek to try & get some volunteers. I fear he will go yet. I don't want him to go. It seems that I could never stand it in the waits. I believe it would kill me. Zona had a fever last night again. Mr. Henry got very wet this evening as it rained very hard.

Sunday 22nd - Zona had a fever last night. Her face broke out with something. Albert Hawkins just left, came after some papers. Mr. Henry about somewhere. I must write some letters today without fail. Jim Parker has been working with the hands as overseer some two weeks.

Monday 23rd - I wrote to Dora, Sister Jane & Lou & want to hear from them soon. It has been some time since I hear from any of them. Mr. Henry, Pinck & I went over in the widening to see the young cattle & back by the hotel place. Cool & foggy this morning. Got the cloth warped by Mrs. Fanning on Saturday last, not put it in today. I did but little work, helped pick wool a little. Zona had a slight fever last night.

Tuesday 24th - Mr. Henry started to Haywood this morning to buy meat. I did but little today. Mrs. Fanning put the cloth through the harness slay, started it to weave. I fear it will do but little good. Dan Hawkins came to work here today.

Wednesday 25th - Cool & foggy. Corn doing but little. Uncle Jimmie Gudger was thrown from a mule & his neck broke today. Mr. Henry will not return to-night. Zona had a slight fever. Old Mr. Boyd is here trying to get the loom a going.

Thursday 26th - I have given over the loom & gone to finish Willie's apron. All are well. I finished heeling some stockings for the children before supper so I sewed till bedtime. Mr. Boyd sits in my room till he goes to bed. Atheline sleeps in the room with me. Mr. Henry came home after eight at night. It has been raining all day, a mist rain but about dark it began in earnest & Mr. Henry very wet when he got home.

Friday 27th 1861 Sept. - It rained last night very hard & this morning the whole earth is nearly covered with branches & creeks. It rained on till near 12 o'clock, not so hard though. The bridge went off about 2 o'clock. It hurt the dam a little, not a good deal. It was higher than I ever saw it get. Trees backed up to the corner of the yard. Very cool this evening. Still cloudy. No mail came today as it rained too hard I suppose.

Saturday 28th - A cool morning but no frost. Cloudy & windy. Mr. Henry went to Asheville, got the mail & some coffee which is selling at 40 cts. per lb. We ought to dispose with it but Mr. Henry won't. Mr. Henry & I went down to the dam this evening. The creek has pretty well run down. It took nearly all the plank off the dam. We took little Zona along with us. The Billy goat was drowned under the old mill house.

Sunday 29th - Some volunteers staid here last night. Cavalry from Cherokee. Capt. Hays Company. Only three going to Cherokee to see their friends so they are to leave soon. Mr. Henry is laying down before the fire, has been asleep. That is his place in winter Sunday. I want to go up to Quinn's this evening to get the last of grapes as we will soon be visited by jack frost. It is 1 o'clock, no dinner yet. Instead of going to Quinn's, Mr. Henry & I went up by the hotel place & down to the spring & tolled some old sows and pigs in the pen. Mr. Henry has run a fence across this corn field above the house & has the killing hogs up.

Monday 30th - Nothing new going on, all are well. Cool mornings. I am doing but little sewing. I actually believe I am getting lazy. Mr. Henry & all hands at work on mill dam. Newton Taylor hired also. Mr. Boyd working at the loom, it is doing very well.

October 1861

Tuesday Oct. 1st - I cut Willie out some dresses but sewed but little. They are short ones. I will have them to make with my fingers as all very fine machine needles are broken.

2nd Wednesday - Col. R. B. Vance's Regiment are going to move over here in the old pine field the other side of the road. I fear they will be troublesome. I expect they will strip every apple at the upper orchard. Four or five of the officers eat dinner here today.

Thursday Oct. 3rd 1861 - I sewed a little on Willie's dress. Fannie has gone to weaving. I suffer a great deal all day with headache, had it all day till bed time. Mr. Henry in Asheville all day. The Regiment began to move today, will all get over soon in a day or two. Mary Rollins brought home some stocking yarn she had to spin. She is busy making clothes for R. W. Candler who is commissary for four or five counties to furnish clothes.

Friday 4th - Mail came but nothing new. The bridges are washed away so badly, had no mail from down the river at all. Turning a good deal warmer. The mill started on yesterday. Cathey's Mill I understand is much damaged, at least the dam & fobay. David Lowry eat dinner here yesterday. He is comissary to this Regiment. I am very sorry they are camped so near to us.

Saturday 5th - I went to the Academy to preaching, heard a good serman from Mr. Byrd. It is a two days meeting. Conference sets before long in Greenville Ten. The ministers are on their way now. Mr. W. Renolds was out today with Uncle Jonnie. Mr. Henry gone off to a muster somewhere. George & John gone after wheat to Bailey's. Finished Willie's dress yesterday. I have done nothing today worth notice.

Thursday Oct. 10th 1861 - Fannie scoured today, not the hall room. I moved the post office fixin upstairs but keep the mail in my room on the little shelves. The press we moved in side room. I helped a little. There are so many volunteers coming down. I hate to see them. They are always wanting something. I worked a little on the second skirt for Willie as I finished one yesterday. All are well, a fair day today. Heard yesterday that Fidilla Jones was dead. Poor fellow, he died in camps of fever. I deeply sympathise with the bereaved family.

Friday 11th - Mail came but nothing new. Mr. Henry went to Asheville, gone all day. Sewed on skirt, got done working it, will finish it tomorrow. We have old Mr. McMahan with us every night. He is a Methodist minister, an old man of 65. I think he had better stay at home as he can't stand the pain. The Government has stopped the rations of coffee. The old man don't like that at all. George & Lige Night both attend the mill. Ham Cannon sawing lumber for the army. The measles still raging in camps.

Typical mill, this one located at Reems Creek, near Weaverville, NC
(Photo courtesy Dry Ridge Museum, Weaverville, NC)

Saturday Oct. 12th 1861 - Nothing new going on. Old David Lowry came here sick or drunk on Thursday night, is still here, was quite sick this evening. Has a little negro of Sam Gudger's to wait on him. He is, or rather was, quartermaster of this Regiment, has been superceded by a man named Nail. I don't know anything about him. Our old man McMahan comes every night.

Sunday 13th - Mr. Henry has gone over to the camps to hear McMahan preach. Mrs. Tutt's funeral is preached today at the academy. I guess they will preach in the yard as there are several sick in the academy of measles. Atheline has gone to church & took Zona, nearly all the negroes have gone. Pinck & Alonzo[33] are rolling marbles on the floor. Willie, dear good child, is sitting on the floor playing. He is a good babe. I must stop & take him up for he is tired. I know & I must see about dinner as it is after 11 o'clock. Mr. D. Lowry a little better this morning. It is quite cool this morning, no frost yet. Atheline gathered the pie mellons yesterday. Mr. Lowry's sister Lurana Lowry & Laura Gudger came soon after 11 o'clock. They took on a great deal. He was much worse than they expected. They sent after Cousin Betsy Gudger. She came after dark. They think it rather a critical case. They sit up nearly all night. Laura Gudger slept with me. Mr. Henry slept with old McMahan.

Monday 14th - Lowry no better. They are stimulating him on brandy but little hope of his recovery. Dr. Neilson to see him twice today. I cut out some shirts for Hanes & Lonzo but sewed but little as I had to be getting up & down getting things for the sick man. He has chronic diarrhea, uses a great many shirts as he is so weak. He can't get up. A good many coming & going, they are very attentive.

Tuesday 15th - Mr. Lowry sinking fast, no hope. He rested very badly, seems willing to die. Mr. McMahan had prayers up in his room Sunday evening. He died today about 20 minutes of 10 o'clock. They took it rather hard. That is his single sister. Cousin Mary Moore spent the evening here yesterday and today after dinner. Also, she brought me a home made apron as a present. I suffered all day with headache, took some pills but got no relief till night. Dr. Neilson & Dr. Reynolds were here this morning after Mr. Lowry died. Cousin Mary staid all night, slept in here with me also (?). The men sit up with the corpse. They laid him out upstairs in the room where he died.

Wednesday 16th - Cousin Betsy & Miss Lowry started this morning to where they are going to burry Gen. Lowry. No one in the house with the corpse but Cousin Mary Moore & I. Mr. Henry gone up to the hotel place. I shall be lonely for some time. I have not seen Gen. Lowry since he came here nor do I expect to. David Plemmons started with the corpse about 2 o'clock to some 20 miles where they burry him. Cousin Mary knit on a sock today for me. I sewed on Hanes' shirt, finished 1 today & some on another. She started home about 3 o'clock. It began drissling rain about 2 and continued all night.

Thursday Oct. 17th 1861 - Rained all day. Fannie cleaned up the room upstairs. There is one bed tick entirely scoured. Col. Vance wants to bring his wife here to board. The branch so backed can't grind at mill. The creek rising did considerable

---

[33] Henry Family slave, son of Sam and Tena

harm to Mr. Henry's mill dam, the dirt work. It will be several days before they grind again. I & Atheline made two shirts for Hanes & Pea. Done all their shirts now.

Friday 18th - Mail came, nothing new. The armies at a stand still. Mrs. Vance came to board. I find her a pleasant lady, has one child, a boy 9 years old. I doubled some thread today, sewing thread, some stocking yarn that old Mrs. Parker sent home. She had only spun 7 broaches, the rest is in wool. Mr. Henry & all hands at work at dam, he superintends but is not stout enough to assist much. I had a letter from Sister Jane too. All well.

Saturday 19th - All well, nothing new. A fair day. I made Willie some shirts out of some of Mr. Henry's old shirts, which does well enough.

Sunday 20th 1861 - Windy this morning. The negroes have gone to the Academy to preaching. I guess they will not preach as the house is full of sick. There is several men here this morning but that is common since this Regiment has been here. Col. Vance comes down every night. This morning he staid till after breakfast. Mr. Henry at sleep. Zona sitting by playing & singing. Pinck at play & Willie gone to church, Aunt Tena & Atheline took him. I must see about dinner. We have turnips today the first. Also possum. Mrs. Vance, Mr. Henry, David, Pinck & I went to the field to see them on dress parade. They did not parade as it looked like rain. Mr. Renolds preached a very good serman in the field. We sat on the ground or rather most of them did. Mrs. Vance & I & some others sit on a rail, when we got back Mrs. Jarvis was here, came to board a week and one child. Capt. Jarvis wife & Atheline had the children upon the field this morning.

Monday 21st October 1861 - All are well, rather a damp day but Mrs. Vance, Mrs. Jarvis, David, Pinck & I went to the camps this evening. I cut out Willie some gowns, nearly made one today.

Tuesday 22nd - Sewed on gowns, finished one but did not begin the other. Gloomy day. Nothing new going on. Mrs. Robertson staid here last night. All are well.

Wednesday 23rd - Mrs. Vance & Mrs. Robertson left this morning for Asheville. Mrs. Jervis spent the day at camps so I was alone. No, Mrs. Jervis was here for dinner, also Leut. Henry & a Roberts (the acting adjutant). We had turkey & duck for dinner. I made some tatting today.

Thursday 24th - Mrs. Vance & Mrs. Robertson come back this evening, staid all night. Cold and a big frost this morning killing potatoe's tops. Our turnips are large enough to eat. Mrs. Jervis at camps today, no one here for dinner but Pinck & I. Made Willie a gown.

Friday 25th - Killed a turkey but did not cook it as all the ladies went to camps. I made Willie another gown out of an old (?) tail. Mrs. Vance went home this evening to stay. Mrs. Robertson stays in her room now. Mr. Henry & I went to the mill dam lake this evening. He has been in Asheville all day. They have got the dam so they can grind. He got some sugar & soda, also two leather belts. Soda is 40 cts. a lb. & coffee 50 cts. per lb. Mail came this morning, nothing new. The Regiment here is to leave on Monday for Raleigh & then to Wilmington they think.

Saturday 26th - Rain all day. I made my apron Cousin Mary Moore gave me. Mrs. Robertson & Mrs. Jervis intended to go to camps but it rained all day. Mr. Henry made 24 sacks for mill. Capt. Creasmon dined here today, had turkey for dinner & duck. Capt. Robertson came tonight, very wet. He was quite sick in the night, had cramp collic. Mill run tonight some time, got our rolls from machine today. Got the sewing machine needles yesterday 8 for 1$, also a letter from Lou. She has lost another babe, miscarriage. I had a letter from Dora & Matt last Monday. All well. They are going to make them some cotton dresses. They sent me a piece of palmetto to wear on my bonnet, & some wild violets.

Sunday 27th – Capt. Robertson not up yet. He had cramp collic last night. Mrs. Jarvis left this morning for home. Mrs. Robertson has just come from the camps. Mr. Henry went with her, he is not come yet. She went to get clean clothes for her old man. I must go and see about dinner as we are going to have duck for dinner. All are well, nothing new going on. No one here for dinner but Mr. Henry & I & the children. Capt. Robertson & wife went to the camps for dinner. Mr. Henry bought a fine chance of chestnuts today for me & the children. The other day Zona came in with a stick saying she was going to shoot the yankees. She is a sprightly child, so is Pinck. Willie is growing finely, very much like Pinck was when he was little.

We all went to the old field this evening to see them on dress parade, had a very good serman delivered by Dr. Chapman, the presbyterian minister of Asheville. It was rather cool up there. They had dress parade after service. It was late when we got home. There was a good many people out. Last ones started, the others went to the camps. He & I only went to the old field. I had to carry Zona part of the way. Mr. Henry over at camps. I did not get back till 1 o'clock. Mr. Henry went to Asheville with the Regiment. It was 3 o'clock before the negroes got dinner as all hands & the cook had to see them start.

Tuesday 29th - Mr. Henry & I went to Asheville to see the regiments leave. It was an imposing sight. Not near so many as there was to see the 25th Regiment leave. I did some shopping, made a bill of some 10$ pale as I went though as I think it is the best way. Got myself a calico dress for which I had to pay 22 cts. per yard, dear enough. I also got some bed ticking. We rode very fast going to Asheville. I went horseback. I was afraid to lope at first but I soon got over that. I rode John & Mr. Henry the gray colt. We got back about 1 o'clock. Mr. Henry got Pinck some boots & a hat. Pinck went with John in wagon. He took some flour. We got three wooden buckets, two for milk & one for me a water bucket.

Wednesday 30th October 1861 - I made Jinnie a bonnet & Pinck a pair of jean pants. Was busy all day. I cut out some shirts for Charley. Atheline sewing on them. Charley is not well today. Aunt Tena thinks it is from eating sugar cane as they have been cutting it down. Stanopher Jones makes it up for half. I have been very sore all day from my ride yesterday.

Thursday 31st - I sewed some on Charlie's shirts & cut out pants for the negro men. Mrs. Fanning got 4 3/4 lbs. of tack rolls on Monday. She has been spinning them. Cloudy, looks like rain. The hands been sowing wheat. George at the mill.

November 1861

Friday Nov. 1st - Cloudy & drisly rain all day. Mail brought no news. There has been a little battle at Leesburg, some 300 killed & wounded on our side & 1000 or 1200 on the other. We got no letters today.

Saturday 2nd - Rained all night. The mill dam broke again, not badly washed this time. We have had so much rain this fall. Every new moon we have a freshet. I made Jim a pair of pants today. Cloudy still.

Sunday 3rd November 1861 - Cool this morning. Jinnie has been sick with sore throat since Friday but is nearly well now. Charlie is still on foot but not well. My little dear ones are very well. Mr. Henry & I went to the mill dam this morning, staid but a short time as it is very cool. This wind blows a spanking gale. The trees will soon be leafless. They are nearly all off, at least they are scared enough to fall. Drearry, gloomy winter is upon us & it is impossible for me to stay here without Mr. Henry. If he goes to the war I will have to break up housekeeping, which I should hate to do for I have things so comfortable in my household. The children are up at Mammy's house. Mr. Henry is down before the fire on a pallet asleep. He generally takes a nap on Sunday. Old Quinn bought us some cider for vinegar last week. I fear it will do no good as it has water in it. I know I must stop & go see my baby. He is such a dear good baby. Mr. Henry got up & went off while I was at Aunt Tena's house, gone till night hunting up hogs. I was alone with my little ones. A fair day & pleasant.

Monday 4th November 1861 - I felt very unwell all day with headache but made two pair pants for negroes and attended to Willie as Atheline cooked. Jinnie & Fannie ploughing trying to get in wheat. All well but Charlie, he has measles. None of the others taken them yet.

Tuesday 5th - I went to Tilda Morris' today, took Atheline & Willie. Took the headache & staid all night. Atheline came home to tell them & brought Zona back with her. All well. A bare frost this morning. Mr. Henry in the field till dark.

Wednesday 6th - Mr. Henry came by to see me. He went on to the election. Henry Thomas & A. Davidson running for Congress. I came to A. B. Jones' & spent the day. Finished my stocking, all the work I took. Came home late in the evening, found all well, the house torn up somewhat. Mr. Henry had a horse brought for me to Jones'. Charlie getting better, Hanes complaining. Heavy frost, high winds all day. Mr. Henry did not get home till sundown as he was one of the judges of the election.

Thursday 7th November 1861 - I began the children some bonnetts today. Willie fretful, did but little at it. Atheline cooks. Fannie did it while I was gone. I got a saque coat pattern from Mrs. Jones for the negroes. Also a cap pattern for little boys. George complaining. I guess 'tis measles. Hands ploughing. Jim Night came Tuesday to plough for Mr. Henry, will work all the week.

Friday 8th - Mail came, nothing new going on. Rained some today. I quilted on the bonnetts, finished Zona's, began Willie's. Mary Rollins & Henry Cook's wife here for letters. Also Mrs. Pettit, Mrs. Norman & Sue Patton. They hear from their husbands every week the two first. Mr. Henry had a letter from Pinck Allen, have some fever & measles in the Regiment. None of the whites have measles here yet.

Saturday 9th - Gloomy day. I made Willie's bonnet. Atheline & I scoured the pantry. I stopped the three gallon vinegar and it broke the molasses all on the floor or at least 1/2 gallon. They were working the course of it. Frank Ellison came here today just from the 6th Regiment. They are doing better than they have been doing. Poor fellows. There is still room for improvement. George getting better, also Hanes & Charles. The measles very light so far. Fannie complaining. Measles I guess. Some rain today, not much. Some yesterday. Warmer than has been. Mr. Henry begins to work on his dam Monday.

Sunday 10th - Pleasant this morning. Mr. Henry, Pinck & I went up to Quinn's. Mr. Henry went to get some rosin to grease his shoes. Did not get any. Came back it was twelve o'clock. Dinner at one o'clock. Mr. Henry has been lying before the fire ever since dinner, has taken a cold. The others all well but negroes complaining with measles. Fannie has them. A hog got sick today, nothing serious I think. A beautiful day, warm & pleasant. Old Quinn is here at this time. Mr. Henry has got up & talking to Quinn. We heard yesterday of a large fleet of yankees going south.

Monday 11th November 1861 - Warm & pleasant. I made Zona a quilt. Mr. Henry bought some jeans from old Mrs. Bates for pants. No other news. The mail boy brought the news tonight that the yankee fleet had landed at Port Royal Beufort Dist. I fear they will be troublesome yet & it really seems our people are dying by doing nothing letting Lincoln's men come among us. Report 13,000 landed.

Tuesday 12th - I made Mr. Henry a pair of pants, those he got yesterday. I was busy all day. Willie a little fretful. Mr. Henry went to Asheville today, got my new shoes. They are a little too large. He got some thread to make some jeans for Mr. Henry. Mrs. Fanning has been working at the new loom doing but little good.

Wednesday 13th - I began Jinnie some chemise. Mrs. Fanning worked at the loom doing no good. Mrs. Stanapher Jones brought my jeans harness home. She has made them for me for which I paid 75 cts. The wind is blowing a good deal. I had a letter from Lou yesterday saying Aunt Sallie was dead. I am very sorry. Today we took the cloth out of the new loom & put it in the old loom. It does very well. We took the same harness & slay. It weaves in flatts. Mrs. Fanning is getting along very well. I was quite unwell in the evening, had to lay down before the fire with cold & headache. Atheline is very unwell, cold I reckon. The wind is blowing a good deal today.

Friday 15th - Mail came this morning. Nothing new going on. I sewed on Jinnie's chemise. Willie fretful, I guess teething. Zona & Pinck are both very well, they are dear good children. They have not taken measles yet. Atheline sick.

Saturday 16th - I finished Jinnie's doings & knit on a very coarse sock for Mr. Henry. I don't think he will wear them they are so coarse. Sue Sutton was here yesterday evening saying Ham Rollins has come back from the wars, they have not been in battle yet.

Sunday 17th - Nothing new going on in the country. Every thing is excitement. We see it reported that Andy Johnston is going to try to come through East Tennessee & steal & plunder what they can. All the time two o'clock & past it is cloudy as if it might rain or snow. It is cold & the wind blowing. Yesterday the wind blew light all day. Matt Crook is here today, he eat dinner here today. He is as funny as ever. After he left Mr. Henry & I went to dam & over in pinto field. It was rather cool.

Monday 18th - Nothing new. I made Hanes & Lonzo a pair of pants out of the cloth wove in new loom as I think will not last long. My dear little ones are well. Pinck a good boy. Zona rather hard headed & Willie is the last child I have had. Atheline does the cooking. There are some three or four hands at mill dam. They grind all the time now. Mr. Henry wants to get his dam secure before cold weather. The others ploughing.

Tuesday 19th - I cut out Jim & John a coat & made Jim's cut of the cloth. Mrs. Fanning wove in old loom. I worked faithful all day and attended Willie. Mr. Henry went to Asheville yesterday also today. Harrie Deaver in Asheville quite sick, relaps of measles. Looks badly.

Wednesday November 20 1861 - I got up with headache. I had it a little last night & eat a harty supper so I was quite sick all day. I sewed a little on John's coat, not much & lay down the rest of the day. Mr. Henry staid in the room nearly all this evening. Hanes took Willie to the kitchen & kept him. He did very well with him. Jinnie got supper. I bathed my feet about sundown but no relief..

Thursday 21st - Head not well yet, some better. I feel very feeble this morning, lay down part of the day. Hanes attended to Willie. The family all well. Mr. Henry in the house part of the day. He seems very anxious if I am in distress. I think he cares a good deal for his Dinah. My head got easy in the evening. I lay down before the fire & took a nap. Betsey McKinnish got 9 1/2 lbs. of rolls today. She is an old woman that lives at the foot of Mt. Yeaden or thereabout.

Friday 22nd - Nothing new. Cold & raining a misty rain. I had a letter from Sister Jane. All are well. A good many letters comes here now as nearly every one about here has friends gone. They have a battle nearly every week in VA., the Confederates gain the day. I made Jim's coat today. Broke my machine, not much only the reel that holds the spool in slipping out. Newt Taylor fixed it this evening so I can go along tomorrow with my sewing. Taylor moved yesterday to one of the cabins on the hill yesterday. I have not seen Mary, nor do I care to see her. That part of Mr. Henry's family have never treated me with any kindred feeling so I shall not trouble myself about them.

Saturday 23rd - Mr. Henry went to Asheville today. Nothing new. He walked as it was so cold. It rained a good deal last night. Not enough to raise the creek. Very cold & windy this morning. I got up at 5 o'clock, rather soon for me. Mr. Henry is an early riser, so are the children. I made Hanes a coat today out of that sleazy cloth. I have no idea how it will look. Got it done by two o'clock & then done Sunday mendings. Mr. Henry came home late nearly sundown. Willie has been fretful today. Hanes attended to him. I made two sacks for mill this morning.

Sunday 24th - Zonnie has the measles broke out all over her this morning. The rest all well. A very cold morning, ice nearly an inch thick in the piazza. Heavy frost but at this time 'tis pleasant in the sun. Nearly twelve. Mr. Henry is sitting here reading, the children up at Murrey's house. Our circuit preacher's name is Smith.

He preaches every three weeks on Tuesday. I expect his congregation will be small. I never know when he does preach till after it is over. I wrote a long letter to Dora & Matt this evening.

Monday 25th - I made Alonzo a coat. Took me nearly all day. Mr. Henry went to Asheville. Cold & windy. Hands pulling turnips in hotel garden.

Tuesday 26th - I made Pinck a pair pants. Went up to the hotel garden after dinner. They are still gathering turnips. I found two five dollar bills some poor volunteer had lost I guess. Rather cool but calm.

Wednesday 27th - I got up at 4 o'clock & took some pills as I had the headache. I had it all day, did but little work or none scarcely.

Thursday 28th - I got up soon after 4 o'clock & actually staid in the kitchen till breakfast was ready to come on the table. Fannie not well yet. Mr. Henry attributes my early rising to the pills & says I must take more. Finished turnips and commenced digging irish potatoes more than half of which was rotten. I began a net for my head. All well.

Friday 29th - Mr. Henry went to Bent Creek after some rent corn from J. H. Green with his waggons. Mail brought no news this morning. The bat'l opened at Pensacola but did not last long. "Nobody hurt" but little damage done to the Confederates. Mr. Boyd brought up the spinning jinnie. We have not learned to spin on it yet. Fannie got dinner today. Mr. Henry came home late in the evening. He went to Asheville yesterday, got the children some dates. I finished my net.

Saturday 30th - Cold & snowing, warm in the first part of the night. Willie was feverish, did not rest well. I still get up soon & stay in the kitchen till breakfast. The negroes had their corn husking last night. Mr. Henry took 45 lbs. of meal & 10 sacks of flour. The meal was the darkies. I covered Pinck's & Zona's stools over & made Mr. Henry a candle screen. Willie fretful. Hands shucked corn. Tena went up to the Baptist meeting on Hominy.

December 1861

December 1st Sunday - The biggest frost of the season. Mr. Henry & I want to go to see Burt Starnes baptised. Too cold to go. Bill Green came to borrow the buggy to go after Amos Green's wife as his remains are to be interred tomorrow at the Willis grave yard. He died at Suffolk of fever, much lamented by the whole company. He joined the second company (Vance's) from Buncombe. Mr. Henry & I went to the dam this evening & then up to see the fattening hogs. He has 46. Some of them very fat & large.

December 2nd Monday - All well. Fannie & I tried to work the spinning jinny but did no good. I quit at about 11 o'clock. After dinner I cut out some shirts for Pinck out of unbleached sheeting. The first of the kind he has had. I sewed some on them. Mr. Henry gone with the waggon to Burt Starnes after corn he owes him.

Tuesday 3rd December 1861 - I sewed on shirts, finished one began another. Betsy McKinish came here this morning, worked at the spinning machine till dinner. No good come with it. Mrs. Tom Cook here today to get some flour for her corn shucking, got it. I took some pills this evening as my head feels badly. Hands ploughing in wheat. Willie has got well, not much sick at all. The other little ones with Newton Taylor preparing waggons & mules to go to salt works. Mr. Henry speaks of going. Amos Green buried this evening, Papa went.

Wednesday 4th - Cold as crout. I sewed on shirts, finished another & began the last one. I intended to go to Amos Green's burial yesterday evening. Went to the mill but it was sun down before they came along with him so I came back. Mr. Henry went. It was dark when he got back. My head feels better today.

Thursday 5th - Finished the last one of Pinck's shirts which makes three. Cut out one for Mr. Henry as he will need one or more if he goes to the salt works. Began him another pair of socks which I must finish by next Tuesday. Willie fretful.

Friday Dec 6th 1861 - Mail came earlier than usual. Nothing new. They are making every preparation for a big battle at Manassas. The 6th Regiment has gone there. Poor fellows, they have had a hard time in Western Virginia. I hope their lot will be success in the coming struggle. They well deserve a glorious victory. G. W. Peake is in the Regiment. I felt very unwell all day, was sick at night with headache. Matilda Morris spent the day here, helped me on Mr. Henry's shirt. I got his done about 4 o'clock & went to bed soon after. I got no letters today from any of my friends.

7th December Saturday - Sick all day with headache. Mr. Henry went to Asheville with waggon. John drove, took some meal & flour for volunteers. Came back at night. I knit a little on his sock, felt too bad to work much. Jinnie sick with headache all day. Killed three hogs yesterday, let Tom Hendrix have one small one. The sausage meat & lard will lay by till Monday. Had the Stines loom taken down today or rather Elijah Knight & Peter Guy took it down tonight. My head nearly well. Mr. Henry got me some cephalic pills today at Asheville.

Sunday Dec. 8th - A beautiful day. I came down on the branch to write, the sun shines very warm & pleasant. I hear the rippling of the branch whilst I write. It is music to my ear. I left Ham Cannon in the room with Mr. Henry so he will not miss me much. Aunt Tena has taken the children

Gen. Robert B. Vance
(Courtesy of the North Carolina Office of
Archives and History, Raleigh, NC)

down to Elijah Knight's. Willie too. Atheline & Charlie gone to see their Aunt at Mrs. Miller's. It is such a beautiful day. I want to be out walking. I think Mr. Henry & I will take a good long walk after dinner if he does not take his afternoon nap. I am owing several letters which I must answer today. Mr. Henry heard yesterday that W. B. Neilson was shot & Charlie Neilson a prisoner by the Union men of East Ten. R. B. Vance's Regiment is reported to have been in a fight near Newport Ten. I reckon Sister Jane is in a peck of trouble. I feel very sorry for her for I guess she has but few to sympathise with her in her troubles. Oh war is an awful thing to contemplate & we are in the midst of a cruel one. Winston Smith came here today to look at Mr. Henry's hogs. He thinks he will take them. Mr. Henry & I went down to Mrs. Fanning's this evening. She has just began that cloth & then we went up by the stable & back by the hog pen. Some of the hogs are nice & fat. It will soon be bed time. Mr. Henry wants me to fix Willie to bed now as he has him in his lap so good night this time.

Monday 9th - I knit all day on a sock for Mr. Henry. He wants to start to the salt works Wednesday. He is gone to Asheville today. Pleasant day. Bets McKinnish brought 9 1/2 lbs. of wool today. It made 25 yards, & got more wool 13 3/4 lbs. to spin coarse. Mrs. Norman here this evening also Mrs. Fanning a little while. Willie not well, has a cold. Finished one sock, only knit the foot & part of the heel. I can't make my living by knitting.

Tuesday 10th - Mr. Henry heard yesterday no salt at salt lick. The government bought it for two months so going to try some other market. I began to turn my old calico dress bottom side up to make them last a little longer as calico dear to purchase now. Willie a little pill. Hanes can't do anything with him.

Wednesday 11th - Finished one dress today began another. Willie won't let me sew half the time, so cross. Nothing of interest going on. Fannie is cooking. Jim Parker had to thrash some of the negroes yesterday evening & Jim ran away last night. Jim Parker started after him this morning. Ground the sausage Monday & rendered up the lard. I emptied it this evening or helped Fannie do it. Mr. Henry held Willie. Cool today.

Thursday 12th - Sewed on old dresses, not done yet. Will not get through this week. Mr. Henry sent Taylor & Jim Night on Turkey Creek for apples, will be back tomorrow night to (?) & to Augusta Saturday. Nothing of interest going on. Fannie went to Miss Tutt's this evening to borrow her wheels to spin her stocking yarn and Tena washing. The hands still sowing wheat & gathering corn.

Friday 13th - Mail came & nothing new. Rather cold. I got no letters. Finished another old dress today in the evening. Fannie cooked some meat & baked biscuits for them to take on the road. Taylor & Knight got back at dark to start tomorrow. Jim Parker came also but no Jim yet. Fannie cooked some chitlans this evening. Mr. Henry is very fond of them.

Saturday 14th - I knit all day, got the last sock done. Nearly sun down, knit the foot today. Willie is getting a little better. I had the headache yesterday & the day before but did not go to bed with it. Took some cephalic pills Thursday evening which perhaps prevent a severe attack. The waggon tongue broke yesterday evening just as they started so Taylor will not get off till Monday, middle of the day. Had everything ready to start, the provisions all packed.

Sunday 15th - A heavy frost this morning but pleasant after. Mr. Henry & I went down to the mill then to Mrs. Fanning's to see the jeans. He don't like it much because there is too much hair in the wool. It is the mixed he don't like. It is made of the wool Mrs. Parker sent home, was poor. I guess she picked out all the fine & left the coarse. Mr. Henry went up by the stables to Mary Taylor's. She lives in one of the cabbins. She has two children Pinck & [Mollie?], very nice little ones.

They resemble their father a great deal. Jim Parker went after Jim again this morning. I don't much think he will get him. We took breakfast in my room this morning as it was so cold. Mr. Henry eat a hardy meal of chitlans. He is going to Augusta, starts a few days after the waggons. Says he is going to camp out with the waggoners. I fear he will get sick. Old Mrs. Capt. Moore called here yesterday evening & staid an hour or so to see some of her friends that is sick on the other side of Asheville. Willie getting better of his cold. Pinck & Zona went with me this morning in our tramp. They are sweet children & dear little Willie was so glad to see me when I come back. Nothing of interest the rest of the day. Bill Petitt staid till late in the evening. Ham Cannon was here after dinner.

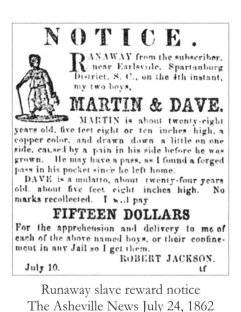

Runaway slave reward notice
The Asheville News July 24, 1862

Monday 16th 1861 December - Bright & frosty. The waggons started about 12 o'clock. I did but little work till they got off. Began to turn my side stripe dress upside down. Capt. Davidson's daughter & two other men eat dinner here today after we were done. One of the men has had John Smith's horse. Mrs. Common came here yesterday evening with negro Jim. Jim Parker met them on this road. He came home that night. Mary Taylor was here this morning after some cards to bat cotton for a quilt, got George's from the mill. Mr. Henry about the farm & mill.

Tuesday 17th - Finished my dress this evening. All are well. Mrs. Common left this morning. Cold & frosty. Sarah Jarrett called here yesterday & mailed some letters for Mrs. Matilda Morris. No one here today.

Wednesday 18th - Mr. Henry went to Asheville today, got some dates for children & 6 lbs. sugar. It is selling at one dollar for 6 lbs. Mr. Henry started this morning about nine o'clock going to market. I hated to see him leave for I doat on him so much. Things don't go well when he is away. George is troublesome when he is not here & all the negroes in general. They don't like to obey me. Old Parker brought three hogs from old Cochrum yesterday, one weighing 83 the other two 94. Quite small. Mr. Henry will nearly overtake the waggons tomorrow if not quite. Mrs. Fanning will stay with me at night. Atheline staid in the house today till dinner, swept the yards. An old man named O. Kelly stays here tonight. He came to see Mr. Henry about making some rye whiskey for Dr. Hardy. Nothing of interest going on. Reuben Fulbright is dead. He belonged to Bob Love's company from Haywood. I had a letter from Dora & Matt yesterday. All are well. They sent me a sample of their new cotton dresses. It looks nice, rather coarse. They said Gad Thomas was dead, died in the hospital in Charlottesville Va. Our poor soldiers are dying from disease terably. I saw in the paper the other day that they had burried 1900 in western Virginia in the place where the 6th Regiment was. They had a hard time of it, poor fellows.

Thursday Dec 19th 1861 - I put velvet round the skirt of Atheline's dress yesterday & across the bosom. Sue Sutton came here today to twist some thread for Mary Taylor. She is staying there while Taylor is gone. She came here last Tuesday to get some needles. They must need a heap of the comforts of life. I feel sorry for Mary, she once seen better days. I don't think she will get much work out of Sue as she is lazy enough for anything. Jim Parker moved in the other cabbin up there yesterday & Peter Guy in his house. The place is lousy with people.

Friday 20th - Mail came today, no news of consequence. I expected a letter from Sister Jane but was disappointed. Several letters came but none for me. Both divisions of the army are quiet now, no fighting. I cut out Zona's red flannel dress yesterday. I am trimming it with red checked velvet. The skirt & a little sack sewed in with the body. I finished it today by twelve. I sewed some on it last night. I have commenced Willie's clouded stockings, red & white. Fannie ground sausage yesterday, put in two hams, the lean of them. She has made it too hot & today she ground another ham to mix with it of the little hogs. I had the headache all day a little & after dinner. I took a nap in the little cradle but found no relief. It pained all night. Atheline sleeps in the room since Mr. Henry has been gone. I did not put the hooks & eyes on Zona's dress as my head pained me so badly.

Saturday 21st - I finished daughter's dress though my head pains me yet. Jim Parker & some of the hands killed eight hogs today. The fattest of them. They are very nice. They only split them open, will cut them up Monday. I knit a little on Willie's stocking. Mrs. Fanning knitted at night on one & I on the other. She narrowed hers too slow so I had it to take out today. My head got easy after supper. It is so lonesome here when Mr. Henry is gone. That old crazy Herrel staid here last Tuesday night. I fear he will come while Mr. Henry is gone & it would frighten me to death nearly.

Sunday Dec. 22nd 1861 - This is a cold cloudy morning, looks like snow. The city of Charleston was burned on the 11th & 12th inst. About six hundred houses. What a fearful calamity to the inhabitants. It seems to have been an accident. Far better to be that way than an incediary. I pitty them for we once had a destructive fire here. I shall have to stay in doors all day as Mr. Henry is not here to go walking about with me. I miss him a great deal. He is so kind to me & the little ones. I had to send for George this morning to come & get us some meal, also wood. He has not got it when he should. He will be a heap of trouble while Mr. Henry is gone. I fear he is not too obedient when he is at home & now he thinks he is free. I must now go out about dinner as 'tis going on 11 o'clock & I have nothing of interest to continue. Mrs. Fanning will be here I guess as she said she would soon. Betts McKinnish brought home the spun thread of 13 1/2 lbs. wool yesterday. Got some hands to find me some stocking yarn, black & 5 broaches of white. Mrs. Fanning did not come till after she eat her dinner so no one to eat but Pinck, Zona & I. Obazena came with her to get some apples. It sprinkled rain a little in the evening. Very cold wind from South East. Five volunteers came after we had eat supper, staid all night, left before breakfast & paid a dollar for staying & supper. They frightened me for I thought it was old crazy Herrel. They were from Clay Co., this state. One of them said he knew Mr. Henry. They said old Mr. Henry was well as they had seen him.

Monday 23rd - Mail came along this evening. Nothing new. Fannie & Atheline scoured today. The wind blew from the north. Very, very cold. The piazzas both froze after they done them. Aunt Tena rendering up lard, got a nice chance. Jinnie getting dinner. I knit on Willie's little clouded stockings before dinner, got one done. I also helped cut up some fat. I arranged the room after dinner. Hanes attended to Willie. Atheline & I fixed the flower vases up, put cedar in flour & made flower pots. I made Zona a doll at night. I had rockers put to a box for a cradle for her Christmas gift. They talk all the time about Santa Clause coming.

Tuesday 24th - I was sick all day with headache. I eat some apples after supper last night which I think was the cause. I had it very badly. I hemmed some three hankerchiefs out of old table cloth in the morning & went to bed about 11 o'clock. Fannie got dinner & ground sassauge meat. Aunt Tena finished lard. Jinnie shucking corn. All hands getting ready for Christmas. Jim & John went home today. Very cold but not so cold as yesterday. Very still. It rained a good deal Sunday night but not enough to raise the creek. Clear at day by Monday but snowed a little through the day. This has been a bright day all day, sun shines warm. At night Mrs. Fanning made Jinnie & Atheline a horse head. They gave Charlie a skin & then went up to frighten Mary Taylor & Jim Parker's folks as they both live in the cabbins on the hill. They did frighten Mary Taylor & Jim Parker, give them a race with a dough face & sheet. It was after 11 o'clock before Atheline came in but the clock is too fast. We went to bed just before 11. I put some chestnuts & dates in the children's stockings, a knife & ball in Pinck's, also some fire crackers. He hung one of his socks up for Obazena as she staid here last night. I fixed Zona's doll in the cradle. My head got better in the evening. Mrs. Night got a lb. of butter here this evening. I gave it to her as Mrs. Fanning is kind enough to come & stay with me at night while Mr. Henry is gone. She also got 1/2 gal. molasses. The children well. Atheline attending Willie. She put up the window curtains today in my room. They were washed last week. I must stop now & write for Christmas day as I am writing this on the 25th late at night 12 o'clock.

December 25 Wednesday 1861 - Christmas day. The children were up by 6 o'clock to see what Santa Clause had brought. They enjoyed their good things fine.

Zona don't seem to care much about her doll, says that don't matter when Pinck showed it to her. Pinck is affraid to shoot his crackers. I got a few from Uncle Sam for him. I ironed some this morning. My head well. Abbe Parker came here this morning to borrow a sley but did not get it. Jim Parker here today. I regulated the clock while he was here, it run too fast. Fannie made the liver pudding today & fixed the guts up to dry & some for chitlins. Andy went to Asheville. I sent by him & got 25 cts. worth of candy, a paper of crackers & 1 lb. of coffee at 80 cts. a lb., a dear drink. I cut out a new dress this evening for myself, took the frills down to Mrs. Fanning's after dinner & hemmed them while I staid. No one here for dinner but Zona & I. Fannie made us some nice coffee, her own. I eat hearty of it & brains & corn bread. Fannie cleaned the sausauge grinder this evening.

This day one year ago Tilda Jones & her mother spent the day here. Now Till is married & her brother Dilla dead. Many a poor soul has passed away in the last year in camps. Jinnie, Atheline & Charlie went to Asheville this morning. Jinnie to come back tomorrow evening & the others Friday. Fannie is to cook two days & Jinnie two. I give Fannie 15 cts. for her day's work today. I have sewed up my dress skirt tonight & it is now going on 11 o'clock so I must quit & put something in the children's stockings as they think Santa Clause is coming, so good night.

Dec 26th Thursday - The children had some candy & crackers in their stockings, even little Willie had cake & some candy. Pinck cracked some of his. Jim Parker, one of Johnston's negroes worked today, also Peter Guy ploughing in wheat. Mr. Henry is putting in a great deal of wheat. I made the sleeves of my dress & hemmed the skirt on the machine. I sewed some at night on the waist. I swept the yard this morning & repiled the shingles at the end of the house. Hanes attended to Willie. I helped Fannie make some cake this morning. She has company today, Andy's children & mother-in-law. It was late when we went to bed. The children's stockings up again. Obazena staid here last night & is here tonight. Mrs. Night not at home. Zona is anxious to see her Pappa, says she can go tot a tot down to "Souf tallisia" after him. I have heard from him last Saturday. All well, getting on finely. I hope they may have fine weather & dispose of the apples to unadvantaged. I paid Miss Peggy Tutt the money that Capt. Creassman left for her today. Jinnie slept in the house.

Friday 27th - I had a letter from Mr. Henry today. He was in Greenville, was well. Taylor had broken his waggon tongue again but had them started on. I had a letter from Sister Ell also. Fowler[34] has gone to the war down about Beaufort. Matt & Sallie were with her when she wrote. They were all well. She said Pa was in a heap of trouble. I guess about the war. I sewed some on my dress. Finished it at night. Atheline & Charlie came home this evening. James Patten Sr. died last night in Asheville. He has been an invalid a long time. Pinck had a fever last night & Zona is feverish tonight. Willie well. The children got a little candy & cakes in their stockings last night. I guess Santa Clause is getting tired of coming. I told them if they hung them up tonight he would carry them off so they go to bed contented. Fannie gone to Morris' so Jinnie & Atheline both sleep in the house. Andy began

---

[34] Gasaway Fowler, husband of Elmira Ann (Ell) Smith

to fix the chimney. Tim Starnes helping him. Parker & Guy ploughing in wheat. Cold & windy.

Saturday 28th - I went to church today at the Academy, was the first one there. Got frightened at A. B. Jones, thought he was old Herrel. The circuit preacher Smith delivered a tollerable fair sermon. Not many out, though it was a bright day. Some what cold but we had a fire. When I got back it was nearly two o'clock. Bets McKinnish was here, brought home my stocking yarn. She took 12 lbs. of wool home with her. I am glad Christmas is done for the negroes for I can't get anything done by them. Mrs. Fanning got the jeans out this evening, near twenty nine yrds, a good piece as I have seen lately. Her & I finished Pinck's sock tonight. She has been knitting on them. It was ten o'clock before we lay down. I knit some on Atheline's stocking also. I wore my new calico dress to church today. It is surplus neck with a frill around. Zona has a sore hand. She knocked up a piece of skin with the hammer before Mr. Henry left & has caught cold in it I fear. She cries all the time. I am dressing it.

Sunday 29th - This is a cold clear morning. Very calm & sun shines warm. We had late breakfast. Rach Allen here this morning to get her letter, came while we were at breakfast. Willie is asleep at this time. Pinck & Zona rather noisey running through the house. I hope Mr. Henry will be here before next Sunday. I shall look for him on Saturday next. Willie got up on his hands & knees last Monday, his first attempt to crawl. He gets down on his stomach since & before & gets along some. Now he has just woke up. I must stop & take him to Atheline & get out dinner for it is nearly 11 o'clock.

I went down to Mrs. Fanning's after I got out dinner, only staid a short time. Came back & sent Charlie to feed those hogs in the pen down at the mill for George don't half feed them. No one here for dinner but Pinck, Zona & I. We had ribs for dinner. I eat heartily. I wrote a long letter to Lou before dinner & began one to Dora & Matt. Mrs. Fanning came up after two. Her & I went up to see Mary Taylor. Staid till nearly sun down. Jinnie had wretched coffee for supper. I sent her after some hickorys intended to flog her but got too tender hearted when she came back crying so I could not whip her. I have finished Dora's & Matt's letter tonight & read some in my bible. I have read it nearly through the second time. I am reading in Corinithians now. It is getting on near bed time so I will soon stop. Mrs. Fanning is reading in the bible now. My dear little ones are all asleep. Willie the last to go to sleep. He is a dear good babe. There is none of them bad children. Oh may they be as much pleasure in my old age as now. I will raise them up the best I can & I pray they will reward my trouble I have had with them when they were little. I now close for tonight, will write soon again.

Monday 30th - Cool & a heavy frost. I went to the mill. George wanted me to look over E. P. Knight's account. He thought Knight was getting along too fast. I guess it will be all right when Mr. Henry gets home & how I want to see him. Emaline Murray spent the day here, had a nice dinner & even coffee for dinner. I made me a course skirt of shirting on the machine today. It worked finely. I sprinkled the jeans this morning. All are well. Jim set in the morning to work. John not come.

Tuesday Dec. 31st 1861 - The last day of the old year dawned fair & frosty, warm when the sun got up, balmy like Spring. There has many a promising youth began this year full of life & vigour, that have not lived to see the old year out. God grant them peace is my prayer. No prospect of peace soon. England is kicking up a pompus about the capture of Mason & Slidell. I hope Lincoln may hold on to them & then woe be to the North.

I cut Pinck a jeans coat but did not make it all today. Hanes nursed Willie. He attends to him now every day. Atheline works out. Fannie does the cooking.

Page from Cornelia Henry's journal dated
December 31, 1861 and January 1, 1862

Pisgah View from hotel site
(North Carolina Collection, Pack Memorial Public Library, Asheville, NC)

1862

"...We are determined to be a free people ... we have got our freedom to fight for a second time..."

January 1862

January 1st Wednesday - New Year's day. Spring like all day. We have had no cold weather of any consequence this winter. I finished Pinck's coat & began a vest for Uncle Sam. Mrs. Fanning went to Asheville. I sent & got some coat buttons for Mr. Henry's coat. They were not good but a pretty button. Tilda Morris here a few minutes today. They have had a skirmish on the Potomac. Several of our men killed. We retreated.

Thursday January 2nd 1862 - I finished the vest after dinner & helped Fannie empty lard. I blistered my hand. My head aches a good deal tonight. Mrs. Fanning spooled here half the day & warped after dinner the jeans for negro's clothes. All are well. A beautiful day. Nothing of interest going on. Dr. Hilliard sent & got two turkeys here last Monday. He is on furlough. P. H. Thrash is expected home soon.

Friday 3rd - Mail came, no news. I had a letter from Mr. Henry today. He is quite well. Was in Greenwood S. C. the 25th, going to Augusta the 26th. I suffered all day with headache, in bed part of the day. Read all the papers but nothing new. The children all well, staid out all day on account of my head.

Saturday 4th - I was busy all day. I swept the yards in the morning & began to sew about 9. I made 11 double napkins for Willie. One side good cloth, the other old table linnen. I hemmed one after night & Mrs. Fanning & I doubled some thread out of thumbs. Atheline & Jim married tonight. They did it on the sly order. Mrs. Fanning & I went down to Fannie's house to see it. No one but Fannie & Jinnie for witnesses. We took Zona as she was up. Pinck & Willie asleep. Aunt Tena & Uncle Sam hostile about it. They did not know it till it was over. I feel sorry for them. They are faithful servants. I don't know what Jim & wife will do for a bed as Parker has gone to J. R. Love's after more hands. He started this morning. John not come yet, will be here tomorrow. I think I did not get to sleep till near 12. Jinnie slept in the house tonight & Jim & Atheline had her bed. Got done sowing wheat today. The corn not in yet. Rather cool today.

Sunday 5th - Jinnie got up very soon before 5 this morning & Willie woke soon after. I called Atheline just after 5, also Fannie. We eat by candle light this morning. A wonder for the cloudy & misty rain today. Mr. Reynolds preached to the negroes today at the Academy. I shall not go. 10 o'clock I must see about dinner soon. Pinck going to church with Jinnie. Cool & misty rain all day. Pinck & Jinnie went to church but few out. It has been a long tiresome day for me. Mr. Henry came this evening, did but little trading in Augusta as everything was up so high. Salt $16.20 for each. He was offered twenty five dollars per sack in Greenville. Very dear, I think. He got no coffee at all as it was selling at 70 & 75 cts. per lb. I think people should quit now & drink rye. We will soon be out of coffee & then we try the pure rye till it gets down. Mason & Slidell have been given up. I wish old Abe had kept them & then perhaps we could have had peace or England would have given the North a decent thrashing. The children were rejoiced to see him. I was as glad as they were. No one suits me like him. Mrs. Knight came up after dinner. I was down there this morning & Mrs. Fanning & Obazena came up with me.

Monday 6th - I cut Mr. Henry a pair pants this morning but did not get them made today. There was several here this morning hunting salt. Some got & others did not. The waggons came today. Jeff Davis (my dog) was glad to see me. Jim Knight is tired of his trip. Mr. Henry went to Academy.

Tuesday 7th 1862 January - I finished Mr. Henry's pants today. The hands are going to kill hogs tomorrow. A good many here this morning hunting salt instead of yesterday morning. I had to give my room up to them & go to the kitchen. All are well. Willie can crawl anywhere, will soon be walking. Atheline & Jim stay in the kitchen loft. John & Peter came today & set into work. The corn not in yet.

Wednesday 8th - I cut Mr. Henry a coat today. Mixed jeans like his pants. Sewed a good deal of it on the machine. Went to Knight's after dinner. Very cold & cloudy. Hands killing hogs today. Turned warmer at night. Killed 29 but did not get all the innards done. My head feels badly. Mr. Henry went with some men to take Francis Starnes as he is a deserter. Took him with no trouble. They stay here tonight also Esq. Thrash, the latter wanting salt but have got none to spare & Mr. Henry has let too much go already. He is too kind to all. The old black cow has a calf, more milk for us.

Thursday 9th - I was sick all day with headache, did nothing at all. Took salts last night but they did me no good. Those men with Starnes left this morning. Uncle Sam cut up the meat & salted it today. The women finished the guts. The children quiet all day, they behave well when I am sick. Mr. Henry in the house nearly all day. He stays with me when I am sick. He is a fond, kind husband. My head got nearly well after supper.

Friday 10th - My head entirely well. Mail came but nothing new. We got no letters, though a good many came to the neighbors. Uncle Sam had a severe attack of the cramp collic today so I sewed but little but will finish the coat tomorrow if nothing happens. Aunt Tena & Fannie at work at the lard, did but little as Uncle Sam was very bad off for a while. Fannie got part of the sassauge ground. Jinnie is cooking now. Atheline in the field.

Jim Parker & George spread out the meat as it is warm like spring & Mr. Henry is affraid it will spoil.

Saturday 11th - Willie is 10 months old today. I finished the coat this evening about 3 o'clock. I went to the stables this morning with Mr. Henry. He has gone to Asheville court this week. In Asheville he has only been two days including today, not much business done this court as nearly everybody in the war. He came back at night. I scoured the candle sticks at the branch. Helped Jinnie wash out some hanks of yarn. The lye has eat up two. I also helped Fannie wash some guts for sassauge. Mrs. Fanning cut out 16 1/2 yds. of coarse jeans this evening. Jim Knight got 7 yds. of it. I must make Uncle Sam a coat this incoming week, also Charlie. Got the lard all done by working after night a little. I went into the new sugar this evening. It is very white, nice coffee sugar but no coffee to put it in. Mr. Henry got 3 sacks of salt & a barrel of sugar was all he got. Uncle Sam well this morning. Jim Parker salted the meat down again, took all the salt I borrowed from Mrs. Knight for the sassauge.

Sunday 12th January 1862 - A beautiful clear warm morning. Spring like. I almost listen for the birds & frogs it is so pleasant. Nothing new going on in the country. All are well. I want to take a long walk this evening with Mr. Henry it is so pleasant. I must stop now as dinner will soon be on & I heard Willie crying just a minute ago. I am writing down on the branch. The rippling of the water is music to my ear. Old Smith & Mr. Henry are sitting on the back piazza reading newspapers.

Mr. Henry & I went to Capt. Moore's after dinner, had a pleasant ride as it is so warm today. We came back about sunset. He rode Zona up to the stables. Pinck & Hanes rode John.

Monday 13th - Jinnie & Atheline cleaned feet & head to make souse & made liver pudding today. Drisley all day. Mr. Henry made out his P. O. returns. I moulded candles & done about generally. Willie not at all well. Teething I think. I have headache slightly tonight.

Tuesday 14th Jan. 1862 - My head pains badly. Cool & cloudy. Nothing of interest. Fannie made souse today, got all the lard put away. Jinnie & Atheline began to stuff sausage this morning, get along very slowly. By night I was sick with headache. Mr. Henry gave me ipacach to vomit and I was quite sick till 10 o'clock. I lay on the floor vs. a bed till 12 & then went to bed. He is so kind to me. I am very thankful. I have such a fond husband.

Wednesday 15th - Sick all day with headache. Mr. Henry gone to Asheville. He got me some blue moss. I took two large pills of it. I will try that for a while as nothing seems to relieve me as yet. Negroes doing but little in the way of stuffing sassauge. Willie still fretful.

Thursday 16th - I was quite sick this morning for a while as the pills were operating but got better after breakfast. Jinnie & Atheline fixed the rooms upstairs. I superintended. Harrie is coming over after dinner to stay a few days.

Harrie came in the evening, looks like a shadow but is improving a good deal. He has rheumatism now. Willie not well yet, very fretful. Was sick & vomiting some today.

Friday 17th - Willie threw up a good deal last night. I had to get up & change my & his clothes. Harrie coughed a little last night. He has a bad cough & I fear 'tis consumption that ails him though he thinks not. Mail brought no news. I had a letter from Dora & Matt Wednesday night. Mr. Henry took it out at Asheville. All are well down there. The negroes finished stuffing sassauge this evening. Mr. Henry gone to old Case's to try to get him off that land.

Saturday 18th - A beautiful morning but cloudy in the evening. I did some mending for the children. Mrs. Jones was here this evening & got 4 lbs. wool. Harrie & the children went to the mill after dinner. We had turkey today for dinner. Bets McKinnish & Milla Penland eat dinner here. Bets got 19 1/4 lbs. wool on Thursday last to spin. She brought Jinnie some stocking yarn today. Tom Tidwell brought his mother up to Taylor's this evening. Tom has been in nearly two weeks. Taylor started to the salt works last Tuesday & came back this evening. Heard on the road he could not get any so he turned & came back. I hope Eliza may not stay long on the place. Willie was a little sick last night, vomited some but did have to get up with him. The other little ones well. Mr. Henry at the mill all day.

Sunday 19th - Cloudy, looks like rain. Harrie wants to go to Asheville this evening, seems to be doing very well. Willie's bowels still loose & he's fretful. Dinner will soon be on & my book is nearly through. I hope to preserve this journal 'till my dear little ones get able to read it. We have turkey for dinner. I hear the children calling me so I must go to them. No news at this time. Harrie left after dinner. Mr. Henry & I went to old Quinn's. I fear we have seen Harrie the last time as I fear he has consumption.

Monday, January 20th 1862 - I now begin a large book for a journal. Shall I live to write it through God only knows. I hope I may be spared to raise my dear little family. I made or rather began Uncle Sam a coat. My head pained me a good deal in the evening so I did not finish it. Willie is very bad in his bowels. Teething I think. Hanes can't do anything with him. I must have Jinnie or Atheline to nurse him.

Tuesday 21st - Atheline in the house today. I finished Uncle Sam's coat & cut Charlie one. Willie fretful, his bowels no better. I took a nap in the arm chair this evening & my head got better. Warm weather. It seems like Spring. I sent Sister Martha Arthur[35] & Jinnie a pan of butter by Harrie. He leaves Asheville tomorrow. Poor fellow. I never expect to see him again. He has gone to Columbia to renew his shattered health.

Wednesday 22nd - Willie still sick. I keep giving him teas and attending to his diet. Jinnie in the house as she has sore throat. Finished Charlie's coat & made Sam a pair pants. Still warm. Last Monday evening we had a real summer shower, it thundered & lightened like a warm summer day. Mr. Henry sent for me to go to the mill this evening to take a long walk. Zona would not go so I only went to the mill. Mr. Henry came back with us.

Thursday 23rd - I made Uncle Sam a pleat-bosom shirt today. Jinnie helped a little. Willie no better. A beautiful day. The hands are making a new road down near the house. Mr. Henry at the mill all day. It saws faster with him to stay there.

Friday 24th - House full of people come to hear the news. The mail brought nothing of importance, no letters for us. I doubled some sewing thread & Jinnie knit on her stocking. Willie no better yet, the others all well. A cold, drisly, damp day.

---

[35] Martha Ann Henry, sister of William Henry

Saturday 25th - I did nothing of any consequence but attended to Willie all day. He is no better yet. Fannie made the children some ginger cakes this evening. A cool day.

Sunday 26th - Staid at home all day, Mr. Henry & I. Willie seems better today. Betsey McKinnish come here to see if Mr. Henry would let her go in the house with Peter Guy. She moves in tomorrow. Polly Jengle & daughter stay here tonight. My head pains me a good deal. I shall be sick tomorrow I fear.

26th January 1862 Sunday, a beautiful day - These lines were given to us by our father R. Henry on last August (1861). He was in his 95th year. He was born 10th Jan. 1767. His mind is perfect yet, retains his memory well, though his eyesight is beginning to fail.

One Hundred Years Hence

Let us drink & be merry, dance, joke & rejoice,
With Claret canary & echoing voice.
This changeable world to our joys is unjust,
All pleasures are ended when we are in dust.
So in mirth let us spend our spare hours & pence,
For all shall be in pot one hundred years hence.

The beautiful damsel with garlands so crowned,
She kills with each glance as she treads on the ground.
Her glittering dress doth cast such a splendour,
Like nothing was fit but the stars to attend her.
All tho she is pleasant & sweet to the sence,
She will be cold & mouldy one hundred years hence.

The greedy old miser gains hundreds of twentys,
And stares on his riches & pines among plenty.
He lays up great treasures he never will see,
The year of two thousand nine hundred & three.
He will leave all his savings his lands & his rents,
For a worm eaten coffin one hundred years hence.

The true hearted soldier a stranger to fear,
Calls up his spirits when danger is near.
He labors & fights great honors to gain,
Not doubting but that he will ever remain.
His courage and valour is of vain pretence,
For to flourish his standard one hundred years hence.

The merchant who ventures his all on the main,
Not doubting to grasp what the India's contain.
He hussels & bussels like a bee in the spring,

Not knowing what harvest or Autumn will bring.
All tho fortunes great gain may lead him with pence,
He will ne'ar reach the market one hundred years hence.

The plush coated Dr. his fees to enlarge,
Kills people by license & at their own charge.
He lays up great treasures of ill gotten wealth,
The drugs of his pots the ruins of health.
The pleasures of health he pretends to dispence,
He will be turned into mummey one hundred years hence.

The rich brawling lawyer with fool wrangling strife,
Will plead you a tune to the end of your life.
He will plead you a tune while the client's in slavery,
The pleader makes conscience a cloak for his knavery.
He boasts of his cunning & brags of his sence,
He will be non est investrist one hundred years hence.

The Priest tells that heaven is a happy place to dwell,
Compared with the pains & torments of hell.
He lives on the tithes of other men's labor,
And thinks that his blessings are viewed as a favor.
He talks of the spirits & bewilders the sence,
Knows not what will become of us one hundred years hence.

Why do we time all our trifles with cares,
Converting all our joys in sighs & to tears?
While pleasure abounds let us ever be tasting,
And drive away sorrow while vigour is lasting.
Let us kiss the brisk damsel that we may from thence,
Have heirs to succeed us one hundred years hence.

Monday Jan. 27th 1862 - I did not get up this morning till after breakfast as my head pained me so badly. I got no easier till after supper. Willie is some better. A cool damp day. There were several women here today. I was so wearried with them. I went in the side room, it was very cold in there.

Tuesday 28th - My head has got well. I made Mr. Henry lapped pants today. Atheline in the house. He is going to Hendersonville tomorrow, to be gone several days. He has gone to Asheville today, got me 1 1/2 yds. of green gingham to trim my scoop with. We have had another battle with the yankees in which Gen. Zolli-coffer was killed & our men badly whipped. Willie is doing better.

"Bethel Regiment to be Re-organized."

EXECUTIVE DEPARTMENT, NORTH CAROLINA, }
ADJUTANT GENERAL'S OFFICE,
Raleigh, Jan. 27, 1862. }

THE first Regiment of N. C. Volunteers being disbanded, a Regiment of Volunteers for the War will be formed, to take its place.— All the companies of the old Regiment about to re-organize for the War, are requested to report to this Office without delay, with the view of going in this Regiment, which will receive the "Bethel Flag."

Additional Volunteer Companies for the war will be accepted, to whom a bounty of fifteen dollars per man will be paid by the State and fifty by the Confederate States. When a full company is tendered four Officers will be commissioned; with a less number appointments will be given as follows: A Captain for forty men; First Lieutenant for twenty-five; Second Lieutenant for fifteen.

The Militia who have been ordered on duty, and to be in readiness, can still avail themselves of this opportunity of getting into the Volunteer service, and the number so doing will be credited to their respective counties.

By order of Governor, H. T. CLARK.
J. G. MARTIN,
Adjutant General.

The Asheville News, February 20, 1862

Wednesday 29th - A dull cloudy day. Uncle Sam & Peter making krout, made one barrel yesterday for Martha Arthur & today for ourselves. I cut out pants for Charlie, Lonzo & Hanes. Finished the two little ones. My head pained me so this evening. I had Atheline to make me a cup of coffee. It feels better since. Willie is a good deal better but wants to stay out in the yard all the time. Is very cross. Mr. Henry started this morning. The hands have finished the road. It is now near 9 o'clock & bed time. Mrs. Fanning is here tonight, also Tom Tidwell. Pinck is sleeping with him. Zona wants to but the candle was out & she would not stay in the dark. I must call Atheline & go to bed. She sleeps in here tonight. John Branton has moved back from Cherokee, wanted to get a house of Mr. Henry, but Mr. Henry thinks he is too drinking. My little ones are all asleep & I must go too.

Thursday 30th - Atheline & I made Charlie's pants & I cut out Peter's coat & finished it at night. Mrs. Fanning came up to stay with me. Willie is getting better, the others are well. Cloudy today.

Friday 31st - Mail came but nothing new. I got no letters. The several came for others. I made Fannie a sack & put up the sassauge. Atheline made her saque. Rained all day. Mr. Henry will be back tomorrow if it does not rain. Willie getting well & I am glad of it, for it distresses me sadly to see my little ones suffer. Two men stay here tonight. They came to the mill (from Transylvania Co.). Tom Tidwell not gone home yet. Branton is staying in the Academy.

February 1862

Saturday Feb. 1st 1862 - I began Jennie a saque & Atheline finished it. I made some cake & dried apple pies after dinner. Willie is doing finely. Mr. Henry came home late in the evening. Cloudy all day & rather cool. Nothing of interest going on. Rumor says J. L. Henry's negro Bob was hung yesterday. I hope it may be true for he certainly deserves death. He committed rape on an old woman some three years ago & effected his escape.

Sunday 2nd - Cloudy & cold. Mrs. Reynolds & Smith preach at the Academy today but we are not going. My tooth aches a little & Mr. Henry has consented to stay with me. He is very kind. Willie was fretful last night. His bowels pained him I think. The negroes have gone to old Daniel Jones' buriel. He died Friday night with dropsey. Fannie is getting dinner. Atheline has Willie. Old Mr. Boyd is here, will stay for dinner I think. I must stop as I want to write to Ell today. I made a pallet before the fire. Mr. Henry, the children & I lay down awhile. It rained some this evening so we did not take our accustomed walk.

Monday 3rd - I cut Jim & John a pair pants today. Atheline is to make them. I heeled Mr. Henry some socks. Willie has got well but very fretful. The others all well. Mail came along but nothing new. Old Jim Night is to attend the mill as E. P. Night is going to Geo. Willie coughed a good deal at night.

Tuesday 4th - Mr. Henry went to Asheville, came back about 2 o'clock. Jim began to lay the hearths, finished the hall room. Only began after dinner, will lay this one tomorrow. I began Mr. Henry's overcoat today, did but little to it. Warm & pleasant. Uncle Sam & Charlie hanging the meat.

Wednesday 5th - Jim laid this hearth today & the kitchen hearth also & fixed the floor in kitchen. A beautiful day. Three men stay here tonight hunting volunteers to form the 1st Regiment again. I sewed some on Mr. Henry's coat, it is very tough sewing. Willie is very fretful, pure crossness I think.

Thursday 6th - Mr. Henry went with those men to Asheville this morning. Not back till night. I have the headache very bad this evening. He brought me a letter from Lou & he got one from Barry Hogan. Fannie & Atheline scoured my room, the dining room & back piazza. Willie has a very bad cold, taken it today from staying in the hall room I think. The others are all well. Rained a little today but broke off in the evening but clouded again towards night.

Friday 7th - Mail came but nothing new. Mr. Henry went to Hendersonville today, to be back tomorrow. I finished his coat today. Atheline finished John's pants today. Tom Tidwell stays with us tonight. All are well. Cloudy all day. I fear it will rain before Mr. Henry gets back. I do think I have got the kindest husband in the world. I think so much of him & he is such a kind father. Cousin Mary Moore was confined with a daughter last Sunday the 3rd inst.

Saturday 8th - Mr. Henry came back late in the evening & is to start to Grahamville in the morning with 3000 lbs. bacon to the army. He sold it today in Henderson to be taken to Grahamville. I made George a coat & patterned a pair pants for Pinck. Atheline helped some. Willie is very cross. It rained a good deal last night & this morning also. I was affraid Mr. Henry would not get home.

Sunday 9th - I feel sad & lonely this morning for Mr. Henry has gone & will be away some three or four weeks. I shall miss him so much. He is always so kind to me & the little ones. It is quite cold this morning, the wind from the North. They loaded the waggon this morning with 3,000 lbs. bacon & a barrel of krout. They had some trouble in getting up the hill the other side of the mill, along the old road. The oxen had to pull up for them. It is cloudy & dull today. I am going to send Charlie to Starnes' after Sue Sutton to stay with me while Mr. Henry is gone. I wish him a successful trip & a safe return home. I can never wish him anything too good for him, for he is a dear good husband. Old Smith the tanner & Peter Guy eat dinner here. I have written a letter to Dora & Matt & Pa in one. It is now after four. I will take Willie awhile as I have nothing more to write.

Monday 10th - A cold unpleasant day. Jim Parker went to Moore's tan yard in Henderson got two sides of leather upper & sole. N. Taylor came back late in the evening, the waggon got to Hendersonville at 11 o'clock. Mr. Henry started off driving. I guess it will be a great drive he will do. I was mending up old clothes & will be at it all the week I reckon. Atheline is knitting on my stockings. I began it last Friday night. Willie is not so cross as he has been, yet wants to go out often. Pinck is trying to spell. Harrie sent him some books & he is anxious to learn all in them before he returns. We have not heard from Harrie since he left. I hope he is improving. Uncle Sam & P. Guy killed a beef today & will slaughter another to-morrow & the next day old Charlie.

Tuesday 11th - The mail did not come last night. A boy came along this evening with the mail. Vic the mail carrier is sick. Louise McKinnish staid with me last night. Sue Sutton was not at home & I don't expect will be soon. I am not affraid to stay alone, yet I feel very lonely at night till bed time & then I soon go to sleep & forget that I am alone. I miss Mr. Henry so much. He will never know how much I miss him when he is gone, when night begins to close in, yes 'tis then. I miss his welcome footstep & his dear familiar voice. I cut out some shirts for Jim & John. Atheline is to make them. I am still mending up clothes. A little warmer than yesterday. The hands are cutting coal wood above the Branton house.

Wednesday 12th - Nothing of interest going on. Uncle Sam & Peter Guy finished slaughtering the beefs. I still mending. Warm & pleasant.

Thursday 13th - Atheline finished a shirt today, began another. I'm still patching. I have been fixing Zona's old drawers so she can wear them. Cloudy in the morning but cleared off before noon. Warm & bright. Sam & Guy finished cutting the hogs this morning. All are well. Jinnie has been ailing a little but up again.

Friday 14th - Mail came. I see the yankees are landing in Alabama on the Tennessee River. They are a tricky set of dogs. I wish this unholy war at an end. L. McKinnish came again last night. She is all gab. My dear little ones are well. Pinck sprained his ankle last Wednesday & lay by a day for it. He limps a little yet with it. The others are well. Willie can push a chair all over the room but does not try to walk alone. It has been a cloudy dull day, rained at night.

Saturday 15th - This has been a changeable day. It first sleeted & then snowed, then nearly all the snow melted & it took a fresh start to snow & snowed on after night. I mended some & moulded some candles. Aunt Tena finished spooling the cloth for some jeans to sell. Atheline ironed the children's clothes. Fannie made some ginger cakes for the children today. We finished the hog heads today. They began to smell a little. I have not heard from Mr. Henry since he started. I hope he is getting along well. I look for him next week & hope I may not look in vain. Things are going on very well at present.

Sunday 16th - A still cold morning. The snow (though not much fell) is melting. I slept till very late this morning as breakfast is generally late on Sunday. N. Taylor was here this morning after tobacco. The children, Pinck & Zona, are throwing across the bed playing & they can't get out. They must amuse themselves some way. They are very noisy in the house. I dread for a rainy day to come in the winter. Now they are rolling the large glass marble. I must stop for my feet are very cold. I began a story last night in the Courtiers of Charles III. The book belongs to Mary Moore but has been here some three years. Mrs. Fanning came up before dinner & the children & I went down with her. The roads are very bad, nothing but mud. Louise McKinnish is here tonight. Pinck is asleep & Atheline is getting Willie to sleep so I must stop & put Zona to bed. She has been combing my head since supper. She wants to go to sleep in my lap. Mr. Henry nurses her to sleep when he is here. It is still cloudy with a South East wind. Snow nearly all gone, only on the mountains. I want to write to Lou tonight & perhaps Sister Frank so I must stop. Louise McKinnish stays with me tonight. She is a great thing to talk about nothing. I wrote to Lou & Sister Frank. It has been a cold cloudy day, wind blowing from South.

Monday 17th - Cloudy & began to rain about 10 o'clock. Aunt Patsy Jamison spent the day here. I cut out some aprons of blue checks for Willie & Zona, did not get one done. Atheline moulding candles. I want my summer supply moulded now. The children well & very noisy as they have to stay in the house all the time. The creek up a good deal. They took some planks off the dam. Mr. Henry has been so engaged he has not finished the dam yet.

Tuesday 18th - Cloudy but no rain. I finished Zona's apron. Had the headache in the evening. Aunt Tena rendered up the tallow today. Atheline moulding candles & will be all this week. Willie will soon be walking, can get up by anything & walk.

Wednesday 19th - Mrs. Fanning warped the cloth today in the hall room as the wind blew very hard. I made Zona another apron today. My head ached very badly in the evening. I took a nap in the side room. When I woke (5 o'clock) it was raining very hard. I made out to get out supper but went to bed early, eat nothing at all. Zona was asleep so Pinck eat in my room before the fire.

Thursday 20th - I got up with headache this morning & suffered all day with it. Mrs. Fanning came & got some filling this evening, black. Caladona Jones was here a short time this evening, wanted to get some flour & brought a letter to the office. Louise McKinnish came this evening after an egg or two to make salve to go to her little sister's eye. I sewed a little this morning on one of Willie's aprons but my head pained so badly I had to lay down. I got two tubs & a pig pen from Matt Cook today for which I gave one dollar & thirty-five cents & a comb for Pinck at 10 cts. but I can't find the comb since. This evening Zona would have me to lay my head in her little lap for her to rub & comb & I have not seen the comb since. The mail came along tonight, it was due here last Monday but Vic has been sick.

Friday 21st - Mail came, no news. The federals have taken Roanoke Island with some 2500 of the Confederates prisoners. They have taken Fort Henry on the Tennessee River also, with 50 prisoners. Things begin to look dark. The state of N. C. has a draft out. Oh! how can I give up my devoted husband, 'tis death to contemplate such a thing. I had a letter from him today. He was in Columbia, had been detained two days. I had a letter from Dora & Matt saying all were well. The people about here are volunteering at a rapid rate to avoid the draft. I wish they would take the Parker boys & T. Hendrix for they are doing no good here.

I made Willie an apron today & began another for him. I went to Mrs. Fanning in the evening to see the cloth, it looks tollerable well. It is cloudy again. Aunt Tena is dying blue. Mr. Henry got the indigo in Henderson at two dollars a lb.

Saturday 22nd - Washington's birthday. What a trouble the once happy United States is in. We are determined to be a free people & we have got our freedom to fight for a second time.

Rain again today. I finished Willie's apron & made myself one like it. Atheline finished the candles today, enough for one year I think. Fannie made some dried apple pies & molasses custards for the children. I mended some late in the evening. I washed Pinck & Zona tonight as usual & put them on clean clothes. Raining very hard, a real summer shower. Fannie in here patching.

Sunday Feb. 23rd 1862 - Sitting in my room by a small fire for there is no need of a large one this beautiful Spring morning. The sun shines warm & pleasant. I have nothing to write so I will wait till evening. Willie is asleep & Zona is standing at my knee begging me for custard so I will give it to her. I took the children & went down to Mrs. Fanning's. They were not at home so we went on over to the new mill dam & back by the old one & then by the goose nest by way of the meadow where Jim & Guy have been ditching. We had dinner at 12 o'clock & a long evening. Atheline took Zona & Willie up to Taylor's after dinner. Jesse Jarrit was here a short time in the evening. Pinck, Jinnie & I went up to the Sulphur Spring. I had the headache very bad so I went to bed about dark & went to sleep.

Monday 24th - This is a very blustery day, the wind very high. The children are at Aunt Tena's house as Fannie & I are scouring my room. She will keep on cleaning up till she gets all the rooms cleaned. My head is nearly well. I took some salts this morning before breakfast. Charlie & Jinnie are ploughing in the garden today. Atheline getting dinner. I have nothing more to write at present. I pieced up Willie an old flannel out of the other children's old ones.

Tuesday 25th - I made nearly two aprons today. One of Willie's & one Zona's. Finished Zona's at night. I would have got it done before night but Harrie Deaver came. He is looking a great deal better, has a cough yet. Is helping raise an artillery company. He brought Zona a doll, Pinck a ball & Willie a marble. Jennie Hopson sent Pinck some glass marbles & the children some candy. Mrs. Fanning staid with me at night as Elijah Night has got home.

Wednesday 26th - Harrie went to Asheville this morning. It rained some today. I finished the aprons today, made two. Atheline sewed on one for myself like the children's. I finished it at night. Mrs. Fanning knit on my stocking. Fannie finished cleaning yesterday.

Thursday 27th - I fixed some marsailes cuffs to undersleeves & ripped my brown woolen sleeves out. I am going to change them to another fashion. The children combed my head for me this evening. I had the toothache badly for awhile after dinner.

Friday 28th - Mail came. I got a letter from Mr. Henry which should have come two weeks ago. Nothing new. The little ones very well. Rather cold. I finished my sleeves but have to take up the waist a little. Atheline cleaning the yards. Willie fell out the back door twice this evening, bruised his head a little on both sides. Uncle Sam hanging up the beef.

March 1862

March 1st Saturday - A. B. Jones went to Asheville & got the mail. No letter for me. I finished my dress & swept part of the yards this morning. It looks like rain. Stewed some fruit which I made into pies and custards after dinner. Atheline finished the yards. I did some mending in the evening. Louise McKinnish brought a little apron for me to cut for her little sister. Her mother is going with the child to Asheville Monday. It has very sore eyes.

Sunday 2nd - I had a dreadful headache all day, took some salts but got no relief. Preaching at the Academy today. The darkies all gone or nearly so. Aunt Tena is not well. Atheline did not go nor Fannie either. Pinck went with Jinnie. I slept nearly all the evening. Cloudy all day.

Monday 3rd - I have had headache till about 4 o'clock this evening. I eat a hearty dinner & it made it worse. Aunt Tena is sick with rhumatism. Atheline & Jinnie milked. They are drawing the coal today. Rain this morning but now near 9 o'clock at night the wind is blowing very cold from the North. The children are asleep. I must wash tonight & put on clean clothes as I was sick yesterday & did not do it. Mail came tonight but nothing new. I began some tatten today for a chemise for myself. Mrs. Fanning is here. She comes every night. I must now stop.

Tuesday 4th - I made some tatten till near dinner & then cut me out two chemise. I went to Mrs. Fanning's in the evening. I hemmed a frill for one chemise. I heard today that Mr. Henry would be home tonight with a corpse from the 25th reg. unit, a young Chris Coffle of Haywood. He leaves a wife but no little ones to mourn his loss. Tom & Frady, the man that hauled him came this evening. Mr. Henry will be at home the last of the week. They brought in my pretty statue for little Cora's grave. All are well. Nothing new going on.

Statue at the grave of
Cora Aletha Henry

Wednesday 5th - I sewed on my chemise, nearly finished it at night. Cloudy but no rain. Atheline sewed some on one of the chemise.

Thursday 6th - Cold & a real snow storm, the wind blew all day. It snowed a good deal. Fannie washed. Atheline got dinner. Willie made his first step alone this morning. He is very proud to try to walk. He is very large to his age. Pinck & Zona will play in the snow. All I can do. They are very fond of seeing their little tracks in it.

Friday 7th - Mail came but no news. Mr. Henry came home about 4 o'clock. I was very glad to see him, so were the children. He brought me a very nice nail brush, Pinck a small hair brush & Zona a very pretty little ring. It has been a very cold day. I did not expect him. He came up by home, they are all well. Dora sent the little ones some flowers. I finished my chemise & cut out Willie some pinnie fores. Got them basted, will sew them on the machine tomorrow & finished off button holes.

Saturday 8th - Atheline ironed. I finished the pin fores. Stewed some fruit & baked some molasses ginger cake after dinner. Muster here tomorrow. Mr. Henry did not eat till after we did. John is hauling manure in the garden. A very pleasant day. Harrie came here this evening, has been to Haywood hunting volunteers for an artillery company. Made but poor speed. Oh! I almost fear we will yet be whipped. The yankees have possession of Nashville, Tennessee & I very much fear will soon be among us. Willie will soon walk alone, he is improving wonderfully every day. Harrie was telling us that Bob was dead (Jim Henry's boy). He got out of jail & they shot him before they could take him. He died of the wound.

RECRUITS WANTED !

TO ARMS---FREEMEN !

PATRIOTS OF THE MOUNTAINS AWAKE! Your country calls and needs you. Already you have acted nobly in this contest for freedom and independence. Your brave sons whom you sent out in the commencement of the war, and who are still standing as a living wall between your homes and the vandal enemy, are re-enlisting for the war, but in this hour of peril to your country, after they have stood the brunt of battle for nearly twelve months, they call upon you to come to the rescue and stand shoulder to shoulder with them in the final fight and triumph. Will you let their call go unheeded and permit them to fight the last battle unaided and alone, against an enemy who has gathered up all his strength for the deadly conflict and for your subjugation. You cannot act thus and be freemen. Come then to the aid of those who are already in the field. A BOUNTY of

One Hundred Dollars

Will be paid to each recruit to the "Jackson Rangers" for the war. I shall be in Webster, Jackson county, until the 26th March, when I shall return to my Regiment. In my absence report yourselves to Private John S. Keener, who is fully authorized to receive your names.
J. R. LOVE, Lieut. Co. A,
16th N. C. T. and Recruiting Officer.
March 6, 1862. 3t

The Asheville News, March 13, 1862

Sunday 9th - A warm pleasant day, wind from the South. Zona & I went to the goose nest (on the hill across the meadow) this morning. I sent Atheline to get her. When I came back, the house is nearly full of men or at least the fire place is crowded, so I write down near the branch in my "studio." Harrie is still here. Mr. Henry got a sack of coffee in Charleston at 53 cts. per lb. Dear coffee. I fear he will not get it at all. He is so kind to me. I love him more & more every day. May God bless him is my prayer. Dinner will soon be on so I must stop. Harrie left soon after dinner.

Monday 10th - I cut out three shirts for Mr. Henry, sewed some on one. Atheline sewed one of the shirt tails. All are well. Willie took his first steps alone last Friday. He is a very fleshey babe, is very proud he can step alone. Nothing new going on.

Tuesday 11th Willie's birthday- I finished a shirt today & began another. Mr. Henry went to Asheville. There was to be some salt & coffee sold today but it was not sold. (Government stores). Mr. Henry bought a horse today, an iron grey. He needs another yet which he will get from Steph Jones.

Wednesday 12th - Cold & cloudy. Mrs. Common came here this evening. I finished another shirt & began the last one. Willie is improving in walking, is affraid of falling. Nothing new going on in the country.

Thursday 13th - Rained all day. I finished the last shirt. Mrs. Common knit one of my stockings. Atheline on the other. She finished one & I the other that night. All are well. Pinck is growing finely. Zona & Willie are dear little creatures. Zona says she is Papa's pet & that Willie is my pet child. I believe Mr. Henry pets her more than he did the others because she is a girl & we lost our other little daughter. Little Cora was a lovely child but it was best that she died. He doeth all things well.

Friday 14th - Mail came, nothing of interest in the papers. Mrs. Common went to Asheville. Cloudy with a little rain. I made a bed tick in an hour & a half on the machine and cut out my gingham bonnett after dinner, nearly made it.

Saturday 15th - Finished my bonnett & done sundry patching. Made some pound cake after dinner, 2 1/2 lbs. It did not bake well. Mrs. Common left for home this morning. It rained a very hard shower about 10 o'clock, heavy thunder for the season. After that shower it cleared off warm & pleasant.

Sunday 16th - I had headache this morning when I got up. Pray meeting at the Academy today. Em Murray was here this morning to see if there was any letters for Mrs. Hawkins but got none. Till Morris & Miss Sumner came here from preaching for dinner & staid till nearly sunset. I had the headache very bad at night. I was very sick at my stomach. Mr. Henry was very attentive, he bathed my feet for me. He is the kindest of husbands.

Monday March 17th 1862 - I was nearly free from headache. I changed some feathers after dinner. Atheline helped. We filled up the new tick & emptied some pillows. I took a long walk with Mr. Henry in the evening, went over in the J. Green field to see the wheat. I had the headache badly when I got back. I think I eat too much dinner. Mr. Henry has three hands working on the mill dam today. Rather cool but bright & sunny.

Tuesday 18th - I had the headache all night & no better this morning. Mr. Henry went to Asheville this morning. Mrs. Tom Cook spent the day here. Mr. Henry got us some apples today at one dollar & 75 cts. per bu. He also got me some magnesia pills & lemon seeds for my head. He is ever thoughtful of me. Willie still keeps trying to walk.

Wednesday 19th - My head felt very badly this morning. Mr. Henry sent to P. Presley & borrowed some coffee which he said cured my head. My head got easy soon after I took some coffee. He always thinks of my comfort. I will have no one to love & caress me if he goes to the war. God grant he may not have to go. Oh! that we could once be a free people & grant us peace most High, the wish of many a sad heart this day. I cleaned up the small goblets. I sent Atheline after them this morning to the store house. There are 52. I cleaned up the pantry generally. After dinner about 4 o'clock I got through & then cut out a dress for myself. Began to hem the frills for the neck. Atheline is making Uncle Sam a shirt.

Thursday 20th - I made some apple preserves today & the sleeves of my dress. Mr. Henry went with the waggon after some bridge sills. They bought one. He was very wet, it has rained nearly all day with wind from South East. Willie can walk across the room & not fall. He will soon be running anywhere. Fried apple dumplings for dinner.

Friday 21st - Nashville has been surrendered to the Federalist. The yankees took Newbern the 14th & took a good many prisoners. The Merimack has done considerable damage to Lincoln's navy during the last week or so. I would rejoice if all their fleets could be done in the same way. Rumour says J. Woodfin is either killed or a prisoner. We got no letters today, that is Mr. Henry & I.

Saturday 22nd - Cold disagreeable day. Some snow fell but melted. There is snow on the mountains. I finished my dress soon after dinner. I then darned some stockings & fixed some to heel for Pinck. I heeled one pair & another ready to pick up the stiches for Pinck. Mr. Henry has promised him to take him with him to see his grand Pa. He is delighted with the idea of going. I want him to go. Zona says she is going too. Willie has a very bad cold & loose bowels. Got the third & last bridge sill today.

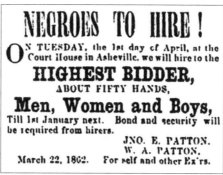

The Asheville News, March 27, 1862

Sunday 23rd - J. Frady staid here last night. He came to settle about hauling that corpse. Cloudy & cold with a little snow occasionally. Atheline is down with toothache. Willie is up at Tena's house. I must go & make Mr. Henry some apple dumplings for dinner. He is sitting here before the fire reading a cultivator. Pinck & Zona are out at play somewhere. Old Mr. Boyd's little boy staid here last night. He came to mill & it was too late for him to get home. It will soon be 12 so I will go to make the dumplings. Jinnie's Sunday to cook. Mr. Henry eat hearty of dumplings, said I must not make any more for he indulged too much. We did not take a walk this evening as it was so cold.

Monday 24th - Cloudy. I made Pinck a pair pants & began another pair. I cut them out this morning. One a jeans pair the other summer pants. I made them for him to go to South Carolina in. Atheline carded bats for her quilt which she will put in tomorrow. Willie still continues to try to walk, improves slowly. He is so large is one reason he can't walk better. The other little ones are very well. I made both pair pants today. I was very busy, the machine did the most of the work. They kill three hogs tomorrow.

Tuesday 25th - Mr. Henry went to Asheville this morning. Nothing new over there. I got a letter from Sister Jane, also one from Lena. I have not heard from either in some time before. Sister Jane will be confined soon. I hope she may pass safely through. I began Pinck a pair drawers but did not finish them. I helped Atheline put in her quilt. Cold & cloudy yet.

Wednesday 26th - I got up with headache this morning. Finished Pinck's drawers & Mr. Henry & I took a long walk up the meadow, hunted for turkey nest but found none. There was two men to see him when he got here. Fannie came after us. He came on. Fannie & I picked some sage for sausage meat. Aunt Tena done up lard today. I parched & made me a little coffee for dinner. My head got well. Finished drawers & cut out two pair of pillow slips for my pillows. One pair I will fringe, the other work with turkey red. Nothing new going on. All are well. I made one pair.

Thursday 27th - I went to the mill this morning to get Mr. Henry to make a fringe paddle. Took Willie. Began my fringe & made enough to go on pillow slips by dinner. Sewed it on & Fannie & I went up to hotel place to get some shrubery to plant out in the front yard. I planted it all out after we came back. Peter Guy's child died this morning of sore throat. They came here for a sheet to lay it out on.

Friday 28th - I began the other pair pillow slips. Made both on machine & began to work one. Spent the evening at Mrs. Fanning's. Warm & pleasant, took the children with me. Willie was delighted with the trip. Newbern has been taken by the yanks, our people were defeated.

Saturday 29th - I got up with headache, took some pills. It got well after dinner. I finished working one pillow slip. Washed Willie's & Zona's head & put them on clean clothes. Atheline got her quilt out before dinner. Mr. Henry started to New Found this morning. Will not be back tonight & perhaps not till Monday. Warm & pleasant. Peach trees will soon be in full bloom, they are not killed yet.

Sunday 30th - Cloudy with occasional sunshine, very warm. Sam has been gardening some for the last week. I staid alone last night. Atheline slept in the house. Jinnie is getting dinner. She has been staying with Ruth (George's wife) since last Tuesday. She has been confined. Fannie is sick with headache. The negroes gone to prayer meeting at Academy. Tena has Willie. Pinck gone up to Taylor's with Tom Tidwell. He came back with Taylor last Thursday.

Monday 31st - My head felt very badly before dinner but after dinner Atheline & I went up to hotel place & got some shrubery & planted it out that evening. I began to work my other pillow slip after dinner, did nothing at it. Atheline hemmed on her quilt before dinner. Warm & pleasant. Mary Taylor came down with us.

April 1862

Tuesday April 1, 1862 - Charlie ploughed down one side of the walk. Atheline & I worked in the yard all day turfing around the piazza. E. Night & Guy began to put up the hen house yesterday. I was very tired at night. Pleasant & fair.

Wednesday 2nd - Stanafer Jones' wife spent the day here & all the Night's were in the yard as a young man by the name of Norris has come for Dick Night. He is a deserter from Lt. Col. Coleman's battallion. They went to take him last Friday night. He says he is not going & Tom Hendrix encourages him in not going. Dick Night married his (Hendrix's) sister last Sunday evening. Mr. Henry officiating as Esq. We had a very hard rain in the evening. Zona & I took a walk to the mill dam while they were marrying. A good deal of hail fell with heavy thunder. Some men staid here that night. They came to the mill from Transylvania, been buying wheat on New Found.

Thursday 3rd - At work on hen house. Old Mr. Boyd here helping. I forgot to say that I finished my pillow slip yesterday or nearly. Fannie scoured the room over mine upstairs yesterday. I had a very bad headache in the evening. Warm, looks like rain. It did rain late in the evening a little. We fixed the walk today, hauled the dirt or threw it with spades down in the low place of the walk. I intend turfing the upper side.

Friday 4th - Mail came but nothing new. We got no letters. Fannie & I scoured all down stairs today except the dining room & side room. I was real tired. Rained a little in the evening. It was late before we got to work as the mail generally brings a good many men after news.

Saturday 5th - Rain in the morning. I turfed some but Mr. Henry had me to come in out of it. He went to Ham Moore's after dinner as it cleared off. Atheline & I turfed the upper side of the walk, a good evening's work at that. Hanes attended to Willie. He is rather troublesome. Hanes is not large enough to manage him. We brought the dirt out of the garden on which we turfed.

Sunday 6th April 1862 - We all attended church. Mr. Reynolds preached a very good sermon. Fannie had dinner nearly ready when we got home. As usual, I had headache. Mr. Henry & I went up the road by the hotel garden. We took Pinck & Zona with us. Zona has on her red flannel dress, the first time she has worn it. Mr. Henry lay before the fire all the evening. The old tanner Smith was here part of the time. I forgot to say Mr. Henry married another couple, Morris & one of old Jim Night's daughters on the 3rd inst. They came after him at 10 o'clock at night & he went. I was vexed. I did not want him to go.

Monday 7th - I fixed some window curtains out of some old sheets for the room upstairs over the hall. I cut out a shirt for Sam & one for Peter. Mr. Henry got a bolt of cloth. He had to give 25 cts. per yd. Dear cloth I think. I had a letter from Frank last Saturday. They are all well. Rained a little today.

Tuesday 8th - Atheline & I cleaned upstairs. Fannie scoured the room over the hall, I scoured the steps. They are clean this time. Atheline is very unwell, took her bed before we got through cleaning. Rain in the evening. Mr. Henry went to Asheville, got me two padlocks, 1/2 yd bed ticking, 10 yds. celicia brown, some garden seed.

Wednesday 9th - I had headache till dinner. Mr. Henry staid in the house & helped with Willie till dinner. Atheline is sick. After dinner it got well, that is my head. I finished Sam's shirt & attended Willie. Rather cool. Uncle Sam at work in the garden. I got a letter from Dora or rather Mr. Henry did. He sent after the mail by L. Case. They were all well.

Thursday 10th - I made Peter's shirt, got done soon after dinner & then began to turf the lower side of my walk. Brought dirt out of the garden, Uncle Sam is working in there. John went Tuesday after wheat to R. P. Wells & got back today. Parker went after him this morning. Fannie helped me in the yard after she came back from D. Ledford's. She went to get her soap kit. He has been hooping it. We got the turfing nearly half done. Atheline not very well. She attended Willie. Mr. Henry got us two lbs. of coffee in Asheville today. He is so good to me.

Friday 11th 1862 April - Mail came this morning but no news. We have had a terrible battle at Corinth Miss. Loss heavy on both sides. I cut Peter a pair pants this morning. Atheline at work on them. I went on with my turfing. Mr. Henry came & helped me some & then called Jim, who is ditching in the meadow by the spring. He helped me finish it. We turfed up the chimney a piece, got done about two o'clock. I sewed a little on Peter's pants. I was very tired. Atheline not well yet. Willie can run all over the house, can get up alone when he falls.

Saturday 12th - Muster up on the hill. Mr. Henry up there. Cloudy all day. Ma Crook & A. B. Jones eat dinner here today. We had eat before Mr. Henry & them came down from muster. Had coffee for dinner, our sack of coffee got home to-day. I was fearful it would never come but it has. After dinner, Atheline & I cleaned up the kitchen. Fannie went to get some sweet potato seed of Mrs. Norman. She (Fannie) made some pies & custards this evening. I swept the yards. It sprinkled rain a little. I finished Peter's pants before dinner with Atheline's help. Mr. Henry & I went up to the hotel garden this morning. He wants some rose bushes, lilac & that flowering almond in the garden brought down here. It is in full bloom now. He did not come back with me as they were collecting for muster. The children ran away & came after us & Atheline after them. They were double quicking it when they got to us. Zona said "Papa help me over, Atheline is coming". He said "no". She said "yes". I seen her coming & in a minute Atheline come in sight. I brought down some cuttings of snowball & woodbine. I fear they will not live. It is quite cool, the wind from the South. A man & his little son from Transylvania Co. after flour. They stay here tonight. His name is Heath. Flour is selling at four dollars a hundred without the sack.

Sunday 13th - Rain. We have had so much rain it seems the farmers will not get their crops in. Wheat looks well. Dick Night & N. Norris started to their company on last Friday & the torries on Laurel took them up & treated them very badly. I hear the stage has stopped running down the river. They are doing considerable damage down there stealing & so on. Mr. Henry went with Knight & Norris to Asheville & did not get back till night. I had the headache very bad all day. Took some pills, it got better on well after supper. Mr. Heath has been here all day & here tonight. Mr. Henry starts in the morning to Asheville & the company is then going on to Marshall. I hope he may return safe to the bosom of his family who love him so fondly. It has rained all day. Fannie & Jinnie baked some biscuits & boiled a ham for Mr. Henry to take along. I parched the coffee & had it ground. I want him to be as comfortable as possible & I pray God to watch over him & take care of him.

Monday 14th - Mr. Henry left today. He did not tell us good bye. Oh! how I dreaded to see him leave but I feel that the great Ruler will work everything out for the best. He doeth all things well & I do pray He may spare my own dear husband. He is all the world to me. Life would be but a blank without him. I love him as no other woman loves. I fixed up some skirts for the children. Willie is a good child. Pinck & Zona are bad to fight. Atheline is very well. Nearly all the men have gone or will go tomorrow. I hear this evening that the militia of this county is called out. I wish the tories could see the error of their ways. Tom Tidwell, Daniel Moore and Mr. Heath are here tonight. It has rained all day a slow rain. I fear the men got wet. I hope Mr. Henry may sleep in a comfortable bed this night as good as he is used to & all the others too & bring them back safe is my earnest prayer to Almighty and most Merciful God.

Tuesday 15th - I have been fixing up some more skirts for the children. I forgot to say that Friday night a man staid here & took off all the old castings, scrap iron &c. to make cannon balls of in Asheville. He got near a 1000 lbs. Heath left for home today. Rained all day. I have not heard from Mr. Henry today. I would like to hear. Mrs. Fanning has got the last piece of jeans in the loom for us, she was up here after some filling. Nearly all the stillhouse volunteers went, drunk at that. Louise McKinnish is here tonight. George is fiddling in the kitchen for the children. They are dancing. They know not what a sad heart their mother has. Let them enjoy life. Cares will come soon enough to their young hearts. God bless my husband. Help him from all harm is my constant prayer.

April 16th 1862 Wednesday - I cut two pair drawers this morning for Mr. Henry & cut some for Jim of his cloth. I nearly finished Mr. Henry one pair. I spent the evening at Mrs. Fanning's. Before dinner I helped Uncle Sam put in some glass in the dining room. He has put the sash in & hung the blind today. I tacked in some glass upstairs also today. It has rain a little all day with occasional sunshine. Atheline has pieced the sleeves of Uncle Sam's shirt. I cut them too short. I have no word from Mr. Henry. Oh! the horrors of war. I want to hear from him so badly. No telling when he will be back. Shield him from all harm is my constant prayer. Almighty & merciful God spare my own dear husband to me & my loved ones I pray.

Thursday 17th - I went up to the hotel garden & got some lettice for dinner. It is a beautiful, warm, bright morning. Brought down some lillies & a few other things to set out in the yard. I made Mr. Henry's drawers, got done before night. Atheline sewing on her chemise. Willie running about generally. The other little ones joyful & happy. I hope my own dear husband is getting along well. May he be happy & protected is my daily prayer.

Friday 18th - I had a letter from Mr. Henry today by Hendrix. The stillhouse company nearly all came back. The militia is not to go but a company leaves Asheville today made up out of the militia, mostly married men. The Night's are determined not to go. Mail came this morning but nothing new going on. The yanks have taken Fort Paleski near Savannah Geo. We are nearly surrounded by the vandals. I did not work much today for I did not feel well. I mended up some old clothes & my hoop. Mary Taylor spent the evening here. She had nothing to say. She is a strange creature. Louise McKinnish has staid with me at night since Tuesday night. Mr. Henry sent his blankets home by Hendrix. He has been out on picket one night so he wrote me. Said he was not cold. I fear for his dear life & well as health but God that takes care of us at all times will, I feel, take care of him.

Saturday 19th - I have felt very sad all day. I am not well, I think is one reason I did nothing of note today. Fannie & Jim Parker had a difficulty this morning. He thrashed her a little. I hate to see them abused. If Mr. Henry was to stay long I fear we would have a bad time of it. I do hope he may soon return unharmed. Fannie baked some ginger bread for the children this evening. It rained a good deal after dinner. My little ones are well. Uncle Sam made some steps down by the pantry last Thursday to the piazza. Tom T. stays with us at night since Mr. Henry left. I am not much affraid of the tories. I finished Atheline's chemise this evening. God protect my dear husband.

Sunday 20th - I got up with a severe headache. Took some pills before breakfast & felt a great better when they operated. It has rained nearly all day. I hope Mr. Henry has not been in it. I have had a long lonely day. Mr. Norman came this evening & sit awhile, brought a letter to mail. Louise McKinnish did not come last night but Tom Tidwell staid with us. Atheline sleeps in the house every night while Mr. Henry is gone. Pinck is laying before a wee fire (it is not cold). Zona & Willie in the kitchen with the negroes. It is 1/2 past 5 & soon supper time. I hope Mr. Henry will be at home by next Sunday. He has been gone one week tomorrow, a long week to me. I ought to have written to Dora & Sister Frank today but I felt so little like writing. I also owe Sister Lena a letter. I must stop & mend up my fire & see about supper. May the Lord of Mercy look down on my dear husband & shield him from all harm is the devout prayer of his wife.

Monday 21st - No news from Madison. I hope things are going on well. I cut out some three skirts for Willie today, made one & began another. The sewing machine is doing fine. I will trim two of them with the trimming Dora & Matt made last summer. The other with tatten (plain). Atheline has been helping a little, she is not well, has headache every day. The children are well. I have toothache nearly every day after eating.

Tuesday 22nd - I finished Willie another skirt & began the last one. We had a freshet Sunday night, took the dirt work of the dam. Two men staid here last Sunday night, came to the mill. They went on to Cathey's. Lou did not come, neither did Louise McKinnish on Sunday night. I ask God's blessings on my dear husband this night.

Wednesday 23rd - I spent part of the evening at Mrs. Fanning's yesterday. Mary Taylor came after some meat & Hanes came after me. I heard from Madison today. They are taking the tories prisoners. Oh that they could see the error of their ways before it is too late for them & their families.

Thursday April 24th 1862 - I finished off Willie a dress today. Atheline had made the skirt. I finished his last skirt yesterday. Fannie made some dried apple pies this afternoon. Atheline very unwell, not able to attend Willie. I clean up all the house myself. E. P. Knight got home last night, says Mr. Henry will be at home soon in a day or two. I hope he may soon return to his family, whose every thought of him & who prays God to take care of him while he is gone.

Friday 25th - Mail came but nothing new going on. Cloudy dull day. Mrs. Fanning staid with me last night. The hands are at work on the dam, will soon have the mill going again. I did nothing scarcely all day but read the newspapers generally. No letter from Mr. Henry. I made some tatten in the evening. We had a good deal of rain this evening & heavy thunder. Tom Tidwell stays here tonight also Mrs. Fanning. I hope Mr. Henry is not out in this rain. God bless him is the prayer of his fond wife.

Saturday 26th - Mr. Henry came home after 9 o'clock. We had gone to bed. I was so glad when I heard his dear familiar voice. 'Twas then I knew he was well & I thank Thy all Wise for returning my husband to his family. Cloudy all day. He went to Asheville this evening. I put some tatten on Willie's skirt, cleaned the candle sticks & done about generally. Fannie made some pies this evening. Atheline not better. Jinnie has been sick two days, is well this evening. Dark when Mr. Henry got back from Asheville.

Sunday 27th - Cloudy this morning but bright now in the evening. Mr. Henry gave Atheline an emetic this morning, she is a little better. Jim has Willie & Zona & Mr. Henry are asleep. I am in my "studio" down by the branch. I must stop as I want to take a long walk this evening. No more at present. Mr. Henry & I took a tramp through the wheat & then out to Quinn's. I got me a nice bunch of flowers, lilacs at Quinn's. We left the children with Fannie. It was late when we got back, dark.

Monday 28th - I cut out myself a chemise this morning, going to trim it with pointed tape trimming, some Dora gave me last summer. Did but little to it. Atheline still sick, not able to do anything. Jinnie is not well this afternoon. She attended to Willie & Mr. Henry & I went to turn the goats in the Murry field. Dark when we came back. He has been to Asheville today, got home about two o'clock. Willie has a cold, is very cross.

Tuesday 29th April 1862 - After cleaning up the house, which I done by 8 o'clock, I sewed on my chemise till after dinner. I then took Fannie & Pinck & went to the hotel yard & got some shrubery. I fear it will not live. Old Quinn is grafting some in the nursery up there in the garden. Mr. Henry got up some things for one. We set them all out before night. I was up in the garden this morning & gathered some lettice for dinner. Went down to see Mary Taylor, she is poor in house hold goods certain.

Wednesday 30th - Finished my chemise today. Fannie made some pies after dinner. Atheline no better. Hanes attends to Willie, he goes where he pleases & when he pleases. Can go up the stair steps rapidly. Nothing new going on. A. B. Jones was here this morning taking in taxes. Took in consideration everything about & in the house. Old Nancy Night was here also trying to get one of the Murray cabbins. They have already moved in. They are a trifling set, no account at all.

BOGGS' BATTALION
OF
LIGHT ARTILLERY!
BREECH-LOADING ARMSTRONG FIELD PIECES!
RECRUITS WANTED
FOR
CAPT. GREGORY'S COMPANY

THE CONSCRIPT LAW HAS PASSED, and all white males, not legally exempt, between the ages of 18 and 35 will be detailed and put into the different arms of the service, without a voice in the selection of their officers, or the corps in which they shall serve. This is the time for those liable to CONSCRIPTION to volunteer.

Pay, Bounty, Subsistence and Clothing furnished from the day of enlistment. Pay better and service lighter than infantry.

Those who desire to join this popular and splendid Battalion will apply to

W. H. BAILEY,
Swannanoa, N. C.

or

T. W. ATKIN,
Asheville, N. C.

April 28, 1862.   4t

The Asheville News, April 29, 1862

May 1862

Thursday May 1st - Cloudy & rained a little till 12. Rained but little after that. I cut out Willie some dresses out of some old ones of mine, also Zona one. Made Willie one after dinner. Mr. Henry went to Asheville after dinner. The yanks have got up to New Orleans but have not landed yet. Willie very cross. The other little ones well.

Friday 2nd - Mail came. I got a letter from Sister Jane. She has a daughter born 8th April, is not doing so well, is going home as soon as she is able, wants me to go with her. I would like to go if it is compatable with Mr. Henry's interests. Atheline still sick. I read till dinner & then made Willie a dress. I have made two of an old gingham skirt & am going to make one of my pink calico dress I brought from Salem, also Zona one of that & Willie one of yellow muslin, a part of a skirt Lou gave me for Zona & me of a skirt Matt S. gave me to fix a dress of one with & there was some left.

Saturday 3rd - I mended Mr. Henry's pants this morning & made Willie a dress of the pink calico & then finished hoeing out my yard. I did some Thursday evening. Fannie made some pies. The children never get tired of them & then they are

77

made very cheap so I keep some for them nearly all the time. Mr. Henry went to Asheville this morning. I sent for some things but only got one paper of needles, had to give 15 cts. for them. Nothing else that I wanted was there. Fair & pleasant.

Sunday 4th 1862 May - Cloudy & rain up to this time 2 o'clock. We had fish for breakfast (Mr. Henry bought them) the first we have had. The hands began to fix the trap this week but did not finish as the water was too high. Beginning to grind at the mill again. Preaching at the Academy today, also yesterday. The negroes all went today, all but Tena & family. Atheline still sick. Charlie went after Dr. Nielson. He will be here in the morning. Sent some pills by Charlie. We have not had our dinner yet 2 o'clock. It will soon be ready. Tanner Smith has been here all day. Willie has taken a good nap. Perhaps he will not cry so much this evening. He has just woke up. I must write to Sister Jane this evening if Willie is not too cross. I owe two or three others which should be answered today or soon. I have not received a line from Lou in a long time. Pinck & Zona are both asleep & Mr. Henry has just woke up. I will stop for I am hungry. It looks now as if it would clear off. Dinner is coming in so I stop. Mr. Henry & I took a long walk this evening, went the old road way past the old Joe Green house. We over took Joe Green just as we came out the lane. We went on with him till it began to rain & then we had several races before we got to the mill. I got a little damp. It rained a very good shower after we got in the mill. Atheline is no better.

Monday 5th - I began Willie a dress but did not finish. Hanes attends to Willie. It is warm & pleasant today. I stay in the hall room every day. I did not work very steady for Hanes is very thoughtless with Willie. The Dr. did not come over today. I hope will come tomorrow as the negro is no better.

Tuesday 6th - I finished that dress & began another, a yellow muslin for Willie. Jim came up from the mill dam at dinner & told that old Mr. Reynolds had found a dead man in the creek about his place, just below about 1 mile. Mr. Henry went soon as dinner was done. They got him out & think it was an old man that staid here a month or more ago by the name of Serratt. It is thought he fell off the bridge & was night. I expect he was coming here to stay all night again. He was swollen very tight & Mr. Henry said smelled awful. Poor old man. No friend is by to see that he is lain away decently. He stays alone this night in the old Hendrix house. They hold the inquest tomorrow. Dr. Neilson came this evening, left some medicine for Atheline. She is no better.

Wednesday 7th 1862 May - Frost this morning but nipped nothing. I finished Willie's dress & began one for Zona of pink calico, some of my old dress. Hanes dropping peas, began planting corn today. I am attending to Willie myself. He goes where he pleases & when he pleases. Pinck gone with Mr. Henry. They burried the old man in an undressed box, had not time to make a coffin as he was so decayed. They think he has been dead 2 weeks yesterday as he passed Sandy Bottom that day. Sam Green saw him & says he seemed very feeble. The creek was up at that time. Fannie took some dinner over to the Willis Grave yard for Mr. Henry & Pinck about 3 o'clock. Frost this morning.

Thursday 8th - I finished Zona's dress just after dinner & cut out a pea green chambra dress for her, one Sister Jane gave her when we were down there. Dr.

Neilson was here this evening, thinks Atheline a good deal better. He staid some time. Mr. Henry went to Asheville this morning, came home to dinner, is at the dam this evening. Hanes out in the field. Lonzo attends to Willie today. Hanes stays till 9 o'clock or till after I get the house cleaned.

Friday 9th - Mail brought no news this morning & battle is expected at Corinth & another at Yorktown soon. I sewed on Zona's dress. It is very tough sewing & dreadfull rotten. Warm & pleasant. Our garden is getting on slowly. The fly or something has destroyed all our cabbage plants.

Saturday 10th - I finished Zona's dress before dinner & washed the children after dinner. Got Pinck's summer pants & fixed them & put them on. Some men came home with Mr. Henry from muster & eat dinner about 3 o'clock. Mr. Henry went to Asheville with them, did not get back till we were done supper. No one here to supper but the children & I. We have beautiful moonlight nights. Hugh Johnston got 200 lbs. of lard & 200 lbs. bacon here last Monday. Mr. Henry got a horse of him. Atheline improving. I have not felt well today. I had the headache last night right badly.

Sunday 11th - Warm & bright. Mr. Henry & I & the children went to the mill this morning to feed the hogs. Pinck weighs 47 lbs., Zona 31 lbs. & Willie 27. I, 118 my usual weight. Dinner is now ready. E. P. Night in here for dinner. Mr. Henry speaks of going to Henry Hanes' this evening. I hope he will not go as I will be alone. Mr. Henry is not going off this evening. R. Boyd is here. He has just eat dinner. M. McKinnish is now at work fixing some banisters for the piazzas. It is very warm this evening. Seems like summer. I must write to Sister Jane as I did not write to her last Sunday.

Monday May 12 1862 - I began Willie a dress, one Sister Jane gave him last summer, purple calico. Did not finish it as I did not begin it till 12 o'clock. I attend to Willie. Jinnie is sick with headache. The others all well. Mr. Henry & I started to walk yesterday evening but he stopped to talk with some men & I came back. Hanes & I went to the mill this evening to meet Mr. Henry & Pinck. Mr. Henry carried Willie back, he walked nearly all the way there.

Tuesday 13th - I finished Willie's dress. Mr. Henry started to Uncle Dillard Love's this morning, will be gone about a week. Hanes out dropping peas today. Jinnie not well yet. She attended to Willie after dinner. We had heavy rain & thunder this evening. Atheline is improving very slow. The mail carrier says they are fighting at Corinth again. We have had a battle at Williamsburg Va., in which we were victorious. God help our course is my prayer.

Wednesday 14th - George Jones' wife spent the day here, came after some ploughs. I made some sleeve loops for Zona & Willie of brilliante. Wiley McKinnish & S. Jones put up the banisters to the front piazza today. The hop vine is growing finely. I wanted columns of plank put in but they have no plank suitable. It rained several showers today but cleared off in the evening.

Thursday 15th - I made Zona & Willie some stockings today. I have tried to get them some. Mr. Henry brought some from Asheville last Monday but they are socks and too large for the little ones. I think Pinck can wear some of them. There is no children's shoes in Asheville at all. Fannie washed some clothes this evening for the children. She will do the washing for awhile as I want Aunt Tena to spin all she can. She has began spinning cotton for the negroes pants. Mrs. Fanning has staid with me at night since Mr. Henry left & will continue I suppose.

Friday 16th - Mail came but no news, only they are fighting still at Corinth. Our forces have evacuated Norfolk & Portsmouth & the yanks have landed there the 12th. We burnt the navy yard, blew up the dry dock & destroyed things generally. Also burnt the Merimac, all the efficient vessel we had. Such is war. I mended Mr. Henry's socks & iron the children's clothes this evening. It rained some this evening. Fannie washed a few more pieces. McKinnish banistered the back piazza today. Willie has staid at Tena's house some today. Uncle Sam began to clip the sheep today. All are well. Atheline improving.

Saturday 17th May 1862 - I had the toothache very badly this morning for a while. It was 9 o'clock or after before I got the house cleaned. I went up to the garden & got some lettice for dinner, also some flowers for the vases. I eat a hearty dinner of onions & lettice & felt drowsy and headache all the evening. Did no work today. My head ached badly at night. Smith the tanner staid all night. Fannie ironed some this evening & made some ginger cakes for the children. I washed Zona & put her on clean clothes. Pinck took a long nap this evening.

Sunday 18th - Cloudy & dull this morning. I slept very late. My head not entirely well yet. Breakfast late. Mrs. Fanning brought up a kitten last night. Willie & Zona think a great deal of it & Pinck is as anxious about it's good treatment. Zona has been trying to get it to eat some molasses cakes. I will stop for this time as dinner must be got out & my head feels badly. No one here for dinner but the children & I. My head ached very bad after dinner. I went to bed soon after supper. Mr. Henry got home about 8 o'clock. Mrs. Fanning slept in side room. All are well at Uncle Dillard's & Aunt Welch's. I was so glad to see him for home is not home without him.

Monday 19th - I began to turn Zona's scoop today. Hemming the frills of brilliente, did not finish it. Mr. Henry & I went to the Murray fields in the evening. We took the yokes off the goats. Some of them are rather wild & hard to catch. There is three young kids & will soon be several others. Pinck was along with us. Mr. Henry went to Asheville this morning, got me steel for a hoop which I have to put together. He also got some shoes for Willie but they are too small. Mail came along this evening but nothing new.

Tuesday 20th - I finished Zona's scoop before dinner, it looks very nice & began on the frills for me. It is pea green gingham, very stiff & hard to sew. Warm & pleasant, needing a little rain for corn & plowing. The wheat is taking the rust a good deal. Some people will not make half a crop. I see in the papers that the planters in some of the southern states will not make their seed wheat.

Wednesday 21st - I finished my bonnett after dinner. I put some tattin on some sleeve loops this evening. I seamed three beds today. Bright & warm, the wind from South. All are well. Atheline has got so she can attend to Willie. Very weak yet.

Thursday May 22nd - I began this morning putting my hoops together with cord. Will put on tape when I can get them in shape. They are very troublesome.

Heavy thunder with very hard rains & hail. Several showers. I eat some molasses custard for dinner & I was sick all the evening with headache from it. I was very sick at my stomach. Clear & warm.

Friday 23rd - Mail came, nothing new going on. I received a letter from Matt. Some of the children are sick & Ell's children have whooping cough. She also wrote that Cousin Harriet Neilson was dead. I am very sorry to hear that. She has been ailing for many years. She died sometime in April. I finished my hoop after dinner. Dovey Jones spent the evening here. I darned some cotton stockings for myself. J. Branton & R. Boyd stay here tonight.

Saturday 24th - I have done no sewing today. Worked out my flowers. Fannie helped some, washed the children & put them in clean clothes & washed & cleaned myself. It has rained a little several times today. Two men stay here tonight that have come to mill. Tinsley is one of them. Willie is running about all over the yard just as he pleases. A good child but shows a little too much temper.

Sunday 25th - My head aches badly this morning & I feel very little like writing. Pinck has just started to church at the Academy. Byrd preaches there today. The negroes, some of them are going. I had a good laugh at Zona a little while ago. She wanted Pinck's pants on. I put them on & she looks so funny. I had to laugh. Her hoops in the pants too. She is crying now, she is so vexed. Mr. Henry has gone to the mill. Willie is out with Atheline. I must see about dinner, as it is after 10 o'clock. My head got easy after dinner & Mr. Henry & I started to Betsy McKinnish's to get her to help wash wool. We saw her little girl at Jim Parker's so we went down there. She said she would come tomorrow. We went out & looked at the wheat the other side of the store house. The Dixon wheat is getting in bloom. The rye in full bloom. The walker & white wheat in root. I came back & left Mr. Henry, Branton & old J. Night looking at the wheat near the stables. It has the rust a good deal. Mr. Henry has from the Murray fields (including them) clear to the Green field including that in wheat. It looks finely & will make a good deal if it is not injured by rust.

Monday May 26th 1862 - It was nearly 12 o'clock before I sit down to sew. I ironed & mended some of the children's clothes, began a blouse coat for Pinck, did but little of it as my head ached badly after dinner from eating onions & lettice for dinner. Mr. Henry & I wrote to Dora & Matt this evening. I done up the mail. He brought no news. The yanks have taken possession of New Orleans some time ago. Betsy McKinnish & Tena washed wool today. Fannie helped after dinner, got nearly done. Tena will finish tomorrow. I had it all taken in the evening & put upstairs, it is not dry yet. My head got better before supper.

Tuesday 27th - I did not get ready for breakfast as Mr. Henry did not wake me. I have not done much today. Sewed some on Pinck's coat, got it ready for the trimming (velvet when I get it). Took a nap after dinner & my head aches a little since. Zona & I went with Mr. Henry down to where he is making fence above E. P. Night's. He is fixing a pasture there for some sows. That was before dinner. He came back with us after he laid up a good many rails & dinner was nearly ready. I got some raddishes & we eat some before dinner. They are very nice now. I feed my little chickens every day twice. We have some 60 or 70 & three little ducks &

two others setting so perhaps we will have more soon. We have some 18 turkeys, young ones. I am sitting on the back piazza steps writing at the pantry door. The kitten is playing around me. Pinck off with his Papa. Zona at the branch as Fannie is washing since dinner & Willie, my pet, is up with Atheline at Mama's house. She is spinning cotton for the negro's clothes & has been sometime. The sun is getting low & I must begin to take in the wool. This has been a beautiful day.

Wednesday 28th - I have mended up some today & sewed some buttons on some old vests. After dinner I had headache very bad. Took a nap. Betsey McKinnish & daughter helped picked wool today. Tena & Atheline picked too. It then dried a good deal in the evening but no rain. I got up in time to get out supper. My head a good deal better.

Thursday 29th - I took a long walk with Mr. Henry. Went through the wheat & came back by the Guy house. There we got some french pinks & set out in the flower yard. We also got some honey suckels & sweet williams (wild) for the vases & Mr. Henry got some ivey after. We came back from somewhere. It was quite a pleasant tramp to me. After dinner I cut out Fannie a worsted dress & made the sleeves & sewed some on the waist. She wants it to wear Saturday night to Jim Moore's wedding. Bets McKinnish & girl & child staid all night. Will finish the wool by tomorrow at dinner. We have several work hands now. A boy by the name of Jones is plowing. Branton & Night at the mill dam.

Friday 30th - Mail brought no news. I finished Fannie's dress before night, got done the wool. Very warm & dry.

Saturday 31st - Very busy all day cleaning up the yards. Zona & I went to the Academy to preaching. The circuit rider Smith preached. It was very warm going & coming. Mr. Henry went to Asheville today. Got me one bunch of tape for tape trimming. I emptied a kit of lard that was leaking after dinner. Cleaned the smoke house behind the kitchen & I was very tired. The negroes all went off to the wedding. I cleaned up the dishes. Had supper before dark. Mr. Henry went up to Cole's to see about sending for salt. It was near 10 o'clock when he got back. I sit up till he came. Zona too, for she took a long nap this evening.

June 1862

June 1st Sunday - Everybody gone to church at the Academy. Mr. Henry took the children. I was too tired to go. My day's work yesterday wore me out. I have been up to Aunt Tena's house a good while. It is very warm today, the wind from the South, a strong breeze. Aunt Tena has just brought Pinck & Zona home. Mr. Henry sent them back. She has gone back so has Pinck. It is just after 12 o'clock. Willie is sitting down here on the floor playing with Zona's little basket. Nothing new going on. Mr. Henry sold the gent cow Friday for 50$ to Bishop in Asheville & yesterday he sold the heff cow to E. P. Knight for 35$. Dear cows I think but money is easy these times. Mr. Henry came back & T. Cook came with him. It was 3 o'clock before we had dinner. We had a cold ham & Fannie baked some bread. Mr. Henry & I took a long walk over in the wheat. It has fallen down a good deal. About the Green house it is very high. It was nearly dark when we got back & as I had not given out supper, it very late supper.

Monday June 2nd 1862 - I have done nothing of importance today. I mended some old dresses. It is very warm today. Mail brought no news. They have had a fight near Richmond. Terrible slaughter on both sides.

Tuesday 3rd - Had toothache all day. Did nothing till late in the evening. Began a bonnet for Zona, some that was left of Willie's dress Sister Jane gave him. Willie will have one like it. Rain all day. Mr. Henry staid with me all day.

Wednesday 4th - Mr. Henry went to Asheville. The battle at Richmond was fought on the 31st May & Sunday 2nd June. Terrible slaughter on both sides. I made Zona's & Willie's bonnetts today. All are well. Warm & fair. No news.

Thursday 5th - Mr. Henry went to Asheville this morning, took Pinck & Zona. They were delighted. I ironed some today & mended up the ironed clothes. Mr. Henry went after something that is broken at the mill, now in Asheville to be mended. He got back after dinner.

Friday 6th - I had the toothache nearly all night. I did not get to sleep till after 2 o'clock. Mr. Henry was very kind, doing all he could to me. It was late before he & I got up & did not eat till the hands were out & gone. Mail came while we were at breakfast, brought no news. I made some tape trimming. Mr. Henry got me 7 bunches of tape in Asheville.

Saturday 7th - I did nothing of consequence this day. Atheline has got tollerable stout again. Mr. Henry & I took a long walk this evening through the wheat & by the Guy house. The blades on the wheat are all dead from rust. He thinks the wheat not injured yet. We went by the hotel place. Mr. Henry is having the dirt dripped where the smoke house was to try to make salt of the water. It tastes salty. Fannie baked some pies & custards this evening & boiled a ham. There is preaching at Sardis tomorrow, quarterly meeting.

Sunday 8th - Mr. Henry & I went to preaching at Sardis. House full. Rather cool today. We had a lunch along but eat dinner after we came home. We took a long walk this evening, went up to see the little kids. We have seven. We also called at Bets McKinnish's as she is not well. Had supper soon after we got back. Jinnie cooked today. John took the children, P. & Z., to ride. They got some flowers at Mr. Reynolds. They were delighted with their ride.

Monday 9th - Cool this morning. I have done no work yet. Atheline is sewing on Peter's drawers. She made him one pair last week. They are some I cut for Mr. Henry & they are too small. I have been cleaning up all the morning. I scalded a bed of ants last Friday in the strawberry patch, back of garden. There was nary a one. I picked some strawberries for Mr. Henry's dinner. He went to Asheville, the first we have had. I must stop now & eat some raddishes Mr. Henry has just gathered for me & I must wash some straw berries & put sugar in them for his dinner. I wrote to Frank, Ell & Lena this evening. The mail brought no news. I made some tape trimming. Capt. Moore eat dinner here today. Caladonia Jones spent the evening here. She came to bring letters to mail. Capt. Moore starts to Richmond tomorrow. Mr. Henry is going with him. I don't want him to go.

Tuesday 10th - I made Mr. Henry a pair pants today. Did not get them done before he started as he came home at dinner & said he was not going so I did not try to finish. But Capt. Moore came on about 3 o'clock & he went on. Mrs. Lance eat dinner here today, brought some plows to the shop. We had a very heavy rain & a good deal of hail yesterday evening. Mrs. Fanning stays with me tonight. All are well. Cool today.

Wednesday 11th - I made some tape trimming today. Spent the evening at Mrs. Fanning's. Pinck & Zona went with me. Atheline sewing on Peter's drawers. Mr. Henry came home in the evening. I was glad of it. I know he wanted to go on but I am so selfish, I want him always near me. I would have liked for him to have gone, yet I wanted him at home. Dora & Matt stay in Asheville tonight on their way to Tennessee. Mr. Neilson is taking them over. Mr. Henry saw them. I would have been glad to have seen them. All are well at home.

Thursday 12th - I cut out some pantletts for Zona & myself today. Did not work much at them. Mr. Henry & I took a long walk, went to where Johnston's negroes were at work to get Mr. A. B. Jones' Carolinian, to hear the latest news of the battle. We got it & sit down under a tree to read the most of it. I have the headache a good deal this evening from eating onions at dinner. It was late when we came back.

Friday June 13th - My head ached all night & this morning it feels no better. I eat no dinner today. Mr. Henry complains of headache also. He has been with me all day. I have been in bed the greater part of the day. Mail brought no news. I got a letter from Ell. They are all well. Fowler has a discharge from the army. I know she is glad. I have done nothing this day but read a little.

Saturday 14th - My head is easy but I am feeble. Sewed a little on Zona's pantletts, put in the trimming tape insertion & bottom tape trimming point on one side only. I fixed Zona's hoop as the tapes have been washed. We had turtle for dinner, a very large one. Mr. Henry caught it yesterday. He is not fond of it. I like only tollerable. It is rather inciped meat to my taste. I washed & cleaned the children this evening. Very warm today about noon.

Sunday 15th - Late breakfast this morning. Had fish, stewed chicken & etc. I eat a good deal of fish, they were small. Mr. Henry has taken the children off somewhere. I was not in when he left or I should have gone also. It is a beautiful morning, not too warm. E. P. Night made his cow trade so Mr. Henry has taken her back. I have nothing more to write. I am writing in the hall room. My chickens & ducks are growing finely. I have about one hundred young chickens & fourteen young ducks & about thirty young turkeys. Mr. Henry sold two hundred lbs. of lard to Winslow Smith in Asheville at 30 cts. per lb. last Wednesday. That is getting along considerably in price I think. Matilda Morris spent the evening here. She is very good company. It was late when she left so Mr. Henry & I did not go to walk.

Monday 16th - I sewed some on Zona's drawers, did not finish them. Mr. Henry went to Asheville this morning for the mill spindle. He did not get it. I assisted some about dinner as Atheline is the cook now. She is not very stout. Mrs. George Jones was here a short time this evening, brought a letter. The mail comes along before night now. He brought no news. Quite cool today.

Tuesday 17th - I finished Zona's drawers & began a pair pantletts for myself. Did not sew a great deal as I helped about dinner & I read a greater portion of the afternoon, a novel "Confession of a Pretty Woman." It was very interesting. The wheat is badly damaged with spot. The Dixon is almost a failure. Mr. Henry thinks the Clingman wheat will do tollerable well. I am very sorry it is so injured for Mr. Henry has such a large crop in.

Wednesday 18th - I finished my pantletts by dinner & sewed them on the drawers. I put tape trimming on them & tucked them. They look very nice. Mrs. Fanning warped the thread for the boy's pants today. I did not help about dinner any. Cool. I have had a slight toothache all day, not much.

Thursday 19th - I cut out some night caps but sewed but little at them. I finished the novel this evening. I am going to work one with turkey red point & tuck one & tatten & tuck the other. Mrs. Fanning brought me two small waiters from Asheville today. I gave 75 cts. for the two.

Friday 20th - Mail brought nothing new. We got no letters. I sewed some on my worked cap, did not finish it as I assisted about dinner. Willie is not so well today, his bowels are very loose. I have been feeding him on panada. The others all well. Mrs. Jessie Smith spent the evening here. She is a nice lady.

Saturday 21st - Mr. Henry went to Asheville today after the mill spindle. Did not get it but got three bunches of thread. No. 7 for negroe's dresses. He went fishing in the afternoon. There are some jack fish below the dam & he has tried several times to catch one but has not succeeded yet. We have small fish frequently. I cleaned the yards with Hanes' help & had the headache very badly at night. Cool all this week.

Sunday 22nd - Mr. Henry has had some wheat cut, it is not much account. Pleasant this morning. We intended to spend the day with Till Morris today but Willie was sick last night & is not well this morning. I want to go after dinner if Mr. Henry is willing & take all the children. Mr. Henry is laying down in side room but not asleep. Dinner will soon be on so I must stop & make Willie some panada. I am upstairs writing in room over mine. We did not go to see Till. Mr. Henry slept nearly all the evening & I went to Mrs. Fanning's in the evening. Did not stay long. I took Zona & Pinck. There was company there. Mrs. Fanning was not at home. Mr. Henry took a long walk. I did not go for I did not feel well. I read. It was dark when he came back.

Monday 23rd - I sewed some on my pointed night cap. Spent the evening at Mrs. Fanning's. Pinck & Zona were along. She is weaving the cloth for the negroe's pants. Mail brought no news. They have been fighting at James Island near Charleston but all quiet now. Oh how I wish & pray for peace once again on us as a free people.

June 24th Tuesday 1862 - Finished my cap today. I do not get much time to work for Mr. Henry is cutting his wheat & has a good many hands. Our vegetables have not come in yet, only lettuce & onions so we are up to all we know to get something besides bread & meat to eat. Mr. Henry sent George to Mr. W. McDowell's after a goat. Pinck went too. He got a little damp as it rained. We were at supper when he came back.

Wednesday 25th - Mr. Henry went to Asheville this afternoon. Got me a beautiful knife, pearl carved handle. He got himself two barlows. He says he loses so many knives, he will try barlow awhile. I made my last cap today for this time. Put tatten on it & began a skirt for Willie out of some pieces of flannel I have. His bowels are a little loose yet. He has four jaw teeth partly through. He does not decrease any in flesh.

Thursday 26th - I sewed on Willie's flannel. Working it with a dark wood shade. Mrs. G. Reynolds was here a while this afternoon. She is a very pleasant lady. Very pleasant but needing rain. Nothing new. Bushel of salt from Capt. Moore last Wednesday. Very nice Virginia salt, it is very white.

Friday 27th - Mail brought no news. I expected a letter from Sister Jane or Dora & Matt but was sadly disappointed. They have not written since they went over there. It has rained nearly all day. A very good season & badly needed. The negroes have set out a good many cabbage plants. Our cabbage are large enough to prune, some of them. I finished Willie's skirt today & made him an apron. I finished the apron after supper. I cut him out two after 4 o'clock this evening. Jim Parker, Mr. Henry, Mont Stradley & others robbed a bee gum tonight. Part of the honey very nice. Stradley stays here tonight.

Saturday 28th - I put away the honey after cleaning up the house & made a jar as Mathiglem for vinegar, a glass jar. Then scoured the bucket which had the honey in it & got to my sewing Willie's apron about 10 o'clock which I finished soon after dinner. Col. Moore & T. Harkins were here this morning. They are speaking of going to the salt lick, also Mr. Henry & Co. I washed & cleaned all the children this evening & washed myself at night. Tom Tidwell stays here tonight & Pinck sleeps with him. Pinck thinks a great deal of Doc. R. Boyd stays also. Tom has come out to move Taylor's family to Cherokee. I am glad of it.

Sunday 29th - Very pleasant this morning. I have picked our first mess of beans this morning, they are well grown. Mr. Henry & Pinck are gone to T. Harkins, will be back to dinner I think. Zona is in the hall room with me eating a biscuit. Willie out with Atheline. Old R. Wells has just left here. He called to mail some letters. Uncle Sam & others killed a hog Wednesday evening. Mr. Henry has the sides rendered up in lard. It was not very fat. I must stop now & get out dinner & string the beans for dinner & Fannie must make some dried apple pies for dinner. The cherries are getting ripe. Mr. Henry & I went up to the Murray place to see the goat (McDowell's). He is a very fine one. It was late when we got back.

Monday 30th - I mended up some old flannels for Willie. He is not very well, his teeth I think. I cut myself out a skirt of selicia & boiled down some brine after dinner, made near 4 qt of salt. It is dark. Mail boy says they are fighting at Richmond again. God grant us a victory & peace. Fight began last Thursday the 26th June 1862. Slaughter terrible on both sides. They were still fighting last account.

July 1st Tuesday - The heaviest rain fell this evening that any one remembers ever to have seen. It began about 5 o'clock & rained on till after we were asleep, 10 o'clock. We like to have had no supper it rained so hard. Some of the mills have been seriously damaged by it. Jesse Smith's & Miller's sustained considerable loss by their mills. The water gaps are all gone on this place. They will fix them tomorrow. Wheat & oats are badly blown down. They will have it to mow. I finished my skirt today. Hemmed it on machine. I don't get much time to work as Willie is not well & needs a heap of attention.

TO THE CITIZENS
OF

NORTH CAROLINA!

I HAVE been authorised to raise and muster into the service of the Confederate States, a Regiment of

INFANTRY,

To serve for three years, or during the war. Each Company must consist of at least sixty-four privates, and as but

TEN COMPANIES

Can be received, those first reported will constitute the Regiment.

Persons between the age of EIGHTEEN and THIRTY-FIVE will see that it is to their interest to volunteer in this Regiment, as each Company will be allowed to

Elect its own Officers,

Whereas, under the Conscription Act, they are liable at any time to be attached to Regiments or Corps ALREADY ORGANIZED.

The Regiment, when organized and equipped, will be assigned for duty under

GEN. KIRBY SMITH,

Whose military department consists of East Tennessee and Western North Carolina.

IMPROVED ARMS

Will be furnished as soon as practicable, but at present all must furnish their

OWN ARMS,

As far as possible, which will be valued and paid for by the Government.

Raise your companies at once, and I will immediately muster you into the service, and place you in CAMPS OF INSTRUCTION.

Captains or others can report to or correspond with the undersigned, at Waynesville, N. C., or to Capt. G. N. FOLK, Asheville, N. C.

R. G. A. LOVE.

June 19, 1862.

The Asheville News, June 26, 1862

July 1862

Wednesday 2nd - Cut Willie two skirts off the sheeting today. Hemmed both on machine & but little else. Hanes is gathering cherries every evening. They are ripening fast. Fight still going on at Richmond. The hands are saving wheat.

Thursday 3rd - Finished Willie one skirt before dinner & picked some cherries after dinner, after reading the papers Mr. Henry brought from Asheville. I got a letter from Lena. They are all well. Old Mrs. Hancock is dead. Mr. Henry gathered a good many cherries this evening. The first paper of the South Carolinian came today.

Friday July 4th 1862 - Mail brought nothing but war news. The papers are filled. The Confederates have the best of it so far. The yanks are retreating. I finished Willie's other skirt today. The bees swarmed yesterday just before dinner. Parker hived them, a large swarm & the only one so far. Old Mr. Boyd stays here tonight. He says George Jones is dead. I am so very sorry for his poor destitute family. God help them I pray.

Saturday 5th - Mr. Henry went to Asheville this morning. The battle still raging. The 1st July loss great on both sides. Mr. Henry came home for dinner & old Mr. Boyd also. Mr. Henry & I went to the burrial. A great many people. He was burried with Military honors. They fired about one dozen times twice. It was sundown before they burried him & dark before we got home as then we had moonlight. I do really sympathise with his poor wife. Oh! may she never need a friend. Jones was very kind to his wife & a fond father. He came home two weeks ago tomorrow, buoyant in hope & now he lays beneath the clod.

Sunday 6th - I had headache all night. Breakfast late this morning. Mrs. Common & her son Jimmie came yesterday evening, just as I was starting. We took Pinck & Zona to the burying. There is preaching at the Academy today. Mr. Henry & Zona have gone, also Willie. Mrs. Common & I are here. I am writing in the front piazza on the round table. We are going to have beans & irish potatoes for dinner & chicken. Cherries are good, ripe now. They will soon return from church & I have nothing more to write. Willie's bowels are loose & he is very cross. The others are well. Ham & Mary Rollins came home with Mr. Henry for dinner. They staid till late in the evening.

Monday 7th - I cut out some of the negroe's pants today & finished Uncle Sam one pair. Very warm today. Mr. Henry went to Asheville this morning, took Pinck & Jimmie Common. He got two bunches of thread No. 12. Gave $3.00 a bunch. No news from Richmond. They had a terrible battle last Tuesday.

Tuesday 8th - Mrs. George Jones spent the day here, also Mrs. Tom Cook. I made George's pants & sewed some on Charlie's. Very warm today. We heard today that David Moon was killed in a later engagement. Jim Welch passed through Asheville last night. He has a finger shot off.

Wednesday 9th - Mrs. Cook & Tom Cook staid all night & till 11 o'clock. The bees swarmed today, a large swarm. Mr. Cook hived them. Mrs. Cook helped me sew some. I finished Charlie's. Made Hanes' & Pea's. Atheline helped some after dinner. I finished Lonzo's after supper as Harrie Deaver came late in the evening. Mr. Henry went to Asheville this evening, will wait for the mail. He will be late getting back.

Thursday 10th - Mr. Henry came after one o'clock. P. Roberts is dead from sickness. His remains will be burried in Asheville as soon as they come & they are on their way. His wife started to see him but missed the corpse some way. I helped about dinner, gathered beans & after dinner sewed on Jim's pants. My teeth have been troubling me again, aching. Harrie will spend several days with us. He is improving a little.

Friday 11th - Mail brought but little news. Watson Cannon is wounded severely in the breast & some others. I do not know them. I finished Jim's pants by dinner.

I feel very badly today as I had toothache so bad last night I did not sleep well. I took a nap after dinner. My teeth pained me a good deal late in the evening but after supper they got easy. Harrie & Pinck go fishing after dinner & after breakfast every day. They are fishing for the jack, said to be just below the dam. Willie is not at all well.

Saturday 12th - Sewed some on John's pants, did not finish them as I had headache & toothache both after dinner. I took a nap in the evening. It has been very pleasant today. McDowell's Battalion is ordered to march next Thursday. Harrie belongs in that, also Jim Parker & a great many of the neighbors. Poor things. I pitty their families.

Sunday 13th - I feel very unwell today. My head aches & I feel badly every way. My head ached all night. Willie is not at all well. There has been several here this morning for news but we have nothing new. It is reported that there was another engagement last Wednesday. I can't say how true it is. We have turkey for dinner. We had our first cucumbers last Thursday & have had a few since. I lay out in the front piazza nearly all the afternoon. Harrie was sitting out there reading. Mr. Henry took a nap. Willie sucked this evening. He has not nursed in several days. I am weaning him.

Monday 14th - Harrie & Mr. Henry went to Asheville this morning. I expect I have seen Harrie the last time. He has a dreadful cough & expectorates a good deal. Very bad looking mucus. I felt badly all day, did not sew much. I finished John's pants. My head felt badly & I felt weak. Harrie sent a can over to put some coffee in. Atheline & Hanes ground some this evening. Mail brought no news.

Tuesday 15th - Made Peter's pants, cut out the others for our own. Willie a good deal better, frets but very little. He has three jaw teeth partly through & his stomache teeth all through. I have not examined his gums in some days. His eye teeth were nearly through a week ago.

Wednesday 16th - Got to sewing about 9 o'clock. Made George's & Uncle Sam's pants. Spent the evening at Mrs. Fanning's. E. P. Knight leaves tomorrow with the others. We had a shower before dinner today & a little rain after dinner. Pinck & Zona went with me to Mrs. Fanning's. Atheline & Hanes finished Harrie's coffee. 14 lbs. can & all. Mr. Henry settled with Jim Parker yesterday evening. Rained a shower yesterday.

Thursday 17th - Mr. Henry took the children to Asheville today to see the battallion leave. They took Harrie a basket of June apples & his coffee. The apples are ripening very fast. Mr. Henry got Zona a long comb & Pinck a pair boots. They are very proud of their things. I made Charlie's & Hanes' pants & sewed a little on Lonzo's. Atheline helped after dinner. Ham Cannon started yesterday to see his son Watson. J. Snelson staid here last Tuesday night. He is a deserter from the 16th Regiment.

Friday 18th - Mail brought no news. I finished Lonzo's pants. Mrs. Fanning warped the negroe's dresses today. A little rain this morning. I did nothing after dinner. I began a sock for Mr. Henry this evening. Willie got his foot burnt yesterday by treading on a coal Jinnie dropped in the kitchen floor, not very badly. The others all well. My teeth have been troubling me a good deal at night for several nights. Willie sucked his last time today.

Saturday 19th - I made Jinnie, Fannie & Atheline an apron sack, some left of the pants Tena got me too. I also made Peter a pair suspenders & Pinck a pair. Wound some yarn late in the evening. Mr. Henry went to Asheville this evening, got back after dark. Got me 16 lbs. of cotton for 2$. Mr. Boyd went & came with him. Newton Taylor stays here tonight. Also Mr. Boyd. Harkins & Night got back from the salt lick with 23 bu. salt. I swept the yards this evening. Nothing of importance going on. Sam killed a kid this evening. Our garden is getting on finely. Our potatoes are nearly all gone. Beans bearing finely.

Sunday 20th July 1862 - Late breakfast this morning. I gathered the beans for dinner, also some cucumbers & onions. It is after 12 & we will soon have dinner. We have our first apple dumplings today. I am upstairs in Harrie's room writing. Mr. Henry down stairs in piazza reading. He has taken a nap since breakfast. Pinck has gone with Atheline & other darkies to hunt huckelberries. Willie is with Tena & Zona playing about generally. Willie's foot looks better this morning. No one here for dinner but our family & N. Taylor. Pinck did not get back till about 3 o'clock. Mr. Henry & I took a walk this evening up by the sweet potato patch & by the spring & then up by the hotel place. We called in a few minutes at Bets McKinnish's. She lives in the cabbin Taylor did. It rained a little before we got home. Not enough to dampen us.

Monday 21st - Mr. Moore & Harkins came this morning & divided the salt. I have been very unwell all day indeed. I have not been well for a month. Willie's bowels are bad off. He is so fretful I can't do anything scarcely. I cut Hanes two aprons today. Sewed a little on one. Mail brought no news. Mr. Henry made his return today. P. O. business.

Tuesday 22nd - Sewed on Hanes' apron. Finished one. Was very sleepy after dinner but did not indulge in a nap. Mr. Henry went to Asheville after dinner, did not get back till dark. He brought a wounded soldier home in the buggy & three discharged soldiers. Joyce was wounded in thigh & foot. He walked on crutches.

Wednesday 23rd - Mr. Henry took Joyce home today, did not get back till dark. I have the headache very badly this evening. Willie is no better & very cross. I have a dreadful cold, I think from being up with him so much through the night. I finished Hanes' apron this evening & sewed a little on Uncle Sam's pants.

Thursday 24th - Finished Sam's pants. My teeth trouble me a good deal. They have not been easy long at a time for a month. Willie is no better. My head aches badly this evening. No news from Richmond. All quiet.

Friday 25th - Mail brought nothing new. It has been reported for several days that Watson Cannon is dead. H. Cannon started to Richmond last week. I hope he is not dead. His mother was here today. She is very low spirited about him. I sewed some on Charlie's pants today.

Saturday 26th 1862 July - I finished Charlie's pants before dinner and after dinner cleaned up the smoke house. Emptied the salt in barrels. Mrs. H. Cook & Cordelia Cook were here a short time this evening. Little Bill Cook has a discharge from the army. He is too young & has been sick of late a good deal. Is sick now.

Mr. Henry went to Asheville this morning, got a lb. of soda for 1$ & 1 lb. of Spanish brown 50 cts. No news from Richmond. I see in the papers that Jack Scaife of Unionville is a prisoner.

Sunday 27th - Rather cool this morning. We had catfish for breakfast. Mr. Henry got a very nice one yesterday from one of Smith's negroes at the bridge. He let the negro have some wire & he is to get one third of the fish that is caught. Atheline was sick yesterday evening & is not well this morning, headache. Jinnie has taken the children to Mrs. Night's. Willie is no better. Mr. Henry has gone up to see Mrs. Cook. He wants to send some work to T. Cook by Cordelia so I am alone. I am writing in the hall. I must now see about dinner & then I must write to Dora & co. I want some dumplings for dinner. Mrs. W. Johnston sent here last night for some coffee. Mr. Henry will let her have 5 lbs. for 5$. He sold 5 lbs. for 5$ last week. That is a dear drink. We have had dinner, had black berry dumplings for they were very nice. We had honey & cream with them as sugar is getting to scarce. It is selling at 40 cts. per lb. in Asheville. I took a nap before dinner & now Mr. Henry is taking one. Old Mr. Boyd & daughter eat dinner here today. She is going to stay down at Ratliffe's where Mr. Boyd is at work. Mr. Boyd's family are not doing well. One of his daughters leads rather a loose life at home.

I want to take a long walk this evening. Willie seems right better today. That is, he is not so cross. My teeth have been aching all day. Mr. Henry got me hot ashes twice last night. They ached very badly for a while. We have not been up with Willie for several nights. I have written to Sister Jane & co. today.

Monday 28th - Made Hanes' pants & sewed some on Lonzo's. Willie very fretful. Mail brought no news of importance. A clear warm day. Mr. Henry went to Asheville, brought no news.

Tuesday 29th - I finished Lonzo's pants & sewed some little on Fannie's dress. Took Willie to ride this evening on John. Went past the Murray place. Mr. Henry was up in the Murray fields, the hands were mowing there. I rode Pinck & Zona a little after I came back. They were delighted.

Wednesday 30th July 1862 - I sewed some on Fannie's dress. Took Willie to ride on Jent (Hutsell mare). She is very lazy. I had to whip all the time. I only went on top of the hill towards Quinn's. It looked very much like rain & did rain soon after I got back. I had promised to ride Zona when I came back but she was not at the house & when she came it was raining. She was very angry about it, cried a good deal. Willie's bowels bad all day. Mr. Henry went to the carding machine today, took Pinck. It was dark when they got back.

Thursday 31st - Willie bad off all day. Rained all day. Jinnie sewed some on her dress. I finished Fannie's dress. I don't work half the time as I have to nurse Willie so much & attend him other ways. Mr. Henry was in the house all day. I am giving Willie white oak steeped in water & a strong tea of red & white oak to bath his bowels in. He has fallen off a great deal.

August 1862

Friday August 1st - I got a letter last Thursday from Dora. They were all well at Mr. Neilson's. They will be over some time this month on their way home. I would like to go with them if I can conveniently. I see nothing new in the papers. I sewed some on Jinnie's dress. Mr. Henry & I went to Till Morris' this evening. T. Morris got home last night. He says Tom Night is dead. Old W. Night got a letter today confirming it. Poor fellow. There was some other men went along with us. J. Tinsley & another man from Transylvania came to buy wheat. Jim cut his foot right badly last Wednesday. Stepped back on the scythe blade.

Saturday 2nd - My teeth & jaw pained me very badly all night. I slept but little from 1 o'clock. They ached on till after dinner & got easy before night. Louise McKinnish stays here tonight. Her mother is not at home. I finished Jinnie's dress before dinner & took a nap before dinner. A. B. Jones sent & borrowed 6 lbs. sugar this evening. I knit some after dinner. Willie's bowels very loose today. Mr. Henry cut his gum of eye tooth Thursday.

Sunday 3rd - A very pleasant morning. Preaching at the Academy but we are not gone. Pinck went with Tena & children. Willie's bowels are a good deal better this morning. We have roasting years[36] for dinner, our second mess. I had some last Wednesday. Jinnie's Sunday to cook. Old tan Smith is here, he comes too often. I must go now and see after dinner a little. Mr. Henry went up Hominy yesterday, bought some molasses. They are very nice. We have apple dumplings for dinner & lasses dip. Mr. Henry took a nap after dinner & we took a long walk. Went over to old Parker's (at the Tom Jones' place). Staid but a short time. I was very tired when I got home & had the headache very bad.

Monday 4th - Willie's bowels well. I hope they may remain so. I faced the hem of an under skirt today. Nothing of interest going on. Very dry & warm, needing rain badly. Jim's foot mending slowly. He is mending up some old chairs. Mail brought no news.

Tuesday 5th - Mended some stockings for Mr. Henry & myself & mended Mr. Henry a pair flan pants. Spent the evening at Mrs. Fanning's. Very warm & dry. Mr. Henry went over on Newfound today. Got some jeans & a coat to sell again.

Wednesday 6th - Faced another skirt today. Mr. Henry gone up Hominy today. We had a little rain this evening, not enough to do any good. Mr. Henry will not be back tonight as it has rained. Atheline sleeps in the house tonight. I sold some butter last Friday at 25 cts. per lb, 4 lbs. I was up a good deal last night with my teeth, had to smoke them before they got better.

Thursday 7th - Mr. Henry came this morning & brought us a basket of peaches, very ripe soft peaches. He is a dear kind husband to me & such a fond father. He has gone to Asheville today, did not get back till we were at supper. He brought me some smoking tobacco for my old teeth. I cut & sewed some on a shirt for Jim today. Very warm.

---

[36] Refers to ears of corn

WAR DEPARTMENT,
Adj't and Inspector Genl's Office.
Richmond, July 14, 1862.

GENERAL ORDERS,
No. 49.

ALL persons engaged in enrolling Conscripts, are hereby authorized and required to arrest deserters from the Army, and to deliver them to the commandant of the nearest Camp of Instruction, or to lodge them in the nearest jail, and to return their names, company and regiment, to the Adjutant and Inspector General.

Jailors are requested to detain them, and will be allowed the fees and charges for the detention of prisoners, prescribed by the laws of the State in which the jail is situated.

Enrolling officers are also required to report to the Adjutant and Inspector General the names and address of all persons absent from the Army, without leave, whether by the expiration of their leave of absence, furloughs, details or otherwise; and when this unauthorized absence exceeds the time required to correspond with the War Department, the enrolling officer will arrest the person and send him to the nearest Camp of Instruction, reporting the arrest to the Adjutant and Inspector General.

Commandants of Camps of Instruction are required to forward deserters and persons absent without leave, to their regiments, and have the powers of arrest conferred upon enrolling officers.

By command of the Secretary of War.

S. COOPER,
Adjutant and Inspector General.

July 31.   3t

☞ The Register, Wilmington Journal, Standard, Iredell Express, Salisbury Watchman, Charlotte Democrat and Asheville News 3 times.

Call to arrest deserters
The Asheville News, August 7, 1862

Friday 8th - Mail brought no news of importance. The Confederates fired into the yankee fleet a short time ago at night & did them some harm. Stonewall Jackson has gone to the Valley again to attend to Pope. I finished Jim's shirt & began Atheline's dress. Mrs. Fanning cut out the cloth yesterday. Jim & the children began to cut fruit today to dry sweet apples.

Saturday 9th - I finished Atheline's dress, washed the children & put them on clean clothes & cut some apples. We have out now what will make two bushels when dry, I think. Mr. Henry went to Asheville this afternoon. Late when he came back. We had had supper. Jim Parker is home on a short furlough. Mr. Henry had a letter from Harric yesterday. He is well & speaks in high terms of his coffee. He is Maj. Deaver now.

Sunday 10th August 1862 - Very warm this morning & dry. Mr. Henry will start to Richmond sometime this week with some substitutes, Branton & a man named Sutten. He is here now. He is from Transylvania Co. We have mutton for dinner & sundry other things too tedious to mention. Mr. Henry has just came back from bathing in Mill dam. He is laying down in side room. Willie & Pinck went with the negroes to bathe. I want to go to Steph Jones' after dinner. We would have gone this morning but Mr. Henry expected some men to see him. We did not go to Mr. Jones. We both eat such a heavy dinner, we took a nap. It was a very warm evening. Pinck & I went down to Night's a short, did not stay long.

SUBSTITUTE WANTED.

I WANT a substitute, to go in Capt. West's Company, Col. McDowell's Battalion, and will pay a liberal price. Apply at my residence on Swannanoa, 13 miles East of Asheville.

MILLINGTON LYTLE.

August 14.   3t

The Asheville News, August 20, 1862

Monday 11th - I changed a dress waist. It had a draw string & I put a belt in. I made it too tight. I will have to change it again. Very warm today. Jim is still drying fruit, gets along very well. Mr. Henry got two apple peelers Saturday in Asheville, gave 75 cts. a piece. They do very well. Tena & the children cut up. Mr. Henry & I were up at the hotel orchard & threw over a good many apples to the hogs. We went over in the peach orchard, got a few peaches that eat very well. They are just beginning to ripen on one tree. I left Mr. Henry at the old store house chatting with Dr. Thrash. I forget whether I have mentioned in my journal that G. W. Candler & his son Charlie are both dead. They both died sometime in July in Va. near Richmond. He had gone to see his sons & took sick & died. Charlie Candler was in the 14th Reg. N. C. V.

Tuesday 12th - I sewed some on Jinnie's dress. Very warm, needing rain badly. The garden looks as if it would parch up. The cucumber vines are doing but little good & the forward beans & potatoes are out.

NOTICE.

THIRTY DOLLARS REWARD will be paid for the arrest of the following members of the 16th Regiment N. C. Troops, if delivered to any Confederate officer, or Fifteen dollars if lodged in the county Jail. Jailors shall receive their fees.

Co. "A," Jackson Rangers.

James Bryant, Private, from Yancy Co., N. C.

Co. "B," Madison Rangers.

Thos. Brooks, Private, from Madison Co., N. C.
Abner Brooks,   "   "   "   "   "
Thomas Ball,   "   "   "   "   "
Thos. Stuman.   "   "   "   "   "

Co. "C," Black Mountain Boys.

E. Banks,   Private, from Yancy Co., N. C.
M. Ray, Corporal,   "   "   "   "
S. B. Ray,   Private, "   "   "   "
J. L. Ray,   "   "   "   "   "
J. W. Higgins,   "   "   "   "   "
J. D. Young,   "   "   "   "   "
E. M. Shepherd,   "   "   "   "   "

Co. "D," Rutherford Riflemen.

J. L. Millard, Priv., from Rutherford Co., N. C.
D. P. Lancaster, "   "   "   "   "
George Harris,   "   "   "   "   "
W. D. Huntsinger, "   "   "   "   "

Co. "E," Burke Tigers.

Henry Cannon, Corp'l, from Burke Co., N. C.
D. E. McPuett, Private, "   "   "   "
C. J. Copeland, "   "   "   "   "

Co. "F," Buncombe Sharp Shooters.

Jas. Smith, Private, from Buncombe Co., N. C.
S. W. Hutchison, "   "   "   "   "
Wm. Lunceford,   "   "   "   "   "
Louis Parris,   "   "   "   "   "
Wm. Sutton,   "   "   "   "   "
T. C. Reaves,   "   "   "   "   "
B. R. Lewis,   "   "   "   "   "
E. Chambers,   "   "   "   "   "
W. F. Dover,   "   "   "   "   "
J. B. Dover,   "   "   "   "   "
C. M. Green,   "   "   "   "   "
D. H. Fehant, Corp'l, "   "   "   "

Co. "G," Rutherford Volunteers.

Jas. H. Carrier, from Rutherford county, N. C.

Co. "H," Jeff. Davis Guards.

A. F. Morgan, Private, from Macon Co., N. C.

Co. "I," Henderson Guards.

W. H. Povey, Private, Henderson, Co., N. C.
J. H. Bryson,   "   "   "   "
Richard Liverett, "   "   "   "
J. M. Lytle,   "   "   "   "

Co. "K," Columbus Riflemen.

W. B. Mills, Sergeant, from Polk county, N. C.
D. M. Lankford, Private, "   "   "
Wm. Knight,   "   "   "   "

Co. "L," Haywood Rangers.

J. R. Chambers, Private, Haywood Co., N. C.
Samuel Clarke,   "   "   "   "
W. T. Clarke,   "   Caldwell   "
W. A. Presnell,   "   Haywood   "
J. C. Reinhardt, "   "   "   "

H. D. LEE, Major,
Comd'g 16th Regt. N. C. T.

August 21.   6t

Thirty dollar reward for deserters
The Asheville News, September 4, 1862

Wednesday 13th - Finished Jinnie's dress & began that man Sutton a shirt. Will finish it tomorrow. Willie is very cross. I don't know whether he is sick or spoiled. At any rate he makes good use of his lungs.

Thursday 14th - I finished the shirt & made a napsack after dinner. Mr. Henry has concluded to start Saturday. The children are all well. Pinck started to school yesterday morning but got sceered for fear the teacher (Miss Nelly Jones) would whip him. It is a free school & there are a great many scholars. Pinck can spell a little & prounounce only a little. He likes his book tollerable well. He does not spell every day for I forget it.

Friday 15th August 1862 - I have made another napsack & sewed some on Fannie's dress. Mrs. Fanning sent the last of the cloth here this morning. Fannie baked two turkeys & some crackers & ginger cakes, also boiled a ham for Mr. Henry to take along with him. He has gone to Asheville this evening, did not get back till after we eat supper.

Saturday 16th - They start to Richmond this morning. Peter goes along to bring the buggy back. I finished Fannie's dress & pealed nicely two bushels of apples in the peeler. Jim & Atheline cut them up. Mr. Henry came back this evening. Jim Parker is trying to hire a substitute & Mr. Henry came back to show the substitute's father the land. I really think Parker would do better business to go along in his place. Mr. Henry will go on the stage Monday. Peter came back & Jim Parker went on with the buggy.

Sunday 17th - Rather cool this morning. The man has not come yet to see the land. It is now dinner time. Mr. Henry is asleep in side room. We have roasting years for dinner & a good number of other things. The substitute man has come at last & we will soon have dinner. The children & I went up those peach trees on the hill to the right of the road. Hanes went along to get them off. Willie is not well this morning. Atheline has gone to Miller's to see some of her relatives & Aunt Tena has Willie. Mr. Henry & Patton went to see the land of Parker's. Mr. Henry did not get back till late so I did not go to walk this evening. A soldier stays here tonight. He came back with Mr. Henry. Willie's bowels are very loose today.

Monday 18th - Mr. Henry started this morning for Richmond. I shall be so very lonely. I miss him so much. He is so fond & loving when with me, which makes such a blank when he is gone. If he should go in the service of the Confederacy, I really believe it would kill me. I have been so dependant on him. I shall often wish for him even this short trip & if he had to stay a year at a time I should be a lunatic I really believe. I trimmed Jinnie's hat today. Before dinner I made Zona a hoop also. Mr. Edd Ham took dinner with us today & went on to Asheville. Dr. Peake's family all well. He is going to join Morgan's men so he said he is not worsted by camp life at all, only a little sunburnt. I have the headache a good deal badly tonight.

Tuesday 19th August 1862 - This day 26 years ago I began life. I have never seen but little of the dark side & pray I never may. Since I have been married, life has moved on as calm as "a summer sea." I have enjoyed life very well so far. 26 years ago & a fond loving mother tended me & 13 years ago the 21st of last April I gazed my last on that loving parent. She sleeps in peace. How little I knew what I had lost, I was a mere child. I have done nothing of consequence today. Fixed a dress that is too small in the band. Willie's bowels very loose & he has some fever all the time. Oh! how I wish he would be stout & healthy. He has been sick a good deal this summer & fallen off a great deal. He is beginning to try to talk, can say dink for drink, bic for biscuit & bon for bonnett. He is very ill.

Wednesday 20th - Willie no better, consequently nothing done by me. Louise McKinnish has staid with me since Mr. Henry left (at night). She is a simple hearted creature & innocent too. I think she is not intelligent for she has never had any advantages. R. Boyd is making the furnice for the dry house. The house is not up yet. We have some 8 bu. of dried fruit & it is very nice fruit. Jim is still working at it as his foot is not well by a good deal.

Thursday 21st - Willie is no better. I staid by myself last night. Mr. Boyd staid at Mrs. Branton's & Louise did not come down. I was not affraid yet I was lonely. Atheline or Fannie sleep in here every night. I have to be up once or twice every night with Willie. How I wish Mr. Henry was at home. I sewed a little on the trimming of Atheline's scoop, will finish it tomorrow. It is a pink cambrie. Very dry.

Friday 22nd - I received a letter from Dora today saying they would be here sometime this month. I wish they would come to chase away some of the long weary days that Mr. Henry will be away. He will be gone some three weeks. I think Dora is a kind sweet disposed creature & Matt is so full of life. I hope they may stay sometime. Nothing of importance only Stonewall Jackson has had a fight in valley in Va. We whipped as usual.

Saturday 23rd 1862 August - Willie seemed better yesterday but still has fever. I sent Charlie after Dr. Hilliard this evening. Willie is not worse nor better. I think it is worms as his bowels are not very loose. We had a good season of rain this evening. I believe it rains every camp meeting here. The camp meeting at Asbury's Campground began last Thursday. I shall not go at all as Willie is not well & the buggy has not come back from Greenville yet. Parker took it there with Branton & co. & I hear today that the horse they worked to it (Hutsell mare) is give out down on the river. I must send for them this week. I have knit a little today, all I have done. I was down at the mill this morning & came by Mrs. Night's. She has a fine son born this morning. She is doing very well.

Sunday 24th - Dr. Hilliard did not come yesterday but said he would come over this morning but he has not come today. I heard he could not get a horse. I looked for him all day. He will surely come in the morning. I staid nearly all day at Aunt Tena's house. She is the only one here, the others all gone to camp meeting. She got dinner. We had a little rain today, not much. Pinck went to the camp ground with Charlie, rode behind him. He is delighted with his trip. It is near 8 o'clock now & I will stop as I want to read. Willie's bowels a good deal better, a health passage today but still has fever.

Monday 25th - Jinnie & I began to scour the house. Cleaned all down stairs, very nice. The mail brought no news. A good many letters went on this evening. Willie seems a little better. How I wish he was well. He is very cross. Jim's mother & sister came here Saturday morning, will leave tomorrow. Sam & the other men putting up the dry house. Tena put in the cloth for Jim's & the other's pants at Mrs. Fanning's. Only 12 yds. She will get it out this week.

Tuesday 26th - Jinnie & I cleaned upstairs today. Moved another bed in Harrie's room. Dora & others will be here soon. R. Boyd has made a large fruit box. Jim is still drying fruit. His foot not well yet. He has a nice chance dried & beautiful fruit. I stay by myself at night, only Fannie or Atheline sleeps on the floor.

Wednesday 27th Aug. 1862 - Jinnie cleaned the dining room & then swept the yards, her & Hanes. Peaches are beginning to ripen a little, clingstones. I have done some mending today, indeed I have done nothing else. Berry Hogan came this evening & another man named Saunders. Berry is on his way to Tenn. Lane is driving a hack, taking a negro woman to nurse Sister Jane's babe down home as she gives no milk. Berry is going to bring some sheep back. Jinnie's brother Jim is along to help drive the sheep. Willie still improves very slow.

Thursday 28th - Berry & Saunders off to Asheville. Mrs. Charlie Moore & niece (Mrs. Clark) spent the day here. I did some sewing for Mrs. Clark on the machine, two shirt bosoms. They had a great deal of work on them. The machine did not sew well at all. It skipped so much. We had our first peach pie for dinner & several other things. I knit a little today on Willie's stocking. Striped red & white. Atheline has been knitting on them.

Friday 29th - I got a long letter this morning from Mr. Henry. It is needless to say it was welcome. I read it several times. He was in Richmond & well. I also received one from Harrie Deaver thanking me for the dried apples & turkey. He seemed very grateful for the farms. I read the papers till dinner & made some tatting after dinner for Zona a gown. I bought 12 1/2 lbs. of sugar of A. B. Jones today at 40 cts. per lb. Not good sugar at that. Berry & co. started soon this morning, will get to Sister Jane's tomorrow evening. Newton Taylor stays here tonight on his way back to camps. Old Mr. Henry tollerable stout so Taylor says.

William L. Henry to Cornelia C. Henry

Richmond Va. 23rd August

My Dear Sweet and Affectionate Wife,

I have not written to you since I left home until now. We are well. Nothing of any consequence happened to us until we got to the place. We got here in the night and the Rail road was so situated that we had to get out on the Rail road bridge. The train being near a quarter of a mile long. Well it was dark when we got off our seats. I told Sitton to follow me and Branton. He did not and we got lost from him and I have not seen him since. That was night before last. All day yesterday Branton & I hunted for him. Branton heard of him. I had to watch him very close all along the road as he would bounce out at every stopping of the cars.

I was yesterday at the Capitol at the meeting of the Congress. I saw our member A. T. Davidson, but did not speak to him. Heard a speech of Mr. Foot of Tennessee upon State's rights. As I came out the hall I met who do you think. The only man that I ever saw before I came to R. except Davidson and I was glad to see him and he almost cried when I spoke to him. We talked 30 minutes and he had to leave and I must confess that I was melancolly when he left.

I am going to the camps of the 23rd this day. I hear that the ambulance train is ordered to be in readiness to go to the Battle expected up the country as the Battle is imminent & will take place soon. Stonewall is trying to get behind the enemy and cut off his retreat.

Richmond is a large city. Some large buildings, some large mills & iron works. The canal furnishes motion power. The iron works are big things for me. One of them are turning out one cannon per day and any amount of shell and shot. Also making large quantities of sheeting iron for the Virginia No. 2. I went to see the No. 2 yesterday. She is a flat looking critter and monstrous stout. I think she is pierced for 3 guns on each side and one before & behind. She will be ready for sea in a month or less time. The men say 2 weeks.

There are a great many ladies on the streets and very gaudy. I don't know how many thousand I saw yesterday of the F. F. V's. Some are very fond of their persons and are grinning & tittering as though the world was on a pleasure trip. I will give you something of the prices paid here. Board from 2 to 4 dollars, common sized watermellons 3 dollars each, peaches $1 pr. dozen, apples 3 to 10 cents each. Other things in proportion, butter, milk 25 cents, the glass extra.
I will quit now.
Kiss the children all around for me and one thousand kisses for my dear wife.
I am as ever,
Wm. Henry

Saturday 30th - Taylor left this morning. I sent Peter with him to get the horse & buggy left at Chuns bridge. He will get back tomorrow I think. I have been making tatten today. Cleaned the children after dinner, washed their heads. Willie is a great deal better. Tena got the cloth out this evening. Fannie baked some ginger cakes this evening for the children. She has done the washing & ironing this week. I was at Mrs. Fanning's a short time yesterday evening. Mrs. Night getting on finely.

Sunday 31st - Cloudy this morning. We need rain very badly. There was rain on the mountains yesterday evening but we got none. This will be a long, long day to me. I expect spend it on reading. I hope Mr. Henry will be here before another Sunday. I shall look for him the last of this week. We have had several watermelons. We have two nice ones I want to save till Mr. Henry, Dora and them comes. They are not pulled yet.

September 1862

Monday Sept. 1st 1862 - I cut & made Jim's pants today & sewed some on John's. Billie Sutton spent the day here. He is a deserter from the 16th Reg. I don't blame them much as they have had a hard time this war. We had a little rain this morning, not enough to do any good. Willie is improving a little. Mail brought no news. A good many letters went on this morning.

Tuesday 2nd - Finished John's pants & made Peter's & sewed a little on Pinck's. He has some like the negroes. In the evening late I went to Bets McKinnish's to see some chickens she got from Dub.[37] I knew the chickens very well. They were once mine. Louise came home with me. All are well.

Wednesday 3rd - Finished Pinck's pants & made the women an apron each like the boys pants. It kept me busy all day. Louise stays with me tonight. I read every night & knit. Very dry with cool mornings & evenings. Feels almost like frost.

Thursday 4th - Made Atheline's other dress & John a pair pants, suspenders, besides patching Pinck's coat. Louise stays with me tonight. All are well. The negroes are drying peaches for me, not peeling. The dry house is not done yet.

Friday 5th - Mail came but brought nothing new. They have had another fight near Manassas. The Confederates whipped them back. Oh God grant us peace once again is the pray of many a heart. The conscript bill has passed taking men to 45. I fear Mr. Henry will have to go & then farewell to happiness for me. I had a letter from Mr. Henry. He is well. He will be home soon. He said by the 5th of this month. Oh! how I wish he would come. He is needed at home now on business.

William L. Henry to Cornelia C. Henry and children

Richmond Va. 27th August 1862

My dear Wife & children
My dear Boy Pinckney
My dear little Arizona
My dear Baby Willie

I write to say that I am well and Mr. Branton is well. Say to his wife that he is harty & will not gone as a substitute yet. I saw Perry Gaston & several other boys, Old Mr. Webb's son Harrison and have been for four days trying to get a furlough for them. They are sick and not able to be of service to the Army.

A great bustle in the city. Any amount of escravigance shown here. I saw M. Gaines the other day. Nothing happening. Stonewall is driving so far before him. The conscript bill will pass taking conscripts to 45 or 50 years. I will then have to go. I intend trying to get an office here as clerk or some other indoor officer as I have a great dread to laying out on the ground and the exposure of an Army.

[37] Slave owned by James L. Henry

I dreamed last night that Harry Deaver was dead!!! Winslo Bergan has lost a leg and is gone home. This is a great city of Captains, leutenants & officers as one half of the men you meet have the bars or stars on the coat collar. All officers and great in their own estimation. There are at least ten thousand men and officers here loafing generally.

I have nothing to write. You see that by the short note above. If you want to write to me at Simsville, S. C. I would like to find a letter there from you. I will be at home soon, say by 5 Sept. I think.

My love to the children & ten thousand kisses to my Dinah Dear. I am, Wm. Henry

---

Saturday 6th - I have done nothing of importance today. Let down a skirt that was too short & read a good deal & knit. Sister Jane & the others came this evening. I was very glad to see them. Miss Eliza Neilson came over this evening with them. She is going to school in Asheville. She is a very pleasant girl. We enjoyed the evening finely. I do enjoy my friends very much & my sisters are very pleasant good girls & Sister Jane is so kind & motherly. She is devoted to her babe. It is a sweet little delicate thing. It sucks the negro woman very well.

Sunday Sept. 7th 1862 - A very pleasant day. Rather cool this morning but pleasant through the day. We eat our large watermellon today. It was very nice & ripe. We also had a nice dinner. Peaches & cream for dinner & the day has passed very pleasantly. 'Tis now late in the evening & Miss Eliza, Dora, Matt & the children have gone to Sulphur Springs. I do hope Mr. Henry will come this evening as he is needed badly at home to attend to some business. I hope he may come tonight. If he don't come before the mail leaves tomorrow evening, I must write to him at Simsville but I do hope he will come. It is now time to get out supper. Sister Jane is upstairs with her babe & I am alone in the hall writing.

Monday 8th - I have done nothing today but knit on a sock for Mr. Henry. I sent for the mail this morning by old Parker. No letter for me. We have enjoyed ourselves very well this day. Sister Jane & I, as Matt & Dora went with Eliza Neilson to school. They came back late in the evening & rather cool.

Tuesday 9th - I cut out Peter & John a shirt each. Matt helped me. She finished one. I sew some on the other, did not get it done. The day passed very pleasantly. We had turkey for dinner today. We had the same one yesterday but Fannie did not get it done so we had it again today. Very nice.

Wednesday 10th - I finished the shirt today & knit after dinner. All are well. Sister Jane's little babe has had a very bad cold but is now nearly well. Willie my pet is getting better, fattening every day.

Thursday 11th - Mr. Henry came home about 1 o'clock last night. I was rejoiced to see him. I was getting uneasy about him. He has been very well since he left, came up by Pa's. They are all well down there. Nothing new. Col. Gadberry was killed in the last engagement at Manassas. No other casualties that I know. At least I have not seen any in the papers. I have done nothing today but knit.

Friday 12th - Mail brought no news more than we have heard. A good many letters came to the office today but none to us. I read a good deal & knit some. We took a ride this morning up to the grave yard. Zona & Willie went also. It was very pleasant. The sun shone rather warm as we came back. Pinck staid with his Papa. Bob Tidwell came this evening. I did not know him.

Saturday 13th September 1862 - Berry came this morning, had not had breakfast. They got some 80 sheep. Very warm today. Sister Jane has concluded to go to Asheville tomorrow, also Matt & Dora. Mr. Henry, Matt & I went to get some peaches this evening below the hotel garden in the hollow. They are very nice. It was a very warm walk. Mr. J. Common stays here tonight.

Sunday 14th - Sister Jane, Dora, Matt & old Jinnie went to Asheville this morning. They thought of going to church. We had a very good season last night & it has sprinkled a good deal today & still cloudy. Willie is not so well today, frets a good deal. The hack has just started to Asheville with the baggage, it is well loaded. Berry will start early in the morning. I am writing upstairs. Mr. Henry is up here lying on the bed. Berry down stairs with a man from Columbia by the name of Skipper. The children there also. I expect it shall be rather lonely for a while now they are all gone, but I will get used to it soon. Mr. Henry is so kind, he stays with me all he can. No one knows how much I love him for he is ever kind. Old Mr. Common stays here tonight. I wish he would go home for he is a great bore. R. S. Tidwell is here also. He leaves for Cherokee in the morning.

Monday 15th - Breakfast very early. Berry got a good start. Skipper & Mr. Henry went to Asheville today. It is reported that our forces are in Maryland. I do hope we may soon have peace. I fixed some shirts for Willie today, at least one & will fix the other two tomorrow. Cloudy & looks like rain. I fear Sister Jane will have a bad time for traveling with her babe.

Tuesday 16th - I fixed the other two shirts today & knit some. Mr. Henry went up Hominy Creek today, did not get back till late in the evening. Fannie does the cooking now. Atheline has a sore foot. She cut some fruit. Peaches are nearly all gone. Uncle Sam got done shearing the sheep today. The wool is very short.

Wednesday 17th - I sew up a lining for a quilt. I want to quilt it soon (my cactus quilt). I made some peach butter today & knit some. Tena & Bets McKinnish washing the wool. Willie's bowels are quite loose again.

Thursday 18th - I have been knitting nearly all day. I began to crochet Zona a net today of coloured cotton, did but little at it. I got some sweet potatoes for dinner today. The thrashers came today to thrash Mr. Henry's wheat, Hendrix & Co. The wheat turns out but poorly. Flour is now selling at 12 1/2 cts. per lb.

Friday September 19th 1862 - Mail brought no news this morning, we got no letters. I knit after dinner. I commenced a pair cotton socks for Mr. Henry. They are very fine & smooth. They are the first I have ever knit him. Willie is still loose in his bowels. I attend to him as Hanes is helping about the wheat & Atheline is not able to walk on her foot much. Mr. Henry contracted for two wheels & a reel the other day. They are to be done in a month.

Saturday 20th - We have had a little rain today. I finished Zona's net today & grabbled a basket of sweet potatoes. I got a little damp as it rained some while I was up there. I changed my clothes soon after I came back. Rather cool & fire feels comfortable. I reckon Sister Jane & the others got home this evening. I would like to be with them. I know they are glad to get back once again.

Sunday 21st - Cloudy & warm this morning but no rain yet. We have turnip salad for dinner. Our first mess. The turnips will be few this year as it has been too dry for them. Sam killed a kid yesterday evening two weeks ago today. The hogs like to eat up old Jim Knight. He was drunk & lay down in the road, not far from Gudger's Mill on Hominy & they suppose it was the hogs. His face is badly cut up & both ears smooth off. I have not seen him. I will soon stop as it is dinner time. Mr. Henry down stairs reading. Willie & Pinck gone with the negroes chinqueapin hunting. They are opening a good deal now. Zona upstairs with me. It seems like fall of the year to look out today. The wind blows mournfully like it. How I wish I was at home this day with Dora & them. I want to go badly.

Monday 22nd - I have been fixing some napkins for Willie today. His bowels are still loose. We have cool mornings & evenings & I fear we will soon have frost. J. Cannon & Co. are still thrashing here, the wheat turning out badly. Aunt Patsy Jimison spent the day here. I was glad to see her. I did nothing but knit while she was here & after she left I fixed two napkins.

Tuesday 23rd - Finished the napkins today. Willie's bowels getting a little better. The others well. Mr. Henry went to Asheville today as the mail carrier told us last night that there had been some hard fighting at Harpers Ferry. Our forces have taken it with terrible loss on both sides. The conscript bill has passed one house of congress. If it should pass both houses it will nearly ruin this country as there are so many poor men with large families of that age.

Wednesday 24th 1862 September - I have been carding bats today to put in my cactus quilt. Atheline helped some. I got it in & quilted a little on it. The thrashers got done here today late this evening. Willie is getting some better. Dyptheria is raging through the country at a fearful rate now. I pray God my little ones may escape.

Thursday 25th - I gathered some potatoes for dinner today & then quilted the rest of the day. Atheline will begin to cook tomorrow. Mrs. Garman spent the day here. She came to see Mr. Henry about selling some jeans to him. She asks 3$ pr. yd. He went to Asheville this morning, did not get back till night. He will not take the jeans at that price.

Friday 26th - Mail brought nothing of importance as Mr. Henry brought the mail yesterday. There has been some terrible fighting within the last week. We have been victorious so far. It seems God has been with us. I have been quilting since I read all the papers. Hanes attended to Willie. Mr. Henry went to Jim Sutton's sale, everything sold very high. He did not get back till after supper. R. Boyd stays here tonight.

Saturday 27th - I have done sundry mending today. Have not taken down the quilt. Made Zona & Willie a doll each & knit & read some in "Vallette," a novel. I have read it once before some years ago. Mr. Henry went to Asheville today, late when he came home. Cloudy & cool all day.

Sunday 28th - Mr. Henry got some oil cloth yesterday, some he sent to Columbia for by Mr. Skipper. He wants to have the long talked of carriage finished so I can go home this fall. Cool this morning with a bright sun. T. Cook is down stairs. His children has had sore throat & one (little Laura) died. I will stop now as I want to have sweet potato pudding for dinner & I will grate the potatoes & sweeten with molasses. After dinner I want to pick some chinquiapins. Some soldiers took dinner here today, two sick & Mr. Inman. He was carrying his son home. He looked very badly. Mr. Henry sent them home, at least loaned them a horse. Mr. Skipper stays here tonight. Mrs. Common came here this evening.

Monday 29th - Mrs. Common went to Asheville this morning, will return this afternoon. I have spent the day quilting, got along very well. Willie is still very loose in his bowels. Jeff woke us up last Friday night by barking incessantly. The dry house was a bright blaze. It burnt the top off. Left the walls standing. There was some 8 bushels of fruit nearly dry in it.

Tuesday 30th September 1862 - I have quilted all day. I can't quilt more than half a side a day. It is very tedious work. Atheline does the cooking. Hanes attends to Willie. His bowels get no better. The other children are very well. Charlie has had the sore throat, it is getting better. A good many cases of dyptheria in the neighborhood. I trust & hope my little ones may escape. Mrs. Common left this morning for home.

October 1862

Wednesday October 1 - Quilted all day. Nothing new going on. There has been some terrible battles lately. Our troops have been victorious & I sincerely hope may continue so. I have not heard a word from Dora & them since they left.

Thursday 2nd - I have quilted all day again. Only mended Willie's gown where Jeff had torn it trying to get if off the nail to lay on. Willie's bowels are getting a little better. Pinck spells a little nearly every day. Zona runs about & makes herself generally useful.

Friday 3rd - Mail brought nothing new. The Asheville News failed to come. Mr. Henry was in Asheville yesterday & got a News. I quilted after reading all the papers.

Saturday 4th - I quilted till dinner & got ready to roll and after dinner Mr. Henry helped me to roll. I washed a little after dinner. I have been attending to Willie yesterday & today as Hanes is picking beans. Zona stays with him when he gets in the yard.

Sunday 5th - Willie slept very badly last night & I had the toothache a good deal. I think he was too warm as it was a very warm night. I slept without cover. His bowels have got nearly well. I got some potatoes for dinner, had a pudding very nice sweetened with molasses, fried cabbage, kid sweet potatoes and other things. A Mr. Morgan eat dinner here. He has gone. Mr. Reynolds preached at the Academy today. Mr. Henry & I did not go. The negroes, all but Jinnie, went. She got dinner. It is now near 3 o'clock. Mr. Henry has gone to pick some chinquiapins. Zona is asleep. Pinck & Willie went off this morning with Atheline to the old Hendrix house to see some of Catherine's kin that lives there. I must write to Lena this evening & there are others I ought to write to so no more time to my journal now.

Monday October 6th 1862 - Mr. Henry & I took a long walk. Zona was along also. Yesterday evening we took a letter to Mrs. Branton. Mr. Henry sent Peter to Asheville yesterday after the mail. Nothing new in the papers. I have been quilting today. I get along very well as I attend to Willie & have to get up often to wait on him & Zona. Mail brought no news.

Tuesday 7th - Quilted again today. No great deal. We are all well. Nothing new going on. I wrote to all my sisters last Sunday & hope I may soon get a letter from some of them. They don't write often.

Wednesday 8th - Mr. Henry went to Spring creek this morning, will be back tomorrow evening. I stay tonight with my little ones & Atheline. I am not at all afraid, yet I feel lonely when he is gone. I have quilted a little today. Mrs. McDowell & Mrs. Mont Patton spent the evening here yesterday. Mr. Henry went to Stan Jones' yesterday evening. He is quite sick.

Thursday 9th - Mr. Henry came home before night. He is broke down in the back again. I made him a nice cup of coffee. It helped his headache a good deal. He strained his back throwing up one of the children yesterday morning. He first strained it in 1852 moving a cross tie, & then again some five years ago a horse threw him & his back has been weak ever since. The conscript bill has passed.[38] I hope Mr. Henry will not have to go. If he does, what is to become of me & my children?

Friday 10th - Mail brought no news, only Price & Vandorn have had an engagement with the yanks not far from Corinth. We whipped them good. That is all the news up to this time. I quilted after reading the papers. Mr. Henry's back is improving slowly. I bathe it good at morning, noon & night in mustang linement. I hope he may soon be restored to perfect health.

Saturday 11th - I quilted some little today. Pinck was sick all the evening, had some fever & complained of his throat being sore. Zona had some fever also. They lay before the fire all the evening. I was really alarmed for fear they were taking dyptheria. Willie has got well once again. Mr. Henry started Hanes to Asheville after the mail this morning but he got frightened at some men they were taking to jail from Jackson Co., so Mr. Henry went after dinner. We had to retreat from Corinth with a heavy loss of men.

Sunday 12th October 1862 – Cool, cloudy & has been raining. It rained a good deal yesterday evening & last night. I did not rest well as Pinck called for water several times last night & I was sick myself. We had a very nice fat opossum yesterday for dinner & I eat too much. I was up a time or two. Pinck & Zona seem well enough this morning. It is quite cool & the wind feels like Autumn is upon us. Mr. Henry is laying down in my room. He lays down a good deal with his back. I am in the side room writing, my hands & feet are getting very cold so I will soon stop & it is getting time for dinner as it is one o'clock. I want to write to Lou Davenport this evening. I did not write to Lou. Mr. Henry & I started to walk this evening. Pinck & Zona saw us & started after us. We came back to them as Zona took one

---

38 The Confederate Congress passed the Second Conscription Act September 27th, 1862, authorizing the President to draft men between the ages of 35 and 45

of her staggery spells. I think they are caused by worms. We went up to see the fattening hogs. There are some very nice ones among them. Mr. Henry has near 90 to slaughter this year. It sprinkled rain a little before we got back. Zona was with us.

Monday 13th - Court in Asheville this week. Mr. Henry went. He is not at all well. Joe Russell & Mr. Furgerson came home with him & stay all night. It was late when they came (dark). We had not had supper. Very cool this evening. I have been quilting a little today. Mr. Henry had a chill after he got home & a high fever. I fear he will be sick.

Tuesday 14th - Mr. Henry a good deal better but not able to attend court. He has laid down nearly all day. Sent after Dr. Thrash this evening, he was not at home. I have quilted some today, got along slowly. Rolled this evening for the third & last time.

Wednesday 15th - Mr. Henry went to the top of the hill this morning with J. Russell & Fergerson as they staid here last night again. It fatigued him a good deal. He waited up there to see Dr. Thrash till near 11 o'clock. I have quilted a little to-day. Mr. Henry went to the mill this evening & took a chill. He was freezing for awhile with the fever. It alarmed me a good deal. He was sitting before the fire & I had to call George to help him to bed. It soon wore off. A man came to stay all night about 8 o'clock. I was ready for bed but put on my clothes. He got his supper & went to bed. He is from Haywood.

Thursday October 16th 1862 - Mr. Henry very feeble all day, has not sit up any. Hanes attends to Willie today. I finished Mr. Henry's cotton socks today & began some for Zona. Striped red, black & white. Have knit but very little as Mr. Henry is not well & I can't work well. Dr. Thrash came this morning, recommended blue pill. He says 'tis Mr. Henry's liver that is not doing well.

Friday 17th - Mail brought no news. Mr. Henry some better, can sit up. Aunt Patsy Jamison spent the day here. Cousin Mary Moore was here a short time in the evening to see Mr. Henry. He sit up nearly all day today. I hope he will soon be well. Sam & some of the others killed a beef this evening, a young one. It is very nice & fat. I have knit a little today. Aunt Patsy took some wool home with her this evening to spin stockings, yarn blue mixed.

Saturday 18th - Frost this morning in low places. It did not kill the pepper. I pulled up a good deal of it yesterday evening to let it dry on the stalk. We have saved a fine chance of ripe pepper this summer, more than usual. I have knit a little in the evening. Mr. Henry & I went down to see the hogs. They are in pens not far from the mill. We then went by the mill to the sawmill where Wiley Knight is mak-ing a molasses mill & then to the dam. Mr. Henry did not seem to be fatigued much. He is improving slowly, does not eat anything of consequence. This has been a bright warm day after the morning was off.

Sunday 19th - Rather cool this morning but bright & warm now. Mr. Henry still improving. I hope he will be well soon. He had a very slight chill yesterday evening & complained of headache a good deal when he first got up but it is better now. Dinner will soon be on. I must stop & draw off the P. O. return. Mr. Henry as-sisted me with the return, got it ready to leave with the mail tomorrow. Old Tanner

Smith was here part of the day. Nothing new going on in the country, all quiet along the Potomac.

Monday 20th - Mr. Henry improves very slow, is not able to go to the mill without resting. I do hope he may soon be well. He frets so much about staying in the house all the time. The others are all well. George Peak eat dinner here today. He left about 2 o'clock for Asheville. Said he was going to Hendersonville tonight. Rather cool all day. I have quilted some today, will get it out in two more days, I think. Mr. Henry & Zona went to the mill this afternoon. He still has slight chills & fever every day. George Peak was telling us of a battle in Kentucky. Our forces were victorious completely as Gen. Bragg commanding the Confederates. We took a great many prisoners, Army stores &c. The mail carrier says the same is reported in Greenville S. C.

Tuesday 21st - Quilted after the cool of the morning was over, will get it out tomorrow. I sold 6 lbs. of butter yesterday evening for 3$. Dear butter surely. Mr. Henry continues to improve very slow. Has no appetite for anything. I hope & pray he may soon be restored to perfect health. He is a dear kind husband to me & a fond father to his little ones.

Wednesday 22nd - I finished my quilt today. I have been four weeks lacking one day at work on it. I have not quilted every day. I have missed four days besides several pieces of days as it has been so cool for the last three days. I have not commenced work till ten o'clock. Hanes has attended to Willie for a week so he is no trouble to me. Mr. Henry still improves. Atheline put mud on the grease spots in my room so I want to scour tomorrow. Three soldiers stay here tonight. One had his arm shot off at the Richmond battles, named Hunter.

Thursday 23rd - Mr. Henry says he feels a good deal better this morning as he sweated very freely last night. He took some sulphur. He is salivated slightly & his teeth are sore. Jinnie & I scoured my room & she scoured the back & front piazza, also the dining room. Mr. Henry & I took a short walk this evening, went nearly to the mill. He did not complain of fatigue when we came back. The children were at the mill. They came back with us. Willie was there also.

Friday 24th - Mr. Henry a good deal better. Mail brought several letters but none for us. The report of the battle in Kty. is true. The Confederates whipped them badly. I cleaned upstairs today as I hear Sister Jane will be in Asheville tomorrow evening. I think she will be here soon after she gets to Dr. Neilson's. I hope she will stay some time with us. I did not scour, only moved the wool & arranged things generally. Mr. Henry, Pinck, Zona & I went to the mill dam this evening so he is getting well.

Saturday 25th October 1862 - I have made me some cloth shoes today. I was not needing them but made them to try the pattern. They do not fit very well but are very easy. I put some old soles to them. They are very warm as I made them of jeans out & in. Mrs. George Jones was here a short time this evening wanting leather for shoes. I feel very sorry for her, she looks so desolate & I think she feels so too. Mr. Henry is a great deal better & I am very glad of it. He has got so he can eat with some relish. His mouth has got well. He sent Hanes to Asheville yesterday for the mail. No letters at all came & the papers have nothing new in them.

Sunday 26th - We had some rain last night & it is raining & snowing a little now. Very cold & unpleasant. I very much fear the sweet potatoes will spoil as they dug them yesterday & Friday. They are covered with straw & boards. I have saved a nice chance of pepper & that I pulled up is ripening very well on the bush. Mr. Boyd staid here last night & is here now & will stay till after dinner. The snow I see is laying on the kitchen. I don't think it will snow much, at least I hope it won't for it will ruin the sweet potatoes. We are all in my room by the fire. Mr. Henry & Mr. Boyd reading. Pinck & Zona eating chesnuts, some George gave awhile ago. I am going to get two Gall & 1/2 for 1.00 from him in the morning. Mr. Henry says he is well this morning, only a little feeble. Oh! how I pity the poor soldiers this cold day. They are suffering for clothes & shoes at this time & we are so comfortable around our hearth. I do indeed pity them, may we soon have an honorable peace is my prayer & the pray of every true Southerner. I must stop soon as I want to read some. I have been reading "Mothers Recompence" for some two or three weeks at odd times & want to finish it today. It is now soon after 12 & dinner will soon be on. We have had a big snow & very cold at night. The snow was two inches deep where it lay & would have been a big snow if all that fell had not melted so fast. The ground froze in the evening. The wind from the North & very cold. Poor soldiers you will suffer this night. Boyd went home after dinner. Mr. Henry wants him to put a chimney to the dining room soon as it is so cold in there. I hope will do it before long. Mr. Henry is much better today, will be able soon to go any where.

Monday October 27th 1862 - Cold with wind from North. Fannie & Jinnie picking & breaking the black wool. The other hands getting fire wood. Mr. Henry at the mill nearly all day. He is about well, has a good appetite. I have bound my new quilt today with red. It looks very well. Mail brought no news, only a little fight at Pocataligo on the coast in S. C. Our forces drove the yanks to their boats. We lost some 20 killed & 60 wounded & missing. The yanks lost a great many more. I cut Mr. Henry five shirts this evening out of sheeting. In three of them I put bleached bosoms. Other two linen.

Tuesday 28th - Sewed some on one shirt today. Fannie & Jinnie at work at the wool. Mr. Henry staid at the mill nearly all day. Much warmer today than yesterday, the snow will nearly all melt today except on the North hill sides. My little ones are barefooted this cold weather. Pinck has boots but has a sore toe & can't wear them. His toe looks very bad. Willie has some old shoes for he has worn shoes all summer but little Zona is perfectly barefooted. We have some nice goat skins to make them shoes but don't know when I can get them made as old Presley is making for the negroes. Peter went to the machine today after the soles. He tells us that Sister Jane stays in Asheville tonight & will leave in the morning for Ten. I think she might have given us a call. Mr. Henry has been out all day riding. Steph. Jones starts Thursday to sell Mr. Henry's hogs for him or buy corn to feed on.

Wednesday 29th - Mrs. Jamison spent the day here. I have not done much on the shirt. The machine stitched the bosom very well. Aunt Patsy brought home some light mixed stocking yarn. It is very nice, blue & white. A great deal warmer today. The leaves are crisped up on the apple trees from the cold. We have had heavy frosts every morning for several days.

W. B. Tidwell to William L. Henry

Camp near Warrenton, Va.
Oct. 29th 1862

Dear Capt.

I will write you a short note to let you know the different proceedings. News came to this place on yesterday that McClellan had drawn his forces from the Potomic supposed for suffering. If so we will be ordered imegrating to Richmond. Col. Payne secured a dispatch from Gen. Lee yesterday stating that McClellan had disappeared from the Potomic. He ordered the Col. to send a party to Manassas and as far in the direction of Centerville as practible. Capt. Randolph with one hundred men starts on the seventh taking from our company 12 men for an advance guard. It is very probable that they will have a skirmish before returning. Gil is now on picket and will be relieved this morning. I was out night before last with a squad of 50 men in the direction of Brustor station. I found nothing and returned safe.

I sent in my application for a leave of absence yesterday. I do not know whether or not I will get it. But if I do you may look out for me in Murphy before long. Lt. Guilford has sent up his resignation. I am greatly in hopes that you will hire a fine inf. and get all the clothing and shoes and other things that your men need. The boys are very anxious to see the boots. I am fearfull that some of our boys will be compelled to suffer this winter for need of warm clothing. I do want you to try and get the company with Thomas in Tenn. I am truly in hopes that you may affect the move. I. J. Slaughter wants you to bring a man in his place.

Be shure to write me how Miss Laura is coming on and if you can hear from Brother Bob let me know where he is. If there is any good or bad news in old Cherokee let me know. Write me how you enjoyed yourself getting home. How is Sallie F. coming on?

I had like to forget telling you the news that Capt. Hugh our comissary had resigned. He is going to Europe on business for Gov. Zeb. Dr. Thomas is talking of going also. There has been more yankees in this neighborhood since you left. My Yankee horse is all right. His legs is getting as limber as drum sticks. I will look to hear all the news from you. I have not heard from your horses since you left. I imagine they are all right and so I close hoping to hear from you soon.

I remain with profound esteem and respect
Your true and devoted friend,
W. B. Tidwell

Thursday 30th - Finished one shirt today & made bosom & wristbands for the other linen one. Mr. Henry went to Asheville today. No war news of importance. He got a set of cups & saucers, also six very nice mugs with covers. The children are delighted with them. We eat in my room now and have all this week as it is too cold in the dining room for the children. The wool that was mixed at the machine is not done very well. It is blue & white, one third blue. It makes a very pretty light suit. Mr. Henry had a suit last winter.

Friday 31st October 1862 - I had neuralgea in my jaw last night. I sit up before the fire from three till four o'clock & this morning it is not near easy. Mail was late coming. We got no letters & but little mail matter & Mr. Henry brought it yesterday. I have done nothing today. I took a nap before dinner & my teeth & jaw are nearly easy. Mr. Henry & I went to the mill this evening. He has taken a long nap since dinner. Wiley Night is at work on our sugar or rather molasses mill, says he will get it done sometime next week. Tom Hendrix was at the mill considerably excited on whiskey. He don't like the idea of having to go to war as the conscripts are called out from 18 to 40. I think Mr. Henry will be exempted as a miller. I do hope he may.

Special Exemptions.

Cn. E. O., Asheville, N. C., April 8th, '64.

ALL persons in Buncombe county who have made applications for exemptions as Tanners, Millers, &c., will report at this Office, that I may get their *descripthd lists*, which are required before their applications can be forwarded.

D. T. MILLARD,
Lieut & Enrolling Officer.

The Asheville News, April 21, 1864

November 1862

Saturday Nove 1st - My teeth & jaw pained me a good deal last night but I did not get up. They are not easy today. I have made the wristbands & collars of the three domestic loomed shirts today & tried to make a bosom on the machine but it would not stitch it so I stitched it myself & run two or three pleats & sewed some on it at night after repairing two of Mr. Henry's old shirts. As I had no knitting I finished Willie's third pair stockings last night & now I must knit for Zona next as she needs worse than Pinck. Pinck's toe has got a great deal better. Willie has been loose in his bowels this week again. Hanes attends to him. I have a nice quantity of walnuts out drying for winter use. The children have gathered them. This has been a warm bright day. Hanes has cleaned the yards very nicely today.

Sunday 2nd - Cool this morning but pleasant now at twelve o'clock. I suffered a great deal last night with my jaw & teeth. Mr. Henry got up & sit with me by the fire. I put some mustard to it & got some relief till I got to sleep. I felt very badly this morning for awhile but feel as well as usual now. Mr. Henry is so kind to me, 'tis such a help to me. I can bear the pain better when I see he sympathizes so much with me. It is now 12 o'clock & dinner will be on before long. We have apple dumplings for dinner. Mr. Henry is very fond of them. I want to take a walk this evening if Mr. Henry is willing so I will stop for this time. Mr. Boyd came just before dinner & says he heard that E.P. Night was accidently killed a short time ago by a gun. Mr. Henry & I took a long walk this evening over through the widening & around by the store house. We went in the store house & got a few apples, some Quinn gathered for him. Some are very nice. I brought a few large ones to the children.

Monday November 3rd 1862 - I went to Mrs. Fanning's this morning to get her to weave some flannel for us. Mrs. Knight looked very sad. She has heard the report of Knight's death. I made two shirt bosoms today, did not get quite done. Frosty this morning but warm after the sun got up. Bets McKinnish got some rolls to spin this morning for flannel. Several letters went off this evening from here.

Tuesday 4th - I began a shirt for Mr. Henry this morning, did not get it done today. All are well. Willie does not try to talk yet, is very backward as much so as Pinck. Zona could say several things at Willie's age. Mr. Henry & I went to the mill yesterday evening. Night will soon have the molasses mill done.

Wednesday 5th - Mrs. Jamison & Betsey spent the day here. Rather cool & windy with rain in the evening. Mr. Henry went to G. W. Candler's sale, got wet coming home. Things went very high. He bought nothing, only a chain. Betsey took home some rolls to spin, white for linsey for the children, some dresses & sacks for me & them. I finished the shirt after dinner & began another one. Mr. Henry sent for the mail yesterday by old J. Night. He got a letter from Harrie saying E. P. Night was dead. They were cleaning guns in the ordenance Dept. & a gun in the hands of another man went off killing Night instantly & wounding another man after passing through Night's head. Mrs. Knight takes it very hard. I felt very sorry for her & her little ones.

Thursday 6th - Very cold this morning, wind from the North. Mr. Henry & Joe Russell started to the sale this morning. Russell staid here last night. I finished another shirt this evening which makes three & two more to make. The bosoms, collars & wristbands are done of the two. Mr. Henry says things went very high today at the sale. Old Mr. Corn stays here tonight. Mr. Henry is not so well tonight. He has caught cold I think as it was very cold this evening.

Friday 7th - Mr. Henry well enough this morning. Corn stays part of the day to sharpen some mill picks. Mail brought no news. I got a letter from Dora & Matt. They are all well. Pa has had an attack of Rhumatism but is better. The others all well. Dora wrote that Bill Santos was dead. He was wounded at Sharpsburg fight & died from the wound. I began Mr. Henry another shirt today after reading the papers. Mr. Henry took Pinck with him to the tan yard this evening. It began to snow some after they started so Pinck was very cold when he came back. Zona & I went to Mrs. Fanning's a little while. I promised to take her to keep her from crying after Mr. Henry & Pinck. The wind blew very cold & snowed on till night.

Saturday 8th - Very cold this morning with a slight skift of snow on the ground but clear. Warm after the sun got up. Wind all day from the North. Fannie & Jinnie breaking wool all day, at least till time for them to go to wash. Sam & others slaughtered a beef this morning. Mr. Henry gave John a thrashing this morning for some stealing from a waggoner that camped up at Mrs. Branton's last night. Mr. Henry went to Asheville this morning, did not get back till sun down. Mr. George Peake came just before he did. He stays here tonight. Very cool this evening. Fannie cleaned the tripe after dinner. Mr. Henry will start Tuesday with his hogs over the Mountain to feed them at Blythe's. He got 1000 bu. corn of him for 1200$. He will stay over there a good part of the time I expect. He bought twenty of A. B. Jones today.

Sunday 9th - A heavy frost this morning but the sun shines warm out of doors. George Peake left this morning. Mr. Henry has gone a short distance with him. He will be back to dinner I think. George Peake is going to the salt works in Va. He has five waggons along. He is going to haul some for salt if he can get it that way. I am alone in my room, the children are at play. It is very cold for little Zona's feet as she has no shoes & I can't tell when she will get any. Willie's are old ones. Pinck can wear his boots on only one foot as the other is not well yet but improving very fast. We have turkey for dinner. Mr. Henry says we must eat one every Sunday that Fannie cooks as she is so much better to prepare such things than Jinnie. I will soon stop as I want some walnuts. We have a quantity this fall laid away for winter. Mr. Henry came home to dinner. A man from the armory in Asheville came here a short time before Mr. Henry got back. He staid till after dinner. He wanted to see the patent loom. Mr. Henry & I took a walk, at least he went up to the spring with the loom man & I met him at the old store. There was some men with him so I went down to Bets McKinnish & staid awhile then we came home.

Monday 10th - I began the last shirt this morning for Mr. Henry, did not finish it. Mail brought Mr. Henry some papers. Nothing new in them. Mr. Boyd is here at work on a loom for us, just an old fashioned one. Uncle Welch stays here tonight. He came with Mr. Henry from Asheville this evening. He has been to the salt works in Va. to procure salt for the people of Haywood Co. Succeeded in getting some. Mr. Henry wants to start with the hogs in the morning.

Tuesday 11th - The hogs got as far as E. Glenn's. Mr. Henry came back tonight. I was glad to see him. He goes on again in the morning. Dr. Sam Love came here about 8 o'clock. He brought John back as he ran away last Sunday. Dr. Love is on his way to Raleigh as he is a member of the legislature. I finished Mr. Henry's shirt soon after dinner & cut out some other work. Sam two shirts, Mr. Henry a pair drawers, myself two pair & two pair of pants I am going to give the soldiers. Poor fellows, a great many need clothes & shoes.

Wednesday 12th - Mr. Henry started early this morning, will be gone some two weeks. I shall miss him a great deal. He is such a kind husband & father. I will stay by myself. Boyd will be here most of the time I think so I will not be affraid. Atheline will sleep in my room. I have began reading "Children of the Abby." I have read it several times but it is a book that will bear reading again & again. I made one of Sam's shirts & began the other today. Mr. Boyd is not here tonight but I am not at all affraid for I feel that my Father in Heaven will take care of me & my little ones.

Thursday 13th - Jinnie scoured my room, the hall & front piazza today. I assisted a little in washing the windows &c. It has been very pleasant today. Mr. Boyd came back this evening. I have done nothing of importance today. Hanes attends to Willie & picks a little wool occasionally, not much as he is lazy. Willie tries to talk, can say something very plain, can call "Mur" almost as well as Zona.

Friday 14th - I sit up till after 9 last night reading & knitting so it was late when I woke this morning & consequently late breakfast as the negroes never get up till they are called. I wrote to Mr. Henry this morning. The mail came before I finished it but I put it in. Mr. Boyd is cutting out a window in dining room as we are going to have a chimney added to it & have to move the windows. I sewed a little on Sam's shirt, did not get it done. Mrs. Jamison & Betsey spent the day here. I tacked some pieces of glass in dining room window to mend the holes. Did nothing after dinner.

Saturday 15th 1862 November - Mr. Boyd made me some comfort needles (wood). They were too large. He trimmed them down last night. I got up very soon this morning before 4 & had breakfast about day. I began a comfort before breakfast to try my needles. They do finely. It will be a small one scarcely broad enough for me. I think of knitting Mr. Henry one of single yarn. This one I am knitting now is very coarse, double & twisted yarn. I have at last finished Sam's shirt & then knit on my comfort. I finished it after night & patched Pinck's pants after washing the children & putting them to bed. I did not go to bed till near 11 as I got to reading & knitting. Atheline came in a while before ten & greased & worked at my head till I finished reading the "Children of the Abby." It is a very interesting work. Charlie & Peter came home yesterday evening. They went with the hogs. Mr. Henry wrote me a little note by them. He is not going to take his hogs to Blythe's as the hog cholera is too bad, even then he has stopped at Mr. Heath's some 36 miles from here in Transilvania Co. Gallion started this morning to Spartanburg with 15 bu. apples, is going to bring back some wheat Mr. Henry has there. Also some cloth Mr. Henry bought over a year ago at the factory if he can get it & I hope he may as our people need shirts badly.

Sunday 16th - Cloudy & looks very much like rain. A little cool this morning. We have had some very pleasant days. I was down at Mrs. Fanning's yesterday morning to see the flannel she is weaving for us. It is not thick enough I fear. I sold two turkeys one day this week for three dollars. Dear meat I think. Mrs. Rankin bought them. This is a dull, gloomy day. We have potatoe pudding for dinner sweetened with molasses as we are out of sugar. It is selling at 75 cts. per lb. & I will not give that. I will do without first. I will not go to walk this evening as Mr. Henry is not here to go with me. I can't enjoy anything unless he partakes of it too. I think of writing to Lou, also Dora this evening or tonight but I dislike to write a letter so much, 'tis a perfect task. I write in my journal because it will be interesting to my little ones when perhaps I am in my narrow bed of clay. I took a walk this evening around the road & then up by the stalls. Atheline was along with Willie & Zona. Rather late when we got back, getting dark. This has been a long day to me. Sunday generally is when Mr. Henry is gone. I wrote a long letter to Lou at night after the children went to sleep & then read some in my bible.

Monday November 17th 1862 - I woke early this morning & had breakfast by candle light. Made a pair of pants for some poor soldier. Got them done by three o'clock & then fixed some yarn for Mr. Henry's comfort. Twisted part myself to knit tonight as Tena is at the cow pen. Very pleasant today. I have not needed much fire. I was sadly disappointed this evening in not getting a letter by mail from Mr. Henry but heard from him this morning by Mull (the man that attends the hogs). He came here this morning. Left Mr. Henry yesterday morning, says he was well & started to Spartanburg to meet the waggon Sunday morning. Sam went to Asheville this morning to get a one horse waggon Mr. Henry bought of W. Smith, did not get it as it was broken badly. Mr. Henry sent Mull after the waggon to haul corn as he can only get it in small quantities. Mull leaves soon in the morning.

Tuesday 18th - I wrote a short note to Mr. Henry by Mull this morning. I have made the other pair of soldier's pants today, got done before night & knit on Mr. Henry's comfort. I sold 8 lbs. of butter today for four dollars. Two horse drivers stay here tonight. Boyd has not come back yet. I wish he would finish the loom, he began it last week. Nothing new going on. Rumor says France Starnes is dead. Poor fellow, he was very loath to go. I fear a great many will die this winter. Oh God who art never out of hearing, grant I pray Thee, grant us an honorable peace is the prayer of one that offers it up nightly.

Wednesday 19th - I made Pinck a pair pants today & knit on the comfort after I finished them. I will finish the comfort tomorrow. Very pleasant weather now. The hands mostly gathering corn, will soon be done. It is reported that Pinck Allen is lying in the woods as he is a deserter. It would be much better for him to go to his Regiment. He belongs to the 25th Reg. He was no use when at home & now he is no use to his country. Not at home as I hear of a good many hen roosts being robbed.

$30 REWARD.

THE above reward will be paid for the apprehension and delivery at the Head Quarters of the 25th Regiment N. C. Troops, of each of the following named deserters from company "I" of said Regiment:

WASHINGTON CURTIS, who was enlisted in March last, is five feet 10 inches or six feet high, dark complexion, black hair and eyes, is *hump shouldered*, and about 34 years of age, and at the time of enlistment resided on South Hominy, Buncombe county, N. C.

WILLIAM KNIGHT, enlisted May 12th, 1862; about five feet 10 inches in hight, dark complexion, black hair and blue eyes—about 32 years old; and at the time of enlistment resided on Hominy Creek, Buncombe county, N. C.

PINCKNEY ALLEN, enlisted in July, 1861, is about 25 years old, five feet 8 or 9 inches high, swarthy complexion, light hair and blue eyes, and at the time of enlistment resided near the Sulphur Springs, Buncombe county, N. C.

The above reward will be given for the apprehension and delivery of each of the above named deserters either at the Head Quarters of this Regiment, or the Commander of any Military Post, so they can be had, or 15 dollars each if lodged in the county jail at Asheville, N. C. Jailor's fees will be paid.

By order of Lt. Col. Bryson, Comd'g Reg't.

WILLIAM Y. MORGAN, Capt.,
Comd'g Co. "I," 25th Reg't N. C. T.

Sept. 11.   2t

Notice of reward for deserters. Pinckney Allen was often hunted by
William L. Henry, leader of the local Home Guard
The Asheville News, September 11, 1862

Thursday 20th - I finished Mr. Henry's comfort this morning. I wish he had it. It is a very nice warm one and large. I made Zona & Willie some jeans shoes. They look very well. They will not stand wet weather, neither will they last long but perhaps they will do till they get leather shoes. Some of the negroes are barefooted, Fannie, Jinnie, Hanes & Lonzo. Sam & others killed a beef this morning, a cow Mr. Henry got of Bates. It is very nice beef. I made some sweet potato custards this evening sweetened with molasses. They are very nice. We are out of sugar.

Friday Nove 21st 1862 - Mail brought nothing new. I expected a letter from Mr. Henry but was sadly disappointed. A good many letters came today. I done some mending before dinner & made some beef sausage in the afternoon. It is very nice. It was very hard to grind. Atheline helped some. Turned a good deal cooler since Wednesday as we had a good rain then at night. Fannie breaking wool today as it is too cold out for bare feet. Jinnie has some old pieces of shoes she wears. Pinck's toe is not well yet but healing very fast. Mrs. Fanning brought our flannel home this evening. It is not at all nice. Too thin by a good deal & very coarse at that.

Saturday 22nd - Done Sunday mending before dinner & knit some after dinner. Mrs. Jamison & Betsey came here about 12 o'clock & staid till late in the evening. They are spinning for us. I want the children's linsey got ready for the loom next week. Mrs. Fanning is to weave it. I want her to make better cloth than she did in the flannel. I intend having it red & black & the warp solid purple as I want to make me & the children some sacks on it. That is if it suits me after it is made. Not so cold today as yesterday as there is no wind blowing. I made some peach pies this evening. Fannie has been breaking wool today.

Sunday 23rd - Very late when I woke this morning so we had late breakfast. Cool but little frost. I went to the mill this morning to look into some of George's boxes but the key would not fit to the box lock. Charlie, Pinck & Zona went with me. The children would bring the old rocking chair to the house, the chair Matt Smith broke several years ago. It has never been entirely repaired yet. They think as much of it as though it was a mohair seated one. It is now nearly 12 o'clock, dinner will soon be on. I wish Mr. Henry would come today. I will look for him this evening. I dreamed he came last night. I want to see him. Atheline is cracking the children some walnuts now. I must stop & help them eat, which I did & picked some for Zona & Willie. I have read the book of Leviticus in the bible today & some of Numbers. I am reading my bible through for the third time in my life. I am also reading Josephus' complete work of the bible. It is very interesting. Mr. Gallion came home this evening, left Mr. Henry at Spartanburg last Thursday. Mr. Henry went down to Pa's that day. He will be home in a few days. Gallion brought home the wheat, also a bale of thread. I am glad to see the thread as we need some. Mr. Boyd came this evening. I hope he will finish the loom before he leaves. Quite cool tonight. I am writing on my lap. This last, the children all asleep at 7 o'clock now.

Monday November 24th 1862 - I woke very early this morning & had breakfast soon. Atheline & Fannie both unwell so Jinnie got dinner. Atheline helped me sew on the children's flannel we made there today. Fannie began mixing wool this morning, black & white. Mail boy saw Mr. Henry. He says he will be at home tomorrow. Mail brought no news. Very cold today & clear.

Tuesday 25th - I made a little flannel today for Willie. Atheline mixing wool & Fannie doing the cooking. I cut out two other little skirts for Willie this evening, cotton ones. I took the children to the mill dam this evening to meet Mr. Henry. Waited till nearly dark. He will not come tonight. Hanes had Willie along too. Cold & cloudy today.

Wednesday 26th - Made Mr. Henry a flannel shirt today. I fear he can never wear it as it is so coarse & rough made of homespun goods. Very cold with wind from the North. Mr. Henry came about sun down. I was very glad to see him, so were the children. He has had a very cold day to ride in. He was at Pa's, they are all well. Pa sent me a pair of cotton cards, also Dora. They are very acceptable these times. Dora & Matt sent the children some pinders. Pinck is very fond of them but Zona & Willie don't like them much. Pa's family were all well. Fowler (Ell's husband) is in the army. I am sorry for Ell. Oh how I wish this war would end. God grant us a speedy & honorable peace is my daily prayer.

Thursday 27th - I have done but little today. They killed a hog this morning & salted it by a new process. Scalded it in brine that would float a potato. The meat to stay in three minutes & then hang & smoke till cured. The meat looks very nice. I sewed some on Mr. Henry a pair flannel drawers. He wants to try some. They are like his shirt, coarse. I cut two pair out. Atheline & I made some sausage this evening, it is very nice. I took one ham & ground up. Also Mr. Henry went to the tan yard & Mr. Penley's. To the latter to see about some wheels. We are to get one next Wednesday by sending for it, also leather at the tan yard. He did not start till after dinner so it was dark before he got back. Boyd is getting along very well on the loom, will nearly finish it this week. Mr. Henry is very much pleased with his comfort. He is a dear good husband, so kind to me & the children. Truely I am blest in him. I believe it would nearly kill me for him to go to the war. He is the best of men.

Friday 28th Nove 1862 - We over slept ourselves last night or this morning. I intended to get up at 4 as Mr. Henry thinks of starting back again to the hogs this morning & I wanted to finish his drawers. I sewed some on them before breakfast & finished them before the mail came, nearly nine when he got here. Mr. Henry spoke of going with the mail carrier but did not get off. Several people came in to the P. O. & about 11 o'clock Mrs. Winslow Smith & Mrs. Slagle came. They staid till near one. They came to get some turkeys. Got three at 1.50 each. Young ones. Mr. Henry eat dinner. I had him a nice cup of coffee for dinner. He started soon after eating. He will not get further than Mills River tonight. It is only 27 or 28 miles to where he is feeding. He thought he would be back here by next Wednesday anyway. I do hope he may get back. I miss him so much when he is gone. Mr. Henry sent Boyd to Asheville this morning to get some shirting. Had to give 55 cts. per yd. I cut Jim out a shirt of it. Some one stold the only good shirt the negro had a week ago.

Saturday 29th - Jinnie washed out my room this morning. Fannie put the fat on to render up as Tena will be ironing & fixing the thread for the children's dresses. It is a very pretty deep purple. Fannie then mixed wool. Mrs. Jamison & Betsey spent the day here today. I finished Jim's shirt today. Some one took the mill key out of the door yesterday. I went to the mill & got Boyd to put on another lock, a very good one. Cool & cloudy today. I made the children another pair cloth shoes last Tuesday, Zona & Willie as Pinck has boots. His toe is nearly well.

Sunday 30th - Late this morning as usual in getting up & late breakfast. Boyd went to Asheville yesterday for himself, did not come here till this morning. He got the mail. Mr. Henry got a letter from his sister Martha to which I have replied today. Boyd's little son staid here last night. He got 6 lbs. of wool. Poor little fellow. He needs clothes. Cloudy & cold all day. I have just eat a very hearty dinner of sweet potato pudding, back bone & other things & am too lazy to write much more. The children are all at play. I am writing in my room by a little slow fire. It was ten last night before I got to sleep as I wanted to finish Pinck's sock. I began it Thursday night & have only knit at night on it. This is a gloomy day & has been a long one as Sunday generally is when Mr. Henry is gone. It is now nearly three & I will stop as I want to read some in my bible.

December 1862

Monday December 1st 1862 - I cut Charlie, Hanes & Lonzo two shirts each this morning. Made one of Lonzo & began his other one. I got a letter from Mr. Henry this evening written in a pamphlet. Vic brought it. He is very well, wants the waggon to start up there to him Thursday. It has been raining a slow rain nearly all day. Atheline at work out today. Fannie does the cooking. Mr. Boyd came this evening. He has not done the loom yet. He is a very slow workman but a good one.

Tuesday 2nd - Made 10 sacks for the flour Mr. Henry wrote for. Finished Lonzo's shirt & began Hanes'. Finished Hanes' after night & sewed some on Charlie's so that was a very good day & night's work. A good deal cooler today. Nothing of interest going on. Boyd at work at the loom. George grinding the flour. The other hands putting in wheat. Old Jim Night is going with the waggon.

Wednesday 3rd - Raining this morning. Mrs. Jamison came to help me make a set of 700 harness. She did not come till 10 or after. I made a fruit sack this morning & put up 6 bu. of dried apples & 5 of peaches to send to Greenville by the waggon. I also weighed the tallow, 120 lbs., to send off & I intend sending a jar of lard, 10 sacks of flour & 25 bu. of green apples which makes out the load. We worked at the harness till about 4 & then Mrs. Jamison started home. Jinnie & Atheline mixing wool today. Quite cool this evening. I wrote a long letter to Mr. Henry tonight. We sent to the tan yard today for some leather, got a side of sole leather, very wet & one of upper leather but little better. Old Smith is a mean old yankee. Jim went after the wheel, did not get it but will get it Saturday.

Thursday 4th - Mrs. Jamison came soon this morning but not till we had breakfast as we generally eat by candle light about day break. She eat her breakfast & we got to work about 9. The waggon loaded up & got off by 12. I sent to Jarrett's yesterday & got 50 lbs. of salt for 5$. That was doing very well I think. It is county salt. Very cold this morning & hard freeze. Mrs. Jamison warped the children's dresses today & I finished Charlie's shirt. Tena will not wash today as she attends to the spools.

Friday 5th - Mail brought a good many letters but nothing new. Burnsides has taken McClelland's place as commander of the feds. All quiet along the lines now though. They expect a battle soon about Nashville, Ten. God give us a complete victory is my prayer & grant us an honorable peace. We finished the harness today by 2 o'clock. Raining all the morning & sleeted & snowed some in the evening. Mrs. Jamison went home this evening through the rain. It was raining this morning when she came. Jinnie & Atheline mixing wool today. Tena washed some for the children to be dried by the fire.

Saturday 6th December 1862 - Finished Hanes' shirt that I sewed some on yesterday & made Charlie's so I am done shirt making for them for a while. Very cold today. High wind from the North, the coldest day this or last winter. Jim got the wheel this evening, a very nice one at that. I made a pair pantletts after supper & put them on the old cotton flannel drawers. Got done by 9. This will be a cold windy night for certain. Boyd went home this evening. I will not wash the children tonight as Willie is sleepy & I have to take him.

Sunday 7th - Water froze in my room last night, the first time in two years. It was a dreadful cold night & but little warmer yet though the sun shines bright. I pity the poor soldiers this cold weather. So many of them needing clothes & shoes. The sawmill caught on fire last night about 1 o'clock from fire left there yesterday as Jim was sawing. I intend going down soon to see the damage that is done. The negroes say 'tis but little. Mrs. Fanning came up & told Sam of it. I knew nothing of it till this morning. I will stop now as I want to eat some walnuts & apples & after dinner I will go to see the sawmill. It was so very cold I did not go to the mill. The wind big all day. Boyd came this evening.

Monday 8th - Very cold today. Boyd put up the loom in the hall room as the chimney is not commenced to the dining room yet. I made Mr. Henry's flannel drawers today. It was so cold I could not half sew. Fannie & Atheline spinning on the new wheel. It does very well. Jinnie doing the cooking. The other hands fixing up the cow pen here above the house. The ground frozen so hard they can't plow.

Tuesday 9th - Mrs. Jamison came today & fixed the cloth in. I sent Hanes to Asheville today to get some alum, got none. I wanted to dye them madder red for the children's dresses. I will now have to have some other colour as alum is not to be had. I had to try the new wheel last night, spun over a cut I think. I got a letter from Mr. Henry saying he would be at home the last of this week. I hope he may for I want him to get through with his hogs soon. He was on his way to Greenville. I made Willie an unbleached selicia today. Hanes brought the mail. I got a letter from Lou & one from Sister Frank. They were both very well. Some other letters came to soldier's wives. I know they are glad to hear from their husbands.

Wednesday 10th December 1862 - I made Willie's other skirt today. I sewed some on it last night. I went to Presley's this morning to get him to make the rest of the negro shoes. Hanes went along with the sole leather. He says he will make them as soon as he can as he has a sick child. A heavy frost this morning but no wind. Betsey Jamison came this morning & began to weave. The stripes run round the skirt. It is blue mixed (light) & black. She is weaving now. I want to get the children a dress each made this week if she gets enough wove to cut it out. It breaks a great deal. Boyd did not get the temples done till late this evening. An old man named Hunter stays here tonight. He is nearly dead with cancer. He is an awful sight. I could not look at him. He is hunting a cancer Dr. that is in this country about Cathy's Store I think. He will leave soon after breakfast in the morning.

Thursday 11th - Betsey gets on very well with the weaving. I fill quills. Jinnie & Atheline spin every morning till it is warm enough to plow & haul corn. Jinnie has no shoes yet, only pieces. Betsey stays here at night whilst she is weaving. I made some tape trimming today for me a pair pantletts & some for Zona a pair & finish the pantletts after supper (my own).

Friday 12th - I cleaned upstairs today. Much warmer than it has been for several days. Hanes carried down the faulty apples. Boyd will have to sleep up there when Mr. Henry gets home & Betsey in the side room. Mail brought no news this morning of importance. Mrs. Branton sent Branton clothes by the mail carrier (Vic). I wrote her a letter this morning to send in the clothes. Betsey cut out the two dress patterns this evening. I dampened it & dried it & her & I made the skirts & sleeves by 9 o'clock. I can finish them easy tomorrow. The next two dresses will be red & black stripe, red dyed with sassafras bark, plum bark & alder buds. 'Tis not a pretty red, too dark & the next dresses will be red broom sedge dye & black. They will none of them be pretty as the colours are nothing extra but they will keep them warm. Bets McKinnish brought home some thread today, the rolls she got 3 weeks ago. She is doing no good spinning this fall for us.

Saturday December 13th 1862 - Finished the dresses & washed the children & put them on in the evening. They look very well for the colors. I looked for Mr. Henry all the evening. He did not come. I wish he would. Betsey did not weave any. After dinner went home, will be back Sunday evening or Monday morning. I am very tired this evening. I have done sundry mending tonight & knit some. Sam & the others have killed three hogs this week. They were not very fat.

Sunday 14th – Warm this morning, wind from south. I am going to meet Mr. Henry after dinner. I hope I may not be disappointed. The darkies all gone but Jinnie. She is getting dinner. We have sweet potato pudding for dinner. Willie is up with Tena as Atheline is gone someplace. The other children at play. I will stop as I have to mix the pudding & I have nothing else to write.

I eat a hearty dinner of back bones, irish potatoes & pudding. I took Zona & went down to the mill. Took my bible. I read while she played around me. We went down about three o'clock & waited for Mr. Henry till near sun down but he did not come. Three men stay here tonight from Transilvania, two of them soldiers. They are on their way back to Love's Reg, the 62nd. I have read the book of Deut. today, 34 chapt. I do wish Mr. Henry was at home. I live on hope, always hoping he will come tomorrow. The heart would soon sink in despondency if it was not for the bright hope of another day. Very warm tonight. I think it will rain soon. May God have mercy on our soldiers & protect them through this war & grant us, I beseach Thee Oh merciful God, a speedy & honorable peace is my prayer morning, noon & night.

Monday 15th - I made myself a pair drawers today & filled quills for Betsey. She gets along slowly, it breaks very badly. Not very cold in the morning but cloudy & cold in the afternoon. Jim Night came home about 11. Mr. Henry wrote me a letter on a newspaper. He wants some of the hogs sent for to kill. I can't send as I have no money. He is well. Gone down home on business, will be at home the last of this week. I do hope he may for I would be very glad to have him near me all the time. He is so kind to me & the little ones. Jeff went with the waggon. He was glad to get home. He is very lean.

Tuesday December 16th 1862 - Cut Pinck three shirts of sheeting. Sewed some on one. I can't sew steady as I have to quill for Betsey. She gets along slowly. I doubled & twisted a cut of stocking yarn this morning. Sent for the mail by McParker, got nothing new. There has been a fight at Fredericksburg Va. No particulars yet. We whipped them soundly. No letters came since the fight which commenced last Thursday 11th inst.

Wednesday 17th - Finished one shirt & began another. Nothing new going on in the country. The children well. It is rumoured that there is a case of small pox near Garmen's bridge, some 4 miles from here. I hope it is not so, yet I fear it is so, it is raging in the army considerably. Very cold today.

Thursday 18th - Willie is very loose in his bowels & very fretful. He grows very fast & tries to talk. Can say some things very plain. I finished Pinck's shirt before dinner & made myself an apron partly after supper. I sew every night after the children get to sleep. Till Morris was here a short time today, borrowed my comfort needles to knit Tom Morris a comfort on. She is looking very well.

Friday 19th - Mail brought but little news. I got a letter from Sister Jane. They are all well. I made myself another apron & sewed some on Pinck's last shirt of the three. Betsey got the cloth out this evening & went home. The children have three dresses each & then some plain linsey, for me some saques & coat lining. I sewed some after supper. Mr. Henry sent little Cora's other tomb stone home by the waggon from Greenville. It is a very nice one, quill letters.

Saturday 20th - I finished Pinck's shirt before dinner & mended the children's old shoes by putting new soles. Twisted a little sewing thread & several other things. Jinnie & Atheline scoured my room this morning. I replaced the things. Willie's bowels still loose. It does not stop his running about. Mr. Henry came home just at dark. We were all glad to see him. He was gone three weeks & one day this last time. I will be glad when he is done with his hogs so he may stay at home all the time. Sam Peake is dead. I am sorry to hear it. He was a good hearted young man. He died rather than be taken a prisoner. He sold his dear. He fought as long as he had a bullet & then was killed. I sympathise with the family. They thought a great deal of Sam.

Sunday Dec. 21st 1862 - Late breakfast this morning. Quite cool but pleasant, now one o'clock. We have not had dinner yet. It will be on before very long. Fannie made some dried peach pies yesterday evening. They are very nice. We eat in my room when it is cold. Boyd has not commenced the chimney to the dining room yet. I don't think he intends to this winter. Mrs. Fanning warped the cloth for the negro's jeans last Friday. It will be away long in Jan. before they get their clothes. They are not very needy yet awhile. Mr. Henry is sitting here before the fire. Boyd is here & rather about, out in the house. Willie is out with Atheline. Pinck is out with the little negroes. Zona is in the room with us. Mr. Henry vacinated the children this morning. Pinck & Zona bawled awfully. He has not vacinated Willie yet. Mr. Henry has a very good scab on his arm, put in at Dr. Peake's. Boyd's two daughters are here, just came in. Also Steph Jones. I must stop and see a little about dinner as it is going on two o'clock smartly. Mr. Henry & I went to the mill this evening & then up by the stables. The children, Pinck & Zona, were along with us. Pleasant this evening.

Monday 22nd - I made the skirts & sleeves of Zona's & Willie's linsay dresses. Mr. Henry went to Asheville today, got a letter from Harrie. He wants two pair socks and a pair gloves. I put on a sock tonight on the needles. Will get Mrs. Mathies to knit the other pair. Fannie spinning the mixed for Mr. Henry's clothes black.

Tuesday 23rd - Finished Zona's dress & knit some on Harrie's sock. Mrs. Jamison came here today & Betsey. Warped a piece of flannel & blankets & got it in the loom ready for weaving. Betsey is to weave it. Nothing new going on. All are well. Willie's bowels loose.

Wednesday 24th - Killed three shoats today. Cured them in brine (boiling). Got the sausage meat made & lard rendered up as tomorrow is Christmas & the negroes then go frolicing.[39] I finished Willie's dress before dinner & knit in the afternoon. I weighed the meat to see how much salt it would take. Mr. Henry scalded it. John & Peter went to Asheville this morning. I gave the children a few fire crackers this evening, some Pinck had last Christmas. Willie was delighted as much as the others. They can't be bought now as there is none in Asheville. Fannie made some peach pies this evening.

Thursday 25th - Christmas day. Many changes have taken place in our short year. A great many have given their lives for their Country in that space. Oh! God I beseech Thee to grant us a speedy & honorable peace is my pray.

I knit all day. Betsey weaving. Till Morris spent the day here. We had turkey for dinner & several other things. George Peak came in while we were at supper. He is just returning from the salt works. He got salt enough to save his bacon. I felt very sorry for him when Mr. Henry told him Sam was dead. Their family is very much attached to each other.

Friday 26th - Till Morris left this morning soon after the mail came. Her & I slept together last night & Mr. Henry & Mr. Peake, Till & I did not go to sleep till after 11 o'clock. Betsey went home yesterday evening. Fannie has been cooking yesterday & today. Jinnie will cook tomorrow & next day. Atheline gone to Haywood to see the Common Negroes. She went yesterday. Mail brought no news. Mr. Henry & Mr. Peak went to Asheville after dinner, dark when they came home. The children have no shoes yet. The negroes all shod.

Saturday 27th - Mr. Henry started this morning to the hogs, going to drive some home to slaughter. Mr. Peak left with him. Rained all day. Betsey did not go home. She finished the last one of Harrie's socks. I began to crochet the gloves today, got the thumb started. I wish they were done as they are troublesome & my other work is needing me so badly. Mrs. Fanning has not got the negroes jeans in yet & will not soon I think. She has acted badly about that piece of cloth I think.

Sunday 28th - Betsey left this morning. It is clear & pleasant. The children all at play. I don't feel very well this morning as I have a dull headache. It was nearly 11 o'clock before I got through cleaning the house. Jinnie getting dinner. I don't feel as if I wanted any. Betsey will not be back in several days as she has to spin some blanket filling. I intend having the blankets carded on both sides. I think they will be very nice. The flannel is very nice. The warp is No. 11 & put in the five hundred sley. Betsey is a very good weaver, takes a great deal of care to clip the knots. I fill quills & Mr. Henry fills some. I will not take my walk this evening as the ground is wet & my shoes not a protection as they are my own make of cloth.

---

[39] Traditional Christmas Holiday for slaves

Monday 29th December 1862 - Old Mr. Parker died yesterday morning. He has been to see his son in the 60th Reg. & came home sick. Only lived a few days after he returned. Tom Parker died whilst he was there. George Boyd died a short time ago in the same Reg. I crochet some on Harrie's glove today & went to Parker's burial, but few people there. I went in the buggy. Charlie drove. The children rode as far as the mill & then came back. Zona cried a little to go with me. Miss Mathies brought home Harrie's socks this evening not knit as I directed, so I only paid her 50 cts.

Tuesday 30th - Worked at Harrie's glove. Finished one last night & began the other this morning. Nothing new going on. Willie is not at all well, worms I think. The negroes mostly gone to George's breaking up Christmas frollic. Atheline & Fannie here, also Sam's family. Willie has high fever tonight & is very scary in his sleep.

Wednesday 31st - Mr. Henry came this evening after dinner. The hogs will be here tonight. Tomorrow they begin to slaughter 100 head of hogs. It will be some time before they are done. Very cold & windy today. Mr. Henry got very cold before he got home.

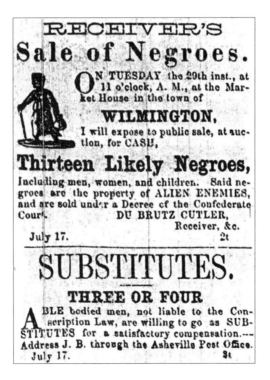

The Asheville News, July 16, 1862

Top: View of Paint Rock, North Carolina
Bottom: Swannanoa River and Black Mountain
(From "Land of the Sky, Views on the Western North Carolina R.R.," published by Chisholm,
North Carolina Collection, Pack Memorial Public Library, Asheville, NC)

1863

"...They have caused some of our best blood to flow & I never want to live under their rule again..."

January 1863

Thursday 1st - New Year's day. I hope another new year will not dawn on us with war & it's horrors. 'Tis awful to contemplate. The hands began to kill hogs today, kept them busy to get 16 done. Betsey came this morning & began to weave. She will soon get the cloth out & then the negro's jeans goes in. Mrs. Fanning has been down with sore throat this week & no better yet.

Friday 2nd - I received a letter from Dora this morning. They are all well. No news of importance. There has been a fight of Murfreesboro. We thrashed the yanks soundly. Killing hogs today. Mrs. Parker came here last night at 2 o'clock to get Mr. Henry to go & cup Abbe. She is sick. He went & Betsey slept with me till day. I got up very soon this morning, soon after 4 & had breakfast by candle light. Two soldiers staid here last night. Very uncouth fellows.

Saturday 3rd - Mr. Henry went to Asheville this morning, staid all day. Got a bolt of shirting, had to give 75 cts. pr. yd. Done up some lard today & made the sausage meat. Sam cutting up the hogs. Killed none today. Mrs. Jamison spent the day here. She & Betsey went home in the evening. I helped to make the sausage & I made myself a pair shoes today. They fit very neatly. The children have got no shoes.

Sunday January 4th - Rained a little last night but fair & windy now. Several men have been here today to see Mr. Henry. I have had headache all day, a little better now 3 o'clock. Willie is very cross, cries half the time. He is not well. Worms & loose bowels I think. The others all well. I want to walk some this evening if Mr. Henry has not gone off. I left him & Ham Cannon in the house. Zona is calling me now & I must go. I am writing on the branch in my "studio." Mr. Henry & Cannon gone to see Abbe Parker. She is very sick, pluresy I think. I did not get to take my walk but went to the hog pen. Met Mr. Henry there & we came back together.

Monday 5th - Mr. Henry went to Asheville this morning, did not get back till night. Nothing new. We have had a terrible fight at Murfreesboro. Our forces victorious as usual. Nothing else of importance. Bob Henry came here today. He wants whiskey very badly. He is one of the prisoners of the 62nd Reg. Mrs. Jamison & Betsey came this morning. Mrs. Jamison to help me make some jeans harness & Betsey to weave. I think she will get the cloth out tomorrow. There is 14 yds. of flannel & 14 yds. of blankets don't card up as I want them to.

Tuesday 6th - We finished the harness this morning by 10 & I made Willie's Linsey dress today. Atheline helped a little on it. Sam cutting up hogs today the hands killed yesterday. Nothing done at the lard today as it rained nearly all day. Atheline is very weakly, not able to do much. She has a dreadful cough. Mr. Henry got her some medicine of Dr. Hilliard yesterday. I fear she will never be well again. Mrs. Common came this evening, brought another boy to work, Henderson. Betsey got the cloth out this evening. Mrs. Jamison still here, will put in the negro's jeans tomorrow & then leave. Mr. Henry & several other men left here this morning to arrest two deserters up on Hominy. He got back at night. They did not get them.

Wednesday 7th - Mr. Henry & I emptied some lard this morning. I sewed some on Zona's linsey dress. They are killing hogs again today. Bob Henry left this morning for Franklin. Mrs. Common spent the day here. Very cold today. Tom Cook cut me out some shoes today. The children all have shoes at last. Pinck also. Dr. Hilliard's Tom is hired here this year at 75$.

Thursday January 8th 1863 - I have been knitting some muffs to the top of Mr. Henry some gloves. They will be very nice when they get done. The hand & fingers crochet. He wants them to wear to market. He thinks of starting next week with apples & some lard. He speaks of going to Columbia. Old Jim Night is to drive one waggon & Jim or Charlie the other. The negro women doing up lard today. They will get done this week. Mrs. Common left this morning. Very cold all day.

Friday 9th - Mail brought no news. We heard yesterday that Harrie was wounded in the battle of Murfreesboro, only a slight wound so we hear. I finished one of Mr. Henry's gloves & began the other. I want to get it done tomorrow. Betsey is weaving on the jeans. It is not good cloth at all. I want the sley changed as I think it is too fine for the thread. Hanes does the quilling mostly. Mr. Henry does some of it. He is so kind to me.

Saturday 10th - Rained nearly all day. Mr. Henry in the house nearly all day. Betsey went home this evening. Abbe Parker was burried yesterday. She died Wednesday morning. Mr. Henry went to the burrial. Mr. & old Tom Jones came after Mr. Henry last Tuesday night. He did not go. The wind blew very hard while they were here. The vaccine matter has done finely in the children's arms. Jinnie made the sausage meat today & washed a little for the children. Tena finished the lard today. Atheline not well.

Sunday 11th - Clear & cold this morning. Turned some warmer since morning. Mr. Henry speaks of going to Asheville this evening to hear the news if there is any. I shall have to make out the P. O. return if he goes. Mrs. Night brought Savannah & Obezana up this morning to be vacinated. Old Mrs. Parker is here now. Poor old creature. She looks very sad & lonely. I sympathise with the family. 2 o'clock two men called here while we were at dinner. Wanted Mr. Henry to go with them to call out the militia as the tories are doing some mischief in Madison again. I do wish they would behave themselves. I don't know whether Mr. Henry will return tonight or not. I hope he may. Mr. Henry came before supper. The militia is ordered to start Tuesday next. Mr. Henry is going though he does not belong to the militia. Creasman came this evening. He is to set in to work for Mr. Henry at

10$ per month. He is only a boy. I made out the P. O. return this evening. Mr. Henry will finish it off to send tomorrow. He will go to Asheville in the morning.

Monday Jan 12th 1863 - Mr. Henry off to Asheville. I made a blanket today for him to take with him. Had cooking done for him & some for old Jim Night. They start to market tomorrow with the apples & lard. Two waggons. Atheline is sick again. The others all well. Mrs. Jamison here today changing the sley in the loom as the jeans is not good cloth.

Tuesday 13th - Dr. Thrash here this morning to see Atheline, thinks it is her liver. Left some medicine for her. Mr. Henry sold some pork to the militia, taken away this morning. Mr. Henry got off about 10. Tom Cook brought my shoes this morning. They are very nice. I put them on right away as I have worn cloth shoes till I am tired. Mr. Henry came home tonight. They did not get off. Charlie & Night started this morning. I cut out Hanes & Lonzo a pair pants each & sewed a little on both pair. Got one pair ready for the machine & some on the others. Jinnie scoured my room & dining room today. The jeans does better since the sley is changed.

Wednesday 14th - Finished both pair pants today & cut them a coat each but did not sew any on the coats. Mr. Henry came home tonight. I was so glad to see him for I did not look for him at all. They don't know when they will march but in a day or two certain.

Thursday 15th - Willie very sick this morning vomiting, worms I think. Mr. Henry took Hanes to Asheville with him & sent some vermifuge back by him. Also an almanac for 1863. Willie got well by dinner. Mr. Henry came home at night, says they leave tomorrow at 8 o'clock. I have sewed some on Lonzo's coat but did not finish it. Rained nearly all day. Mr. Henry's coat wet. I made him a tent this evening after he came home. He wants a cape to his coat. I will make that in the morning. I am very sorry he is going. I shall be very uneasy about him all the time he is gone. I made two oil cloth covers last Monday, one to lay on & the other to cover a tent.

Friday 16th - I got the cape done about 9 o'clock & he started before the mail came. Very cold this morning. Nothing new in the mail. I finished Lonzo's coat & sewed some on Hanes'. Mr. Henry came home tonight. The militia went on today but he staid with Gen. Erwin as one of his staff. I am glad he has got a position.

Saturday Jan 17th 1863 - Mr. Henry & Pingrie Plott started early this morning for Asheville. Plott staid here last night. Very cold this morning. I finished Hanes' coat this evening & cleaned up both rooms upstairs. Sorted the apples that were on the floor. Hanes parched some coffee this evening. I am very tired tonight. I am knitting Mr. Henry a nice comfort when I get it done. I only knit at night on it. I wish he had it to wear to Madison. Mr. Henry & young Plott came back about 5 o'clock. Mr. Henry thinks he will go on tomorrow with Erwin & others of his staff. I do hope they may have no trouble with those lawless people.

Sunday 18th - Very cold last night, ice in my room. Plott left for home this morning & Mr. Henry went to Asheville. I hope he may return tonight yet I fear he will not. May heaven protect him is my prayer. I must write some letters today. I want to subscribe for the Field & Fireside today & write some other letters. I did not write any letters. I only sent on for the paper & read part of the evening. The other part I spent up at Tena's house. Atheline not well but improving slowly. Till Morris came over this evening. I sent Hanes after her & to take a paper to Mrs. Jones. She has a felon coming on her right fore finger. God bless my husband while he is gone with life & health is my prayer.

Monday 19th - Mrs. Morris did not leave till 11 o'clock. I then cut Mr. Henry's flannel shirt & sewed some on it. Did not finish it. Cloudy & turned cold today. Betsey came this morning to weaving. She is not at all well. Mr. Henry went to Marshall yesterday. Kind heaven protect him.

Tuesday 20th - R. Boyd & daughter stayed here last night & will not leave before morning as the ground was covered with snow & still snowing very fast. Turned a good deal warmer than yesterday. I finished Mr. Henry's shirt & made Uncle Sam a pair pants & cut my blue mixed saque. Boyd put an old lock to the side room. It does very well. He also put rockers on the little rocking chair. The hands killed the last of the hogs yesterday. Sam & Jim cutting up & salting the meat today. Jim was taken down with his rupture this evening, is in a great deal of pain. I have heard nothing from the Laurel war yet. Hope to hear soon of the tories being exterminated.

Wednesday 21st January 1863 - Jim is up and about this morning free from pain. I made my saque today, faced it around with black doe skin. It fits very nice. Atheline is sewing on the children's flannel skirts. She will make the skirt & I will put on the bodies. Betsey was not able to weave today so she made two blankets. Snow is going away very fast. The days seem as if Spring was with us. I hope Mr. Henry is getting on well. I would be glad to hear from him.

Thursday 22nd - I cut Zona three pair drawers today of sheeting, made one pair trimmed them with tatten. Jinnie at work in the yard. She has the pot in the kitchen. Aunt Tena is carding the blue mixed over enough for Mr. Henry a suit of clothes. Fannie does the cooking now. Atheline sews a little. I cut my flannel skirts this morning. She will make them & I will put the bands on. Jinnie made the sausage today. Mrs. Jamison spent the day here today. Very muddy, the ground very full of water. I heard from Mr. Henry today. He was well yesterday & they had all gone over in Yancy Co. We have killed some 30 tories & taken 16 prisoners. We have a force of over a thousand men in the tory region.

Friday 23rd - Mail brought no news of importance. The armies all quiet now. A good many of the militia have come home, all under 40. I wish Mr. Henry had come. I do hope he may soon be permitted to return in health. Ham Cannon came home last Tuesday quite sick & gets no better. I hope Mr. Henry may not get sick or hurt any way. I can only pray for him & that God may keep all harm away from him. This life would be a blank to me without him.

Saturday 24th - I fixed some more yarn for Mr. Henry's comfort. I have knit 1 1/2 cuts & it is not more than half long enough. Jinnie twisted it, also some sewing thread. She finished the lard today. I put bands to my flannels & bodies to the children's skirts. Atheline helped some. Betsey went home this evening. Till stopped here a few minutes this evening. I tried to persuade her to stay all night but she expected company & had to go home. She went to Asheville today.

Sunday 25th January 1863 - Cloudy & warm this morning. I staid by myself last night, only the children & Jinnie slept on the floor. Breakfast very late this morning as I had Pinck & Zona to wash. I did not wash them last night. Till promised to come over here this morning if her company left. I guess they did not leave as it is now nearly 12 and she has not come. I will stop now & eat some apples. How I wish Mr. Henry was here to help me enjoy them. I doubt if he has any today. I hope he may be at home in another Sabbath. Grant him long life & good health is my humble prayer.

Mr. Henry came home about 7 o'clock. A man named Lance came with him. He is has enjoyed the trip finely. A good many tories have been killed by Col. Allen's Regiment. I hope they may exterminate them this time. Till Morris stays with us tonight. She came over this evening soon after dinner.

Monday 26th - I cut Henderson two shirts today & pair pants. Atheline is to make them. I sewed some on the sleeves of his shirts as they were to piece. I tried to stitch some collars for Till this morning but the machine would not do it nicely so I gave her some tatten to trim one with. She gave me some button moulds, 1/2 yd. linen lining & 8 spools of thread. She is very kind to me. She comes to stay any time I send for her. She left soon after dinner today. Betsey came to weave today. She will get the coarse jeans out this week. I counted out the fine jeans today for Mr. Henry's clothes, No. 12, 26 yds. in the piece. Mail brought nothing new. Fannie not at all well. She be confined soon I think.

Tuesday 27th - Mr. Henry married Foster Johnston & Mollie Glenn today at old Bob Hughes', a run away match I suppose. I made Pinck a pair new drawers today & finished Mr. Henry's comfort at night. He wants it tomorrow as he is going to old Mr. Wells' sale. He & his wife are both dead. They both died in about one month. Mr. Henry is ordered to go to Marshall with some prisoners next Thursday, some 30 prisoners & about thirty Cavalry to guard them. They are deserters from the army. Nearly all the militia have come home, a good many of them hired substitutes & the substitutes got home nearly as soon as they did.

Wednesday 28th January 1863 - Mr. Henry started very soon this morning. It is very cold today, snow on the ground but melting a little. He wore his comfort. I hope he may not suffer with cold. Betsey went home this evening. It was late when Mr. Henry got home. The children were in bed. I made him a nice cup of coffee. I feel very unwell tonight. I have a very bad cold. I commenced to foot up some stockings tonight for myself. I heeled some for Mr. Henry today & cut Pinck's coat & pants of light blue mixed. I let Polly Guy have some cotton to spin today. She is to get some soap grease to make on the shares. Mrs. Fanning made some on shares. Her's is not so good. Willie is getting so he can say anything he wants to. I can understand him very well.

Thursday 29th - Mr. Henry left early this morning, took a ham and a good many crackers. I had them cooked yesterday. They were very nice. He thinks he will be back tomorrow night. I hope he may. I sent Hanes to Ham Cannon's to ask Mrs. Jamison to come tomorrow to warp the fine jeans as it will be ready in that time. It is a very dark purple dyed with maple bark & chinquapin root. Ham Cannon is very low with liver complaint. Not much sickness in the country. I finished

Pinck's coat & began his pants this evening. Old Boyd & a soldier stay here tonight. Betsey is sick tonight with headache.

Friday 30th - Mail brought a great many letters. I got one from Matt & one from Harrie. Harrie was slightly wounded by his horse throwing him but up & going again. He is very grateful for the things we sent him. I think he appreciates a kindness very much. Matt said she would come up this month if Mr. Henry would come for her. They were all well. Mr. Henry will meet her in Spartanburg in a week or two. I got my first papers of Southern Field & Fireside today. Three in one package. It is a very good paper I think. Mr. Henry came home after night. I was glad to see him. Home is not home without him. Jim got the sheep home today. He brought them part of the way yesterday, some Mr. Henry bought of at Wells' sale. He got some hogs, also some hay. Charlie & Tom will go after the hogs tomorrow in the waggon as they are too wild to drive. Very cold today but thawing some.

Saturday January 31st 1863 - I finished Pinck's pants yesterday. He has them on today. Mr. Henry gone to see Ham Cannon. He is not better. He will go to several places today. Mrs. Jamison is here today. She was here yesterday & warped the cloth. Mr. Henry did not get home till dark. Boyd stays here tonight. My cold no better. Snow nearly all melted. I began to fix an old dress today but come to the wise conclusion it was not worth the trouble. Jinnie is doing the cooking, Fannie mixing wool & Atheline sewing. Sam & others put a sill under Fannie's house today.

February 1863

Sunday Feb. 1st - Cloudy & warm, snow all gone. Preaching at the Academy today but few went from here. Mr. Reynolds preaches the 1st Sunday in every month. Mr. Henry & Boyd are sitting here reading my paper. The children playing hide & seek in the yard. Willie is sitting in Mr. Henry's lap. It is dinner time, 2 o'clock. We had very late breakfast this morning. Tom Morris is at home. He came after Pinck Allen who has deserted again. I read all the evening my papers & read some in Ernest Linwood. I have read it before but it is a book that will bear reading again & again.

Monday 2nd - I cut Jim, Charlie, Hanes & Lonzo's pants. Atheline helped sew on them. We made Jim's and sewed some on the others. Mr. Henry went to Asheville today, it being court week in Asheville. Nothing new going on in the army. It is reported that the blockade is raised at Charleston. I fear 'tis not true but hope it is.

Tuesday 3rd - Cold & snowing this morning. I am tired out of snow. We have had a great deal of snow this winter but little rain. Mr. Henry did not go to Asheville today. Sam Murray & Steph Jones eat dinner here. I made Mr. Henry a vest today. It is not a very nice one but will do better than his old one. Ely Glenn eat supper here tonight. The snow is two or three inches deep. Not so cold tonight since the wind has lay. Betsey weaving, will get enough to cut Mr. Henry's suit out this week. It is very nice jeans. It breaks very badly.

Wednesday 4th - Mr. Henry went to town today. The snow melted a good deal but turned colder at night. The ground froze very hard. Jesse Morgan & a soldier stay here tonight. I made with Atheline's help, Hanes' & Lonzo's pants & cut Sam's & George's. The soldier brought home John horse that Bob Henry took off 3 weeks ago.

Thursday 5th - This morning there is the deepest snow I ever seen or ever want to see again. It is about 16 or 18 inches deep when it is not drifted. Everything is shut up now, a complete blockade. Snowed occasionally all day. Morgan started home this morning & the soldier left about 11 o'clock. One of Dillard Love's negroes is waiting here till the snow leaves a little. He is a white nigger. We have done nothing today but sit by the fire. I finished Sam's pants. Atheline sewing on George's. Fannie spinning some stocking yarn to foot me some stockings. It is a difficult matter to keep the children out of the snow. They can't walk in it for it is too deep. I had the chickens caught & put in the hen house cellar & chaff house. The turkeys have not been out of the trees today. I began some tape trimming this evening, only made a little. I am sorry for our poor soldiers if they have such weather as we have. May God temper the winds to the shorn lamb is my prayer.

Friday 6th - Mail brought nothing new. He went back from here. Mr. Henry gave him a certificate so the mail will not go through this week. Vic left the mail here but took the log. Cold north wind today. Snow not melting any of consequence. Negroes getting wood. Very cold time to do it, it is true but we are out & have to have it or freeze. I made some tape trimming today & dampened dried & cut Mr. Henry's coat this evening. Betsey cut 7 yds. out this morning for coat & pants. I am footing up some old socks for Pinck, some of his last winter socks. I do my knitting at night mostly. Not many people came to the office today as it is almost impassible along the road. Mr. Henry went to feed some sows & pigs this morning, he rode. He says 'tis nearly impassible for a horse to get along. 'Tis dreadful on the stock. We have a yearling choked on straw. I expect it will be dead by morning. We have had three nannie goats to die this winter & our lambs have nearly half died. We have had a dreadful winter on stock of all kinds.

Saturday 7th - Got the sleeves, tarts & breast of Mr. Henry's coat done. Worked all day at it. Sewed the seams with the machine, it done finely. Betsey went home this evening. She walked. She was affraid a horse would fall down with her. Dr. Love of Hendersonville dined here today. Snow melting a little, dripping off the south side of the house. A bright sunny day but cool.

Sunday 8th February 1863 - Cloudy with occasional sunshine. The report that the blockade was broke at Charleston is confirmed, so Dr. Love was telling us yesterday. I hope 'tis true. Sam Murray was here yesterday & begged me out of a little coffee for his wife who is sick. I do wish they would let me alone about coffee. I must stop now as I want to eat some apples, walnuts & peach leather. It is now after 12 & soon dinner time. Snow melting very slowly. Mr. Henry staid in the room all the evening as the snow is too deep to travel much.

Monday 9th - I finished Mr. Henry's coat today after working faithfully all day. It suits him finely. It looks very well. Mrs. Jamison & Betsey came today just after we had eat dinner. They eat here. They say it is very bad walking. Snow melting some faster. Mrs. Jamison stays here tonight. I do not feel so well tonight. Mrs. Jamison reeled some this evening for us on Mrs. Fanning's reel (a count reel).

Tuesday 10th - I cut Mr. Henry a pair pants this morning like his coat. Did not get them done. Snow melting rapidly. Mrs. Jamison went home after dinner today. Nothing new going on. All quiet along the line of invasion. Fannie is breaking black wool. Jinnie does the cooking & Atheline is sewing a little. She is very lean yet, does not seem to gain any flesh.

Wednesday 11th - Finished the pants by dinner & cut a little gown & two little shirts. Trimmed the gown with tape trimming & the shirts, one with hand stitched frills, the other crochet edging. I sewed little on the gown. Sold two turkeys today for three dollars for Mr. Latta in Asheville. He is a refugee or rather an invalid from Columbia S. C. Snow going rapidly, very wet under foot. Mr. Henry out most of the day. Capt. Moore dined here today. Mr. Henry went off with him, did not get back till night.

Thursday 12th - Finished the gown & sewed some on the shirts. Made the sleeves of both. Warm & bright, snow nearly all gone. Old Jim Night started yesterday after a load of corn to Dr. Kilgore's in Transylvania Co., some Mr. Henry has there. He gave two dollars a bushel for 1000 bu. Corn is very scarce about here, now selling at any price. Poor soldier's families. How are they to get along, no one can tell. I hope none may suffer for the staff of life yet I fear some will.

Friday 13th - Mail brought no news. A. B. Jones brought the mail out yesterday. I finished the shirts by dinner & had them washed. Tena washing today. Cut some gowns for Willie & Zona of old stuff. Nearly made one for Willie. Several people here today for letters but none came this morning.

Saturday 14th - Made two other gowns today. One for Willie & one for Zona besides finishing the one I began yesterday. Laura Gudger was here this morning a short time. She wanted to buy some goblets. Mrs. George Jones spent the day here. She came to see Mr. Henry on business. He went to Asheville this morning & did not return till night so she did not get to see him. Snow nearly all gone, only an occasional speck on the north sides of hills. Betsey went home yesterday evening. She had no more filling. She wove in what Tena had spun of the blue mixed. It makes beautiful cloth, prettier than the black mixed. A traveler staid here last night, an old man named Shipman.

Sunday 15th - I washed the children last night & put their clean clothes on & then darned some stockings of Willie's and a pair of Zona's. They wear their stockings very fast. Cloudy this morning & warm. Seems as if Spring was with us. I will stop now as I want some apples, walnuts & peach leather. The apples will soon be gone. Mr. Henry is sitting here teaching Willie to talk & mawking me. The negroes started a rabbit while I was eating apples. It ran through the yard & under a drain in the road down by the old cow pen. Mr. Henry, I & all the children had to go & see the negroes dig it out. Mr. Henry & I read after dinner. I read a good deal in my bible. I will soon go to bed as Willie is sleepy & I am tired of doing nothing.

Monday 16th - I did but little of anything today as I have not been well. Jinnie & Atheline scoured my room & dining room today. Cloudy & looks like rain.

Alston's negro came here today & got 53 lbs. lard. Mr. Henry up at the old hotel place. They are fixing up the old hen house to roll down here.

Tuesday 17th - Betsey came today through the rain. She will get out the cloth in a day or two. Mr. Henry in the house all day as it is raining. I cut some little aprons today, two brilliante & two bleached. Sewed some on one. I am fixing it around with green chambre. It will look very well.

Wednesday 18th - Finished that apron & made another. Still cloudy. Atheline making some napkins. All are well. Mr. Henry went to Asheville today. Alston's negro got 6 turkeys yesterday at 1.50 each, is to get four more tomorrow. Willie is trying to talk, can say any word but can't frame a sentence.

Thursday Feb. 19th 1863 - Betsey got the cloth out & went home this evening. Alston's negro got the turkeys today. Old Dave Alford stays here tonight. Jim Cannon & old Night started to slaughter the hogs today. I made another apron today. Mr. Henry went to Asheville today. Nothing new going on. They have not got the hen house here yet & I fear they won't unless they tear it down & then we have no nails to put it together with.

Friday 20th - I finished the last apron today, faced it around with yellow brilliante. I read all the papers. I received a letter from Sister Ell yesterday. She is doing finely with her little twin boys. Mr. Henry started this morning to attend the slaughtering of the hogs & is then going down after Matt as she has promised to come & spend some time with us. Mr. Henry will have to hire a buggy as he went horse back. He thinks he will be back in a week or two.

Saturday 21st - I made some cushions for the chairs in my room & cushioned a stool also. They will do better than nothing these cold days. Rain nearly all day today. I sent by Jim Nichols to Asheville today for the mail & some button moulds. They are very small. I gave 50 cts. for 60 buttons at Merriman's.

Sunday 22nd - I have the heart burn badly this morning. It is some better now as I have been vomiting. I have had it for a week, more or less. Rained very hard last night & cool this morning & cloudy. The children are all in the kitchen. I hear their little laughing tongues a going. Fannie is not so well this morning. It is near her time of confinement. I do hope Mr. Henry will get back before she gets down as it is her first one.

Monday 23rd - I have been crocheting today on a cover for the candle stand. Mrs. Jamison & Betsey came this morning to warp a piece of jeans, 50 yds. They put part of it in the harness today. Betsey is to weave it. I send after Mrs. Andrews today as Fannie was complaining a good deal. She stays here tonight. Warm & pleasant. I got a letter from Matt tonight by the mail. Pa is not at all well. She says she can't come if Pa gets no better. The others are all well.

Tuesday Feb. 24th 1863 - Mrs. Andrew's went home today, also Mrs. Jamison. They both staid till after dinner. Fannie got better. I have been crocheting all day. Nothing new going on. Julia Bonner, a niece of old Mr. Reynolds is expected to die every day. She has consumption. Betsey began weaving today. Night & Cannon got home today, brought some offal of the hogs, not much.

Wednesday 25th - Finished the cover of candle stand today & made fringe & put it on & began the tidy for the rocking chair. Mrs. George Jones & Mag Morris took dinner here. Mrs. Jones came to see Mr. Henry on business. Warm, looks like Spring was with us.

Thursday 26th - Crochet on tidy. Raining & cloudy all day. Celia Hampton burried an infant today at Sulphur Springs Academy. Miss Bonner died this morning. Ham Cannon's wife is down with fever. I hear of but little sickness in the country.

Friday 27th - Mail brought no war news. Harrie wrote to Mr. Henry. The letter came today. He is in Columbia on sick leave. Poor fellow. I fear he will soon leave this bright, beautiful world to try the realities of the dark unknown future. My paper does not come regular. It is quite a treat when it does come. A good many people here after letters &c. today.

Saturday 28th - I have done but little at my tidy yesterday or today. Till Morris came just after dinner today, from preaching at Academy & Tom Morris called for her this evening. He had kin to muster on Licks Creek to get recruits. He has not heard of Pinck Allen yet. Cloudy. We have had a good deal of rain. It washed the garden considerably as it was broke up this week. The hands got the hen house moved down this evening after so long a time working at it. It looked very strange to see a house on a waggon & drawn by oxen.

March 1863

Sunday March 1st - Clear & windy this morning. We had some rain last night. Mr. Reynolds preaches at the Academy today. The negroes mostly gone. Tena has the children. I am going up to her house soon as I get tired of being alone. I wish Mr. Henry would come this evening. Jinnie sleeps in the house at night. Betsey went home Friday evening.

Monday March 2nd 1863 - I have crocheted some today, not much. Mr. Henry & Matt came this evening. I was very glad to see them. They left home last Wednesday. They left all well down there. The buggy broke down a time or two on the road. They staid two days at Erwin's on a break down. It was dark when they got here. We were eating supper. Betsey came this morning. Warm & pleasant today. Nothing new going on.

Tuesday 3rd - Finished my tidy today, put the edge on. Matt & I have enjoyed the day finely. Mr. Henry went back today to hunt Matt's hat. They lost it, the band bow, yesterday out of the buggy. He will not be back tonight. I hope he may find it. The little ones all well.

Wednesday 4th - Crocheted some today from some patterns Matt has. They are very pretty. Very cold & disagreeable today. Mr. Henry came just after dinner, came by Smith's tan yard. Got two sides of sole leather & sent Tom after another side at the tan yard. Fannie still spinning some. Betsey getting on very well with her weaving.

Thursday 5th - Mr. Henry went to Asheville today. Took about fifty yds. of jeans, 18 yds. of it very fine. I have been knitting some today, footing some stockings. Matt making some tatten for Zona & Willie's gowns. Turned some warmer.

Friday 6th - Mail brought nothing new. We all read generally nothing new in the papers. All are well. I have knit some today. Fannie baked some molasses bread this evening. Matt & I cut them out. They taste very well.

Saturday 7th - Knit some today. Nothing of importance going on. All are well. Betsey went home yesterday evening. Mrs. Cannon getting no better. Warm & pleasant with clouds. Fannie still on foot. The others all well. All quiet along the lines. Oh! that we could have an honorable adjustment of affairs & stop so much blood shed. Hope, the anchor of the heart, still keeps looking from one month to another for peace to be declared but I fear that day is far distant.

April 1863

Sunday April 19th 1863 - Six weeks has passed since I wrote in you, my dear old journal. I have been confined in that time & got up again to health. My babe was born 8th March at 23 minutes after 8 o'clock in the morning. A fine healthy boy.[40] He gave us some trouble at first by having us up at night till he was two weeks old but since he has been no trouble at all at night. He is like the most of children, loves nursing. The children think a great deal of it. Pinck can nurse it a short time but he soon tires of it. Matt has been very kind to me. I shall ever remember her kindness to me & my little ones when I was not able to attend to them myself. Aunt Patsey staid with me till the babe was nearly a week old. She would have staid longer but Mrs. Cannon was very sick with typhoid fever at that time and is not well yet. I was confined upstairs & did not go down till the babe was two weeks old. We have had a great deal of company for the last six weeks.

Mr. Hosea Linsey has a contract for gun stocks. They are going to get them out here at the mill. He has one hand here & he stays himself through the week. Old Mr. Cagle is here now. He has dispepsia. He is drinking the sulphur water, thinks it does him a great deal of good. Charlie & Lonzo have been very low with pneumonia fever. They are both up again but not stout. Matt & Zona had a slight attack. Zona was right sick several days. Thanks to a kind Providence he spared them a while longer. Fannie was confined a week after I was with a girl, a healthy child. It cries a great deal more than mine. My babe weighed eight lbs. before it was dressed & 13 3/4 lbs. when it was a month old. Our garden is getting on very well. Rather late as we have had so much rain. Harrie Deaver came here yesterday evening. He looks very badly. Poor fellow. He can't last much longer. He only weighs 102. He weighed 112 last Spring when he was here. He is nothing but a shadow. He is on his way to his Regiment. He is Col. of the 60th Reg. now since Col. McDowell's resignation. Harrie is very feeble. He says he is not going to stay in the Regiment long. They expect a fight soon at Tullahoma. He is going to resign after the fight if he is not killed. I hope almost against hope that he may recover. I fear he has consumption. I pray God to spare his life yet awhile longer. He is in the bloom of manhood & if it is Thy holy will, spare him to old age to be a useful member of society.

---

[40] Gustavus Adolphus (Gus) Henry

Harrie made a present of a beautiful dress, the one he brought from Columbia. Also a paper of needles & a spool of thread. Needles and thread are selling at one dollar each now. I shall prize that dress very highly as coming from him. The yanks attacked Charleston, at least tried to pass the forts on the 7th & 8th of the month but they left with some of their best boats badly crippled & have not renewed the attack. I believe I have written all of any importance for the last six weeks. There has been a great deal of sickness in the country. Old Mr. Quinn died some three weeks ago leaving his family very destitute. Have mercy on the poor in these trying times is my prayer. There has been a pressing officer through the country. We have a fine chance of bacon up in the loft now. Mr. Henry was not at home & I had it put there. He is going to sell to them at the market price. Very warm today. I must soon stop. I am writing upstairs in Harrie's room. Looks a good deal like rain.

Oh! God I thank Thee that I passed through my confinement & Thou saw fit to spare my life. Spare me I beseech Thee to raise up those little ones Thou hast given me. Give me wisdom to rear them as seemeth good in Thy sight. Bless us as a nation. May we at length come out conquerors if it is Thy holy will. Grant us a speedy peace on honorable terms & Thine shall be the glory.

Monday April 20th - I have done nothing of interest any importance today. Knit a little. Harrie & Mr. Henry went to Asheville this evening. I never expect to see Harrie again. Poor fellow. I fear his days are few on this earth. He is very feeble & coughs a good deal. He is still cheerful. I don't think he will last long after he goes back to camps. He is Col. of the 60th. He says he is coming back after the next fight we have at Tullahoma if he is alive. Ah! yes if he is alive, I don't think he would be able to be in a battle if he was there.

Tuesday 21st - Matt & I spun a little today. Fannie cooks. Atheline spins some and waits on the children. Willie is a very cross child. He tries my patience sorely. Zona is not well nor hasn't been for sometime. Worms I think. Pinck is a stout healthy child. We have not named the babe yet. He grows very fast, notices a good deal & laughs. Does not cry much yet. Love's nursing. I shall miss Matt a great deal when she goes home. She speaks of going next week.

Wednesday 22nd April 1863 - Aunt Patsey spent the day here. Betsey went home this evening. I have spun a little & reeled some after dinner. Atheline has nearly enough for her dresses. Mr. Henry & Matt intended to go to Asheville today but it rained. I wanted to send some things to Harrie but Mr. Linsey came over today & said he started today at 12 o'clock. I am sorry he did not get his things before he started. I wanted him to take some butter, brandy, candles & some soap but the soap was not done, at least it was not hard. Aunt Tena has been working at it yesterday & today.

Thursday 23rd - I have been crocheting on a little sock for the babe today. It will be very nice when done. Mattie is knitting Zona a pair rail road stockings. We spin a little occasionally through the day. Zona is not well yet, has a little fever nearly every day but still keeps going about. Matt & Betsey sleep upstairs. Pinck on his trundle bed. I moved one of the beds out of Matt's room into the other room for Boyd & Moore. They are getting along slowly with their gun stocks.

Friday 24th - Mail brought no news of importance. The conscripts are called out to 40. Oh! if Mr. Henry should have to go, I don't see how I could ever stay here. I hope he may not have to go. He is the best of husbands & then so kind to the children, so patient. Life would be a blank to me without he was near me. The conscripts have to be examined next week in Asheville. I pray he may not have to go. Mr. Henry & Matt went to Asheville this morning. Mr. Henry came back at night. Matt stays with Mrs. Dr. Hilliard till Monday. Nothing new in the village.

Saturday 25th - I finished one of the babe's stockings yesterday & began one for Mr. Henry today. His are knit (cotton). A beautiful day, warm & bright. Betsey went home this evening. Zona still unwell. She has fallen off a great deal. Looks pale & lean. Mr. Henry, Pinck & I took a long walk this evening. Went to see the little colt at the Stradley place. The Luther mare's colt. It is a very fine colt. So large & well made. I was very tired when we got back. It was sun down & I had to get out supper after I came. I bought 8 lbs. of honey yesterday of old Jim Case. It is not very nice. Gave a lb. of bacon for a lb. of honey. Bacon is selling at 75 per lb. Corn from 4 to 6$ a bu. & flour 25 cts. per lb. Dear living to those who have to buy.

Sunday evening, April 26th 1863 - This has been a lovely day. The apple trees, some of them in bloom. Some of the peaches have been killed by frost. The grass in the yard is getting green fast & other things in the front yard. What the calves & hogs have not destroyed is putting out finely. Mr. Henry & Mr. Moore have gone up towards the Spring. Mr. Henry thinks Mrs. Hutsell is having rails made on his land & he has gone to see. Atheline has the baby off on his first visit away from the house. Jim has Willie along also. Pinck is going about at his pleasure. Zona is setting in my room with me clipping paper. She looks thin. I have nothing more of interest to write. Warm this evening. Mr. Henry & I have made out the P. O. returns today. I gave out & he copied. Nothing more. I have promised Zona a walk this evening & will take her when it gets cool. Mr. Henry & I went with Zona to the mill. Met Mr. Cagle. He came back this evening. He thinks this water helps him a great deal. He is a dispeptic.

Monday 27th - I crochet the babe a stocking today. Cloudy some rain. Mattie came home with Mr. Henry from Asheville this evening. She enjoyed herself finely, staid at Mrs. Hilliard's all the time. They are examining the conscripts in Buncombe at Asheville this week. They take nearly all they examine. When will this war cease? Echo answers "when?"

Tuesday 28th - Matt began Zona a pair pantletts today, will put on some edging she crocheted. Matt Tidwell came back today. Three years ago she went to Mississippi with her father. She came alone. Poor girl, your mother has caused her family an ocean of trouble. Why was she spared? Matt did not hear of her grandpa's death till she got to Asheville. She has seen a heap of trouble since she left here. Old Mr. Henry died some time in Jan. 1863.

Wednesday 29th - I cut out a chemise each for the negro women & a table cloth. I made the table cloth. Matt Tidwell is sewing on Atheline's chemise. Sister Matt & I read a good deal this evening. She is going home next week. I am very sorry of it. I shall miss her sadly. We take a long walk every evening. She is a good girl. Her & Dora think of spending some time in Ten. this Summer with Sister Jane & return by here. I want to go down home with them this fall as it has been nearly three years since I was there. Willie is not well, has a cold & wheezes like he was threatened with croup. Others all well.

Thursday 30th April 1863 - Mr. Henry went to Asheville today, staid all day. Sister Matt & I went up to the stables to meet him this evening. He had come but we did not see him as he had the mare eating grass in the garden. I sewed on Jinnie's chemise some today. The baby will not lay in the chair when he is awake & I nurse a part of my time. Zona has got well but looks badly. Atheline is spinning. Fannie cooks.

May 1863

Friday May 1st - Mail brought no news. No letters for our family. This is a beautiful day. Mr. Henry went to Asheville this morning. We met him above the stables & rode to the stables, had a merry short ride. Matt Tidwell was along & we met Pinck at the stables too. Mr. Henry led the horse, the Cagle horse. He seemed rather factious because Pinck touched his tail, Mr. Henry said. Mr. Henry got three packs of envelopes for 1.00 today, brown. The people of Asheville had a May party today on the mountain, back of the College.

Saturday 2nd - I have done several things today. Finished Fannie's chemise, first parched some coffee. Sam & others killed two hogs yesterday. Atheline done up the lard today. Fannie baked some loaf bread & molasses bread this evening. Sis Matt & I went to meet Mr. Henry this evening. He went to Asheville after Matt's earring this evening. He forgot it. We rode down to the stables. He got 5 lbs. of sugar today for 7.50, 1.50 per lb. Dear sugar. Harrie is in Asheville, gave out at Knoxville, Tenn. Poor fellow, he has come back to die I fear. The two Matts went to church at the Academy today but did not stay for preaching as they saw a cloud coming. It did not rain any of consequence here. Our garden is backward, needs rain. Betsey went home last Thursday evening. The two Matts sleep upstairs in this room. Pinck & Willie on the trundle bed & Mr. Henry, Willie, the babe & I on the big bed.

Sunday 3rd - Both Matts gone to church at Academy. Cloudy with occasional sun shine today. Mr. Henry down stairs asleep. I am in Matt's room knitting. Willie & Zona are with me. Willie wheezes a good deal yet. Zona is well. Pinck gone to church & all the negroes but Fannie & Atheline. Fannie getting dinner & Atheline has the babe. Old Mr. Cagle is quite unwell in bed in the other room. He is giving the children some sugar. Poor old fellow, he is fond of little ones.

Monday May 4th - I have been lonely today. A sad long day. Mr. Henry & Matt started home today. I wish I could have gone too but I could not conveniently. My place is at home with my little ones. I felt so lonely all day. Matt has been so kind to me & the children, attended to my housekeeping when I was not able to do it myself. I love her a heap. I will try to repay her kindness some day. She is a good girl. So is Dora. They are both lovely. Dora is so mild & gentle. Matt has a generous heart. I made Mr. Henry a pair drawers today, got them done before night. Matt & Atheline spinning. Sister Matt & I went to the Sulphur Spring yesterday evening, met Mr. Henry at the hotel place. Matt got her shoes this evening. They are very nice ones. We brought a bucket of water for Mr. Cagle. It will be some time before I walk with my baby sister again.

Tuesday 5th - Jinnie scoured my room & the dining room today. I took one bed out of my room & changed the furniture a little. Matt & Pinck will sleep on the little trundle bed & Zona, the babe & I in the bed. Willie in the crib by the bed. I have done nothing of importance today. Helped arrange the things in the room. Mr. Cagle no better.

Wednesday 6th - Atheline cleaned upstairs today as I expect Harrie this week. Poor fellow. I fear he will not live long. He is very feeble. I have knit some today. Cloudy & raining this evening. Willie still wheezes a good deal. One of I. Mathew's children died this morning of fever, typhoid pneumonia, and another child very sick.

Thursday 7th - We arranged the room upstairs for Harrie today. Put up another bedstead (single one). We got the single bedstead from J. Green's two or three weeks ago. We put the single bedstead that was in my room in the side room & took the corded stead out as it was too large for the size of the room. Matt & Betsey will stay in there when Betsey comes.

Friday 8th - We have had another victory at or near Fredericksburg Va. Gen. Jackson had an arm broke. We lost one Gen., killed. Paxton & Gen's A. P. Hill & Heath were wounded. I have not seen the casualities yet. The loss on our side not so great as on the yanks. Oh that they would see the error of their ways & turn from their wickedness before too late. I would ask Thy blessing Oh Ruler on high on us as a nation, give our soldiers courage & endow our rulers with wisdom from on high. May they be enabled to govern the men with kindness & grant us a speedy peace on honorable terms is my prayer Oh! most merciful God.

Saturday 9th May 1863 - I fixed my hoop this evening. Made some flour sacks this morning. A bright, beautiful day. This is the most backward Spring ever known here. The trees are putting out a little now. Last Sunday the woods looked nearly like the dead of winter. They are putting forth very fast now. I lined Pinck's straw hat yesterday. Mrs. Willey Knight made it. He got it last Sunday. Mrs. Bob Moore was here a short time this afternoon, wanted to see Mr. Henry on business. Mr. Cagle sent a horse for his wife yesterday by the mail boy. He is no better. He expects her today. I hope she will come. He is able to come down stairs yet. The whip o wills came & lit on the piazza Tuesday night & Wednesday night this week. I dislike to hear them very much about a house. Not that I am superstitious but they make such a plaintive wail. Aunt Patsey spent the day here today. She says Betsey will be here Monday. Old Jim & Bill Knight got home today with a load of bacon from Dr. Kilgore's. They bought 151 pieces & 21 joles. They will go after the other next Tuesday.

Sunday 10th - A beautiful bright day. Excellent growing weather. Our people will soon be done planting corn. Our lettuce is just getting large enough to eat, very late at that. We had some last Sunday. It was very small. I wish vegetables would come in fast for I am tired of dried apples & meat. I have not heard anything more of Harrie. I think of writing to him tomorrow by the mail. I have looked all week for him & Mrs. Hilliard as she sent word she was coming over with Harrie this week. My babe's ear still runs. Poor little fellow. I fear it pains him. It is inflamed on the out side this morning. Jinnie is getting dinner. I guess it will soon be ready. Atheline has the baby & Zona off somewhere. Willie is down with Jinnie & Pinck off with the negro boys. I want to write some letters this evening. One to Lou & one to Sister Jane. Mrs. Cagle has not come yet. Matt spent the evening at Mrs. Willey Knight's, staid till dark. Three men stay here tonight. Not soldiers.

Monday 11th - I began to crochet a pair socks for the babe today. Did but little at it. Harrie came over in the evening. He looks some better than he did when he left but I fear he will never be well again. The sun shines very warm today. Betsey weaving. Matt spinning for her some dresses. Atheline spinning for the negro's pants. I received a letter from Mr. Henry by the mail today. He & Matt were in Greenville. Last Friday they went up on Crayershead Mountain.

Tuesday May 12th 1863 - No more news from the fight yet. I have worked a little on the babe's stocking. I took the toothache after dinner, not very badly. The baby's ear still runs, smells rather offensive. I hope it may not injure his hearing but I greatly fear it will. Willie still wheezes some. The other two little ones very well. Harrie has been to the mill today. Oh! how glad I would be to see him once again in health. I would ask Thy blessing on him this night & may that blessing be health if it is Thy holy will.

Wednesday 13th - I did not sleep well last night as my teeth ached very badly all night & not much better this morning. They are very sore. I almost wish sometimes I had no teeth, they ache so much. I finished one little sock today. It looks very nice. The yarn is so very fine 'tis tedious. Nothing of interest going on. Harrie brought back his box of hams & butter that we started to him. They are very moldy. We have lettuce beautifully now.

Thursday 14th - Harrie went to Asheville this morning. It rained a little but cleared off before dinner. I had the headache all day & was quite sick after dinner with it. Harrie came back about 5 o'clock. He got the papers which give a full account of the & Fredericksburg fight. Gen. Jackson is dead. Died from pneumonia & his wounds. He was wounded by our men through mistake. We have lost one of our best Generals. A nation now mourns his loss. Harrie complained of his lungs some after he came back. He says he can't ride horseback.

Friday 15th - Mail brought nothing new but four letters as Harrie brought the mail yesterday. My head not entirely well but a great deal better. I took some pills this morning. Aunt Patsey spent the day here. Warped the thread for the children's dresses. It is 4 of purple (dyed with Willow root) & 1 of white. I crocheted some after dinner as my head was easy nearly.

Saturday 16th - I finished the other little sock tonight. Rather cool tonight & last night too. Old Jim & Bill Knight got home last night with the bacon. The trash of Bent creek pressed five hundred lbs. of it. The women did it. They paid 50 per lb. for it. Old Jim Knight brought the money home. I wish Mr. Henry could stay at home to attend to his business but he has other business that perhaps is of more importance. He wrote me that he would go to Columbia before he came back to get hands to work at his gun stock contract. Too many irons in the fire. Some will surely burn up. It has always been so & ever will I reckon. He carries on too much business for his means.

Sunday 17th 1863 - Clear & windy. No preaching near today. Fannie will soon have dinner ready. Atheline has the baby. The other children downstairs. Harrie sitting in front piazza reading. Matt asleep in side room & I am upstairs in Harrie's room writing. I expect to spend the evening in, reading my bible. I am reading in 1st Kings. I am also reading Josephus' works on the Bible. I read one & then the other so as to keep them on the same subject. Dinner is nearly ready so I will stop for the present. I spent the evening in reading.

Monday 18th - I got a letter from Mr. Henry tonight by mail. He was in Columbia the 12th ult. He had seen Martha Arthur, Virginia & Mollie H.[41] They were all well. I look for him this week. I began the baby another pair stockings. I get along very slow crocheting. Harrie thinks he is improving.

Tuesday 19th - Dry & warm needing rain badly. Our garden gets on slowly. No cabbage plants out yet. I worked some on the stocking. Handed threads to Betsy after dinner for the children's dresses. She will put it through the sley tomorrow. Atheline spinning but gets along very slowly.

Wednesday 20th - Betsey got the cloth started today. It looks very well. Aunt Patsy came this morning to put it in. She went back before dinner. She is not very well. She fell on the fence the other day & hurt her ribs. I finished one stocking & began the other today. They look very nice. Mr. Henry came home this evening. We were glad to see him. Pa sent me a little negro to nurse for me. Rose, one of Clois' children. He brought me a calico dress for which he paid $32 1/2 dollars, 9 yds. at 3.50 pr. yd. I did not know he was going to get it. It is very nice calico.

Thursday 21st - Mr. Henry & Harrie went to Asheville today. They came back late in the evening. Nothing new going on, all quiet along the lines. Mr. Henry says Mollie looks very badly. Poor woman, she is too good for Jim if all reports are true. They were all well at home when Mr. Henry left.

Friday 22nd - Mail brought no news of importance. Mr. Henry got a letter for me yesterday from him. He beat the letter home. The baby's ear has quit running. Willie still wheezes some. Mr. Henry gives him squills night & morning. Mr. Henry went to Asheville today with a load of bacon for which he gets $1.00 pr. lb. He sold to the armory.

William L. Henry (Bill) to Cornelia C. Henry (Dinah)

My Dear Dinah

I will start home in the morning. Sold Bacon at $1. Mr. Lopez will try to get some hands and will write.

I have bought a knife apiece for the children. Please speak to them of Papa and the knives with string holes.

The leaves were full grown when we got over the mountain while the buds were just bursting and many trees not showing life. I eat green peas

---

[41] Martha Ann Henry, sister of William Henry. Molly Henry, wife of James L. Henry

yesterday. I saw strawberries but did not relish them!!!

You see the certificate. I send it so as to stop the sale of bacon or any other disposition.

Feed in Columbia is tolerable, only $6.00 per day, women extra.

Tell old man Cagle narry a pound of coffee for sale in Columbia that I can find. Stores have check striped country domestic at $2.00. How do you like it? Flour is selling at $12 1/2. I think that is lower than for Buncombe.

Nothing to write. I will fill with wishing myself home to enjoy things that are not on this side of home nor no place else. I will bring you and Willie a negro girl from Grand Papa. Hope to stay at home when I come "a few days." Love to the children and to their Mother my highest esteem & purest love. I close by subscribing my name as your lover.
Bill

W. A. Lonergan to William L. Henry

Columbia May 13th 1863

This is to certify that Wm. L. Henry has sold to me as agent of the Government all Bacon he may have up to the above date. Said Bacon to be delivered to the most convenient R. R. point from his residence (as soon as ordered).
W. A. Lonergan
Govt. Agent

Saturday 23rd - Tax giving in day, a good many people here. Betsey got out the children's dresses this evening. It looks very well. Mr. Henry sent three thousand (3000) lbs. to the armory again today which makes 5,307 lbs. in all. He did not go today himself. I fixed some sewing thread today. I finished the babe's stockings yesterday, put bows on them.

May Sunday 24th 1863 - Very warm this morning & very dry, needing rain badly. Harrie & Mr. Henry & Pinck gone to church at Academy. Mr. Reynolds preaches F. M. Starnes' funeral today. Matt & I did not go as it gives me the headache to walk so far & it is very warm today. The children all well. Jinnie getting dinner. Matt rocking the babe in the cradle. Lane left here this morning. Pa sent him here after the jack. He came here Friday night. It took him 4 days to come. He rode a mare. Mr. Henry & Harrie & Pinck went to Capt. Moore's from church. Matt & I went on the hill to see Mr. Cagle & others. We staid till Mr. Henry came up after me. It was about sundown when we got back.

Monday 25th - I cut Mr. Henry two pair pants today & Pinck three pair of the cloth Betsey wove, cotton jeans. I did not get one pair of Mr. Henry's done. Mail carrier says Vicksburg is holding out against the seige. Nothing new going on.

Betsey will put Rose's dresses & aprons in the loom this week. Rose does very well nursing. The baby's ear has quit running a week ago.

Tuesday 26th & Wednesday 27th - I have had headache for two days, yesterday & today. I have had a very bad spell of it. Bill Miller came here yesterday. He & Harrie went to Asheville yesterday after noon. They did not get back till this evening. I took some pills today & my head is nearly well this evening. I slept part of the day yesterday & a good deal today.

Thursday 28th - Our forces still hold Vicksburg. They have repulsed the yanks nine or ten times. Mr. Henry in house nearly all day as it is raining. I finished Mr. Henry's pants & made Pinck a pair today. W. Miller staid here all day, his wife has a young boy babe some three weeks old. Betsey & Aunt Patsy spent the day here yesterday. She warped the thread for Rose's dresses & got it started & Betsey is weaving on it today. Nothing new going on. We were needing rain badly. We have a good season now yet I think we will have more from the looks of the clouds.

Friday 29th - Mail brought no news more than we have heard. I received a letter from Mollie Henry last Monday. She seemed very desponding about Jimmie. She is devoted to him. I cut Zona & Willie a dress of the homespun today, got Zona's done & sewed some on Willie's. Her's fits beautifully. She is delighted with it. I trimmed it with buttons. The sleeves & front, the waist & sleeves are all together. Rain & sunshine alternately today. Mr. Henry went to Asheville today. He came home in the evening very wet. We had a very heavy rain this evening. He got 41 lbs. of sugar & at 1.50 pr. lb., not very nice at that. Mr. Miller left this morning for home.

Saturday May 30th 1863 - Betsey went home this morning. We have had some rain today, not much. I finished Willie's dress soon after dinner & put it on him. He is very proud of his homespun with buttons. I washed Pinck's head after dinner. George cut his hair today. It is shingled very close but looks very well. Mr. Henry out about the farm & mill. Wiley Knight moved the loom this evening in the back piazza. He put the rollers on the trunnel bed also. The children are delighted with it. Mr. Henry got the rollers when he was in Columbia. He is ever thoughtful of his wife & children. He is such a good man.

Sunday 31st - Cloudy & sunshine this evening. Looks very much like rain if the wind don't blow too much. Atheline is not well today, has headache. Rose is rocking the baby in the cradle now. Strawberries are beginning to ripen a little. Old Goodlake & Margaret were over here this morning. They brought Matt's shoes, one pair. She will get the other pair soon. Margaret looks badly. She breaks very fast, has two living children & one dead. Old Goodlake would start before dinner. Margaret wanted to stay till evening. There was a wounded soldier stopped here for whiskey. I think him an imposter. Mr. Henry gave him some brandy. He says he was in the Fredericksburg fight, the last one they had. I will stop now as my baby is fretting. He laughed out yesterday, the first time. Harrie came up to take a nap. I am in his room writing. He is lying on his bed.

June 1863

Monday June 1st - I made Rose a dress today & cleaned out the pantry & smoke house. Atheline spinning. She gets on very slowly as she is slow at any & everything. Mail brought no news more than we have heard. We are closely beseiged by the yanks at Vicksburg. God grant us a victory.

Tuesday 2nd - I am not so well today but took some pills before dinner & my head feels better. Willie still wheezes a good deal. I made Rose two aprons & a chemise today. I have done very well to be taking pills. Nothing new going on. Wiley Jones left here some three or four weeks ago. Rumor says he has gone to the yanks or tories in East Tenn. He left his family. He is a conscript that comes under 40.

Wednesday 3rd - We had some rain last night & some this morning but cleared off up in the day. Aunt Patsey & Betsey were here this evening after meal & meat. Mr. Henry out on business all day. Willie still rattles in his lungs. I cleaned up the wool upstairs this morning so it was late when I got to work. I began a dress for Willie but did not finish it. Harrie seems about as usual. He has been a little unwell for a day or two but seems to be doing better now. I don't think he will ever be well again yet I hope he may. Oh! to be cut down in the bloom of manhood is sad indeed.

Thursday 4th June 1863 - Mr. Henry & Harrie went to Asheville today. It was late when they got back, at least sunset. We still hold Vicksburg & our prospects are bright. Our forces are confident of holding it. I finished Willie's dress & began Zona's. Pinck Allen is still a deserter, also his brother in law Bryson. Allen says he will never go back to the 25th Reg. & Bryson says he don't intend to go the 60th or any other. Rachel Allen came to see Harrie yesterday about Pinck. Harrie told her he could do nothing for him.

Friday 5th - No news today but one letter came as Mr. Henry brought the mail yesterday. I made or rather finished Zona's dress & sewed some on Pinck's pants. I sewed them up on the machine. I made six sacks Wednesday evening on the machine. They were made of the tent cloth, the one I made Mr. Henry the time he went to the Laurel war. They are very dirty. He is going to send after some wheat to Haywood. He gives six dollars & a half for wheat & sells flour at 25$ a hundred.

Saturday 6th - Harrie went to Asheville today but got no news. All quiet, only at Vicksburg we are annoying the yanks some there yet. I finished Pinck's pants & turned Willie's hat. It looks very well, better than I thought it would. He is very proud of it. I washed & cleaned all the children except the baby. Pinck has an ugly sore on his foot, 'tis getting better now. Mr. Henry gave Willie an emetic yesterday morning of ipacac. It made him vomit a good deal, yet has not stopped the rattling in his throat. He is giving him one this evening. I hope this one will do him good. We bathe his chest with spirits turpentine. The babe is growing finely. Matt & Dora passed through Asheville last Wednesday on their way to Tenn. I think they might have given me call but they were with Neilson & his visits here are few & far between.

Sunday 7th - Rather late breakfast this morning as all are lazy & sleepy every Sunday. Mr. Henry has gone up on Mt. Yaden to look after the fence as he wants to sow some buckwheat up there. Harrie in the front piazza reading the Bible. Willie off in the strawberry patch with Rose. Atheline has the baby in the strawberry patch. Pinck I guess is there too. Zona is down stairs going around generally I suppose. I am writing in Harrie's room. The horses are grazing in the yard as it is getting a good pasture. There is preaching at Sardis today but none of us went. Aunt Tena went yesterday to the baptist church on Homeny. She will be back this evening. She began to dye the wool this week, will be sometime before it all gets done. She has none black yet. She is dying with white & black walnut bark. Jinnie is getting dinner. Pinck has some frogs for dinner. I wish potatoes & beans would soon come in. I am tired of so much onions & salad but 'tis all we can afford yet awhile. I will stop now as 'tis after 12 & dinner time.

Monday 8th June 1863 - I made Mr. Henry a pair cotton jeans pants & fixed up the mail. Nothing new came tonight from Vicksburg. Willie still wheezes. Mr. Henry & Harrie went to Asheville this morning. Harrie has not come back tonight. He will come tomorrow.

Tuesday 9th - I made Pinck a pair cotton jeans pants & sewed some on Zona's dress. Harrie came over this evening. Mr. Henry went to Asheville this morning & back this evening. Nothing new going on.

Wednesday 10th - I finished Zona's dress today. The baby's neck is sore, chapped I think. I hope it will soon be well. He is a good child. His neck has been sore several days. Harrie has strawberries for lunch once every two or three days when he can get the berries.

Sunday 14th - Several days I will put under one. On last Thursday I got up with headache. It got worse so I took some pills about 10 o'clock. They did not relieve me any. Betsey Jamison staid all night here Thursday. William Tidwell, Tom & another man also so the house was full. I did not eat any supper. A workman came here last Monday to saw out gun stocks. He is boarding here too. Friday morning my head felt some better but pained me some all day. No news came of importance. I received a letter from Lou last Monday. She is well & doing finely.

Saturday morning my head pained me a good deal & all day it did not get easy. Eugenia Hopson[42] came Saturday morning to see Harrie. I was glad to see her. She is looking thin. Her little Fannie is growing off very well. She is a pretty child. Harrie was glad to see her I know. She will not stay long. She is a kind, good creature. Sunday has been a long rainy day. The children gathered some strawberries for dinner. They are very nice. Eugenia, Harrie & I loved them. Mr. Henry will start off tomorrow to So. Ca. & then to Charlotte N. C. I am sorry to see him go. I would have him ever with me if I could. He is such a devoted husband to me & so kind to the children. I love him more each day. Mrs. Rutherford came here today. She is to make soap or at least learn Aunt Tena to make hard soap without salt. Dr. Thrash was here this evening to see Willie. He recommends squills for the wheezing. It is now supper time & I must get out supper. I am down in my studio on the

---

[42] Daughter of Mary Louise Henry and Reuben Deaver, sister of Harrie Deaver

branch writing. I left Eugenia, Mr. Henry & Mrs. Rutherford in my room with the children. Mattie & Pinck strawberry hunting. Nothing more this evening at this time. Jinnie, Hopson & I went to the mill also Mrs. Rutherford went to the dam. We saw Pinck Allen as we came back. He looked very sheepish. Mr. Henry went down to see him. We met him at the mill. It was dark when Mr. Henry got back as we had eat supper.

Monday 15th June 1863 - Eugenia & Matt, Pinck & Rose went to the View after strawberries today. Got back for dinner. We had cream & strawberries for dinner & some for supper. I have done nothing today. Mrs. Rutherford working with the lye to make soap. Mr. Henry started this morning. I was sorry to see him go.

Tuesday 16th - This has been a very warm day. Atheline went & gathered some strawberries. We had some for supper. They were very nice. William & Tom Tidwell stay here tonight. William starts in the morning or after dinner, back to the army. God protect our poor soldiers I pray. Help us in this fight.

Wednesday 17th - Eugenia & I went to the mill this evening. She wanted to have a dough board made. Wiley Night made a very nice walnut one & sent it up this evening. Fannie made Eugenia a pie to take with her of strawberries to eat on the stage. Harrie went to Asheville yesterday & he & Jinnie go today as she wants to leave on the stage in the morning. Harrie will be back tomorrow evening. I finished Willie's dress today. Eugenia gave Zona a very nice muslin dress & me a nice cap & some other little things.

Thursday 18th - We have had some rain today. Harrie came over in the evening. I crocheted a net for Matt today & fixed tassells to Zona's old net. Eugenia got off on the stage. Harrie said it was crowded. She will have a rough time of it. I fear nothing from Vicksburg yet.

Friday 19th - Mail brought no news. Till Morris spent the day here. I sent Atheline to Mrs. Jones' to borrow some lard as old Night failed to bring any from Transelvania. He went after corn last Monday & did not bring any lard. I mended an old calico dress today & began to fix another one of my old Salem dresses. It is a good dress but too short in the skirt.

Saturday 20th - Finished my dress today. Nothing of importance going on. The militia is called out the first of Aug. & then my own dear husband will have to go. Oh! what will become of me & my little ones, God only knows. I wish I could see one ray of hope in the future. It would lighten my heart of a great load but I see not the faintest hope for my poor sinking heart to cling to. Oh God I beseech Thee to grant us an honorable peace before more blood is shed. If we have not been sufficiently punished, when, oh when will our trials cease? I shall be very lonely if my own dear husband goes. I love him so much but every wife loves their husband but I have no one else to love me but him & my little ones & I do hope against hope. I fear that he may have to go. Oh! for peace is my daily prayer morning, noon & night.

Sunday 21st June 1863 - Cloudy & dull all day, a little rain. We had our first chicken this morning for breakfast. They are small yet. We had mutton last week, very nice lamb. Willie is getting better of his wheezing. The baby's neck is very sore. It is running, also behind his ears. He does not fret much. He is a dear good baby. The others are all very well. Linsey moved his hands to Mrs. Fanning's for her to cook for them last Monday. I am glad of it. They will sleep in the old store house as Cagle moved back home last Monday. It seems a long time since Mr. Henry left & it is not a week yet. I hope he may get back this week but I fear he will not. Harrie is upstairs. Zona & Willie in here with me. Pinck off at play. Aunt Tena has the baby as Atheline went to Asheville yesterday evening. Mrs. Rutherford left last Thursday morning. I paid her three dollars for coming down & making soap. I ought to write to Lou this evening but I am so troubled about the militia call I can't compose myself enough for anything. I hope he will not have to go but I greatly fear he will. My life will be a blank without him. He is so dear, so dear to me. I did not write to Lou. Aunt Tena attended to the baby part of the evening. He is fretful. I think his neck hurts him as it is very raw.

Monday 22nd - Mail brought no news at all. Harrie is mightly out about Vicksburg, fears we will surrender. I expected a letter from Mr. Henry but was disappointed sadly. Willie getting better of the rattling. I washed the baby's neck in borax water today. It does not seem to help any, still raw. I began to fix an old dress for myself today, did not get it near done. It is the one Sister Jane gave me three years ago when I was last at home. I put a belt in it & am going to face the skirt as 'tis too short.

Tuesday 23rd & Wednesday 24th - Headache for two days. I took some pills before dinner yesterday but they did not relieve my head any. It got easy this evening. I have been in bed nearly two days the most of the time. I have it very bad of late & it last some two or three days. The baby's neck is better. It has a greased cloth to it now. It does better than anything I have tried. Harrie getting on as usual. The others all well.

Thursday 25th - I finished my dress today. I sewed a little on it Tuesday morning before my head got so bad. Nothing new. Rumour says Lee's army has gone to Pensilvania. 'Tis not confirmed yet. Rain, rain. It rained yesterday & all day today. Tom Tidwell started home yesterday. Jinnie spinning. This evening I hoed out my flowers in the front yard. They needed it badly. Aunt Tena getting the web ready for the boy's pants. They need them now. It is ready to warp.

Friday 26th - Mrs. Fanning warped the cloth today. It rained nearly all day. The thread did not get wet to hurt it. Betsey Jamison here today, will come back in the morning to put the cloth in. I began Atheline's calico dress today, made skirt & sleeves. Her & Jinnie spinning. No news this morning. I received a letter from Matt saying Sister Jane had another daughter born 17th ult. Little Dora is only fourteen months & a few days old. She is rearing another youngster in a hurry. Harrie still at a standstill, his cough is no better.

Saturday 27th - Finished Atheline's dress soon after dinner & reeled some. We had a very hard rain this evening & heavy thunder. Betsey got the cloth started. Tena dyed the felling today copperas. The chain is maple dye (purple). Old Bill Knight came home this evening, brought a little note from Mr. Henry. He will be at home in a few days. He is well. Got 11 sheep & paid 300$ for them, a high price I think. A. B. Jones went to Asheville today, got no news. Harrie received a letter from Eugenia this evening. She got home safe.

Sunday 28th - Some rain this morning but clearing off now. We have beans for dinner, our first mess & irish potatoes. We have had potatoes several times. We had chicken stewed & fried for breakfast. They are rather small yet to eat. Betsey staid all night last night, is here today. Harrie reading in front piazza. My paper came last Monday, the first time in two months as they were out of paper. 'Tis rumoured that the yanks made a raid into Knoxville, Ten. the 20th. I fear they will come to Asheville yet. I want to write some letters so I will not write any more now. I wrote a long letter to Lou, also one to Sister Matt & a short one to Pa. I spent most of the evening in writing. We had a shower today.

Monday 29th - Betsey began to weave on the boys pants today. I fixed a calico dress of Rose's. The mail brought no news. I got a letter from Mr. Henry & one from Sister Frank. They are all well at Frank's. Mr. Henry was in Columbia, said he was coming by Simsville to get my letter. I am so sorry I have not written to him. He will be so badly disappointed. I will do better in future. I was not aware he valued my insignificant letters so highly.

Tuesday 30th - Warm & some rain. We have had rain for nearly two weeks every day. Things are growing finely. Beans & potatoes, plenty cherries & June apples ripening. Also raspberries. Strawberries gone. Matt began to fix her thread for the loom. Atheline spinning. Nothing new going on. Willie has nearly quit rattling. The baby's neck gets no better. He is fretful with it. I look for Mr. Henry a little this evening. Hope he may come. I began to fix my old purple muslin dress, turn it up side down & face it. Did not get it done.

July 1863

Wednesday July 1st 1863 - Finished my dress before dinner & put it on. Made some paste board & after dinner warped Zona's hoop & went to meet Mr. Henry. Pinck, Zona & Willie waited at the dam a good while for him & just as I got set down in piazza to eating some cherries that Harrie had gathered, Betsey saw him coming by Mrs. Fanning's. We all, that is the children & I, ran & met him way down the road. He was glad to see us & we him. He asked the first thing, why I did not write. I was so sorry I had not. He went up expecting to get my letter at Simsville, lost some time. I am very sorry I did not write. I was affraid he would not get it. I never thought of his coming up there for my letter only but that was all the business he had there. I shall not cease to regret that soon. I made an apron for myself this evening of an old gingham dress I have had ten years & cut another out of it. I had it before we were married. It is worse for wear.

Thursday & Friday 2 & 3 - Had headache all day yesterday. I felt it a little Wednesday. Mr. Henry & I did not go to sleep last night till 12 o'clock. We have so much to talk about when he gets home. We talk nearly half the first night he gets home. He bought a beautiful silver cup with glass bottom. I tell him I must claim it. He says 'tis for little Hooker as he calls the baby. He is so kind & good to me & the children. He stopped at Rach Miller's, they are all well. He saw Mollie Henry at his Aunt Miller's. She is spending sometime there. I gathered some beans today for dinner & strung them. My head got well Thursday evening after I eat some cherries. They certainly helped it as my stomach needed an acid. We had beets (our first) for dinner & apple dumplings today. I did but little work. The baby fretful with his neck. We began to cut wheat last Wednesday. It is only ripe in spots, not generally. Wheat is very good, also oats. The sheep Night brought home are doing well. I began Harrie's other sock this evening. They will be very nice when done. I have one done. It is fine yarn & tedious to knit. No news this morning. My bowels have been running off this evening, paining me a good deal. A swarm of bees went off yesterday after they settled.

Saturday 4th - Betsey cut 20 yds. of the cloth out today & went home before dinner. Willie is not well, has a cold. The baby fretful, won't let Rose nurse it any scarcely. I fixed Harrie's linnen coat today & watch pockets for Mr. Henry's pants. They are too shallow so I will have others to make next week & made my other apron of the old dress. Dr. Kilgore's overseer stays here tonight. I went to meet Mr. Henry, he was at the mill. Zona went with me. She thinks a heap of her Papa almost as much as Mother so she thinks, but I know differently. Willie is wheezing some this evening.

Sunday July 5th 1863 - Cloudy this morning & began to rain about 1 o'clock. Rained a good shower & then stopped but began again about 3 & now near 4. Looks as if it would be a wet evening. Old Mr. Reynolds preached Tom Parker's funeral at the Academy today. I did not go as Willie is not well. Mr. Henry & Kilgore's overseer went. Zona went with Atheline. Jinnie got dinner, had apple dumplings among other things for dinner. Matt has her thread seamed but not through the harness yet. The baby's neck is some better today though it still looks red. Atheline has the baby. Mr. Henry is asleep in side room. I have just been reading to him till he went to sleep. Harrie is upstairs asleep & Kilgore's overseer is in front piazza reading an old paper. Willie is not well today, was sick vomiting last night. His bowels are loose today. Matt is sitting here in my room with me. I am writing on my lap. I hear Zona playing in the rain, trying to catch water in a bucket in front piazza. I had the cloth shrunk yesterday. I will go to work on it tomorrow if nothing happens. I do hope Mr. Henry may not have to go in the militia. Oh! how I wish this unholy war would stop. Grant us peace Oh! Ruler of the Universe.

Monday 6th - Mail brought no news. I received a letter from Eugenia. They were all very well. I made Henderson's pants today as he is needing them very badly & cut the others out. I blistered my finger as the scissors were very dull. Atheline weaving. Tena helping or rather attending to her. Matt has her cloth started. Willie nearly well of the rattling. The baby's neck seems to be healing slowly.

Tuesday 7th - I made Sam a pair pants today & made some rasberry pies for dinner. They were very nice. Mr. Henry & Harrie gathered the berries. Uncle Welch staid here last Sunday night. There is a deranged woman in the neighborhood. I fear she will come here.

Wednesday 8th - I made Charlie's pants today & began Hanes'. I made the pies for dinner of rasberries. The hands are cutting wheat. It is very fine. We have rain nearly every day. The June apples are ripening fast.

Thursday 9th - I finished Hanes' pants & began Jim's. Did but little to them. Mr. Henry gathered rasberries yesterday evening for pies today. W. Shields & another man of Columbia were here today. They did not stay for dinner & I was not sorry as we had not prepared for them. We had a very nice dinner, vegetables &c. Cherries will soon be gone. Nothing from our forces. They are in Penselvania. No news of Vicksburg.

Friday 10th July 1863 - I made Lonzo a pair pants today & went with Mr. Henry after rasberries. We gathered a nice chance. Mail brought no news. We hear this evening that Vicksburg has fallen & we are all sorry of it yet we feared it sometime. This war will last a long time I fear. Very warm today & bright. Our garden is doing finely. Beets large enough to eat & plenty beans & potatoes.

Saturday 11th - Mr. Henry sent Tom to Asheville soon this morning after news. Vicksburg surrendered the 4th July being in a starving condition. We hear it rumored that New Orleans is taken back by Gen. Taylor & McGruder but it's not confirmed. Also that Gen. Lee has taken 40,000 prisoners in Penn. We have heard none of the particulars of the fight yet.

I made Tom's pants today, fixed Zona's hoop & washed the children this evening also baked some pies for dinner tomorrow. Atheline baked the pie for dinner. Mr. Henry went up the creek this morning, did not get back till late this evening.

Sunday 12th - Late breakfast this morning as usual on Sunday & late dinner too. Mr. Henry has gone off to the Stradley place. Harrie is asleep. The children at play. My head feels badly. I am affraid I shall have another spell of sick headache soon. I suffer a great deal with it. I generally take pills. Sometimes it relieves me, at others does no good at all. The babie's neck is healing some I think. It still looks red & raw in some places. I think we will have rain this evening as 'tis cloudy. We had a shower yesterday evening & some heavy thunder. I will stop now. I want to read my bible some.

Monday 13th & Tuesday 14th - Headache very badly all day Monday. Got a little easier towards night & this morning. I feel very feeble from it. I done nothing till after dinner today then finished Sam's pants Atheline has been at work on yesterday & today. No news of importance. We still have a heap of rain. We sent off the mail return yesterday.

Wednesday 15th - I began a vest for Mr. Henry made of my watered silk mantilla. Did but little at it as I made the pies for dinner. Tena is weaving as the baby has a bile on it's breast and is so fretful. Atheline has to nurse all the time nearly. It looks very red & hard. I have a wilted cabbage leaf to it now. Atheline is sewing on Charlie's pants, what she can. She gets along slowly as the baby is fretful. Fannie does the cooking, her baby is a very good child. They finished cutting wheat today. The wheat very good.

Thursday 16th - Mr. Henry went to muster today on Licks Creek. They enroll the militia today. Oh! will the cruel war never stop! I made the dumplings for dinner of apples & sewed some on Mr. Henry's vest. Nothing new going on. I received a letter from Matt & Dora today. Sister Jane is improving slowly.

Friday 17th - Mail brought no news. I finished the vest today & darned some old coats & one for Harrie. They were fighting at Jackson Miss. the 11 inst. & at Charleston also. I fear they will take Charleston.

Saturday 18th - I have done several things today, odds & ends & patching. Mrs. Jamison here for dinner. I fixed a shelf for the dishes & curtain around it in the dining room. Mr. Henry & Harrie went to Asheville this evening, also Pinck. They got no news.

Sunday 19th - We will have cucumbers for dinner today, our first. They come off of Aunt Tena's vines. Some rogue stole all our butter last night out of the spring house. I think it was George. Matt Ray of Haywood Co. staid here last night & left this morning. Harrie has gone to the spring. Mr. Henry to the Hotel orchard as the Knight women are beating off his fruit so badly. They are a bad set of people. Tena got out the cloth yesterday of the pants. Matt's dresses look very well. She will get them out next week. Mr. Henry, the children & I went after some rasberries. Pinck & Zona had a fine time of it. We left Willie & the baby with Tena. Very warm this evening. This is the first dog day.

Monday 20th - I have done some mending today, not much as I helped some about dinner. I made the pies. Jim Patton of Asheville & William Candler is tax paying day today. They meet at the mill. George is not well at all. The others all well.

Tuesday 21st - I made Lonzo a pair pants before dinner today & began Hanes' but did not do much on them as I have the headache. The baby has a tooth. I found it this evening. He is not 5 months old till the 8th of Aug. He has cut this one earlier than any of the children. The others had two when they were 6 months old. He is not so fretful this week.

Friday 24th - I have had the headache ever since Tuesday. I sewed some on Wednesday on Hanes' pants & took a nap after dinner. My head got worse & at night I suffered a great deal. On Wednesday night could not sleep. I was so sick at my stomach & Thursday I was very feeble all day & not at all well & today not much better till after dinner & then I got well. I finished Hanes' pants today. Atheline has sewing on the pants for two days. No news. Jim Parker had his arm shot off at the fights near Jackson Miss.

Saturday 25th July 1863 - I took a long walk this morning before breakfast. Went up by the stable & then down to the house. Breakfast was ready when I got back. I have been cleaning up in the smoke house today. Got things arranged very well. I want to wash & put the children's clothes on this evening. I have done some mending today. We are all well. The baby's neck & other sore places healed. I must stop now as Gus is fretting.

Sunday 26th - Warm today with a good deal of thunder this evening but little rain here yet. Mr. Henry & Tom Cook gone to see the sheep Mr. Henry got of Bob Williams in S.C. Nothing new. Several deserters in the neighborhood. They ought to be sent to the army if possible & that soon as they are stealing of honest people. Harrie is asleep. The children at play. I am going to write a long letter to Dora & Matt this evening so I will stop in this.

I wrote to Dora & Matt & a sheet to Sister Jane. Mr. Henry & I went to walk this evening up to the hotel orchard. It rained a little but we stopped in the old store piazza.

Monday 27th - I strung the beans for dinner. The children helped. Stephens came in the time we were in the front piazza. Mr. Henry hired some negroes of him today, is to give two bushels of grain for five hands one week or 8 hr. a

month. There are two women & three men. They are to come tomorrow. I
mended two old under bodies & put a yoke & sleeves in a gown for the baby. 'Tis
an old long gown of his & that makes a short gown. I will put a yoke & sleeves on
two old underskirts that were made for Pinck when a baby to make short gowns
for the baby. The skirts have never been used much. I will fix the others tomorrow
or next day. Mail brought no news.

Tuesday 28th - Did but little today. Fixed one gown. Very warm today. We
heard Jim Parker had his arm taken off, poor fellow. I fear he will die. Nothing
new. The yanks have not taken Charleston. They are on Morris Island. I very much
fear they will.

Wednesday 29th - Finished the last of the babie's gowns today. They fit very
well. Atheline is working in the field as the grass is growing very fast. Stephen's
hands came over today or rather yesterday evening. Some rain this morning, showery. We have had a great deal of rain.

Thursday 30th - I began Zona a bonnet today making it of yellow quilt calico.
Did not finish it. Sam & others killed a hog this evening & scalded it in brine. It is
very large meat. I hope it may save well. We cured one that way that done finely.

Friday 31st July 1863 - Mail brought no news of importance. Our little colt got
its leg broke in the old bridge. It died this evening. Zona & I went up to the orchard & stopped to see that sick negroe, one of the Stephens' women. They live in
the old store house. We came by the stables & saw the dead colt & then to the
house & then Mr. Henry, I & the children went to the mill as they have got the
new wheel started. Boyd made it. It goes finely. The bucket machine does only
sorty. Harrie went to Asheville this morning, will not be back before tomorrow
night. I have not felt well at all today.

August 1863

Saturday August 1st - I have been gloomy all day. My spirits are below zero
smartly. Harrie came home this evening. Nothing new from the war. I finished
Zona's bonnet yesterday & began one for myself of green quilt calico. Betsey Jamison spent the day here today. Our people are nearly done laying by the crop. Very
warm today.

Sunday 2nd - Matt, Zona & I went to church at the Academy. Mr. Reynolds
preached & administered the sacrament to the negroes. Not a great many people
there. I had headache all the evening. Stephens dined here today, had nothing extra. Harrie went to Asheville this evening. He starts to Columbia in a hack in the
morning. This has been a very warm evening & indeed all day. Mr. Henry took a
nap this afternoon after Harrie & Stephens left. The family are all well. The sick
negro going about.

Monday 3rd - I fixed my hoops, both sets today & made up the mail. Nothing
new. Very few letters. I received one of Eugenia. They are very well & very warm.
She says she heard the cannon at Charleston & thought it thunder. Nothing more
this time. Jinnie, Jane, Atheline & Tena spinning. Fair & warm today.

Tuesday 4th - I began Zona's brilliante dress today, a white one Sister Jane gave
her the last time I was at home. I am going to put two rows of pink pointing on the

skirt. It will be tedious but I have nothing much to do now. Very warm today & dry. We need rain especially for the garden.

Wednesday 5th - The thrashers began on Mr. Henry's wheat yesterday. The machine is not a good one & old one Mr. Henry got of Green & Morgan. I think it a poor excuse. Mr. Henry is not much pleased with it. They have nine hands & seven horses to work it. Very warm & dry.

Thursday 6th - I went to see the thrashing machine this afternoon, also Matt & Zona. A little shower of rain fell while we were there. Not enough to do any good. They get along slowly thrashing. Nothing new going on. All are well. I get on slowly with Zona's dress. Mr. Henry stays about the thrasher pretty close. Our people are done laying by the corn, some of it is sorty grassy.

Friday 7th August 1863 - Mail brought no news of importance. Our army is quiet. I sewed some on Zona's skirt today & read the papers generally. Very warm & dry. We have a little sprinkle of rain nearly every day but not enough to do any good.

Saturday 8th - The baby is five months old today, has two teeth & can nearly sit alone. He is smarter than any of them have been & a pretty little hazel eyed boy. The other children are very well & growing finely. I finished the skirt of Zona's dress today & made Fannie's baby a dress of an old calico coat she got somewhere. Mrs. Hutsell gave me a short call this morning. She is quite fashionable in her manner. Very warm & fair today.

Sunday 9th - Warm this morning. Stephens is here in the piazza with Mr. Henry. I see Mrs. Till Morris coming so I will stop for this time. She will spend the day I think.

Till staid all day. I had the headache very bad in the evening. Went down to the mill, or the pasture just the other side of the mill to see the sheep. Till went also & then went on home. It was after sunset when I got back.

Monday 10th & Tuesday 11th - My head has ached all yesterday & is not well today. I have been sewing some on Zona's dress today, got all the pointing done. The belt & sleeves are small points. I have felt a great deal better since dinner. The others are all well. The mail brought no news but four letters came. Betsey Jamison staid here last night. I wrote to Jim Henry yesterday evening. I want to buy his piano. I hear he wants to sell it. 'Tis a very nice one. Mr. Henry fixed the mail this evening.

Wednesday 12th - Jinnie began to scour the house today. Scoured upstairs & scalded & scoured the side room, hall & front piazza. I finished Zona's dress before dinner & helped Jinnie some after dinner. Matt helped her some.

Thursday 13th - Jinnie scoured & scalded my room today, the back piazza & the dining room & we fixed the things upstairs, some of them. The window curtains are not washed yet to put up. Mr. Stevens dined here today. We had our first roasting years today for dinner. Mr. Henry sold the Johnston horse to Stevens today for four hundred & fifty dollars. $450 a big price I think considering he is a small horse. Very warm & has been all this week. We need rain badly.

Friday 14th - The mail carrier (Vic) brought the wrong mail so we got no mail at all nor won't get any till next Friday. Vic took it back to Asheville. Mr. Henry went to Asheville today but got no mail. He came home for dinner. I washed the hearths today. They look very well. The thrasher is going again. It breaks down every few days. The baby's bowels very loose.

Saturday August 15th 1863 - I finished arranging the things in the house today. Every thing is clean & nice. Jinnie washed yesterday & moved today. Atheline had the headache yesterday. I put pine bushes in the fire places today & done some mending on stockings & socks. Mr. Henry sold the last of the jeans today for 5$ five dollars a yd. He has sold 26 yds. to Stevens & 16 1/4 yds. to Dr. Cain. I want to buy a piano with the jeans money.

Sunday 16th - This will be a long day to me as Mr. Henry started this morning to So. Ca. to the factories. He expects to be gone a week. I hope he may get back that soon for I am so lonely when he is gone. The baby's bowels are no better. I got some peaches yesterday, nearly ripe. They taste very well as they are the first we have had. Mr. Henry took some off with him & some coffee. He told me not to put in the coffee but I did. This will be a very warm day. We had a very hard rain here Friday which was badly needed. We had a very hard rain this evening. Atheline combed my head & got the dandruff out. Some of the negroes went to prayer meeting at Miller's Meeting house. This has been one long day.

Monday 17th - Mended a dress & began a night cap for myself of the scraps that were left of Zona's dress. It will make a nice cap. I will trim it with jackonet edging. Aunt Patsey Jamison spent most of the day here today. Bill Sutton (a deserter) was here today. He looks badly, poor fellow. This is the second time he has deserted. He is very tired of the war.

Tuesday 18th & Wednesday 19th - This is the 19th, is my birth day. I was born in 1836, 27 years ago today. Many changes have turned up since that day. My own dear mother has passed away. I can't wish her back when I certainly believe she is at rest. She is free from all the cares of this life. I had headache yesterday & today, not one of the worst sort as I was able to sit up. I finished my cap & knit some on Pinck's sock. I am knitting him some cotton socks. Matt Tidwell will knit one pair for him. Today I took some tea, a garden plant commonly called Old Man. I think it done me some good. It is very bitter. I took a nap after dinner & my head was well when I woke about sundown. Harrie came over yesterday. We sent to Asheville for him. He brought my mantilla, it is died black & looks very well. He brought the children some candy & Fannie sent Zona a home made duck. Eugenia's family were well when he left.

Thursday 20th - Mrs. Jamison & Betsey warped the thread for the women's dresses today. I made a shirt bosom today of domestic for Jim. It looks very well. I cut some shirts for Pinck of sheeting, also a pair drawers for Zona. Nothing new going on. The baby's bowels have got well. We made some cider this evening. Dr. Cain & Lady were here a short time this evening. He was wanting jeans.

Friday 21st - I was sadly disappointed this morning in not getting a letter. I thought certainly I would get one from Dora & Matt but no letter for me. We got but few letters for any one. I began a shirt for Pinck, did but little at it. Mr. George Peake came here today about 11 o'clock. He is looking badly. He tells me his brother Glenn is going to marry Narcissa Beaty. I would not have thought it. People have strange taste when a heap of property is at stake. Very warm today. Betsey began the dresses this morning. They look very well.

Saturday 22nd - I finished Pinck's shirt after dinner & helped Harrie make cider. He got the press up & it done finely. We made a fine chance. Mr. Peake left this morning for Greenville, Tenn. He is going to buy salt. He will be back in a week or so. I have heard nothing of Mr. Henry since he left. Wish I could hear something of him. Uncle Sam & others killed a beef this evening. A very nice young beef. We have had some watermellons this week. They were not very good.

Sunday 23rd - Warm this morning & clear & still. This will be another long day as Sunday generally is. I wish Mr. Henry was at home. My little ones are all well. We have a corn pie for dinner. I am affraid I shall hurt myself eating the pie & beef. I have some letters to write today. One to Eugenia & one to Sister Frank & one to Sister Lena so I will stop. Wrote two letters, one to Sister Celena & one to Eugenia.

Monday 24th - Harrie fixed the mail. I received a letter from Sister Elmira saying one of her twins died. She was uneasy about it when she wrote. I feel sorry for her. Mr. Fowler is in the army & I know she feels sad and lonely. Nothing new going on. Cloudy today but no rain.

Tuesday 25th - I went down to the orchard this morning to see about the apples as Betsey Knight claimed one tree. I got very angry with her. She is a lazy woman. When I came back, Mr. Stevens & lady was here. They only staid a short time. We made some cider today. I fixed an old dress that was too long. No news from Mr. Henry yet. I wish he was here.

Wednesday August 26th 1863 - George Peake came here today just before dinner on his way back from Greenville. He was surprised to hear Mr. Henry had not got home. My baby is very unwell, had a hot fever last night & very fretful today. I have done nothing but attend to him. It is his teeth I think. Some men stay here tonight, soldiers I think.

Thursday 27th - Several people here today as it is tax giving day. Sam Gudger is Confederate tax collector. They did not annoy me any as they done their business in the piazza. I have done nothing but knit today as the baby has been no better. He had a very high fever last night. I was up with him several times. Betsey & Matt sleep in here on the floor. I do wish Mr. Henry would come.

Friday 28th - I got a letter from Sister Frank today saying Pa was very unwell & wanted Dora & Matt to go home. I hope 'tis nothing serious. No news came today. They were still fighting away at Charleston. My papers come very regular now but they have very little news, though they contain a good deal of reading matter. I trimmed the baby's hat this evening. It is very pretty. He looks so sweet in it. He is some better. I was not up much with him last night.

Saturday 29th - I trimmed Zona's hat today. It looks very nice. Mr. Henry came this evening. We were all glad to see him. We met him at the gate. He is a dear good husband. The negro women have been drying fruit since Wednesday. They have fixed the dry house this week & are drying in it. Sam killed a nice mutton this evening. Our bacon is running low. Mr. Henry tells me that Ell's baby is dead. I am sorry for her. She will take it so sadly I know. He says Pa is improving. I am glad to hear it as Sister Frank's letter made me uneasy.

Sunday 30th - Rather cool today indeed. It has been cool for several days. Matt & I went up to the peach orchard to get some peaches. They were not ripe so we got some apples in the garden & came back. We had our first peach pie today for dinner. It was very nice. Mont Stradly eat dinner here today. 'Tis evening now & Mr. Henry & Harrie are asleep upstairs. Matt is in the front piazza. I must soon stop as I want to write to poor sorrowing Sister Ell. I sympathize with her deeply.

I have written a long letter to Ell consoling her as well as I could. I know nothing can alleviate her grief.

Monday August 31st 1863 - I mended up some of Zona's old drawers for Willie today. They fit finely & look very nice. Still cool morning & evening. Nothing new going on. They still keep up the fight at Charleston. I fear it will have to surrender at last though the commanders are confident of holding it. Gen. Beauregard has orders to burn it so Madam Rumour says.

September 1863

Tuesday Sept. 1st - I have been mending drawers for Willie again today. Nothing of interest going on. We are needing rain very badly. Turnips are doing no good at all & the dry weather has cut the corn short.

Wednesday 2nd - I spent the day at Mr. A. B. Jones. Went to see Matilda Morris as she is sick, had a miscarriage last Wednesday. It was dead. She is doing finely. They had some fine watermellons. I enjoyed the day finely. I rode John & took Rose behind me to attend to Gus. He was no trouble. I think I shall go again soon to see Mrs. Moore & Mrs. Alexander.

Thursday 3rd - I ripped Harrie's old soldier coat apart today. I am going to make Pinck one of it. I sewed a little on it. We made some cider in the evening; Harrie, Mr. Henry, Matt & I. Mr. Henry has been to lay off Mrs. F. M. Starnes' dower today, he got back about three o'clock.

Friday 4th - Very little mail today, nothing new. They still keep fighting at Charleston. Nothing going on about Richmond in the way of a fight. Both armies are quiet. Gen. Bragg has fallen back to Chatanooga. I fear our forces will retreat too far in Tenn. I sewed some on Pinck's coat, did not finish it.

Saturday 5th - I finished the coat today. It fits beautifully. Mrs. Jamison spent the day here today. She is spinning some for us, black mixed jeans. I want to take it to Lena when I go, if I do & if not I will send it by some one. We made some more cider this evening.

Sunday 6th - Mr. Henry & I went to the View today. He & some other men went to hunt a deer lick thinking perhaps it was salt. Why they licked it & eat the dirt. They had not found it when we left. I was very tired when we got back as we rode up the mountain. I rode the Cagle horse & he rode John bare back. We came by Gallion's & got some water. I was very thirsty & then down by Ham Cannon's. Dora & Matt were here when we came. They did not get off on the train as we were told so they are going home now. They came to Asheville on the stage from Warm Springs.

FRENCH BROAD LINE

OF

FOUR HORSE STAGES,

From Asheville, N. C., to Greenville, Tenn., running down the French Broad River through the grandest scenery of the world, crossing the Mountains in full view of the Painted Rocks.

This line of stages, said by all who travel upon it to be one of the best in the Union, leaves Asheville daily, Sundays excepted, at 5½ o'clock, and connects with the train upon the East Tennessee and Virginia Railroad, at Greenville, at 7½ o'clock. Passengers can breakfast at M. A. Alexander's, and dine at the Warm Springs,—both eating-houses unsurpassed in this country. Fare from Asheville to Springs, $8; to Greenville, $6.

W. P. BLAIR,
Proprietor.

Advertisement from "Mountain Scenery," by Henry E. Colton, W. P. Pomeroy publisher, 1859

Road from Marshall
to Warm Springs,
along the French
Broad River
(North Carolina Collection,
Pack Memorial Public
Library, Asheville, NC)

Monday 7th September 1863 - Some refugees from Tenn. came here last night with some negroes. They are all running out of Ten., scared to death nearly. Dora says the road is thick with them up from Warm Springs. Mr. Neilson came up with Dora & Matt. I have done nothing today. Some more refugees camp below the house here tonight. Capt. Collins has his negroes there & then some white men. They are from Kentucky. They would all do better business in the army. Two others came here this evening so now we have a house full.

Tuesday 8th - I have done nothing today. The negroes are cutting fruit. Those refugee negroes are at work here, the women picking wool. They will get done today. Their Master is hunting some place to take them to. I cut Jinnie's & Atheline's dresses today. Dora & Matt sewed a little on them. I have done nothing. The militia is called out to go & fight or at least keep the yanks & tories back from Asheville. Mr. Henry went to Asheville this morning. Mr. Neilson came over here this evening. The house is full. The girls have to sleep in my room on the floor. The mail brought no news last night.

Wednesday 9th - Dora & Matt went to Asheville this evening. Harrie went with them. They take the stage tonight. They are anxious to get home to see Pa. Capt. Collins & the others with him left this morning early. Neilson & others went to Asheville. Mr. Henry did not go. Eighteen of Morgan's Cavalry dined here today. Their dinner was cooked after ours was. There was eleven here for supper. Some went to Capt. Moore's.

Thursday 10th - Only 18 took breakfast here this morning. They all left soon after breakfast. The men that had the negroes here took them off yesterday. They bought some land of Col. Evans in Henderson Co. I made Jinnie's dress today or rather finished it. Our forces abandoned Morris Island the night of the 7th ult. I am very much affraid that Charleston will yet fall. Our force has perfect confidence in holding it. Only one refugee here tonight. He came Tuesday night. He is a paroled prisoner from Vicksburg.

Friday 11th - Mail brought no news. I got a letter from Sister Lena yesterday. Mr. Henry got it out of Asheville. The militia starts tomorrow. I had Mr. Henry some nice crackers baked this evening & a chicken smothered. Charlie & Pinck went up to Murry's on Mills River after some bacon. He baconed one of Mr. Henry's hogs that got away when they were feeding up there last winter. It was dark when they got back.

Saturday 12th 1863 September - I finished Jim's shirt before dinner. I began it yesterday. Mrs. Jamison warped a piece of white cloth today, near fifty yds. 'Tis for shirts & coat lining. Mr. Henry left this morning. I hope he will be back tonight. Yes he has come, they say they will start on Monday. Some refugees stay here tonight, five. We hear the tories have been to Mr. Neilson's three times hunting him. He is in Asheville yet & had better stay till he can get some more refugees to go back with him.

Sunday 13th - Two men left this morning. The other three are still here. 'Tis near dinner. I must go out & see about it a little. Mr. Henry is lying in here (the side room) asleep. The others are lounging about generally. Aunt Tena went up Homeny to preaching yesterday, will be back this evening. The baptist has an association. A beautiful day. Mr. Henry caught a negro in the orchard yesterday evening. He gave him some impudence & Mr. Henry corrected him. He hurt his foot & one hand smartly. He can scarcely walk, his foot is swollen & hand too.

Monday 14th - I cut Fannie's, Jennie's & Atheline's dresses this morning & made the waist of Fannie's. Mr. Henry went to Asheville this morning. Tom Cook came by him after we were done dinner & said Mr. Henry & the other mounted militia had gone to take up some soldiers that are going through the country stealing horses & other things too numerous to mention. I am affraid they will get into trouble. I pray God to take care of them & may my dear husband return in safety to his family. The mail brought no news. They are massing the Confederate army near Chatanooga. 'Tis reported that Gen. Ewell is in East Tenn. with a large force. Burnsides is at Knoxville, that is his headquarters. Things look gloomy indeed.

Tuesday 15th - No news from Mr. Henry today. I wish I knew where he was. I have had the headache all day. I took a nap in the front piazza on the lounge & it feels better now. I had some cider made this evening, 'tis very nice. Betsey is weaving, gets on slowly as she has it all to scise back as she goes.

Wednesday 16th - No news from Mr. Henry today. They went out through Burnsville. I finished Fannie's dress today. I did but little at it yesterday. Very dry & needing rain for turnips. They are very scattering. I hope we may yet have rain to make some. No news from Charleston. They still keep fighting.

Thursday 17th September 1863 - Capt. Collins & Co. left this morning. They have been here since Saturday night. Two came Saturday evening & the other two Sunday evening. No news from Mr. Henry yet. I would be so glad to hear from him. He is so very dear to me, so good & kind to me & the children. May kind Heaven protect him.

Friday 18th - Considerable excitement going on in the Country. We hear the tories or yankees have burned Waynesville. I don't believe it. They are warning in the militia. In a hurry Charlie took some flour to Asheville today & when he came back to the bridge, they had torn it up so he left the waggon & forded the oxen over. Harrie went to Asheville this morning & took Pinck. They will not get back tonight. I have been breaking wool today for Mr. Henry, some stocking yarn. I sewed some yesterday on Jennie's & Atheline's dresses. I made the skirts & Matt is to finish them. She got them done today.

Saturday 19th - Mr. Henry came home last night after supper. I was so glad to see him. I thank the Oh! my heavenly Father for taking care of my husband. My prayer was answered. They took those men prisoners. They numbered 38 & our forces only 17. They surrendered without a word. They are deserters from a Va. Reg. They put them in jail in Asheville yesterday evening, only two that made their escape. Frank Boyd & Bill Cook came home with Mr. Henry last night. They went with him to Asheville this morning. Very cool today. I think it will surely frost to-night. Pinck came home with Mr. Henry this evening. We were glad to see him. The little fellow was cold when he came. Mr. Henry has to go to Marshall tomorrow. I made myself an apron & Pinck some suspenders today.

Sunday 20th, the first frost - A big frost last night. The potato tops killed. The negroes cut their tobacco this morning before the sun got on it to try to save it. Mr. Henry left about 9 o'clock. I do feel so lonely. I don't know when he will come back again. I hope & pray no ill may befall him whilst he is gone. I pray God to watch over him, protect him & let him return to the bosom of his wife & little children. Fair & bright today but cool. Neither tories or yankees have been near Waynesville. What tales we do hear. They are fixing up the bridge again. I think Harrie will be over this evening. Harrie has not come but eleven soldiers eat supper here. They are part of a detail from the 25th Reg. to get up deserters. I heard that a little boy named Jones was taken up today. He was carrying news. Some money, 1900$ was found in the pad of the saddle, also a letter. He was carrying the news to Tenn., to Willey & Doc Jones, both tories.

Monday 21st September - Sixteen soldiers took breakfast here. They did not stay at the house last night but camped at the old store house. Old Mathew Common staid here last night. Twenty soldiers took dinner here. I cut three chemise for myself this evening & done a little on one. I intend pointing one, put tape trimming on one & frill the other. Joe Parker was taken up yesterday evening as a deserter but they let him loose again. I think he has been persuaded off by Wilk Bryson as Bryson came with him. No news from Mr. Henry today.

Tuesday 22nd - I have felt very gloomy today. Matt & I went up the peach orchard, got but few peaches as they are all gone or nearly so. We sit down by the old store house under a tree & staid there some time. I love to go on the hill where once stood our hotel but I feel so sad when I look at the ruins of the old house. I sewed some on my chemise today. Did not get it done. We had a big frost Monday morning. I saw some after I got up. The sun was an hour high. We had some frost this morning but 'tis more pleasant today. Indeed I got quite warm as Matt & I were going up to the orchard. It was about 11 o'clock when we went & dinner was nearly ready when we got back. Harrie came over this evening. The bridge is not up yet, he forded. Betsey has been sick all day, wove but little.

Wednesday 23rd - I finished my pointed chemise about three o'clock this evening. Betsey better & weaving today. No news from Mr. Henry yet. I am very anxious to hear from him. I do hope he may soon return to his home well & will not have to go out again soon. If it was not for hope, I don't know what would become of me. 'Tis the anchor of the heart with me. I hope to hear of him every day. I ask my Maker to take care of him whilst he is gone & I feel He will. Not done the wool yet. I want them to get done this week but Jane & Atheline are very slow. Rose & Jennie are cutting tops. We will begin the sugar cane soon.

Thursday 24th - The hands began the cane today, grinding. The mill does very well. We have not commenced to boil yet. Mr. Henry came home last night. We were all glad to see him. He brought no news. The tories were leaving Madison, going over to Tenn. to keep off the conscript or away from it. They are a lawless set over there. I began my frilled chemise today, did but little at it. The children all well.

Friday 25th September 1863 - Mail brought no news of importance. Mr. Henry went to Asheville this morning. We made some very nice molasses today, the first we made are too thick but the others are splendid. I sewed some on my chemise today but did not finish it. Mr. Henry came home this evening. No news.

Saturday 26th - Betsey went home yesterday to go to church today at the Academy. They have quarterly meeting there this time instead of at the camp ground. I think I will go tomorrow. John & Peter came here last night. They live in Haywood this year. I finished my chemise today. My dear little children are all well & growing finely & I am very thankful for it. My baby has been sitting alone for over a month. He has only two teeth. He is a dear good baby. Willie is a little stubborn at times but I hope he may out grow that. Pinck is a good child & so is Zona. They are so affectionate to their Papa & I. We are truely blessed with good children. I am thankful of it. I will try to raise them the best I can.

Sunday 27th - I went to church today & heard a good sermon from the Rev. Baldwin. The house was full. I had a chair carried up for myself. I kept Zona & Atheline had Gussie. I call my baby Gus, that will be part of his name. I came away before they were done sacrament. It was 2 o'clock when I got home. Mr. Henry did not go with me. He & I took a walk this evening, Pinck & Zona too. We did not go far.

Monday 28th - Mr. Henry & Harrie went to Asheville this morning. It was dark when they got back. We made some molasses today. I began to make some tape trimming for myself a chemise. Made enough for the neck or band. I got two letters tonight, one from Dora & one from Lou. They were all well at home, also at Lou's. Bragg has gained quite a victory below Chatanooga. I hope he may be able to rout Rozencrantz effectually.

Z. B. Vance to J. L. Henry

Executive Department
Raleigh, Sept. 24th 1863
Capt. J. L. Henry[43]
My Dear Sir:

I have appointed you to the command of a cavalry company in the mountains, where is nearly complete for the state defence.

The occupation of East Tennessee has opened all western N. C. to destructive incursions of the enemy & I am raising troops & arming them as fast as possible for it's defence. Please report promptly, if you can get your resignation accepted, as I have no competent man in that country to command cavalry except Maj. Woodfin who commands the Home Guards.

Respectfully Yours, Z. B. Vance

J. L. Henry to Gen. S. Cooper

1st No. Ca. Cavalry
Baker's Brigade
28th Sept. 1863

Gen S. Cooper
Adj. Genl

Having been appointed Captain of Cavalry for Home Defense, I respectfully tender my resignation as 1st Lieutenant, Company "G" 1st Regt No. Ca. Cavalry. Annexed. See Governor Vance letter.

I am very Respectfully,
Yr Ob Servt, J. L. Henry

Tuesday 29th - I made some more trimming today. Made some molasses today. Mr. Henry went to Asheville today. The militia has gone into camps at Reems Creek camp ground. 'Tis a great pity that the men have to leave home at this season of the year. It will cause them to lose their wheat crop & molasses too for the cane will soon spoil if not made up on account of frost.

Wednesday 30th September 1863 - I sewed a little today. Mr. Henry went to Asheville today. Nothing new. Made some molasses today. Cloudy & warm. We are having beautiful nights. I am up at the furnace where they boil every night till the molasses gets done. My old teeth have been hurting me some. They are decaying very fast. I will soon have none to ache.

---

[43] James L. Henry letters courtesy NC Dept. Archives and History, Raleigh, NC

October 1863

Thursday October 1st - Rained all day, a sprinkling rain. Sam & Jennie made some cider for apple butter today. Mr. Henry staid at the furnace all day. He has a very bad cold. I don't think his sitting out under that shelter will do him any good whatever. I got damp today attending to the cider making. Mr. Henry made some apple butter today, it is very nice. He sent Tom to Asheville this evening to get some news. He got nothing new. I was up last night with my teeth. They did not ache long. I have done nothing towards sewing today. I attended to the cider making, empting molasses &c.

Friday 2nd - Mr. Henry is down with his back. He went to Asheville today & came home for dinner. It rained very hard all night last night & the dirt work the other side of the dam gave way. The mill will not run any more for a week if not more. Mr. Henry & I went up to the hotel orchard this evening. I got some late peaches. They are very nice. I lost my net. He waited till I went back & found it. He is a dear good creature. His cold is some better but his back is not. The mail brought no news at all.

Saturday 3rd - Mr. Henry started to camps this morning. He only went as far as Asheville & came back in the evening. Charlie took a load of flour over to the armory today. Mr. Henry supplies them with flour. Mr. Henry says 'tis reported that the yanks had left Knoxville. I hope 'tis so. Cool & frosty. I finished my chemise today. Betsey got the cloth out yesterday. 49 yds. of it.

Sunday 4th - Cool all day. Bob Henry took dinner here. He rode off one of Mr. Henry's horses & was to send it back from Knight's shop but he sent Charlie back saying he intended taking the horse on so Mr. Henry has gone on after the scoundrel for such he is. He is drinking some but not drunk. I do hope & pray there may be no difficulty about it. Mr. Henry's back is not nearly well yet. I put a plaster of Quin wax to it last night. I hope he may get home tonight all safe is my prayer. He came before dark, got the horse.

Monday 5th October 1863 - I cut some shirts for the negroes, made one for Lonzo. The negro men at work at the dam. The dirt work washed away last Friday. The creek was up a good deal. Uncle Sam & the women folks still working at the cane. Mr. Henry staid at the dam all day today. Mrs. Widow George Jones spent the day here. Jennie has been dying the warp of a piece of jeans today. Her & I made some cider today. Harrie went to see Lt. Col. Roy today. He has got back but did not see his friend. Mail brought no news.

Tuesday 6th - I made a shirt today. They killed a hog this morning, very nice. We were out of lard, why we killed it. Mr. Henry stays nearly all the time at the dam. They get on slowly. Nothing new going on. Corn is selling at seven dollars a bu. & wheat at ten dollars, sugar three.

Wednesday 7th - Made another shirt today & attended to the pots some, they get on slowly making molasses. Atheline & Matt spooling today. Very cool & frosty mornings. Too cold for my little ones to be barefooted, if I could help it. The negroes have no shoes yet.

Thursday 8th - Mr. Henry went to Asheville today to hear the men speak that are running for Congress. 'Tis M. Erwin & J. D. Hyman to speak today. He came home before night. I made some peach preserves of molasses today. They are very nice. The peaches were late ones. I made a shirt today. Matt & Atheline finished spooling about 2 o'clock.

Friday 9th - Aunt Patsey & Betsey came to warp the cloth. They stay here tonight. Her & Mr. Henry settled tonight. We owe her 14.30 cts. Jim Parker took dinner here. He looks strange without his arm. Mr. Henry gave his wife a bunch of thread, also Mrs. Tom Parker & Mrs. Jones, George's widow & Elie, Jamison's wife & Mrs. Isreal one. They beamed the cloth this evening & got part of it in the harness. I made a shirt today. The mail brought no news of importance.

Saturday 10th - I made the last shirt today. Betsey got the cloth started. Matt made some candy for the children this evening. Mr. Henry went to Asheville this morning with Branton. He has deserted so we all think he was at home some two months ago & then went back, at least he left this neighborhood. I don't think he ever went back. He says his Reg. has disbanded. A tale of his own I imagine. Mr. Henry came back this evening & old Mr. Lundy with him. Lundy is a Tennessee refugee.

Sunday 11 October 1863 - This has been a long day. It was near 11 o'clock before I got the house cleaned up as Atheline is sick & since dinner I have washed three of the children & put clean clothes on them. They went off with Henderson before dinner & did not return till after we were done our dinner. They are all gone again. Little Rose has the baby. She has gone to Tena's house with it. She has nursed today. Jinnie got dinner today. We had sweet potatoes & turnip salad for dinner & several other things. I got a few sweet potatoes Saturday. They have done no good this year at all. Neither have our turnips. It has been so very dry. Corn is hurt, some by the frost & badly by dry weather. Mr. Henry is asleep in the room on the trundle bed. Harrie is sitting in there reading. I am writing in the side room. Matt is not well today, eat no dinner. She has gone down to Mrs. Fanning's now. Tena has been a little sick this week but nearly well now. Jinnie washed & Atheline ironed this week. Jinnie will wash all the time now I think, at least till warm weather comes. Tena is getting old & can't stand exposure. Mr. Henry wants to take a walk this evening. I don't think I can go as I will have to attend to feeding Gus before he goes to sleep. I must go to see Atheline as I have not seen her today. Mr. Henry slept till nearly night so he did not go to walk.

Monday 12th - No news this evening by the mail. Mr. Henry at the dam all day. Mrs. Petit & Mrs. Parker got some wool here today. Mr. Henry sent the wool today to a carding machine in S. C. by old Jim Knight & Tom Hendrix. They take a load of apples down. Clear & pleasant today. Harrie went to Asheville this morning & returned this evening. I made two coarse bolster cases for the trundle bed & hemmed a coarse towel. The towel is a yd. of cloth Mr. Henry got of Mrs. Peter Presley for a goose. I cut out some shirts for Fannie's baby, also some aprons & made one of the shirts. I also fixed two little old flannels for it.

Tuesday 13th - Mr. Henry started to the camp this morning. It was raining when he left. I begged him not to go but he said he felt it his duty. I made Gus a saque today of my old drab flannel one. It was worked very nicely with crimson cruel. I cut it so it is all worked around yet. Betsey weaving. Rose made some cider today.

Wednesday 14th October 1863 - Atheline finished little Mary's clothes yesterday. I cut her out a dress of the cloth Betsey wove last, some of the first. It was filled on with remnants. I also cut Tena & Atheline an apron of the remnants & cut Jane & Rose a chemise of the white. I have not heard from Mr. Henry since he left. I wish I could hear. I do hope he is well & doing well. I ask the O! Lord to watch over my dear husband whist he is out in the service of his country. Keep & preserve him from harm & bless me & my little children with health is my nightly & daily prayer. Bless my husband I beseech Thee.

Thursday 15th & Friday 16th - I have had a very bad spell with my head yesterday & today. I took a nap since dinner & it is nearly well. Harrie went to Asheville this morning to take Mr. Henry some clothes, at least to seek an opportunity of sending them to him. He left them to be sent by the first opportunity. He sent me word by Mr. Page to send him some. Willy Jones, that run from the conscript law, has got home cured of toryism, so I hear. Harrie got some sugar in town for me. I paid three dollars a lb. Got seven lbs. for twenty dollars. Dear sugar. We got done the molasses today. Uncle Sam has a little cane of his own to work up yet. Will get it done tomorrow.

William L. Henry to Cornelia C. Henry and children

French Broad, N. C.
Head quarters Western Division
Marshall, N. C.
16th Oct. 1863

My Dear Wife and Darling Babies,
    I write a few lines to say that I am well & all of our "army" are well. Some of our horses need shoeing. We may be busy in a day or two as we are in forty miles of the enemy and I think we will see a few of them by the time you get this letter. I need a shirt, my double filled pants. Have shoes made for our people. Rankin will let you have leather. Harry can get it. Send a boy to bring it.
    We have about 160 mounted men and will not be idle. We may bring down wrath on our country for to stir up their wrath. We are determined on visiting their lair. I hope nothing will be wrong until I get back. I see you have had a hard rain. We have had nothing more than a sprinkle. The river is 3 or 4 feet up. Provisions are scarce. Solgering is tolerable fair.
    My love to the children and a good night kiss all round. Ten thousand kisses to you my Dear.
    From Wm. Henry

Saturday 17th - My head entirely well this morning. I made Pinck a cap today as I can't get him a hat. I tried to cover an old one for him but did not succeed very well. It is too small & looks sorty. Willie wears it & thinks it a beauty. Harrie sent Hanes to town this evening after the news. Sluder wrote him that tories made a raid on Warm Springs last night & killed old Mr. Garrett, took all his horses, all Runbow's & all Blair's (the stage contractors at Warm Springs). They took 11 men of Capt. Robert's men prisoners. Oh! how long are we to be so persecuted? How long Oh Lord, how long? I pray O! so fervantly for an honorable peace. Grant us one I beseech Thee. Oh! Lord of love & mercy. I suppose Mr. Henry is down there now. I have not heard from him since he sent after the clothes. Matt got her cloth started today after so long trying. Betsey went home sick Thursday. Nothing serious I think. My little ones all well. The militia gone to Warm Springs.

Sunday 18th 1863 October - A beautiful morning. Every thing looks cheerfull & happy only I am sad. Yes I feel gloomy this morning. My dear husband is out I can't tell where, yet I have asked my Heavenly Father to take care of him & return him safely to his family & I believe He will do it. Help Thou my unbelief I pray.

I will write to him today & send it by Billie Cook as he goes back in a day or two. I will write to Eugenia today too I think or perhaps wait till tomorrow & write to Lou too. They put the water on the dam yesterday. It washed under the spilling so in one place they had it to turn off again. They have nearly another weeks work on now by not fixing it right at first. I may write more in this after dinner. I did not write to Lou & others. Harrie & I & Zona & Willie went to the dam this evening.

Monday 19th - I have done but little today. Sewed some on Jane's chemise. Atheline & Jinnie scoured my room, the dining room & back piazza. Jinnie made some cider this evening, the last we will have this season. I heard Mr. Henry was well. I am glad of it truly. Oh! that he may be spared is my earnest prayer.

Tuesday 20th - I went to T. Cook's today. Took Pinck to get Cook to make our shoes. I had headache when I came back. I was very tired. I rode Paddy. No news from Mr. Henry today. The yanks or tories are supposed to be at Warm Springs now. I wrote a long letter to Mr. Henry Sunday evening, thinking Billie Cook was going back soon. As he is not, I will get Harrie to take it to Asheville in the morning. I had Atheline to make me a cup of good coffee & now my head is nearly well.

Wednesday 21st - I took one of my old flannels & made Gus three short skirts of it. I did not get them done today. Harrie took the letter today to Asheville but heard nothing of Mr. Henry. I am uneasy about him. Oh! that this war could stop honerably. I do pray so fervantly for my dear husband & for all the Confederacy. Help us Oh! Lord, I beseech Thee, help us.

Thursday 22nd - I finished the little skirts before dinner & cut out three dresses of my old ones for Gus. I sewed some on one. No news of Mr. Henry today. I would be so glad to hear from him. I do hope he is all well & getting on well soldiering.

Friday 23rd 1863 October - I received two letters from Mr. Henry today. He was well. The 21st, one letter came in the mail, the other by hand. I was so glad to hear from him. Tom Cook began to make shoes this evening, made Willie a pair. It has rained nearly all day. I made Gus a dress & began another. Jinnie is cooking.

Fannie got to be so triffling I could not stand her any longer. She, Jane & Rose are gathering beans. They started the mill Wednesday morning but it broke in another place so all hands are at it again.

William L. Henry to Cornelia C. Henry and children

Ream's Creek Campground
21st Oct. 1863

My Dear Wife & Children,
   I write only to say I am well. I have had several trips and will only say that I get back from Madison in a few hours. I now have orders for the night thus I will be all this night on horse back. I have enjoyed soldiering finely. I met with a great many things to make me laugh and many other things to make me sad. 'Tis sad to see Madison County nearly all now in the biggest scare you ever saw. Bob Farnesworth & Mother have moved out & old H. Barnet has been completely robbed of everything last night. We will go by Spring Creek & look over on Tenn.
   I will say I thank you for the clothes. I have not got them yet as they are in Woodfin's trunk & he is gone. Tell Pinckney that I love him & I want him to be obedient to his Mother & kind to his sister & brothers.
   Tell Zona to be a good girl & mind her Mother & love her brothers. Tell her I love my daughter.
   Tell William & Robt that they must grow fast & do the best they can to be good boys. I love my boys.
   To Wife, the object of my love & who richly deserves all my best wishes and kindness, take good cheer. Be kind to the poor & needy. Have the fam. attended the best you can. Continue the mill dam to the hill if it broke around at the end or do the best under the circumstances.
   Have Sam to sow wheat & soak the in blue stone. I want the corn on the Joe Green field & sow wheat. Then sow in the land joining Johnston's corn. The land in where Johnston's corn.
   Have a pasture spend for the dry cattle. Close the fence above the houses including the oat field. I will write to you soon from somewhere else.
   I am as ever,
Your Husband,
Wm. Henry

Saturday 24th - Mr. Henry came home last night about 8 o'clock. I was so glad to see him but when I heard of his narrow escape & having to go back this morning, my heart almost stopped to beat. He & others had a skirmish with the tories or yanks at Warm Springs Thursday evening. Mr. Henry thinks Maj. John Woodfin is killed. A ball brushed Mr. Henry's arm, it is an ugly place & very sore. His horse was shot in the fore leg. They had to run up a mountain. Mr. Henry was near Woodfin when he was shot. He fell off his horse soon after they started up the Mt. & 'tis supposed he was dead. Mr. Henry's horse run under a bush & pulled him off. He then run about 100 yds. & Maj. Woodfin's horse & another horse came along so he got Davis' horse. Davis was shot in the hip. He got back to Marshall by the time Mr. Henry & them did. There was only twelve in the squad. They were sent around by Woodfin to see the strength of the enemy. The others, about 100 men, were a quarter of a mile behind. These others were Capt. Harris' Cavalry. Two men were killed in Capt. Harris' company. Mr. Henry & these others slept in the Mountains that night. He left his horse as he was too lame to travel. It was the Cagle horse, a good one. Mr. Henry says he could run very fast. They got to Marshall yesterday about 12, had not eat anything since Thursday morning. He lost his overcoat, hat & cape & left his bridle & saddle on poor John Cagle when he left him. He woke me this morning about 1 o'clock. We did not get up till near three. I felt miserable indeed. I slept but little last night thinking of his going this morning. It kept me awake a long time. It may be the last night I shall ever sleep in his dear arms. Oh! I have felt so sad all day, so miserable. I told him goodbye in the front piazza. He eat breakfast a little after 4, he and another man that was going with him. It was raining when he started. Oh! that the Lord would hear my poor petition & spare my dear husbands life. I ask & beseech it of Thee Oh Lord. Stay Thy wrath on us as a nation I pray & grant us peace.

Stevens sent after his negroes we have hired, they went. The people of Asheville expect a raid every day from the tories or yanks one. Stevens is going to move his family, white & black too. I have felt so sad all day. I have done nothing of importance. I finished the dress for Gus. Cook got Pinck's & Zona's shoes done today. Fannie is spinning. I want to make Mr. Henry an overcoat as soon as I can get the filling spun. He wants it lapped. Betsey will help spin it. She has quit weaving till she gets the filling ready. There is about ten yds. to weave yet. She will be here Monday after rolls. The waggon got home with the rolls Thursday night. They are very nice, most of them mixed. I did not get the fine wool carded. They brought it back. They would have had to wait two days for it so they said so they brought it home. Take care of my husband whilst he is out I ask of thee O Lord. May our forces come out victorious I pray. They expected a fight with them today. They sent the cannon down yesterday from Asheville.

Sunday 25th - I would be so glad to hear from Mr. Henry, to hear he was well & unharmed. We have heard nothing of them today. This has been a long day to me. I hope he may come home tomorrow. He said he would if he could. I do hope he may come. This has been a cool day all day & little cloudy this evening. Preaching at the Academy today. None of the whites went. Harrie is upstairs asleep. The children at play. Gus looks very sweet in his short dress. He has two other teeth above & the two in front above are nearly through. He cut the ones on each side of the two upper ones before the two in front. Rather a strange way I think. May Heaven protect my dear husband and may he soon return to his family is my earnest prayer.

Major John W. Woodfin on his horse "Prince Hal."
Woodfin was killed near Warm Springs, October 20, 1863
(Courtesy of the North Carolina Office of Archives and History, Raleigh, North Carolina)

Monday 26th October 1863 - I made another dress for Gus today. No news from Warm Springs. The fight was to come off today but Gen. Vance did not attack them on the road leading from Asheville to Warm Springs as the program was but sent a courier to Col. Sam Bryson who was in the Spring Creek road. The courier did not get there before Col. Bryson had fought & had to fall back. We lost 5 killed & two wounded. Our forces fought well. The loss of the enemy not known. The men who did most of the fighting were a detail from the 25th N. C. Reg. as brave men as ever drew a trigger. They were under the immediate command of Lt.

Welch of Haywood. Harrie went to Asheville today. Mr. Cook making shoes. Nothing from Mr. Henry today. I hope he is safe.

Tuesday 27th - I cut out a good deal of work today. Willie three shirts, Zona two night caps, myself one, Gus a new dress & Pinck a pair drawers of the cloth Betsey wove. I sent & got 10 yds. of shirting, unbleached, for which I paid twenty dollars & two lbs. of soda for 10$. That is certainly a big price. Harrie got them today in Asheville. Mr. Henry came home this evening. I was very glad to see him. He has to go again in the morning. I am sorry of that. I have asked my heavenly Father to take care of him & I feel He will. I sewed some on Pinck's drawers today. Cook still making shoes. He will go off with Mr. Henry in the morning. The children all have shoes & some of the negroes.

Wednesday 28th - Mr. Henry & Mr. Cook left about 8 o'clock this morning. I felt very sad but such is the fate of the war. Henry Cook & his mother took dinner here today, also Aunt Patsey Jamison. I finished Pinck's drawers soon after dinner & began a haversack for Mr. Henry of oil cloth. Four soldiers (Vicksburg prisoners) stay here tonight. They say Mr. Henry left Asheville just after three o'clock today. He wrote me a note by them telling me to take them in if I liked. They are very genteel looking men.

Thursday 29th & Friday 30th - I had the headache very badly yesterday evening & last night. I was very sick but got better after vomiting. I finished the haversack just after dinner & my head pained me so badly I did nothing else. 'Tis a nice haversack. Harrie went to Asheville yesterday, heard no news. Lt. Welch brought the bodies of the killed to Asheville yesterday evening, all but one. He is burried in the garden at Warm Springs & they did not know it till after they left the Springs. The yanks have all left the Warm Springs. 'Tis reported we have whipped them near Greenville. I do hope it may be so. In the fight last Monday they fought hand to hand, knocked each other down with their muskets. Our forces fought well. Harrie got Pinck a hat yesterday in Asheville for which I paid ten dollars. Tom Cook came by here this morning & says Mr. Henry was well yesterday evening. I am always so glad to hear from him. Cook took some leather & Mr. Henry's old boots home with him to fix. He is to make me a pair shoes also. He has to go back on Monday or Tuesday. My head has ached all day, a little better since supper. I began a cap for Mr. Henry. It is too small. I shall have make another crown. Tena & Atheline spinning for Mr. Henry's overcoat & pants. I cut the jeans out of the loom last Wednesday, 15 1/2 yds. I will make Mr. Henry a coat & pants next week & Pinck some clothes as I want to send him down to Pa's for Dora to teach. I wrote to Dora today. I sent Mr. Henry's haversack by Russell Jones' on this morning & put some molasses bread in that Atheline baked yesterday evening. She got dinner yesterday & Jinnie washed. May kind Heaven protect my husband I pray.

Saturday 31st - My head entirely well this morning. I finished the cap today. Harrie thinks it will fit. I hope it may please him. No news from Mr. Henry today. We have got all our apples put up & a fine chance of them. They are upstairs. Matt is not well nor hasn't been for several days. The others all well. Gus has four teeth above & two below.

November 1863

Sunday Nove. 1st - A beautiful morning. A. W. Cummings preaches at the Academy this evening. I don't think of going. He is our preacher next year. I don't like the appointment much. I hope he may do us good. The children are all at play. Harrie has been out walking & just returned near 12 o'clock. I am up in his room writing. Dinner will soon be in I think. I will not write much more now. I expect to spend the evening in reading my bible. May Thy kind protecting hand be over us & over my dear husband through out the coming week is my earnest prayer. Oh! Father of Mercy, hear my supplication.

Monday November 2nd 1863 - I began a pair pants for Mr. Henry this morning, did not get them done. Harrie went to Asheville this morning & stays there tonight. Vick brought no news. Matt Tidwell is not at all well. She fell & hurt her back last week. She was weaving at Betsy McKinnish's & the bench fell with her. Betsy began the weaving of Mr. Henry's overcoat today. 'Tis lapped & then carded very thick & nice. My little ones are all well. How happy I would be if Mr. Henry was at home & the war was ended but I fear it will be years yet.

Tuesday 3rd - I finished Mr. Henry's pants before dinner & cut Pinck two pair after dinner & sewed a little on them. I began to crochet Pinck a pair gloves this evening. Harrie came home this evening & brought no news. I thought certainly I would hear from him this evening. I live on hope when one day goes by. I hope to hear of him the coming tomorrow but when the day wanes away & nothing of him, I feel so sad & lonely. May kind Heaven protect him is my prayer.

Wednesday 4th - I sewed on Pinck's pants today, did not get either pair done. Mrs. W. Reynolds & Miss Kate Hickey spent the evening here yesterday. No news from Mr. Henry today. I am so anxious to hear from him. The yanks have been gone nearly two weeks from Warm Springs but 'tis thought they will come again there. I would be very glad if they would stay away. Jinnie washed up the floor of Harrie's room this evening. Poor fellow, he spits a great deal & coughs a good deal every night. I don't think he will live long though he don't think he has consumption.

Thursday 5th - I finished Pinck's pants, both pair today. Matt getting a little better. Mrs. Willey Knight took dinner here today. She came to see Matt. Gus is not at all well, his bowels are loose. I am up with him every night. Betsy & Matt make their bed on the floor in here so we are not affraid.

Friday 6th - Harrie went to Asheville today, heard nothing of Mr. Henry. Betsy got the cloth out today, 10 1/2 yds. I sent Henderson to Mrs. Rutherford's for the soap she has been making, got 32 lbs. That was Wednesday. Pinck went along. On Thursday, Henderson went to Cook's & got my shoes. Tom Cook is to come this week & finish making shoes as Harrie got some leather in Asheville last Tuesday. Henderson has had a very sore heel, the oxen tramped on it. It is better now.

Saturday 7th November 1863 - This has been a lovely day. I looked for Mr. Henry all day but night closed in & he has not come. I will still hope he may come tomorrow. I finished Pinck's coat this evening. I began it yesterday. I fixed an old port monie for him this evening. He is quite proud of it. I put some old postage stamps in it for money. It does him finely. Atheline has been sick nearly all this week. She has been spinning yesterday & today for Rose some stocking yarn. Tena will dye my dress piece next week.

Sunday 8th - Cold & clear this morning. Nothing new going on. I do wish Mr. Henry would come home tonight. I hope he is well & getting on well. Matt is sick today. Willie was not well last night, his bowels loose. Gus has not eat anything today. His bowels are deranged some. I think 'tis his teeth. He has four above & two below. The children are all at play. Atheline has Gus. The wind from the North & very cool for Nov. I will stop as I want to read some. I am reading in Ezra in the Bible.

2 o'clock & 20 minutes. I spent the evening in reading. Harrie took a nap this evening. The chimney caught on fire this evening & burned out. I was alarmed about it for awhile but it done no harm. I received a letter from Mr. Henry this evening. It had got to Mollie Henry some way & she sent it to me. Mr. Henry was well last Sunday, said he would try to be at home this week as it is court week. I hope he may come.

Monday 9th - I cut Mr. Henry a coat today & sewed a little on it. Very cold with wind from North & cloudy with occasional spits of snow. No news of importance. My little ones all well. Tena dyed the chain of my dresses today a light lilac of willow bark. It will freeze tonight I think.

Tuesday 10th - Tena spooling today. Atheline spinning filling for the lining of Mr. Henry's overcoat & cape, also Pinck's cloak. It will be filled on first in my dress piece. Harrie & Pinck went to Asheville today, heard nothing of Mr. Henry. Very cold today but a bright sunshine all day which made it more pleasant. I sewed on Mr. Henry's, the machine did not do well.

Wednesday 11th - Finished the coat, all but button holes & buttons. I shall have to cover some buttons. I am affraid the coat is too small across the shoulders. 'Tis a nice warm one. I intend carding it before I put the buttons on. Tena & Atheline spooling today, nearly finished it. Tom Cook making shoes, came this morning.

Thursday 12th November 1863 - I finished the coat before dinner. Betsy helped me card it. Her & Aunt Patsey are here today to warp my dresses. I spent the evening at Mrs. A. B. Jones, took Zona behind me on John Smith. Pleasant all day. Mr. Cook got the leather all worked up this evening & went home. He is to finish Mr. Henry's boots this week & then make Pinck a pair shoes, the baby a pair & Matt a pair. I want to start Pinck soon to Dora to school. Mrs. Hutsell is teaching at Sand Hill Academy but 'tis too far for Pinck to go. Nothing at all from Mr. Henry. I hope he is well & getting on as well as I wish him.

Friday 13th - The mail brought no news. Gen. Ransom had a fight at Rogersville, East Ten. in which we got the best of it. Lee is fighting nearly every week in Va. but not a general engagement. Oh that this war could stop on honorable terms. I cut Mr. Henry a pair pants of the lapped today & sewed some on them. I wish Mr. Henry could come home & stay till I could make his overcoat. I know he needs it badly. My little ones are well. I have to be up with Willie nearly every night as his bowels are loose. Betsey began the cloth today, filling in wool, first for coat lining and other things. Atheline has not been so well this week but better yesterday & today. Sam killed a hog this morning as we were out of lard. Our hogs are improving very fast now.

Saturday 14th - I finished the pants today. Jinnie made some sausage this evening. Harrie went to Asheville today, heard nothing of Mr. Henry. I would like so much to hear from him. He has been gone two weeks last Wednesday. I have only received one little letter from him. There are two hospitals in Asheville. Gen. Vance has one & the Ladie's Hospital. I expected Mr. Henry home tonight but he has not come. Matt stays at Mary Knight's tonight, a bad place for a young lady but she is determined to keep no company but the lowest. I can't do anything with her at all so I just let her alone. I will be glad when she gets off to Cherokee. I will then have no responsibility resting on me. I wish her well & would be glad to see her do well as she is a relation of my own dear husband & anything he cares for is dear to me. May Heaven protect him is my prayer.

Sunday 15th November 1863 - Atheline slept in my room last night. Clear & cold this morning. I sent some clothes to Mr. Henry this morning. Winslow Smith is to take them from Asheville. I expect he is good dirty in this time. I hope he may soon be at home to spend some time. I feel so lonely when he is gone. If it was not for my dear little ones I don't see how I could employ my mind but they keep me thinking how I can best do for them & their Papa's interest. Oh! That this war could stop. I pray Thee O God, stay the wrath of they hand upon us. Grant us a peace that seemeth good in Thy sight, in Thy own good time, should that time be far distant give us courage & patience to await it's coming with humble hearts. May we as a nation not fall into the hands of our enemies. I would ask Thee Oh Lord to take care of my dear husband. Protect him, spare his life & preserve his health. May he not fall into the hands of our enemies who seek our ruin & this I ask for Jesus sake, Amen.

William L. Henry to Cornelia C. Henry and children

In the road near W. P. Blair below Warm Springs
Sunday 15th Nov. 1863

My Dear wife & cubbs,

I am well. Nothing of any importance to write. Last night we made a recognisance of the enemy's camp at Cedar Creek & found our forces too weak to attack so we came over the mountain to wait, the result possibly to be in motion again today. We were in two miles of the enemy. They were well posted and some 400 to 600 strong. The news we got was that the enemy had fallen back to some station above Greenville & were in strong force on the rail road. I heard of Sister Jane. She is well. Wife, I will not be at home for some time. I will be at court in Asheville. I may be home on duty. If you can I think you had better have the corn in the Joe Green field gathered & have one load of shucked corn hauled to Asheville as tythe then feed the stears & cows that you intend to kill a little meal or corn & pasture them well. Please see to these things. I will

continue to write to you by every courier. We are as merry and as cheerful as cricketts. The morning is pretty. Nothing to say. Love my children & treat them as kind as possible. Be good to the poor. I send my love to you & all the family. Ten thousand kisses to the Mother & Babies.
Yours,
Wm. Henry

Monday 16th - I sewed some on a shirt for Willie today. I received a note from Mr. Henry this evening saying he wanted several things. I began to fix some yarn for him, some gloves & began the gloves this evening. I am going to knit them. Betsy will knit the top like a galles. Nothing new. Vance's men had a little brush with the enemy in which we lost one man. They recaptured a part of the hogs, only 80 I think. I wrote to Mr. Henry by the man this evening & sent him some paper, envelopes & stamps. I hope to hear from him soon.

Tuesday 17th - Harrie went to Asheville this morning to get Mr. Henry's overcoat cut. He came home late in the evening. No news from Mr. Henry. I finished one of his gloves & began the other. They will be very nice I think. I have headache tonight & fear I will have it tomorrow.

Wednesday 18th & Thursday 19th - I have had headache yesterday & today till since dinner. I took some pills this morning & it is nearly well tonight. Matt & I have nearly finished Mr. Henry's coat & cape. Only a few button holes which I will finish in the morning. I have suffered a great deal in the two last days. My head has pained me so badly but I could not put by my work for I was affraid my dear husband was needing his coat so I sewed on. He is so good to me. I can never do enough for him. Father of Mercy, take care of my own dear husband.

Friday 20th 1863 - The mail brought me no letter from Mr. Henry. I was sadly disappointed. I finished the coat this morning. I want to get nice buttons to put on it if I can. Put on some large buttons for the present. I began a cloak for Pinck but did not finish it today as there was tax giving in day. I paid 73.31$ tax today to Joshua Roberts as Harrie did it for me. I gave 75$ yesterday for two bu. of salt. Dear salt. Mollie Henry & little Bell came here this evening. Mollie is looking thin. Bell is a large healthy child. She is delighted with the children. Harrie was in town yesterday, heard nothing of Mr. Henry. He brought me a wee note from him saying he was well. Aunt Patsey stays here tonight.

Saturday 21st - Aunt Patsey & Betsey went home before dinner today. I finished Pinck's cloak today. We killed a hog yesterday, one of our fattening ones. The other hogs abused it so 'twas necessary to kill it. I have knit some on Rose's stocking today. I finished Mr. Henry's gloves on Thursday last. I only knit on them at night. Raining & cloudy today.

Sunday 22nd - My heart was made to leap with joy last night for Mr. Henry came home. It was after supper. I was so glad to see him. He only stays a day or two & then goes again to serve his country. We talked half the night. I feel so dull today.

Five soldiers dined here today. They are of Capt. West's camp, the same as Mr. Henry. I took a long nap in Mr. Henry's arms on the trundle bed. I felt badly when

I woke. I have a slight headache this evening. He & I went to the hog pen this evening. The hogs are improving very fast. Tom Cook brought his boots & my shoes today. His boots are too small. I am very sorry of it. My shoes do better than they did but not a nice fit yet. Betsey & Aunt Patsey stay here tonight. Mr. Henry leaves in the morning. I am very sorry. I ask Heaven to protect him & shield him from all harm.

Monday 23rd - Mr. Henry started this morning. Billie Cook & Fayette Jones went with him. I feel so sad today. I have nothing of note today. Knit a little. Mollie Henry went home this evening. Henderson took her in the buggy. I sent by her to get me some buttons (brass) for Mr. Henry's coat. They are very small. I gave eight dollars for two dozen. The mail brought no news. I wrote a long letter to Dora this evening.

Tuesday 24th 1863 - I began a vest for Mr. Henry today, did not get it done. I am knitting him some socks. I sit up till 9 o'clock at night & then rise between four & five. My little ones are all well. Gus has three teeth below & four above. He tries to pull up by a chair. I think he will walk when he is a year old. Pinck will start to Pa's next week.

Wednesday 25th - I finished the vest today. 'Tis a nice one like his overcoat. I hope it may suit him. I do try to please him & make him comfortable & he more than pays me for all my kindness. He is the best of husbands, so kind to me & the children. I shall miss Pinck sadly for a time. He is a good boy. Little Zona & Willie will miss him too I imagine. We have paid 60 bu. of tithe corn & one load of hay.

Thursday 26th - I sewed some on Willie's shirt today. I began it some two weeks ago but had to make Mr. Henry some clothes so I laid it away for a time. I have headache this evening so I did but little sewing. No news from Mr. Henry this week. I hope he is well. May a kind Heaven protect him is my daily prayer.

Friday 27th - My head ached badly today till since dinner & now 'tis nearly easy. I took a nap before dinner in the rocking chair & felt better. I began a stocking for Gus this evening of white yarn. Mr. Cook sent Matt's, Pinck's & Gus's shoes yesterday evening. Gus's fit very nice, so do Pinck's. No news came this morning of importance. Betsey got my dresses out this morning & put in the flannel for Mr. Henry's shirts. It very dark purple chain & black mixed filling. Looks very nice.

Saturday 28th - I finished Willie's shirt today & did a great many other little things. Put up Pinck's clothes in his carpet bag. He & Harrie think of going Monday. Mr. Henry came home this evening. We were all very, very glad to see him. I was not expecting him but was Oh! so glad to see him. This is a cruel, cruel war to take my own dear husband from his little family yet I look forward to a better time when this war is over & I would be glad if it could be over very soon. Grant us a peace I pray Thee Oh Father of Mercy in Thy own good time. Give us patience to await that time.

Sunday 29th - Mr. Henry started back this morning. 'Tis very cold. The wind from the N. He was highly pleased with his vest. I am affraid he has suffered with cold today. I wish he could have taken dinner with us today as we had a nice turkey for dinner. How I wish he had it instead of us. Fannie made some molasses bread for the children yesterday evening.

Monday November 30th 1863 - I cut one of the dresses today, making it infant. Waist is mutton leg sleeves. Nothing new going on. All are well. I would be so happy if Mr. Henry was at home & we had our independence. He says he is going to stay in the army till peace is declared. That seems very distant to me. Very cold today. Betsy came yesterday evening. Aunt Patsey stays here tonight. Mail brought no news.

December 1863

Tuesday Dec. 1st - I finished my dress today. It fits very neatly. No news today from Mr. Henry. Pinck will wait till Harrie goes down to Columbia & then go in the waggon with Mr. Hanes. I shall miss my little boy sadly I know but 'tis for his good I send him. Zona knows all the alphabet. She wants to learn. Willie is growing finely. Gus is trying to pull up by a chair. I think he will walk when he is a year old. This has been a very cold day but no so unpleasant as yesterday. Sam & Charly killed two beeves today. They are very nice fat oxen. Jim is helping gather the Johnston cane. Some rogue stole two of the fattening hogs last night. I think it was George & Steven's Boston. Harrie wrote Stevens a note this evening concerning it. He will be over in the morning. May kind Heaven protect my household from harm & Oh! God of love & mercy, preserve my dear husband. May he not fall into the hands of our enemies. Grant us a speedy peace & one that seemeth good in Thy sight is my daily prayer. Amen.

Wednesday Dec. 2nd - Mr. Stevens was over today, seems to think Boston had no hand in the hog stealing. Betsey cut out the cloth for Mr. Henry's shirts yesterday. I began one today. Fannie is rendering up the tallow today & moulded some candles. A fine lot of tallow out of the two beeves. A pleasant day after the morning.

Thursday 3rd - Harrie & I went to old Smith's to get some leather or rather to see when we could get some but did not get the promise of any. It was dinner time when we got back. We came by Mrs. Pettit's to see about some cloth she is to make for us. She will have it done soon after Christmas. Atheline finished the tallow today & moulded some candles. Fannie washed today. I did not get Mr. Henry's shirt done today. It seems a long time to be at work on one shirt. Oh how I wish he was at home. It really seems to me I can't stand it to have him in the army.

Friday 4th - I received a long letter from Mr. Henry today through the mail, all concerning the farm. I finished his shirt before dinner. The hands killed ten hogs today. I went to old Mr. Presley's this evening & started to Branton's & met with Mr. Henry. He came up the turnpike just after I passed it & called to me. I was so glad to see him. I had Pinck behind me. He has been to Haywood to carry a dispatch & then another back to Asheville. This evening we went out nearly to Jim Jarrett's with him & then turned back & went to Branton's. He was not at home. I went to see him to get him to put up a bridge below the dam. Mr. Henry said perhaps he would come home tonight. I hope he may. Yes he came just after supper. I made him a nice cup of pure coffee. I am always glad to see. I love him more & more each day. Oh Merciful God spare my dear husband's life & preserve his health I pray, for unto Thee & Thee only can we look for success in this our time of need. "Bow down Thy ear, Oh Lord and hear, hear Thou me, for daily I will call. Yes, I will call Oh Lord on Thee." Hear my poor petition, I ask for Jesus sake, Amen.

Saturday 5th - Mr. Henry took Charley & the waggon & went to the tan yard (old Smith's). Mr. Henry says he intends to have his leather. He was gone all day. I had a nice dinner for him thinking he would be home for dinner but he did not get back till supper. He got a fine lot of leather. He & old Smith are now even. Mr. Henry left for Marshall about seven o'clock. I hated to see him go. No one knows how badly. He has to be in Marshall tomorrow morning as they are going to make a raid into Ten. about Newport. I went with him to the gate & told him good bye & Oh! the bitter tears that I shed, to think he would be riding till one or two o'clock tonight in the cold & me & our little children would be snugly in a warm room & beds so comfortable, that he has prepared for us. This is a cruel war. My poor heart will surely break with trouble. Mr. Henry did not sleep well last night. He said it was the strong coffee. He did not get to sleep till nearly one o'clock. He will get sleepy tonight before he gets there & no chance to sleep as his horse is a little wild. Oh Merciful God, take care of my dear husband I pray.

Sunday morning 11 o'clock December 6th 1863 - This is a beautiful morning. I hope Mr. Henry did not suffer with cold last night. My first waking thoughts this morning were of him & very last thought last night was a prayer for the husband of my choice. He has always been so kind to me & the children which makes him doubly dear if possible. He has always made home the most desirable place to me on earth & now he can't share that happy home with me. Oh it really seems 'tis more than I can bear. I know there are thousands of women left in a heap worse condition than I am but Mr. Henry is all the world to me. Life would be a blank to me without him. "May God temper the wind to shorn lamb." Unto Thy kind protecting care do I give my husband. O! Lord, watch over him & care for him. When danger is near will Thou protect him. Give our soldiers brave hearts & willing hands to drive the invader from our land. Stand by them in time of need for "Thou hast said the battle is not to the strong nor the race to the swift." Have mercy on the poor widows & orphans of our land. Lead them to the only source of comfort. Teach them how to pray, for unto Thee only can we look for help & Thou hast said "knock & it shall be opened unto you, seek & ye shall find." Give our rulers wisdom to act as seemeth good in Thy sight. May our enemies be led to see the error of their ways & leave off persecuting us. Bring confusion on their counsels and O Lord I beseech Thee, stay the wrath of Thy hand upon as a nation. Stop this cruel bloodshed & make the hearts of a nation glad by restoring us a speedy peace & one that seemeth good in Thy sight. Should Thou see fit in Thy infinate wisdom to make that peace far distant give us patience & courage to fight the battles before us. Be with us O Lord and we will come out all right. Our soldiers who are languishing on beds of suffering have mercy on them. Give them patience to wait Thy own good time when Thou wilt say it is enough. Oh God of love may we not fall into the hands of our enemies. Be with my husband through the coming week. Protect and preserve him & Thine shall be all the Glory for Christ sake, Amen.

Monday 7th December 1863 - Matt & I took a walk yesterday evening, went on top the hotel hill. Zona was with us. We called at Mrs. Knight's to see her babe. It is two weeks old today. She said it was very unwell & today we hear it died last night. I finished the shirt I began last Friday, a colored one for Mr. Henry. Matt & I went up to the old store house this evening & brought down a sack of old papers, as some one has broke off the back of Bob Henry's desk & they are partly his papers & other old papers no account to any one. We were not down at Mrs. Knight's as we heard her babe had been burried. The militia is called out again.

Tuesday 8th - No news from Mr. Henry since he left. I would be very glad to hear from him. I suppose they went over into Tenn. Harrie went to Asheville yesterday with Charlie. He took the leather we got of old Smith to Rankin's Tan yard to be finished off. I sent by Harrie & got 7 lbs. of sugar & paid 21.00, three$ pr. lb. & got 1 paper of needles & paid 1.50, a paper of pins 1.25 & one card of agate buttons for 4.50. I really think speculators will whip us sooner than the yanks. I made Willie a shirt today.

Wednesday 9th - I made Willie a homespun apron, some I had filled on the last end of the flannel. 'Tis purple chain & filled two of white & two of purple maple dye. I will make him two & Zona two. All are well. We are having a pleasant winter so far. I hope it may continue so for our poor soldiers are but badly clad & will suffer.

Thursday 10th - Mrs. Bob Gudger & Cousin Laura Gudger spent part of the day here. Mrs. Gudger wanted some wool, got 4 lbs. She did not pay for it. I made another apron for Willie today. Jinnie cleaned up the upstairs floor yesterday where the apples had been. John Love's son Dillard staid here last night.

Friday 11th - Mail brought no news. I received a letter from Sister Dora last Monday. They were all well. Dora & Matt had just returned from a visit to Columbia. Pinck & Harrie will start down there next week, I think now. I hope they may have favorable weather. My head feels badly tonight. I fear I shall have headache soon again. No news from Mr. Henry. May Heaven protect him I pray.

Saturday 12th December 1863 - Cloudy & raining all day, a slow misty rain. I have been in bed part of the day with my head. It is much better now at 4 o'clock. I have knit a little today. I made Zona an apron yesterday & intended to make her other one today but have been too unwell to work much. Newton Taylor is here this evening, just from the 60th Reg. He brings no news. Mary & family are all well. He is looking well. I will stop as the children are getting too obstreperous. They are a happy cheerful set. They know not of my trouble. Let them be happy while they can. Cares will come soon enough to their young hearts.

Sunday night 13th - My head entirely free from pain this morning. Heavy fog & then clear but clouded up before dinner & now after 8 o'clock raining. The dam washed around last night. I hope it will not stop the grinding long. Some one broke in the mill last night, took some two bushels of wheat, some two weeks ago they took two of our fattening hogs. It really seems they will steal us out of house & home soon. Oh! That the Lord would grant us peace. Yes one that seemeth good in Thy sight. May Heaven protect my dear husband is my earnest prayer.

Monday 14th - I done but little today. Made Pinck a housewife, a small one & fixed some needles, thread & buttons in it for him. He is delighted with it. They will start sometime this week. No news from Mr. Henry. All quiet along the lines. My little ones all well & I am thankful of it. Five soldiers stay here tonight. They are from Texas. Aunt Patsey warped the cloth for the boy's pants.

Tuesday 15th - Harrie went to Asheville this morning & brought me a letter from Mr. Henry. He is at Paint Rock & well. Betsy & Aunt Patsey put in the cloth & began it. Aunt Patsey went home this evening. Jinnie scoured my room & the dining room today. I have been fixing up Pinck's things & done nothing of importance.

Wednesday 16th - I have got everything ready for Pinck to start. We looked for Mr. Hanes all day. I will hate to see my little child leave me. I love him so much. He is a good child. I hope 'tis for his good I send him away from me. He ought to be at school every day. I shall miss him Oh! so sadly. May Heaven protect him I pray.

View from Paint Rock, printed in "Land of the Sky, Views on the Western North Carolina R.R.," published by Chisholm
(North Carolina Collection, Pack Memorial Public Library, Asheville, NC)

Thursday 17th December 1863 - I have been in bed part of the day with headache but some better this evening. Rained all day today & a good deal last night so the dirt work of the dam is gone & will not be repaired soon again as there is no one to help build it again as the militia is all out. Hanes has not come today. Joe Russell stays here tonight. He brought me a letter from Mr. Henry. Capt. Russell is sent here after the waggon. He will not get it. He brought me a letter from Mr. Henry. He is at Paint Rock. I have knit a little today & only a little.

William L. Henry to Cornelia C. Henry and family

Wm. L. Henry
Private Co. B, 14th Batt.

Paint Rock, 13th Dec.
My Dear Dinah & Babies,
    I only write you a few lines to say I am well & enjoying myself as well circumstances will admit of. I cannot enjoy things away from my home under arms for the destruction of my race as well as I could at home with my wife & the war over but peace has not come nor will it show us it's smile I fear for some time. Gen. Vance has come to take charge of this district. I like him & his course better than the course Col. Palmer. Tell John Hendrix & Albert Knight to come to camp. Have their horses shod & come on & not wait to be brought in as a hound with a guard after them. Send me a shirt or denim, which I need I do not know. I think some of our men will be at camp ground Reams Creek.
    My Dear, don't sell anything to eat. Store if possible as our friends will all have to move from Tenn. I have nothing to write. I hope you are getting along well. Kill your hogs & cattle.
I am as ever yours. Ten thousand kisses & fine wishes to my wife & babies.
Wm. Henry
    Wife, please let the bearer have five pounds of blue stone if you have that much. I know you ought to have more if not wasted.

Friday 18th - Mail carrier turned back from Sandy Bottom today as the river was up so he could not pass so we will get no mail here till next Friday. I wrote to Mr. Henry by Capt. Russell this morning. Harrie took 1 3/4 lbs. of fine wool to Asheville to be sent to Coleman's to make Mr. Henry & him a hat each. Mr. Hanes was here today & says he will start in the morning. I had some fresh crackers & some fresh green apple pies baked this evening. I had some baked last Wednesday for them & a nice ham boiled. Sam & the others killed nearly all the hogs, 22, today. Mr. Henry came home this evening & a heap of soldiers come & eat supper here & the negro's cooked for the others. Fannie & Jinnie were baking bread all night long. Fannie washed Mr. Henry's clothes tonight. They think of leaving early in the morning for Cherokee as it is reported the yanks are in there & have burned Murphy. Fanny cooked Mr. Henry some beef, crackers & molasses bread. The house is full of soldiers & some camped at the old store house.
    Saturday 19th - The soldiers stay here all day, having their horses shod. Nine o'clock before we got our breakfast. Pinck & Harrie started about 11. I was so sorry to see my child go away. God bless him with health & contentment. I never expect to see Harrie again. He took all his things to Columbia. I sent a box of apples for Pinck & had another one fixed up for Eugenia but they could not take it. It

is very cold this morning & last night. I fear Pinck will suffer with cold. I hope he may get there all right. Harrie had the toothache very badly when he started. He will suffer all day with it I fear. The house full of soldiers all the time. I have done nothing today. My heart feels sad & lonely for my oldest child is gone. If he was back I would not send him. I love my little ones so devotedly. God bless him I pray.

Sunday December 20th - A very cold night & no better this morning. Zona & Willie slept on the trundle bed last night, part of the night, as Mr. Henry had to get up in the night & put Willie with me & he slept with Zona till day. I miss Pinck so much when night closes in. I want to see my little boy come into the fire but he will not come for many a long weary month. Yes they will be long months to me. Mr. Henry & all the soldiers started today about 12. I was sorry to see Mr. Henry go as it is so very cold. A heap of them will suffer with cold today as a great many of them are thinly clad. Betsey did not weave any yesterday & she is here this evening. She did not go home as there was so many soldiers about. Aunt Patsey has just left. She came here since dinner to see what kept Betsey. She will get very cold. Zona & Willie are talking about Pinck now. They speak of him often & Zona cries for him often. I wish he was here. I must go & get out supper as the sun is nearly down. I hope Mr. Henry is well & not suffering from cold. God bless him & spare his dear life to his family & bless my little boy with health & contentment is my sincere prayer.

Monday 21st - I have done nothing of importance today. Jim put the back in Bob Henry's desk & moved it in my room. I then spent the remainder of the day looking over some old papers Matt & I had brought from the old store house. I found nothing of importance among them as they nearly all belonged to R. Deaver. Of no consequence to any one so I burned them. The negroes at work at the lard today, did not get it done. No mail this evening as the mail carrier did not go up the river Friday.

Tuesday 22nd - I made Zona an apron today & went to Mrs. McKinnish's after some thread. She will bring it in the morning. Very pleasant this evening. Sam got through with the hogs this evening & we got done the lard. Nothing new going. Wiley Jones (the only open mouthed tory we had in the neighborhood) died last week. No one grieves after him much.

Wednesday 23rd - I began my lapped dress today. Betsey is weaving a blanket for Mr. Henry on the coarse jeans & carding it. It looks very well, will keep out cold. I would like so much to hear from Pinck. I am very anxious about him. I am affraid he will not be contented yet I hope he may. Two men called here today & say the Battalion did not go to Murphy but turned off through the Cataloocha Mountains yesterday.

Thursday 24th December 1863 - I finished my dress about 8 o'clock tonight. Betsey & Matt made Zona & Willie a doll each & hung them up on their little stockings. They will be delighted with Santa Clause's present. I put some molasses bread & a large apple in them too. One of Mr. Neilson's little sons was here today. Sister Jane is in Asheville living at John Woodfin's house. She will spend the day here tomorrow. The boy wanted some corn & flour. I sent some of both, 3 lbs. of flour & 1 bu. of corn. I gave Matt a skeer tonight. She made a dreadful noise hollering.

Friday 25th Christmas Day - I remember this day ten years ago very well. I remember this day nine years ago well. Sister Jane & her children & Mr. & Mrs. Black spent the day here. We enjoyed it finely. Had an eggnog before dinner. Dinner was late. We had turkey & several other things too numerous to mention. They all went back soon after dinner. I felt so sad & lonely. I have not felt cheerful & happy in a long time & then to have Sister Jane with me such a short time. I am going to spend the day with her next week. I miss Pinck so much. I wish he was here tonight. He is a good child. Little Dora is a little bit of a child. The baby is large enough to its age, six months old. Mrs. Black has a boy babe the same age of Sister Jane's. This has been a beautiful day but rather cold. The mail brought no news of importance. Betsy went home this morning. She cut out the cloth & I began Mr. Henry a blanket. Did but little to it before Sister Jane & them came.

Saturday 26th - This has been a dull gloomy day, sleeting all day. I finished the blanket today & helped Matt make a coat for Jim. We finished it before night. A soldier stays here tonight. He says he is a courier for Gen. Longstreet. He is full of talk, a boy about 19, married Tucker from Milligeville Geo. No news from Mr. Henry yet.

Sunday 27th - Cloudy & raining this morning. Gen. Buckner's headquarter waggons passed here today. They are going to Longstreet. They have come a long way as the communication is cut off between Longstreet & Bragg. The last news we had was that Longstreet was pressing on Knoxville. I do wish we could get the yanks out of Knoxville & any great wish absorbing all is to have peace, yes an honorable seperation from the North. They have caused some of our best blood to flow & I never want to live under their rule again. Oh that God would grant us peace at an early day & protect my dear husband I pray.

Cornelia C. Henry to Pinckney Henry

December 27 Sunday by the fire in my room

My own dear little Pinck,

How are you getting on at Grand Pa's? Very well I hope. How did you spend your Christmas? I thought about you a heap & wished you were here to hang up your sock. Zona & Willie hung up theirs & Zona got a big doll, some molasses candy, some ginger bread & a big apple & Willie got the same. So you see the yankees have not got Santa Clause yet.

How did you like your Christmas letter? You must be very smart & learn to read so I can come after you. I want to see my little boy & Zona talks about you a heap, says she will be so glad to see you. She don't comb my head often as she did when you were here to help her. Willie's sore finger is nearly well. He wants to see little Pinck too & little Gus will jump & crows to see Pinck.

I have not seen Papa since the day after you left. They all left on Sunday after you left Saturday. Aunt Jane spent Christmas day with me. Little Dora & the baby too. She is living in Asheville at John Woodfin's house. I am going to see her this week. She has been run from her home by the mean old yankees & tories. They are mean people to do that way.

You must be a good boy & Papa & Mother will love their child so much. You must never tell a story & tell Aunt Dora good night every night for Mother & Papa. I kiss Zona & Willie every night for you. Hanes & Lonzo send howdy to you. Rose says tell Pinck she will be glad to see him when he comes. Mother sends a heap of love & kisses to her little Pinck. Gus, Zona & Willie send love & kisses to you. Be a good boy & write to us often. God bless you with contentment.

Your fond Mother

Mother dreamed of Pinck the other night. Does Pinck dream of Mother?

Cornelia C. Henry to Dora Smith

December 27, 1863

My Dear Dora,

I have just finished Pinck's letter so will write you a letter in it though I have nothing to write of importance. Sister Jane spent Christmas day with me. I was very glad to see her. The yanks have treated her badly. She looks old & case worn. I am so sorry for her. She had both children & Mr. & Mrs. Black & Mrs. Black had her babe. They only staid all day. I was sorry she could not stay longer but she had to go back as Mr. Neilson had to leave in a day or two. Little Dora is very small but tollerably well. She is teething which makes her fretful. I am going to see Sister Jane this week if the weather will let me. We have had some very cold days of late & sleet & rain in abundance. She is living in John Woodfin's house. I am glad she had got out of Tenn.

I have not seen Mr. Henry since the day after Pinck left. I heard last Tuesday that he was well. Oh! Dora if this war lasts one year longer I shall be prematurely old. I have seen so much trouble since Mr. Henry has been out, it really seems to me sometimes I can't stand it. I am afraid I shall be a lunatic when the war is over. I won't suffer myself to dwell on it. I try to throw it off but when night begins to throw it's mantle over the earth, I want to see Mr. Henry coming but days will run into months before he can come at leisure & perhaps he may never come again. Oh! 'tis perfect agony to me, my life is no pleasure to me at all.

Talk to Pinck of us often. Teach him to be a good obedient child. Love him for my sake & his Papa's. Let me hear from him after every week. I shall want to hear.

Your devoted sister, Cornelia

Monday 28th - Matt & I made Hanes a coat. A very pleasant day. Some soldiers stay here tonight. They were cut off, belong to Forest's Cavalry. Jinnie is cooking today to let Fannie have her Christmas. I received a letter from Mr. Henry this evening. It came by hand. He thinks he will be at home by New Year's Day. I hope he may. I am very lonely when he is gone. I wrote to Pinck & Dora yesterday, also Lou. The mail brought no news.

Tuesday 29th - I spent the day with Sister Jane today & enjoyed it finely. The roads are very boggy. Hanes drove me. I took Gus. He was delighted with the ride. I got home about dark & found Mr. Henry here. I was very glad to see him. He will stay at home several days as the Battalion is going to camp up at Hominy Camp ground. Jim Henry & some other gentlemen took supper here tonight. They go for hunting early in the morning from here. Quite cool this evening but clear. I got a letter from Harrie last night saying they got to Greenville the 24th & he was going to take Pinck on to Columbia with him. Mr. Haines called here today & said Pinck was satisfied with the trip. He did not fret any about home & Mother. Bless my child Oh Lord. Bless him with health & contentment.

Wednesday 30th - I cut out a good deal of work today but did but little sewing. Mr. Henry at home all day. I enjoyed the day finely for I would be so glad if he could stay at home all the time. They, Mr. Henry & others, had a little brush with the bushwhackers on Cosby Creek in Ten. last week. None of our men were lost. I am glad they were so fortunate & particularly so as Mr. Henry was one among the number. I am very thankful.

Thursday 31st - I have done nothing of importance today. Sewed a little on Lonzo's pants. Sam & others killed two beeves today. Cloudy & warm. Mr. Henry at home all day.

1864

"...may we not fall into the hands of our enemies..."

January 1864

Friday Jan. 1st 1864 - Mr. Henry sent George to Asheville today to sell some beef. He went in the buggy so as to bring a goat from Bill McDowel's. He did not get the goat but contracted the beef to be delivered tomorrow. I sent Sister Jane some cabbage & some dried apples & sent Mollie Henry 8 cuts of mixed yarn to knit Jim some shirts. Rained all day today.

Saturday Jan. 2nd 1864 - Very cold this morning. It snowed some last night but rained on it & it all melted by 10 o'clock. Clear, windy & very cold this morning. Mr. Henry went to Asheville today & went down to see Sister Jane. They are all well. It was dark when he got home. I began to crochet some gloves for Zona & Willie today, did but little at it.

William L. Henry to Pinckney Henry and Dora Smith

Sulphur Springs, N. C. 2nd Jany 1864

My Dear Little Son,

I write this the first letter I have ever written to you. I can not express how much I want to say on paper. The day after you & Cousin Harry started to South Carolina, I started with my company on a trip to Cosby (a little creek in Cocke County Tennessee). I suppose you know how cold the weather was, as you were out in the day and I was out day and night, and two days & two nights without anything to eat and only two bundles of oats for each horse. I recon you think we were hungry. Well some of the men complained a good deal.

We traveled through the Catalucha Mountains from Haywood County in the direction of New Port and on the morning of the 24th Day of December, we met a lot of the enemy in the woods. They were acting as bush-whackers (that is men fighting in the woods & behind logs, stones & trees). We were engaged in shooting at each other about two hours & then the enemy ran off in the mountains and our men following for two or three miles shooting at each other occasionally when they would get in sight. None of our men were hurt. A few of the enemy were killed, some wounded & some taken prisoners. We got all their breakfast as they had not got done cooking it, and all their cook vessels and something like 30 horses & such things as are about a camp. We then came home by way of New Port & the French Broad river.

I got home a few days ago and found your mother & the children all well. We have some little lambs, pretty little fellows. The branch is covered over with ice and the weather is very cold. Willie and Zona feed the chickens and ducks & talk of brother Pinckney & send a good night kiss to Pinckney and pray God to bless their brother & bring him safe home to his mother, Papa & little brothers & sister. Zona takes a little spell of crying occasionally about little Pinckney.

Well sisters Dora & Mattie, I have not written to you for some time as I had some little riding around to do. I have been practicing soldiering for some time & I find that I can commit pretty well. I suppose you have long since heard that Sister Jane had moved to Asheville to avoid as much as possible the calamities of her own adopted country. I saw her yesterday. She is in the John W. Woodfin house near Dr. Neilson's house. She is well but she looks very case worn. I am truly sorry that she had to leave her home as I fear we people of the mountain country will have to move out next summer unless the enemy are driven out of East Tennessee, as we will not have enough stuff to support the contending armies that will have to pass through this mountain country, and that must be quartered on our section, as I hope we may be able to stop the enemy in the mountains.

The enemy will try in the months of May & June to push our armies to the wall as several thousand will be at home from expired time, whose service will have expired by that time. Our darkest days will be next Spring & Summer but then we will be able to push the enemy back to their own cold northern home. Oh! that the war might be broat to a successful close and our men who are yet alive be able to come to their different familys & avocations. I hope to weather the storm & be at home not to be called away for the defense of all that I hold dear & love best.

I want you to love my boy and be kind to him. Try by kindness to teach him his duty. I want both of you to write to me as your letters to wife are not to me & I want to hear from you in letter to myself. I know you have very little to write of and little inclination to write. I want you to say to Mr. Smith that my family & Mr. Neilson's familys are well. Love to all.

Love, Respectfully

Wm. Henry

Mother, Gus, Willie & Zona all send love & a heap of kisses to Pinck. You must be a good boy & ask God to bless your Papa every night. Zona sends you this button. She says keep it till she comes.

Sunday 3rd - Mr. Henry went to Asheville this morning & came back this evening. We started to meet him. He called us back Friday night, was very cold. The ice in the room was nearly an inch thick on the bucket. Last night was not so cold & today 'tis mild enough. The Cavalry has moved to the camp ground.

Monday 4th - I crochet some today, finished one glove & began another. They are striped red & mixed light blue making a grey. I made some ginger cakes this evening. Mr. Henry & I took a walk. Went up to the old hotel garden. The hands are making a sheep & cow house on the hill above old Tena's house. Branton helping. They are making it out of the old crib as it fell down. No mail tonight. I don't know the reason.

Tuesday 5th - I have copied the Post Office return today. I will not do anything else as I have headache badly. Mr. Henry went to the camps this morning, said perhaps he would come home tonight. I hope he may. He & I went up to the stables this morning. We came back & he started about 10 o'clock. My head aches so bad. I will stop this time. Mr. Henry came home this evening. 'Tis very cold at this time (evening).

Wednesday 6th & Thursday 7th - I was sick all day yesterday with my head. Crocheted some on Willie's gloves. Mr. Henry at home all day. I was so glad of it. He is so kind & attentive to me when I am sick. Gus is not at all well & Willie is quite sick today with a cold. He has been lying down nearly all day. Mr. Henry went to Asheville today. They have orders to march in the morning. I am very sorry of it for Mr. Henry will have to go. I quilted Gus & Zona a bonnett today. Matt helped me. We sewed some on them but got neither one done. I had Mr. Henry's rations cooked today. Aunt Patsey stays here tonight. Very cold this evening with a little snow occasionally.

Friday January 8th 1864 - I finished the bonnets with Matt's help & then we made Willie a cap. It looks nice. Mr. Henry started this morning. I was so sorry to see him go out in the cold wind. Oh! this cruel war, when will it end? Echo answers "when"? This has been a cold day. The sun come out about 10 o'clock. We had a little snow last night. It did not cover the ground entirely. I think it was too cold to snow much. Mr. Henry & the whole Battalion went towards Haywood. He thought they were going out into Ten. again on Causby Creek where they had that other little skirmish. I do hope they may return soon all safe. I pray God to watch over my dear husband & shield him from all harm. Be with our forces in the conflict. Stand by & give them courage. "Thou hast said the battle is not to the strong." Help us I beseech Thee in this our time of need. Help us Oh Lord I beseech Thee.

Saturday 9th - Willie seemed better yesterday but in bed nearly all day today. Gus is getting better. I have done but little of anything today, only wait on Willie. I cut Sam's & Charlie's coats today. Matt & Atheline made Charlie's & did some to Sam's. I washed my net & put some tassels on it. Betsy went home with her Mother yesterday before dinner. She cut out 17 1/2 yds. of jeans before she left. Some rogue cut the skirts off of Mr. Henry's saddle last Tuesday night. There is a great deal of stealing going on about now. The mail came yesterday morning but had but little for this office. The mail carrier did not go through last Friday on account of high water so that accounts for his not coming on Monday last. Very cold today, thawed but little all day.

Sunday 10th - Matt & I were up till nearly one o'clock last night with Gus. He had something like the colic. I gave him some oil about 12 o'clock. He got better after it opperated & slept well till morning. Willie rested very well last night & seems some better this morning but not able to sit up long. Gus is fretful today & Zona is not well. It really seems we will all get down. I have a very bad cold. I sent Charly after Dr. Thrash this morning. The Dr. will be here this evening or early in the morning. I wish he would come this evening as Willie's throat is sore & inflamed a good deal. He is crying for me to take him so I will stop this time. Betsy came this evening. Willie has a high fever & very cross. No one can do anything for him but me so it keeps me busy.

Monday 11th January 1864 - Willie is a little better this morning. The Dr. came this morning & gave him a powder. He is sitting up this evening & has but little fever. I hope he will be well soon. I have made some hankerchiefs today. All the work I have done was with Willie in my lap so it is not much. I am sadly disappointed tonight by not getting a letter from Harrie or Dora. Very little mail came tonight.

Tuesday 12th - I made eight hankerchiefs today. Willie is a heap better. George took some honey yesterday evening to make Willie some cough mixture. He & Gus have a dreadful cough. Zona has a cold but is not so bad off as the other two. I have a cold myself.

Wednesday 13th - I finished Zona's gloves today. I had one done & she left it on the hearth last Saturday night & it got burned so I had to ravel it out to save the red. It hurt my eyes to crochet at night so I finished it today. No news from Mr. Henry. I nearly made Zona a night cap tonight, pointed it.

Thursday 14th - Jinnie scoured my room & Harrie's room today. I worked Zona a night cap today with turkey red. It looks very nice. I hope to hear from Pinck by tomorrow's mail. I would like so much to hear he was well & well satisfied. I hope Mr. Henry is well. May a kind Heaven protect him I pray.

Friday 15th - I received two letters from Dora & one from Harrie. I was very glad to hear from my dear little child. They were all well. Harrie took Pinck to Columbia with him. Eugenia put some little trinkets in Pinck's shoe. I thank her very much for remembering my little boy's shoes as Mother was not there to do it for him. They got to Columbia the 24th & went up to Pa's the 28th on Monday Dec. 1863. They gladly welcomed my little child. My Field & Fireside came today. I hope it may come on regular as it has been stopped since Sept. on account of paper. Some soldiers stay here tonight. They say our men that went into Tenn. were taken prisoners. I am affraid it is true. If so, it will be a long time before Mr. Henry gets home. I hope 'tis not so yet fear the worst. Atheline & I fixed the rooms upstairs this morning. I then finished Zona's cap & began one for myself, working it with turkey red. It looks very nice. No news in the papers today.

W. H. (Harrie) Deaver to Cornelia C. Henry

Col. Jny 7th 1864

Dear Aunt,

    I have looked into every nook and cranny of Columbia that looked anything like scissors in search for a pair for you and I can not find a pr. even as good and as large as the ones you have. I will still keep an eye out & if I see any will be certain to get them for you.

    I think the property heretofore spoken of would bring over 4500$ in this market now. Property is very high. I suppose there is a fear of the money.

    It has been cold ever since I came down. It is freezing here today. I can't see what the poor do. Wood is 35$ a load. I tell you fives are small. Apples are 25 to 50 c. each. Eggs 2.00 dz. and other things about the same. We are all very well and Fanny can talk more than Zona and you know that is no little. Pinck poor little fellow I know you miss him & he must be well cared for indeed if he does not miss you. The cars run off the track the day after I came down from Union and smashed up generally. I am glad Pinck & I was not on it.

    There is no news here, rather a gloomy feeling in regard to the war. I hope the tories will leave you alone.

    My Love to all.

Affectionately,

W. H. Deaver

Saturday 16th January 1864 - This is Matt Tidwell's birth day, twenty today, so she says. I finished my cap today. It looks & fits very nicely. Aunt Patsey here today mightly distressed about our forces being taken prisoners. She heard that the Confederates had given up all Western N. C. She is greatly distressed about it. Old Presly made George a pair of shoes today. He will be back on Monday to make Fannie's & Atheline's. He cut out Aunt Patsey & Betsey some today. No further news of the prisoners. I have a right bad headache tonight but 'tis better since supper. I hope it may be well by morning.

    Sunday 17th - My head is nearly well. Preaching at the Academy today but I will not go for fear my head will ache again. I sent Charlie to Asheville with a note to Mollie Henry to hear the news. I hear this morning that Jim Henry & nine others made their escape. I do wish Mr. Henry could have been one among the number but I fear 'tis otherwise ordered. If he is a prisoner I hope he may be well treated, yes, just as well as I wish & he will be well cared for certainly. Willie is about well. Gus is fretful, cutting teeth I think. This is a beautiful day. I want to be out walking as we have had some of the coldest weather this winter we have had in a long time, none since 1856-57. The ground has not been thawed well for three or four weeks. Charly got back about 3 o'clock. Mollie wrote that Jimmie's command was not captured, only Gen. Vance & 150 of his men. They had taken a wagon train & the yanks recaptured the waggons & Vance & his men, so I think Mr. Henry is not a prisoner. Gen. Vance & a great many of his men made their escape. I hope 'tis all true. Oh! That God would grant us a speedy peace & let no more hearts languish in pain. Stay the wrath of Thy hand upon us as a nation I beseech Thee & nation will praise Thee, yes, turn our hearts to praise if we have sinned in Thy sight. Lead us to see our errors & help us turn from them for unto Thee alone can we look & hope for help in this, our time of need. Unto Thy kind protecting care do commit my husband. Watch over him & shield him from all harm. Keep us from all harm this coming week is my prayer.

Monday 18th 1864 January - I sewed some on my dress today. I made the sleeves, trimmed them with some dark goods & put buttons on the point at the back of the arm. I finished the waist & sleeves today. I put a dark coloured belt, like the sleeves. The mail brought no letter for this office tonight. I received a letter from Mr. Henry this evening. He was in Parrottsville, Ten. yesterday morning. I am so glad he is not a prisoner & I hope he may never be one.

William L. (Bill) Henry to Cornelia C. Henry

12th January
My own dear wife and children

We and the horses passed the top of the Smokey Mountains about 11 o'clock. The mountains are lightly covered with snow. A great deal of ice in the road and fords on the branches & streams. No accident to any person or horse has happened since we left home. We are jolting along the stream. Have much ice all day Sunday. We have had very little feed for our horses. I will write again tomorrow or some other day.

14th I did not write anything to you yesterday. I was prowling around about 16 miles from Sevierville. My company on picket last night, all but five men who were sent to hunt J. L. Henry as he did not come to Tenn. He came in about 10 o'clock last night but the men sent to communicate with him did not find him and are out yet 3 o'clock in the evening.

General Vance took about 100 horsemen & went to Sevierville & captured about 19 Yankey waggons and teams & drivers and two negroes and was trying to run them to the mountains in the direction of Cosby. I saw the men who were present at the capture. Jimmy broat in twenty odd horses & mules. We have played smash if we can get away all sound. Our scouts are now looking for the enemys. I do not expect a fight in this locality, of any moment we may skirmish a little but not a regular hand to hand tilt. I think the enemy are too busy to look to little things and are closely watched by Longstreet so it will not surprise me, either a fight or no fight.

This 14th is a beautiful day and the ice is thawing a little. Yesterday was a little cloudy and warm but not so warm as this day. It did not thaw much yesterday.

I will tell you how the waggons and artillery down this mountain. The horses were unhitched & everything turned loose. Artillery went over the ice and snow and did not break anything or lose anything of any account.

Near Parrotsville, Tenn.
Sunday morning 17th Jany.

General Vance is certainly a prisoner & some men I do not know. Five men of my company are, I expect, among them. They were sent to carry a dispatch to Genl. Vance.

I and Co. B. are in good health and spirits and would like to see home and it's comforts. Oh that I was at home this Sunday to roll about with my wife & babies as I once did, as I always do when at home (Dear word). We were in the hearing of cannon all day yesterday. Please give the bearer a good dinner or something nice to eat. I have some of the bread & meat you cooked for me & I will only eat when I need it.

We are camped in one mile of Parrottsville & will go to church this day if permitted. I now see the church steeple.

Write to Pinck & tell him & my children of their father's love for them. Remember the poor soldier. Work on mill dam & keep a warm & cheerful heart. Never despair. Longstreet is in 6 miles of Knoxville, west of Smokey mountain, on the road from Webster to Sevierville Tenn..

I want to see you. Good bye my Dear Wife & Dinah & ten thousand kisses to my wife.

Bill Henry

Tuesday 19th - I finished my dress this evening & put it on. It fits beautifully. I trimmed the bias seams at the sides with buttons. Matt made nearly all the skirt last night. This has been a very cold day, high winds from the North. We eat dinner by a candle as the wind blew in the dining room so. Old Presley is making shoes here, will get done this evening.

Wednesday 20th - More pleasant today than yesterday. No wind & warm & bright all day. Sister Jane sent Paddy horse. She has had him near a week to mill on. I made some bolster cases longer this morning. Made myself an apron & sewed some on one for Willie. No news from Mr. Henry. I would like so much to hear from him. I can only pray for his safety & leave him in the hands of my Heavenly Father. He doeth all things well.

Thursday 21st - Matt & I went to Asheville today. I spent the day very pleasantly at Sister Jane's. I called at Mrs. Jessie Smith's & Mollie went with me down to Sister Jane's. Mrs. Smith sent the horse down. I left Matt this evening unintentionally. She was very angry when she came home. Tom Tidwell came here this morning. He wants to see Mr. Henry. I wrote to Harrie tonight, also to Dora & Pinck. I am very tired.

Friday 22nd - I received a letter from Harrie this morning saying he could not find any scissors in Columbia such as I wanted. I finished Willie's apron & began a dress for Fannie's baby of the cloth Ruth Pettit brought home this morning, some they made for wool they got. Made 15 yds. of good cloth for 5 lbs. wool.

Saturday 23rd - I finished Mary's dress this morning & spent the day at Ham Cannon's. Mrs. Jamison is sick there. I took my knitting. I got home a while before sundown. Mr. Henry came this evening. We were all glad to see him. I was very glad. Home is not home with out him. Oh! that this war was over & my dear husband at home to stay, I would be so happy. I feel that we will be successful in the end. God grant us peace at an early day I pray.

Sunday January 24th 1864 - This is a spring like day, so pleasant. Matt has gone to Mrs. Green's to spend the week with Sarah Jane Kurkendol (Case, used to be). Hosea Linsey of Asheville has been here all day. He & Mr. Henry have gone down to Mrs. Fanning's now. I hope Mr. Henry will soon be back as I want to take a long walk with my dear husband this evening. I do wish this war was over & he at home. I wish Pinck was at home. I miss him so much. He is a good boy. Zona & Willie are both a little inclined to be stubborn & pout. It grieves me to see them so. Gus is a very good child. I must go & take him awhile now. Mr. Henry & I went up to hotel garden this evening. We met Ham Cannon up there. I left Mr. Henry & him & came down home. I met with Atheline & the children soon after leaving him. She head to the Spring & came back by the stables.

Monday 25th - I went with Mr. Henry to Asheville today. I spent the day very pleasantly at Sister Jane's. We left Asheville about 3 o'clock. It was nearly sunset when we got home as we rode slow. I never tire of being with my dear husband. I rode Matt & he the Well's horse. This has been a beautiful day, a real Spring day.

Tuesday 26th - I have been riding nearly all day with Mr. Henry. We first went to Capt. Moore's. Staid a short time and then to the Camp ground where the soldiers are. I suppose there was a hundred there. I did not get down. Mr. Henry staid but a short time. We then went to old Mr. Thrashes & got out dinner & then by Henry Hanes' to get some cotton but he had sold out. We came on back by Russell L. Jones & then home about sunset. I enjoyed the day finely because I was with Mr. Henry. Very pleasant today. I forgot to say, we went to old Billy Penly to see about getting a wheel. Mr. Henry has the promise of a spooling wheel & a reel.

Wednesday 27th - Mr. Henry at home all day. Charlie hauling manure in the garden. We had a nice turkey for dinner. Fayette Jones, F. M. Corn took dinner here. I can't bear Corn for I believe he had a hand in the burning of the hotel. He is mean enough for anything I think. I took Zona & Willie a short walk this evening. Branton, George & Fannie working at Mill dam.

Thursday January 28th 1864 - Mr. Henry went to the Camp ground today. They all leave there tomorrow. I am sorry of it. I finished a dress for Gus today that I began yesterday. Eliza Neilson & young Martin spent the day here. Pres Jones & Mag Morris were here a short time this evening. I had Mr. Henry's & Tom Tidwell's rations cooked this evening. I am so sorry to see my dear husband go. Oh! that this cruel war would cease is my prayer.

Friday 29th - Mr. Henry started about 9 o'clock. I was very sorry to see him go, not knowing when he will return to his comfortable home. I made myself a cape today like my lapped dress. It fits neatly. I cut some collars (three) this evening for myself, sewed some on one. Mr. Henry received a letter from Pinck last Monday. We were very glad to hear they were all well at home & that my dear child was well satisfied. May a kind Heaven protect my dear boy & may he enjoy life till a good old age. Kind Heaven protect my dear husband in his wanderings I pray.

Saturday 30th - Mr. Henry wrote to Pinck yesterday before he left. Tom T. came back today as he could not get a bridle or saddle in Asheville. The command left Asheville about 12 o'clock yesterday. Mollie Henry came out to the farm today but did not come down as Jim is in Asheville & she wanted to stay all she could with him. I re-covered Pinck's & Zona's stools this evening. Willie claims Pinck's now. I fixed some cushions in two chairs in my room & finished my collar today.

Sunday 31st - I went to Sardis to a quarterly meeting today, took Zona. Charly drove the buggy. Heard a very good sermon from the P. E. Taylor. I was quite sick with headache all the evening. A little cloudy today but pleasant. Hanes went after Matt today. She came this evening.

February 1864

Monday Feb. 1st & Tuesday 2nd - I was very unwell all day yesterday with my head & only knit some. I sent some wool to Ham Cannon's yesterday for him to exchange for cloth or thread at the factory. He starts today. I made one collar today & began another. I bound one with pink gingham, put tape trimming on one & bound one with yellow gingham. I went to H. Cannon's this evening to see Mrs. Jamison who is very low with typhoid fever. 8 o'clock high, North wind, cloudy & turning cold fast.

Wednesday February 3rd 1864 - I finished my collar this morning & hem stitched a little frill for the neck of Zona's dress & cut Zona a calico dress this evening & sewed some it. Made yoke neck & infant waist, 'tis some calico I have had sometime. I had a dress like it some five years ago & it is what was left of mine & Sister Matt's dresses as she had one like it. Cool this morning but bright & pleasant. Tena & Atheline fixing a piece of jeans for the loom. Mrs. Fanning will weave it here. She is owing Mr. Henry some.

Thursday 4th - I finished Zona's dress this evening. It fits neatly. Sam has got all the onions & buttons planted, about a bushel of buttons. He & Hanes are making krout today, will not finish before tomorrow. Mr. Branton, George, Fannie & Charlie at work at the dam, will have it done in a week or so. The militia is called out again as the tories & yanks have made a raid to Franklin in Macon Co. 'Tis reported they are advancing on Asheville. I hope it is not so. I have not heard one word from Mr. Henry. I hope he safe & well. I hear the yankees captured a part of Thomas' Legion & killed a good many of his Indians. I don't give much credit to the report as we hear so many things. Mrs. Fanning warped the cloth today & beamed it. I received a letter from Matt & Pinck last Monday. I was glad to hear Pinck was well & satisfied. May kind Heaven watch over my child & protect him &

may Heaven shield my dear husband & may he soon return to home in peace is my fervent pray Oh! Lord of love & mercy.

Friday 5th - Mail brought but little news. I received a letter from Eugenia saying Harrie was quite sick with a pain in one eye. I never expect to see him again. He seems so hopeful of being well again but he will die in the prime of manhood, I think. 'Tis sad to think one so young should be cut off in his bloom. I went to Asheville today, tried to exchange a tissue dress for calico but could not. I got two lbs. of soda for twenty dollars, four lbs. of sugar for twenty dollars & one card of agate buttons for two & a half dollars. I gave 4.50 last fall for a card of the same sort. I got some pants buttons, 50 cts. a doz., got 4 doz. I spent the day at Sister Jane's. I took Lonzo along as I took Sister Jane a coffee pot & some eggs. Late when I got home. The children, Zona & Willie & Matt with me at the stables. Zona & Willie rode down.

Saturday 6th February 1864 - I saw the cannon yesterday. They have it placed so as to sweep the bridge this side of Mrs. Cunningham's on the other side of the river. They were throwing up breast works. I hope it may be a false report about their advancing on Asheville. I called in at Mrs. Smith's yesterday in Asheville. She is scared good. I did not see Mollie. She was at her house packing up to leave Asheville. Big fraid was after them. I made Zona a long saque today, faced it round with red spotted flannel. It fits nicely. We have had rain & snow today but none of consequence on the ground. Some soldiers stay here tonight from Longstreet's command. They are very nice men from Georgia. Three staid all night & one other one eat breakfast. Their bill was $9.50. They seemed perfectly satisfied with it & seemed very grateful. They had a waggon along & corn & hay for their horses.

Sunday 7th - Cold & N. wind this morning. The snow nearly all gone, melting now 11 o'clock. The sun comes out occasionally but plenty of snow on the mountains. I would be so glad to hear from Mr. Henry. Oh! that this cruel war was over. I do hope & pray for peace most fervently. Surely the Lord will not turn a deaf ear to all the prayers of the South. I have written to Sister Lena & Sister Ell. Preaching at the Academy today. There has been quite a revival at Sardis. The meeting lasted till Friday night, had several to profess & a good many mourners. I hope they may hold out faithful for there is many out of the church yet.

Monday 8th - I made Willie a long saque today like Zona's. It fits very neatly. Trimmed it around with some pink flannel. Mrs. Fanning weaving today. Cold & windy. The mail brought no news of importance. Gus can push a chair all over the room. Willie can talk right plain.

Tuesday 9th - I went to Johnston's firm this morning to pay for some tin I had mended yesterday, & today I had Gus two napkin pins mended. Very cold going there as the wind was in my face. I took Zona behind me on John. Lonzo took the pans and other tin. Mr. Baker from Mr. Henry's Co. eat dinner here today. He brought me a letter from Mr. Henry. I was very glad to get it. He was well. I went to Jim Brook's this evening on business of Harrie's. Accomplished nothing by going. Pleasant this evening.

Wednesday 10th Feby 1864 - I cut Gus two aprons. One a calico apron, the first I ever made of calico for one of my children. The other a blue checked one,

Yankee checks. Made the calico one & nearly finished the other one. Sam & Hanes hanging the meat. Nothing new going on, all are well.

Thursday 11th - Mr. Henry came home last night. We were very glad to see him. He got here about 7 o'clock. Zona & I were sitting here by the fire. Matt in the hall room as usual. She does not stay with me when there is fire any where else. She is a strange creature. I finished Gus' apron today, mended the fingers of Mr. Henry's gloves. Had his clothes washed. I don't know when he has to leave. He & I went to see Mrs. Jamison this evening. She is getting better. We rode very fast going there. I rode Paddy & he the Well's horse. A soldier stays here tonight. Some three or four are camped near Mrs. Cook's on the road. I am so glad to have my dear husband at home again. I do hope he may get the gun stock contract & then he will leave the army. They put the water in the dam today to try it. It leaks some.

Friday 12th - Mail brought no news of importance. Mr. Henry at home till after dinner then went to G. W. Owensby's to get seed oats, is to send tomorrow after them. Quite pleasant today. Mrs. Fanning getting on very well with the jeans. Gus stood alone today for the first time, did not try to step. Willie can wash his face & hands very well. He will be three years old the 11th March. Gus one, the 8th & Zona five the 21st March. I have been mending socks for Mr. Henry today, marked his blanket in two places & made some soft ginger cake this evening. It is not nice at all. Two soldiers stay here tonight from camp by Mrs. Cook's.

Saturday 13th - Those soldiers that staid here last night were arrested about ten o'clock. I was frightened when the men came after them as I had just got to sleep. They all went off very quietly. They were arrested for taking Johnston's corn, pressing it. Mr. Henry & I went to Asheville today. I spent the day very pleasantly at Sister Jane's. Her family all well. Got home about sundown. He rode Willie & I Zona, down to the road opposite Mrs. Fanning's. She has not wove any today, washing & doing other things for herself.

Sunday 14th Feby 1864 - I rolled the cloth off the beam & cut some off for Pinck a pair pants off the first end. It is very nice jeans. I did not fix it back on the beam. Mr. Henry started to Pa's this morning, rode John. Cloudy & looks like rain. I fear he will get wet but hope he may have good weather. He will go to Col. before he returns. He only has 10 days to go & come. I do hope he may get a government contract. I tried to play on the piano at Sister Jane's yesterday. I have forgotten all about it. I am so sorry. I once played very well but 'tis all gone now. I scarcely know the notes. I am going to give Mollie another trial for her piano. I will give 1200$ for it if she will sell it. I am sorry I have forgotten. This cruel war, when will it end? Oh! that the Lord would grant us peace. Have mercy on us Oh! Lord. Stay Thy hand upon us as a nation & grant us peace I pray.

Monday Feby 15th - Rained nearly all day today. The mail brought no news of note. My little ones are all well. I made some pinafores for Gus today. Matt hemmed a frill for Zona's chemise. I cut two for her today of bleached domestic. Mrs. Fanning weaving today. She is making very nice jeans, better than any Betsey has ever made.

Tuesday 16th - I spent the day at Capt. Moore's. Daniel Moore has been very low with typhoid fever but some better now. I wrote to Mr. Henry from there by request of Dr. Neilson as he wanted Mr. Henry to bring up a horse his brother Charlie has at Pa's. I hope Mr. Henry may get the letter as he can bring Pinck home if he wants to come. I would be so glad to see Pinck, & Zona & Willie would be delighted. Zona & I were very cold this evening when we got home as the wind was very high. There has been some drunken soldiers here today, vomited on the floor in my room & stole Matt's comb. She just got it yesterday by Vic. He got it in Greenville at four dollars.

Wednesday 17th - I fixed the band of Zona's chemise today & sleeves. Sewed the frill in & began Mr. Henry a pair gloves in the evening. Matt will make Zona's chemise. Very cold today. I could not keep warm by the fire & we have very good fires. Fannie spinning. Atheline knitting, heeling the children some stockings. Nothing new going on in the country. Negro Jim Common set into work this morning at the same wages he did last year.

Thursday 18th Feby 1864 - I finished one of Mr. Henry's gloves today & began the other. I finished "Morgan's Raids & Romances" this evening. I have read it & knit. 'Tis very interesting. I don't like to knit at day but if I have anything to read I don't mind it. My little ones are doing very well. Gus will soon be walking. Willie is a very stout healthy child. He can talk nearly plain. Zona can begin to read a little in the first lessons in her primer.

Friday 19th - I received a letter from Harrie this morning. He is not so well. I am sorry to hear it. He has had erysipalus in the head. I have not heard from Pinck in two weeks. I expected a letter today from him. I hope my child is well. Nothing from Mr. Henry since he left. 'Tis rumoured the yanks have left Knoxville. I hope 'tis so. Warmer today than the two last days. Very cold yesterday & Wednesday. Ice 1/2 inch thick in the room & ice all day on the wash stand.

Saturday 20th - I finished the gloves yesterday evening & plushed part of one cuff last night. Finished them today. They are very nice. I hope they may please Mr. Henry. I put the band on Zona's chemise this evening. Mr. Cannon came here today. He exchanged my coarse wool for thread, got 4 1/3 bunches for 13 lbs. wool. The fine wool he brought back as he could not get it carded. Two soldiers dined here today, going to Longstreet. A good many waggons & soldiers passed today. They said a long train of waggons & about five hundred men are to come on tomorrow. I hope none of them may stop here. Some soldiers are so rude. Betsey was here today, says her mother is better.

Sunday 21st - Pleasant today, a little cloudy & has snowed a little. Not much. Willie was not at all well last night, has a sore tongue & said his throat pained him. I put some ointment on it & he does not complain of it today but his tongue is still sore. Wiley Knight moved last Thursday. I am glad they are gone. He is so lazy. Mr. Henry had Charlie to move old Mrs. Presley out of the store house last Sunday. She went to Johnston's farm & they sent her from there last Tuesday so she is now in the house with old Presley. She is no account at all. Zona & Matt gone to Mrs. Fanning's this evening. Willie sitting by me cutting a stick with my knife. Gus sitting on the floor & Rose playing with him. I hope Mr. Henry & Pinck will be at home by Tuesday. I bought all of Uncle Sam's chickens. He is affraid the passing soldiers will steal them. He brought them down last night. They did stay at the stables.

Monday 22nd Feb. 1864 - I worked some on the band of Zona's chemise today. Very pleasant today. No news of importance. I received a letter from Dora last night saying they were all well. Mr. Henry had not got there when she wrote. Mrs. Fanning got the cloth out today. Tena will fix another piece this week.

Tuesday 23rd - I finished Zona's band & sleeves today. Jinnie washing. Matt got our dinner. The negroes got none today. Atheline is not at all well, headache & pain in her side. Matt, Zona, Willie & I went to meet Mr. Henry this evening but were sadly disappointed as he did not come. Willie almost cried because we did not go on. It was nearly dark when we got back.

Wednesday 24th - I finished the chemise today & cut an apron for Zona. 'Tis brilliante & pointed with yellow. We went a short piece to meet Mr. Henry. The wind blew so hard we did not go far. Rather cool this evening. Matt is knitting me some gloves of single yarn. They will be very nice. They are a good deal of trouble.

Thursday 25th - I finished Zona's apron, all but facing around the neck. Mr. Henry came tonight just after we eat supper. He brought me several pieces of music, late music. He is a dear good husband. He got a knife for himself, gave 12$. A very good knife. We were all very glad to see him. He left Pinck well & satisfied. He took Pinck to Columbia with him. Pinck was delighted with his trip to the city.

Friday 26th - Mr. Henry & I went to Asheville today. He took the jeans, got 28 yds. of drilling for 7 yds. jeans & exchanged 26 yds. for 9 bunches of thread, three No. 8, 3 No. 9 & 3 No. 10. Sister Jane's family all well. Rose burnt Gus' hand today. I gave her a good thrashing for it. Mrs. J. Lusk stays here tonight. Mrs. Fanning helping spool today. They nearly got it ready to warp. I got a letter from Sister Frank this morning. They are all well. Very windy today.

Saturday 27th - I finished Zona's apron today & did some other little things. Some soldiers eat dinner here today. One stays all night. They were wounded, most of them in the arm. Mrs. Fanning warped & put the cloth through the harness. Mrs. Lusk left this morning, went to Mrs. Hutsell's. There has been several men here today to see Mr. Henry. 'Tis always so when he is at home, one continual string of men. I get awful tired of them.

Sunday Feby 28th 1864 - Smokey all day. Mr. Henry & I went up to the hotel garden this morning. I went down to see Betsey McKinnish. Louise has been sick but is up again. I left Mr. Henry talking to some men. I came back by myself as I did not see Mr. Henry. He came down soon after I got here. He swapped Paddy & the Wells' horse yesterday & got two mules. One a very large one. He some boot. Gus is not at all well. He frets a great deal. His hand pains him. I think the others are tollerable well. Willie a little unwell at night, worms I think. We gave him some vermifuge last Friday night. Since then, he has been better. Zona & Willie sleep on the trundle bed. Mr. Henry is asleep on the little bed. I do wish he could stay at home all the time. He is such a good husband. Oh that the Lord would hear our prayers & grant us peace. We have been sorely punished as a nation.

Monday 29th - I began fixing an old calico dress today. Did not finish it. Very pleasant. Mr. Henry started the ploughs today sowing oats. Nothing new going on.

I hope my dear husband will stay at home a while. Atheline & Matt are doing the cooking, dinner & supper. The mail brought no news tonight.

March 1864

Tuesday March 1st - Mr. Henry & I went to walk this morning up by the flax patch by the spring & then by Betsey McKinnish's & then to where they were plowing back of stables & got back about 10 o'clock. I finished my dress today. 'Tis open in front with facings in front. A soldier stays here tonight, also Cousin William Henry of Henderson Co. We have had some rain this evening. It is needed for small grain.

Wednesday 2nd - I began to plush Mr. Henry's tops of his gloves last night. The first ones are too small so I will take them & put others to his. He went to Asheville today. No news. Gus is not at all well, has a cold & very cross. The others are all well. Mr. Henry will start soon I fear. The command is in Jackson Co. He is ordered up.

Thursday 3rd - Tax collecting day. A good many people here. Dinner late after one. I finished mine & Mr. Henry's gloves today & put on some cotton knitting. Footing some cotton stockings for myself. Cool mornings & evenings but pleasant when the sun gets up. Cousin William H. still here. Gen. Martin's cavalry passed through Asheville yesterday. I wish I had been there to see them. Two soldiers stay here tonight.

Friday March 4th 1864 - Some rogue went into our smoke house last Tuesday night & took two sides of bacon. They drawed the staple. There is a great deal of stealing going on through the country by deserters. I think some one goes in the mill occasionally & takes what they want. We don't let any grain stay there. I made myself a linsey saque today, trimmed it (facing) with dark coloured flannel. It fits neatly. Gus still very cross. He cries every time I dress his hand. 'Tis getting well fast. I got all the missing No. of the Field &c. today. I will subscribe again soon. I wrote to the editor some two weeks ago telling him his paper was not coming regular so he sent me the back No.

Saturday 5th - I have done some mending today. Mr. Henry went to Asheville & Cousin William. An old friend of Mr. Henry's called here today for dinner & two other men. They are refugees from Ten. McBee was his name. He is badly crippled from fever falling in his leg when he was young. I sewed my papers together this evening. No news from Longstreet's army. Gus some better. Mr. Henry got some leather today at Rankin's tan yard, some nice goat skins. He got dinner at Sister Jane's today. They are all well. Mr. Neilson is at home. Cool and windy today. Betsey Jamison was here today, says her mother is very low, taken worse last Thursday. I am affraid she will never be well again. She has been very kind to me. I am sorry she is sick. Matt & Atheline made some molasses bread this evening & boiled a ham for Mr. Henry as he expects to start tomorrow but he says he will not go soon. He received other orders today from Hd. Qts.

Sunday 6th - Mr. Henry & Cousin William gone to church today at the Academy. Mr. Reynolds preaches. I want to go to see Aunt Patsey after dinner if they can get the horses up as they have been turned out. Matt will go with me. This is a beautiful day. Atheline sick this morning. I was quite unwell all day yesterday but some better today. My side pains me a good deal from my liver I think. Gus is crying so I will take him. Matt & I went to see Aunt Patsey this evening. I took Gus. He tired my arm a good deal. He was delighted with the ride. Aunt Patsey is some better. I hope she may get well. She said to me when I told her good bye "I wish I was well enough to go home with you." We took her a little lard.

Monday 7th March 1864 - I have mended up some burnt holes in my homespun dresses today & some other odds & ends. Cousin William went to Asheville this morning, did not get back till after dinner. Matt got dinner & supper as Atheline is sick. Mr. Henry went to hunt some of his men today. He will not be back before tomorrow. The mail brought no news of importance. Pleasant today.

Tuesday 8th to Thursday 10th - I have had a severe spell of headache Tuesday, in bed nearly all day & was no better Wednesday & not much better today till 10 o'clock. I suffered a great deal, nearly blistered my temples with mustard. Mr. Henry came home Tuesday evening. I was so glad to see him. He is so kind to me at all times & especially when I am sick. Sister Jane & Mr. Neilson were here a short time Tuesday evening. I scarcely know how Wednesday passed as I slept part of the day. Mr. Henry staid with me all day. Today I have felt a heap better since morning & this evening I am entirely free from headache but still feel weak. I have knit some today. I made up some flour dough for some of Mr. Henry's Co. this evening. There will be some 5 or 6 here for supper. Matt baked it. Fannie helped to get supper.

About 9 o'clock, Mr. Henry & the men started. They will be out all night hunting deserters. They go up Homeny Creek too as old Andey Bell marries tonight & the deserters are to give him a serenade. I hope they may all return safe.

Friday 11th - Matt & I sit up till near 11 o'clock last night. The wind blew very hard in the night about two. It frightened me. Two of the men that went off last night with Mr. Henry came here for breakfast this morning. Mr. Henry will be on soon, he stopped at Capt. Moore's. Atheline very unwell this morning, sent after Dr. Thrash, could not come then. After Neilson he could not come & then after Mrs. Anders. She came about 12 but the babe was born sometime before. A boy, very small. Mr. Henry came about 10. I cleaned upstairs & the smoke house this morning, did not finish the smoke house but Rose did. I heard this morning that Aunt Patsey died yesterday evening about sunset. I was surprised as I thought she was getting well. I am sorry she is dead. I hope she is at rest. I wanted to go there this evening but had nothing to ride as Nell is rode down & Mrs. Anders went home on John. This is Willie's birth day. He is three years old this evening at fifteen m. after six o'clock & Gus was born a year ago last Tuesday 8th at 23 m. after 8 o'clock in the morning (Sunday) & Willie was born on Monday. Zona was born the 21st of this month, on Monday 25 on after 9 o'clock on Monday 1859. Cora was born ten m. after three Nove. 17th Tuesday 1857 in the evening & died Sept. 10th, 25 m. of 9 o'clock in the morning Friday 1858, aged 9 months & 23 days. I thought my heart would break when I seen my baby was dead. Oh God may I never have to have another such a trial but He doeth all things well. I felt it then & do now. Our eldest born, Pinck, come into this beautiful world 20th July 5 m. of

12 o'clock in the morning, Sunday 1856. He will be 8 years old in July. I am getting very anxious to see Pinck. He is a dear good boy. I had a letter from Lou last Monday. She has a fine daughter, weighed 12 lbs. at its birth, born 10th Jan. 1864. She is very proud of her babe. The mail brought but little news this morning.

Saturday 12th - I doubled some cotton stocking yarn this morning. Matt sit up at Ham Cannon's. She says Aunt Patsey looks very natural. We went to her burying soon as we got dinner. Willie & Zona went also. A good many people there. Till Morris came home with us this evening. She went home late this evening. We got here about 3 o'clock. Tom Morris came on with Mr. Henry about 4 o'clock. Tom Cook brought Willie's & Zona's shoes today. They are very nice. Willie was needing his shoes badly. An old man named Young stay here tonight from Transilvania. Very pleasant today.

Sunday 13th - High winds today. Atheline doing finely. Gus can take a few steps alone. He is a dear sweet child. He is out somewhere with Rose. Mr. Henry is sitting reading the news to Branton. He has Willie in his lap asleep. Zona is out at play. I paid Sam nearly all for his chickens tonight. I got 31 of him. Poor Betsey. I sympathise with her. She has lost her best friend. She takes it very hard. May God temper the wind to the shorn lamb. I staid in the house all day. Mr. Henry took a long nap after dinner. Aunt Tena's Elvira came to see her yesterday evening. She is a good negro. I wish she was mine.

Monday 14th - I made Jim a shirt today. I went with Mr. Henry up to the hotel garden after dinner. He went to the Murray place. I came on home. Rose took Zona, Willie & Gus to the Sulphur Spring this evening & came back by Betsy McKinnish's. I have a cold & feel badly. Lonzo & I cleaned out the cellar today & fixed some hen's nest in there.

Tuesday 15th - I made an under body with sleeves today for myself. I feel very badly this evening as my head aches. 'Tis from my cold I think. Mr. Henry at home about the farm all day. They are sowing oats. Matt does the cooking.

Wednesday 16th & Thursday 17th – My head ached badly all day yesterday. I was in bed part of the day. I sewed a little on my under body & finished it today. Mr. Henry went to Asheville yesterday & today, also Col. Ray is selling off. I have made two towels today since I finished my under body & wrote some letters. One to Sister Frank, one to Lou & one to Stockton & Co., proprietors of Field & Fireside. I sent 8$ to Stockton for the paper. Fayette Jones got some leather here this evening to make a pair boots. He has gone to have them cut now & will return the leather that is left. Billie Cook is here waiting for Mr. Henry. 'Tis supper time so I will stop this time.

Friday 18th & Saturday 19th - I was sick again yesterday all day with headache. I took a nap after dinner & it felt better. Capt. Thrash got our bacon today. He took some beef also (dried). He is to give 2.25 a lb. for bacon & 90 cts. for beef. 'Tis a fair price I think. Old Mrs. Lance was here today wanting to get off a 100$ bill she had as she don't want to fund it & all money above 5$ bill has to be funded by first of April or lose 33 1/2 per ct on the dollar. Eliza Parker was here today. I had a letter from Pinck & Dora last Wednesday. He was very well. I have done sundry mending today. I did nothing at all yesterday as I felt so badly. Mr. Henry received a letter from Harrie yesterday. He is not improving any. I had a letter from Eugenia in it. She says Harrie is failing very fast, getting very feeble. She seems very uneasy about him. I parched some coffee this morning, cleaned the silver & other things.

Sunday 20th March 1864 - Pleasant but a little windy this morning. Goodlake was here this morning after some government flour as Morgan's men are to pass through Asheville tomorrow. I hope none of them may come this road, they are such rogues. Mr. Henry & I will go over in the wheat in the Joe Green field. He thinks 'tis nearly all froze out. If so, I don't know what we will do for flour another year. The children are out at play. Gus is not improving any in walking. We have turnip salad for dinner & dinner will soon be in. Mr. Henry went off with some men soon after dinner so we did not take our walk. He went in the wheat. It is nearly all froze out. I fear the people will suffer for bread. God grant us peace & bread.

Monday 21st - I cut some pillow cases today of drilling. Made one pair & fixed the warp of the fringe. I intend to fringe both pair. The mail brought no news tonight. Seven cavalry soldiers stay here tonight. The upstairs is full. Several of Mr. Henry's Co. stay here tonight as they go to hunt some deserters in the morning. Mr. Henry went to Asheville today. No news.

Tuesday 22nd - Snow four inches deep this morning when we got up. It continued to snow till 12 very fast. About 9 or 10 ten inches deep. Mr. Henry & others went to hunt P. Allen this morning, saw nothing of him. He got back about 2 o'clock tired out as they walked & the snow was so deep. I have done but little at my fringe today. Mr. Henry in the house all the evening.

Wednesday 23rd - I finished one pair pillow slips today. Mr. Henry & some of his men out tonight hunting deserters. They started at 1/2 past 7. I hope none of them may get hurt. Old Mr. Burgin was here a short time tonight. He came after his wheat that is here. He sleeps at Mrs. Fanning's tonight. T. Taylor is at work here. He stays here at night.

Thursday 24th - Mr. Henry & the men got home about 1 o'clock. They were very cold. I made fringe for a pair pillow cases today. The snow nearly all gone off the south side. Mr. Henry at home all day. No news of any importance. Gus is improving a little in walking. He tries to talk. He is a sweet child, goes about talking. He looks like a gosling as he talks about as plain as me. I had a letter from Harrie last Monday. He has got us 11 lbs. coffee for 100$.

Friday 25th March 1864 - Snowed again last night but melted nearly as fast as it fell. Mr. Henry left here yesterday evening hunting deserters again. He came home this evening. They took two men to Asheville this evening. Mr. Henry did not go as I am quite unwell with headache. Millie Jones spent the day here today. She came to swap horses with Mr. Henry. He let her have old Nelly & got 5 1/2 yds. jeans & 35$ to boot. A good trade for him as I think the horse he got from her is better than Nelly. 'Tis a mare. I finished the pillow slips this morning. My head pains me badly tonight. Snowed some today. Melting now at 8 o'clock very fast.

Saturday 26th - My head has pained me a good deal today but better this evening. It ached all night last night. I have knit a little today & parched some coffee since dinner. Mr. Henry had Jinnie to get me a nice bunch of ham, batter cakes, biscuits & coffee. I eat a good deal as I have eat nothing of note since yesterday. Newton Creasmon stays here tonight. He belongs to Mr. Henry's Co. Sgt. Lance left three horses here yesterday. They are sent back from Cherokee (the command). They are going to dismount them. They are taking up deserters out there. Mr. Henry sent Hanes & Lonzo to Asheville today to get some oats he had got of Cains. Pleasant & warm, the snow going fast.

Sunday 27th - Warm, the snow melting rapidly. Mr. Henry will go out this evening after deserters again. I hope he may not get hurt. Two of his men are here now. They go with him. Dinner will soon be on so I will stop. I feel very feeble today. I have not been well for nearly four weeks. I think I miscarried yesterday three weeks ago. I have not been well in nearly 4 weeks. I fear I won't be again soon. Mr. Henry did not go out this evening as he is ordered to report at Asheville tomorrow. He went to R. L. Jones' this evening & sent a dispatch to J. L. Henry. He is in Clay Co. I think. Goodlake came to mill today for the army at Asheville. Margaret came with him & brought her two children. She looks badly. It was nearly sundown when they started back & dark long before they reached Asheville. Gus can walk all over the house & get up when he falls & can say Papa right plain. He is a dear sweet child.

Monday 28th March 1864 - Mr. Henry went to Asheville this morning & some of his men came home with him this evening. He brought no news. I made a pair drawers for myself today & wrote to Harrie, also to Sister Lena. I fear Harrie will not live long. Eugenia is very uneasy about him. I expected a letter from Dora & Pinck tonight but was disappointed sadly. But little mail came to this office tonight. Some soldiers stay here tonight of Mr. Henry's Co. They are nice genteel behaved men.

Tuesday 29th - I have done some mending of pillow slips today. Mr. Henry out nearly all day after deserters. Found none. Disagreeable all day, a cool rain. No news of importance. I am not at all well, blooding some, it gets worse every day. I must do something for it. Gus is delighted because he can walk. Willie has got to stammering a good deal in talking. I must try to break him of it. Zona is growing finely & learns her lesson only occasionally. She is not very fond of her book. I wish I could hear from Pinck. He is a good child. May Heaven protect him I pray.

Wednesday 30th - Finished the mending & cut a skirt for myself. Sewed some on it. I am not at all well today, worse than yesterday. Some of Mr. Henry's Co. came here tonight with a prisoner. They sleep in Harrie's room & lock the door tonight. Mr. Henry has been out all day, came in after we had eat supper, he & two others. They have been looking for Allen today but saw nothing of him. He lies in a cave I think. I do wish they would or could find him for he is always stealing something.

Thursday 31st - I finished my skirt before dinner & cut Mr. Henry a pair pants. I am still very unwell, feeble & no account generally. We have had a good deal of rain this week so Jinnie has done most of the cooking & Fannie spinning. No news of importance.

April 1864

Friday April 1st - Cool this morning. I don't feel any better. I have been taking teas all day & applying cold cloths & camphor. It helped me a little while & then 'twas as bad as ever. I finished the pants this evening. Mr. Henry went to Asheville today & consulted Dr. Hilliard. He gave him some tincture of iron to give me. I take some tonight. I hope it will help me. I would hate to leave my little children now for some one else to rear. I hope I may be spared to raise them. God grant my husband & myself long life to raise our children. Give us wisdom to raise them as seemeth good in Thy sight I pray.

Saturday April 2nd 1864 - I have been in bed part of the day but am a good deal better this evening. I hope I may get well soon. I have done nothing today, only knit a little. All the soldiers are gone & I am glad of it for the house has not been clear of them for a week till tonight. They are all nice men, genteel in their deportment. I received a letter from Dora yesterday saying they were all well. Pinck has learned to knit & Dora is learning him to write. I would be so glad if he could write. I had a letter from Eugenia also. Harrie was not improving any. Jennie wants me to get her ten yds. of white flannel made. I fear it will a bad time to get now as every one has made up their wool. Cool & cloudy this evening.

Sunday 3rd - Warm & bright today. Some of Mr. Henry's Co. been here today to report but all gone now. He is asleep in the room on the trundle bed, his place every Sunday when at home. Mr. Reynolds preached at the Academy today but none of the white folk went. Atheline's baby not well today. I think it ruptured as it looks like it. I am nearly well once again & I am very thankful of it. Willie is here by me trying to write & ruining the pen I think but he has to do something to keep him still. Matt & Zona have gone to the Sulphur Spring & taken Rose with Gus. I want to walk about some this evening so I must go & wake Mr. Henry up. We went up to the Spring & then up to Betsey McKinnish's. I am very weak but nearly well of some of my ailments. Matt had Zona & Rose & Gus up there. Willie went with Mr. Henry & I. We had quite a pleasant walk. I always enjoy a walk with Mr. Henry & the children.

Monday 4th - I mended some pants today & cut Gus a saque & nearly finished it. I stopped to write a letter to Pinck or I would have got it done. I face the saque around with a piece of plaid. Old Mrs. Parker stays here tonight. She had her house & everything she had burnt up yesterday. Poor old creature. I am really sorry for her. She has but few friends. I think the neighbors will give her something to live on. She has had a full share of trouble in this war. The mail brought no news of importance tonight.

William L. Henry to Pinckney Henry, Dora Smith Powell and Matt Smith

Sulphur Springs, N. C. 4th April 1864

My Dear Son & Sisters,
   I write only to say that we are all tolerable well at this time. Your Mother has been rather poorly for a month. She is I think better now

and I hope may remain better. The children Zona, Willie & Gus are hearty and doing well. I must tell you of the big snow, it was ten inches deep and now the big mountains are covered with snow. It looks pretty at a distance but oh the idea that is associated with the snow, the suffering of our brave troops and the suffering of our poor people and the suffering of cattle, hogs & other animals on account of the winter being so long and grass being slow in coming. I really think that some, a great many, of our poor will suffer & perish for bread in this country. Our crops are short and the winter has been the longest ever known, having frost the 18th of Sept. to kill all vegetables and grasses so from that time to this, cattle, stock of all kind has had to be fed.

I have been at home nearly all the time since I was down there. I am with thirty of my company to hunt up some deserters that are in the mountains & other bad men of our country that need watching & making them behave. There were three horses stole in this neighborhood two nights ago. One belonged to Mr. Newton Penland & two to Silas Morgan. Penland lived three miles & Morgan four miles from this place.

I have nothing of any importance to write. My people work only tolerable for the last two weeks. The snow has prevented all plowing which puts our farming a little late. My wheat froze out so bad that I have to plow it up. Oh! how I hate to lose a wheat crop.

Dora & Matt, are you coming up to the mountain country this summer? If so what time? Please answer in the affirmative. We would be glad to see you all. Tell Mr. Smith I must buy corn for my people. Wife will write a little on this page & close up the letter to our little son who is learning so fast. I wish I could stop in some night & see you knitting & making your abc's and see what a nice quiet boy you are. I know you are a good boy & doing as well as you can. I hope to get a letter from you soon. Has Mattie got over her trip "artu spun truck"!
I look for a letter soon.

I am as ever your Father & Brother,
Wm. Henry

Cornelia C. Henry to Pinckney Henry

My Dear little Pinck,
The mail will soon be on but I will write a little as Papa left this for me. Papa has told you all about the big snow. Atheline's baby is growing finely, about as big as a rabbit. She asks about you a heap of times. Let me tell you something. Gus can walk all over the house & not fall & when he does fall he can get up hisself. See I told you he would walk before you came home. He can say Papa right plain. He will run & meet you at the gate when you come & call you Pinck. Now see if he don't. He has got to fighting of late. He pulls Rose's wool good for her when

she don't please him.

Zona has grown a good deal since you left. She spells her lesson every day & Willie wants to spell too. They often speak of you & want to see Pinck come home. You must learn fast so you can read your paper when you come.

Tell Aunt Dora to send me the measure of your head. I want to have you a straw hat made by the time you come & tell her to send the measure of your foot to have you some shoes made to travel home in. I am affraid Mother can't come after you as Papa can't stay at home & if we all leave the soldiers & deserters will steal all we got. We will send after you next month I think. I would like to come so much but can't this time. Be a good boy.

Mother has been sick for a month but I am a good deal better now. I have not weaned Gus yet. Papa wants me to wean him. I am so lean. Love Aunt Dora & Aunt Matt. They are your Mother's sisters just like Zona is your sister. Be kind to them. They will love you for you are a good boy. Mother & Papa love you dearly. Knit me something & send in a letter so I can show it to Zona & Willie. Good bye. God bless you my dear child.

Your fond Mother

Zona, Willie & Gus send kisses to Pinck, Aunt Dora & Matt. Dora give my love to Pa. It seems he cares nothing for me.

Tuesday 5th - I finished Gus' saque today & began to put a body to my gown. Did not get it done. Mr. Henry & his men have gone to hunt Pinck Allen tonight. They intend watching his house for several days. He has so many friends, I fear they will not find him. Tom Cook stays here tonight. I had some rations cooked for the men this evening.

Saturday 9th April 1864 - I have suffered a great deal with my head in the past four days. I was in bed nearly all day Wednesday. Thursday it was a little better. I eat some dinner & I suffered a great deal that night. It was near 12 o'clock before I got to sleep. It really seemed my head would burst. Mrs. Snelson & husband spent the day here. Friday I was in bed nearly all day. Mr. Henry staid with me all day. He had a leather bottom put in the rocking chair yesterday for my comfort. He is the best husband in the world, so kind to me & my dear children. I hope I may live to raise them but I fear unless my health improves, I will have to leave them for some one else to raise. 'Tis a sad thought to me. I feel much better today. Sat up all day & knit some & finished my gown I began last Tuesday. Mr. Henry went to Asheville today & all his detail. They go to Marshall on Monday. I hope Mr. Henry will not have to go. The tories have been robbing some down there again. The men lay around Allen's house till Friday evening. Mr. Henry came home Wednesday when he heard I was sick. Rained all day yesterday. It seems we will not get much work done on the farm as 'tis too wet to plough. They are still sowing oats. We have had a great deal of rain in the last two weeks.

Sunday 10th - Wind from the North today. Cool. Peach blossoms getting out & the grass in the yard beginning to look green. Miss Ruth & Ellen Jones spent this day here. They are nice girls. Mr. Henry is asleep in my room. Willie & Zona at play. Matt, Ruth & Ellen out talking. My head feels unwell yet. I fear I shall have another attack. I am lean & feeble. Oh! that I could enjoy good health, I would be so thankful. We did not go to walk this evening. Matt & Zona went a piece with Ruth & Ellen. It was dark when they got back.

ENROLLMENT OF THE "RESERVE CLASSES."

CIRCULAR.

CH. EN. OFFICE 10TH CON. DIST., }
ASHEVILLE, April 14th, 1864. }

IN compliance with Circular No. 18, Conscript Office, Raleigh, N. C., April 6th, 1864, issued in pursuance of Circulars No. 13 & 14, Bureau of Conscription, Richmond, *all* White male persons between the ages of 17 & 18 and 45 & 50 years, are hereby requested to appear at the Court House of their respective counties on the 30th day of April, 1864, for Enrollment in the "Reserve Classes."

Such persons will present themselves to the Enrolling Officer should their names not be called, and be enrolled, otherwise they will be placed in "the general service."

All persons between the ages specified above will be enrolled and allowed to return home until orders are issued for their organization into Companies and Regiments.

All claims to exemption from service, on any general tour of the Enrolling Officer and Examining Board.

When companies have already been organized under the Act of Congress authorizing the Enrollment of this class of persons, the Captains thereof will immediately furnish this office with certified rolls of such Companies. No Volunteering will be allowed after the 30th inst., and officers elect furnishing Rolls will append a certificate on honor that no Volunteer has been received since the 30th April, 1864.

In counties where the Enrollment of this class has already been ordered, persons liable to Enrollment in said class will appear on the 30th instant, for Enrollment and also on the days previously appointed for the General Enrollment for Examination by the Medical Board, and the investigation of all claims to Exemption.

J. H. ANDERSON, CAPT.
and En. Officer, 10th Con. Dist., N. C.
April 21, 1864.

Conscription order for all males
between ages 17-18 and 45-50
The Asheville News, April 21, 1864

Monday 11th - Mr. Henry at home all day. The hands still plowing in oats. they are at work in the field up here above the house. Our flax needs taking up but it has rained nearly ever other day for two weeks & it is too wet. I have fixed Gus a gown today of old stuff & went up to the top of the hill this evening after Willie. He went up there with his Papa. He would not come down with me. Mr. Henry & two men came down soon after I did. One man stays here tonight. The mail brought no news of importance. Capt. Tom Candler & his men were turned back from Greenville S. C. They started to join Morgan. They are to be conscripted so rumor says.

Tuesday 12th April 1864 - I made another gown for Gus today of old stuff. It will last awhile & such times as these we have to make everything count that will. Mr. Henry does not have to go to Asheville for a few days. He went to Asheville today. No further news from Laurel. I do wish we could once again have peace. We surely would do better than we did before this war but I fear that day is still far distant. God grant us peace I pray.

Wednesday 13th - I have done some mending today. Mrs. Fanning is here helping to spool a piece of cloth, mine & Matt's dresses. 'Tis one & one of pine bark dye & pale copperas. A crazey woman was here today named Rogers from Haywood Co. She has some sense, not much though. Mr. Henry at home today. I wish he could stay all the time.

Thursday 14th - I got a hat of Mary Tutt yesterday evening for Willie, gave two dollars for it. Mary spent the evening here. I knit some yesterday evening on Mr. Henry's cotton sock. I began it last Monday evening. Mrs. Fanning warped & beamed the cloth yesterday evening & put some of it in the harness. Mr. Henry went to Asheville today & sold the jeans. 40 yds. at 16$ a yd. A good big price. No further news from Marshal. A big battle is expected to come off before Richmond in a short time. I hope we may be able to whip them successfully & may that be the last one is my earnest wish. I began to piece up a quilt today of old dresses, mine & the children's. Mrs. Fanning got the cloth started today. It does not make good cloth as it is too light in the sley.

Friday 15th - I was sadly disappointed this morning in not getting a letter from Pinck, but little mail this morning. Rain all day. Mr. Henry had some cherry scions set out in the yard today. He got them of Mrs. Quinn. He had a good many grafted scions set out yesterday in the garden. I hope they may grow. Mr. Henry speaks of resigning. I would be so glad if he would, then he could stay at home all the time. I worked some on my quilt today. Mrs. Fanning getting on very well with the cloth, 'tis very fine & nice. I fill some quills occasionally. My little ones are doing finely. Zona does not like to learn her book much. I don't hear her spell, only occasionally as I don't want her to get a distaste for it. Willie stammers some in talking. I hope he will out grow it. Gus can walk any where & can go & shut the door. Oh! so smart a child is seldom seen.

Saturday 16th April 1864 - I sewed some on my quilt today. Mr. Henry went to Asheville today & says he has to go to the Mouth of Ivy tomorrow, 'tis about 18 miles from here. This has been a day of all sorts of weather. This morning fair & then cloudy & after dinner, cold & blowing snow. A very unpleasant evening. Mrs.

Fanning warped a piece of cloth this evening for herself. I fear this cold night will kill all the peaches, if not apples. Mr. Henry has had some of the fruit trees pruned about the yard & garden. We had some beans & beets planted this week. I do wish the weather would turn warm so vegetation could grow. Our wheat is no account at all, froze out. I fear we will need bread next summer before corn comes. One of Mr. Henry's men stay here tonight. Some one stays in the mill every night as P. Allen has threatened to burn it. He is a bad man & I wish he was out of the country.

Sunday 17th - Mr. Henry started about one o'clock today. I had some crackers & molasses bread cooked this morning & some ham fried & then had him a nice kid ham for his dinner & a nice cup of coffee & other things. George killed that little white goat Friday. It is very nice meat. Fayette Jones goes with Mr. Henry today. Stimp Case eat dinner here. He started off with Mr. Henry. I hope Mr. Henry may be back soon. May a kind Providence take care of my dear husband whilst he is gone. Spare his dear life I pray. Matt & I took the children & went up to the Spring & then up by Mrs. McKinnish's. We did not stay long. Very windy this evening. I fear all the peaches are killed. I hope Mr. Henry got along well. Kind Heaven protect him & spare his dear life I pray & may the same kind Father watch over my dear little Pinck & bless him with content.

William L. Henry to Cornelia C. Henry

Marshall, April 17th 1864

Dear Wife,
    I write to let you know that the war is progressing very well. Nobody scared nor no person hurt.
    Maj. Erwin is sending off his various companies in several directions. I go with him. I am ordered to be ready at any minute. I have been out on picket one night. I can only describe picket duty by saying a party goes to a place and stays to prevent passing, or passing either way. I was not cold the night of picket. I was out yesterday and found the cabin at which Knight & Morris was shaved. I will tell all about it.
    I am as ever, yours. To the children, remember me & to your self all the love of your husband.
Wm. Henry.

Monday 18th - I have sewed on my quilt today. Fayette Jones came by here this evening from Mr. Henry. He left him at the camps, two miles this side of Marshal at the Mouth of Ivy on the state road. He was well. Fayette came back after the muster rolls. He goes back in the morning. Mary Moore was here this morning. She got a lb. of fine wool to make hats & is to pay coarse wool in return. She only staid an hour or two. Mrs. Fanning gets on very well with the cloth. Matt & I fill most of the quills. I was disappointed tonight in not getting a letter from my dear little Pinck. I do hope he is well. No news of importance tonight.

Cornelia C. Henry to William L. Henry

Monday night April 18 1864

My own dear husband,

I send all the papers I know anything of. I hope they may be the ones. Yesterday was a long, long evening after you left. You know time lags mightly with me when you are gone, especially on Sunday. I took the children & went to the spring but did not enjoy the walk, as if you had been along. I miss you so much. How I wish you were at home & the war over so you could stay all the time. I would be the happiest creature in the world, I know. I do hope you will soon return home to stay.

I have nothing of importance to write but thought I would have a little confab with you tonight on paper. We have had some rain today. The hands have been taking up flax & plowing.

Stimp Case came by this evening & says the tories & our folks had a little brush on Spring Creek yesterday. He said the woods was full of tories & he could not get across after your horse. I expect big fraid was after him. I will send you all the papers that came tonight. I did not get a letter from Pinck but expected one. I send you some paper. If you stay any time, write to me often. You know your letters are highly prized by your Dina.

Well Papa, 'tis nine o'clock & I am still up. Better be in bed, I think I hear you say "You will not be up for breakfast in the morning." Yes I get up right soon & do about generally.

Mr. Henry, don't you want your oil cloth? I fear you need it tonight as the ground is so wet. I am tempted to send it by Mr. Jones. If you want anything, let me know. My absorbing wish is to have you at home. Come as soon as you can. Yes I know you will do that. The children sent a good night kiss to Papa & ask God to take care of him. May a kind heaven watch over you & protect you is the prayer of your loving wife, Dina

A heap of sweet good night kisses from me. I will give them to you when you come. Yes a bushel of 'em.

Tuesday 19th April 1864 - I have sewed some on my quilt today. I wrote to Mr. Henry last night & sent it this morning by Fayette Jones. He passed about 11 o'clock today. I had a letter from Mr. Henry this evening. He was well & thought he would be at home this week. He sent a fine stable horse home this evening, also some seed corn, an early sort. Lt. Posey is to bring his horse home (John). Matt is still cooking.

Wednesday 20th - I have nearly finished my quilt. I did but little to it after dinner as my head ached. I knit & read Falkner. 'Tis an old book of Mrs. Rachel Miller's but very interesting. I have heard nothing of Mr. Henry today. I have one hen with 16 little chickens. She had more but they have died. I have several hens sitting & one turkey.

Thursday 21st - My head ached till dinner but I finished my quilt & then had a nice cup of coffee for dinner & it relieved my head. I have quilled some this evening & knit & read some. Zona & Rose have been trying to learn to sew today. Zona does very well to be so small. Willie wants a needle too to sew & Gus plays about generally. They are a lovely set of jewels.

Friday 22nd - This is a beautiful day & so was yesterday. It looks more like Spring than any days we have had lately. We have had a very wet Spring so far. I fear we will need rain this summer. The apple trees are putting out & peach trees in full bloom but the woods look like the dead of winter. I think a few such days as this will start things to growing. I received a letter from Sister Frank this morning. They were all well & Pinck too. Mr. Henry sent two small oxen home yesterday. Charley Presley brought them. Mr. Henry was well when Charlie left. He left last Tuesday.

Saturday 23rd - I planted my moss this morning. A little cloudy today. I finished Falkner, also Mr. Henry's sock (cotton) & began to foot a pair woolen ones. I also twisted some sewing thread this evening & doubled some. Mrs. Fanning got out the cloth before dinner, 33 1/4 yds. I will make me two dresses, I think. Matt has one dress on the piece & then some for Willie & Pinck some pants. Mrs. Fanning warped the piece for the negroe's pants, 25 yds. Louise McKinnish will weave it. I have parched some coffee tonight & Matt knit for me. 'Tis raining now at 9 o'clock. The children are all asleep. No one here tonight but Matt, I & the children. May Heaven protect us & Papa & Pinck.

Sunday 24th April 1864 - Rained all night & nearly all the morning till now at 11. Turning cooler. I expected Mr. Henry yesterday but he did not come. I will keep looking for him till he does come. Betsey McKinnish is here. She has just told Matt that her mother is very sick & wants her to come & see her. If I was Matt I would not go. She has not treated her as a child & I would let her alone. May she be a better woman than her mother is my wish.

Monday 25th - I cut Willie two pair pants this morning, got one pair done & then fixed up the mail. We are all very well. Atheline's breasts are but little better yet, she is very feeble & I fear will never be stout again. Her babe grows some but very small yet. I received a note from Sister Jane today. She sent Billie after some peaches & some sage. Her children are very well. She wrote me that Dora was married on the 12th ult. to Capt. J. M. Powell. I hope she has made a good choice for she is a dear good sister. I hope he make her happy. I feel confident she will be a good wife. That leaves Matt very lonely if she does leave home. May she be contented is my wish.

Tuesday 26th - I received a letter from Sister Frank last Friday saying Pinck was well. I have not had one from Dora in three weeks. I suppose marrying has so engrossed her mind, she has forgotten her friends. I made Willie a pair pants today. Rose has been cleaning up the yards this week. The grass is very green & the apple trees begin to show their bloom a little yesterday & today have been beautiful Spring days. I can scarcely stay in the house. The warm sunshine & green grass seem so inviting. Mull brought me a letter from Mr. Henry this evening. I was very glad to hear he was well. They are still at the Mouth of Ivy doing nothing in the way of fighting. He will be at home soon.

William L. Henry to Matt Smith and Dora Smith Powell

Camp 14 N. C. Cavalry
Mouth of Ivy, N. C.
April 26, 1864

My dear Sisters Mattie and Dora,
    I have nothing that will interest you to write, only the continued bad news from East Tennessee. The tories and bad men of that section are having everything their own way and theirs is a reign of terror. A man came through our lines a day or two ago and tells of the horrors of that devoted region. I understand that but a few real Yankee soldiers are in that country, not over three or five thousand, and a few native tories in Yankee service. Several of the best citizens have moved out and many are paying dearly for their temerity in remaining in their homes and trying the Yank reign of terror again.
    This mountain is terribly perplexed by the almost constant raids of the enemy in our different sections of Western Carolina. Several horses have been stole and houses robbed in these raids. The road on this river has suffered a great deal. The tories have robbed Mr. Garrett's house once or twice. The Warm Springs Hotel has been deserted by the Rumbeau family, they having moved over about Rutherford County. Barnett's, Gudger and Smith have all left the road. Thus all the people have forsaken the river from Paint Rock to Alexander's except a few at Marshall. The tracks of the waggons have all washed out and it is with caution that you approach each turn in the road not knowing whether you meet a friend or your death by a Tory sentinel. Mattie and Dora write to your brother and let me hear the news.

Wm. Henry

Wednesday 27th - I made Willie a drawer body today & did some other little jobs & cut my dress in the evening & sewed some on it. I went to Betsy McKinnish's this evening to learn how the cloth was doing, 'tis too thin. Sleyed it, will have to be cut out & put in another sley. Zona went with me. Betsey is planting potatoes in the hotel garden on the shares, we got half. Betsey says the Hendrix women & Hannah Cook drove my turkeys up in the woods in front of her house this evening & then in a few minutes she heard four guns & this evening the big gobbler & young black one is missing. Tom Hendrix, a rogue, killed them.

Thursday 28th April 1864 - I sewed some on my dress today. No news from Mr. Henry. I hope he is well. Matt is making her dress this week. She still does the cooking. Taylor started to Mr. Henry yesterday. I sent him some clothes & some molasses bread & wrote a long letter to him. He richly deserves all my love. He is the best man in the world I think. May heaven protect him I pray.

Friday 29th - I received a letter by hand from Mr. Henry this morning, also his saddle bags & dirty clothes. He is very well & will be at home by the 5th of May. I will try to wait patiently till then. Mrs. Hutsell was here a while this evening. I finished my dress this evening. It has cuffs of a dark stuff, also belt & pockets trimmed of the same & the buttons up the skirt. It fits beautifully. Betsey McKinnish got another sley today of Mr. Norman to weave my cloth in. I think this one will do. I wrote a few lines to Mr. Henry this morning by Mull, telling him about Hendrix killing them.

Alexander's Inn, located on the French Broad River along the Buncombe Turnpike. Photo from "Land of the Sky, Beauties of Western North Carolina," published by Taylor and Jones.
(North Carolina Collection, Pack Memorial Public Library, Asheville, NC)

William L. Henry to Cornelia C. Henry and children

Mouth of Ivy
28 April, 1864

My own dear Wife and Babies,
 I rec'd your very kind letter of yesterday by Taylor. I was glad to hear that you were all well. I will be at home for a few days in a short time as I have been one of the Court Martial to convene in Asheville on the 2nd May and will be able to stay at home at night until I hear from my resignation.
 I have the least news to write, not the least thing in the world to write of. Mrs. Black went down the river yesterday on the way to Kentucky. She had a negro man, two mules and a (barouch?). I wonder what is the matter? I really fear she will be robbed of all her effects before she passes the Warm Springs and that she will come back without anything but her baby. I think it is the extreme of folly for her to go. A "screw loose, I trow!" I think Mr. Black will follow.
 I will write you a few lines in a day or two. Ten thousand kisses to the wife and children of
Wm. Henry

Saturday 30th - I have felt badly all the morning. My back pains me a good deal, also my side. I have done nothing today. I think I shall take a nap this afternoon.

May 1864

Sunday May 1st - I lay down yesterday evening & did not get up again as I had a severe headache & all night & till after dinner today. Mr. Stepp of Mr. Henry's Co. was here this morning. Mr. Henry sent me two nice fish by him. Stepp left him yesterday evening. He was quite well & will be at home on the 5th as he is on a Court martial to convene that day. I will be so glad of it. I do hope his resignation may be accepted & then he can stay at home. Stepp took off the Stallion. Mrs. Corn got her filly last Monday that was here. Mrs. Fanning came up & spent the day with me today as Matt went to Steph Jones'. Mrs. Fanning & I & the children went up to old Betsey's this evening to see the cloth. I think it will do in that sley. The children got some lilac flowers this evening. They are not full bloom yet. They got some cherry blooms too. The apples will be in full bloom in a day or two. I don't think the apples are injured much yet but the peaches are nearly all killed I fear. Ruth Jones came home with Matt this evening. She stays here tonight. She is a very pleasant lady. Matt lost her keys today. She will go in the morning to hunt them.
 Monday May 2nd 1864 - Very windy today. Zona went with Matt & Ruth this morning to hunt her keys. Mrs. Dr. Hilliard sent some cotton here today to ex-

change for chickens. I sent her ten chickens for ten pounds of cotton. I have done nothing of note today. I will do some mending this evening I think & perhaps spin a little. The hands planted the sugar cane last week & the forward corn Mr. Henry sent home. Matt & Zona got back just after dinner. She did not find her keys. She had my big scissors Saturday evening & we can't find them anywhere. I think they must be in her trunk. I spun a little today & mended some. No news of importance tonight by the mail.

Tuesday 3rd - I cut some quilt pieces today of old dress skirts. Atheline will piece it if she gets able. She mends very slow. I fear she will never be well again. She has a dreadful cough. Her baby grows some, it does not suck her at all now.

Wednesday 4th - I cut some quilt pieces today till dinner & then lay down as I had the headache. When I woke about 3 o'clock, Mr. Henry was standing by me. I was so glad to see him. Lt. Posey was here this morning & said he thought Mr. Henry would not be at home before tomorrow. He has come home on a court marshal. They are going to try Capt. Parker for stealing & other things. My head is nearly well since he came.

Thursday 5th - I spent this day very pleasantly with Sister Jane. Her & family are all well. Mr. Henry went with me. 'Tis so pleasant to be near my dear husband. He is the best man in the world. I hope his resignation may be accepted so he can stay with us all the time. We received a letter from Pinck today. He is very well. I am very tired tonight. I shall retire soon. My little ones are all well. Gus has been a little loose in his bowels but better now.

Friday 6th - Mr. Henry went to Asheville today. No news of importance. Very cool this morning, feels like old winter was with us again. I am affraid it will nip my beans. I have knit some today.

Saturday 7th - Mr. Henry went to Asheville today. Nothing new. Zona, Willie & I went up to Betsey McKinnish's yesterday evening & then went up the road & met Mr. Henry. He let the children ride. They were delighted. I have done several things today. We received a letter from Pinck today. It has been some time on the road. He sent me a garter of his own knitting. I prize it highly. He sent Zona one some time ago.

Sunday 8th May 1864 - This has been a beautiful day. Tilda Morris & Lou Shuford spent the day here. Also Tom Cook & wife. We had our first lettuce today for dinner. Mr. Step was here for dinner. He has been carrying Mr. Henry's stallion about. He has been here several times in the last two weeks. Mr. Henry & I took a long walk this evening over in the widening. It thundered some this evening but we had no rain. We are needing some now. I am very tired. My back always gives out in walking.

Monday 9th - Mr. Henry went to Asheville today. Allen Edwards began to clip the sheep today. I spent the day very pleasantly at A. B. Jones'. Zona went with me. Till came home with us. She expected a letter from her husband tonight. She is very anxious about him as he has been in a fight at the taking of Plymouth. I have the headache tonight, I think 'tis from fatigue. The mail brought no news of importance. 'Tis reported that the fight has commenced at Richmond. I pray God to crown our forces with success.

Tuesday 10th - I began my calico dress today, did but little to it. The sleeves are made after a pattern I got from Till yesterday. I will frill the cap & around the waist. It is gathered on top. Mr. Henry got the dress last Spring in Columbia, gave $3.50 a yd. I thought that high, but now calico is selling at ten dollars a yard. Mr. Henry received his resignation accepted. I am so very glad, now he will stay at home. He did not go to Asheville today as he is relieved from the court marshal. An old man stayed here last night, night that Capt. Parker robbed in Cherokee. Mr. Henry knew him, named Draper. He will stay here till Thursday & then he has to go to Asheville again.

Wednesday 11th - I sewed on my dress today, finished the sleeves. They look very nice. Rained nearly all day today. Several men here tonight. Edwards will finish the sheep tomorrow. Old Bently has been here this week breaking flax, still at it. The fight began at Richmond the 6th. We are victors so far. I hope we may be able to whip them good there & that peace may soon dawn on our bleeding country. Oh Lord help us in this our great conflict. Give our men courage & our Generals wisdom. May we come out conquerors & Oh Lord I pray Thee grant us a speedy peace.

Thursday 12th 1864 May - I made the waist of my dress today & sewed some on the skirt. 'Tis very tough sewing, has so much starch in it. Mr. Henry at home in the farm all day. They will nearly finish planting this week. Things are growing very fast. The woods begin to look green. My children are all well. I am contented when they are all well & Mr. Henry at home. I would be so thankful if peace was made. Pinck will soon be at home. I want to see my child. He is a good boy & I hope may make an honorable man. Willie is a very affectionate child & so is Zona. They kept my spirits up all winter while Mr. Henry was gone. They are all dear good children. I hope I may live to raise them & their Papa, may long life be granted him I pray. May they grow up to useful members of society, honorable & virtuous is my humble prayer.

Friday 13th - We heard this week that Gen. Jenkins is killed & Gen. Longstreet wounded. It was done by our own men, the same (Mahoney's) brigade that killed Stonewall Jackson. I fear there is some one in that brigade that is not all right. I finished my dress today. It fits very neatly. Mr. Henry went to Wiley Knight's this evening. I went up the meadow a piece to see Heff's calf but not find it. I came back by myself. We have a good many young chickens but they are dying a good deal with gapes & the hawk takes one nearly every day. It wearys me a good deal to see the old hawk take them off & they crying so pittifully.

Saturday 14th - I have done some mending today & after dinner put up some of the winter clothes & got out some summer ones. Mr. Henry has laid aside his flannel & coloured shirts & is wearing white ones again. He looks like his self again. I have not taken off homespun yet but have left off my flannel & yarn stockings. The children have been barefooted for nearly three weeks. Gus was not at all well last night. I slept but little. His bowels were loose & he is taking a cold & I think cutting some teeth. Mr. Henry went to Asheville today & got the coffee Harrie bought in Columbia. He sent it up by old Mr. Linsey. I had a letter from Harrie yesterday saying he was no better. I fear he never will be again. There is 11 lbs. of coffee for $100, 9$ per lb. Some one stole some of Mr. Andy Jones' wool last night. I expect it was Pinck Allen. He is a terrible rogue. A bright day. Fannie cooked today & baked some molasses bread this evening.

F. M. Corn to William L. Henry

May 14, 1864

Capt. Henry Sir
    You will please send me the old Enlist papers of the Co. by the Earliest Entelegence by the request of the Col. and you will oblige me.

Yours very respectfully
F. M. Corn
2nd Lt. Co "B"

And also send all the Papers of the Co. that you have in your charge. Mr. Parker objects to going in as a recruit for Mr. Step as there was no understanding about it between them.

Sunday May 15th 1864 - Cloudy this morning but faired off and clear till about one & now 2 o'clock we are having a nice shower. Mr. Henry & some other men have gone to hunt Mr. Jones' wool. I hope they may find it. They went this morning & have not got back yet. I hope he may not get wet. Our friend, Lt. England, staid here last night. He has gone to Mike Luther's now. He is a nice boy. No one here for dinner but Matt & I & the children. Mr. Henry & F. Boyd have just got in. They are very wet. They found nothing of the wool. Part of the men went in towards the bend of the river. Mr. Henry & Frank went up in the Starnes settlement. There is a good deal of stealing going on. I am so glad Mr. Henry is at home. I have been affraid they would break in the smoke house or mill. I do wish they could catch some of these bad men that are stealing & doing other mischief. Willie was not at all well last night, has a dreadful cold. Gus is nearly sick with a cold too. I made them some hoar hound candy today. They eat it very well. Mr. Henry is asleep on the trundle bed. Frank Boyd in my room & the children at play upstairs except Willie who is asleep. I have just finished a letter to Harrie & Eugenia & now 'tis near supper time. Still cloudy.

Monday 16th - I wrote to Sister Frank & Sister Ell today & knit some on Willie's sock. I am knitting him a pair cotton socks for Sunday. Mr. Henry went to Jake Starnes' this morning after hay. Charlie & Jim also. Lt. England took dinner here today. Betsey Jamison spends the day here & stays tonight. She is cheerful enough now. The mail brought a good deal of news from Richmond tonight, all favorable to us. Frank Boyd & Lt. England stay here tonight. Bently still at work at the flax. Edwards grubbing.

Tuesday 17th - I have done nothing but knit a little today. My head aches some this evening. Betsey left here this evening. There was a man found dead in the Starnes settlement this morning, said to be Pinck Allen.[44] Mr. Henry went up this evening to see him. They have taken him to Mrs. Norman's. He is shot through the body under the arms. His sisters & wife take it very hard. He has been lying out nearly a year & stealing generally. He will steal no more in the world. May God temper the wind to the shorn lamb. Help his wife bear her great trouble.

Wednesday 18th May 1864 & Thursday 19th - I suffered a great deal with my head yesterday (Wednesday). In bed all day. Mr. Henry went to Asheville & got some sugar. No news further than the news of Monday is confirmed. Banks has surrendered our forces in Va. victors. P. Allen was burried yesterday at Sardis. Mr. Henry in the farm today. Mary Tutt spends the day here. Jinnie & Matt cleaned the side room & one room upstairs after dinner, scoured & scalded. My head not well this morning but now since dinner nearly easy. I had a letter from Sister Lena Monday. They were all well. I finished Willie's socks today & began a pair cotton gloves for myself of thread I have had ever since I was married. I bought it from home, some coloured thread I had left of knitting stockings. May Tutt was going to stay all night as it looked like rain this evening but her mother came after her. I suppose she was uneasy about her. Mary brought my hat & Gus' today. They are very nice.

Friday 20th - Mr. Stepp & Charlie started with the cattle to Black Mountain this morning. A good deal of mail today. Louise McKinnish brought home the cloth last Tuesday, 26 yds. I have done no cutting on it yet, will begin next week. Jinnie & I cleaned my room before dinner & Matt & her scoured the hall room, the front & back piazza. Mr. Henry went to Asheville today. I am very tired tonight. Rose a little sick yesterday evening but well enough to attend to Gus today. He is very cross, has a cold. The others all well.

Saturday 21st - I cleaned upstairs this morning & then down stairs generally. Matt helped. I scoured the buckets, pans, dippers & tub before dinner & after dinner done some mending & knit some. Mr. Henry walked to Asheville today as the horse is not well but a good deal better. Mr. A. B. Jones came by about 12 & told me Mr. Henry said if he was not at home tonight, not to be uneasy about him as he had some business with Mark Erwin that would keep him late, but he came after dark. I was glad of it as there was no one here but me & the children & Matt & she is so easily frightened. Old Bill Knight, Ingle & Ron & Bently have been at work at the flax all this week, got some ready to hackle. I want to get some spun for Mr. Henry & Pinck some clothes before he goes after Pinck. I will be so glad when he

---

[44] Local resident Jim Holbrook writes that Pinck Allen was shot near the current location of Speedy's Junk Yard by a gunman on the hill east of Starnes Cove Road and north of the McKinney Road intersection, close to the present day Starnes Cemetery. Pinck had apparently been hiding out in a nearby cave. There was once a large rock in the field where the junk yard now exists where Pinck would come down, and his wife Rachel would meet him with food. (Pinck Allen essay compliments of Old Buncombe County Genealogical Society and Jim Holbrook.)

gets home. Matt, Zona & Willie went up to hotel garden this evening & got some flowers.

Sunday 22nd May 1864 - This is a beautiful May morning. Matt & Zona gone to church at the Academy. Mr. Henry out walking about. Willie & Gus in the yard with Rose. I am writing in the side room. Mr. Henry & Mr. Stepp moved the loom to the back piazza last Thursday & I had the press that was in here put in the hall room.

Nothing new going on in the country. Allen's sudden & inglorious death has ceased to be a theme of conversation. I think it has give some of the deserters in this neighborhood a big sceer. Mrs. Nichols was here last Friday wanting Mr. Henry to get Nichols a transfer. Mr. Henry was not at home. I hear Bryson has written to Col. Palmer on the subject of going back too. I wish they were all back at the command. Mr. Jones has never heard anything of his wool or meat yet. Till sent me some of Tom Morris' capture at Plymouth, some raisins & candy yesterday. She was here a short time last Friday & went to Asheville. Mr. Henry & I had a very pleasant walk up to Mrs. Quinn's this evening. 'Tis always pleasure to me to be near him & very dear little children. I hope Pinck may soon be at home.

Monday 23rd - I cut eight pair pants today & nearly made George's. 'Tis very narrow cloth but tollerable thick. Matt spinning for her dresses. I have had the wool commenced on today. Fannie & Tena washing it. The other hands planting potatoes in the meadow. Billie Ledford is at work here. Bently still working at flax. Mr. Henry thinks he will not raise any more as it costs too much. Not much news tonight. The fight still goes on at Richmond in our favor.

Tuesday 24th - I finished George's pants, made Lonzo a pair & began Sam's today. I wrote a long letter to Pinck, Dora & Matt yesterday evening & sent him some raisins & candy in the letter. He will be delighted & know he is a good boy, so affectionate. I think Willie will be a good deal like him. Zona is very affectionate also. Gus is a lovely baby, tries to talk. Atheline is not improving much. She sews a little every day on a quilt of mine. Her babe does not nurse her at all, only the bottle. It is growing some. I fear she will never be well again. I fear she has consumption. She has been a faithful nurse to my children.

Wednesday 25th May 1864 - Sister Jane sent here Monday & got a two horse load of hay. Mr. Henry was in Asheville last Monday, sent five sacks of flour but did not sell it. Sister Jane sent today after two pigs & wants to hire a negro woman for her feed. I don't want to hire the woman but will try to hire her to Mrs. A. B. Jones.

I finished Sam's pants & Charlie's that Matt sewed on yesterday. Fannie & Tena finished the wool today & Fannie washed some cotton. Rained this evening. I took off the large wheel of my sewing machine & washed & cleaned it well. It runs some lighter but still heavy.

Thursday 26th - I made Sam's other pants today & sewed some on Hanes'. Mr. Henry went to Asheville today. Charley took the waggon & some flax seed. Sam & George went. George is implicated in trading with one of Hugh Johnston's negroes, something about stolen corn. They gave George about fifty licks. I hope it will do him good. Johnston said it was Sam & Charlie first but the negro said

George. Johnston has a spite at Sam & wanted to get him into trouble. I am glad he is clear. It wounded his feelings a good deal to think he was accused of stealing.

Friday 27th - I had a letter from Harrie yesterday. Mr. Henry got the mail. He is no better. I finished Hanes' pants, made Lonzo's & cut & sewed some on Jim's. I went up late this evening to see Mr. Bently break flax. Mr. Henry had Willie & Gus up at the store house & Rose, Matt & Zona went home with Mary Tutt this morning & staid all day & Mary stays here tonight. Mrs. Andrews & Mary Blanchard staid here last night. Mrs. Andrews brought the net she made for the cradle. 'Tis very nice I think. I shall send it back to her as she asks too much for pay.

Saturday May 28th 1864 - Betsey McKinnish picked wool here yesterday & today. It is not quite dry as it has rained nearly every day since it was put out. Yesterday was bright, rather cool mornings & evenings. I had the toothache last night, neuralgea I think. I have had it several nights this week.

I finished Jim's pants & washed the children & cleaned them. Matt & Mary Tutt went to Mrs. Joe Green's this morning, a long walk I think. Blair was to sell Mr. Henry's flour at auction but Pat Thrash pressed it for the government. I think he acted badly. Mr. Henry's fine horse Clarion is improving some. He thinks he has been foundered a little. We took in all the wool this evening as it rained. Jinnie hoed out the flowers in the front yard, cleaned the candle sticks & baked some molasses bread for the children. George seems very much chagrined at his strapping. He has not been to his meals since.

Sunday 29th - This is a beautiful morning. Mr. Henry brought me some strawberries this morning, the first I have seen. Jinnie & Rose took the children up to the hotel garden. Mr. Henry has been asleep upstairs. I went up & lay down till he went to sleep, then slept. He has just come down. Tom Cook and him are in the front piazza. Dinner will soon be on. Fannie cooking today. Our garden getting on very well considering it is so cool. Fires are comfortable morning & night. I had George to cut Zona's hair some three months ago. She had long hair & I kept it pulled but it was so uneven, I thought it best to keep it short a while. Mary Tutt brought Willie's hat home Friday. She made one for Gus & sewed Willie's together for 10$. I got the plat of Willie's from Louise McKinnish.

Monday May 30th 1864 - I cut some quilt pieces this morning & done some mending & after dinner I trimmed my hat & Gus'. Mine I trimmed with silk & velvet & Gus' with yellow & white ribbon. They both look very neat. Mrs. Lance was here today & took home some tow to spin for bread. The poor of country have a trying time for bread now. I hope they may get through & not suffer. I was sadly disappointed tonight by not getting a letter from Pinck. I hope he may be at home soon.

Tuesday 31st - Mr. Henry & I went to the Murray place this morning to salt the sheep. I got back about 9 o'clock & trimmed the vases & made Gus some cloth shoes. Jimmie Henry, Jess Smith & Lt. Gibson took dinner here today. Also old Mr. Linsey. They all left soon after dinner.

I lined Willie's hat this evening. One for every day wear. The hands are going over the corn & replanting. Sam sowed the hungarian grass seed last week. The clover in the hotel garden is beautiful. They cut it for the horses. Our horses are very lean as we have no grain to feed them on. We live on the toll of the mill. Bently is at work in the farm. Billie Ledford also. Billie works for a bu. of corn a week. He has been here two weeks, the last of this week. Matt & Mary Tutt got back Sunday evening. They complained of being very tired. Mary staid here Sunday night.

June 1864

Wednesday June 1st - Cool this morning but warm in the middle of the day. I cleaned up the wool upstairs today. 'Tis not picked yet, some of it is. I want the other picked next week. I want to send the fine wool off to So. Ca. by Mr. Henry when he goes to have it carded. I want to make some flannel & Mr. Henry & Pinck & Willie some jeans of it. 'Tis very nice & white.

Mr. Henry at home all day in the farm. Things go on better when he is at home. I do hope he will stay at home all the time. Oh! that we could have peace. I do hope the day is not far distant when peace will once again smile on our bleeding country. Grant us an honorable & speedy peace Oh! Lord I beseech Thee.

June 2nd 1864 Thursday & Friday June 3rd - I was sick in bed all day yesterday with my head. I sit up a little & finished my gloves & put on Zona's stocking. I am going to knit them lapped stitched. My head was a good deal better yesterday evening. This morning my head was better but still not well. I lay down a while this morning. Charlotte was here today, came after the winding blades, sley, shuttle & quills.

The mail brought no news of importance. Mr. Henry went to Asheville yesterday, was gone nearly all day. I lay in the side room & slept a good part of the day. Mr. Henry says he hates to see me go in the dungeon, as he calls it. I darken the window with the cradle quilt so the flies don't annoy me.

William L. Henry to Pinckney Henry

June 3rd 1864
Sulphur Springs, N. C.

My Dear Boy,
    I will come for you soon now. I hope you may be a good boy and learn to read and write. I hope your health may be good & that you may be able to come to see your little brothers & sister. They are playful & speak of Pinckney, and Willie always when he has anything that is nice is going to save it for Pinckney. I gave him a little sugar and he was going to save it for Pinckney. He wrapped it in a paper and kept it some time. The children are nice little fellows.
    Your Mother was very sick with headache yesterday and the night before. She is now up but feeble. Poor woman. She has some bad spells of headaches and toothaches but soon gets up after a sick spell.
    Aunt Dora & Mattie, I was at the village yesterday & Mr. Wm. Neilson had just got home from Tenn. He had a very hard fight near

Greenville and lost some four or five of his men killed & wounded. He lost his negro man Mose after a race for six miles. He thinks the negro will come in. The yanks can't persuade his negro Sam to follow them. He is at home at Wake. Mr. Neilson's family are all well.

I have nothing more to interest you. I will come to see you in a short time.

I am as ever yours,
Wm. Henry
Write soon & often

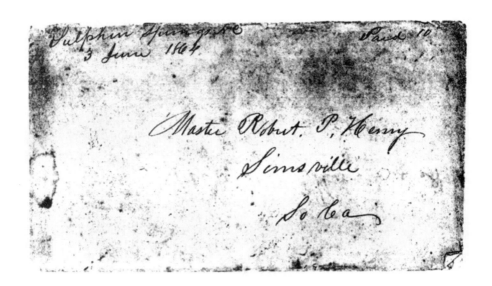

Saturday 4th - Rained nearly all day. Mr. Henry at the mill nearly all day. He is going to start the bucket machine again. I hope it may do good service this time. I picked some wool this morning & knit some. Tena went to see her daughters, Betsey & Leizana this morning as they are both very sick. Mr. Henry brought me a nice paper of strawberries. I gave the children some. They are ripening very fast now. I got Zona's stocking in the heel this evening. I took off a hen with fourteen chickens this evening & one turkey. We only have 10 young turkeys & about 100 chickens. The chickens have died up with the gapes. I put three hens under pots this evening to keep them from going with one chicken each. I first tied two of them but they soon got loose. Mr. Henry sent Charlie up to Mr. Stepp (where the cattle are) last Wednesday. They are about the Black Mountain. One of the oxen have died since they were taken there. Mr. Henry will sell his beef to the government at one dollar a lb. & he gets hide & tallow. Troops are gathering in Asheville. 'Tis thought they intend going to Tennessee. I hope they will not find the way here for some soldiers are very troublesome. Jinnie made some sweet cakes for the children this morning of molasses.

Sunday 5th June 1864 - Cloudy this morning but little rain. Matt & Zona went to church to the Academy. Mr. Reynolds preached. They have just got back. Mr. Henry & I & the children, Zona & Willie, will go to the Murray place this evening. I attended to Gus this morning & Rose went to church. He is very little trouble but a great deal of pleasure to attend my children. I am weaning him. He sucked Thursday morning & then not till Saturday morning. I don't think I will let him suck any more. I do feel so sorry for him when he begs to suck. I hate to turn away & try to amuse him as he soon forgets it & goes to play. He is no trouble at night as he has not sucked any at night for a month. This has been a very wet Spring. Farmers are all behind with their work. I hear the clover & grass seed sown this Spring are doing very well and the clover in the Hotel garden is very nice and is the only feed for our work stock as all the grain is given to the needy for bread. The need of grain is very great and it will be very hard for all to get bread this season. We went to the Murray place, had a pleasant walk. It was rather warm going. We came back & got some strawberries this side of the spring. Nearly sundown when we got back. Two men stay here tonight. Old Draper is one. He is the same man that was here about a month ago. Capt. Parker robbed him & the man that is with him. Rained some this evening.

Monday 5th - Mr. Henry walked to Asheville today. His horse is nearly well. The bees stung him last week, last Tuesday. He still has little swollen places on him when they stung him. This is court week in Asheville and I got a basket of one of the Guy women with a cover last week. I gave sixteen lbs. of flour for it. I have knit some today. Very warm.

Tuesday 7th - I have done several things today, fixing some dresses for Gus, tucking them. Mr. Henry went to Asheville today, rode Clarion. No news of importance. They are still fighting around Richmond & at Dalton. Our forces successful so far. I do hope we may be able to thrash them good so they will let us alone. Oh that we could have peace. I would be so glad. This is enrolling week again. I think they will soon have all the men & boys too.

Wednesday 8th June 1864 - I made Gus a gingham bonnett & fixed Zona's hoop today & knit some. Mr. Henry at home all day. Dan Smith is at work at the bucket machine. Bently & Billie Ledford in the farm. The weeds & grass are growing rapidly as 'tis so wet. I had a letter from Lou last Monday. She is very well.

Thursday 9th - I am very tired this evening as Matt & I & Zona have been to Mr. Reynolds field (the other side of the widening) after strawberries. We got a basket & bucket full of nice ones. We went soon after dinner. It was very warm but cloudy. We got back at three. Mr. Henry & Mr. A. B. Jones came soon after we did. They had been to Asheville. No news of importance. I covered Zona's scoop with brown linnen before dinner. It looks very nice. It was nearly worn out. I had Mr. Henry & Mr. Jones a nice cup of coffee for their dinner as Mr. Jones had the headache. I have a slight headache this evening from fatigue I think. I must go about supper as I expect Jinnie is waiting on me. Gus nurses one breast every day. I hate to wean him. He has not sucked the left breast since last Thursday. Mr. Henry wants me to wean him entirely. He is a dear good child, tries to talk & pouts so sweet. Willie is inclined to pout too. They are all good obedient children.

Friday 10th - I did not get a letter from Pinck this morning. I think Dora might write every two weeks any way. We have not got a letter in over a month. Dora is coming up this summer. I wish she would come on & bring Pinck. I sewed some on my bonnett today. 'Tis pea green calico. It will fade when washed but I had nothing that suited any better for a bonnett & calico at ten dollars a yd. is a little too much for me. The first swarm of bees came out today. Mr. Bently hived them, a nice swarm. A soldier eat dinner here. He came to the mill with corn for the government. He got some milk in his jug. Poor soldiers. Their rations are short & I fear will still be shorter. Nearly every day some one comes here for bread. I feel sorry for them. Poor women. I hope none of them may suffer for the staff of life.

Saturday 11th June 1864 - I finished my bonnett this morning & reeled six yds. for Matt & put some tobacco in the woolen clothes & knit some before dinner. A woman named McRea was here for bread today. She eat dinner here. Her little boy eat at dinner like he was nearly perished & I expect was hungry. Mr. Henry let her have a little flour. After dinner I & the children & Matt finished picking the fine wool. The wool is all done now. I knit some on Zona's stocking this evening. We had a heavy rain this evening & heavy thunder. We are not needing it at all now. The grass & weeds grow very fast in the corn when 'tis so wet. Rather cool this evening, fire feels comfortable. Jinnie went to Asheville this evening to see Charlotte, will come back tomorrow evening. Aunt Tena's Betsey (that she went to see last Saturday & came home Monday morning) is dead. She died yesterday morning. Dr. Logan came to see Atheline for the first time yesterday. He thinks it is cold. She is nothing but a skeleton. Her baby cries a great deal at night. It is very lean & ruptured & that makes it cry some I think. I had a nice plate of strawberries & cream for Mr. Henry's dinner last Thursday. He gave them nearly all to the children. They enjoyed them finely. I wish Pinck was here to get some.

Sunday 12th - Cloudy & cool this morning. Matt & Zona have gone after strawberries up towards the spring. Willie is out at play. He loves to play by himself. Rose has Gus & Mr. Henry is asleep in my room & I am writing in Matt's room. Atheline is some better but still feeble. She sits up part of the time. I do wish she could get well once again but I fear she will never be stout again. She has been a good nurse to me & the children. Mr. Henry sent Billie Ledford to Asheville for the mail yesterday evening but got none of importance, only one letter & no papers. I must go & give out dinner as Fannie, I expect, is waiting. The evening passed pleasantly as it always does when my dear husband is near. Mr. Henry & I went & gathered a few strawberries this evening, brought some to the children. We went up to the spring & then up by the hotel garden & got some flowers. It was near 5 o'clock when we got back & rather cool for June.

Monday June 13th 1864 Very cool this morning, fires are comfortable. Old Mrs. Thrash was here this morning & got five of the sheep Mr. Henry got of Capt. Thrash, government sheep. He is to pay for them in beef. I mended some today & sewed some on a quilt. It is of old dresses & other odds & ends. Matt spinning for her dresses yet. She gets on slowly as she only works part of her time. Atheline is not doing so well, very feeble.

Tuesday 14th - Sewed on my quilt all day. Sarah Jane Kurkendol & Ellen Jones staid here last night. They left this morning. Mr. Henry at home all day in the farm. Oh! God I beseech Thee, spare my dear husbands life. I know that the bad men of the country thirst for his life blood. I know that the issues of life & death are in Thy hands & I pray Thee keep my dear husband under Thy kind protecting care. Spare his dear life. Oh! Lord I beseech Thee and Thine shall be all the praise.

Wednesday 15th - Sewed some on my quilt, got all the squares done. Perry Gaston was here this evening. He & Mr. Henry sit under the apple tree in front of the house and the children played around them. I am so thankful to the Giver of every good and perfect gift that my dear husband is at home. Oh! that this cruel war was over. How long O! Lord how long! Hasten the glad day when peace will once again smile on us, in their hot displeasure remember mercy, I pray Thee O! Ruler of the universe.

Thursday 16th - I tore out the squares for my quilt to put it together but sewed but few of them. Till Morris eat dinner here. She went to Asheville after the mail. Marion Knight is killed. I pity his mother. She takes it very hard. He is her third son that has given his life for his country. May God temper the wind to the shorn lamb. Bryson & Nichols started to their Regiment last Tuesday. They have been laying out for six months or more. Henry Jones, who deserted the hospital at Raleigh, went with them also. Henry's family are very much grieved about it. Matt & I made some pound cake this evening & sweetened with molasses instead of sugar. 'Tis very nice. Jinnie had to help about the clover hay as they are cutting it this week.

Friday 17th and Saturday 18th & Sunday 19th - I will have to write for three days in one. Friday, Mr. Henry & I went horse back to Asheville & heard two excellent speeches from Dr. Deems who is raising a fund to educate the orphans of soldiers. His was an able address. Gov. Vance followed. His was a very good one also. We left Sister Jane's about 11 o'clock & got back to her house just after four. I never was so fatigued in my life & had a dreadful headache. We started soon after we eat our dinner (at 4). Mr. Henry had to walk as the Authorities at Asheville pressed his horse. I came nearly all the way alone. I suffered a great deal on the road. It was sunset when I got home. I went to bed as soon as I got in. Cousin William Henry, Anon Jones & Capt. Russell staid here all night. Mr. Henry got home about dark. I woke up at 9 & took a cup of good coffee my dear husband had fixed for me. He is so kind to me. He & Sister Jane wanted me to stay all night in Asheville but I could not leave my dear little children. I was not able to sit up any scarcely Saturday. I lay in the side room all day, the dungeon as Mr. Henry calls it. He hung something over the window to keep the flies from annoying me. Mrs. Tom Cook spent the day here. She brought home the flax. She has been spinning seven yds. of flax & three of tow. It rained a little nearly all day. Mr. Henry in there part of the time. He fixed a fish hook to catch a large jack fish that stays in a deep hole just below the dam. I don't think he fished much. Anon Jones left this evening. He is flying round Matt. Cousin William & Capt. Russell left this morning. Sunday evening, Tom Tidwell & another soldier staid here last night. They left this morning. I lay upstairs till about 11 o'clock & then came down & dressed. I feel very feeble but my head is nearly well. Mr. Common has been here all day, came before breakfast this morning. The children are at play. Mr. Henry upstairs asleep & Matt in the front Piazza talking to Mr. Common. Gus has not sucked since last Thursday. I don't think I will let him nurse any more as my milk is about dried up. Rose let him fall off the logs into the branch last Thursday. I was frightened nearly to death. I was near her when he fell. His clothes were very wet. I received a letter from Sister Ell last Thursday. They were all well. Her husband is in the army. She is greatly distressed about him. I have not heard from Dora & Pinck in a month. They treat us badly I think. I must stop now & go clean upstairs, make the beds &c. I did not clean upstairs as I felt too feeble. Old Mr. Commons stays here tonight. He is a great talker.

Monday 20th - I cleaned up this morning & then cleaned the smoke house. Everything gets out of order when I am sick a day or two. Cousin Bob Love of Haywood was here today. I had early dinner & he & old Mr. Common started soon after dinner. I pieced my quilts today. It is pieced in single irish chain. I received a letter from Dora tonight saying they were all well. I was very glad to hear it. Mr. Henry will go after him next week.

Tuesday 21st - I sewed on my quilt today & finished it & intend piecing two like it for the crib. The tories & deserters killed Andy Johnston of Henderson Co. a few weeks ago. There are a great many in Henderson & Transelvania Co.'s. I hope they will never come here. I do hope & pray we may never fall into the hands of our enemies. Mr. Henry at home all day.

Wednesday 22nd - I sewed on the crib quilts today. Dr. Logan was here today. This is his 4th visit to Atheline. I don't think he does her any good whatever. She is very feeble. I fear she has consumption. Mr. Henry at home all day. Wiley Knight is fixing up the buggy. One of Mrs. Quinn's children died last night of diarrhea. I hear of a good many having it. Gus has been unwell all week with it. He is very fretful. I think he is teething. I let him suck today for the last time I think. He has not sucked since last Thursday & then only the right breast as the other is dried up. He did not get anything when he sucked of consequence but he begged so for it.

Mr. Henry said let him have it. He has been no trouble to wean. He is a good child when well.

Thursday 23rd 1864 June - I finished both cradle quilts today before dinner. After dinner I made some kerchiefs for Rose to wear on her head as I had Jinnie to cut her hair off very close this evening. Jinnie baked some molasses bread this evening. Mr. Henry went to Asheville this morning & got his horse Clarion. He also got a nice lot of his leather from the tan yard, some beautiful calf & goat skins. Mrs. Norman was here this evening. She is an incessant gabber. Matt made Rose a bonnet of old stuff this evening. My head feels badly this evening. I fear I will have another bad spell with it.

Friday 24th - Mail brought no news of importance this morning. Mrs. Tom Cook staid here last night & went to Asheville today & back to dinner. She is a good woman I think. I cut & sewed on a pair pants for Charlie today. I also cut Jinnie & Fannie an apron each. Matt made Fannie's this evening. We are having some very warm days but still cool mornings. Cool enough to make fire feel comfortable. Mr. Henry took the buggy tonight to Hawkin's shop today & the harness to Blanchard's to have them mended. He brought Gus' shoes home. They are full small. He is very proud of his new shoes. He is some better today. I have given him smart weed tea and I think it helps him.

Saturday 25th - Very warm today. I finished Charlie's pants this morning & made some paste board. Anon Jones spent the day here. He & Matt enjoyed themselves finely. Matt & Zona went to Miss Peggie Tutt's this morning to get some flowers but got none. Zona is not so well today, her bowels are loose. Mr. Henry at home all day. I made Jinnie's apron this evening & put splits in Rose's bonnett. I am still giving Gus smart weed tea. He drinks it very well. Rose is not well this evening, looseness of the bowels.

Sunday 26th - Very warm this evening, so warm no need of a fire. A little rain this morning but now nearly clear. Mr. Henry asleep upstairs. The children at play. I must go and give Gus some of his tea. Zona better this morning. Mr. Henry & I went to the Murray place, also Zona. We got a few cherries. They are nearly ripe up there & scarcely turned down here. Zona was delighted with the little kids we have. Two, late when we got back. Matt & Anon Jones went to preaching at the Academy but they were too late as preaching was over. We came back by the Spring & then up through the flax patch. Zona complained a good deal of being tired. My back pains me a good deal tonight. It generally does when I walk much. I am lean & not much account any way. Jones left soon after we got back. Willie did not like it at all because we left him. He said he wanted to see the little kids too. He was asleep when we started.

Monday 27th - I cut some shirts today for the negroes out of sacks & sewed some on Charlie's. No news of note tonight. Gus some better. This has been a very warm day, so was yesterday. Till Morris was here a short time this morning. Mr. Henry in the farm all day.

Tuesday 28th - Mr. Henry went to Asheville today. Thrash paid him in part for his bacon. Mr. Henry thinks of starting tomorrow. I had the headache this evening but it got better after I drank a cup of good coffee. Mr. Henry went to Blanchard's this evening. He is nearly done the shoes & harness. My head nearly well by supper. The coffee I think cured it. Mr. Commons stays here tonight. Bently is still working here. Billie Ledford has not been here this week.

Wednesday 29th - Mr. Henry took Willie on John after the buggy this morning, got back just before dinner. Mr. Commons left soon as he eat dinner. Mr. Henry has concluded not to start till tomorrow. He got his shoes. They are very nice. I read nearly all the morning in a book Mr. Commons had, "The Annals of Newbery" by Judge O'Neal. 'Tis very interesting. I fixed up Mr. Henry's clothes & some cakes & some coffee for him to take with him this morning. I sewed a little on Hanes' shirt after dinner. I made George's yesterday & Charlie's Monday. Mr. Henry & I went to the Murray place this evening & got a basket of cherries. We came back through the oats. They are splendid. Mr. Henry says he never saw nicer oats in his life. Sundown when we got back. Matt had given out supper & it was nearly ready. I am not very tired this walk but fatigued some. I have not felt well all day but feel better this evening. I enjoyed the walk finely. I always do when my dear husband is along. I am blest with a kind husband & loving good children. Gus is getting better. I hope he may soon be well. I will be so glad when Pinck gets home. I am going to try to teach him & Zona this summer. It requires a good deal of patience to teach children properly.

Thursday 30th June 1864 - Mr. Henry started this morning. I shall miss him so much. He will be gone ten days or longer if he goes to Columbia. Harris is to come up this summer & board at Dr. Hilliard's. Lt. Gen. Polk is killed. I am truly sorry of it. He was a good man & a first rate general. He was killed near Marietta Ga. I sympathise with his bereaved family. They reside just in the suburbs of Asheville in the Foster house. I finished Hanes' shirt before dinner & after dinner cut Gus some skirts of one of my flannels. It was softer for summer than home made flannel & I did not need it as I have two homespun linsey ones. I began to work one with blue silk, some of the fringe of Lou Deaver's blue mareno shawl. She gave me the shawl long ago & I made Pinck a cloak of it & Zona (she was the baby) a little talma & saque. The skirt looks very neat. Matt made the other two this evening, all but putting on the waists. She will make & set them on tomorrow. 'Tis reported that the tories made a raid into Camp Vance (at the head of the road two miles from Morganton) & took all the conscripts that were there. They were boys, about 150 I think. They surprised them.

July 1864

Friday July 1st - I finished Gus' skirt this evening & mended some. Till Morris & her little sister Sallie spent the day here & stay tonight also. Till, Matt, Sallie & Zona went to the Murray place this evening & got some cherries. They are ripe up there but not here. I have a headache this evening. I gave my head a good washing last Tuesday, also Zona's & Willie's head. A good deal of mail this morning but little news.

Saturday 2nd - Bently drove some bees last night, the comb in no account only for wax & no honey of importance. The bees swarmed today. That makes 5 swarms this season. Dr. Logan was here last Tuesday, his fifth visit. I can't see he does Atheline any good at all. I think there is very little hope of her ever getting well. I feel so sorry when she asks me how long before she will be well. I tell her before long I hope, yet I have no hope of ever seeing her well again. She has been good & kind to me & my children. I hate to see her pine away & think she must die. I will never have another such a nurse. She was so kind to the children. Rose is very careless. I have done a good deal of mending today. Matt helped me some or I would not have got done.

Sunday 3rd July - Anon Jones staid here last night, left soon after breakfast. I & the children went to the Academy today to church. Rose carried Gus & Zona & Willie walked. Mr. Reynolds preached. I sit by the window near the door & my thoughts wandered back over the past. I thought how often I had been there & seen Atheline come with Pinck (she always kept the children in church) & then in year or so she carried little Cora & then not long till she carried Zona & then Willie. But I think she has been to church her last time. I felt so sad to think of what she had been & what she is now but we must all die sooner or later. She has been good to me & I love her & pray she may be restored to health. Her baby grows slow. She stays up at Tena's house now & Jim keeps the baby. She can't walk alone, her feet and legs are swollen. She is nothing but skin and bones. I expect Mr. Henry is at my old home this evening. I wish I could be there a while too. I love my old home. Many tender recollections cling around it. I don't know when I shall see it again, perhaps never. I will stop as I want to go up & sit awhile with Atheline.

We have had a big fight near Marietta Ga., have not heard the casualities yet. I hear Jim Nichols is wounded slightly. We had a very hard rain this evening indeed. It has rained since three o'clock.

Monday 4th - Matt & I quilted one of the cradle quilts today. I bound it this evening. No news of importance by mail tonight. Atheline is not improving any. I think she will soon leave this bright beautiful world & try the realities of our home above. She seems to think she will be well again. I wish I could anticipate such bright hopes but I can't.

Tuesday 5th - We quilted the other cradle quilt today. I bind it this evening as I have a slight headache. Anon Jones spent the evening here. Gus has got a good deal better. I hope he will soon be well. He is cutting his jaw teeth, two are partly through. I knit some this evening. Atheline is not improving any.

Wednesday 6th - I did some mending this morning & knit in the evening. Matt & Jinnie scoured the side room & hall & front piazza. Gus sick at the stomach this evening, vomiting. Rose has let him eat green apples. The June apples are turning a little. Cherries will soon be gone. Currents & raspberries ripening.

Thursday 7th 1864 July - Gus quite sick this morning. I was up with him several times last night, vomiting & purging. He has some fever this morning. Mrs. Andrews spent the day here. I bound my old palm leaf fan this morning & nursed Gus & knit in the evening. I go up & sit awhile with Atheline every evening. She loves company. I don't think I will sit with her long. She can't walk alone, her feet are badly swollen. She is nothing but skin & bone.

Friday 8th - I received a letter from Eugenia this morning. Harrie is quite unwell, confined to his bed. Poor Harrie. I expect to hear is no more soon. Gus some better this morning. He slept very well last night. A good deal of mail this morning. I have knit & nursed Gus nearly all day. Till Morris did not get a letter from her husband today. She is very uneasy about him as 'tis rumored he is killed. Mr. Mark Erwin was here this morning & got fifty lbs. flour.

Saturday 9th - Jinnie scoured my room, the dining room & upstairs today. Matt & I helped some. We did not get the things arranged upstairs this evening. Gus a good deal better today. Rachel Jones stays here tonight, also Dr. Baker, surgeon of Capt. Peter's Artillery. He is very polite & an incessant talker. He bored me awfully. Jinnie fixed a bed for him upstairs. Things were torn up generally.

Sunday 10th - This is a very pleasant morning. Cloudy with occasional sunshine. Dr. Baker left early before breakfast. Rachel will stay till evening I suppose. Atheline was down at the kitchen yesterday evening. Jim brought her down. I think she will never come again. He took her back to sleep at Tena's house. She is a good deal worse this morning. I fear she will not live through the week. They are very uneasy about her. Gus still improving. Matt, Rachel & the children hulling peas. We have plenty of peas, beans & fine potatoes now. Mr. Henry & Pinck came home this evening. We were very glad to see them. Pinck has improved a great deal & grown a heap. Mr. Henry staid at Mr. Bill Miller's last night. They were all well at home when he left. Dora and Matt speak of coming up this summer. Sister Frank sent me a sack of nice cotton. I am certainly greatly obliged to her for it. Mr. Henry & I went to the Murray place this evening. We have eight nice little kids, only four goats have kids yet. Four others to have kids. We had quite a pleasant walk.

Monday 11th July 1864 - Mr. Henry & I & the children went to the Murray place this morning to see the kids. They were delighted with them. Gus was along. It was so pleasant to be walking with my husband & dear little ones. Willie got tired as we came back & fretted some. Very warm today. I have knit some today. Rained nearly all the evening, a slow rain. Atheline no better.

Tuesday 12th - I spent the day at Mr. R. L. Jones'. Mrs. Jones is very low. Her & two daughters are also down with typhoid fever & some of the negroes are sick. She sent me word to come. They have but little company. Till Morris is staying there now. Every one is affraid of the fever. Mrs. Willey Jones has a little daughter very low with flux. I got a little damp as I came back this evening, at least my skirt did. I had my parasol & Laura Jones loaned me her shawl. Mr. Henry went to town today but no news.

Wednesday 13th - I mended some this morning & then cut Pinck's pants of the cloth Dora gave him. Did not finish the pants. They are open in front, his first pair made that way. Anon Jones spent the day here. Tom Tidwell came up this evening from the camps. Some of the 14th Batt. called here last night about 9 o'clock to get some bread & milk. We were abed & asleep. He got up & had them some bread baked. There was ten, only two staid all night. Dr. Baker staid here Monday night.

Thursday 14th - I finished Pinck's pants & began his coat. Mr. Henry & Pinck went down on the creek yesterday evening & gathered a pan full of nice raspberries. We had two pies for dinner & will have enough for two tomorrow. Jinnie baked them this evening & some molasses bread. I sent Lonzo to town this evening after the sley. Mrs. Fanning warped the thread Tuesday. Tena spooled it Tues-

Tuesday & cleaned the flax. 'Tis only ten yds. to be filled with flax & five tow for Mr. Henry's pants & coat. Atheline seems to be sinking very fast. She is very feeble, can't sit up any at all. She seems perfectly resigned to die. Jim Henry, Joe Russell & Jim's orderly staid here tonight. A very hard rain this evening & 'tis reported that Gen. Early has burned Washington City & had captured Harpers Ferry. I hope 'tis so.

Friday 15th July 1864 - I sewed some on Pinck's coat today, would have finished it but went up to sit with Atheline awhile. She is still in her right mind. She told me this evening she was going to die. I hate to think she will soon be gone but 'tis best. He doeth all things well. Mrs. Fanning got the cloth tied in this evening. Sister Jane sent a seven hundred sley instead of a six after she had put it in she had to take it out. I borrowed a seven of Mrs. A. B. Jones. No further news of the burning of Washington City. There is a great deal of sickness in the country & town too. Typhoid fever. Edom Cole & four of his children have died in a month. Lord bless us with health & guard us from our enemies. May we not fall in their hands I pray.

Saturday 16th - Atheline died this morning about half past eight. She went very easy. She died very easy. She was 19 years old last December 21st day. Jim takes it very hard. I have had the headache all day very bad but 'tis some better this evening. Mr. Henry went to Camps this morning to identify his horse that was killed at Warm Springs last fall. I have done nothing today. I made a white bow for Atheline this morning. Mrs. Fanning, Betsey McKinnish, Fannie & Jinnie dressed her very neatly. I had a pair of my fine stockings & a nice pair of gloves put on her & gave her a sheet. She has been good and kind to me & my children. I loved her for loving them. She died perfectly in her mind, told them all good bye last night. She was willing to go. I am glad she was resigned. She was nothing but skin and bone, looked almost like a skeleton. I think she had consumption. She asked for her baby this morning. It was asleep so she did not get to see it & when it awoke they took it to her but she did not notice it. She asked Jim this morning if he was not glad her soul was happy. Tom Tidwell went to Asheville today. Got me 5 lbs. of sugar for fifty dollars. Very dear. I don't use it, only when I have headache. Mrs. Fanning got the cloth started this morning but wove none after Atheline died.

Sunday 17th July 1864 - My head not well this morning. I lay down on the lounge & tried to sleep but could not. Matt kept the flies off me. We sit up till 11 o'clock last night thinking perhaps Mr. Henry would come. The moon shone nearly as bright as day. They sung & prayed all night I think, at least every time I was awake. Yesterday & today have been beautiful days. They started to burry Atheline about half past one I suppose. She smells a little. There was a heap of negroes went on from here. They had plenty of company last night. Matt, Tom & the children went. I was affraid to leave the house in such times as this. I sent for Mrs. Fanning to come & stay while I went to the grave yard but she has the headache & could not come. I then sent to know if Arbazena might stay with me & she sent her. They had not been gone long till Mr. Henry came. I was so glad to see him. I felt so lonely. I got him some milk & fixed his dinner for him & he is now upstairs asleep. Arbazena went up to the hotel place a while ago with Nance Warren. Nance came after her letters that Tom brought out yesterday. Everything looks very lonely. Atheline will never come to me again and ask what she will do. No never. They have come back from the burrying. I received a letter from Sister Matt yesterday evening written the last of May (the 30th) a long time on the road. Mr. Henry took a long nap this evening. Old Boyd is here tonight.

Monday 18th - Mr. Hopson brought Harrie Deaver's body here yesterday evening late. He died last Thursday 14th in the morning at a quarter past one. He was confined to bed about three weeks, suffered a great deal. He was willing to die. He left all his stuff to Eugenia. He thought a heap of her. She was so patient waiting on him. Mr. Hopson left soon after breakfast this morning. We all went up to see Harrie burried, a good many there. It was one o'clock I suppose before they were done. Till Morris came here this morning & went with us. Anon Jones staid here last night. He went with Matt. Very warm today. Harrie's box smelled some, he was in a coffin & then in a box with charcoal. Poor Harrie hated to leave this bright beautiful world, I know.

Tuesday 19th July 1864 - I cut out my muslin dress today & sewed some on it. Matt has made the skirt today. I am going to make a garibaldi waist. Mrs. Fanning weaving. I have filled her quills today. I sent some ten coarse to Johnston's to be mended this evening but did not get it done. I was amused at Willie. He had the coffee pot & Gus wanted it. I told Willie to give it to him. Willie said "Mother Gus might put he head in it." He wanted an excuse to keep from giving it to him. That reminds me of Pinck when he was a little fellow. I was putting some cologne on him he said "sugar in it Mullie lasses in it." I suppose he thought it had sugar and molasses in it to make it smell so sweet. I was much amused at the children & geese some four years ago. It was late in the evening & old Sam was trying to catch two little lambs he was raising by hand. (He put them in the chaff house every night). The lambs ran in among the geese (where they had stationed themselves for the night) & Sam after them. The geese flew in every direction. One came between the kitchen & the house. The children said the geese said one to another "Where am you" & another one would say "git along, git along." They had awful squawking saying something. I teach Pinck & Zona every day. They both learn very fast.

Wednesday 20th - This is Pinck's birth day. He is eight years old today. I remember this day eight years ago very well. Mrs. Peake & Dr. Peake were there. They came the evening of the 7th Saturday & Pinck was born five minutes of twelve on Sunday morning. The house was full of boarders. We had many things then to what we have now. The burning of that hotel nearly broke us up. I hope to be as comfortably fixed some day again. A great many changes have come over us since then. We burried one of our darling children since & now have three younger than Pinck living. Pinck is well grown to his age. The summer he was a year old, 1857, I thought he would die. He was sick three months with diarhea. He was nothing but skin and bone. I have dressed him many a morning & never expected to undress him alive. I nursed him nearly all the time. Sometimes Atheline would walk him some. We rode him out every day. Sometimes Sister Jane & I would ride him but mostly Mr. Henry and I. We had a nice buggy then & a gentle poney we worked. I am thankful my child was restored to health. May he make an honorable high toned man & a useful member of society. I wish all my boys the same. May they all be useful to their country & piously inclined. Lead their young hearts unto Thee Oh Lord I pray. I wish my dear little daughter may grow up a virtuous chaste woman. May she never err from virtuous faith & when they come to die may they "dread their graves as little as their beds." Mr. Henry out in the farm all day. I finished my dress this evening. It fits very neatly. Mrs. Fanning got the cloth out today. No news from the army. They are expecting a raid on Asheville every day. They are fortifying there now. I do hope & pray the enemy will never get in. Like David I ask Oh! Lord may we not fall into the hands of our enemies.

Thursday 21st - Tena washed today and shrunk the cloth for Mr. Henry's pants. I made Pinck a cotton coat today & cut Willie a pair pants of the one & one like my dress only 'tis filled on sollid pine bark dye. Matt helped me some. Atheline's baby grows very slow. I don't think they will raise it. We had a very hard rain & wind this evening. It blew the oats badly. They are cutting oats now. Mr. Henry stays with them all the time.

Friday 22nd - A good deal of mail but little news this morning. Edney the P. M. at Asheville has been succeeded by Capt. Good Roberts. I hope the mail matter will get on better now. I finished Willie's pants & cut Mr. Henry's this evening. He has to go out in the militia next week. I hope he may get off.

Saturday 23rd - Cool this morning. This is tax paying day. A good many men here. I give up the front piazza to them. Winslow Burgin is the collector. He has one leg off just below the knee, lost in battle. Mrs. Hutsell here a short time today. I finished the pants this evening. Matt helped me some. Albert Hawkins cungured the Clarrion this evening to cure fistula. I hope it may do good. He is a very valuable horse & I wish he was well. Pingree Plott staid here last night. He & Tom Tidwell started to camps since dinner. Jinnie baked some cakes for Tom to take with him.

Sunday July 24th 1864 - Very cool this morning. I had the pines taken out the fire places & fire this morning. Mr. Henry has gone to see Capt. Jones to try & stay at home to save his oats. Mary Tutt is here. Her & Matt go to church this evening at the Academy at 2 o'clock. Dr. Cummins preaches. Dinner will soon be in. We have our first cucumbers today. We have had apple dumplings several times. I sent Lonzo to Sister Jane's yesterday with a basket of apples. They are getting ripe (the June apples). Mr. Henry did not get home till nearly sundown. He will go to town in a day or two to get his leave of absence. We did not go to walk this evening as Mr. Henry was tired.

Monday 25th - I fixed my new muslin dress today. It was too long in front & fixed Jinnie's old muslin. No news of importance tonight from the army. Some men robbed old Mr. Fulton about ten miles from here last week. I am affraid they will be here before long. The robbers were blacked. They took money & clothes of Fulton's. Mr. Henry in the oats all day. They are very ripe, need cutting faster than we can possibly cut them. Some government waggons here today for oats.

Tuesday 26th - I have been quite unwell all day, a dull headache. Mr. Henry went to town since dinner. We had eat supper when he got home. He got a furlough for ten days. I am so sorry he has to go out again. I do hope no ill will befall him. I have done nothing but knit today. Matt finished a shirt for Sam today, began it yesterday.

Wednesday 27th - I began Mr. Henry's flax pants today. Anon Jones spent the day here. Mr. Henry in the oats all day. Cloudy today with a little rain this evening. Corn is needing rain a little now. The children are learning very fast. I teach them morning & evening. Zona can read in three letters & Pinck can read & spell very well.

Thursday 28th - I finished Mr. Henry's pants & mended some this evening. My head aches a good deal this evening. I think 'tis from eating black berry pie at dinner. Anon Jones here for dinner today. He has just left. We are having a very good shower for the corn but I fear it will injure the oats. Tena is spinning wool to make Eugenia's flannel of the mareno wool. It is very fine & soft. Mr. Henry sent Pinck & Lonzo to town last Tuesday after a newspaper. They staid all day as Pinck loaned Mollie Henry John to come to the farm. They took Sister Jane some apples & brought back a white rabbit in the basket. William Tidwell sent it to Zona. It is a beautiful pet. It stays upstairs. I am going to have a cage made for it. The children are delighted with it.

Friday 29th - A good deal of mail but little news. I cut Pinck two shirts today but did nothing to them. Some rain today. Mr. Henry went to town this morning, came home for dinner. They are expecting a raid every day on Asheville. Still fortifying. I mended some today. Till Morris spent the evening here. Matt & I went to Betsey McKinnish's this evening. She promised to help spin the wool for Eugenia's flannel, is to send after it in the morning.

Saturday 30th - Mr. Henry and I went to the Murray place this morning to salt the sheep. I frequently go with him. I love to be with him. He is very dear to me. I came back by myself as he stopped with R. L. Jones to chat so I came on as it was getting very warm. He did not come to the house till dinner as he went where they were cutting oats. George finished the rabbit's cage yesterday & he is in it. I cleaned upstairs where the rabbit staid this morning & scoured the buckets, pans & dippers. Matt got dinner. Fannie has been cooking this week as Jinnie can tie oats faster than she can. Fannie tied till dinner today. I mended some since dinner & washed the children & cleaned them. Mr. Henry slept nearly all the evening. He has headache since he got up. Very warm today.

Sunday 31st - This is a very warm morning. Mr. Henry killed Pettit's dog this morning. It killed one of his fine rams. I am very sorry. We have only three fine rams now. Tom Cook is here today. He & Mr. Henry are in the front piazza. Dinner will soon be in. We have apple dumplings for dinner. We have them or some other kind of dessert every day when Mr. Henry is at home. He is very fond of dumplings. I am so sorry he has to go out again. How long Oh! Lord, how long before we will be blessed with peace? Hasten that glad day Oh Father of mercy & love I pray. Tom Tidwell came this evening. He is looking badly. He is a good soldier & a clever boy I think. No news of importance.

August 1864

Monday Aug. 1st 1864 - Tom is broke out with the measles very thick this morning. His face is swollen a good deal. I have sewed some on Pinck's shirt today. Matt upstairs with Tom nearly all day. Mr. Henry out in the oats all day. He wants to get done cutting this week. No mail of importance tonight.

Tuesday 2nd - I finished Pinck's shirt today & knit some this evening. I think of going to see Sister Jane tomorrow & stay till Thursday evening. Mr. Henry at home all day. they are getting on finely with the oats. Mrs. Patsey Jones & Lou Shuford called here this evening. They brought the mail but nothing new. Mrs. Jones is a very fast woman, disgusting in my eyes.

Saturday 6th - I went to Asheville on Wednesday, spent the day very pleasantly. In the evening, Sister Jane & I went up to see Mollie at Mrs. Jessie Smith's. She was not there. We sit awhile and called at Bill Johnston's and Mollie & Mary Johnston went with us to the fortifications, just above Jim Henry's house. I met some of my old friends there, Billie Jeter & Davey Thomas. They belong to the battery. Mollie went with us to Sister Jane's. I had the headache & was very nervous. Mollie & Sister Jane did all they could for me. My head ached all night & all day Thursday. Mr. Henry came over Thursday as it was election day. I was very nervous all the morning. Sister Jane made me some strong coffee & that quieted me some. I sit up but little all day. Mr. Henry came home. I took all the children with me. We went in the buggy & Lonzo rode Clarion. Rose carried Gus on the seat with me. Mollie staid with me till Friday morning, her & Billie. I wrote a note to Matt Friday to have something cooked for Mr. Henry as I expected him to start this morning. I felt a good deal better on Friday morning & wanted to come home but Mr. Henry did not come down to Sister Jane's till so late. He brought Willie home on Clarion. Pinck & Lonzo came this morning. I started from Sister Jane's about 10 this morning. Capt. Jeter called to see Sister Jane this morning which detained me a little. Sister Jane gave me a pretty muslin dress and Gus a nice calico one & several other little things. We were all glad to get home again. Mr. Henry does not go till morning. I have done nothing since I got home, only look around generally. The June apples will soon be gone.

Sunday 7th - I went to church at the Academy. Mr. Reynolds preached. From church I went to Mr. A. B. Jones' to see Mrs. Tilda Morris who is sick. Mr. Henry went to town this morning prepared to go to Burnsville to the militia but got to come home for a week longer. I am very glad of it. Hanes came after me on John. He sent Gus & Rose and sent me word to stay all night but I came home. Tom is going about everywhere.

Monday 8th - Tom gone to see about the cattle. Anon Jones here all day. I made a jar of pickles this morning, have been doing odds & ends all day. Mr. Henry got done his oats last week. The mail brought no news of importance. We had a terrible fight at Petersburg a short time ago. The yanks sprung a mine & killed about 100 of our men & then took our breast works. Our forces rallied & recaptured them. Capt. Jim Cathey was instantly killed, also Lucious Welch. I know Aunt Welch will grieve herself nearly to death about him.

Tuesday 9th - I washed all the children & myself this morning & greased ourselves with sulphur & lard to cure the itch for we all have it some. I have sewed some on Pinck's other shirt today. I am now sitting on the hill, back of the house, under the big locust, writing. The children are playing near me. Rose has Gus in the house. Very pleasant this evening. Tom got back about three o'clock this evening. Mr. Henry in the farm somewhere. 'Tis time for the children's lessons so I must stop. I received a long letter from Sister Frank today. They are all well. Mary wrote some in the letter. She writes very well.

Wednesday 10th - Finished Pinck's shirt today & cut Zona & Gus a bonnett. Matt helped me. We did not get them done. No news of importance. I hope Mr. Henry will not have to go out in the militia. I do wish this cruel war was over. The children learn very fast. Zona can read & spell in three letters. Gus & Willie go to play while the children are reciting.

Thursday 11th - We finished the bonnetts today before dinner. Very warm today. The hands cutting hay at Starnes. Fannie is cooking. I don't like her at all as a cook. She is so contrary but Mary is not at all well & she stays in to attend her. Anon Jones is here tonight. He leaves for the army on Sunday. Tom is still here. He got the furlough lengthened for fifteen days.

Friday 12th - Mr. Henry married Mrs. Fanning & old Boyd last night. I would not have thought it. He has been trying to get her some time. I fixed one of my old homespun dresses for Fannie today & cut Rose an apron of part of it. Matt made the apron. I cut me a body of celecia this evening, low necked. I intend putting tattin around the neck. Mr. Henry went to town today & staid all day. No news.

Saturday 13th - I finished my under body today. Billie Neilson was here today and got some apples. Sister Jane's family are all well. I have done some mending this evening. Tom made the children a check board & a puzzle on the other side of the board. They are delighted with the puzzle. Three soldiers staid here last night. Mr. Henry killed a beef this morning, 'Tis very nice. Tom & Charlie took the fore quarters to Asheville this evening. He gets one dollar a pound for net beef.

Sunday 14th - I spent the evening in reading "Zaider," a very interesting story. Sister Jane loaned me the papers. This has been a very warm day. Mr. Henry & Tom gone to Ruff Miller's (he lives at Tom Jones' old place) to buy a cow. Aunt Tena went to Asheville yesterday evening. Pinck & the little negroes have gone to take the goats to the Murray place. They got out and came down here. They go nearly any where they want to. Gus is asleep out here on the piazza & Zona & Willie are playing out here also. Sunday is a long day to me. This has been a very warm day. Mary has got well. I want to read some in my bible so I must stop for the day.

Monday August 15th 1864 - Very warm today. I hemmed the frill for Zona's bonnet that Sister Jane gave her. Sister Jane will roll & whip it. No news tonight by the mail.

Tuesday 16th - I finished Zona's bonnet today. I teach the children every day. They are learning very fast. Gussie tries to talk but can't say anything. Willie is a very affectionate child, thinks there is nothing in the world like his Papa. Mr. Henry thinks a great deal of his children and I am very glad of it.

Wednesday 17th - Eliza Patton came here Monday & spooled. I had the piece of flannel ready for the loom Tuesday. Eliza Patten worked till Tuesday at dinner. Her & Tena got through spooling both pieces. She then went home. I began today my muslin dress Sister Jane gave me. Matt helped me some. It is made garabaldi waist. Mr. Henry went to town today & got his linnen coat cut.

Thursday 18th - I have had a slight headache all day & yesterday too. I finished my dress this evening. Matt has sewed some on Mr. Henry's coat. Betsey Jamison was here this evening, only staid a short time. The children learn fast & are a dear good set of wee ones. Mrs. Fanning gets on slowly with the flannel as she has warped a piece for us and one for herself this week.

Friday 19th - I am twenty eight years old today. Getting up in years smartly. I finished the coat this evening. My head has not been easy since Tuesday. Matt fills quills for Mrs. Fanning. No news of importance this morning. I do hope we will be able to whip the yanks good at Atlanta.

Saturday 20th August 1864 - Matt & I cleaned upstairs today. We expected Sister Jane this evening. Mr. Henry went after her after dinner but Dora was sick & Mr. Nielson got home last night so her nor Eliza either came. It was dark when Mr. Henry & Pinck came. I have done several things today. I washed all the children & put on their clean clothes this evening. Gus is a little loose in his bowels.

Sunday 21st - Rained a good deal today & still raining. Jim is very unwell, his rupture hurting him. Tom is still here & another little soldier named Sanderson from Cherokee, one of Tom's acquaintences. Preaching at the Academy today. Rev. Byrd. None of the white family went but nearly all the nigs. Pinck & Zona have gone off with Sanderson. I fear they will get wet. Willie is asleep on the bed with his Papa. Mr. Henry is reading "Gerald Gray's Wife." Eliza Neilson sent me three books last week. "Elenor's Victory" & "Master William Mitten." I have only read Gerald Gray. It came out in The Field & Fireside some months ago. Jim seems to be suffering a great deal. I can hear his groans & moans in my room. I am sorry for him. Jim got some easier before night.

Monday 22nd - Jinnie scoured my room today & dining room. I have knit some today. No news tonight by the mail. Very warm today. The children have had no lessons today.

Tuesday 23rd to Friday 26th August - I went to town last Tuesday to see Dora. She is quite sick. I enjoyed the day finely. I went and came alone and as usual, came home with a severe headache. It was not entirely well this morning but now all well once again. I have knit some in the three past days, only a little of that. I am knitting Zona some stockings. Eliza Patton got the cloth started last Tuesday for the negro's dresses. It looks very well. Mrs. Fanning got out the flannel Monday evening. Matt's books came today. "Lady Audley's Secret" & "Robert & Harrald." I have spent most of the day in reading "Robert &c..," 'tis very interesting. A good deal of mail this morning but little news. 'Tis reported that Wheeler is in Sherman's hair. I hope 'tis truc.

Saturday 27th - I have odds & ends as is my usual Saturday's work. Charnes Scaife & a Henderson dined here today. I have not seen Charnes before in twelve or fourteen years. He resembles his father a great deal. Henderson is a stranger to me. Pinck slipped off to town with Lonzo this evening. He was very dirty. I did not know he was gone till he came back. Mr. Henry sent Lonzo after the mail.

Sunday 28th - Mr. Henry & I went to Sardis to Willey Jones' funeral. We took all the children but Gus. The house was so full we could not get in. I sit out in the grave yard & read Hymns till preachinig was over & then we eat our dinner & came home. Pinck & the little soldier (Joe Sanderson) came sometime before we did. Pinck was delighted riding a horse by himself. He took a cry this morning when I told him he had to ride behind Charlie but he rode all alone. The other children were delighted with the trip. I finished reading "Robert and Harold" this evening. It was not very interesting.

Monday 29th - I began Willie a body of orange colored calico. Did not finish it. No news tonight. All are well.

Tuesday 30th - I finished the body today & began two shirt bosoms this evening. Mr. Henry went to town this morning, came back to dinner. Mr. Neilson & Lt. Farnesworth came back with him. No news.

Wednesday 31st - Finished the shirt bosoms & made another bosom. I cut three shirts for Mr. Henry this evening. Mr. Henry out with the hands cutting hay. Fannie & Tena drying fruit last week & this.

September 1864

Thursday Sept. 1st - Cool mornings all this week. A little fire feels comfortable. I began one of the shirts this morning. Sarah Jarrett spent the day here. Mr. Henry went up the creek to a sale today, did not get back till night. Bought some cattle. He is pasturing a good many cattle for the government.

Friday 2nd - No mail of importance this morning. I finished the shirt before dinner. Mr. Henry took Jim, Charlie & Hanes & went after the cattle he bought yesterday. Got them all safe home this evening. I have been reading "Lady Audley's Secret" & knitting. It is very interesting.

Saturday 3rd September 1864 - I have knit & read part of the day. Davey Thomas from Union spent the day here. He belongs to Jeter's Battery. Sargt. Bunch came with him. Bunch lives near Dr. Peake's. We had some nice peaches today & our first watermelons. Mr. Henry sent Pinck to town today after the mail. He could not get in so we got no mail. Dora is getting well. Sister Jane says she will be here next Tuesday, if all well. A very hard rain today. Pinck did not get back till late. I finished "Lady Audley's Secret" this evening. Very well pleased with it as a novel.

Sunday 4th - Mr. Reynolds preaches Lige Night's funeral today at the Academy. None of the whites went from here as it was raining this morning & so damp. Two men came here last night, soldiers to attend the government cattle. I slept so long this morning, I feel very dull today. We generally have very late breakfast on Sunday morning. Lizzie Boyd died Friday night of flux & typhoid fever. A great deal of sickness in the country. She lay nearly six weeks. I hope she is at rest. Old Mr. Common staid here last night. He is one tiresome old man. William Tidwell & Cousin Ann McClure came about three o'clock. I had dinner prepared for them & old Mr. Common. They went up to the Academy to preaching before coming here. She is a very nice girl. She is living with Mrs. John Woodfin now.

Monday 5th - Cousin Ann and William went to town this evening. Mr. Henry went this morning. The news that Mr. Vic brings tonight is rather bad. He says we have fallen back from Atlanta. I am sorry of it indeed but I still hope 'tis for the best. I mended some this morning & then sewed on a shirt some. We had a nice watermelon yesterday evening & a nice musk mellon this morning.

Tuesday 6th - I finished the shirt today & began the last one. Mr. Henry did not go to town today. Court in Asheville this week. Some warmer this week than last. Fannie & Tena drying apples. Elsie weaving. She gets on very slow. I wrote a letter for Matt this evening to A. H. J. She coppied it. Sister Jane sent word by Mr. Henry yesterday that she would be here tomorrow. I hope she will not disappoint me as she has done two or three times before.

Wednesday 7th September 1864 - I did not get the shirt done today as I washed the children this morning & after dinner fixed some thread to make up the negro's dresses. Elsie cut out 26 3/4 yds. yesterday. Sister Jane did not come today as it has been cloudy all day & some rain this evening. Bad time to save hay.

Thursday 8th - I finished the shirt this morning and cut Jinnie's & Fannie's dresses. Made the waist of Jinnie's. Matt has some boils of her arms, very bad ones. I think 'tis from the itch. She has been spinning some this week. Zona got through her primer today. She is very proud of it. Pinck is learning very fast. Mr. Henry promised Zona he would take her to Asheville & get her a new book. She is anxious to go. Willie & Gus amuse themselves at the swing under the cedar trees while I am hearing the other children.

Friday 9th - Mr. Vic brought the wrong mail this morning & took it back so we got no news. I finished Jinnie's dresses & began Fannie's. Jim's baby died today about 12 o'clock. It has been sick for three weeks. It was very poor. I crocheted a little sheet & made a pillow for it. This has been a beautiful day, the first bright day we have had in several.

Saturday 10th - They burried the baby at the middle of the day. I finished Fannie's dress today and began Mr. Henry a pair socks. Matt is going to knit one. This day six years ago, my dear little Cora died. I know it was best that she died but 'tis hard to think so even now. I often think of her and almost wish her back again to this troublesome world but I can go to her but she can never come to me. May I be ready & willing to go & be with my friends that have gone before.

Sunday 11th - This day six years ago we burried our dear little Cora. Her features are indellibly imposed on my mind. I will never forget how my child looked in her narrow bed. None of the other children look anything like her. She was so fond & affectionate. I never knew how much I loved her till she died. This is a warm pleasant morning. Prayer meeting at the Academy today, a negro meeting. The two soldiers still here as cattle guard. I want to go to Steph Jones' this evening as the family is sick. We have our first peach pie for dinner today. Tena cut some peaches too. Dry last week. It was so damp they rotted a good deal. I staid in doors all day today.

Monday 12th - I made Rose's dress today. Elsie got out the cloth, 20 1/4 yds. No news of importance. Gen. Morgan was betrayed & killed at Mrs. William's in

Greenville Tenn. Mrs. Joe Williams betrayed him. I can't wish her anything but an untimely end. I wish our forces had her about one hour & then lose her.[45] Tuesday 13th - I sewed some on Rose's apron & made George a coloured shirt today. Matt is helping me make up the negro's clothes. The children are learning very fast. Zona is going through her book the second time. Gus is trying to talk & Willie loves his Papa as much as ever.

Wednesday 14th - I and Matt went to Henry Boyd's burrial at Capt. Moore's burrying ground. Three of Wilson Boyd's family have died in about ten days. One of his sons was killed in Tenn. & Sam died of fever, so did Henry. He has another son sick with fever. That family has been sorely afflicted. May God comfort them in their bereavement & may they look to Him for comfort, who has caused their wounded hearts to bleed so often during this war. I had headache all the evening but sewed some on Jennie's dress. We got home to dinner. I had some coffee made after dinner and my head got better.

Thursday 15th - Finished Jinnie's dress after dinner. Sim McDaniel took dinner here. I have not seen him for ten years, I reckon before. He belongs to Jeter's Artillery. He has changed but little. Capt. Thrash & two other men came about three o'clock & got dinner. Thrash is to take part of the cattle off tomorrow to exchange for bacon, about 100 I think.

Friday 16th - Mail brought but little news. Mr. Henry went to town today, came home to dinner. Tax giving in day. Old Mr. Reynolds received a good many in the front piazza. They did not annoy me any. Mrs. Norman came in & had a chat. There are three soldiers here attending cattle. One came last Wednesday. The other two have been here some two weeks. I finished Fannie's dress & began Rose's apron. Fires feel comfortable. I have put on a feather bed, I fear it will frost.

Saturday 17th September 1864 - Old Mathews peeling apples yesterday & today. Pinck peeled yesterday & he cut up & today Hanes peeled till dinner & Lonzo after dinner. Fannie ironed this morning. Tena sized some thread today for the shirts. I finished Rose's apron & knit after dinner. Mr. Henry at the mill dam all the evening as it has a leak. They are trying to fix it. He has headache tonight. We had peaches & cream for dinner & peach pie. Mr. Henry got a gal. of honey from Lac Case this week for a bunch of No. 9. 'Tis very nice. I sweeten the pie & peaches & cream with it. It is better than sugar for that I think. Jessie Smith's babe died last Tuesday night. It has been sick since May.

Sunday 18th - Cloudy & raining this morning. Rained some last night. Bad time on fruit that is cut. We have a good deal out. Tena has made some nice peach leather this week. Peaches will soon be gone. I will not try today any more. This is a dull gloomy day. Rain, rain. Mr. Henry upstairs asleep. The children in the front

---

[45] Mrs. Williams did meet her end when John Dowdy, present when Morgan was killed and later captured and sent to an Ohio prison, escaped and returned to the scene of Morgan's death. Confronting Mrs. Williams, he was quoted in "A Civil War Treasury of Tales, Legends and Folklore," edited by B. A. Botkin, as stating he told her "You have five minutes to talk … when the five minutes were up my gun went off – she was dead. I laid her on the porch, crossed her hands, rode off, and I ain't been back there since."

piazza playing. Cordelia Cook (an unmarried woman) had an illegitimate child this week. I am sorry for the family. I must stop now & get out dinner as it is 11 o'clock.

Monday 19th - I made an under body for myself today. Matt made Jim a coloured shirt. No news tonight. The children all well. Pinck & Zona learning fast. Elsie came this morning & began to spool the shirting piece.

Tuesday 20th - Matt & I made Mr. Henry a pair of jeans pants today. Elsie finished the thread by dinner. Mrs. Boyd warped it this evening. No news of importance. The soldiers still tending cattle here.

Wednesday 21st - I mended my hoops today, both sets. Elsie put in the cloth but did not get it started. I knit some after dinner. Rained all day. The fruit I fear will rot that is cut.

Thursday 22nd - I went to Mr. Blanchard's this morning after Gus' shoes. I took him in my lap. My arm got very tired. He enjoyed the ride finely. I did not get the shoes as they were not done. I went over to Cousin Mary Moore's & rested awhile & eat some nice peaches & got home in time for dinner. Gus is not at all well, his bowels are very loose. I fixed the cloth for weaving this evening. Tena & Matt helped. I wove some. Mr. Henry went to town today. A soldier came home with him named Ball. They went to Blanchard's this evening to get Mr. Ball a pair boots made. Mr. Henry brought Gus' shoes, they are too small. He can't get them on. I am very sorry as he is needing shoes. Warm & bright today.

Friday 23rd - Very little news this morning. Till Morris was here a short time this morning. Rained nearly all day. Mr. Henry in the house all the morning & at the mill in the evening. Matt & I made a shirt for Mr. Ball today. He stays here today waiting for his boots. He lets Mr. Henry have a pistol for the boots. He is a nice little soldier. Tena has been making some starch this week. She has not put it to sun yet as it has rained so much.

Saturday 24th - Tena put the starch to sun today. We had one little shower & then fair. Mrs. Emaline Luther spent the day here. She came to see Mr. Henry. He was gone to town. She waited till he came home. He got back about three o'clock. I have knit all day. Elsie weaving today. Aunt Tena wove yesterday. 'Tis said that Gen. Early met with a defeat near Winchester the other day. I am sorry if 'tis so. Mr. Henry brought the mail today. I received a letter from Ell & they were all well. Dora had gone to see Powell's relations. Fowler was at home on furlough.

Sunday 25th - Clear & cool this morning. Matt & I & Zona & Willie went to get some chinkapins, did not get many. Mr. Moffet, one of the cattle guard, left Friday night on big furlough. Two other militia came this evening to tend the cattle. Mr. Henry has gone to see Marsh Williams this morning. The children are at play. Willie out here in the back piazza playing. I am writing in back piazza as the sun is warm & pleasant. I am very tired of having soldiers here. They are a great annoyance to me but what can't be cured must be endured. Such is life & a rugged one it is to some of us.

This is a cold , unfeeling world. When will I be called to my home in Heaven?[46]

Monday 26th September 1864 - W. Henry began this journal over three years ago. War has desolated our happy land sadly since then. I do hope the glad tiding of peace will soon smile on our bleeding country, "how long Oh! Lord how long" is the burthen of our praying.

I made Mr. Henry a flannel shirt today. This has been a lovely day. We have had so much rain of late a bright day is appreciated. The mail brought no news of importance.

Tuesday 27th - I fixed some Willie's flannels today for Gus, his bowels are some better. I knit in the evening. No news today. Some rain.

Wednesday 28th - Mr. Henry went to town today. Maj. Roberts was mortally wounded yesterday by some bush-whackers. Our forces killed the three that had a hand in it, but their lives does not compensate for such a man as Maj. Roberts. Jimmie Henry's little daughter is very sick. I want to go & see her soon. Mrs. A. B. Jones spent the day here, she is a very pleasant lady. Rained a little this evening. I wove a yard this morning & knit after Mrs. Jones came. Elsie not here today. Matt dying the thread for her dresses, I have a dress on it & some aprons for Zona, 'tis four of willow dye & one of white.

Thursday 29th - Mr. Henry off to town today. I intended going but it rained. I have made Charlie a vest today. A basket meeting begins at Hominy Camp ground tomorrow. I do not expect to attend as I have no way of taking the children & I dislike to leave them so much, I love them very dearly. When I go they all want to go, I stay with them, 'tis more pleasure then to go and leave them. Pinck & Zona are learning very fast.

Friday 30th September 1864 - Mail brought little news. Maj. Roberts is dead. I spent the day in Asheville with Mollie. Belle is very sick. Jimmie is in town. Mr. Henry went over today, he went before I did as he had some business to attend to. Fair and warm today.

October 1864

Saturday October 1st - Mr. Henry out about the cattle today. Rain nearly all day. A bad time for preaching. I have read & knit all day, some books Eliza Neilson loaned me.

Sunday 2nd - Mr. Henry went to preaching today, he said a large congregation but a little excitement, they wait till night for that. Matt & I and the children at home all day, I read nearly all day. Rose went to church & I attended. Gus, he is very unwell today, his bowels loose again. Two of the cattle guard here for dinner. Jennie got dinner. I forgot to say that the children's books came in the mail last Friday. Zona a Dixie primer & Pinck a Dixie Reader. They are delighted with them. The Captain's Bride came also. I sent for them to Raleigh, at least I wrote & they came in the mail. I received a letter from Sister Frank yesterday. They were all well.

[46] A separate, single entry made in the journal margin

242

I received one from Sister Matt last Monday. Dora is spending some time with Mr. Powell's relations.

Monday 3rd - I moulded some candles & knit & read today. Mr. Henry went to preaching at Camp ground. They break up tonight. He is going tonight again. Mr. Robers Joice & Mr. Larkin Reeves, two of the cattle guard, went last night & they & Mr. Shroat, the other guard, go tonight. Two soldiers stay here tonight, several stayed here last Saturday night & took off some fifty cattle.

Tuesday 4th - Nearly 12 o'clock when Mr. Henry came last night. Matt & I sit up and waited for him. Gus rested badly last night & Sunday night also. His bowels are very loose. He looks sick, a large worm came from him this morning. I must go down stairs and get out dinner and hear the children's lessons as it is 9 o'clock.

Wednesday 5th October - I put in a quilt today & got some quilted. I am reading a very interesting novel "Bertha Percey," 'tis very good. Elsie not here today as her child is sick.

Saturday 8th - Very cold today. High wind, no frost yet. I have done nothing but knit and sit by the fire all day. Mr. Henry & Pinck went to town yesterday. Pinck staid all night & he and Eliza Neilson came out today got him just at dinner.

Sunday 9th - Cloudy & windy last night so no frost. Mr. Henry took the keys off in his pocket to Starnes so no dinner till nearly three o'clock, wind still blowing from the north.

Monday 10th - A heavy frost this morning, the first one we have had. I have knit and read today "Bertha Persey," she was a good mother. I wish I was as good as she was. Pinck went home with Eliza this evening & stays there tonight. They have a tableaux in town tonight.

Tuesday 11th - Some warmer today. I spent the day in town. Bell is very sick, I fear she will not recover. I pity Mollie, her life is devoted to Bell. I took Zona behind me. Pinck & I came home this evening & Zona. Mr. Henry went to town after dinner he came home before we did. Betsy Jamison came here today, will spend several days. I think a great deal of Betsy, she is a good woman.

Friday 14th - I had the headache some when I came home Tuesday. It has pained me a good deal for two days but today it will once again. I knit some & fixed a dress today. Matt & Betsey went to Ham Cannon's to borrow a sley, they got one. We beamed the cloth this evening & Matt & Betsy began to put it in. No news of importance this morning.

Saturday 15th - Betsy not well this morning. Matt & I finished the cloth before dinner, she put it in the sley and got it started. I fixed Gus a linsey dress this evening, one of Willie's old ones. I am reading a novel "Macarie." 'Tis only tollerable. Eliza liked it very much. I am knitting Mr. Henry a pair mits double cuff. Somebody stole his gloves with plush tops. I am sorry of it they were very nice gloves. 'Tis reported the yanks are on their way to Asheville. I hope 'tis a false rumor.

Sunday 16th October 1864 - Mr. Henry had toothache all night last night but better this morning. Betsey still here. She has got well. Preaching at the Academy this evening her & Matt speak of going. Tom Glenn preaches. Betsey will go home this evening. Mr. Henry & Jack Kerkendoll gone off somewhere on the farm. This is a bright beautiful day, the children at play in back piazza. I gave them some chestnuts a while ago, they enjoy them. Pinck went to the tableau in town last Monday. He has a heap to tell about it to the children. Betsey and I went to the Academy to church this evening. Tom Glenn preached. Mr. Henry came up after preaching to come home with me. 'Twas after sunset when we got here. It was so kind in him to come after me.

Monday 17th - I made Willie a pair pants & Gus an apron today. Mr. Henry in town nearly all day, he says Bell is no better. Mr. Henry suffers a good deal every night with neuralgia in his face. I can sympathise with him as I have had it once very badly.

Tuesday 18th - I have knit and read today. Reading "The Deserted Wife," 'tis very interesting. I thought of going to see Belle today but Mr. Henry's teeth pain him so at night I will not go till they get better. He is so kind to stay with me when I am unwell. I will wait on him & try to get him well.

Saturday 22nd - I went to town on Wednesday & came back Thursday evening. Mr. Henry took Willie, Gus & I. Rose walked to the bridge. We worked the Neilson horse to the buggy for the first time, he seems to be gentle. Hanes came after me, brought Zona so we had a buggy full of children. Rose rode behind, I sit up till two o'clock at Mollie's Wednesday night. Bell is getting better. Eliza & I went up after supper. Willie & Gus were both asleep. Rose carried Gus & Bill Willie. I had the headache all day Thursday, took a long nap at Sisters Jane's. Mr. Neilson came home Wednesday night. I had headache all day Friday but did not go to bed for it. I knit and finished reading "The Deserted Wife." Matt is weaving. I have been doing odds & ends today and nothing generally. Mr. Henry bought Starnes lien last Thursday, he came this morning. Gave 3000$ in Confederate money.

Sunday 23rd October 1864 - Mrs. Joe Green spent the day here & stayed here tonight. She has her baby with her, a large child for only nine months old. Joe Green died some time in June. This has been a bright pleasant day. I have headache a little this evening. Mr. Henry in the house all day, his teeth not well yet.

Monday 24th - Mr. Henry went to town this morning, staid all day. Mrs. Green left this morning. I mended some today & sewed some on Hanes' shirt. Mail brought no news of importance. The children are all very well & learn fast.

Tuesday 25th - I finished Hanes' shirt and made Charlie's today. Quite cold all day. The hands are at work on the road & some making molassess. We make this years in a large box. I don't like it near so well as I do pots. It makes a quantity at a time is one advantage but then they are not thick. I paid Wiley Wells, Mrs. Green's little boy, four hundred dollars today borrowed money.

Wednesday 26th - Some soldiers stay here tonight, they have Jim Mathews, a prisoner. He had been lying in the woods for several months, he says there are some 40 deserters to meet in Haywood on next Monday to go the Yankee land. Cousin Robert Welch came here this evening on his way to Richmond. Going into service. I made Zona's shirt today & cut some chemise for Fannie & Jennie.

Some soldiers stay here tonight from Henderson. The tories killed Mrs. Joe Bryson & wounded two of her daughters one night this week. Oh! This is a cruel world & cruel people in it.

Thursday 27th - They took Mathews to jail this morning. Mr. Henry went to town with the Muse boys. They have been lying in the woods but came in. Mr. Henry came home to dinner. I have been quilting today.

Friday 28th - Jim Henry was here yesterday evening. Cousin Bob Welch still here. Jennie moulded some candles this evening. I finished my quilt today & Matt & I bound it this evening. Cousin Bob went to town this morning intending to go on but missed the stage. It leaves again on Sunday morning. No news of importance. They will soon be done the molasses. I will be glad of it.

Saturday 29th 1864 October - I cleaned up the pantry this morning & emptied some molasses & cleaned up the smoke house & then wove a little. Matt finished her dress yesterday. I went to see Betsey Jamison in the evening to get her to weave the cloth out. She will be here Monday. Cousin Bob left this evening, went to Waynesville.

Sunday 30th - A bright beautiful day. Mr. Henry gone to R. L. Jones' since dinner. The children at play, have not been to dinner yet. I must stop. I coppied the P. O. return this evening. I wanted to get it ready so Mr. Henry could send it off tomorrow before he started to Waynesville, he thinks of starting in the morning.

Monday 31st - Jennie scoured my room & the dining room today. I helped some. They killed a hog today. I am very glad as we were out of bacon and lard too. Jennie made the sausage this evening. Fannie got dinner. Jane Parker & Betsey Jamison staid here last night. Betsey has come to weave.

November 1864

Tuesday Nove 1st - Mr. Henry started to Waynesville yesterday after dinner. I have done some mending today & began a gingham bonnet for myself. Matt & Jennie scouring the front room & piazza today. Jim Henry was here this morning. He is going to move Mollie out to the farm. I don't think she will be satisfied, but such is life women is soon tired of. When the charm of youth is past, man's love is of short duration.

Wednesday 2nd - Betsey cut out Willie's bodies yesterday, the cloth. I finished my bonnet this evening. Cloudy & rain all day. No news of importance.

Thursday 3rd - Matt & I sewed on Willie's bodies today. Finished one & began the other. Cloudy & rain today. Betsey gets on slowly weaving.

Friday 4th - Finished both bodies today & knit some after dinner. Mail brought us no news. Fair & pleasant today.

Saturday 5th - Clear & cool. I have been mending all day. Mr. Henry came home this evening. We are all well.

Sunday 6th - Preaching at the Academy today, Mr. Reynolds. None of the whites went. Betsey & Matt have gone to prayer meeting tonight at the Academy. I hope it may do them good. Till Morris spent the day here.

Monday 7th October 1864 - Cloudy & gloomy this morning, it well accords with my unhappy temper. I must write several letters today. Mr. Henry has gone to town this day. 'Tis reported there was a fight at Spring Creek yesterday. I can't believe it. No news in town.

Monday 14th - A week has past since I wrote, nothing of importance has transpired. I sometimes think I will lay aside my journal forever, but then again I think it may afford my little ones some pleasure when I have passed away from this cold unfeeling world. 'Tis nothing but trouble & vexation of spirit here below. Surely there is rest for the weary in the world to come. Mollie came out to their farm last Friday to stay awhile. Bell is improving very slow. Mr. Henry is very unwell, something like gravel. He has suffered a great deal since last Thursday. Very cold this morning. I am quite unwell today with a pain in my right side, I feel very little like writing so I will stop for today.

Tuesday 15th - I cut out a dress for myself today, sewed some on it. I am making it saque waisted. It will suit me better for awhile now. The children have lessons every day. Zona is learning very fast. Pinck has but little taste for his book. He ought to be kept at his books all the time. He will be nine years old in July. I will soon be an old woman. Mr. Henry is not improving any. I am sorry of it as he suffers so much. I hope he may soon be well.

Wednesday 16th - I sewed some on my dress today but did not finish it. I have a severe pain in my side today. Mr. Henry in bed nearly all day. He is not improving any though he is taking medicine all the time from Dr. Hilliard.

Thursday 17th - Mr. Henry went with some men last night to arrest a deserter, they took him to Asheville. Mr. Henry & Mr. Norton did not get back till eleven o'clock. Matt & I sit up till they came. I sewed some on my dress last night. Mr. Henry is not so well today from being out last night.

Friday 18th - I finished my dress today. It fits very neatly. No news this morning. I had two letters from Eugenia last Monday. She has received the flannel. I intended to go to see Mollie this evening but it rained. I knit some. My side is not entirely well yet but better.

Saturday November 19th - Last Thursday was little Cora's birthday. She would have been seven years old. I almost wish she could have lived but God saw fit to take her to himself, 'tis best that she died. Rained nearly all day. Gus can say any word but does not try a sentence yet. He is a dear sweet child but shows a little too much temper. Willie is very quiet, loves to play alone. Pinck & Zona make enough noise for a whole family. They are full of life and mischief.

Sunday 20th - Rained all day. Mrs. Fanning moved today. I am glad Mr. Henry has got rid of one of his women renters. Sam & others killed the cow that Hannah Cook claimed last Friday. She is a bad woman. Mr. Henry had her driven home last Friday morning. Hannah took on a good deal about it. The cow certainly belongs to Mr. Henry, she was very fat.

Monday 21st - I crocheted Zona a net today. Turning cold. We have had some snow tonight. Mr. Vick brings news that Sherman is burning things generally in Ga. & is now marching on Atlanta. I do so wish we could capture his whole army. Mr. Henry still suffers a good deal but some better than he was a week ago.

Tuesday 22nd - I cut my dress this morning but sewed but little on it. This has been a very cold day a little snow on the ground. Fannie will get down the wool today mixing & then she will spin. Tena is spinning but gets on very slow.

Wednesday 23rd - Sewed some on my dress today. Still very cold, snow not all gone yet. Mr. Henry still goes about. He ought to be very still, he improves very slowly. I wish I could keep him quiet for a week & in that time he would be nearly well.

Thursday 24th - Some warmer today than yesterday. I finished my dress today. Mr. Henry & Matt went to Mr. Blanchard's this morning. Mr. Henry came home to dinner but Matt staid till nearly night. Mr. Henry went to Mrs. Jim Cowen's this evening, did not get home till nearly dark. Sam & others killed four beeves & two hogs today.

Friday 25th - I finished my dress yesterday. I spent the evening very pleasantly at Mollie's. Bell is improving, she has measles now. Pinck staid all night. Zona came home with me. Snow nearly all gone. Mr. Henry sold one of the hogs to Mr. Stevens at three $ a lb. Dear meat.

Saturday 26th November 1864 - I made some hair grease today of beef marrows perfumed with cologne. Tena rendered up some of the tallow and lard. Willie Alexander, Mollie's brother, spent the day here. He is nearly 15 years old. Sam & Jim cut up the beef today. Sister Jane got one beef weighing 313 lbs., 'tis very nice. They slaughtered six head of cattle.

Sunday 27th - A detail of fifteen men (going towards Haywood) came here last night & cooked their rations. Mac English was along but I did not see him. They left about 12 o'clock. Mr. Henry & I went to sleep long before they left this morning. This room was full of dirt nearly. Matt went to Mr. Steve Jones' yesterday morning, I expect her this evening. Jim Henry, Willie Alexander & three other men here this morning. They all left before dinner. Mr. Henry has been lying down nearly all day, he is a good deal better this evening. I am very glad of it. Cloudy nearly all day but now 4 o'clock nearly clear. I hope we may have some pleasant, dry weather now for awhile.

Monday 28th - I did some mending & made Gus an apron. We heard today that Jim Ballew was dead. He has been sick near a month of fever. He is to be burried at Sardis tomorrow at 12 o'clock. I feel very sorry for his wife, she has three little children. May God temper the wind to the shorn lamb.

Tuesday 29th - Mr. Henry, Pinck & I went to the burial today. We rode very fast going for fear of being too late, we got there in good time. He looked very natural. His wife seemed almost inconsolable. I did nothing of note today. Cut Zona a dress of one of my old waisted skirts.

Wednesday 30th - I sewed some on Zona's dress today. We are all well & I am very grateful for health.

December 1864

Thursday 1st - Matt, Pinck & I went to prayer meeting last night at the Academy. Not much excitement. I spent the day with Sister Jane very pleasantly, dark when we got home. Mr. Henry was with me. He is improving slowly.

Friday 2nd - I finished Zona's dress today. It does not fit so I will change it a little. Warm & pleasant today. Not much news this morning.

Saturday 3rd - I fixed Zona's dress today, it fits very neatly now. I have done several things today. Cloudy nearly all day. Tom Glenn's babe was buried last Thursday.

Sunday 4th - I went to church at the Academy today, took Zona & Willie. Mr. Henry staid at home as he had a pain in his back. Mr. Reynolds preached. Till Morris, Mary Curtis & Henry Jones took dinner here. We all went to prayer meeting. They had a great excitement among them. Mr. Henry staid at home. Old Boyd & his wife are here tonight, this is a beautiful moonlight night.

Monday 5th - Mr. Henry, Till Morris & I went to town today. Till & I done some shopping. We took dinner at Sister Jane's. Night when we got home.

Tuesday 6th - Till staid here last night, left early this morning. 'Tis rumoured that [Pers?] Jones married Peter Rich tonight. John Thrash & a Miss Luther married Sunday night. People still marry though the war is going on. I sewed some on Gus an apron today, made some apple butter after dinner & some molasses candy. The candy will not be done enough to pull this evening.

Wednesday 7th - Fannie washed up my room this morning. I must go now & give out dinner. Mr. Henry went to town yesterday & today. N. W. Woodfin's overseer was killed Monday evening by a drunk man. They are trying the man. I must pull the candy this morning. The candy is not very nice, scourched a little. I finished Gus' apron this evening. Fannie scoured the hall room & front piazza this evening. Matt helped her.

Thursday 8th - This is tithe giving in day. I knit some & fixed my net. Pinck is complaining some, I expect he is taking the measles. Very cold & windy today. Mr. Henry at home all day, he is not at all well. I hope he will soon be well.

Friday 9th - Pinck in bed nearly all day. Mr. Henry has neuralgia in the face last night. Did not rest well, his face very sore this morning. No mail of consequence, very cold, wind from North & sleeting & snowing all day. I have done nothing but knit on Pinck some socks. Jennie is sick, I suppose 'tis measles she is taking. Fannie does the cooking. This is a bad time to have measles, so cold, the dead of winter. I hope they may all get through well. I do hope & pray for health for my family. I am so grateful for it.

Saturday 10th December 1864 - Mr. Henry in bed nearly all day. His mouth so sore he can't eat anything, only a little soup or coffee. Pinck is broke out thick with measles this morning & doing very well. Mr. Henry sent Tim to town this evening to get five lbs. of sugar for sixty dollars & one lb. of crushed sugar for 15$. Dear sugar. No news in town. Snow melting some today.

Sunday 11th - A bright sunny day with wind from North. Quarterly meeting at Miller meeting house going on today. Snow melting very fast. Mr. Henry is no better. Pinck some better, Jennie broke out with measles this morning. Some soldiers staid here last night. I must stop this time. Till Morris stopped here this evening. She had been to Miller's meeting house to church. It began to turn cold about 12 o'clock today & now at night very cold. Matt and Betsy Jamison gone to prayer meeting at Mrs. Caroline Jones. I think they will suffer with cold. Old Mr. Blackwell will stay here tonight.

Monday 12th – Mr. Henry's jaw very painful. I think it will beal. I have knit some today & waited on him and Pinck. Pinck is doing finely. Betsy warped the jeans today. Very cold all day. I suffered more with cold last night than I ever did I think. We kept a fire all night.

Tuesday 13th – Mr. Henry has eat nothing since Saturday. He suffers a great deal with his jaw. Pinck sit up a good deal today. I have done nothing but wait on them.

Wednesday 14th – Pinck up all day. Some warmer today. I made three hanker-chiefs today, one for Willie, one for Zona & the other for myself. Mr. Henry no better. He can't eat anything. His jaw is swollen so he can't get his mouth open. 'Tis very painful to swallow as 'tis swollen inside. Betsey began to weave today.

Thursday 15th – Mr. Henry sent after Dr. Thrash today. He came tonight. Thinks 'tis from his teeth. I poulticed it yesterday & today. We will still continue the poultice till it breaks. Pinck is about generally, a difficult matter to keep him in the house. I have knitted a little today & waited on Mr. Henry. He has not eat any-thing but a little soup & coffee since Saturday & very little of that. He is getting very feeble.

16 December 1864 – Mr. Henry's jaw broke in the morning and run a good deal. It has been running some all day. Mrs. Hawkins was here this evening. I went to Blanchard's this evening to get Zona & Willie some shoes made. Pinck took some leather. Zona rode behind me. We went on with old Mrs. Hawkins. Mr. Henry is some better this evening & I am very glad of it. He has not eat anything yet.

Saturday 17th - Mr. Henry's jaw still running. He is very feeble, does not eat anything. 'Tis rumoured that Kirk[47] is coming up the river to attack Asheville. I hope 'tis not so. Cloudy & some rain today. Cousin William Henry stays here to-night. Betsy is weaving upstairs, her & Matt stay up there all the time. She is afraid of getting the measles.

Sunday 18th - Cloudy & raining this evening. Brother Jimmie took dinner here. Miss Ellen Jones has been here all day. Matt & Betsy went to Cannon's this morn-ing. I sent for Matt, she was at Mrs. Norman's. Marcella Allen came home with her after dinner. Betsey has not come yet, the girls are upstairs. Mr. Henry is lying down, he sits up but very little. I sent some tallow to town by Uncle Sam last Thursday to exchange for cloth. Got twenty yds. of nice sheeting for 25 pounds of tallow. No news from Kirk. Lord hear this my humble petition, may we not fall into the hands of our enemies and Oh! Father of mercy, hasten the glad day when peace will once more smile on our bleeding country, and may my dear husband soon be restored to health is my prayer.

Monday 19th - Betsey has not come yet. Matt & Marcella Allen went to prayer meeting at Albert Hawkin's last night, they were late getting home. Matt has had toothache all day. Louise McKinish stays with her tonight. I made a pair drawers

---

[47] Col. George Washington Kirk, leader of North Carolina Union regiments who con-ducted raids into western North Carolina

Col. George Washington Kirk with his wife, Louisa Jones Kirk
(Photo courtesy Leon Kirk and Joey Woolridge)

for Zona today & waited on Matt some. Rose is not at all well, Jennie is improving very fast, Pinck still keeps going.

Tuesday 20th December 1864 - I received a letter from Eugenia last night, they are all well. Matt slept very little with her jaw last night. Zona is not well today. I cut some shirts for Pinck today & skirts for Zona also some drawers for her, sewed but little. Capt. Russell & brother took dinner here. Sherman got through to the coast, I am sorry he did.

Wednesday 21st - Zona still unwell, measles I think. Mr. Henry is not at all well but improving. I finished another pair of Zona drawers today. An agent for a Georgia hospital was here today. The yankees robbed the hospital, he is trying to get supplies. Betsey same today. Matt's jaw better. Gus is not well. Rose & Jennie breaking wool. No war news.

Thursday 22nd - Cold & snowing. Zona & Gus still unwell. Fannie hurt her back this evening. That throws us out of a cook. She is not very stout at this time. I sewed some on Pinck's shirt today. Jennie & Rose breaking wool today.

Friday 23rd - Gus quite sick all day, sit in the large rocking chair all day, can see some measles on his face. No news of importance. I finished Pinck's shirt & knit on Mr. Henry's gloves. He did not like the mits so I have taken them out & knitting fingers. Rose is down today, measles I think. Mary has measles. Jennie & Jim cooking today. Not so cold today as yesterday. Some snow yet. Tena washed today.

Saturday 24th - Tomorrow is Christmas. I will not make any cakes or anything. I have my hands full attending to the sick. Zona is down & Gus broke out very well with measles. Some warmer today. I finished Mr. Henry's gloves today. Jennie & Jim cooking. Rose is doing very well with measles. Fannie & Mary both doing well.

Sunday 25th - Christmas Day. This day one year ago Sister Jane & Mrs. Black took dinner here. Today we had a common dinner. The agent for the hospital Mr. Botts called here again. The people up the creek contributed largely, all but Ham Moore. He gave five dollars. Mr. Henry gave two sacks flour, 2 bu corn, 1 gal brandy, 1 bu dried apples, 2 gal. syrup & 2 dozen (24) candles. Zona is broke out very well with measles. Willie is not well and has not been for several days. Matt & Betsey at home all day, Matt is afraid to go out on account of her jaw. She suffered a great deal with it. I think the negroes will enjoy their holiday but little as Fannie has to wait on Rose & Mary and Jennie has just got up from measles. Mollie Henry sent the children a basket of cakes last night. They were delighted this morning at Santa Clause's visit. Zona & Gus could not eat them but Pinck & Willie enjoyed them finely. Mr. Henry stayed in the house all the time, helps me with the sick, he is not well at all. I don't see how I would do without him, he is ever kind to me & the little ones & I love him for it.

Monday 26th - The children all seem to be doing well, Willie is still complaining. I hope be well. The measles will soon come out on him. Mr. Henry in the house all day. Pinck helps me wait on the sick very well, he is very willing to do all he can. I sewed some today not much.

Tuesday 27th - Mr. Henry went to town today, no news. He took dinner at Sister Jane's, they are all well. He borrowed some coffee of her as we were out. I have sewed some today on Zona a skirt. I did but little as I had three sick children to attend to. Willie in bed nearly all day. Zona is improving but Gus gets up slowly, his bowels are very loose.

Wednesday 28th - I finished Zona's skirt today & sewed some on another one. Matt is helping me. Betsey gets on very slowly with the jeans. Pinck is needing a coat badly. He has been a great help to me since they have been sick. Zona sit up a good deal today. Gus some better. Rose & Mary doing well. This is the negroe's last day of Christmas, I am glad of it. Mr. Henry in the house all day, he is not entirely well yet can't get his mouth open much. It has been nearly three weeks since he did open it. He does not suffer any pain now. The glands are swollen in his jaw yet. Ellen Hawkins spent the day here & here tonight as 'tis snowing this evening. No news of importance from the war. Pinck & I got up soon this morning & parched coffee, dressed the children & cleaned the house before breakfast.

Thursday 29th 1864 December - Mr. Henry sent Ellen home this morning. The snow melting some. I finished the last one of Zona's skirts today. The children improving. I fear Willie will not get along well as he was not broke out so well as the other children. I hope he may do well, he took teas very well & is anxious to get well again.

Friday 30th - Mrs. Benson & husband spent the day here, she has three children. She had her babe with her, a boy. She is looking very well. But little mail this morning. I sewed some on a shirt for Pinck today. Gus is very cross. Zona is running about the house generally. Willie does not seem so well. Mr. Henry in the house all day. Till Morris was here this evening.

Saturday 31st - The last day of the old year. It has had no great trouble for me. I wonder what 1865 will bring. I hope it may bring peace. The yankees have commenced the fight on Wilmington. Willie is able to go about but still droopy. Gus is improving but very cross. Zona about well. Very cold & snowing some nearly all day. Mr. Henry at the mill part of the day, the first time he has left the house any time since Tuesday. He is so kind in helping me attend the children. Rose staid in my room all day. Her first since getting over measles. Fannie spinning, Jennie cooking. I finished Pinck's shirt today & made Zona & Gus some garters, they are delighted with them. I did some other things.

1865

"... 'Tis so sad to think we are subjugated..."

January 1865

Sunday January 1st 1865 - Very cold this morning but a beautiful fair day, snow melting some. Willie does not seem well at all. Gus nearly well. Zona out in the kitchen, her first time since getting well. Willie & Gus are both asleep. Willie has some fever this evening. This is the first day of the new year, may it be a happy one to me & my dear ones. May this year close the bloody struggle & may we come out victorious. I do hope Mr. Henry may not have to go into service again. O! Lord hear this my simple prayer. Grant us a speedy and an honorable peace. Deliver us from our enemies; unto Thy kind protecting hand do we give our lives our country. Help us in this great hour of need. Be with us in the coming conflicts and ere many months roll around may Thou see fit in Thy infinite wisdom, to say it is enough lay by Thy sword, and unto Thee shall be all praise. Amen.

Monday 2nd - This has been a beautiful day, the snow melting very fast. I made Willie a pair drawers today & cut him two shirts. Mr. Henry went to town. No news. Mr. Neilson is quite sick with fever.

Tuesday 3rd - I made Willie a pair drawers today. Matt made one of his shirts. Mr. Henry went to Mr. George Owensby's burrial today, he died of relaps of measles. I sympathise with his bereaved family.

Wednesday 4th - I spent the day with Mollie. She is sick but getting better. Late when I got home. A very pleasant bright day, snow nearly all gone. Bell can walk a little with some one by her side.

Thursday 5th - Betsey got out the jeans yesterday. I cut Pinck's coat today & sewed some on it. Mr. Henry went to town today. Cousins John Love & Lucius Welch came home with him, they are here tonight.

Friday 6th - But little mail this morning & no news of importance. I finished Pinck's coat & cut his pants. Bob Luther spent the day here, came to see Matt. Rained nearly all day.

Saturday 7th - Matt & I finished Pinck's pants & made Willie a pair. This has been a very cold windy day. Mr. Henry at the mill most of the day.

Sunday 8th - Pleasant to yesterday. Mr. Henry & Pinck went to the camp ground as the battallion is forging there now. I read all day. Betsey warped a piece of cloth yesterday, forty three yds., two dresses for myself the other for the children.

Monday 9th - Cloudy & looks like rain. I fixed the cushions over in the chairs this morning. I think I will write to Dora & Matt after dinner, we have not heard from them in some time. I wrote to Dora today, also to Lou & then coppied the P. O. return. Fayette Jones & Capt. Deaver stay here tonight, also Tom Tidwell. Cool & some rain this evening. We heard some time ago that Tom was a prisoner but I am glad 'tis not so, he is a nice boy.

Tuesday January 10 1865 - I bound one of my homespun dresses as 'tis too short. I cut Mr. Henry a pair pants and Willie & Pinck a pair. I sewed some on Mr. Henry's. No news by tonight's mail. The children are all well of measles. Pinck and Zona learn very fast.

Wednesday 11th - I did not finish Mr. Henry's pants yesterday as I was fixing in the cloth. Matt will weave some this week as Betsey has the measles. She has been complaining some days but only broke out this morning.

Thursday 12th - Finished Mr. Henry's pants today and began Pinck's. Cousin Louise Gudger called here this morning, she only staid a short time. Matt began the children's dresses today. Wove Mr. Henry a coat lining on the first end. I filled some quills.

Friday 13th - We had a heavy rain last Monday night & thunder Tuesday morning. The creek was very high but it did not injure the dam any. I finished Pinck's pants & began Willie's today. The people of Asheville give the soldiers a dinner tomorrow. No news by the mail this morning. This has been a bright cold day. Betsey improving rapidly. Matt still weaving.

Saturday 14th - Matt, I and Rose scoured my room today. I did some darning in the evening on the children's stockings, they wear them out almost as fast as I can knit them. Matt cut out the children's dresses & Mr. Henry's coat lining today. We heard this evening that Anon Jones was dead. He was wounded two months ago. I sympathise with the family. He was a nice young man.

Sunday 15th - This has been a beautiful day. Pinck fell off the mill steps yesterday evening but did not get hurt much. It is a wonder it didn't nearly kill him as he fell from the top step to the ground. Mr. Henry & Pinck went to Mrs. Quinn's this morning. We had four soldiers here for dinner. Tom Tidwell was here a while this evening, he heard Pinck was badly hurt & came to see him. Till Morris & Mag Morris came here this evening, they & Matt have gone to preaching tonight at the Academy. I don't know whether they are coming back here tonight or not. The children are all asleep. Mr. Henry sitting here reading.

Monday 16th January 1865 - I finished Willie's pants today & cut the children's dresses. Betsey weaving today. No mail tonight as the bridge over Broad river washed away by the freshet.

Tuesday 17th - Matt & I made Zona's dress today & sewed some on Gus'. The children are learning very fast. Gus can talk nearly plain. He can say any sentence of three words. He speaks nearly as plain as Willie. Willie is a good quiet child, talks but little.

Wednesday 18th - Mr. Henry went to town today to get his coat cut but forgot it. He speaks of going tomorrow. I finished Gus' dress this evening. Their dresses fit very neatly, made infant waist with pockets. They are delighted with their pockets. The hands killed six hogs yesterday weighing 888 lbs. I am very glad as we have been out of lard some time.

Thursday 19th - Mr. Henry went to town today, did not get his coat cut but left the cloth to be cut this week. He bought an oven lid today & a skilit & lid for which he paid 79.50. It seems incredible. Matt is weaving Zona & Gus a spotted dress each. They are spotted with red, they look very neat.

Friday 20th - I made Zona an apron today & Betsey made one. I made Gus an apron yesterday. No mail of importance today.

Saturday 21st - I done several odds & ends today. Rained all morning but clear in the evening. Charlie is to marry a negro of Stephen Jones tonight. He is very young to marry, just 18.

Sunday 22nd - Gloomy all day with some rain. Mr. Henry at home all day. Mr. Julius Alexander was here awhile today. I had a long hunt since dinner for the nutmeg grater. After looking all over the pantry I found it in the P. O. shelves. Charlie & wife came over today to see the old folks. Tena does not like the match much. I want to write some letters this evening so I will stop. I wrote to Sister Frank this evening.

Monday 23rd - I hemmed frills for my gowns today & cut the gowns. Cold today. No news of importance. Mr. Henry about the mill. We have had a very severe winter. A great deal of snow & rain, the roads are very bad. Vic has not come home tonight. The children are learning very fast. Gus is improving in talking very fast as he can say anything nearly as plain as Willie. Willie is a very quiet child.

Tuesday 24th January 1865 - Mr. Henry went to town today but did not get his coat. Matt helped me sew on my gowns today. Mr. Vic (the mail carrier) came this evening. He had been water bound. No news. He got me a pound of copperas at Greenville for ten$. 'Tis very dear. We used to get it at 5 cts. per lb. Very cold today.

Wednesday 25th - Finished one gown today. This has been a very cold day. Mr. Henry at the mill most of the day. Tonight I told Gus to warm his feet before he went to bed. He sit in his little chair with his feet stuck up to the fire. Mr. Henry told him to take them down. He said "Muppa told me." I cherish up all their little sayings, they will be men some day if they live. I pray they may be honorable men & high toned. May my daughters be virtuous & mild & may they all have good & active minds is the wish of their mother.

Thursday 26th - I finished my other gown today, they look very neat. Very cold today. I fixed a gown this evening. Mr. Henry at home all day.

Friday 27th - I have knit nearly all day. I have to heel Pinck's socks after he wears them two weeks. I put in every night in knitting & some times knit in the day, it takes a heap of knitting for four pair little feet. The mail brought little news. Still very cold, the coldest spell we have had this winter. It has been cold since Monday. The ice is very thick on the branch & in some places frozen over.

Saturday 28th - Mr. Henry went to town today. The Court House took fire soon after he got there and burned down. It was an accident. 'Tis thought no other house was injured to any extent, though several took fire. Lt. F. M. Corn, Dr. Murdock & some of the soldiers went to the yankees this week. I am not at all surprised at Corn as I have a very contemptable opinion of him.

The new moon tonight lies flat on her back, I am no star gazer so can't tell what sort of weather it indicates. I hope we may have some pleasant weather now. This has been a very cold day, wind from the north. They got nearly all the county papers out of the Court house and all the prisoners, some fifty. I am glad no lives were lost. I have knit & darned stockings all day.

Sunday 29th January 1865 - Matt spotted the children a dress each, Zona & Gus. She finished weaving them last Monday. Betsey will finish the piece now. This has been a cold day but not near so cold as any other day this week. The ice on the branch not melting any, very thick this morning. Tom Tidwell was here today also Capt. Joe Russell. Tom is looking very well. I played with the children some tonight blind fold. They enjoyed it finely & so did Mr. Henry, they are all asleep now. Mr. Henry is sitting here reading the Testament. I finished reading through the Old Testament today the third time. I read it through once at school in Salem & have read twice since I was married. I find it nearly all very interesting. 'Tis near bed time (eight o'clock).

Lord keep us safe this night. Guard us from all harm. Bless us with health and contentment and deliver us from this cruel war and O! Merciful Father I pray that we not fall into the hands of our enemies.

Mr. Henry tells me to say that the black sow he got of old Billie Knight had pigs last week. He lost two sows just at the time of pigging. We think some one eat the sows. One of the sows lost her pigs a few day's since. Hogs are very scarce through the country.

Monday 30th - Matt & I made Rose two chemise today. Betsey is weaving. This has been a very pleasant day. No news of importance.

Tuesday 31st - Warm & pleasant today. I made a cradle tick cover, Matt made a pair pillow slips. I cut Mr. Henry a pair of pants & sewed some on them. Killed four hogs today, we only have 10 hogs for bacon this year. We will try to make it do us. Pork is very scarce through the country. I hope no one may suffer for bread. The meat is not in the country for all.

February 1865

Wednesday Feb. 1st - Matt & I finished Mr. Henry's pants today. I began Zona's hood this evening, knitting it on large wooden needles. Mr. Henry went to Starnes' this evening to see about some hay, he did not get back till dark. Betsey got out the cloth this evening. I had the children's dresses shrunk. I want to make them this week.

Thursday February 2nd 1865 - I cut the children's dresses today, sewed some on both but did not finish either. Betsey warped the web for the negro's pants. Her & Matt beamed & began to put it in. Matt is going to wear it as 'tis linsey instead of jeans. Mary Blanchard was here today. She brought my shoes home, they fit very neatly.

Friday 3rd - Not much mail this morning, there is a great rumour of peace. Commissioners have gone to Washington City for the purpose. I do hope & pray daily for an honorable peace. I finished Gus' dress today. Matt got the cloth started. This has been a pleasant day for Feb.

Saturday 4th - Very pleasant all day. I finished Zona's dress today & mended some & then knit. I have the head piece of her hood done and am knitting the border, Matt wove all day. Miss Ruth Jones stays here tonight. We hear this evening that the yankees & tories are fighting our forces on Johnathan's Creek. Mr. Henry had some rations cooked this evening, he is going on with the forces. The courier has gone to Asheville for reinforcement. I do hope they may not get here. I see something on the next page that Mr. Henry has written this evening. It makes my heart ache to read it. 'Tis I do pray to God with a trusting heart that He will spare my dear husband's life. May he soon return to this family safe and well.

4th February 1865 - As the enemy are reported to be on Johnathan's Creek and I am going with the command to meet them, I will only say that all or any of my property that my be left after paying my just debts, I want my wife Cornelia Catherine to have and to hold and dispose of to suit herself either by sale or gift.

The claim Robert M. Henry holds against me is fraudulent and injust & I have employed my old friend Mr. N. W. Woodfin & Judge Baily as atterneys & I wish every evidence searched for.[48] Sister Eliza was a witness in all the agreement I ever had with Robt. M. H. & that was about keeping the Hotel & settlement was demanded on all and everything outstanding between us in the year of 1855. The witness G. W. Peake was present & J. L. Henry knows we quit all business together.

To my wife & children I hope to return shortly in peace & the country I hope may soon be free from war and its terible consequence.

Wm. Henry

Sunday 5th - Mr. Henry went to Asheville last night, started at 8 o'clock & got back about 12. A courier staid here last night on his way back to Haywood, he is sent on with amunition. Mr. Henry says there is very little excitement in town. One Co. is ordered to Waynesville so Mr. Henry is not going, I am very glad of it. I packed up his provisions ready to start and sit up and waited till he came home. I do hope they may not come here. Col. Jarrett & Mr. D. Blackwell were here today. They say a courier came in this morning & reports that Waynesville is burned. I hope 'tis not true. Matt, Betsey & Miss Ruth went to church at the Academy today.

---

[48] Robert M. Henry, brother of William L. Henry filed suit against William claiming there had been an agreement between them to equally divide any property willed by their father on his passing. William Henry disputed this claim. The case eventually made its way to the North Carolina Supreme Court.

Mr. Henry slept nearly all the evening. I feel very sleepy but will try to sit up till night.

Monday 6th February 1865 - Mr. Henry went to town today. Got his coat cut, I will begin it tomorrow. Matt still weaving, she gets on very well. Betsey went home this morning, she has been here near two months. I made Zona's hood today, 'tis very pretty. Willie insists on having a comfort & Gus wants a hood. I reckon I will have to make them something to please them. I made Zona an apron today. Cold but bright today. The children played in the yard nearly all day. Dark when Mr. Henry got home.

Tuesday 7th - Sleeting & cold this morning. We had a letter from Mr. Hopson last night saying their little Fannie was dead. I know that nearly killed Eugenia, she was so devoted to her. We had a letter from Dora yesterday. Pa was not well, the others very well. I will begin Mr. Henry's coat today. I intend to cut the pattern as ten$ is too much to give for having a coat cut. Vic brought no news. He brought mine & Matt's knitting needles. He gave 5$ a set. Very dear I think & then they are entirely too large. I cut the pattern & sewed some on Mr. Henry's coat.

Wednesday 8th - I sewed all day on the coat but got but little done. Robert Tidwell came here last night. He says Uncle Welch is dead, had an apoplectic fit Sunday night & died nearly instantly. He was at his son Bob's, had ran there from the yankees. Robert says the Kirk band are making their way back to Tenn. I wish our forces could have caught them. Mr. Henry went to town today. Very cold all day. Mr. Henry has some lambs. This is bad weather on them.

Thursday 9th - Very cold today, blowing and snowing all day, too cold to snow much. I have sewed on the coat today. I think I will finish it tomorrow. No news of importance. Mr. Henry got the children some new books, they are delighted with them. Willie does not want to learn his a. b. c.

Friday 10th - Snow thawing some today. Mr. Henry at home all day. He boiled the beef brine over today, the beef looks very nice. I finished his coat today, it fits very neatly. The tails are very long. It has very nice buttons on it. He gave twenty$ for one dozen buttons. Everything is very dear. Salt $2.25 a lb, sugar 15$ a lb.

Saturday 11th February 1865 - I have knit some & mended some. Finished the comfort today, 'tis very nice. I began Pinck another pair of suspenders this evening, knitting them. I had a note from Sister Jane today saying Billie Kelly was dead. I am sorry to hear it. I heard sometime ago that he was wounded but getting better. I hope he is at rest. She wrote that our forces had given up Branchville and the troops were at Columbia. Our peace commissioner did no good at Richmond. They have returned. I did hope they would fix up an honorable peace but peace is not to smile on us yet. How long O! Lord? How long is our punishment to last?

Sunday 12th - Yesterday was cold but calm & today the wind from the north & very high, almost a March wind. Mr. Henry has gone to Tom Cook & old Cockrum's, will be gone all day. Robert, Matt & Pinck gone to church at the Academy so Zona, Willie & Gussie & I are alone. Zona has been reading to me & Willie looking at the pictures in his little primer. Gus is asleep. I think I will write some letters this evening and read some. Dinner will soon be on so I will not write much more. The children all sleep upstairs but Gus, he wants to go up every night &

sleep in Mattie's bed as he says he is a very sprightly child. Mr. Henry & I think a great deal of our children. I hope they may repay our tender love for them. Mr. Henry came home late this evening. He has spent the day at Capt. Moore's. Very cold all day.

Monday 13th - Mr. Henry went to town today. Cold but not so windy as yesterday. I began a vest for Mr. Henry today & cut Pinck a coat. I do not think of making the coat this week.

Tuesday 14th - I finished the vest today. Matt got out the cloth. Very cold and snowing this evening. The mail carrier reports that they are fighting near Branchville. We have also had another fight at Petersburg, Va. Oh! Lord send us peace. Help us in this our great time of need.

Wednesday 15th - Matt & I sewing on the negro's pants. Mr. Henry about the farm, turning some warmer this evening & began to snow. Tom was over here last Monday and told us of the soldiers treating their Col. very badly, some one is greatly to blame I think. The Col. has gone back to Raleigh. No news of importance.

Thursday 16th Feb. 1865 - Snow on this morning three or four inches deep. It is nearly impossible to keep the children out of it. Gus wants to play snow ball as well as the others. He can talk so I can understand everything he says. He is a very sprightly child. Willie is a sober, matter of fact sort of fellow & Pinck & Zona, as full of mischief as they can be. They have kept a great deal of noise today as Bell was here. Mollie & her spent the day here. She can walk alone but limps some.

Friday 17th - Mr. Henry went to town today. No news. 'Tis rumoured that Sherman is in four miles of Columbia, but 'tis not believed. Mrs. Commons here today, wanted to see Mr. Henry so she stays here tonight. She says that tories took a good many horses from Haywood & robbed some houses. Aunt Welch they robbed a good deal. I am so sorry for her.

Saturday 18th - Mr. Henry at home all day. Mrs. Common left this morning. Snow nearly all gone, some cooler this morning. Matt and I have made up all the pants, only three pair we will finish next week.

Sunday 19th - Matt, Robert, Pinck & Zona went to church at the Academy but no preaching. Willie cried to go but I gave him an egg so he soon hushed. Mr. Henry and I took a long walk this evening, went to see the lambs. We have twenty very large ones. I was very tired when we got back. I went to the mill after the children. They were all down there playing, Gus too. Mr. Henry came on up to the house as we saw a man at the gate. It was Willie Alexander hunting Mollie. Mr. Henry came back down to the forks of the road to meet us. This has been a beautiful day. Snow all gone but plenty on the mountains around. I feel better since I have got rested. The children all abed. I hear Pinck & Zona laughing upstairs. I don't think they are very sleepy.

Monday 20th - I began to make up some little things today. This has been a beautiful day. Matt & the children and I went up to the hotel place & then down by the spring. I was very tired when we got back. Mr. Henry out on the farm all day. Hanes & a Patten, Mr. Henry has hired, are scutching flax.

Tuesday 21st Feb. 1865 - Matt is making pants for negroes. The weather is so pleasant I feel like we ought to be gardening. Mr. Henry out all day. Matt & Fannie are scouring today, got all the house cleaned. Tom Tidwell stays here tonight, he is on his way to Cherokee. Robert is to go with him.

Wednesday 22nd - Bob & Tom started today. Cloudy & looks like rain; 'tis rumoured that Columbia is in the hands of Sherman & that Charleston has been evacuated, things look gloomy indeed. The Editor of the "Asheville News" who has always been a Southern man seems now to be changing his politics. I suppose he is scared into it. Oh! that the Lord would hear my prayers for peace day & night do I call on Him. Oh! Father of mercy I beseech Thee and grant us a peace that seemeth good in Thy sight.

Thursday 23rd - Rained all day. The ground is very wet. We have not been to walk since last Monday. I promised Mr. Henry to walk every day when the weather was fine, but it fatigues me so much & my back pains me when I walk much.

Friday 24th - Cloudy and some rain today. Mr. Henry at home all day, a soldier staid here last night just from Macon and says that Sam Love is dead. Found dead, killed himself drinking. I know it nearly broke his Mother's heart, they have no children at all. Sam was a very wild drinking fellow. His wild career is ended at last. Not much news this morning, 'tis reported that Wilmington is evacuated.

Saturday 25th - Mr. Henry went to A. B. Jones' today to lay off Pinck Ballew's dower. Rained all day & this evening, a real summer shower with thunder & lightning. Mr. Henry got wet coming home this evening. I hope this rain will settle the earth as 'tis in a loblolly nearly. We hear today that a hundred men had run away from Asheville last night, going to the yankees so thought, but I can't believe it.

Sunday 26th - Clear and pleasant this morning. Tom Cook is here today. Mr. Henry & him have taken a walk. The children at play. They are glad to have a bright day so they can get out. Mr. Henry bought two bu. of very fine buff apples last Friday, we appreciate them highly. He gave 20$ a bu., very high. He is so kind to me and the children. May a Kind Heaven protect him and spare his dear life, is the sincere wish of his devoted wife. I took the children & took a walk town to the mill dam & over to see the young kids. They were delighted with the kids and played on a bank down there. Gus & Willie enjoyed it finely. A soldier stays here tonight who has been a prisoner for nearly two years. He looks to be in fine health.

Monday 27th - Very pleasant. I began to work a little skirt today. I want to get through with little things this week. No more news from Sherman's army.

Tuesday 28th - Mr. Henry at home all day fixing up the farm. He went to town yesterday. This warm weather makes one think of gardening but the garden is too wet to plough.

March 1865

Wednesday March 1st - Cloudy & looks like rain. One of Capt. Collin's negro women came here last Monday hunting her a home. She is here yet, has two children. I would not feed & clothe her and her children for her work but some one must keep her. Her master is a prisoner.

Thursday 2nd - Rained all day. Fannie & Jennie spinning & Celia[49] cooking, she is a very poor cook. Zona is perfectly carried away with Celia's babe. 'Tis a white one, she nurses it as if it was something nice.

Friday 3rd - A good many letters came this morning. 'Tis rumoured that we have captured the whole of Sherman's waggon train and about 5000 prisoners. I hope 'tis true. Cloudy & some sunshine today. I am nearly done with the little things. I hope it may not be long before the wearer will come to wear them. I suffer a great deal with my back.

Saturday 4th - Old Lincoln takes his seat again today. I see not the least hope of peace. I hear that the yankees have burnt the bridge at Shelton on the Spartanburg & Union R.R. I fear they will give Pa a call. If they do, they will nearly ruin him I fear. I finished my little things this morning. Matt & Zona went to Mr. S. Jones' this evening. Pinck went too, he did not start till they were a good piece ahead and then the little fellow ran his best. I stood and watched him till he got out of sight. 'Tis rather lonely tonight, no one but Mr. Henry, Willie, Gus & I here.

Sunday 5th March 1865 - This has been a beautiful day. Mr. Henry, Willie & I took a long walk. I was very tired, my back pains me a good deal this evening. When we came back Pinck had come home. One of Mr. Jones' little sons came with him. Zona & Matt went to church at Sardis. I sent after Zona this evening. They have come, Zona is quite tired. Pinck has gone to take the little Jones boy home. Mr. Henry has taken a long nap but has gone now to see old Mathews' son who got away from the guard as they were taking him to Morganton. I don't want Mr. Henry to have anything to do with him. I fear he is a bad man.

Monday 6th - Fair and bright all day. Tim plowed some in the garden today. Matt & I made Pinck a coat today, got done before night. Mr. Henry went to help lay off Mrs. George Owensby's dower. He came back in the evening with a severe toothache, suffered a great deal. I did all I could for him.

Tuesday 7th - I cut Zona a bleached domestic apron today, the first one she has ever had. This war has made us do many things we never done before. Matt is planting out shrubery in the yard. I tell her the hogs will root it up. Pinck, Zona & Willie are out there very busy helping. Also Gus & Rose I imagine. Gus and Willie are more in the way than they help. Matt & Pinck went to Mrs. Blanchard's this morning to get Mary Blanchard to make her a pair shoes. Warm & bright all day.

Wednesday 8th - Rained all evening, some men thrashing oats. Fannie & Jinnie spinning since dinner. Two paroled prisoners stay here tonight. I have embroied the coller and cuffs of Zona's apron today. They look very nice. Mollie Henry got home from Asheville yesterday. She has been in town two weeks. Ruth was confined with a boy babe last Monday. We had very good news by Mr. Vic last night. I hope 'tis all true. He says our forces have whipped Sherman somewhere not far from Chester & taken ten thousand prisoners and that we have whipped Grant at Petersburg. I hope it may be true. My little Gus is two years old this morning. He is a very sweet child, talks nearly plain and is the picture of health & his Papa ask him

[49] Henry Family slave

where he is sweet he puts his finger on his mouth, does fret on his cheek for pretty and says he has Papa's eyes. He is very much like Mr. Henry.

Thursday 9th March 1865 - Mr. Henry went to town today to hear from home as Mr. Neilson has just returned from there. The yankees did not get to Pa's as the river was up. I am very glad of it. Mr. Powell is at home now on furlough. Pa is not well, has sprained his ankle and has to go on a crutch. I am sorry of it. I know he worries a good deal about it. None of our negroes ran away. I finished Zona's apron today, it looks very neat. Rained all evening. Mr. Henry got a little damp. One of those soldiers that staid here last night is going to stay a few days to work in Morgan's place for the government. His name is Hunecut, he is from Kty.

Friday 10th - I have done several odds and ends today. The mail brought several letters but no news. Till Morris was here this morning to the P. O. She got two letters from her husband. This seems like March indeed, cold & high wind all day. They are not done the oats yet as the weather has been so bad.

Saturday 11th - Willie is four years old today. He knows most of his letters. I have tried to learn him a verse of poetry today but has not learned it. Mr. Henry went to town today. No news. I sent by him for some copperas but he forgot it. I have some dye ready for the copperas but can't use it till I get it. Tena is fixing a piece of cloth for Pinck & Willie some pants. I put away all the newcomer's clothes today, fixed up things generally. Miss Emeline Jarrett was here this morning, and Till Morris was here this evening. Cold and windy all day.

Sunday 12th - Cold and frosty this morning and a beautiful bright day. Mr. Henry and Matt have gone to preaching at Sandhill. They have three days meeting there Friday, Saturday & today. I will stop now and give the children an apple, they will soon be gone. Mr. Henry and Matt went to Mr. Jones' for dinner. Mr. Henry came home about three o'clock and Matt came late this evening. Mag Morris came with her & stays here tonight. Rachel Jones was here a short time this evening. Matt is to write her a composition for her examination. Mr. Henry & I took the children over in the widening to see the lambs, they were delighted. Gus enjoyed it as much as Zona & Willie. The walk tired me a good deal.

Monday 13th March 1865 - This has been a very pretty day. The hands finished thrashing the oats. Mr. Henry thinks he will have near 75 bushels. He has not sowed any yet. I began to work on some collars for myself today, cut two linen ones and one marsailes. I intend trimming one linen one with tatten, the other with tape trimming and the marsailles collar with a pink facing. The mail came early tonight but brought no news.

Tuesday 14th - Cloudy in the morning but fair in the evening. Matt went to the hotel place & got some shrubery. Her & Hunecut set part of it out this evening. The hands gardening some today.

Wednesday 15th - We had a very wet night last night, it rained very hard. The branch & creek are up a good deal, the mill can't grind for back water. Some rogue stole Pinck's horse last night. I fear he is gone for good this time. I finished my collars this evening, they look very neat. The ground is very wet, we can't garden any more for a few days.

Thursday 16th - The big white cow fell off the bluff below the mill and shattered one of her fore legs. They killed her. I am very sorry for it, she would have had a calf soon. It seems this is a week of ill luck to us. We have no news from the army at all now. I hope the next we hear will be very good. 'Tis reported that Tom Harkins has written to Jimmie Henry to know if he may come back. I think he got tired of the yankees very soon. He ought to stay with them now. I have crocheted some today on little stockings.

Friday 17th - Some rogue broke in the back end of the smoke house & stole two sides of meat last night. I think it was some of our own negroes. I have fixed some stocking yarn today (cotton). Miss Tilda was here a short time this evening, she is good company. Mrs. Long was here also a short while. She gave Mr. Henry a very nice coat pattern a short time ago and wants to make it up. I am very willing that she should, he gave her two sheep. She seems to be a very nice lady. She says she is going to make me a dress, but I don't want her to do it. I think it very kind of her to make his coat. I have finished one pair little stockings & began another, they look very nice. I would be very glad if the wearer was here to take them but I will have to wait my time. I dread it so much. Merciful Father, be with me I pray. In my hour of suffering give me strength to go through.

Saturday 18th March 1865 - The hands gardening all day. We have a good deal done. We have a fine turnip salad patch, have been using salad for two weeks. Celia cooks and Fannie and Jinnie works out. Celia is nicer about things than either of the others. Matt & Hunecut at work in the yard nearly all day. It will be very nice when they get done. Mr. Henry and Pinck went to town this evening to see if they could hear anything of Pinck's pony. They did not hear anything of it. Three men stay here tonight.

Sunday 19th - This is a beautiful day. Mr. Henry, Zona & Matt gone to the Academy to church, the other children are at play so I am alone. Mr. Henry said when he started he hated to leave me alone. I told him I would not be lonely. They will soon be back I think. I wish I could walk about with more ease, but I will soon be relieved I hope. Mr. Henry & them came home to dinner. We took the children & went down to creek a short distance. Gus threw several stones in the water, it was fine fun for him.

Monday 20th - The hands are putting in oats in the Green field. Mr. Henry stays with them nearly all the time. No mail tonight as the mail carrier could not get through last Friday on account of high water. Matt & Hanes at work in the yard. I have sit in the front piazza nearly all day. It has been very pleasant.

Tuesday 21st - I have crocheted some today, finished the candle stand cover and began a pair of little stockings. Cloudy and some rain today. No news of importance. Some one stole Mr. Henry's fine horse last night. We think it was Honeycut, the paroled prisoner that has been staying here. Mr. Henry is a good deal troubled about it. I do hope he may get him again.

Wednesday 22nd - Mr. Henry has heard from his horse. Capt. Johnston's men took up Honeycut last Tuesday morning at Pigeon River, they will bring him & the horse to Asheville in a few days. Yesterday was Zona's birthday. She was 6 years old. The children prepared their dinner, they enjoyed it finely. May they always enjoy life is the wish of their mother. Mr. Henry took Tim & went up on the mountain to keep the fire from the fence on top the mountain but could not do any good. This has been a very windy day. The big limber twig apple tree down towards the branch blew down today. Hanes' hip is getting some better. He helps Matt in the yard. He has had a slight attack of rheumatism for the last two weeks. The rest of the family is very well. Willie has a cold.

Thursday 23rd - Wind very high today, the fire still burning on the view. It looked very pretty last night. I am afraid to let the children be out for fear a limb or tree may fall on them. No news of importance. Willie is not at all well today with cold & Gus had a high fever last night from cold and worms I think. Matt & Tilda M. went to town today. Till warped my cloth before she started. Sister Jane's family are all well.

Friday 24th - Two men brought Mr. Henry's horse home last night, they put Honeycut in jail. I hope they will keep him there till he can behave himself better. But few letters this morning. We hear Sherman has taken Fayetteville this state. I do wish this cruel war could stop. We still hope on and pray for a better day. Oh! Lord have mercy upon us. Look with a pity eye on our suffering, and stay Thy wrath upon us as a nation.

Saturday 25th - Still windy but not so bad. I have knit some today, am done my sewing for a while. Gus quite unwell all day, from cold I think. Willie is getting some better with his cold. I took off a hen with chickens this evening, these are my first ones. I have had several hens to quit their nests on account of the lice, there are a great many of them in the hen house. I will have it cleaned & scalded next week, I think. George told Mr. Henry this evening that the negroes are going to run away between tonight & Monday morning. They are afraid to go in the army. Rachel Jones stays here tonight.

Sunday 26th - Mr. Steph Jones came here soon this morning & says Charlie & his negro man are gone. Sam & Tena seem to hate it very much. I believe they know he was going. Mr. Henry went with Mr. Jones to town. He got back about 2, says several negroes have gone from town. Mrs. Cook and husband spent the day here & stay here tonight. Rachel left this evening.

Monday 27th March 1865 - Tim has not come home today so he has gone to the yankees too, I think. Mr. Henry went to town today to hear Gen. Vance speak. No news. He & several other men went tonight to take a white man that is to meet some negroes at Patton's shop, but did no good. The Muse boys staid here last night with two prisoners. They took up one man here so they had three. Two paroled prisoners and a soldier from William Tidwell's company staid here also so we had a house full. They sit up all night with the prisoners. Mrs. Cook left here this morning. Jim Henry was here this morning. I believe he is a torry, at least he thinks we are badly whipped. He is the cause of his men deserting so much, I think. About a hundred negroes left Asheville last night & the country around. Poor ignorant things. They believe what the trash of the country tell them sooner than their masters. Tim & Charlie's going will break into our crop a good deal but I hope we may be able to make bread. I think George will go too. Till was here this morning, says her boy John has gone & so has her Papa's Ben. Nearly every one that has negroes have lost some. Our forces shot into them last night, 'tis not known with what effect. I do hope they killed some. Five soldiers stay here tonight, some stay nearly every night. I am very tired of so much company. Pinck has been cutting corn stalks all day, his first day's work. Rose cleaned the cellar today. I helped some, her & Celia began to clean the hen house but did not get it done. This has been a beautiful day. Mrs. Long was here this evening a short time.

Tuesday 28th - Cloudy and gloomy this morning. My back feels badly from stooping about yesterday. The mail did not come last night, I can't imagine the cause. I expect to knit most of the day. Mr. Henry sent Lonzo to town today for salt. Eliza Neilson sent us some books to read, I am reading "The Lamplighter." I find it very interesting, the other two books I don't think are very good. No news of importance.

Wednesday 29th March 1865 - I have read and knit all day. The book is very interesting. Mr. Henry about the farm, they are still ploughing in oats. Mr. Henry hired a woman from Sister Jane, she began today. We had a good rain last night, they are needing it as the earth is very dry.

Thursday 30th - I have knit and read all day. Some soldiers stay here tonight. This has been a fair, pleasant day. 'Tis reported that the yankees under Thomas are coming up the river, I do hope 'tis not so. Celia cleaned the hen house Tuesday & yesterday, I never saw so many lice in my life. I think she has scalded the most of them. My little chickens are getting on very well, I will have some more soon, I think.

Friday 31st - The mail came this morning, said he did not go further than Dunn's Rock last week on account of bushwhackers. He did not call as he went back Saturday evening. No news, only we have given Sherman a good whipping. I do wish we could destroy his whole army. Finished my book & began "The Caxton Family." I don't think it much, I skip a great deal of it. Miss Tilda helped Matt put in the cloth today. I doubled some stocking yarn. Clear & windy all day.

April 1865

Saturday April 1st - Matt got the cloth started today. I filled quills & helped some. Mr. Henry went to Jake Starnes' this morning, came home to dinner. Matt has not finished the yard yet, we intend to plank up the walks as soon as we can get the lumber. This has been a very pretty day, only high winds.

Sunday 2nd - No one at home but Mr. Henry & I. Pinck and Zona gone to Mollie's to see Bell. Matt took Willie, Gus and Rose to spend the day with Tilda. She has moved in the houses Nichols used to occupy on Mr. Jones' land, her & her sister Pinck Ballew. Mr. Henry is asleep on the trundle bed. I am writing in the hall room. I am tired so I will stop for this time. I don't know that I shall be up till next Sunday. I will be so glad when it is all over. Oh! Lord of mercy, be with me in my time of suffering. Give me strength to bear up under the pain is my constant prayer. Rose came home with Willie before dinner. Gus staid with Matt. They came about three. Mr. Henry went this evening to see his sheep. I started but gave out and came back. Pinck & Zona are well pleased with their visit, they got home about sunset.

Union bushwhackers attacking rebel cavalry
(From "Four Years in Secessia," by Junius Henri Browne, p 346, O. D. Case and Company, 1865)

Monday April 3rd 1865 - I have knit some today. Nothing of importance going on. All are well. Mr. Henry about the farm all day, the hands still plowing in oats.

Tuesday 4th - The mail brought no news, he did not come till nearly nine o'clock last night. I have cleaned up some in the house, the closets &c. Rose helped some. Gus is nearly able to take care of himself. The children enjoy this spring as they were housed up all winter nearly. They are learning very fast. Mr. Henry at home, that is, in the farm. He is not very well.

Wednesday 5th - I have done several little jobs today. Zona was quite sick this morning, vomiting worms I think. She did not complain any after dinner. Mr. Henry is not well. I have Rose to bring a bucket of sulphur water twice a day. We are both very fond of it.

Thursday 6th - Mr. Henry went to town this morning. About three o'clock we heard the yankees were in town but did not believe it till about four when George came up from the mill and said some men had come from town & said it was certainly so. Matt & I began to fix up things. Sam came and said Mr. Henry had gone on to the front and sent me word by Mrs. Owensby not to be alarmed. Sam took charge of the bacon. I am very uneasy about Mr. Henry, I fear he will expose himself. Till was here this evening. It has been raining a little all evening. Some soldiers (four) stay here tonight. I think they had better go on to Asheville. May a kind Heaven protect my dear husband this night and all our brave men and turn back our enemies. Oh! Lord, deliver us from our enemies I pray.

Ginnie to Cornelia C. Henry

Columbia, April 6

Dear Aunt Cornelia,

Many thanks for the beet seed and the letter you wrote me on the 17 Feb. asking if I was not afraid of old Sherman (the old dog). You little thought he was so near me, that the very moment you was writing that he and his hosts were entering our town. Oh! Aunt to read about the Army and see and feel it are two things. I do assure you, I feel as if I was 50 years older. It is no use for me to try to give you any idea of what I have seen and heard since I last wrote you.

The Sunday before the yanks came, Aunt's family left for Marion. She ran over before she started & said they were only 15 miles away and she had to leave & I must take care of her things. Well Mr. H. went down street Sunday as it was and tried to get some one to move in the house for we know it would be burned if there were not some one in it and he tried all the week up to Thursday and could not get any one in it, so I went over and had her lard and flour and some other things carried over to our house, but we fully expected to be burned too for the wind blew a perfect tornado.

Friday morning at 11 o'clock they entered the town and then the work began. Sherman gave them 36 hours to do as they pleased only not to abuse the Ladies. They ransacked our house from one end to the other, took everything they could haul. All those doyles you gave me but three that was dirty and I can not begin to tell what all they did take and Harry's nice overcoat, and poured something on my bed that eat up my bed clothes. Oh! it would take six months to write you all. Uncle's house was burned and the things they carried with them was burned at Black-stock's on the Charlotte R. R., so they are left with out a change of clothing and not a thing and all their men went off with the yankees and our boy too.

Uncle and Eddy came down two weeks ago. Uncle is going back next week to bring Aunt & the girls down here and stay with us. Mr. Hopson & his father lost everything at their store, did not save even a tool to work with.

Columbia had 124 squares and 84 was burned so you can see what a fire we had. There is not a house from one end of Main Street to the other. We are on the brink of starvation. I don't see what is going to become of us. The Lord will provide. His ear is not deaf that he can not hear and his arm is not shorter that it can not save.

Many thanks for your kind words of comfort about my little Lamb. Oh! Aunt how I miss her. I feel as if I can never be myself again. Every where I go I listen for those dear little feet after me. I hear them not. When I go to her little grave I feel as if I must dig her up & look at her. Oh this world is so dark without my little sunbeam. A few moments before she died, she was in her Father's lap & she told him to put her in her crib, she wanted to go home. He told her she was home in Papy's lap. She said "No, I want to go home". He laid her in her crib and in a moment her little spirit had gone home. Oh! you don't know how I miss her. I do pray for Grace to say "Thy will be done." It is hard, so hard.

Harry Deaver grows so fast, is a great big boy. Tell Pinck he can throw him down now. Howdy to all. Write soon,
Affectionately,
Ginnie

Willie Arthur had to be put in the asylum in January. His mind is gone & he has lost his voice, is not able to talk.

Ruins of Columbia, SC from the front of the Capitol looking north
(Compiler's scan of original Harper's Weekly, April 1, 1865)

Friday 7th - Mr. Henry came home about eleven o'clock. I was so glad to see him. Matt & I were still up. I felt so distressed I could not sleep if I had gone to bed. Mr. Henry said we repulsed them handsomely. I am very glad of it. He thinks they will fight again today. It nearly killed me this morning to tell him good bye. He went to town this morning and came back about 12 o'clock and says the yankees left last night. I am so thankful. I believe the Lord heard my hearty felt prayer. They took some prisoners at Rankin's tan yard, some four or five. We had two men slightly wounded. We do not know the enemies' loss as they were some six hundred yards apart, they left one leg in a boot. Our men acted well. The artillery played on them all the time. The negroes here heard it but I was upstairs when Matt was weaving so could not hear it. They fought down about Nick Woodfin's farm. I do hope they may never come back again. The soldiers that staid here last night did not go towards Asheville this morning but up the river. I think they wanted to get away from the fight. Till was here today. Mr. Henry sent the children over to Till's this morning & Matt went after them as soon as he came from town. Till came home with them and staid till nearly 4 o'clock. Mr. Henry woke up those soldiers after he came to know who they were. They said they belonged to Capt. Deaver's company. We went to bed about 12 o'clock but Mr. Henry got uneasy so we got up and he went up & woke them up and they all went out to sleep. The first night Mr. Henry has ever slept out and I hope 'tis the last he will ever have to leave his nice warm bed. The yankees killed one of N. W. Woodfin's negroes for running. Old Sam don't believe the yankees would do anything wrong. I hope they may never get here to convince him. Matt and I sit up after Mr. Henry left till one o'clock and then slept very well. She slept on the floor in here. Some one robbed Mrs. Owensby's smoke house last Wednesday night, took some bacon and flour. I am afraid they will give us a call sometime but I hope and pray not. Oh! Lord deliver us from our enemies I pray.

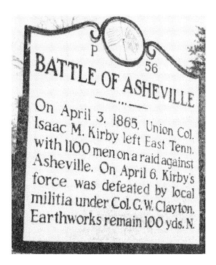

North Carolina Historical Marker located on SR 1781 (Broadway Street) near UNCA in Asheville

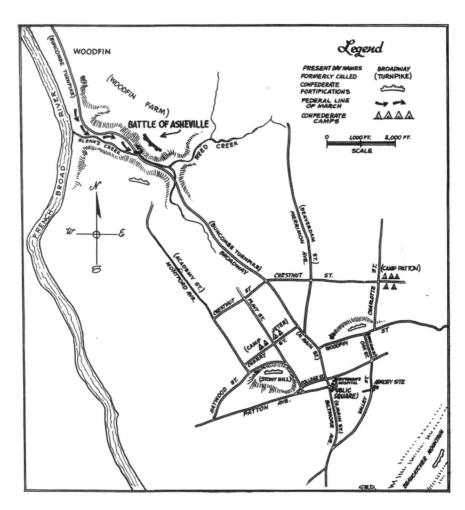

The Battle of Asheville location was near the University of
North Carolina at Asheville, where earthworks are still visible
(North Carolina Collection, Pack Memorial Public Library, Asheville, NC)

Saturday 8th - The prisoners all got away from the yankees, they say Tom Harkins was along with them. We heard today that our forces had evacuated Richmond and Petersburg. We also heard Tom Morris was wounded.

Mollie Henry has a fine son, she was confined yesterday. Jim is in town. I would like to go to see her but can't now. I have made Jennie some little things today, some other little jobs. Bettie Knight was here today. Came to see Mr. Henry on some business. She says the yankees burnt the bridges as they came up the river, Alexander's and Garman's. I do indeed feel very gloomy about our Confederacy at times but I try to put my trust in a higher power.

Sunday April 9th 1865 - Cloudy and raining all day. Till was here this morning, she is greatly distressed about her husband. She left before dinner. Mr. Henry & I thought we heard something last night, we got up and looked around but saw nothing. O! How I wish this cruel war was over. I fear peace is far distant yet. How long O! Lord, how long are we to be persecuted as a nation? Hasten the glad day when peace will once again smile upon us. Spare my dear husband's life. May we live to a good old age. Give us wisdom to raise up our children as seemeth good in Thy sight & when we come to die may we dread our graves as little as our bed. O! Mercifull Father may we never fall into the hands of our enemies is my humble prayer, which I ask for Christ's sake. Amen.

Monday 10th - No news from the yankees. I hope they have gone back to Tenn. and will never molest us again. The peach trees are shedding their blooms. I hope the fruit may not be frost bitten this year. I have been knitting some today. Mr. Henry is not at all well, his back is paining him a good deal.

Tuesday 11th - The hands are plowing, breaking up corn land. They finished the oats yesterday. Mr. Henry is not well though he stays with the hands most of the time. I have been sewing some for Fannie today. Matt is getting on very well with the cloth. Rose quills for her.

Wednesday 12th - Nothing of importance going on in the country, three soldiers took dinner here today. Tom Tidwell was here a while this evening. Rained nearly all day. Mr. Henry is in the house all day lying down, his back is very painful. I have weaved some today. The apple trees are budding, the tree in the upper corner of the yard begins to show the red bud of the bloom a little. The dogwoods are budding some & some of the oaks.

Thursday 13th - Fair and warm. A little frost this morning. Rachel Jones and her little brother were here today after turnip salad. We have had a great deal but it is going to seed now very fast. Our garden is getting on very well, the potatoes are not up yet but the onions, lettuce, mustard &c. are growing very well. Mr. Henry in the room nearly all day abed. I have sewed some & knit some. No news of importance. The children learning very fast, Zona memorizes very readily.

Friday 14th April 1865 - The mail brought a good many letters. Till Morris got one from her husband. He is wounded in the leg just below the knee & 'tis supposed the yankees have him as they took Richmond and Petersburg. I was very much surprised this evening to hear Mrs. Steph Jones was dead, she dropped dead. She had complained some before but not sick in bed. I pity her little children. I hope she is at rest. This has been a beautiful day. Mr. Henry is some better. He has been out some today.

Saturday 15th - Rained all the morning. Mr. Henry eat dinner just after 11 and went to Mrs. Jones' burial at Sardis, they took it very hard. Tom Tidwell is here this evening. I took a nap before dinner today as I got up very soon & had a slight headache. Laura Jones was here a short time today to get some brandy for her mother. Cleared off in the evening. An old man came here this evening hunting a negro he has ran away, Aunt Tena's niece. Tom had gone with the old man to Jim Henry's farm tonight to look for her, she staid there last night. The apple tree in the upper corner of the yard is in full bloom, the other's red buds showing very plain, the pear trees & cherries in full bloom & have been for three or four days.

Sunday 16th - Clear and high winds today. Three soldiers have stopped here to stay till morning. Matt has gone to the Academy to preaching. The children are at play. Mr. Henry is a good deal better, he took a long walk this morning. I hope he may soon be well. He is down in my room talking to Tom Cook. It will soon be dinner time so I will stop for the present. We had some company to dinner today. Laura Jones & Emma were here. Till spent the evening here.

J. L. Henry to Cornelia C. Henry

Asheville 18th April 1865

My dear Sister,
  I send you the protection paper for personal property which will be ample sufficient against all pressing officers & others after corn, meat, provisions &c. Perhaps robbers will not heed it, they seldom do. This will also protect William from all interruption I think, should he come home. I send you the Cincinnati Commercial, the latest paper received here. No news. All well. Thank you for the cow. Will take good care of her & come to see you soon.
Yours truly,
J. L. Henry

I send you also the "Freedman." It's a beauty ain't it?

Friday 21st - We heard yesterday that the yankees were in Asheville. Not much excitement. I hear this morning it is not so. Mr. Henry has been about the farm all the week planting corn. I have done several odds & ends this week, cut out some dresses for Zona & Gus. Miss Tilda was here this evening. No news of importance. The mail don't go up the river any more so we get no news, only as it comes by hand. We have some beautiful weather now. Apple trees shedding their bloom. The garden is not doing much, so dry.

April Sunday 23rd - Mrs. Jones & Pinck Ballew spent the day here. Two men came here this morning, one without a hat, and said the yankees were up on Mills River. Mr. Henry gave him a hat and they went on to town. Tom Muse went to town today & says we have an armistice of sixty days & thinks we will soon have peace. I sent for Betsy Jamison this evening to come and stay a while to attend to my baby. She is here yet.

Monday 24th - Mr. Henry went to town this morning, walked. He did not get home till night, he was very tired. The yankees are to pass through town tomorrow from up Swannanoa. It is a part of Stoneman's command. William Tidwell stays here tonight. They all sleep out for fear of the horses being stolen. Tom Tidwell is here too. William says Lee has surrendered his army. I am sorry for our brave men. "God moves in a misterious way his wonders to perform." My babe cries a good deal all night.

Tuesday 25th - Mr. Henry about the farm till dinner. After dinner took a long nap. He did not get to sleep last night till two. He slept with Gus and I. He brought me some flowers today, the last he may ever bring but I hope and trust all to my Maker.

Major General
George Stoneman
(Library of Congress, Prints and
Photographs Division, LC-B813-1562A)

North Carolina Historical
Marker located on US 25
(Hendersonville Road
south of I-40 in Asheville

Wednesday 26th - The yankees, or rather Kirk's men, came here last night hunting Mr. Henry to kill him, but thanks to a kind Providence, he was gone. I may never see him any more but I feel that God will take care of him. In Thee Oh! Lord do I hope for comfort and to Thy kind protecting care do I give my husband. Preserve his health and spare his life. I beseech Thee.

Wednesday 26th 1865 April - I slept not one bit last night. I spent the night in prayer & I believe the Lord heard my heartrending supplication. Oh! Lord spare my dear husband's life. Preserve his health. Turn the hearts of his enemies from persecuting him. Give them hearts to feel another's woe, turn them back. Oh! Father of mercy, in their wicked ways, give them hearts of flesh instead of stone. May they never feel the agony I went through last night.

Thursday 27th - Tom Tidwell came this morning and says the yankees dashed into Asheville last night at dark and took possession of the town. Tom thinks there is no danger ahead. Tom wants to leave the country. I think he will soon. Two yankees plundered the house today, did not take anything. They frightened me nearly to death when they came. I took a pain in my head on Tuesday night when they come. I thought I would go into a spasm. It got better about day. They have not been in my room yet. I hope they will not come.

Cornelia C. Henry to William L. Henry

My own dear husband,

I am getting on very well and will do finely if you will only stay away from the house day & night. For God's sake don't come to the house nor no house. Oh! you must keep hid and leave the country tonight. They were Kirk's men and said you had drove their hogs away and they intended to kill you. They did not come in my room nor take anything. They asked for blankets. Matt told them we had none but what was on my bed. They said they would respect me. They went to Sam's house and told him they would blow his brains out if he was the one that promised to bring them the stallion. They said it was Tim that brought them Pinck's horse. You must not stay near the road but go way over the mountains and tonight try to get out of the country. Take Doc Tidwell with you and if the enemy occupy the country long I will try to come out to you some way as soon as I am able.

Oh Papa, for my sake and our children's sake leave tonight if you think you can possibly get through. Till says her Papa will pilot you through the mountains. Yes, go and I will come when able. George said there was 15 yankees at the Murray place this morning as he came in. Trust no one but keep away from the house. They won't hurt me. Don't be uneasy about me. God is with me and I feel He heard my heartfelt prayer last night. Yes, He took care of you. Papa if you try to get out of the country tonight do send me word some way. Go and take Doc with you. I will try to send you some clothes today to Till's. You must leave the country tonight.

The yanks up at Murray place asked George if he was just from you. He told them no. They are watching all up there for you. Stay where you are for fear they will catch you. Go lie in some thicket till you leave and try to leave tonight. These yankees are at the Murray place on the watch for you. Try to get out of country tonight. I will not be easy till I know you are gone. May God protect you and watch over you in this trying hour. Stay away from the road. Go way off. I will come to you at Pa's if the yankees stay. Disguise yourself and pass under a fictitious name. Oh yes, leave and try to get out.

The stallion is very lame. No chance to get him out of the way. I will try to hide him out or George will. I am doing finely and will do a heap better when I know you are gone to Pa's. May God watch over you and protect you is the earnest prayer of your own dear wife. Farewell. If we meet no more on earth we will meet in heaven. May a merciful God protect you this day and through your wanderings. Keep clear of the road. They are on the watch for you. I can't quit writing you are so dear to me. Kirk will stay in the country I think and you must go. Tell Lin what you intend to do. I am affraid to send you anything now for dinner. I am affraid they will be watched as these yankees are at the Murray place for that purpose.

Good bye, may God protect you is the prayer of your loving wife.

Cornelia C. Henry to William L. Henry

My ever dear husband,

Your own dear letter was received a few minutes ago. I am so glad you are going to try to get out of the country. May God prosper you in your undertaking. I feel a heap better since I know you are going out. I only send your clothes as I am affraid of your being detected bundled up with clothes. I send all the stuff I have cooked. When this gives out I hope you may meet with good friends who will help you on to your journey's end.

I don't think we could get the mule to you well & if these men leave soon we could not make a crop on one horse. I will try to save the mule. My clothes I will try to save and if I can't I had rather lose all than lose you. Now you must stay there & not try to come back till times are better. I will stay here as long as I live to save our little stuff. You must do the best you can and be contented. Don't worry about me. I shall do well enough. God will take care of me and our babies, I feel and know. Your old shoes are so bad, they are not worth sending. You must stay at Pa's till the war is over or till times get better. You know I cannot be content so long as you are in danger.

None of the children woke last night when the robbers were here. They went to Jerry Riches' last night and threatened old Mr. Riches' life. Took his mule & three saddles. Mrs. Long is here now. They treated her badly in the way of cursing &c. They took nothing from her. Miss Tilda is here also. I shall do very well.

Papa, it was George instead of Tim that got off Pinck's horse Old Sam said. They said it was the miller. That is how come George with so many greenbacks. It really seems that no negro will do to trust. I shall get on very well if you will only stay away. Do let me hear from you as often as possible. I will save your land papers. Mrs. Long & Miss Tilda say they will take most of the things that are in the trunks, if not all so I think I can save all my things. Don't you be uneasy about me. I know I have a friend who will take care of you and me and our dear little ones. Yes, He heard my poor simple prayer. I shall never cease to praise His name in my heart. You may rest assured, you will be remembered in all my heart felt addorations & you must pray too. Ask Him for life. My life would be a blank without you. Now don't you be uneasy about me, I shall get on well.

You must be very cautious till you get out of the country. Change your name should you meet any one. Pass for deserters or anything so you get out safe. I told you all this morning what the deserters done, or tories rather. They said they belonged to Abbott's scouts. They were well dressed, some in Yankee blue & some in Confederate grey. Be very careful how you pass through Henderson Co. Perhaps you had better stop at Bill Miller's and inquire how things are ahead.

Now don't get vexed at anything Pa may say but stay on and at Berry's. I shall be better satisfied when I know you are safe there. I wish I could be a little bird to go along and see you safely landed at home. Tom has come and says he will go along. I am very glad. Now my dear Papa do be cautious. Do you think you will ever read this long letter? It may be the last one you will get in a long time. I shall be very glad to hear from you at the earliest convenience. I do hope you may get away safe.

The children don't know anything of your going. I know they send their best wishes & a heap of kisses to their dear Papa & even little Gus and Eddie send kisses and love and I send a heap more than you would be able to carry if it was heavy. Doc is anxious to get off so I must soon close. Do you think it dangerous to travel tonight? Doc does. Try to get to Bill Miller's tonight anyhow if you can. And now my dear Papa, don't, please don't come back on any account till things are quiet here, if 'tis a year. I can come to you. Till says she will stay in the house, but I am willing to stay if you will stay away.

I send you our daguerrotype. Look at it sometimes and think of the happiness these two faces have seen together & the joy I hope is in store for them at no far distant day. Let's put our trust in God. I don't think the tories will come again soon. I hope not, at least. Good bye. May a kind heaven watch over and protect you and may our loved country soon be restored to quiet and Oh! Papa try to get through. May heaven protect you is the prayer of your loving wife that loves you dearer than life. Farewell till we meet which I hope will not be long. You have the constant prayer for your success from your wife. Ten thousand kisses to you from me & the babies. God bless & protect you I pray.

Yours in love

May 1865

May 5th Friday - Our baby not yet named[50] was born on Saturday morning half past five, the twenty-second (22) of April 1865. May a merciful God protect its father & mother & their little children through all their troubles and dangers, and may they, we, all be happy in this world as we once were. Yes, my life with my dear husband has been very happy and if we never meet on earth he will still be mine in Heaven. Father of Mercy, protect him I pray.

May 11 Thursday 1865 - Well old journal, I have seen a heap of trouble since I last wrote in your dear pages. I will try to give a correct account of how things have gone for nearly three weeks.

Our babe boy was born on Saturday morning, half past five o'clock. I did not sleep any all night Friday night. Miss Tilda came over just after nine o'clock at night. Mr. Henry got her to come. He was uneasy about me. I sent after Dr. Thrash but he was not at home so Mrs. Anders came. I did very well.

May 11th Thursday - I am too feeble to write for every day so I will just put it all under one. The yankees have plundered the house some six or eight times, taken some bacon and some other little things & frightened us a heap of times. We are very thankful we have come off so well. They took everything Mrs. Stevens had. I am sorry for her and her little children. Matt & Pinck Ballew went to town yesterday a week ago and got protection papers. They have not plundered the house since. They took the stallion. The Gen. told Matt to go around and see if she could find him. She looked at their horses but did not see ours. She saw a negro Regiment. She said it was the worst sight she ever saw in her life.

The negroes are all doing for themselves about here. Jennie has gone to Jim Henry's farm. Mollie has moved to town. This is a wretched state of affairs, the yankees are here nearly every day but behave themselves. Some camped up here by Mrs. Cole's (on their way to Haywood), night before last. They were about here all night, some of them. They robbed three of our bee gums. Some came here last night about 9 o'clock and got supper. These said last night that they were just from SC & that the yankees were tearing up things generally. I hope their hearts may be softened before they devastate the whole state. Oh Lord we know the arm is not shortened & Thy ear deafened, that Thou canst not hear. Deliver us O! merciful Father, deliver from our enemies. Turn them back, stretch forth Thy hand and say it is enough. To Thee and Thee alone, do we look for aid in this our great hour of need. Turn them back Oh! Lord, grant us peace, we beseech Thee, and Oh merciful Father, may the day soon dawn on when our friends can live at home in peace.

---

[50] Edmund Lee (Eddie) Henry

May the time soon come when my dear husband can again join us around our one happy hearth stone. Deliver him from his enemies and spare his dear life, I pray. Help us Oh Lord to bear our trials and troubles with Christian fortitude. Give me strength to bear it & may I soon be restored to health and contentment.

I coughed up a pin yesterday that I swallowed before my mother died, about a year I think, so it has been in my lungs for 17 years. I hope it has not injured my lungs as I would be very thankful for health and life to raise my children. The pin was broke in two and rusted till it is rotten. You can't see any brass, only a little about the head. I have a cough, not much. I have taken a little cold in some way. My baby cries a good deal. I think it has hives. It is sleeping very well now and has been ever since I began to write. I must stop, I fear I have written too much already for my eyes. No yankees been here today, it is now past twelve. Betsy helping Tena wash. Matt making Zona's and Gus some dresses. Very warm today but a pleasant breeze sturing. A thunder storm in the evening. The air cool tonight. We have had no yankees today. I hope they may not annoy us any more. Some of our near neighbors have sent them on us to annoy us. I know who they are & will never forget them. I have tried to live in peace with all my neighbors.

Friday May 12th 1865 - Matt spent the day at Till's. Some yankees got milk here today. They had fifteen waggons, been out foraging, they were very quiet. I am not so well today, have headache. I took a long nap this morning but it did not relieve my head. Rather cool today. We needed some rain. Oh! that the Lord would deliver us from our enemies and grant us peace. How long O! Lord, how long is the burthen of our prayer.

Saturday 13th - I began a pair stockings for myself yesterday. I did some mending this morning and took a short nap. Some yankees here since dinner, they have gone. Matt gone out to see them when they come. She is a good rebel. Her & Betsy will finish the children's dresses this evening. I expect they will make Pinck & Willie's pants next week, if the yankees don't get the cloth and then they will have none. The baby is fretting so I will have to stop. Those two soldiers that have just left took off Jeff (dog) with them. Pinck ran after them and asked them not to take his dog but they took him on. I hope they may not kill him. I had to give Pinck a whipping this morning about cutting up Jennie's bed stead. I do dislike so much to whip my children. They are very dear to me and now that Mr. Henry is gone, they have no one to look after them but me. Oh! Lord, help us to bear our cares and troubles. Stretch forth Thy arm O! Lord and save us. In Thee and Thee alone do we put our trust. Take care of my dear husband in his wanderings. May the time soon come when he can return in peace to his happy home.

Sunday 14th - This has been a very pleasant day, no yankees here today. Mr. Sevier was here this morning, wanted to get a wagon to move his family. He married one of Miss Kate Garret's sisters. He says Mrs. Garret has been robbed till she has nothing scarcely. I am truly sorry for the family. Mrs. Long spent the evening here, no one else has been here today. Preaching at Sardis today but none of the whites attended. The negroes seem to enjoy their freedom finely. Fannie is a worrysome one. I wish she was away from here. Oh! good Lord deliver us from our enemies. I pray, hear Thou my daily prayer, I beseech Thee.

Monday 15th May 1865 - Two yankees came here this morning and asked for breakfast. We told them we had only a little. They got very mad and wanted some bacon or butter. One said he was coming back to load a wagon from here, full of bacon. I hope the Lord will give him a better heart and turn them back in their wickedness. No other yankees have been here today, I hope they may not come here any more. We hear Kirk is to come on from Franklin in a few days. I hope they may not trouble us. I cut some pants for Pinck and Willie today, it tired me a good deal. Miss Tilda is here this evening. Betsey is still here, she has the baby now. Miss Tilda stays with us tonight, she is very good company. Oh! when will the time come, when my dear husband can return in peace to his happy home. How long O! Lord, how long?

Tuesday 16th - Nothing of importance occurred today, one yankee here. The Kentuckian, he generally has a bundle of news, but had none this evening only some of the yankees have been poisoned in Asheville on milk. Some of them in the hospital. I reckon they will not drink any more. Matt and Betsy sewing on the children's pants. I sit up nearly all day today. I hope to soon be well. I teach the children some, not much as the baby cries a great deal. It wakes up about three after resting very well all the morning and then he does not go to sleep till about eight at night. I think he is troubled with hives. Charlie (negro) has come back. I wish he had staid away.

Wednesday 17th - Four yanks eat dinner here. We were done dinner when they came. I have went into the table since Sunday. It seems so strange not to see Mr. Henry in there. I hope the time may soon come when he can return home in peace. I went to the smoke house this morning, the first time I have been out of doors in nearly four weeks. I am gaining strength a good deal now and hope I may soon be well. I worked the button holes in Willie's pants, both pair. Some rain this evening but fair morning. Betsy cupped the baby. Since dinner Zona and Pinck had a time of it, they were so provoked with Betsy for cutting the baby's back, Zona cried she was so hurt about it. I went off upstairs. I could not see my baby's skin cut & hear it cry so. I hope it may do him good. He has not rested well all day.

Thursday 18th May 1865 - The yankees robbed Mr. A. B. Jones of meat and corn today, also Miss Tilda. Mr. Jones' Richard sent them there. Till came here this evening and got Matt to go up to the turnpike road with her. She said she intended to kill the negro. There was one yankee stopped here this morning with a chill and the little yankee Kentuckian was here. Kentuck went with them. When they came back they told us they had nearly had a serious affair up at the road. Till snatched the Kentuckian's pistol to shoot the negro but some men ran in between, she did not fire. The Kentuckian stays here tonight. He is affraid of being bush-whacked. Rain tonight.

Friday 19th - Fair and bright this morning. Kentuck left. Mr. A. B. Jones and Capt. Moore here this evening, they have a meeting of the citizens of Buncombe in Asheville next Monday. I hope they may fix up things so people can live at home in peace. No yanks here today. Oh Lord, deliver us from our enemies I pray, and grant us peace.

Saturday 20th - Betsy and I finished Pinck's coat I began yesterday. I can't sew long at a time, my eyes pain me. Press Rich was here this evening. The yankees have not been here today. No news. They took five of our chickens & one turkey last Thursday. They are bad men.

Union Troops in Asheville - Company F, 2nd NC Mounted Infantry
at Camp Jeter following the Occupation of Asheville
(Printed in the Asheville Citizen-Times, obtained from the
University of North Carolina Library, originally from the Library of Congress)

Sunday 21st - Only one yankee here today. The Muse boys came home today. Their house is burnt. They saved a good many things. I am very sorry for them. We once had our house burnt and 'tis threatened to be burned again. My God in His love, give our enemies better hearts. Oh! Lord, turn their hearts from their wickedness, give them hearts of flesh instead of hearts of stone. Rained a very hard rain this evening. Betsy went home this morning, she will come back tomorrow I reckon, as she has not come this evening. The baby has done very well today. I have had toothache all day, not very bad.

Monday 22nd - A yankee came here this morning and took our oxen and waggon. I don't know what we will do for firewood as that was all the chance. I do hope and pray for deliverance. O! Lord hear me I beseech Thee. I had toothache this morning but 'tis better now. Betsy came this morning, she has headache. Betsy McKinish is washing wool here today. I have stopped them now at 12 o'clock for fear the yankees would take it. Tom Muse is here, think he is in a great deal of danger staying here. Oh! this is a cruel war that people can't stay at their own homes. Oh that the Lord would hear our cry for deliverance and peace.

Tuesday 23rd - The yankees all left town today. Mr. R. Murry went over this morning and tried to get our waggon back but could not get it. They are a roguish set any way. My teeth and jaw have pained me a great deal today, they are some easier tonight. No yanks here today, I am very thankful. I believe the good Lord heard my prayer and I feel grateful for it.

Wednesday 24th - My teeth did not pain me much today but not near easy. The children are taking whooping cough. Gus and Willie coughed a good deal. I am afraid it will hurt my babe a good deal but hope it may not. The Muse boys have never been disturbed yet. I wish Mr. Henry could be at home in peace. I have not done anything of importance today. I am very feeble. I have been at the gate twice since I have been sick. That tired me a good deal.

Thursday 25th - My teeth & jaw have pained me a great deal all day, they are some easier tonight. I have done nothing all day. Miss Tilda stays here tonight. Old Mull was here last Monday evening and said Kirk was going to send a detail to burn the house last Tuesday but they never came. The mill is not doing any good so George says. I think he consumes the toll. He is just what I always thought he was, a rascal. Wiley Knight was here this evening. The yanks nearly all left town, only a few sick & some others.

Friday 26th - Goodlake was here this morning & says some of Kilpatrick's men are to pass through town today, some 3000. He is a good yank as any since they got in here. Mr. A. B. Jones started to town this morning but heard of the yanks and came back. My head has pained me a good deal today. I took some salts this morning, it helped me some.

Saturday 27th - Cloudy & some rain last night, our garden looks very well. Onions and lettuce a plenty. Mr. Henry has been gone one month today. I hope in a month more he may be able to return in peace. My head & teeth nearly easy this morning. Till was here this morning. Betsy warped Tena's cloth this morning. I want to write some today to Lewis.[51]

Saturday evening May 27th - I wrote a long letter to Lewis today but have not yet finished it. I gave him a general history of things. I hope to have a mail soon to send it by. I made some flower pots this evening but he is not here to admire them. I don't enjoy life, only with him but I fear it will be many a day "ere he will come back again." We have a good many roses in the yard. Most of the things Matt planted grew. The snow ball bloomed this year for the first year in the yard. Matt spent the evening at Till's. I got out supper for the first time in five weeks. I hope in another five weeks to see my beloved husband again. Pinck told me this evening that Mr. Neilson had gone on home. I wish he had come by the house. He said Lewis was well, we were very glad to hear it. May a kind Providence watch over and preserve his health & spare his life to a good old age is my prayer.

---

[51] William Lewis Henry (Mr. Henry)

Cornelia C. Henry to William L. Henry

At home May 27th 1865

My own dear husband

You have no idea how glad we were to hear from you, and I know you will be equally as glad to hear from us. This leaves all tollerable well. I am still very weak, and have suffered a good deal this week with tooth-ache and jaw, and some headache. Willie and Gus have the whooping cough. The baby has not taken it yet. I am affraid it will nearly kill it. He is growing finely.

Now I will try to give you a correct account of how the enemy treated us. They took Clarion the first week they came in. Matt went to Gen. Tillson (Yankee) to try and get him back, but he was gone so we will never get him. They took some meat, no corn, some oat straw and clover hay, plundered our house some six or eight times. Took Harrie's leggins and some knives and forks. I believe is the most they took out of the house. They started with the mule one time, but Matt begged them out of it.

They come here last Monday and took the two spotted oxen and waggon to move Mr. Jones' Richard to Tenn., that is a very mean negro. These nigs are all working for themselves. Sam still here & family. Char-lie has come back and working with Sam. Jinnie has gone to Jim Henry's farm. They have nearly twenty negroes there. Mollie has gone to town three weeks ago. Old Andy would not take Fannie unless I gave her a cow & some stock generally. I told him I would not do it. He threatened to report me to the yankees but he soon found out the nigs were not such pets with them so Fannie is still here. George is at the Mill still but I am going to rent it till you can come home as it does not now keep us in corn bread. We get no flour at all only some wheat I borrowed of Mr. A. B. Jones. He has been very kind to me and all the other good rebel neighbors.

The yankees have treated Mr. R. L. Jones, Capt. Moore & A. B. Jones badly, taking corn, bacon, hay and horses and mules. A. B. Jones has only one horse left. Till has hers yet. They took her bacon too. Jones' negro Richard sent them there & went with them. The negro has gone to Tenn. now and I hope he may never come back again. You have no idea of how big the nigs feel. Old Sam & Tena there is no difference in, but take care for the others, even Rose, feels her freedom. I wish they had went with the yankees, all but Sam's family.

Nearly all our soldiers about here have come home. Albert Hawkins is a prisoner. Some people think they will force our prisoners they have into the army to fight France. Jim H. thinks they will draft through here in six months. Tom Morris has been sent to Johnston's Island. Lusk nor

Tom Pinck Jones have not come home yet.

I think you can come home in a month if the yankees all get quiet in that time. 3,000 of Kilpatrick's men were to pass through town yesterday, all the first have gone. I mean the ones that came in when you left. We had one friend among the yanks, a man we never saw. I can't help but think a little something of him. He was the main cause of them not robbing us worse than they did. He came to see us every few days and would tell us who reported us. We were reported to the yanks more than any family about and by people we thought our friends. I will tell you some of them when I see you.

Jim Henry is just as we expected he would be, all right on the Yankee question, they did not molest him. Our Yankee friend is gone now. I hope to see him again. They watched the house for weeks after you were gone. Some of our neighbors (Mrs. Hutsell for one) told them you were in the country. Lee Mull, the scamp you have kept from starving, came here last Monday & said Kirk had ordered a detail to come on Tuesday and burn the house but they did not come. Mull thinks he is something powerful.

Gen. Tilson gave Matt a protection paper when they first came in. Maybe that helped us some. They have taken several chickens & robbed three bee gums. I am glad you were gone. It worried me nearly to death and you would have felt like taking to the bushes.

Teague bush-whacked the yanks some in Haywood. They were not bush-whacked any of any consequence about here. They said they intended to kill Teague and all his men if they caught him. They took two of Ham Moore's horses, his black one and another, two of Sam Gudger's, both and all Wilson Boyd's.

Tom Harkins is not at home. The yanks say they sent him across the Ohio River to stay till the war was over. Also F. M. Corn, Dr. Candler & his company. Fayette Jones went to Tenn. with Tom Candler and we hear he has been sent across the Ohio. Jim Cowen is at home, his wife is splurging around generally, more mad than anything I think.

On the whole, the yanks have treated us very well so far and we are very thankful for it. I have not heard from Sister Jane in nearly two weeks. They had only taken a few pieces of meat, then all her negroes were gone. I think 'tis best for them to go as they are so insolent & will tell anything they know & tell a heap of fibs besides. Don't let Pa trust his negroes or they will betray him and cause the yanks to treat him worse than ever. Only two or three yanks came in my room. They were quiet while in here. One Yankee drew a pistol on Matt and demanded her gold & silver. It frightened her nearly to death. They frightened me nearly to death but thanks to a divine Providence I am still alive and hope to cheer your life for many a day and year yet.

Some of the yanks would behave very well and some of them were the worst men I ever heard. They were so wicked. We have not seen a

Yankee since Monday & this is Saturday. Bill Snelson is at home. The Muse boys have not been interrupted since they got here. Mr. Jones thinks you can come home in a month.

The citizens of Asheville met last Monday to put North Carolina back into the Union. J. L. Henry general in chief of the meeting. Jim is not a friend of ours, no indeed. Anything else I think. Oh! how I wish you could come home safely. I have done the best I could. They have taken none of the stock yet. I hope they may not. We have no chance of getting the young cattle or sheep out of the way now so we will trust to Providence as I have for the last month and He has comforted me. If it had not been for prayer and faith, I don't know how I could have lived for the last month.

I have a heap of other things to tell you but will put it off till you come. Mrs. Cole raised a Union flag when the yanks came in. They are good tories. We have found out our friends since the yanks came in. Old Dryman passed here about two weeks ago & wanted Harkins' watch, said he intended to have pay for it &c. He seen Pinck and told him of it, nearly sceered the child out of his wits, saying he was going to burn the house. If the house is burned, I think George will be at the head of it as he wants to get me away, but I intend to stay as long as the land stays. We have had a heap to contend with. Sam has behaved very well, all his family.

Oh! Papa won't you be tired of reading this letter, but I am not tired of writing. I never tire of talking to you. Zona is sitting here nursing Eddie Lee. He is five weeks old today. She is very fond of him. I have been out in the yard a little, to the smoke house twice and to the gate three times. I am gaining strength slowly now and think if the yanks will stay away, I will be well by the time you come. I want you to wait till the army all gets quiet & civil law is restored to our loved country, which I hope will be soon.

The children often ask about you. Gus has not forgotten Papa's eyes yet. He and Willie cough a good deal. Pinck is stout. If I hear anything more from Sister Jane I will let you know before I close. They took her mules & a few pieces of bacon was all they had done two weeks ago. They have taken every good horse out of the country. The baby is crying so I will stop this time.

Cornelia C. Henry to Dora Smith Powell and Sister Matt Smith

May 27, 1865

My own dear Sisters Dora & Matt,

I have given Mr. Henry all the news so I will not have any to write you. You can see how we have been treated by the enemy. As long as Mr. Henry is safe I will not grieve for our losses. I am so sorry to hear my dear old home is in ashes. How did it take fire? Surely no one was mean enough in that country to try to burn you all up. I can sympathise with you in your loss. I do hope the yanks will not get down there. O! Dora you know nothing of how they do till you see with your own eyes and hear with your own ears.

Tell Pa if he has anything of value to put away to burry it himself where no mortal eye can see. The yanks hunted all over the meadow for our meat but as it was not there, they did not find it. Do all your hiding yourselves for the negroes think the yanks are their friends and will tell everything and a heap more besides. That is my experience with them and everybody else's about here. The yanks treated people a heap worse where the nigs told tales on them. They took nearly everything S. N. Stevens had, Mr. Henry knows him, & broke in Tenant's house just across the river & took all his gold and silver & broke up his furniture and smashed things generally. Old Jim Brook's gals are sailing about in Mrs. Stevens' & Mrs. Tenant's fine clothes, took their embroided window curtains & made peticoats of them. 'Tis a shame the way they done. I wrote Mr. Henry about the way they treated Sister Jane. I heard from her last week. They were all well. I hope the garrison, if they come to town, may behave themselves.

I will send an Asheville News if I can get one. I have seen one Yankee paper since they came in here. They are all gone now and things are very quiet. No robbing nor anything of the sort going on. They have been gone nearly two weeks. I do wish Mr. Henry could come in safety. You & Matt must cheer him up as much as possible. Try to make him happy & contented. We are getting on very well and hope the time is not far distant when he can come. I would be so glad to see you all this evening but it will be a long time I think before I am gratified. If things get quiet you, Mr. Powell & Matt come up with Mr. Henry.

Everything is going on in the country as usual but we don't know how long it will be so. I do hope they will not garrison Asheville. We are able to take care of ourselves I think. We always have done it. How is Aunt Rosa getting on? I am so sorry for her. Give her my best love & tell her I would gladly divide my household goods with her if I could get them to her. I am so sorry for Pa. I know he grieves over the loss of his house but he will have to bear it with as much patience as possible. Every bad thing for the better.

Did you get my music book or either of my other books? I hope you lost none of your clothes for 'tis a bad time now to get others. Do you see Ell, Lena & Frank often? Give my love to them & tell them I will write when the mails get to going again. Be kind to Mr. Henry. Cheer him up and I will ever remember you & Matt for trying to make one so dear to me happy in his troubles. I hope he may soon be able to come home in safety. Oh! life without him is nearly a blank. 'Tis so hard for me to bear, yet I try to look on the bright side and think there is a better day coming.

Do you think this war is over? I don't believe that such a corrupt nation as the yanks can stand long. I hope they may feel this war as we have felt it. The French will fight them on their own soil & in Mexico. They are going to draft through here. Don't you know the mountains will be full of men. There is many a man here that will never fight for the North.

Sunday 28th - Rather cool today. I took a nap before dinner. Willie is sleeping now. He and Gus sleep every day since they have whooping cough. The baby does not cough yet, I am afraid it will go very hard with him. No one has been here today. The yanks passed through Asheville quietly last Friday, so I heard. I hope they may not molest us any more. Matt & Betsy have just come in from strawberry hunting. They are ripe now but not very large. I must stop and nurse awhile. Matt has the babe. I finished reading through my Bible today for the third time in my life, and I have read a Universalist sermon today.

Monday 29th - Nothing of interest going on. I have knit some today. I have no heart to work since Mr. Henry is gone and no hope of his coming home soon. Oh Lord help me in my troubles I pray. Take care of my dear husband in his wanderings and may we yet spend many happy days together.

Tuesday 30th - I have knit some today. The children cough a good deal especially at night. Willie's cough is worse that Gussie's. I hope the baby may not get it, I fear it would nearly kill him. Wiley Knight is fixing the waggon, is to make a wheel and tongue. I think he will finish it this week, if he works. Betsy is spinning me some stocking yarn for Mr. Henry some socks.

Wednesday May 31st 1865 - Jim Henry was here today, he is all right on the yankee question. I do hope and pray for a better day for us, surely the Lord will hear my cry. Jim came over to see George about the mill as we have been getting such little grain. Jim thinks he will do better now. I hope he may as there is room for improvement. Fannie was confined with a girl this morning. No one here to do anything for her till Mrs. Anders came nearly an hour afterwards. Granna stays here tonight. Betsy McKinish here yesterday & today helping wash wool, got done today.

June 1865

Thursday June 1st - I wonder if Mr. Henry can come home safely in another month. I fear he can never live here in peace again. My life is no pleasure without him. I pray God to spare his dear life. I cut Pinck a coat and Gus an apron today. Finished the coat, all but button holes. This has been a very pleasant day. My teeth have got nearly well.

Friday 2nd - Finished Pinck's coat this morning & sewed some on Gus' apron. Bob Luther spent the day here, he had an Asheville News giving the proceedings of the meeting they had in Asheville. It was perfectly disgusting to see what an active part J. L. Henry took in it and a good many others, not an original secessionist in the meeting.

Saturday 3rd - Betsy and I went over to Till's this morning to get the Asheville News as I want to send it to Mr. Henry. I know he would be glad to see it. Mrs. Ballew said she would send it over tomorrow. Mr. Andy Jones is very sick, nothing serious I think. We got back near about 12 o'clock. The baby had not woke since I left. That is the first time I have been off the place. I have been going to the back house ever since Tuesday and getting out dinner also I have nearly regained my usual strength. I have finished Gus' apron today.

Sunday 4th - Very warm today. Miss Till & Mag Morris spent the morning & took dinner here, they left soon after dinner. Matt went off with them. I wrote some this evening to Mr. Henry. I wish he could be here and stay in peace but I fear his life will never be safe here again. Oh! 'tis very hard to have to live without him. I wish I could go to him. It really seems to me I can't stay away from him any longer but then I know it has to be so, so I try to submit. I was very uneasy about Pinck yesterday as he was gone all day. I ought to have corrected him but he begged off. He had been fishing with some little boy.

Cornelia C. Henry to William L. Henry

June 4th Sunday

Tom Muse speaks of starting to you in the morning so I will write a little more. Mr. Jones thinks you could come home but I fear for you to risk it. The tories blame you with Allen's death & have hung Tim so they say. I wish you had listened to me sometimes when you did not. Things would have been better for us I imagine but the past can't be recalled. Let us submit to the decrees of a divine Providence. I am affraid you can never live here in safety again. Oh! 'tis hard to live away from you, so hard that it seems I can't stand it. I would not be much uneasy about you in day time, but I know I could not rest at night for fear they would be after you. I think the Muse boys lay all on you about the deserters. They want to clear themselves so all is laid to you.

Mr. Coulter told me the other day, that the Union people of Ten. were suing for damages. I will try to illustrate that you may understand. A poor woman brought a suit against Gen. Braselton (a rebel) of New Market for damages in forcing her husband into the army and he got killed. The United States gave her damages for one hundred thousand dollars, & several others he told of selling their lands to pay the damages of sending their husbands to the army. He thinks they will do that way here after awhile. If so, we are ruined.

The Tory & citizens have drove off all N. W. Woodfin's cattle, milk cows & all. Things are very quiet about here now. Yanks all gone. They expect some in Asheville soon to garrison the place. The citizens petitioned for it, I understand. If they come, I don't think you would be safe at all home. I wish you could come in peace. You don't know how much I wish it.

I will send you the Asheville news if I can get one. You can see what they done at the meeting in Asheville. Not an original secessionist in the meeting. Jim Henry is a great man with the yanks. He was here last week, is going to help the North fight France and I think will try to take his whole Batt. He is a Jim. He says the yanks will draft through this country.

He is perfectly willing to go, says he would not be contented at home. No, he has never been contented anywhere with anything long. Jim says the yanks are going to make the Southern people pay their taxes for the last four years in gold & silver. It will nearly break the confederate states won't it? We are to pay our taxes to the U. S. as in times of peace. You understand for the last four years.

Mr. Neilson has got home all safe. I have not seen him since. The yanks did not treat Sister Jane badly, took a few pieces of meat & her mules. She is doing her own work. Most of the ladies about town are.

The yanks brought one Regiment of nigs to town when they first came but they are gone long ago. They killed five whites in town for ravishing a young lady down on French Broad. Jim Henry says they treat their nigs very badly, are very cruel to them. They intend to send them to fight France. They are at war with France certain. The reason is this. Napoleon placed Maxamillian on the throne of Mexico & Jim says according to the Monroe doctrine, there was never to be a monarchy in the U. S. I do hope & pray that France may make them feel some of this war yet. I told Jim so he said that would do me no good. I told him yes it would. Just think of Jim fighting for a nation he has fought against for four years.

I send you a paper of protection. Jim sent it to me some three weeks ago. He says for me to send it to you. I don't know whether it will do you any good or not. I am affraid for you to come home on my say so. Tom Muse will tell you there is no danger but he is part Yank himself when with them. I think they have laid all their deserter business on you to screen themselves.

Things are going on as usual. George is doing better since Jim came over to see him so I will not rent the mill. Mr. A. B. Jones & Jim were affraid that George would burn it. We are getting plenty of meal and flour now. Our crop looks tollerable well. Corn small. It has been so cool the sugar cane did not come up any scarcely so Sam planted the land in corn last week. The wheat & oats look well, so does the clover. I wish you were here this evening to go strawberry hunting with me.

I am getting quite strong. Went to Till's yesterday morning. Till was here this morning till dinner. Mr. A. B. Jones is very unwell. He has been very kind to me. I will never forget his kindness in my time of trouble. Oh how I wish you could be here. If I was to advise you to come and then you were to get killed I would never get over it. 'Tis so hard to live away from you but I try to be resigned to my lot. Betsy is still with us. The whooping cough is hurting Willie a good deal. Nothing serious though. The baby has not taken it yet. Betsy & I and the children are in the front piazza. I wish you could be here to enjoy life with us. The yanks may part our bodies in this world but they can have no power to part our souls. If we never meet on earth "I will still be thine in Heaven."

The horse the Muse boys rode home, I fear will die. They have had him at their house ever since they came home. Did you tell them to keep him? I think I will send for him soon & get Sam to doctor him. He is very poor & has distemper. I am very sorry you ever had anything to do with those boys. They have caused me a great deal of trouble about you.

We will have no fruit this year of consequence. Our garden looks very well. We have fine onions. I have put out all but five cows. I mean milk cows. The other cattle are all here. Wiley Knight is fixing us a waggon. He will get it done this week if he works. The yanks ordered all this waggon timber to be taken to Asheville. Old Goodlake has come & got most of it. Goodlake is a good Yank as any.

I know you will get tired of reading so much but I can't tell when I will have another opportunity of writing so you just read part at a time & then rest a week or so. Every thing looks as it always did. The yanks have made no great difference in the looks of things but we feel the change, hearing of them coming and seeing them is very different things. How can I stop writing when I know not when you can hear from me again? How I wish I could be with you this evening but it may be months and years and it may be forever. Papa, if you hear of the yanks coming down there, keep out of their way if possible. The Tenneseans have a great spite at you about those hogs Gen. Vance had drove out. Do take care of yourself. We will get on very well. Don't fret about us. I can live any way for awhile if I know you still live or don't hear from us in months. If you were to come home, I fear you would have to stay concealed all the time & you know that would be no pleasure to either of us. Employ your time in some way most pleasant to yourself. If we are whipped we are ruined anyway but if God spares our lives you & I will be happy with each other & I hope we may live a very long year together yet.

If you have a chance write me what is to be done on the farm &c. I will do the best I can. You may be sure I am still teaching the children. Don't trust Tom Muse with any of your secrets or where abouts. Let no man know your secrets whatever they may be. I believe I have written all the news. I may add some more before Muse starts. Eddie is doing finely, grows very fast and just like his Papa.

Mr. Henry, I fear you can never live here again if we are whipped. 'Tis hard to quit one's home forever. Oh! 'tis so hard to live without you near me. God help me I pray to bear my troubles.

Sam says the clover ought to be moved but we have no meat nor bread to hire it done. What will we do about it? Sam says a man told him (he did not know the man) that he intended to kill you if it was ten years before it was done. I fear you can never live here any more if we are whipped and if we are, we are ruined anyhow. We will have nothing by the time they are done for damages & taxes & so on.

Monday 5th - I wonder what Mr. Henry is doing this evening, thinking of home no doubt. I wish I and all the children were with him. Pinck has been gone nearly all day. I am uneasy about him. I hope nothing has happened to him. I must make him stay at the house. Willie still coughs a good deal. The baby is coughing some. I am affraid it will hurt him badly. Gus coughs a good deal but not so bad as Willie. I took the children and went to the Mill this morning to see Mr. Presly and see about the toll. Presly is to shoe the mule and iron the waggon this week. Tom Muse began to mow the clover this morning but his scythe needed some fixing so he will not do anything till tomorrow. I fear he is not very good to work at anything. I have knit some today. My head aches some today. Betsy has gone home for a few days. Rose picks wool and attends to the baby. Matt has him now. My head feels badly so I will stop for this time.

Tuesday 6th - I have done nothing of note today. I have no heart to work. I wish all the negroes were with the yanks, they are a great annoyance. Hasten the glad day O Lord when we can live in peace & safety. I hope Mr. Henry may soon come and can stay in peace.

Wednesday 7th - I have knit some today. I don't do much of anything of consequence. These are times that tries ones souls and body too. I hear the children's lessons every day. My babe has the whooping cough, it strangles a good deal. I hope he may get through it safely. He is growing very fast.

Thursday 8th - We had a very heavy rain today & some hail. No news, only that Gen. Kirby Smith has surrendered & that the yanks have captured President Davis. I hope neither report is true. May God protect us and defend the right I pray.

Friday 9th - This day has passed as all others do now, long and weary. I wish Mr. Henry was here to "solice all the joys of life", the joys are very few now.

Saturday 10th - Mr. Henry came home this evening. We were very glad to see him. I do hope he may be able to stay in safety. I will be uneasy about him at night, I know. Matt and I were sitting in the front piaza talking about him. She saw him the other side of the mill & said she believed it was Uncle Bill. I did not believe it till he got nearly to the gate. I was so glad to see him. He has been gone six weeks last Tuesday, the longest he was ever gone from me since we were married.

Saturday 10th June 1865 - Mont Stradly went down to Pa's & told Mr. Henry the yanks were gone and that they had taken everything we had. He said he was coming any hour and that troubled him so he started. I am so glad he is at home. Matt and Lin Muse scoured the house yesterday and today I paid Lin in bacon. Mont Stradly stays here tonight. Matt, Pinck and Zona sleep upstairs. Mr. Henry did not find things torn up as bad as he expected. He seems a good deal cast down at the turn the war has taken. It is enough to make any one sad to think our brave men have fought and died for nothing. We try to submit to the decrees of an all wise Providence.

Sunday 11th - Mr. Henry, Matt, Pinck and Zona went to the Academy to church today. Henry Jones was here for dinner. Till came this evening, her and Henry stay here tonight. Mrs. Long was here a short time this evening. Mr. Henry took a long nap this afternoon. Mrs. Long was surprised when I told her Mr. Henry had come. The yanks came to town last Tuesday and left last Friday. I hope they may not come back again. Mr. Henry says they have a garrison in Hendersonville.

Monday 12th - Mr. Henry out all day trying to get his clover cut. I had some of it cut by the Muse boys. I am a little uneasy about Mr. Henry at night but I put my trust in the Lord and I feel he careth for us. I cut my dress today. Matt is helping me make it a home spun dress. I am so much happier since Mr. Henry is at home. I pray he may stay in peace and safety.

Tuesday 13th - Mr. Henry is troubled about the way negroes are doing but what can't be cured must be endured. I finished my dress this evening, it fits very neatly. Matt spent the evening at Till's, brought home the things. Mr. Henry went over and helped her and George Jones brought some. Some of the things are damaged a good deal, some of the quilts are nearly ruined.

Wednesday 14th - I went to Till's this morning. Mr. Henry went to Mr. Andy Jones'. Mr. Jones has been very sick but is some better now. Mr. Henry met me at Till's. Pinck & Zona went with me. I got the rest of my things from Till's. We were needing our knives and forks badly. Till came home with us & spent the day. I have knit some today.

Thursday 15th June 1865 - I cut Hanes and Lonzo a pair pants each. Tena finished the cloth this year, she is weaving some for shirts now. Fannie does nothing but loaf about generally. She is one trifeling piece of creation anyway. Tena does the washing yet. I don't know how long she will do it, she has not cut up any yet.

Friday 16th - Mr. Henry at home all day. Some rain this evening. One of Josh Jones' daughters was burried today at Sardis, killed by lightning yesterday. We had some very heavy thunder yesterday & the heavyest rain of the season. I fixed the meat away this morning and finished the pants this evening. I sent some clothes to the branch this morning and Tena sent them back. Her first time of showing her freedom.

Saturday 17th - Mr. Henry has gone to town today, I hope nothing may happen to him. He is very dear to me. There is a meeting of citizens there today for some purpose. This is a very warm morning. Willie & Gus both asleep. They are getting better of their cough but the baby suffers a good deal. I want to put away the winter clothes today and get out the summer ones so I will stop and get out dinner and then to work. Mr. Henry came home late in the evening, nothing done at their meeting. The tories wanted it all their own way.

Sunday 18th - Preaching at the Academy today, Mr. Reynolds preached. Mr. Henry, Matt and Zona went. Mr. Bird took dinner here. Pinck was gone today till after dinner. I gave him a whipping this evening for it. I hate to whip my children but still I must do my duty. Mr. Henry went to Sand Hill to preaching this evening with preacher Bird. Matt spent the evening at Miss Tilda's. I have a very bad headache this evening. Mr. Henry came home about six o'clock.

Monday 19th - I took some pills last night, my head not well yet. I cut two linen shirt bosoms this morning but did but little at them. Fannie has set in to work for her board. She could not work for her food and clothes at first and now she works for her food alone, is to spin five yds. a week and wash one day. She is picking wool now and will be nearly all the week. Rose is helping but she is so trifling I can't get anything out of her. Oh! 'Tis so sad to think we are subjugated, help us Oh! Lord to bear Thy chasting rod.

Tuesday 20th June 1865 - I finished the bosoms this evening. I cut the bodies this morning. Matt is sewing on them. Mr. Henry is staying about the mill this week to see how much toll it makes. We only get about three bu. a week for our share.

Wednesday 21st - I am still at work on the shirts but have neither one done yet. Matt is helping. No news of importance in the country. Everybody looks discouraged at our subjugation. It really seems to me some times that I don't care to live but then again I want life to raise my children. What would they do without a mother? Help me O! Lord life's burthen to bear.

Thursday 22nd - My babe is two months old today. I have seen a great deal of trouble in the last two months, more than I ever want to see again. Sister Jane spent the day here today. Mr. Neilson came to mill and she came over in the waggon. I finished one shirt today. Celia is doing the washing after dinner every day till Fannie gets able.

Friday 23rd - I sewed on the shirt today. No news of importance, no mail yet. It is a great pity this war came on as we had to be subjugated. Life is not so sweet as it once was. O! Father of Mercy help me not to repine at Thy holy will.

Saturday 24th - Lt. T. L. Morris got home last night, he is nearly well. Mr. Henry went to see him this morning. I finished the shirt this morning. One week making two shirts, with Matt to help, that is slow getting on.

Sunday 25th - Rained all day, the creek very full. We all staid at home today. Mr. Henry and Pinck went to the dam this evening & then up to Till's. They got wet as they came home.

Monday 26th - Matt & I made a garibaldi waist today for myself of my old brilliante dress. It fits beautifully. Betsy came this morning, she is going to weave some here for herself. Matt helped her put it in. Mr. Henry is going to mind the mill himself. Jim Cowen, old Randle and George nigger came to his mill this morning and demanded possession, but Mr. Henry would not give them possession.

Tuesday 27th June 1865 - Nigger George went to Hendersonville today to see the General Commander there. He wrote a very polite note to Mr. Henry about it. George misrepressented the case to them. I know he and Cowen are full brothers, both nigs. Two paroled prisoners staid here last night. Matt and I are making the children some bonnets. I have a slight headache today.

Wednesday 28th - My head pained me some this morning but since dinner much better. I have sewed some today. Betsy weaving. Mr. Henry is tending the mill, has made a good deal of toll this week.

Thursday 29th - Col. Moore was at the mill yesterday. He is going to Hendersonville for Mr. Henry about the mill. Miss Eliza Neilson, Miss Lewis and Joe Collins spent the day here. My head has ached all the morning but better now. Till came this morning & staid till after dinner. Mr. Henry at the mill all day, he is miller now.

Friday 30th - We finished the bonnetts today. No news. We have some beans, peas and potatoes every day but not a plenty.

July 1865

Sunday July 2nd - I did several odds and ends yesterday and today. I have tended the baby all day as Rose and Celia have gone to town. Betsy and I took the children and went to walk, left the house alone and some one came in and took Mr. Henry's pistol out of his coat pocket. I am so sorry. I don't think I will leave the house soon again.

Monday 3rd - Mr. Henry staid at the mill last night. I was sorry to see him go off alone with no weapon. My troubles are great. Help me to bear them with Christian resignation. I don't expect to do anything today. I have no heart to work at anything. I do hope Mr. Henry may yet get his pistol but I fear 'tis gone. Think Andy or Hanes one took it as Hanes was in the yard & so was Andy.

Tuesday 4th - Matt and Betsy spent the day with Mrs. Long. They came home late. They did not get anything as their things were put where they could not get to them. Gus lost the keys this evening. I had a long hunt for them and found them in the hall in a chair. This day 12 years ago I made my flounced baraige dress, Sister Jane and I. Things have changed a great deal since then.

Wednesday 5th July 1865 - Oh! This is a peace we little expected and did not want but help us to be resigned. There is a great change in the negroes. They seem not to want to do anything, only as they are hired. I finished my baby's dress today, 'tis made of my robe muslins. It looks very neat.

Thursday 6th - I sewed some on Zona's dress today made of Sister Dora's skirt. Dora gave it to her in 1860 the last time I was at Pa's. Mr. Henry has a bealing on his hand. He suffers a good deal with it. Dr. Holt and Dr. Summey were out to see Willie last Tuesday and Dr. Holt lanced his hand, it run a little. Dr. Summey thinks Willie's left lung is diseased a little. They left some medicine for him. I am very much afraid he will have consumption. Mr. Henry went to town last Tuesday and took the amnesty oath.[52] The country is all quiet. I am sorry this war ever was, as we had to be conquered. But God willed it so and we submit.

Friday 7th - Mrs. Long spent the day here, brought some of my things home. I sewed some on Zona's dress. Betsy is not done her dress yet. Matt ironed till after dinner and Celia finished. Mr. Henry's hand is not improving any, he sleeps but

---

[52] A proclamation for amnesty and pardon was issued May 29, 1865 by President Andrew Johnson

very little at night with it. I sympathize with him but can't do it any good. It first started from a bruise caused by carrying hay.

Saturday 8th - I have done several odds and ends today, finished Zona's dress. Mr. Henry's hand still painful. The wheat crop generally is very short. I don't see what people are to do for bread. Willey Knight is helping Mr. Henry tend the mill.

Sunday 9th - Matt went to Sardis to church. Lizzie Wright went with her, they walked. It has been very warm all day. Andy Miller come here this morning before dinner. Things are getting quiet up in Henderson. He says this war has broke some men up. I am sorry we are subjugated. 'Tis very hard to be resigned. I have more trouble with Rose & Fannie than any. I think Fannie puts impudence in her head. I wish they were all gone from here, every one of the coloured. I hate a nig.

Monday 10th 1865 - This has been a very warm day. Betsy, I and Fannie have secured the house all over. Matt nursed, she got very tired of nursing. Mr. Henry's hand not improving any.

Thursday 11th - Fixed up things generally today. Still very warm. No news of importance. Willie is improving some I think. I will call my babe after our great General Lee. He did us all good service so I will name my baby Edmund Lee. I will ever love Gen. Lee and intend to teach my children to love his name.

Friday evening July 21st 1865 - I have not written in my journal in several days. Nothing of importance has transpired. We have had very warm weather. I have suffered more with heat this summer than I ever did since I have been in the mountains I think. Pinck was nine years old yesterday. There has been a great change in things since then, our country has bled at every pore. 'Tis hard to be sub-jugated after losing so many of our good men, but God so willed it and we have to submit to it. Betsy went home last Thursday, was a week and came back last Monday and her and I made a set of harness to weave Celia's and Rose's dresses. Tena spooled them last week and Till warped last Friday. I spent the day at Till's last Wednesday and took all the children but Pinck. He went home with Mr. Neilson last Tuesday evening from mill. Mr. Neilson says Billie is not improving any, has been confined to bed for ten weeks with scrofula. Mr. Neilson is very low spirited, think he can never live in Ten again. I am truly sorry for him. Mr. Henry's hand is some better than it has been but still very painful, he has had it opened several times. Mr. Henry is done his oats, they were very fine. Mr. Norman is tending the mill, began last week, he is doing very well. I hope he may be honest. Mr. Henry has three nigs hired, one a mute. Matt is weaving Celia's & Rose's dress. I quill. She gets on very well. Betsy still here, she speaks of going to Daniel Ledford's this eve-ning to have her shoes mended. My babe frets a good deal this warm weather. His cough is better, so is Willie's. Gus is as fat as a pig, it did not hurt him. I must stop as I want to make some blackberry vinegar this evening.

Saturday July 22nd 1865 - Matt and Betsy spent the day at Mr. Ham Cannon's. Matt & Betsy and Matt Cannon went to the top of the view. It was very warm and gave Matt the headache so she did not enjoy the scenery. 'Tis a beautiful landscape from the top of the Mountain. I have been there several times and enjoy it every time. I have done several little things today. Mr. Henry brought a bucket of huckleberries this evening, they are very nice. We all eat some and left some for a pie tomorrow. Mr. Henry has a very bad headache this evening.

Sunday 23rd - Mr. Morris and Till spent the day here. Very warm today. Willie is getting a good deal better, has a very good appetite. Gus is as fat as a pig and calls every body a "debil" that don't suit him. I don't know where he learned it, from the little nigs I think. Pinck is getting to be a great big boy and full of mischief. Zona has more temper than I like to see in her but I hope she may out grow that.

Monday 24th - I have doubled some thread to quilt today. Fannie is carding the bats. Matt is weaving, she gets on very well. Very warm, we had a very warm summer so far, the warmest I ever felt here.

Tuesday 25th - Betsy and I put the quilt in today but did nothing at it as I have the headache and lay in bed nearly all evening. Mr. Henry's hand is not improving any. He stays with the hands all day, they are saving hay. This is beautiful weather for that, so hot, so hot.

Thursday 27th - In bed all day with headache all day yesterday. I have quilted some today and since dinner wove a yard and a half. I have the headache tonight from getting too warm this evening, it is very warm upstairs in the evening. Matt & Betsy quilted.

Friday 28th - I quilted some today. No news of importance going on. Mr. Henry's hand getting worse again, he suffers a great deal with it. Mr. Norman is pleasing the mill customers very well now. Betsy got out the cloth today.

Saturday 29th - We have quilted none today. I have done sundry other little jobs and attended to babe as Rose is washing her clothes. I call him Edmond Lee after our good general. I love Gen. Lee and ever will. I think he did all he could for the South and then to think we are subjugated, 'tis very hard indeed.

Sunday 30th July 1865 - Mr. Henry and I went over in the oat field this morning and saw the goats. We have one little kid. I had the headache till after dinner and then I took a nap and it is nearly well. Some rain this evening and rather cool. Old Granna Wiggins has been here all day & stays here tonight. Lizzie Right has spent the day here. A woman stays here tonight, going to see her mother in Haywood. She lives on Little Ivy. Her name is Pendland. She is a good rebel, we love all good rebels.

Monday 31st - Mrs. Penland left before breakfast this morning. Pinck, Willey Wells & Zona started to school this morning. Matt went with them. Zona would not stay, she came home with Matt about nine. I will teach her. 'Tis raining now and looks like we will have a wet day. Rachel Jones is here. Zona is learning her lesson and keeps telling me she knows it. I must hear it and then get out dinner and then to quilting which will be near 11 o'clock. Matt and I and Rose with Eddie, went to meet Pinck this evening. We met Mr. Henry and young Morris on top the hill, they said Pinck had come on to the house. Morris is to board here and go to school, he seems to be a nice young man. Pinck is very well pleased with his school. I am very glad of it, I hope he may learn fast.

August 1865

Tuesday August 1st 1865 - Some rain this morning but Pinck did not get damp. He is still very well pleased. I have made Celia a dress today, she is very well pleased with it. Matt and Betsy are quilting today. Mr. Henry's hand is very painful, it is still running. He stays with the hands all day saving hay. These last two days have been unfavorable for hay making.

Wednesday 2nd - Mrs. Long was here yesterday and had me to promise to spend the day with her today. She came by for me but it was warm. I put her off till next Monday. Betsy and I got out the quilt this morning and hemmed it today. Matt & Fannie are scouring the house today. Cloudy and looks a good deal like rain.

Friday 4th - Betsy, Zona and I and Rose with Eddie spent the day at Mr. Steph Jones' yesterday. I had the headache when I got home and so did Betsy. I went to bed as soon as I got home. I made Jim Patton a shirt today, he needs clothes badly.

Saturday August 5th 1865 - I took all the children to church to the Academy today. It was warm and Gus walked so slow it worried me a great deal. Pinck and I carried him most of the way home. Mr. Henry came to meet us back of the garden. Rose carried Eddie. I have done several things since dinner as this is one time I have been to church and it did not give me headache. I took some lunch along today for my self as well as the children. Mr. Henry says that is the reason I get hungry. Rachel Jones and Laura Owensby came here this evening, they have all gone to church tonight. I am too tired to go. I expect it will be late before they get back. I will not sit up for them.

Sunday 6th - They came very near leaving Pinck last night as he went to sleep and they could not find him. It was 12 o'clock when they got home. They have all gone to church this morning. None of the children but Pinck went. Mr. Henry has gone, his hand pained him a good deal last night. I do wish it would get well, I dislike so much to see him suffer. I expect a good deal of company for dinner so I will stop this time. We had a good deal of company this evening but no one eat dinner but our own family, the others had eat at church as some people carried their dinner. Mrs. & Mr. Long called by this evening. I am to go to her house tomorrow if nothing happens.

Monday 7th - Matt, Betsy and Mr. Arch Morris went to prayer meeting at the Academy last night. I don't think it very prudent in girls to be out till 12 o'clock at night. It rained this morning so I did not go to Mrs. Long's but sewed some on a pair pants for Jim Patton. Betsy and Matt sewing on Rose's dress. Mr. Botts stays here tonight, he is a refugee from Kentucky.

Tuesday 8th - Betsy, Zona, I and Rose with Eddie spent the day at Mrs. Longs. I have a slight headache this evening. Botts is here again tonight. This has been a cool, pleasant day. Mr. Henry met us this evening. He is so fond of his wife and babies, this would nearly be a blank to me without him. I pray God to grant him a long life of health and contentment. His hand is not improving any.

Wednesday 9th 1865 August - I finished Patton's pants today. No news of importance. Betsy finished Rose's dress today. Matt has done nothing of any consequence. Fair and cool, feels like fall of the year was approaching.

Thursday 10th - I lost my knife today in the yard somewhere. I am very sorry. I have had it four years. Betsy and Matt got dinner, I helped some. Celia is washing today. Fannie moved yesterday in the house with Mrs. Quinn. I never intend to associate with a negro for I shall ever consider them my inferiors. I have done but little today. We had several men to dinner. I could not eat much for regretting the loss of my dear little white handle knife. Mr. Henry gave it to me and I prized it so much. I have taken several looks for it but the woods and grass are too high for me to find it. Newton Taylor came in from Cherokee last night, says they are all well. William Tidwell is to be in, in a few days.

Friday 11th - I have been sewing some on Sam's coat today. Betsy and Matt ironing. They go to Sardis to church tonight. There has been a great revival at Locust Knob going on this week and they have moved it to Sardis. Taylor is going with them. I hope those who professed religion may hold out faithful and may do better than they have been doing.

Saturday 12th - Matt & Betsy came home last night about two o'clock. William Tidwell came today. Matt and Betsy have gone to Steph Jones' tonight and then to Sardis tomorrow to preaching. I have sewed some on Sam's coat today, I get on very slow. Mr. Henry's hand not improving any, it pains him up his arm.

Sunday 13th - Lt. T. L. Morris & Till, & Major T. P. Jones spent the day here. Pinck Ballew came over with them but her babe was sick so she went home about 11 o'clock. She left Alice and Wilber. The children had a merry time of it playing. My head aches some this evening.

Monday 14th - Two o'clock when Matt and Betsy got home last night. Late hours I think for prudent women to be out. I have helped Miss Till about weaving our bonnets today. She warped and put them in & wove nearly two yards. We have to get more straw.

Tuesday 15th - I went to Till's this morning to help get the straw and she would have me stay till after dinner. She had a very nice dinner, the first cabbage and sweet potatoes I have seen. Mr. Henry sent for me to come home as Miss Rachel Johnston of Mills River had come down with her father to mill. We have a house full of company tonight as Mr. Freeman & his little son Bobbie are here and then there are some three hands here moving, two Cook boys and Joe Parker. Matt, William and Newt have gone to see Matt's mother. Started this morning.

Wednesday 16th - I finished Sam's coat yesterday evening. William & Newt came back today but Matt is going to stay till the last of this week. Betsy and I have been weaving on our bonnets today, only wove a yd. I went to Till's this evening and got some straw but not enough. Till will be here tomorrow with more straw to finish it. Willie and Zona went with me, it is a great treat to them to go to Miss Tilda's.

Thursday 17th - Till and I got out the bonnets today. Betsy got dinner, rained nearly all day. We had our first musk mellon out of the garden today, it was a very nice one, the children enjoyed it finely. Zona is not learning fast now. She does not like her book. Gus is a naughty boy some times, calls us all nigger and debil. I expect I will have to whip it out of him. I dislike so much to whip my dear little ones.

Friday 18th - I have been fixing up some of Willie's and Zona's old clothes for Soloman and Doug (Celia's children) today, Betsy helping. My babe is not at all well, loose bowels. I think he will cut teeth soon. My head ached some tonight.

Sunday 20th - I had the headache very bad all day yesterday. Sister Jane spent the day here but I could not enjoy it as I was so sick. Betsy ironed all day. Mr. Henry's hand has pained him a great deal this week, but it is a great deal better now. I got part of the core out of one of the places, it is running in three places. He is asleep upstairs now. Eddie is fretting, I must go to him. Nothing new going on, all quiet now.

Monday 21st 1865 August - Betsy and I washed out some five quilts this morning. They are damaged a good deal in the way of stain. Old Mull is the cause of that. I hope he may get his just reward some day. Matt came home today, thinks of teaching a school down there.

Tuesday 22nd - I went to Miss Till's this morning. She came over with me, we brought my thread over. Matt is going to make herself some dresses, I will have one on the web. Till and I cut our bonnets today. I have not made my crown fit very neatly, it is the first one I have tried. Very warm today.

Wednesday 23rd - Sewed some on my bonnet today, it is very unhandy work. Matt and Betsy have got their thread dyed today. Betsy went home this evening, is to be back tomorrow.

Thursday 24th - Mr. Henry's hand is a great deal better. I and Tena got dinner today. Matt is spooling her thread. Mrs. Long spent the day here. We scarcely ever go a day without some one to eat with us. I have sewed some on my bonnet today, not much.

Friday 25th - I ironed till dinner. Matt spooled. Betsy not come yet. Tena is helping spool, she is more willing to do anything now than ever. I think she will find freedom is not such a delightful thing after all. She has behaved very well all the time. I am very glad we are rid of Fannie. She was one troublesome piece of African flesh.

Saturday 26th - I finished my bonnet today after working all week on it, it looks very nice. Pinck went to Sister Jane's today after my seven hundred sley. She had loaned it so I did not get it. I sent to Jim Henry after the cow. He had turned her out and could not find her as she is dry. I had headache this evening but took a nap and it cured me. Mr. Yett of Tenn. ate dinner here today & left a letter for Sister Jane from Vic Peake. She is married to Norman. She is very happy now, so she writes. Two men stay here tonight, came after the still for George Peake.

Sunday 27th - Cool this morning but warm now. We had a nice peach pie for dinner. Billie Cook brought us a basket of nice peaches yesterday and one last Tuesday. Mr. Henry sent him to McAfee's after them. William was to Locust Knob to church today, just got back. I want to go to Tilda's this evening to see if I can get a sley for our cloth. Had some very nice water mellons this evening but don't think I can get a sley.

Monday 28th - Betsy came yesterday evening. She has been sick. She warped the cloth today. I have mended some today and went to Mrs. Steph Jones' and then to Mrs. Owensby's to try to borrow a sley but got none. I will try to get one of Mrs. Norman. Betsy gone home, took all her things. I can't imagine why she left. Something has happened as she expected to make this her home. Till Morris is teaching school at Locust Knob, began today.

Tuesday 29th - Two of the Guy women here today bottoming some chairs. I got a school basket for Pinck and some other baskets of them. They are very poor and indolent people. Matt and I put in the cloth, got a sley of Mrs. Norman.

Wednesday 30th - Matt got the cloth started today, it is very nice. I began to fix my debaize dress but did not finish it, am going to make it longer. Nothing new, only hard times. Oh! this war has taken a heap from us but thanks to a divine Providence I still have my dear husband, my children and a home and I try not to murmer at His Holy Will.

Thursday 31st - Tena and I got dinner, she helps me when I have to cook. We had a nice peach pie for dinner. I finished my dress this evening. Matt and I got supper. This war has learned me to cook. I try not to murmer at the way this war has turned but 'tis very hard to curb my proud spirit.

September 1865

Friday September 1st - I have ironed some today and Celia some. Old Mrs. Muse had two fits at the mill today. Matt and I started down to see her but met Mr. Henry and he said she was better so we went in the orchard, that is Mr. Henry and I, got some apples. When I got to the house, Billie Cook was here with a basket of nice peaches. I enjoyed them finely and Zona it seems, she never gets enough peaches. The children are all very fond of them. It is so kind in Mr. Henry to send and get them for us, he is a dear good husband.

Saturday 2nd September 1865 - I have done several things today. I always have as much as I can do every day. Mr. Henry and I put some bran to soak to make starch this morning. Matt ironed nearly all the evening. She thinks of going to camp meeting, it began yesterday. Mr. Henry went to the camp meeting today to see Sol Luther about a mule of his. The Confederate government got it and gave it to Tom Stradly and he sold it to Luther. I fear Mr. Henry will never get it.

Sunday 3rd - Matt and Zona gone to camp meeting with Mrs. Long in her buggy. Pinck and McParker rode the fillie. Mr. Henry at home all day. Elsie Patton came down and staid all day, she helped me get dinner, we had a nice peach pie. Mrs. Long brought us the peaches and we had our first mess of cabbage. We had a good rain last night, we needed it badly. We have had some this evening. The creek is backed up in the road at the mill a good deal. The old bridge broke in this evening. They will have to fix it up soon. Eddie has been very fretful today. Rose and Celia gone to preaching today. Celia took both her children.

Monday 4th - Very warm today. I began to make some tatten for a chimise but done but little at it. I fill quills for Matt, strained out the starch this morning. Mr. Henry took out the bran for me. Matt helped me. Mr. Henry has had the bridge mended today. I must go to Eddie as he is crying.

Tuesday 5th - I have so many little jobs to do. I get but little work done of any sort. Pinck is at home this week and last too as Mr. Hood has dismissed his school for the boys to save fodder and make up their cane. We will have none to make up this year. Very warm today. I have suffered a great deal this summer with heat. Mr. Henry went to town today. Sister Matt has come up to spend some time with Sister Jane. She does not speak of coming out here so Mr. Henry says. I don't know what she means by it unless she does not care to see us. I have tried to treat my sisters all as well as I was able and I am sure Mr. Henry has.

William L. Henry to President Andrew Johnson

To his Excellency Andrew Johnson,
President of the United States of America at Washington D. C.

The petition of William L. Henry of the County of Buncombe and State of North Carolina, of the age of 41 years and by occupation a farmer, respectfully sheweth unto your Excellency that during the rebellion just closed your petitioner held the office of Post Master at Sulphur Springs, Buncombe County, North Carolina. Your petitioner further sheweth that this is the only civil or diplomatic office ever held by him either before, during or since the rebellion. Believing that the South was right in throwing off allegiance to the general government, your petitioner respectfully acknowledges that his sympathies were strongly enlisted in favor of the success of the rebellion.

Your petitioner held the office of Captain in the 14th Battalion N. C. Troops for the period of five months, but being afflicted by disease and having the care of property which could be rendered more beneficial by his immediate presence, he resigned the aforesaid office & except as aforesaid has in no wise aided by bearing arms in the cause of the rebellion. Your petitioner sheweth that he aided the rebellion further by paying such tithes & taxes as were from time to time required of him.

Your petitioner is advised that by virtue of the first clause of the Amnesty Proclamation issued by your Excellency and bearing date 29th day of May A. D. 1865, he is excluded from the benefits of said proclamation without first obtaining your Excellency's pardon.

Your petitioner further sheweth that he has taken the Oath of Amnesty as prescribed by your Excellency in the proclamation bearing date aforesaid (a copy of which is herewith exhibited) and your petitioner, now that the federal authority is re-established, respectfully swears that he will, as in duty bound, observe the said oath and become a true and loyal citizen of the government of the United States, and obey and respect the law of the Federal government aforesaid and faithfully support, maintain and protect the same.

And your petitioner as in duty bound will ever pray &c.
Wm. Henry, Done at Asheville, N. C., 5th Sept 1865

Many soldiers signed the Oath of Allegiance following the defeat of the
Confederacy. Above is the Oath as signed by William Henry
(Courtesy North Carolina Department of Archives and History)

Wednesday 6th September 1865 - I and Matt strained out some starch this
morning and the hogs got in the meadow and upset the tub so we lost all our
starch. I have done some mending today. I do but little work. I feel disheartened at
this war. Oh! Lord help me to govern my rebelious heart.

Thursday 7th - I and Tena got dinner. Celia is washing. I have never cooked a
meal yet by myself and hope I may never have it to do. Still I am thankful we still
have something to cook, we are nearly out of bacon. It got lost in the hiding of it
when the yanks were in here. I think old Sam and George got a good share of it.
Sam is fixing him up a house to move in out of the yard. I will be glad when the
nigs all get away from us and then maybe we can keep a thing or two without lock
and key.

Friday 8th - I have ironed some today. Very warm. I got so warm I have headache this evening. Matt is getting on very well weaving. No news of importance,
old yank Kirk is merchandising in Asheville. I hate the yanks so bad I don't think I
will ever trade any with them. There are several stores in town.

Saturday 9th - I went over to Till's this morning, had a very nice mellon and
brought one home. I took Till a small basket of peaches, some Mary Rollins
brought us. They are not very nice. We had a peach pie for dinner. I eat a very
hearty dinner. Did some mending after dinner and attended to Eddie. Matt, the
children and Jim Patton went to get some pine this evening, they got a nice chance.

Sunday 10th - This day seven years ago, my dear little baby Cora died. I could
not see it was for the best then, but I think it was now. Oh! this cruel war has

nearly crazied me. I am so rebelious. It is so hard to have our wills so crossed by One who doeth all things well. Help me O Lord to curb my rebelious heart. I am thankful my dear husband is spared to me and my dear children. I ought to be thankful for that blessing and I do try to be. I was in a great deal of trouble seven years ago today. I loved my dear little babe so dearly, but God took her to himself. She is now an angel in glory.

Monday 11th 1865 September - I have headache today but 'tis better this evening. I took a nap since dinner and feel much better. I made some tatten, have enough now. Matt will get out the cloth in a day or two. I have a nice chance of starch. I have not put it out yet. No news of importance going on, some yanks in town but they are very quiet.

Tuesday 12th - I cut two chemise for my self and two shirts for Mr. Henry of sheeting. If it had not been for that bolt of sheeting, I don't see how we would have got along. About under-clothes, it is nearly all gone now. Celia is doing the washing in evenings now and she will do the ironing also.

Wednesday 13th - I finished one chemise this evening. Matt will get out the cloth in the morning. It will not be enough for me a dress. I am sorry of it. I have a nice chance of starch drying and some in soak. Mr. Henry has his hogs up to fatten. We have only ten as they nearly all died up with cholera last spring.

Thursday 14th - We are having some beautiful weather, now fair and warm. Matt shrunk the cloth this morning and ironed some this evening. Pinck and Zona recite to me every day, they are learning very fast. Pinck can cipher some and Zona makes straight marks. Willie knows nearly all the alphabet, all but e and h. They seem to be very hard to him.

Friday 15th - Mr. Henry went to town this morning. Sister Jane's family all well. Matt is coming out before long. Mr. Henry sent Jim Patton to Bob Gudger's today and got one ham of very nice bacon. It seems so strange for us to be out of meat. Our meat went very strangely in the hiding. George and Old Sam hid it. I imagine they supplied themselves out of it. I finished my chemise this evening. We had quite a refreshing shower since dinner.

Saturday 16th - This has been a day of all sorts of work as Saturday generally is. I washed all the children's heads this evening and mine too. Mr. Henry went to Capt. Moore's this morning, did not get home till after dinner. Capt. Freeman's little Willie staid here last night and Thursday night also. Freeman & family start to Texas in a few days hunting a home.

Sunday 17th - Cool this morning but the sun is very warm now. Pinck is off hunting chinquapins, the others at play in the kitchen except Gus who is not at all well, has sore throat. I think he is lying down and has been all morning. He had a fever all night. I hope he may soon be well again. Eddie is getting better of his cough and getting fat fast. Till and Mr. Morris spent the day here. I wrote in Mrs. T. F. Glenn's album today. Gus no better this evening.

Monday 18th - Mr. Henry started to get his horse (stallion). He has heard he was in Henderson Co. Steph Jones went with him. Some rain today. I fear Mr. Henry will get wet. I have sewed some, a shirt bosom today. Gus is much better, his neck is full of little blisters on the outside. I made a mistake and put croton oil on instead of a linamint for sore throat. I hope it may soon be well, he is fretful still.

Thursday 19th - I sewed some on the shirt today. Rachel Jones came here this evening and brought me a note from her father saying Mr. Henry has gone on for his horse and will perhaps go to Pa's. Rachel stays here tonight. Miss Tilda was here a few minutes this evening. I hope Mr. Henry may get his horse and may a kind Providence watch over him and take care of him in his wandering.

Wednesday 20th - I have sewed some on Mr. Henry's shirt. I am uneasy about him but I will give him into the hands of a divine Providence who has cared for us all our lives. Gus' neck is improving but not well. His ears are sore behind them. I think they will be well soon.

Thursday 21st - This day sixteen years ago, my only brother was thrown from a horse and killed. It seems a long time since then. Our hearts were very sad but I think it was for the best. "He doeth all things well." I have sewed some today. My head aches badly this evening.

Saturday 23rd - I had headache very bad all day yesterday. It has got nearly well since dinner. I have done but little today, sewed some. No news from Mr. Henry. I do hope and trust no harm has befallen him. He is very dear to me and our children. How could I live without my own dear husband? God bless him I pray.

Sunday 24th September 1865 - I took all the children to Till's and spent the day. Mr. Henry came over there about dinner. We were all glad to see him. He got his horse, he is very poor. He had no difficulty in getting him. I am glad he got him and no trouble and got home safe. He did not go to Pa's, only went to Spartanburg. Mont Stradly stays here tonight. "Lord keep us safe this night I pray."

Monday 25th - Elsie Patton, Celia and I scoured and scalded the whole house today. Mr. Henry went to town. He has the blues, the worst sort this evening. He is very desponding for fear his debts will break him up. I hope not. He will hate to give up his homestead and mills and everything he has. I hope he may not have to do it. If we do, help us. O Lord to be resigned to Thy will I pray.

Tuesday 26th - Matt got dinner yesterday and her and I put the house in order today. Made some changes upstairs in the furniture. Mr. Henry about the plantation all day. No news of importance. Lafayette Jones has returned home, he ran out when the yanks came in. Things are going on badly at the North. The yanks killing up rebels &c. Will they ever stop their meanness? Lord help us I pray.

Wednesday 27th - I have done my first day's washing. Celia and I got done about three o'clock, a big washing at that. My hands are very sore and raw in several places but everything is clean. I spoke to Tena about washing yesterday but she did not seem to want to do it so I did it myself. I have sewed some this evening. Tired as I was, I could not sit with folded hands idle. I have too many to work for, to do that. Mr. Henry did not want me to wash.

Thursday 28th - I finished the shirt and did some other little jobs. Matt ironed nearly all the clothes. Mr. Henry about the farm. He is having some waggon spokes split. Wiley Knight has moved down to Mrs. Fanning's house at the mill. He and Bob Jarrett are going to work in the old mill house. Jarrett lives in the old store house. He is a cabinet maker. I hope they may do well.

Friday 29th September 1865 - I have fixed a short gown for Eddie today and done some other mending. 'Tis one continued mend and patch. I hope always to have as good clothes for my children as now if no better. Mr. Henry sent Sister Jane some rails for a pig pen and sent her some soap. Ike Hendrix took the waggon & Pinck went along. Matt has never been over to see us yet. I think she is treating us badly.

Saturday 30th – Mending all day. Fair and pleasant cool mornings but no frost yet. Mr. Henry got some hogs from A. B. Jones to fatten on shoats. Put them in the pen this morning. Mr. Henry did not come home for dinner. I sent it to him. They are getting spokes. Jim Patton has left. I am glad of it as he did not earn his bread. He is so indolent. Sam and Henry will leave soon for So. Ca.

October 1865

Sunday October 1st – Cool this morning but pleasant now. Mr. Henry has gone to Tom Cook's today. Will be gone all day so I will miss him a great deal. I must stop now and get out dinner as we have but little to cook. No flour as Mr. Henry wants to sow all the wheat he can get. Pinck gone to hunt some walnuts, the other children at play. Mr. Henry came home to dinner. Dr. Neilson called here to see Matt and took dinner with us. Matt has not been well for some time. I hope she may get well as she is taking medicine from the Dr.'s.

Monday 2nd – Still cool mornings and evenings. I began a dress for myself to-day. Yoke waist and puffy sleeves. It will be some trouble to make I fear. Willey Wells and Arch Morris have come again as school began this morning. Pinck went and I went a piece with him. He is not afraid but I fear he is lonely so I go with him when no one else goes.

Tuesday 3rd – Sewing all day, but get on slowly with my dress. It fits very neatly. Matt fixing up a dress. She speaks of going over on Turkey Creek to teach school near her mother. Mr. Henry about home all day. No news.

Wednesday 4th - High wind all night so no frost but cool enough for it. Pinck wants his shoes. Tom Cook is to make them this week. Did not finish my dress this evening. A young man named Boling staid here last night and has let Mr. Henry have his mare saddle and bridle for ten months tuition, and board to Mr. Hood. He seems to be quite a nice young man.

Thursday 5th - Frost for the first, a good deal. I finished my dress today, it fits beautifully. I will not like to wear it for Mr. Henry says it is so ugly. I do love to please him. Mr. Boling went to school today for the first day.

Friday 6th - A big frost this morning killing things. Generally warm after the morning. Oh! Autumn makes me feel so sad to see the leaves falling and know that dame winter is coming with rapid steps and then we are cooped for the season. I did some repairing on my old debaize dress but did not finish it. My head aches some this evening. Matt and I took a little walk this evening to get some grapes but found none. We have a quantity of walnuts drying.

Saturday 7th - Pinck and Lonzo went to Mr. Cook's and got his shoes, they are rather small. We went and got a basket of nice grapes this evening. Mr. Henry and Mr. Boling went with us. Willie and Zona also. Pinck's shoes hurt his feet so he and Gus staid with Rose and Eddie. I had to get up with Eddie this morning about three, he got cold. Mr. Henry made up a fire for me, he is very kind to me.

Sunday 8th - I took the children to Till's this morning. Mrs. Ballew has moved into the kitchen as her babe is not at all well. Till was not at home, had gone to John Starnes' on business. I came home about 11 o'clock, found Mrs. Tom Morris here. Mr. A. B. Jones and wife & Mr. Albert Hawkins and wife were at Mrs. Ballews when I left. I suppose Mr. Henry has gone over there as he is not at the house. Mr. Boling is down stairs reading. He makes himself quite useful in cutting wood. He only cuts with one hand, the left shoulder has been shattered in this cruel war. It will soon be dinner. We have sweet potato custards for dinner, our first. Celia got some nice potatoes yesterday evening in the garden. Pinck is standing by me trying to write, he makes a very good out of it. Mr. Henry brought us some nice grapes, we have had several this fall as we have no apples. They eat very well.

Sunday 15th October 1865 - Nothing of importance has happened this week. I spent last Tuesday at Sister Jane's. They are all well. Mr. Neilson still absent at the North, gone to lay in goods. Everybody is merchandising, there are several stores in town. Celia has been sick ever since last Wednesday with dyptheria so Matt and I have done the cooking and a hard task it is as there are so many to cook for. This war has changed our circumstances a great deal. I have done more hard work this summer than I ever did in my life. I can't see the good of abolishing slavery. Matt is getting dinner. I have the headache a little. I fear it will get worse towards evening. I will have supper to get and I dread it. Tom Cook brought Zona her shoes today, she is very proud of them. Pinck, Zona & Rose went to get some walnuts. Pinck got the basket in the race. Zona ran to the house & told us of it and then took a good cry. Poor little dear, she was distressed about it. Cool and cloudy today. No news only work, work all the time. Celia is better. I hope she may soon be well and never get sick any more as long as she lives with us. Matt (sister) will come out in a few days to spend some time with us. She is looking badly. I must stop now as I have nothing more to write.

Monday 16th - We got breakfast this morning. Celia is getting better. I like to cook very well. I try to adapt myself to circumstances which is not very pleasant to the inclination sometimes. I sewed some on my dress today and got the waist done. Matt and I went and got us some wood this evening. 'Tis hard on us to carry wood but we go at it cheerfully. I hope there is still a better day a coming.

Tuesday 17th - I finished my dress, only the cord around the hem. I have been at it for nearly a week but have had so much other work to do I have but little time for sewing. Pinck came home yesterday evening with his feet very sore from his shoes, they are too small. I will teach him at home till he gets shoes.

Wednesday 18th - Celia getting better but not able to do much yet. Mr. Henry about the mill all day. They are getting a good deal of work in the shop waggon making or rather repairing. I do hope Mr. Henry may prosper in business.

Thursday 19th October 1865 - We had a great eclipse of the sun today, nearly a total eclipse. I never expect to see such another sight in my life. I finished my dress today and cut Hanes and Lonzo a vest and did some sewing on them. Matt, Willie and I went to get some haws, they were all gone. We got a few walnuts and came back. It made our supper very late. Old Mrs. Justice was burried this evening, she has suffered a great deal with cancer on the face. Mr. Henry went to the burial.

Friday 20th - I finished Hanes' vest today. Matt ironed. Tena washed yesterday. Celia helped get breakfast for the first time in a week. I am glad she is getting up again. Mr. Henry is very busy getting in his rent corn. He will have enough rent to do us I think. The hogs are improving very fast.

Saturday 21st - I have done several things today, odds and ends. Mr. Henry at Hendrix's measuring up corn nearly all day. Rather cool this evening.

Sunday 22nd - Eddie is six months old today. He is a dear good baby, can nearly sit alone. He is very fond of his mother, sleeps in my arms nearly all night. Willie learns very slow. Is spelling in three letters but can't pronounce any. Cool all day. Mr. Henry, Pinck and Mr. Bouldin went to prayer meeting at Locust Knob tonight. They were disappointed as there was none.

Monday 23rd - Some frost this morning, quite cool. Pinck has gone to Mr. Steph Jones' to get him shoe leathers. Mr. Henry speaks of going to town this evening after Sister Matt. I hope he may. I must get out dinner. We have our first turnips for dinner today. They are very large. I have some drawers to fix for Gussie. He is a very fat, healthy child. Willie does not look so stout.

Tuesday 31st - A week has past since I last wrote but nothing of importance has transpired. Sister Matt came over last Thursday and staid till yesterday. Matt Tidwell spent last week at Mrs. Green's. Mrs. Kirkindoll is lying very low with consumption. Willy was not here last week, at home gathering corn. I did several things last week, got dinner Thursday as Celia was washing. Mr. Boling & Pinck went to Sand Hill Academy last Friday night to see the Magic Lantern[53] and some other experiments. Pinck was delighted. He went last night to Till's to a corn shucking, the first he was ever at. A man staid here last night and wants to board some ten days. He is a refugee from Ten. Matt Tidwell went down with Dr. Candler to Turkey Creek last Sunday, is going to teach school. I hope she may do well. I must stop as I have a shirt to make for negro Henry. I made him one last week. Mr. Henry about the mill nearly all the time.

November 1865

Wednesday Nove 1st 1865 - I sewed some on Henry's shirt yesterday and finished it today. I have so many things to do I scarcely know where to begin. We are having some beautiful weather now. The refugee, Mr. Jacobs, is staying here for a week or so. He is a very pleasant young man. I have a great deal of sympathy for refugees as my dear husband was once one. We have a good deal of company and are more scarce of edibles than we ever were. Wheat is so scarce that we get none to grind so we live on corn bread & a good deal of punkin. We do not get butter enough but will soon get more as Heff has a young calf two days old. Our boarders seem very well pleased with our meager fare. We are thankful we are still spared and life goes on very cheerfull with us. Pinck has been staying at home near two

---

[53] Early slide projector

weeks as his shoes were too small but has another pair now and is going again. He learns very fast. Zona is through her first reader. Willie can't pronounce any yet. Eddie has one tooth below, I found it last Sunday. He is a dear good babe. Gussie is as fat as a pig.

Thursday 2nd - Rained all day, a very gentle rain but enough to keep Celia from washing. We have had a beautiful fall, so dry. Every one is done making molasses. We have not had a great deal of frost. I have been fixing up some napkins today. Jeff got them the other night and tore several up. Mr. Henry about the mill most of the time. Pinck did not go to school this morning as it was raining and Mr. Boling went home with some of the students yesterday evening.

Friday 3rd - I made Eddie some pinifors of doilies today. They do very well. Still raining. Elsie got the cloth warped yesterday but has not come yet to put it in. Mr. Henry let Mr. Curtis have some cattle on a debt today and found where some rouge had killed one of his yearlings. Some nig I imagine. I fear they will kill up people's stock a great deal this winter.

Saturday 4th Nove 1865 - Elsie came this morning. Her and I put in the cloth. She got it started. Till & Pinck spent the evening here. Rained till dinner and then fair and windy, turning cold very fast. I got a quill basket from the Guys this evening and Mr. Henry got a feed basket. Uncle Sam moved today, we will miss him a great deal. Mr. Henry used to say he could not keep house without old Sam but now we will have to do it. The war has broken us up. I can't see how we are to pay our debts & still retain a home. Mr. Henry worries about it a good deal. He is prematurely ten years older in the last eight months. The loss of the hotel hurt him a great deal and now the negroes being freed is another blow. I try to cheer him but he is gloomy nearly all the time. I feel so sorry for him. He loves his old homestead so dearly. May God in his love, spare us the trial of giving it up and may we be more prosperous in our business transactions.

Sunday 5th - Cold and windy all day. Ice this morning for the first. We have staid close by the fire all day. Mr. Henry has been in the room nearly all day. I took the trundle bed down last Monday for the children. Pinck sleeps upstairs in the room with Mr. Boling and Mr. Jacob, in Matt's room. Tena will still milk till old Bently comes, he is to move tomorrow. I fear I will not like old Bently's folks but I will try to get along with them the best I can. Elsie wants to live here I think, but she is not neat in her person.

Monday 6th – Bently's family are to move tomorrow. I got dinner today as Celia is washing. She has two weeks washing to do. I did a little sewing after dinner, not much as I was too tired. Hard work breaks me down very soon in the back.

Tuesday 7th - I got dinner again today and very tired tonight. Bently's family came down today. They are to do our milking. I have sewed some today, not much. Things are going on quietly through the country. Nigs are stealing some occasionally. I feared as much since they are too indolent to make an honest living. Oh! that they were removed from among us, they are a roguish set generally.

Wednesday & Thursday & Friday 10th Nove 1865 - For two days past I have been sick with headache but well this morning. Mr. Henry got a few lbs. of coffee yesterday in town. He laughingly says that cured me. It is certainly very pleasant to the taste to have a cup of nice coffee for breakfast. I am very tired tonight. I have ironed all day and then went to meet Pinck this evening, as Mr. Boling went to Madison Co. this morning and I thought Pinck would be lonely coming home from school alone. He is a good boy, learns very fast but a little mischevious.

Saturday 11th - Attended to Eddie nearly all day as Rose is washing her clothes. Eddie has two teeth below. Mr. Henry says he intends to find the first one above and I intend to find it so our fingers are in Eddie's mouth soon in the morning and late at night. I have done a good deal of mending today. Elsie still weaving. When she gets enough for Sam and Henry some clothes, she will cut it out.

Sunday 12th - At home all day. More pleasant then it has been for several days. No news.

Monday 13th - I am so busy I scarcely know what to do first. I have made Celia a bonnet and began to quilt Eddie one today. I want to make him some short clothes as soon as I can. Zona and Willie are learning slowly. I have so many things to do I neglect them. Willie cannot pronounce yet.

Tuesday 14th - Finished Eddie's bonnet today and made Doug a flannel shirt. Elsie cut out the cloth today. Mr. Henry stays at the mill nearly all the time. They are doing a good deal of work in the waggon shop.

Wednesday 15th - Elsie is helping me make Sam's & Henry's clothes. She sews very well, finished one pair & nearly another. We will make Henry a coat. I cut it today.

Thursday 16th - We are still sewing. We got dinner as Celia is washing. Mr. Jacobs has been having some chills but has not had one since last Monday. I hope he may get up well again. He seems to be very quiet. Boling came back from Madison last Sunday evening. Mr. Morris does not stay here all the time, he seems to have a very unhappy disposition.

Friday 17th 1865 Nov. - Finished all the sewing this evening before night. Three pair pants and one coat. Mr. Jacobs went to town today. No news of importance. All are well. Eddie has no more teeth yet.

Saturday 18th - Elsie ironed today till dinner, then went home. I have done some mending today. Till was here this evening. Her and I went up to Bettie Knight's and Daniel Ledford's, had some business with them. Ledford lives where Muses lived. I have the headache some this evening.

Sunday 19th - I went to bed last night before supper and woke up about 9 o'clock. Mr. Henry had put the children all to bed and was sitting by the fire waiting for me to wake. He had me a pot of nice coffee so I got up & he and I drank some & sit by the fire till near 11 o'clock and this morning I am nearly free of headache. I went over after Till this morning. Her and Mrs. Morris came over and spent the day. Tom Cook was here all day also. Mr. Boling and Mr. Jacobs & Pinck went to church today but no preaching (at the Academy). Warm and pleasant all day.

Monday 20th - Raining this morning. Mr. Jacobs has another chill. I expect to make Eddie some short clothes this week. I must stop now and fix a blanket on the side room bed for Mr. Jacobs as he is sitting here by the fire. I began to work Eddie a skirt today of home made flannel. 'Tis very soft and nice.

Tuesday 21st - Finished one skirt for Eddie today and made the body of the other one. No news of importance. Mr. Jacobs missed his chill today. Sarah Jane Kurkendoll died last Tuesday & so Wiley was not here last week, but here this.

Wednesday 22nd - Finished Eddie's skirt before dinner, cut him some dresses and gowns after dinner. All of old goods I am not able to buy. Calico at fifty cts. yd. Pleasant weather now. We have had a beautiful fall so far, no very cold weather.

Thursday 23rd - Finished one of Eddie's dresses today. I put short clothes on him yesterday for the first. He looks very sweet in short dresses. He is a dear good babe, no trouble at all. Will sit in the large chair a long time and play. I could do very well without Rose but she has no one to take care of her so I keep her as an act of charity. She is very indolent and mean with it.

Friday 24th November 1865 - Mr. Henry is forty-two years old today, will soon be on the decline of life. He has broken a good deal in the last five years, begins to look a little old. I tell him he must get young again as the war is over now. Mr. Jacobs went to town today to a tournament, got back this evening. No news in town. I fixed two gowns for Eddie today. I have turned Willie back to the abc's as he can't pronounce. Zona is going through her book very fast the second time.

Saturday 25th - Odds and ends have I done all day, just as I do every Saturday. Very pleasant today. Elsie ironed most of the things yesterday. She has gone to town today, will get out the jeans next week I think. Mr. Henry has had the cows tied up this evening in the stalls of cow house. They cut some (rare shines?).

Sunday 26th - This has been a lovely day. I took the children and went up to see Aunt Tena in her new home. She seems to be very comfortable and contented. After dinner, Mr. Henry took Eddie and we went over to Miss Till's. They were not home so we only rested and came back. Pinck brought Guss and Willie. Zona was with us. Gus did not want to come back. He wanted to go to the house. We met the children just as we started home.

Monday 27th - Mr. Henry is going to put up the bridge below the mill dam today. Bently went to Capt. Moore's this morning and got his oxen. I will be sewing on Eddie some clothes today.

Tuesday 28th - Made Eddie a dress and cut out a worsted dress for him. No news. Very pleasant weather, rather warm for Dec.

Wednesday 29th - I finished Eddie's dress today and cut Pinck a pair pants. I heard tonight that Sister Jane is going to move soon. I am sorry of it. She was company to me though I never saw her often. They go to Spartanburg, I think. Mr. Neilson has gone into business there I hear.

Thursday 30th - I have had headache all day but did not stop sewing. I want to go to Sister Jane's one day this week to spend several days and take all the children. I can't enjoy myself and leave them at home. They are very dear to me. I hope they may reward my watchfulness and care in future years.

December 1865

Friday December 1st 1865 - Headache all day but I have not lay down for fear of making it worse. Mr. Henry about the mill nearly all the time. Mr. Jacobs here still.

Saturday 2nd - My head has pained me all day but nearly well this evening. I have knit some today and been in bed part of the time so feel but little like writing.

Sunday 3rd - Some rogue stole Mr. Henry's gray mare he got of Mr. Boling. Mr. Henry and Boling started in pursuit of the thief today. They think he has gone towards Waynesville. I think George (negro) had a hand in it. It really seems we have the worst luck and the most of it of any one. That was the best horse we had. I do feel so sorry for Mr. Henry.

Monday 4th - Mr. Henry has not come yet. I expected him last night. I ironed some this morning and did some mending in the evening. Mr. Henry and Mr. Boling came just before supper, did not get the horse. I am very sorry of it.

Tuesday 5th - Fixed a dress that was too short waisted. Cloudy and oppressively warm for two days. A light shower tonight with fair prospects of more. We need rain at the mill to raise the water.

Wednesday 6th - My head feels full and bad this morning. Still cloudy and misty rain. I expect to make Mr. Henry some pants today or tomorrow. I sent Zona over and got Mrs. Tom Morris' pattern. I will cut them out soon. I cut them and sewed some on them.

Thursday 7th - I got Lizzie Bently to wash today as Celia is not well. I helped her some but Mr. Henry came down and would have me to come to the house and in a few minutes, Sister Matt and Georgie Neilson came. They start in a few days to Spartanburg Village. I am very sorry for it. Sister Jane was all my relations that was near me. I shall miss her so much. I will feel so lonely and desolate when she is gone. I went over to Till's after Matt left. I think I will go to town tomorrow.

Saturday 9th - I told my dear sister goodbye today. I may never see any of my kindred again. I have no one to look to now but my dear husband and children. I feel sad and lonely. I enjoyed my visit very much but then when I thought I was at Sister Jane's my last time, my heart was sad, so sad. I was so sorry I could not take my dear little ones. They were so anxious to go to see Aunt Jane and the children. Zona said she could walk and Willie took a good cry when I told him Aunt Jane was going to move. He wanted to go and see her but I told him we would go to see her in Spartanburg but when, I can't tell. My arm is very sore today from carrying Eddie as we rode horse back. I rode Clarion and Mr. Henry, Jacob's mule. Rose walked there & rode behind me back. Mrs. Jesse Smith's little daughter Maggie died last night. She is very unfortunate in losing children.

Sunday 10th - I took all the children and spent the day at Miss Tilda's. Mrs. Jones was there. Very pleasant. Mr. Henry came and met us. He is so kind to me and the children. He staid at home with Mr. Boling and Mr. Jacobs.

Monday 11th - Fair and pleasant. We have had a beautiful fall, so mild and dry. It has been a fine time on farmers. No news of importance. We hear Europe has declared war against the United States. If so, I hope their land may be desolated as

Sherman desolated So. Ca. & Ga. as he passed. Surely a just God don't intend them to prosper. They are certainly a lawless set. May they yet meet their just desserts.

Tuesday 12th - Made Mr. Jacobs a pair pants today. Mr. Henry has some hands on the turnpike road. He is going to work it out to the Henderson line. He will not be at home tonight. I will miss him so much. He is a faithful hand with the children, dressing and undressing them.

Wednesday 13th - Made Willie a pair pants today. I have such little heart to work. We are greatly in debt. 'Tis distressing to think of it. The war has laid a heavy hand on us, brought us down from affluence to nearly nothing. Only our land is left. I can't see how we are to get through. I hope we may be able to keep our dear home but things look very dark at this time.

Thursday 14th - Cold and turning colder every hour. Mr. Henry did not, Thursday night or last night, but I think will come tonight as 'tis too cold to work on the road. I have knit some today and made Eddie a saque, it fits very neatly. No news. I expect Sister Jane is in Spartanburg in this time, she has a tollerable pleasant time.

Friday 15th - Mr. Henry came home last night. It was very cold, ice in the room. Gussie had a hot fever all night last night, is very drowsy all day. Worms and cold I think. I have done nothing but read and knit today. Reading "Vale of Cedars." It is very interesting. I borrowed it of Eliza Neilson. Mr. Henry in the house all day as it is too cold to be out much.

Saturday 16th - I have several things too tedious to mention. Mr. Henry and Mr. Bouldin went to town today. No news of importance. 'Tis reported that the Black Republicans will not allow the members to congress from the rebel states to take a seat in congress. Such times as we do have but this will be nothing to what it will be if the U. S. gets into war again.

Sunday 17th - Some snow this morning. The children all up soon to see it. Gus is better but not able to go out yet, he walks about the room some. I gave him some oil yesterday. He took it so well, he is a good child. Snow nearly all gone this evening. Betsey Jamison stays here tonight. She has not been here in some time before. She acts strangely.

Monday 18th - Mr. Henry and six hands have gone on the road today. Jacobs took their dinner. They will be at home tonight. I have fixed a dress I intend to let Elsie have, and knit some. Willie is sick since dinner vomiting. I think he eat too much walnuts before dinner. Gus has been up all day.

Tuesday 19th - I have washed some today. My hands are very sore, the skin off in several places. Mr. Henry does not want me to wash, but Celia had to cook for the hands that are on the road. They take their dinner with them. They will get done tomorrow. I have sewed some since dinner. Warm and looks like rain this evening but fair this morning.

Wednesday 20th - I cut Willie a coat and sewed it today. He is very proud of his first coat. I have dried most of the clothes, some by the fire, till after dinner and then the sun came out. Mr. Henry still on the road but will get done today.

Thursday 21st - Fixed a dress for Rose and knit some after dinner. No news of importance. Two travellers stay here tonight. We have some every few nights but they nearly all say they have no money so 'tis a poor business.

Friday 22nd - Killed seven hogs today, none very large. We will have to be very economical with our meat to make it last. Tena helped with the chitlens. I have moulded some candles today and several other things. Cold and clear today. Very calm.

Saturday 23rd - I am very tired tonight as I have been on my feet nearly all day baking for Christmas. Henry killed the turkey this evening. The children hated to see Peter slain. Two travellers stay here tonight. I think they are yanks.

Sunday 24th - Rained till about 12 o'clock and then cloudy. Mr. Henry has taken a walk this evening. I would have gone also but 'tis too muddy. I expect a few friends to dine with us tomorrow. It seems very little like Christmas to me. I used to look forward to that day with a great deal of pleasure when I was young but that time is past, never to return. This day, one year ago, we all hoped the war would soon end in our favor but it did not. Still we try to submit to the will of the great I Am.

Monday 25th Christmas Day - Bright and clear till noon. Cloudy all evening. Mr. A. B. Jones & wife, Mrs. Ballew, Mr. T. L. Morris and wife took dinner with us. Also Mrs. Rufe Miller but she came unexpected. We had a very nice dinner, the turkey was very fat. I have headache some today. Pinck has gone home with Millard Jones this evening. He was very anxious to go. Celia & Rose have gone Christmasing till Saturday night. I will do the cooking with Henry's help. He is very good to do anything. Things have changed a good deal with us since last Christmas, we still hope for independence but now the last ray of hope is forever obscured. I try to be resigned but 'tis very hard to say "Thy will be done." Mr. Henry is more submissive than I. He is a good Christian I believe.

Tuesday 26th - Up soon and got breakfast. Things have gone on very quietly. Jane Bently is to nurse Eddie till Rose comes home. Headache all day from cold I think. I like to cook very well, though it is very awkward to me. Lizzie Bently helped me some today. My back gives out so quick I am not fit for hard work.

Wednesday 27th – My head still aches some but I got breakfast. No news. Lizzie Bently helped me some today. My back gives out so quick I am not fit for hard work.

Thursday 28th - Elsie has been here today and last night. I had the headache very bad yesterday evening but took a nap and felt much relieved. We have had cloudy weather every day this week but not much rain. Little Jacobs started home this morning. Poor little fellow, I am glad he can go to his friends. His father now lives near Franklin. Elsie goes home tonight.

Friday 29th - I have done everything by myself today, did some sewing on Pinck's coat. I cut him a pair pants and coat last Thursday. Jane is a very good nurse, gets on with Eddie finely. I don't see how I could get on without her. Pinck has holiday this week. He brings me water and does several turns.

Saturday 30th - My left breast is a little sore. I got my feet wet today. A little snow last night, enough to make things sloppy wet yesterday. I think if the days govern the months they will all be wet so far. Finished Pinck's coat today. Elsie staid here last night, ironed and got dinner. Mr. Henry about the mill nearly all the time.

1866

"...Poor negroes, they sicken and die and no one cares..."

January 1866

Friday 5th January 1866 - Since writing in my journal we have entered into another year. What will it bring us? Joy and happiness or sadness and woe. Oh! that is something the future has to unfold, we can't look into future one moment.

I have been quite sick since Saturday. I took a chill Saturday night and had a very high fever all night. Mr. Henry sent for Dr. Hilliard Sunday, he gave me some medicine. I did not sit up any Sunday of note. My head and back have pained me a great deal. I have been improving every day. This is the first day I have sit up all day. I think I will be well in a day or two. My breast is nearly well, does not pain me, only when Eddie nurses. It was the weed in the breast what ailed me, caused by cold. Mr. Henry has been very kind to me in my sickness, says I must not expose myself so any more, but I have to work. Very cold yesterday and today a little snow yesterday but fair today. Ham Rollins moved in the house with Bently till he gets a house built.

Saturday 6th - I have done some little odds today, not much. My breast is still hard one side. No news. The mail came yesterday for the first time. Vick is still on this route. Mr. Henry is very good to get up with Eddie at night and give him some milk. I give but little now as I have no appetite.

Sunday 7th - Bright, rather cold. Mr. Andy Miller and another man stay here tonight on their way to Asheville. I took the children and took a walk up by the stables. My breast pains me some today.

Monday 8th - I finished Pinck's pants this evening. I began them over a week ago. Mrs. Joe Green stays here tonight, she is a nice woman. Mr. Henry about the farm all day. He has Henry hired this year.

Tuesday 9th - I cut and began Mr. Henry's coat today, got the lining of Till. 'Tis very nice brown linsey. Till has been a very good and true friend to me, I will always like her. Cold and clear this morning.

Wednesday 10th - Sewed some on the coat today. Mary Rollins helped me on the coat some today. Ham Rollins is building him a house to move in. Old Mrs. Bently has moved the milk up to the dining room. I think she will wash the pan a little oftener.

Thursday 11th - Mr. Henry went to Sandy Bottom yesterday and put up the toll gate again, some men cut it down a few days before Christmas. Warm and pleasant

313

today. Celia scoured my room today. Elsie got dinner and ironed some. My head ached all day.

Saturday 13th - My head ached badly all day yesterday. I did nothing all day. Mr. Henry staid with me most of the day. My head some better today but I still feel very weak. I have knit some today. I have not finished Mr. Henry's coat yet. I have not got the buttons so can't work the button holes.

Sunday 14th - Warm and fair. My breast pains me some today. I expect I have got a little cold in it. I took a walk with the children this evening up by the stables. Rather cool. Mr. Henry is very kind, he gets up with Eddie every night and gives him some milk. He is afraid I will get more cold. He is as tender with me as if I was a baby.

Monday Jan 15th 1866 - I finished putting the collar on Mr. Henry's coat but not the button holes yet and made Eddie a sack. My breast pains me a good deal today. I fear it will beal & I am putting spirits of turpentine and champhor. It is not so painful this evening as this morning.

Thursday 16th - My breast a good deal better. Eddie up only once last night. Old Bob Boyd at work on the sawmill, began last Monday. Mr. Henry has Boston hired to run the bucket machinery. I have done several things today. Till spent the evening with me. Mr. Henry is sitting here waiting for me to go to bed. It is near nine and eight is our bed time. He is so kind to me. I will stop for this time and an old man from Transylvania stays here tonight on his way to Asheville to see the yankee Capt. about some mules that have been taken from him recently.

Wednesday 17th - I cut some coats and pants for Tena today. I am to make the coats. I have net some on the partridge net this evening. Old Mrs. Bently has been at it nearly three weeks. I think I can net one wing in two days. I will try on it to-morrow. Warm and pleasant today. Mary (a nig) is washing for me today at 25 cts. in green back. She is to spin some for me. Fannie got some wool yesterday evening to spin and Tena got some this evening.

Thursday 18th - I have been netting today. Have had headache all day. I lay down this evening and took a rest and feel much better since. I will finish the net tomorrow if I am well. Bob Jarrett has quit work, is going to Atlanta. He and Mr. Henry settled up today, he owes Mr. Henry some.

Friday 19th - Very warm for January, but little fire needed. I finished the net by two o'clock and cut Mr. Henry a pair of flannel drawers, of flannel of borrowed of Till. I sent to her house this evening but she was not at home. I got very warm. I took Rose and Eddie as I was afraid she would not attend to him well in my absence. Zona took care of the other children. Till was not at home. I rested a little at her spring and came back.

Saturday 20th - Rained all the morning & turning very cold this evening and clear. I have done several things today. John and Billie Cook came today and had a settlement with Mr. Henry for their work last summer. Two men staid here last night.

Sunday 21 Jan 1866 - A yankee soldier staid here last night. He seems to be nearly an idiot. He says he is a Prussian. Very cold this morning with wind from North, fair. The ground thawing a little. The children stay by the fire very well today as 'tis too cold to be out long at a time. Mr. Boyd is nearly done the sawmill. He is very slow but a good workman. My breast is nearly well but still a lump in it, it is not sore any. We will be housed all day as it is too cold for out door exercise.

Monday 22nd - I sewed some on Hanes' coat and helped put sticks in one wing of the net. The wings are not long enough. I will net them about two yds. longer. Mr. Henry about the mill all day. Bob Jarrett's family left today. Going to Atlanta or Augusta Ga. Money too scarce to lay out for furniture. Ham Rollins will move in the old store tomorrow. He is attending the sawmill.

Tuesday 23rd - Sewed some on Hanes' coat and net some. I am teaching Zona and Willie. Willie is very young, not yet five. He does not progress very fast. Pinck has had a slight touch of sore eyes but they are getting better.

Wednesday 24th - Finished Hanes' coat and the net this evening. I went to Elsie's since dinner. She has got my cloth very narrow, almost ruined it. Ham Rollins moved yesterday. Mr. Henry about the mill all day.

Thursday 25th - I have done odds and ends today and nothing much in the end. Eddie's eyes are getting sore. I fear the children will all have sore eyes. I do hope it may not injure their sight any. They are more precious in my eye than gold dust.

Friday 26th - I went to the examination at Sand Hill today. Went by Miss Tilda's and her and I went together, also Rose Blanchard. I came back by Miss Till and got dinner. My head aches this evening. I fear I will not get to go to the exhibition tonight. Zona is very anxious to go. She cried to go with me today and I promised her to go tonight. She is very fond of me, a dear child she is to us. I want her to go to school next session if I can gently. She always says she don't want to leave me, she is devoted to her mother.

Sunday 28th January 1866 - I suffered a great deal with headache Friday night and all day yesterday. Mr. Henry took Zona and Pinck to the exhibition, they rode. They enjoyed it finely. Mrs. Bently and Jane staid with me. Mr. Henry and the children came home about 11 o'clock. They had a bright moonlight night and not very cold. Mr. Henry in the house nearly all day yesterday to be with me. Very unpleasant out yesterday as it was raining and snowing most of the day. Zona is my little housekeeper when I am sick. She is a nice child at anything.

Monday 29th - I was cleaning up the house nearly all morning and after dinner, Mr. Henry and I fixed the net and went bird hunting but caught nothing. The children all wanted to go but we could not take them. I started with Willie but the saddle turned and Mr. Henry thought I better not take him on Clarion. I regretted very much to disappoint him. He cried a little. Gus cried a heap, his eyes are getting sore. Eddie's are some better. I had a very pleasant evening. Time always passes pleasantly with me when I am with my dear husband. Zona will start to school tomorrow I reckon. I hate to give up my little pupils. She has recited her last lesson to me for awhile. It makes me sad to think of it. I had to whip Willie today about his lesson. I dislike very much to punish my dear children but I do it for their good.

Tuesday 30th - This has been a day of trial to me. I had to make Zona go to school. She cried as if her heart would break when I whipped her. She said "I want to stay with you." It grieved me sorely to make her go. I went to Mrs. Ballew's this evening to meet the children. Zona seems a little better satisfied this evening but I fear she will cry in the morning again. If she does, I don't see how I can make her go. She is so affectionate. I have missed her a great deal today. I have attended to Eddie part of the day as Rose washed up my room. Gussie's eyes are very sore. Eddie's are some better. Two yanks stay here tonight. I wish they would stay away. We have no bread for them to eat. I hate the whole tribe of them. Mr. Henry went to town. No news. He and all the children are asleep and as 'tis nine o'clock, I must go to bed.

Wednesday 31st - Zona went to school very well this morning. I have made her a doll today and done but little else. Cut her a dress this evening, expect to sew some on tonight. She is very well pleased with her doll. It is a nice one with feet. Mr. Henry about the mill most of the time. The bucket machine is not fairly started yet. If we don't make money on something soon, I can't see how we are to get along. This war has been very hard on us.

February 1866

Thursday 1st Feb. - I finished Zona's dress this evening. She is very well pleased with school, I think will learn fast. Jane Bently is going. I have a sore finger that worries me a good deal. It has been sore about two weeks from a very small burn. I got cold in it. Willie slips off to the mill every day since Zona has been going to school. Gussie's eyes are nearly well but I still keep him in the house. He worries a good deal about it. Eddie's eyes are nearly well.

Friday Feb. 2nd - I have been sewing on a chemise for Zona today, it is pointed. Rachel Jones was here this afternoon. Came to borrow some things for Ruthes' wedding. She marries Askew Curtis next Thursday. Rach and I went over to Till's to try to get a white wreath. Till had none. Very pleasant today.

Saturday 3rd - Finished Zona's chemise and did some mending. Mr. Henry not so well, has headache from cold. Very cold today, wind from the north. Gussie's eyes about well. Eddie's are a little inflamed yet. No news of importance. Yanks still in town. They do not behave very well but I reckon we must attribute it to their ignorance.

Sunday 4th - Very cold all day. Rev. Doggett and Jess Case stay here tonight. Henry got dinner as Celia went to Mr. Step Jones' today. No one here for dinner but Mr. Henry, the children and I. Mr. Bouldin went off with Henry Jones this morning. Henry staid here last night. 'Tis getting near bed time. Mr. Henry has headache tonight. He is upstairs with the men. I must dress my sore finger and then to bed.

Monday 5th - I worked on Zona a chemise. Some warmer. Mr. Henry and Mr. Doggett went to town. Mr. Doggett stays here tonight again. Also, Mr. Jack Kurkendoll. No news of importance in town.

Tuesday 6th - Finished Zona's chemise and cut Pinck a shirt. Getting more pleasant. Doggett left for home this morning. Mr. Henry and Kurkendoll went to town. Mr. Henry got some upper leather and harness leather. Kurkendoll got a pair of upper leathers for himself.

1871 Harper's Weekly illustration of a
ferry on the French Broad, probably at Alexander's Inn
(North Carolina Collection, Pack Memorial Public Library, Asheville, NC)

ANDREW JOHNSON,

PRESIDENT OF THE UNITED STATES OF AMERICA,

TO ALL TO WHOM THESE PRESENTS SHALL COME, GREETING:

Whereas, *W. L. Henry.*

of Bancombe county, North Carolina by taking part in the late rebellion against the Government of the United States, has made himself liable to heavy pains and penalties;

And whereas, *the circumstances of his case render him a proper object of Executive clemency;*

Now, therefore, be it known, *that I,* ANDREW JOHNSON, *President of the United States of America, in consideration of the premises and other good and sufficient reasons me thereunto moving, do hereby grant to the said* W. L. Henry. *a full pardon and amnesty for all offences by him committed, arising from participation, direct or implied, in the said rebellion, conditioned as follows:*

1st. This pardon to be of no effect until the said W. L. Henry. *shall take the oath prescribed in the Proclamation of the President, dated May 29th, 1865.*

2d. To be void and of no effect if the said W. L. Henry *shall hereafter, at any time, acquire any property whatever in slaves, or make use of slave labor.*

Pardon received by William L. Henry from
President Andrew Johnson after the close of the Civil War.
(North Carolina Collection, Pack Memorial Public Library, Asheville, NC)

318

3d. That the said *W. L. Henry.* first pay all costs which may have accrued in any proceeding instituted or pending against his person or property, before the date of the acceptance of this warrant.

4th. That the said *W. L. Henry.* shall not, by virtue of this warrant, claim any property or the proceeds of any property that has been sold by the order, judgment, decree of a court under the confiscation laws of the United States.

5th. That the said *W. L. Henry.* sh notify the Secretary of State, in writing, that he has received an ___ the foregoing pardon.

In testimony whereof, I have hereunto signed my name and caused the Seal of the United States to be affixed.

Done at the City of Washington, this *First* day of *February.* A. D. 186_, and of the Independence of the United States the *Nine eth.*

Andrew Johnson

By the President:

Secretary of State.

Wednesday 7th - I went to Till's to run off some yarn. Did not get home till dinner. I want to fix some yarn to knit Capt. Bouldin a pair of gloves. I finished Pinck's shirt. Very pleasant, little misty rain. Mr. Henry went to Sandy Bottom to see Mrs. Glenn about the toll gate, she was not at home.

Thursday 8th - I have knit some on Mr. Bouldin's gloves. It is so course and rough. I will not knit it of that thread but get some other I think. My head aches a good deal this evening. A relation of Mr. Henry's stays here tonight, a McClure of Gaston Co. He is out hunting a stolen horse.

Saturday 10th - Sick all day yesterday with my head and nearly all today. It is nearly well this evening. Till spent yesterday evening with me, brought some very nice apple butter. Mr. Henry went to town yesterday. He heard some one had taken some hay of his so he went to see about it. They had taken it through a mistake. Mr. Henry in the house all morning with me, went to the mill after dinner. Daniel Ledford brought up two washing tubs he has made. He is working for Mr. Henry now.

Sunday 11th - Warm and cloudy all day, a little mist of rain this evening. Mr. Henry and I had a very pleasant walk. I enjoy a stroll with him very much. Eddie's jaws have been swollen some for two or three days. I don't know what is the matter. It has nearly gone away now. He does not fret any with it. He is a dear good baby, tries to climb up by a chair. I received a letter from Eugenia last Friday, she is still grieving about her lost children. She has three dead. I know it was a sad trial to her devoted heart. Zona spent the night with Hattie Alexander at Capt. Moore's last Tuesday and Pinck went to Mr. Norman's on Wednesday night.

Monday 12th Feb 1866 - Knit some on a glove for Mr. Bouldin. 'Tis very rough yarn. I will get Lizzie Bently to spin other yarn. Rained nearly all day, very muddy. Mr. Henry gone to Sandy Mush to get some bucket lumber, will not be at home before tomorrow.

Tuesday 13th - Spent most of the day at Till's helping her weave some bridle reins. Mr. Henry came this morning, has headache because he did not get coffee this morning at Dr. Candler's. Matt will be at home in a few days.

Wednesday 14th - Rained after dinner. Henry and Mr. Bently killed two hogs this evening. Mrs. Common stays here tonight. The weather has been very warm for several days, seems like spring.

Friday 16th - I suffered a good deal with headache yesterday but took some salts and feel very well today. Very cold yesterday but some warmer today. Mrs. Common went to town yesterday. Boston has quit work here.

Saturday 17th - Mrs. Green came here yesterday and left this evening. Some warmer today. Mary Rollins has a very sick child. Mrs. Green and I went to see it this evening, it has sore throat. I finished Mr. Bouldin's gloves this evening. He has gone to Marshall today. Mr. Henry in the house most of the day.

Sunday 18th - Rained all day. Matt and Mr. Blackwell came this evening. She is very glad to get home. Mr. Bouldin has not come.

Monday 19th - Knit some and nothing much done. Mr. Henry about the mill. No news of importance. All are well. Bouldin came this evening.

Tuesday 20th - Had the hen house cleaned and made nests. Matt and I made Dan a shirt and Eddie a pair cloth shoes. Fair and warm but very muddy. Celia is sick so Matt & I will have to cook.

Wednesday 21st - Sent Tena the clothes to wash as Celia is no better. Matt does most of the cooking. No news of importance.

Saturday 24th - I have had a very severe attack of headache for three days. Have done nothing. Mr. Henry stays with me a good deal when I am sick. He is very fond of his family. No news. The weather very pleasant.

Sunday 25th Feb 1866 - Mr. Henry and I spent the day at Capt. Moore's. Willie was with us, he got tired of the long walk. Capt. Moore seems on decline a good deal. Old age I think.

Monday 26th - Cut Gussie two shirts of under bases. Times are very hard with us and nothing to buy with. I hope for a better day soon. Mr. Henry went to town. No news.

Tuesday 27th - Finished one shirt and began the other. Mr. Henry has heard from his grey mare. A negro stole her and has her now in So. Ca. He speaks of going soon to look for it.

Wednesday 28th - Finished the shirt. Mr. Henry at home about the mill. No news. Celia still sick. Still having fine weather.

March 1866

Thursday March 1st - Calm and quiet today. Mr. Henry will start in a day or two to S. C. Mr. Hood's school was out yesterday, he begins again first of April. I will be glad when Bouldin's time expires.

Friday 2nd - Celia is getting well, got dinner today. Fannie washed for us yesterday. This has been a beautiful day. Mr. Henry started to So. Ca. this morning. I do hope he may get his mare. We do have a bad time of it, it really seems we were born under an unlucky star. May our Heavenly Father watch over and take care of my dear husband in his wandering.

Saturday 3rd - I have been putting out some shrubry in the yard today and went to the grave yard after dinner and cleaned off my little baby's grave and set out some things. Bouldin went with us, Matt did not go. Her and Bouldin are taking on at a desperate rate. They enjoy it, I guess in their way. I am sure I could not enjoy such familiarity. Warm and pleasant. Had the garden plowed up yesterday.

Monday 5th - I was quite sick yesterday with headache but feel entirely relieved today. I cleaned all the children as I was too unwell yesterday. I will do some little things this evening. High winds and cool.

Tuesday 6th - Jim Nicholds or some one, changed cows with us last Saturday night. Took one we got from Nicholds and brought the one back we had swapped to him. 'Tis a very mean trick. He is a galvanized yank[54] so we can't expect anything better of such people. I have been mending some.

Wednesday 7th March 1866 - Warm and fair. Done some gardening today. All are well. No news from Mr. Henry. Tena here this week making soap.

[54] Term used for Confederate soldiers who swore allegiance to the Union

Thursday 8th - Celia ironed as I hired Maria to wash for a peck of corn. Matt and Bouldin still taking on.

Friday 9th - Mail brought no news. Very pleasant. Did some gardening today.

Saturday 10th - Spent the evening at Miss Tilda's. Received a letter from Mr. Henry, he was at Anderson S. C. last Wednesday, has heard of his mare. I do hope he may get her. I had a letter from Sister Jane and Matt. Matt is still with Sister Jane, they are very well pleased with Spartanburg.

Sunday 11th - This is Willie's birthday, he is five years old. Gus was three last Thursday. Things have changed greatly with us in the last five years. My head has pained me a good deal today but better this evening. Fair and pleasant.

Monday 12th - Till was confined last night. She went to preaching at Sardis yesterday. It only lived a short time, a premature birth. She is doing very well. My head is nearly easy this evening. The children went over to see the little dead babe at Till's, they think it very small. About seven months babe.

Tuesday 13th - I went over to Till's a while this morning, she is getting on finely. Sewed some on Bouldin a shirt. No news from Mr. Henry. I do hope he may get his mare.

Wednesday 14th - Celia washed, Rose got dinner. I finished Bouldin's shirt and cut Zona some pantletts. Spent the evening at Till's. Very pleasant. Bouldin went to town, but I got no letter.

Thursday 15th - Cloudy and warm. Finished Zona's pantletts since dinner. I want to write to Eugenia Hopson this evening. I began a pair of cotton socks for Mr. Henry this evening. I hired the waggon and oxen to a man to haul potatoes at three dollars a day, only for today.

Friday 16th - Made Zona a pair frilled pantletts. Head ached a good deal before supper but some better now. Rev. Dogget stays here tonight, he brought us some very nice cabbage. Late I think for them. Rather cool this evening.

Saturday 17th - High NW wind all day, very cool and disagreeable. My head well this morning. I have knit most of the day. Bouldin in the dumps. Matt can do anything with him, he is nearly crazy about her, is perfectly infatuated.

Sunday 18th March 1866 - Very cool this morning, ice in the dining room and upstairs. Pleasant now (three o'clock). Matt, Zona, Gussie and I spent the morning at Miss Till's, she is getting on finely. My head does not feel very well, I hope it may wear off. No news from Mr. Henry. I do wish I could hear from him. I hope he will soon return. May a kind Providence watch over and protect him is the prayer of his devoted wife.

Monday 19th - I knit some today. Very pleasant. No news from Mr. Henry. All are well.

Tuesday 20th - I had scouring done, nearly all the house. Matt and Zona spent the day at Mr. Steph Jones' yesterday, got some crissanthums. She took them to the graveyard this morning and planted them and some other things. I had headache yesterday. Matt is very kind to me when I am sick.

Thursday 22nd - Mr. Henry came home yesterday, got his mare. Cousin James Robert Love came with him, on his way to Asheville. I had headache all day yesterday. Mr. Henry came by William Tidwell. They are all well. He brought me a beautiful willow basket. He thinks of me when he is away. I have finished my flannel skirt and began one for Zona. Spent the evening at Till's, she is getting on finely.

Friday 23rd - Finished Zona's skirt. Rained all day. Mr. Wm. Miller of Henderson staid here last night, he left this morning in the rain. Mr. Henry and Cousin Love went to Asheville yesterday, he will not leave for home till morning.

Saturday 24th - Matt spent the day at Till's. I made an apron for Rose and finished off Dan's apron. Warm and pleasant.

Sunday 25th - High wind from the north. Matt and I went to Tena's before dinner. Henry Jones staid here last night. No news of importance.

Monday 26th - Cold and windy. Cut Pinck a shirt and sewed some on it. Worked some in the yard. The things are growing finely. Matt and Bouldin have had a split up.

Tuesday 27th - Sewed some on a shirt for Henry. Matt is making one for Edd. Charlie is at work here, he got in a scrape stealing corn of Steph Jones. Mr. Henry took him out of jail. He and Kate are working at eight dollars a month. My headaches some this evening.

Wednesday 28th - Thursday 29th March 1866 - I have suffered a great deal from headache yesterday and today. It is some better this evening. Mr. Henry and I found some turkey nests this evening. Very cool, high wind and spitting snow. Celia washing today.

Friday 30th - Cold and calm. I have made a blanket & will do some gardening this evening. I have made a solemn promise to Mr. Henry this day, to quit snuff or tobacco in any way and I intend to keep it. I know it is injuring me and by God's aid I will keep my pledge.

April 1866

Sunday April 15th - Some time has passed since I last wrote. I have broken my pledge. It seems I can't quit my bad habit though I think it is injuring my health. I will try to use it more moderately. Mr. Henry is so anxious about my health. I hate very much to grieve him but that is a habit that has grown on me so 'tis nearly a part of my self.

Nothing of interest has transpired in the last two weeks. We have had beautiful weather. Apple trees are nearly in full bloom, peach trees have shed nearly all their bloom. Some peaches are killed by the frost of last week but still plenty left so far. Joe Russell and Bently took the cattle to Fines Creek about a week ago, he took the goats last fall. I hope they may do well. Mr. Henry speaks of sending the sheep as soon as they are sheared. I had a very severe attack of headache last week, last three days. Kate does the milking now. We get more milk than when Mrs. Bently milked. Willie found my knife last week, I lost it last summer. It was very rusty but Mr. Henry soon got it open, it does very well now. Willie was so proud when he brought it in. I am teaching him at home. Pinck and Zona are going to Mr. Hood. Mrs. Boyd and husband spent the morning here. Mary Curtis and Jim Presly married today at Mr. A. B. Jones'. A runaway match. She certainly has made a bad selection.

Monday 16th - Knit some today. My head aches some today. Mail brought no news this evening. The children are learning very fast, they like to go. I am glad to see them trying to excell. Pinck is a noble, generous boy, has such a good disposition. Zona is a little pettish and cross. May God bless us in our children.

Tuesday 17th April 1866 - I have had headache all day. Knit some and took a nap in the arm chair after dinner. Mr. Henry laying off some hill side ditches in the land Negro Jim is to tend. Jim and Sam are our best renters it seems.

Wednesday 18th - I cut Rose a dress and Edd a shirt. I made the dress and Matt is making the shirt. Mr. Henry got me some snuff last Saturday. He said he had nearly as soon give me poison. I wish I could quit it on his account. I will take it very moderately. Willie went to school today for the first time. He is very well pleased, says he is going every day.

Thursday 19th - It has rained every day this week, the ground is very wet. I want to do some gardening as soon as it dries a little. Willie gone to school again. I have sewed some on a shirt for Bouldin today. Mr. Henry got the shirting in town.

Friday 20th - Still raining. Zona staid with Mollie Hood last night. She says she cried. I am sorry if she gave them trouble. Finished Bouldin's shirt and cut Eddie some dresses of some of my old ones, did not sew any on them today. Willie did not go to school as it was raining some. Pinck and Bouldin went.

Saturday 21st - I made Eddie a dress before dinner & did some mending in the after noon. Mr. Henry sent and got Matt and I some snuff today, also six lbs. of coffee. Pinck and Zona attended to Eddie this morning while Rose did her washing. They dislike to nurse very much. They planted some sugar cane seed this evening but it rained so they had to quit. The hands then fixed the chaff house for a hen house. There are so many lice in the hen house down here, the hens won't sit to do any good. I have greased the sitting hens this week.

Sunday 22nd - Eddie is one year old this morning at half past five o'clock. Oh! it was troublesome times then. I hope I may never have to go through such again. A kind Providence has been merciful to us and spared our lives for which we are very thankful. Till and Tom spent the day here, also Mary Rollins this evening. Fair and cool today.

Monday 23rd – Cool, fires feel comfortable. I cut Eddie three aprons out of a duster Zona gave me the last time I was at home. Matt made one & I one. Mr. Henry about the farm all day planting sugar cane today.

Tuesday 24th - I made an apron and nearly a dress for Eddie. Bouldin and Morris had a fuss today at school. Arch is a great story teller. I think they are both to blame. Willie still going to school. The hands have all quit work at the mill except Wiley Knight. John Rollins is carrying around the stallion.

Wednesday 25th - Sewed some on Bouldin's shirt, Matt is helping me. Bouldin at school. He and Arch have not killed one another yet. I don't think either very dangerous. Willie's feet are sore from wearing his shoes so he is not at school today. Gussie misses him a great deal as he has no one to play with, he stays a great deal in the house. It was very windy yesterday.

Thursday 26th - Last night one year ago, the yanks came here hunting Mr. Henry. He and I spoke of it last night. That was indeed a night of trouble to me. I pray I may never pass such another night. I have done several things today. Worked some in the yard, hackeled some flax and spent the evening at Mrs. Ballew's partly and partly at Till's. She (Till) came home with us to get some turkey eggs. The hands gardening today. Mr. Henry went to Sand Hill and I went with him to Pinck's. We came back by Till's. Bouldin has gone up to Miller's after his pistol, I reckon he will kill Arch. It is a great pitty too, such a brave man should not get to fight at all. Tom Miller was killed a short time back in Pickens Dist. So. Ca., he was on the scout. He killed a man year or two ago. Justice overtook him at last. 'Tis supposed he was murdered for his money and horse. He was a great drunkard.

Friday 27th - My head has ached some but I took some pills before breakfast and 'tis nearly easy this evening. I have knit some today. Matt finished Bouldin's shirt this evening. Very warm. The ground is getting very hard.

Saturday 28th - I have done several things today. Washed all the children this evening. I had a letter from Eugenia yesterday. She wants to come up to board this summer. I dislike to take boarders. She will not seem so as she is very pleasant and unassuming. I would like to have her.

Sunday 29th - Mr. Henry and I went up to salt the sheep, had a very pleasant walk. Came back by Tena's. Betsey Jamison staid here last night. Her and Matt have gone now to Mary Knight's. Love Muse and Albert Knight were married last Thursday night. Rather cool and looks like rain. Old Boyd is here this evening.

Monday 30th April 1866 - I have done several things. Worked some in the garden. No news of importance. Matt made Edd a pair pants. Willie has got tired of going to school. I will learn him at home. Mr. Henry in the farm all day.

May 1866

Tuesday May 8th - Nothing of importance has transpired in the last week. I feel very unwell this morning from headache and I scoured some yesterday and worked some in the yard. My spine is very sore this morning. I am troubled a great deal with pain in the back. I would give anything if I was stout and robust as Matt. Gussie is not well this morning. Eddie was quite sick last week from sore throat I think. Mr. Henry went to town yesterday. No news of importance. We are having beautiful weather, the trees beginning to put on their summer dress. We still have plenty of fruit, if no more frost cuts it off. Kate and Charlie moved to Fannie's old house yesterday. Bently began to sheer the sheep yesterday. Old Maria shearing today. High winds this morning. I will do nothing but knit unless my head gets better.

Friday 11th - I have had a very severe attack of headache, one of the worst spells I ever had. Threw up some blood. I fear I will have hemorrhage of the lungs some day but hope not. I would hate to leave my dear husband and little children, never to return again. I pray for health and wisdom to rear up my children. I have sewed some today, finished Zona's dress and sewed some on Willie's coat. Matt is making Zona an apron.

Saturday 12th - Finished Willie's coat and did some other little jobs. Kate ironed the children's clothes this evening as it has rained too much to have all the clothes washed. Charlie is working better this year than he ever has. Freedom has helped him. Maria is shearing sheep this week.

Sunday 13th - Till and Mag Morris spent the day here. Very bright and pleasant all day. We have been at home enjoying ourselves. The children went to see Mama this morning.

Monday 14th - Rather cool and fair. I made Gus a coat and picked some wool. Matt making Zona an apron. Celia is going to leave for Kentucky in a week or so. I expect to take Kate to cook then. Mr. Henry about the farm all day. No news of importance going on.

Tuesday 15th - Cut Mr. Bolin a pair pants, sewed some on them. He is going to get Mrs. Jones to cut his coat. Mr. Henry made Willie go to school this morning. He had to whip him a little. He does not like to go at all, says the rocks hurt his feet and makes several excuses for not wanting to go. The hands planting potatoes today. Matt and I cut part of the potatoes. I then cleaned out the smoke house. Rather cool today.

Wednesday 16th - Zona came from school yesterday evening with headache and had a high fever last night. She is at home today. Willie went to school very well this morning. Pinck went home with Walter Moore last night. I finished Bouldin's pants and began his coat. Matt is helping me.

Thursday 17th - I received a letter from Matt. They are all well. It came by hand. We finished the coat before dinner and then picked some wool, just got done. Rained nearly all day. I fear the children will get wet this evening. Zona went today, she looks pale. Gussie is playing about me now. Mr. Henry is sitting here playing with him. Eddie's bowels are still loose.

Friday 18th - No news of importance. Knit some, the children gone to school. Willie does not like to go at all. He will not learn fast I fear.

Saturday 19th - My head aches a good deal this evening. I picked some wool. Celia will start tomorrow for Kty. I think Rose intends going with her. I don't care if she does, she worries me no little.

Tuesday 22nd - I have had a very bad spell with my head, it is nearly well now. Celia and Rose started Sunday. I attend to Eddie myself, his bowels are loose but he is very little trouble. Willie stays at home today as he is not trying to learn. He can notice Eddie some. Kate does the milking and cooking and washing. Mr. Henry went to town today. I went to Aunt Tena's this evening and borrowed some coffee. We have picked wool today.

Wednesday & Thursday 23rd & 24th - Nothing of interest to write. Eddie getting better. Mr. Henry not so well today, kept the children from school to attend to Eddie so I could wait on him. Kate washed today. Matt got dinner. Mr. Henry some better this evening.

Friday 25th May 1866 - Mr. Henry some better, can sit up a little. Picked wool. The children gone to school except Willie. Mr. Henry had a letter from Eugenia this morning, she wants to come up this summer. No news. Warm and pleasant.

Saturday 26th - I have done several things today and am real tired tonight. Rained some last night and till near ten o'clock. Then clear till evening and a shower. Cleaned the children since dinner. Eddie is nearly well. Wonder how Rose and Celia are getting on.

Sunday 27th - Mr. Henry got so he can go out a little. He got me a handfull of strawberries this morning. Zona and Willie went to get some sulphur water, they got a few. Clear and bright this morning but now cloudy and looks very much like rain. (First strawberries of the season.)

Monday 28th - Mr. Henry thinks we had some frost last week. We had some very cool mornings for the season. No news of importance. Some yanks in town attending their coloured brethren's wants. I hope they may get their fill of them. Mr. Henry is getting better.

Tuesday 29th - I cut Pinck a pair pants today and sewed some. Mr. Henry thinks we had some frost this morning, cool all day. Had a fire. The wind whistles like winter. Received a letter from Sister Matt, they are all well. It came by hand. The children all go to school. Willie likes it very well for a few days at a time. He and Pinck staid with Millard Jones last night.

Wednesday 30th - Finished Pinck's pants. Still cool. Mr. Henry still improving. Eddie can't walk yet but crawls everywhere. He does not fret to go out any now. He is a sweet babe. Gussie plays with him.

Thursday 31st - I had headache all morning, took some salts and that relieved me. I have knit some and read some. Matt kept Eddie most of the evening. I would like to get a nurse if I could. Pinck hates to nurse so. He is a noble boy.

June 1866

Friday June 1st - I took Gussie and Eddie and spent the day with Till. Had peas for dinner, the first I have seen. Jane Bently went with me to help carry Eddie. Till came back to the top of the hill with me. Two men stay here tonight from Clay Co. William Tidwell's family are well. Organized a militia co. today up on Hominy, the first since the war closed. Mr. Henry did not go. He has got a great deal better.

Saturday 2nd June 1866 - I made Zona a bonnet of straw, I had it wove last summer. It looks very neat. The children want to go to Sunday School tomorrow. Pinck attended to Eddie. Rained most of the day. Jack Kurkendall stay here at night. Set out some cabbage and tobacco plants this evening. Mr. Henry in the house most of the day.

Sunday 3rd - This has been a beautiful day. Henry and the other negroes picked some strawberries. I will have them a pie for their supper and we will take cream with ours. Mr. Henry off tending the cattle by Wiley Knight's. Pinck has Eddie at play. He is a good boy. I will ever remember his kindness to me. Pinck, Zona and Willie went to Sunday School but did not go in the house. Preaching at the Academy Rev. Baldwin, none of us went except Boldin and Kirkendoll from here. Mont Stradly came back with them and took dinner but has gone now.

Monday 4th - Old Jennie, Tena's sister came today to work some for me, she is picking wool. I cut Pinck a coat of Mr. Henry's old cloth overcoat. Sewed some on it. Eddie hinders me a good deal about my work, he is a very good babe. Gus plays with him and tries to amuse him.

Tuesday 5th - Finished the coat today. Old Jennie picking wool. Matt in the blues. All are well. Rather cool of mornings. Our garden looks fine but we will

327

have but few chickens this summer to fry. I took off nine. For the first we have about a dozen young turkeys.

Wednesday 6th - Began a cap for Pinck of black cloth. I don't get to work more than half my time for Eddie. Mr. Henry about the farm, he has got nearly well.

Thursday 7th - Finished the cap, Pinck is delighted with it and his marbles Mr. Henry got for him today at town. Cousin Sam Gudger and Col. Moore took dinner here today. Mr. Henry came home to dinner. No news in town.

Friday 8th - I have done little jobs all day. Mr. Henry and the children went strawberry hunting, Zona brought me a few. Pinck staid to attend to Eddie. I wish I could get a nurse as Pinck dislikes nursing so much and Zona is too small. The children came home about 2 o'clock as the school had a fishing party after dinner.

Saturday 9th June 1866 - This has been a very warm day for the first one this summer. We had a refreshing shower about 1 o'clock. I suffer with headache as I was ironing. Kate has gone to help them in the corn a few days. Old Jennie got dinner. I did some mending this evening. Mr. Henry washed the children for me, they still have the itch. It is a troublesome thing and hard to get rid of. I fear the children will have it as long as they go to school.

Sunday 10th - Very warm. We had our first potatoes today. Jim Henry took dinner here. Till & Tom spent the evening with us. Pinck and Willie went to Sunday School at the Academy. Zona staid with me. Mr. Boling left this morning. He had a letter from Tenn. telling him to get away. I think he hated to leave.

Monday 11th - I have changed an old dress of Zona's for Eddie. No one here but Gus, Eddie and I. Matt up at Mary Rollins putting in her cloth. She wants to get it out by Thursday. Very warm today. Eddie has been fretful today. Mr. Henry gone to town as 'tis court week.

Tuesday 12th - Aunt Jennie's grand child Harriet came to nurse for me today. She is to stay for her clothes and feed till fall. Matt cut her cloth out as it did not suit her some way. Mr. Henry at town today.

Wednesday 13th - Eddie likes Harriet very well. She is not very sprightly. I cut Pinck a pair pants and Willie a coat. Sewed of the pants. Willie likes to go to school now. We had a very hard rain today, some thunder and lightning. Kate working in the field. No news of importance.

Thursday 14th - Finished the coat for Willie. Matt is going to try Mrs. Bently to weave her cloth. She is in the blues still. Rain again today.

Friday 15th - I have done several things today. Harriet is not very attentive to Eddie, he is a good babe. Children came home early from school. Gus is very quiet every day, no one to make noise with.

Saturday 16th - I am very tired tonight as we have scalded and scoured the house. Pinck and Harriet carried most of the water. Pinck is a dear good boy, does not murmer at doing anything for Mother. I pray for health and understanding to govern my children right.

Sunday 17th June 1866 - Dr. Candler staid here last night. Matt speaks of going down there soon. I don't think she will go. Old Boyd and wife took dinner here, they left soon after. Mr. Henry and I spent the evening with Pinck Ballew. We took Eddie and Harriet. Eddie was delighted with little Hester, wanted to kiss her all the time. Mr. Henry and I stopped to fix a crossing place for the children. I sent Harriet on. I came on soon after but Harriet and Eddie were missing. I started back to hunt them knowing she did not know the road. I ran up on the hill by Miss Tilda's and called. Till came with Eddie, I was very glad to see them. I was really distressed about him. We had gone that way in going to Pinck's. We had some rain this morning.

Monday 18th - I have done several things today. A gentleman came here to get board for himself and two ladies. I told him we could not take them. He is going to try Mr. Henry. Matt is making a calico dress. Mr. Henry got her last week. She is getting over the blues.

Tuesday 19th - The man back again to get board. He did not see Mr. Henry yesterday. The ladies came over with him to the spring. They did not come down here. I have done several things today.

Wednesday 20th - The boarders are to come today. I am sorry for it. Mr. Henry took them in at 75$ a month for the three. I hope they will not be troublesome. We cleaned upstairs for them. I went to Till's this morning to take some indigo wool & thread to dye for Mr. Henry a suit of clothes.

Thursday 21st - Mr. Marshall, Miss Hall & Miss Marshall are our boarders. They seem to be very nice ladies, very social. I have done some little jobs today and very little of anything.

Friday 22nd - Court still in session. Mr. Henry has been every day last week except Saturday & every day this week. I have done some little things. Harriet cleans upstairs. Rained some this morning.

Saturday 23rd - Kate washed for the boarders today. I helped a little. Betsy stays here tonight. I bathed the children in the branch. Zona and Willie cried but Gussie laughed. They still have itch.

Sunday 24th - Mr. Henry, the boarders and Zona went to church at Sand Hill Academy. Very warm this evening. Betsy still here. Harriet went to see her Mother yesterday so I attend Eddie. Mr. Henry has headache, is lying down since dinner. I must stop as I have to churn Sunday as it is.

July 1866

Sunday 15th July 1866 - Three weeks have past since I wrote in my dear old journal. I have been so busy I have not had time to write. Aunt Jennie got so insolent I dismissed her a week ago. She took Harriet with her so I have had my hands full. Eugenia has come up to spend the summer. She staid near two weeks here, has gone to Col. Cathey's now. Sallie Cathey came for her last Monday. Dub has been cooking some for us but he left when Jennie did. We have had some very warm weather & still so.

The boarders seem well pleased. Mr. Marshall is not here now, has gone to Columbia, been gone near two weeks. They, our boarders, are very pleasant young ladies. Eugenia is in bad health. I think she will have consumption if it has not already set in.

Eddie can walk and tries to talk. He is a very affectionate child, so fond of me, wants to kiss very often especially if I scold him. Gussie attends to him when I am out. I need a nurse badly, wish I could employ one. A Mrs. McAfee is here today, trying to get some weaving & work generally to do. Mr. Henry had some hands at Woodfin's farm last week cutting grass to get the seed. He staid one night. They were three days cutting, will go again this week. Our June apples are ripening. I must stop and eat some. Miss Hall, Miss Marshall, Zona & Willie gone to church at Sulpher Springs Academy, soon time for them to return.

Sunday 22nd July 1866 - I have been so busy this week I have not had time to write. I am worn out with drudgery and it seems it will not be any better for some time. Robert Tidwell came here last week. He and Matt went to see their Mother last Wednesday. I kept Zona at home to attend to Eddie. They came back yesterday. I have made Gussie a yellow body & Eddie a dress of the same and done a great many other things. I must go and get supper tonight as Matt is gone to Till's. I don't know whether she will be home tonight. My head pains me a good deal this evening. Kate is so contrary, I think I will have to turn her off. Very dry, needing rain badly. Our beans and cucumbers doing no good. Lord send us rain.

Monday 23rd - Sewed some on Pinck a shirt. Very warm. It is nine o'clock nearly every morning before I get to house cleaned and things done up generally and then I have the beans to string. I cut some pants for Tena's family this morning.

Tuesday 24th - Some rain this morning. We are needing it badly. Finished Pinck's shirt and cut some more pants for Tena's family. The children at home today, they are a heap of help to me.

Wednesday 25th - Mr. Henry, Misses Hall & Marshall gone to Woodfin's Mountain for a view. We scoured the house, the children helped. Miss Addie Banner's (one of my Salem teachers) husband stays here tonight, Mr. Everhart. He is to leave tomorrow.

Thursday 26th - Spent the day in ironing and some mending. Mr. Henry and others came this evening. Some rain tonight, we have not had a good season yet.

Friday 27th - Mending all day & fixing a dress of mine for Kate. Zona at home tending Eddie.

Saturday 28th - Read most of the evening. My head aches and I feel badly. Mr. Marshall came yesterday evening. Cousin Robert Love & Mr. Edwards staid here last night so we were crowded. Bob Tidwell is still here. I wish he was somewhere else.

Sunday 29th - We went to church at Sand Hill. A house full of people. Took all the children but Eddie. Matt kept him. A little rain this evening. So cool and pleasant. Mr. Henry is hurrying me to bed so no more tonight.

Monday 30th - I have sewed some on Willie a shirt. I get such little time to sew. Zona attends Eddie, she is very kind to him. Pinck and Willie go to school and Gus spends most of his time with Henry and Charlie with the waggon.

Tuesday 31st - Finished Willie's shirt today. No news of note. Bob Tidwell got drunk and fighting generally so he is now in jail. He could do well if he would but 'tis hard for him to do right.

August - September 1866

I have neglected you, old journal, for a long time but I have felt so badly part of the time and been so busy, I have not had time to write. I was very busy getting the children ready for the examination. Zona looked very sweet in her swiss. I got them all shoes and hats before the examination. It came off on the 21st inst. and the day after, we started to Pisgah. Camped between the two Pisgahs (big & little). We enjoyed it finely. Eat a heap of huckelberries that evening. Slept but little that night as some of the party were up all night. We had a very comfortable tent. Got up long before day and had breakfast, then started to the top of big Pisgah as soon as could see to walk. We had about 20 in the party. We wanted to see the sun rise but it was so misty, but we had a grand view, staid up there some two hours and took lunch when we came down about 9 o'clock. Eddie did finely. Mr. Henry carried him up the mountain. I know he was very tired but never complained. We took Charlie and Kate along. We came down the mountain after dinner and camped a mile or two this side of Little Pisgah. We all slept that night, we all walked down the mountain. Mr. Henry rode and carried Eddie. I enjoyed the trip down the mountain finely, laughing at Kate and the Jennet. I rode it up, it went on finely. I was very sore when I got home, my legs and hips. We found a man and his wife here to get board when we got back. We took them in. They are very pleasant, no trouble at all. Mr. McGrill & lady. He is old man and she a young lady. They occupy Mr. Marshall's room as he left the 30th of July on business to Columbia. I don't know when he will return. Miss Marshall & Miss Hall want to go to Black Mountain this week. Mr. Henry and McParker started for his cattle and goats at Joe Russell's this morning. Will be gone several days. I hope he may get all of them. Corn crops will be short this year on account of the dry weather. We had a good season last week, the first in six weeks. I think I have let Eddie suck the last time as I have no milk and it is not good for him now. He loves it so good. I do feel so sorry to have to deprive him of it.

Sept. 3rd Monday - Mr. Henry left yesterday for Spring Creek to see after his cattle, will be gone several days. I cut up my old flounce gingham dress and made an apron of it for my self. Cut two others of it. Pinck is going to school to Ellen Hawkins at the Academy. I will start Willie soon. I don't know whether I will send Zona or not as she is such a help with Eddie.

Tuesday 4th - Made an apron. All the boarders and Matt went to town except Mr. McGrill. We had a very heavy rain and high wind this evening.

Wednesday 5th - Made an apron and did some other little jobs. McParker came home this evening, says Mr. Henry will be at home in a day or so. I miss him sadly when he is gone. "The days are sad without him."

Thursday 6th - Began Mr. Henry a shirt. It tires me to sew steady. I will try to finish it tomorrow. We have very nice peaches, the trees back of the garden are breaking down. We have a nice chance out drying, it has been a bad week on fruit, so showery.

Friday 7th - Finished Mr. Henry's shirt before night. I went to meet him but was sadly disappointed. He came while we were at supper. We were so glad to have him home again. The boarders play every night, seem to enjoy it finely. I don't feel like romping now so I read and knit in my room.

Saturday 8th - I have knit some, getting the children's winter socks ready. Mr. Henry went to town and after dinner started back to Spring Creek on business, rather unexpected. He will be out most of the night. I wish I could go with him, home is not home with out him.

Sunday 9th - Miss Marshall, Hall and Pinck gone to church in Asheville, the others out walking. I must soon stop as my head feels badly. I have headache a great deal. I am not as stout as usual at such times. I hope 'tis all for the best.

Monday 10th - Rained all day. Mr. McGrill & lady left this evening. I made some hankerchifs and cut some pants after dinner. Mr. Henry has not come yet. Mr. Sol Blackwell stays here tonight. No news of importance. We had rain yesterday evening. Miss Hall and Miss Marshall staid at Mr. Reynolds' & Pinck at Dr. Hilliard's. They came home this morning.

Tuesday 11th Sept. 1866 - I made Henry a pair pants. Matt is helping Miss Hall. Mr. Henry got home about 3 o'clock, got a horse and waggon on the debt of security for Russell. We were glad to see him.

Wednesday 12th - Mr. Henry went to town as 'tis court week. Mr. Marshall came this morning, a brother of the one that was here. Newt Taylor came this evening on business I think. I wish we were clear of our debts. I made Pinck a pair pants. Kate & Mary washing. I have to hire washing every week. Kate is so lazy.

Thursday 13th - Made Gussie a pair pants and sewed some on Willie's. Mr. Henry went to town. No news. Very warm. We have some very nice peaches. Pinck and Willie go to school, they like it very much. Bently is drying fruit, the peaches are rotting badly, those that are cut.

Friday 14th - Mr. Henry and Mr. Marshall went to town, came back to dinner. I finished Willie's pants. The Marshall Co. will leave next week. They want their clothes this week. Miss Marshall is hard to please in her clothes.

Saturday 15th - I have headache all day. I took a nap since dinner, 'tis better now. I have knit and read most of the day. Mr. Henry and Marshall went to town and back to dinner, they leave on Tuesday next.

Sunday 16th - Rain all day. Camp meeting going on. Mr. Henry and Pinck went, he has come home, Pinck is still there. No one has tented, it is only a quarterly meeting. I sent Charlie after Mr. Henry but he missed him and has gone on to the camp grounds. The children are playing about generally. I will stop and eat some peaches.

Monday 17th - Very pleasant and warm. I have done several things today, nothing of note. The boarders leave for Black Mountain tomorrow, will be gone several days. We had a beef killed Saturday evening, it was very fat. I made some candles this evening.

Tuesday 18th - The boarders left this morning. I cleaned upstairs, it was very dirty under the beds. Matt don't sweep nicely. I have knit some.

Wednesday 19th - Scoured upstairs & down, only my room that was scoured yesterday evening. I am real tired this evening. Mr. Henry very busy trying to get a hack done for Glance as they have come after it and are waiting for it.

Thursday 20th - I have been fixing up the house. My head ached very badly this evening. I took a nap and it helped it. They got off with the hack this evening.

Friday 21st - Cool this evening. The boarders came. Some rain today. I have made a saque for my self of linsey faced with black.

Saturday 22nd - I made Eddie a sacque, trimmed it round with blue, 'tis very neat. Still cool but no frost yet. I think I have done odds and ends since dinner.

Sunday 23rd - At home all day. Mr. Henry went to preaching at Locust Knob, did not return till after supper. The boarders went to the Episcopal church in Asheville. Still cool and fair.

Monday 24th - The boarders have gone to Cedar Mountain &c. Will be back in a week. I will miss them when they leave. Miss Marshall gave me a nice dress pattern this morning and Pinck a knife, Willie a french harp, Gus a ball & Zona and Eddie a dress each. She is very generous indeed. Mr. Henry has started to Spring Creek for his cattle since dinner. Went to town before dinner and got me some bleached domestic, a pair of shoes, some sugar and coffee. I must stop as I want to go to Till's. Spent the evening very pleasantly with Till, they move to Georgia soon.

Tuesday 25th - Matt and I made Mr. Henry a pair pants. Kate washing. Nothing of importance going on. Some of the neighbors making molasses. Rather cool but no frost yet. Should we have frost it would ruin a heap of corn.

Wednesday 26th - Made Gus & Willie pants, Matt helped me. The children are not going to school this week or last as Miss Ellen has given two weeks to fodder. They are full of life, the noise worries me at times.

Thursday 27th - Mended some and then we sewed on Pinck's coat. Eddie frets a heap, I think he has worms. He looks badly but has a good appetite.

Friday 28th - Matt went with Till & spent the day at Mr. Rich's with Press who has a son. I finished Pinck's coat and sewed some on Willie's. The children go gathering chenquipins every day, there are a great many. I string them. they are very proud of their beads as they call them.

Saturday 29th September 1866 - Finished Willie's coat and did some mending. Fair and pleasant. I expect Mr. Henry this evening, hope I may not be disappointed. I have washed the children at night.

Sunday 30th - Cloudy. Mr. Henry did not come last night. I expect him today. I think the boarders will be back this evening. The children all gone to get chinquapins. Matt is attending Eddie.

October 1866

Monday Oct. 1st - I had a letter from Mr. Henry by McParker saying he would not be at home before the middle or last of the week. Mc. came yesterday and brought some of the cattle. Joe Russell has sold some four of them. He was a thief, surely, after all Mr. Henry's kindness to him. So goes the world. Gratitude is seldom found in any class. The boarders came late this evening, they are delighted with the scenery. I think Mr. & Miss Marshall are taking on slightly. I have been fixing an underskirt today, did not finish it.

Tuesday 2nd - The boarders leave tomorrow for Warm Springs. I finished my skirt today. Nothing new going on.

Wednesday 3rd - They left about 10 o'clock. I never expect to see them again though Miss Marshall spoke of coming back next summer. I cut Zona and Willie a pair drawers and sewed some on Willie's. The children are going to school this week, Pinck & Willie. Zona thinks she can't leave her mother. I hope she may always be as affectionate as now.

Thursday 4th - I spent half the day with Till, finished Willie's drawers. She is not so well, threatened with miscarriage again. Mr. Henry came home today after dinner, brought us some chestnuts. We were glad to have him home again.

Friday 5th - Made some tape trimming for Zona a pair pantletts. Matt wants to go and see her Mother soon. She sleeps upstairs with Pinck & Willie. Zona and Gus in my room on the trundle bed. They have a time who will sleep with Mother when Mr. Henry is gone so they take it by turn.

Saturday 6th - There was an agricultural meeting here today, some half dozen men, mostly from Asheville. Kate washed up my room this morning. I finished Zona's drawers today. Was down to see Mrs. Mary Knight this morning who was confined last Wednesday with a daughter and not doing so well. Rather cool but no frost yet to injure anything.

Sunday 7th October 1866 - Mr. Henry went to church at Locust Knob and came home to dinner. Bright and fair today. He and I took a walk to the brick yard. Dr. Candler was here when we came back, he stays here tonight.

Monday 8th - I cut Zona two chemise, worked some on one. The bleached is very hard to sew, so stiff. I am embroidrying one with turkey red, the other will have tape trimming. Mr. Henry went to town, brought a bundle Miss Marshall had left for us. She sent Zona two little vases, very pretty & some other things.

Tuesday 9th - Still at work on Zona's chemise. No news of importance. No frost yet, but cool.

Wednesday 10th - Finished one of Zona's chemise and began the trimming for the other. Matt went home with Dr. Candler this evening to spend a week or so, she does not like to stay down there at all. I don't know why. Mr. Henry went to town came home to dinner.

Thursday 11th - Sewed some on Zona's chemise. Zona attended Eddie. She is a nice little girl. Willie does not like school much. I am affraid I will not raise him, he is rather delicate. I fear his lungs are diseased.

Friday 12th - Finished Zona's chemise and began to fix a dress of mine. Mr. Henry at Clayton's foundry in the morning and at Mr. A. B. Jones' after dinner. Some rain this evening. Tom Morris moves to Ga. in a week or two. Till will not go before spring. Old Mrs. Holloway goes to keep house for him.

Saturday 13th - Mr. Henry went to town, got Eddie a pair shoes. He is very proud of them. I finished my dress this evening & done several other things. I have the churning done in the house & get more butter. I think I take it up myself.

Sunday 14th - Cool but no frost. Mr. Henry gone to preaching in Asheville as Conference is in session, began last Wednesday. The children went to Sand Hill to preaching. Mr. Hood preached his farewell sermon. He goes to Clay Co. Eddie has kept me company. I took him down to Mrs. Knight's to see the baby, he was delighted with it. I expect Betsey Jamison up soon so I must stop. The children have come from church.

Monday 15th October 1866 - I began a dress for myself of the curtain Miss Marshall gave me. I will make a waist of it for my debaize skirt. We have had a little frost, not much. We have no turnips this fall or cabbage either. We have some nice radishes and plenty of dried & green fruit, the hands are gathering the apples.

Tuesday 16th - Finished my dress before night. Zona tend Eddie. She is a very good nurse to be so small. Pinck hates to nurse very much. Eddie tries to say everything any one tells him.

Wednesday 17th - I spent the day with Till, took Zona, Gus & Eddie. Mr. Henry was over there making Mr. Morris' molasses on the new cast mill he got of Clayton. It does very well. I sewed some on my waist. I have headache this evening from eating boiled cabbage I think, for dinner.

Thursday 18th - My head ached some all day. Mrs. Alexander spent the day here. I finished my waist. Fair and pleasant. We have a little frost nearly every morning now. They are still gathering apples. Will soon be done.

Friday 19th - Sick all morning with headache, better since dinner. I began to fix my debaize skirt. Mrs. Parker here shearing sheep skins. Mr. Henry over at Mr. Morris' till after supper. They get on slowly with the molasses.

Saturday 20th - Finished the dress & did some mending. I thought Matt would come this evening but she has not. Pinck is tending Eddie today, he tends him Saturday and Sunday and Zona all the week.

Sunday 21st - The children have been off chestnut hunting. They did not get many. Mr. Henry & I are going to walk now. The children will stay here. Warm and pleasant today. We went to Mr. Wm. Reynolds' and spent the evening. The children kept Eddie.

Monday 22nd - We have cool mornings but pleasant through the day. I made Willie a pair drawers. He and Pinck go to school. Zona tends Eddie, she is very careful of him. Gus plays about generally.

Tuesday 23rd - Nothing of importance going on. We are having very pleasant weather. I have fixed some drawers for Gussie. Matt has not come back yet. I have not heard from her since she left.

Wednesday 24th - Fixed some skirts for Eddie. He can say anything you tell him so I can understand. God bless us and our children with health & contentment is my daily prayer.

Thursday 25th October 1866 - I cut Eddie's linsey dress & nearly finished one. Rather cool all day.

Friday 26th - I finished one dress and began the other, it fits very neatly. Mr. Henry about the mill most of the time.

Saturday 27th - Mr. T. L. Morris had a sale today, he leaves soon for Ga. A great many are moving from Buncombe and indeed everywhere. Capt. Thrash leaves soon for Texas. I finished Eddie's dress this morning and have done other little jobs. A negro was buried at the Academy this evening, the children and negroes went. Kate took Eddie. Poor negroes, they sicken and die and no one cares for it.

Sunday 28th - Rev. Dogget preached at Locust Knob, he staid here last Friday night. He is quite an ordinary man. Mr. Henry went to hear him preach. Till spent the day with me. We had a slice potato pie for dinner, our first and last one I expect. Aunt Tena sent me a few potatoes this week. The children gone to see Mammy except Eddie. Esq. Thrash took dinner here. Dogget is here tonight.

Monday 29th - I cut Pinck some dresses, Eddie some flannel skirts and pillow slips. Made Eddie a skirt. Rained nearly all day. Mr. Dogget left in the rain. Kate twisting some stocking yarn and sewing thread.

Tuesday 30th - I took Zona behind me. Mr. Henry & Eddie and spent the day at R. S. Jones'. Mr. Henry went up to Mrs. Green's and came by for me in the evening. Tom Pinck Jones is in last stage of consumption, can't live long, he looks very badly. He is resigned to death. Zona fell off the plank fence at Mr. Jones' gate and got her leg between the horse block and fence. I was frightened so. I feared it was broke but was very thankfull to find it was not.

Wednesday 31st - I made Eddie a skirt and sewed some on Pinck's drawers. Very pleasant. No news.

November 1866

Thursday Nove 1st - Till spent the evening here, helped me sew on Pinck's drawers, nearly got both pair done. Got the cubboard home. Mr. Henry got Till's, also her spinning wheel & some irish potatoes. Mr. Morris left yesterday. Till says she is lonely at her mother's.

Friday Nove 2nd - They brought the cane home and began to grind today. I finished Pinck's drawers, cleaned the cubboard, washed some wool and made four pillow slips. Some fine wool I clipped from a sheep skin last night. Mr. Henry wants me to crochet some baby stockings for the fair in Asheville which comes off the 13th of the month.

Saturday 3rd - Warm and pleasant. I made four pillow slips and did some mending. They are making mollasses. The children got very dirty at the boiling. Mr. Henry has gone to an agricultural meeting on Reems Creek. Got home after supper. Pinck and the children went up to the Academy for his coat he left one day this week but it was gone. I am sorry, it was a good old coat. Some one took it I suppose. I sent Zona & Willie to Tena's to take the fine wool to spin.

Sunday 4th - Mr. Henry & I went out to see the goats this morning. They are having kids. The hogs have destroyed some. He has taken Eddie and gone now. The children all gone to church at the Academy to hear the yankee preacher. I must stop as 'tis late. Sun down nearly and I have the trundle bed to bring in as Gus wets it nearly every night and then I want to go to Mr. Henry down by the mill to look after the goats.

Monday 5th - Began to point a chemise band for my self. Perry Gaston called here today to get some white China Asters for a wreath for Tom Pinck Jones' coffin, he died last night. I gave him what I had. He is to be burried tomorrow at 11 o'clock.

Tuesday 6th - I went to the burrying alone as Mr. Henry was expecting Col. Hatch. Two o'clock when I got home. I came by Mr. A. B. Jones' to get Till to come home with me. She promised to come tomorrow & spend several days.

Wednesday 7th - Finished the band and sleeves & began to crochet some baby stockins for the fair which comes off next Tuesday. Till has not come.

Thursday 8th - Mr. Henry went to town since dinner. Till came this evening. Mr. Andy Jones took dinner here. I have crocheted all day. Have one pair done, all but balls and bow.

Friday 9th November 1866 - Crocheted all day. Till sewing on my chemise. Mr. Henry went to town. No news.

Saturday 10th - Had headache till after supper, lay in bed part of the day but finished off the stockins. Finished our cane last night. Mrs. Bently moved her things to John Rollins' yesterday evening. Bently is gone, they were about to get after them for adultry.

Sunday 11th - Rained nearly all day. Old Boyd and wife were here for dinner and old man named Freeman from Ivy, Madison Co. He staid here last night and will be here tonight again. He is a rank tory.

Monday 12th – Till's mother sent her word to come home. She left this evening. She and I have been at work on some little skirts for herself. I am to finish them. Mr. Henry went to town as 'tis court week.

Tuesday 13th - Mr. Henry off to town. I sewed on the skirts, got both pointed. They killed a hog this evening. Some men stay here tonight from court, neighbors.

Wednesday 14th - Finished the skirts and began Eddie a quilted bonnett of two sorts of calico scraps. Mr. Henry gone to town. Doc Tidwell came this evening, also little Jacobs that was here last winter.

Thursday 15th - The children, Pinck, Willie and Gus went to Mrs. Caroline Jones' from school. Raining this morning so I sent for them. Willie and Gus came home but Pinck went on to school. Finished Eddie's bonnett and my chemise. All the beds full of men last night. I expect the same tonight. It takes me till 9 o'clock every morning to clean the house. Mr. Henry has been to town every day. I was sorry to see him go in the rain this morning but he had to go.

Friday 16th - Pinck at home today as his shoes are bad. Presley is to make them some next week. Presley began to tend the sawmill last Wednesday. We are to board him two meals. I don't like that.

Saturday 17th - Mr. Henry off to town. Jacobs left yesterday morning. Doc gone to his mother's today. I finished my chemise today. Kate and Mary Jones scoured all down stairs very neatly. No company tonight.

Sunday 18 November 1866 - Cool and cloudy all day. Mr. Henry went to old Boyd's this morning, he lives in the old Hood house near Sand Hill. I expected Mr. Henry to dinner but he has not come yet. I must stop now and make up a fire, he will come soon I think. Zona has four kids in the yard and three old goats. She puts them in the cellar every night to keep the hogs from them. She is very attentive to them.

Monday 19th - Court still going on in town. Mr. Henry gone over. Mr. Bob Hawkins and Rev. Doggett stay here tonight. I have made Zona a short saque today and cut a dress for her. Jack Humpries is still at work here, commenced when they were making molasses. He seems to be a good disposed boy.

Tuesday 20th - The children and I sorted the apples. Pinck has not been to school this week as his shoes are bad. Presley is to make him a pair today. Jennie scoured upstairs this evening where the apples were. I sewed some on Zona's dress. Mr. Henry did not come home last night as he was on the jury of a negro murder case. He will be home tonight. Mr. Penly staid here last night & is here tonight. Doc came back this evening. He says Matt wants to come home but has no way of coming.

Wednesday 21st - Finished Zona's dress. Mr. Henry off to town. Pinck got his shoes yesterday and Zona hers today. Rather cool today. One of those negroes is to be hung, the other branded.

Thursday 22nd - Cut three caps for myself. Will work one with turkey red, one with white and put tape trimming on the other. Sewed some on one.

Friday 23rd - Finished my cap. Very cool or colder than we have had yet. We have had a beautiful fall. People are late gathering their corn. Some one is stealing corn out of almost everyone's fields. That is what comes with freedom.

Saturday 24th - Mr. Henry has not been to town yesterday nor today. Doc went yesterday. They branded the negro, the other is to be hung the 21st Dec. I have done odds and ends all day.

Sunday 25th - Cool and fair. Col. Jarrett and Mr. Alexander were here this morning. The children gone to see Mamma but Eddie, he is asleep. Mr. Henry want to go to Wiley Knight's when Eddie wakes and I am going with him. Doc & Jack gone to church at Locust Knob.

Monday 26th November 1866 - I cut Willie a coat and pants and Pinck a pair pants, sewed some on Willie's coat. No news. Mr. Henry gone with some hands to work on the road, intends to put up a toll gate soon.

Tuesday 27th - Finished Willie's coat and began one for Jack. Mr. Henry comes home at night, the hands stay on the road. No news of importance. Miss Ellen's examination comes off the last of this week. The children like her very well.

Wednesday 28th - Finished Jack's coat. Rather cool today. Doc is still here. I think he will stay awhile and work in the waggon shop.

Thursday 29th - Rained all day, the hands came home off the road. I made Jack's pants and sewed some on Pinck's. Mr. Doggett stays here tonight. I fear he has no pure religion in him.

Friday 30th - Fair and cool. The children all went to the examination except Eddie. He has been very good, no trouble. Mr. Henry about the mill. I made Pinck's pants. Lizzie Bently came this evening to hire to me. I think I will keep her a while at 75 cts. a week. Enough I think.

December 1866

Saturday Dec 1st - Lizzie rid the beef guts and made some sausage and other things. I have done several odds and ends. Mr. Henry over at Mr. Clayton's most of the day. Doc gone to the toll gate. He sent us word he was sick with colic since dinner. Charlie and Jack killed a beef yesterday evening, the one we swapped with

Doggett, for it is very nice beef. I made some hair oil of the marrow. Lizzie has done very well today.

Sunday 2nd - Cold and clear. Mr. Henry & Pinck went up to see Doc. Pinck & Doc came home to dinner. Mr. Henry has not come yet. I expect he stopped at Mrs. Owensby's for dinner. Lizzie gone up to see her mother at John Rollins'. Her & Bently have parted. Rumor says they have never been married. They were about to get after old Mrs. Branton for living with old negro Sie. She ought to be whipped good I think. Negro John has moved back to Buncombe.

Monday 3rd December 1866 - Mr. Henry gone on the road, he wants to finish it this week. I hope he may, we miss him so at home. The children have enjoyed the day finely I imagine, as they have been very noisey. It has been too cold for them to play out so they are have had horses of chairs. Willie is growing some stouter I think. He can reach and put the comb on the mantle piece in my room by tip toeing. He thinks 'tis something wonderful. I am going to teach them till they get a school. Pinck and Zona recite very well but Willie can't keep his mind on it long at a time. Pinck is studying grammer, geography, reading & spelling. He dislikes arithmetic & writing but I have him to try both. Miss Ellen Hawkins stays here tonight. 'Tis very cold & sleeting this evening. I have made a night cap today.

Tuesday 4th - Mr. Henry came home tonight but will leave soon in the morning. I will be glad when he gets done. Home is not home without him. Much warmer this morning. It rained some last night. Ellen went home this morning. The children have done very well with their lessons. I sewed some on a cap.

Wednesday 5th - Pleasantly warm. We have had a beautiful winter so far, no snow and very little cold weather. Mr. Henry will not be home before the last of the week, he thinks. He takes a heap of nursing off my hands when at home, gets Eddie to sleep. It worried me so nurse him. Eddie is a very affectionate babe, thinks no one can nurse him but his Ma. He can say nearly anything he tries. Zona is still very devoted to the goats. I wish they were out of the yard as they have eat nearly all my shrubery.

Thursday 6th - Pinck & Doc went to the toll gate. I thought Mr. Henry would like to come home. Jack came last night and said he wanted to come tonight but Pinck has come and says Papa is not coming. Jim Ledford has a shucking today.

Friday 7th - Matt came back today, she seems discontented some way. I hope she may soon get over it. She is pleasant enough when she will be and makes herself miserable at her will. Doc made me some patent right winding blades. Very well done for him.

Saturday 8th - Christmas will soon be here. Gus tells me he is going to have a knife then. I told him some time ago, if he would not cry till Christmas, I would get him a knife. He thinks he must have it though he has cried every day since I told him. I must try to treat my little school Christmas. I like to see them enjoy themselves. It will not be long that they are children. When I look at Pinck & Zona I think I shall soon be an old woman. I tell Pinck he must quit growing. He says "Mother you will get older if I do stop growing". Mr. Henry came home this evening. Done the road for a while. This has been a lovely day. It rained nearly all night but cleared off this morning & bright & warm.

Sunday 9th - Cooler this morning than yesterday, wind from the North but bright and a warm sun where the wind don't reach you. No news of importance. I will stop as I have nothing more to write and dinner will soon be in.

Monday 10th - My journal is so monotonous I am tempted at times to lay it aside entirely but Mr. Henry tells me it will interest my children at some future day and I wish to live in their memory long after I am in the silent tomb. They perhaps may read these pages with interest after the hand that penned them lies moldering away. If it will add any to their pleasure and content to give them all I can to contribute their happiness.

The hands killed three hogs. We have five more at home and some out to fatten on the shares which will make us plenty of bacon. I have made some bureau covers & cut Zona's and Eddie's dress Miss Marshall gave them. Very cool and fair today.

Tuesday 11th - Lizzie fixed up the lard. I have been at work on Zona's dress. Matt shearing some sheep skins as she wants the wool. Doc is still here, he goes to the toll gate nearly every day. They went after some men yesterday evening for not paying. The gate is giving Mr. Henry some trouble. He went today and the men paid. I helped Jennie make some sausage today.

Wednesday 12th - I am still at work on Zona's dress, got it done this evening. It fits very neatly. Cold and fair. I teach the children every day. Willie is very careless about learning, the others seem to try more than him.

Thursday 13th December 1866 - Sewed all day on Eddie's dress, will finish I hope tomorrow. I am tired of them. Mr. Henry about the place all day. I fear he will have trouble with Jim Ledford about the rent. Ledford is disposed to act the rascal.

Friday 14th - Pinck and Doc went to Asheville to a gander pulling. Doc got one gander head. Pinck is delighted with the trip. I finished Eddie's dress this evening. Lizzie has been ironing some. Mr. Henry went to work on the western pike today. Cool this morning but fair. The negroes are hauling in the rent corn from Jim Moore's. Henry came home last night from hauling at Mr. S. N. Stevens'.

Saturday 15th - Cold & sleeting. I pity the stock as we have no cow house or sheep house either. We will soon get more milk as Muly had a calf last Monday and some of the other cows will be milking soon. I will be very glad as we do not get enough for the table. I have done odds & ends all day.

Sunday 16th - Cloudy & the ground covered with sleet and the trees have a heavy coat of ice. Melting a little now, nearly 12 o'clock. Mr. Henry gone to old Boyd's, he will have a bad time for walking. I want to look at the children's heads so I will stop this time.

Sunday 23rd - A week has elapsed since I wrote. I have had nothing of importance to write. We have had some very unpleasant weather, the yard is very muddy now. I hear no talk of Christmas though 'tis close at hand. The children talk a heap about it. Gus says he will get a knife. I have made some little clothes this week, nothing much. I started to Mr. A. B. Jones' with the children this morning but found it so muddy I came back. Cloudy all day, a little rain tonight. We had no dinner as Jennie has been gone yesterday & today to get some wages due her. Doc and Pinck started to Clay Co. last Tuesday, to be gone about two weeks. I miss Pinck a great deal, he is such a help. Does anything I want cheerfully. He was so anxious to go, I let him go to gratify him. Zona does not do things half as cheerfully as Pinck. May God protect my little boy in his wandering.

Monday 24th December 1866 - I have spent the day in fixing things for the children's Christmas. Baking and decorating. I have fixed a table in the hall with their little presents, cakes, candies &c. since they went to bed. Gus says Santa Claus will bring him a knife. I wonder if Pinck will hang up his sock tonight. This has been a very pleasant day.

Tuesday 25th - The children up early, anxious to see their presents. I took them in the hall after lighting the candles. They are delighted with their knives & the nice things on the table. Eddie thinks a great deal of his rag doll. He is a very affectionate child. I can't scold him. He comes and wants to put his arms around my neck every time I speak cross to him. He is a dear child.

Mr. Henry & I spent the day at Mr. A. B. Jones' as Pet is quite sick. Lizzie has been gone all day. I don't think she will come back again. The children want to shoot their crackers all the time. Eddie is affraid of them. I hope they have enjoyed the day as much as I want them to. I love to see them joyous and happy. Cares will come too soon anyway to their young hearts.

Wednesday 26th - Jennie and Lizzie both gone. Matt and I have everything to do. We did our first milking. Mr. Henry helped us. He had all the feeding to do as Jack is not here. Mr. Henry has gone to town today. I have spent most of the day in cleaning up, generally in the kitchen and dining room as Jennie has left everything dirty. Lizzie has left us, gone to Haywood with her mother to live.

Thursday 27th - I have done but little sewing, mostly out doors work. Matt is very good to help. Very cold this morning. Some snow, wind from the North & light. I got very cold when I was milking. Matt got breakfast. I milked with Jack's & Mr. Henry's help. It tires my hand a good deal to milk but I would soon get accustomed to it I think. Zona can milk nearly as well as any of us, she is very fond of it.

Friday 28th - I sewed some & got dinner. Henry Jones was here so Matt had to entertain him. I fed the hogs at dinner. Jennie has not come home yet. Don't know when she will.

Monday 31st December 1866 - The last day of the old year. The last time I will write 1866 in my dear old journal. The old year has past with its joys and cares. The new year, what may it bring us of life's blessings? I hope we may be more prosperous another year. May a kind Providence show a smiling face. I have had headache for three days, 'tis nearly well tonight. Matt had her hands full till Saturday evening. Jennie came. Cold and unpleasant all day. Farewell old year, you will soon be numbered with the things that were.

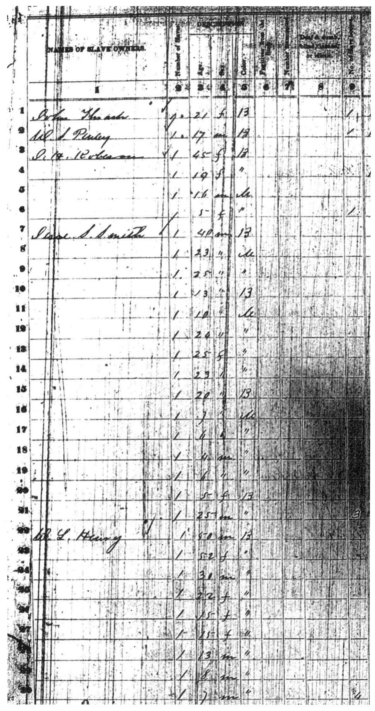

Portion of 1860 Buncombe County Slave Schedule documenting the
number of slaves owned by William L. Henry before the war

1867

"…Oh! that God would give our enemies better hearts…"

January 1867

Tuesday January 1st 1867 New Year's Day - What changes may take place before I date another new year? Or I may not be on this beautiful earth at another year. I trust in Providence I may be spared to raise my dear children. I have cut some little clothes but sewed but little. Now no news of importance going on. We are having some very cold weather, a good deal of snow.

Wednesday 2nd - Still cold. I have sewed some. I tend Eddie nearly all the time as Zona dislikes nursing so much. He is very little trouble. He is such an affectionate little dear. Tries to sing "hop a dudle do." He tries to talk, can say some words right plain. Mr. Henry thinks there never was such a child. The children still have their goats in the cellar. They spend most of their time working & playing with them. Eddie is affraid of the old goats. I sent him to shut the door the other day, he met the old goat at the door. It frightened him, so ever since, when I tell him to go and shut the door, he says "goat" so he don't go.

Thursday 3rd - Sewed some, made two shirts (infants). I had a letter from Matt yesterday saying Sister Jane had twins. I know she has her hands full. They were born 19th Dec. a boy & girl. Mr. Henry about home all the time.

Friday 4th - Still very cold, snow melting a little. Nothing of importance going on. Did some sewing today.

Saturday 5th - I have mended some & ironed some. Still melting, the ground is very sloppy. Jennie does the milking and cooking & some washing. I think she will leave soon. Negroes get tired so soon, they are not contented long at a time at one place.

Sunday 6th January 1867 - Cold wind from North. Mr. Henry at home till after dinner then went to old Boyd's. Jane Jones came this evening. She is going to work with us awhile at 75 cts. a week. She seems to be willing to work. Jack went to Haywood yesterday after his clothes & came back tonight. Matt went to her Mother's today, she sent for her. She only wants to stay a week.

Monday 7th - Jennie left us this morning. She wanted higher wages. I could not give her any more than I gave Jane Jones. I have sewed some on an apron. Helped Jane clean the kitchen since dinner.

Tuesday 8th - Sewed some. Still snow on the ground & has been for near five weeks. Snowing some this evening. Mr. Henry about the mills all day. Two negro woman have been washing for me today. They only washed half the day and are to come tomorrow to finish.

Wednesday 9th - Fair all day, snow melting off the South sides rapidly. I have made two infant shirts today. Mr. Henry about the mill. No news of importance going on. Some movers stop here tonight from Transelvania by the name of Queen.

Thursday 10th - Mr. Henry gone to Joe Green's sale of land. His widow has married a McBrian recently. The movers stay here today. Some snow this morning but faired off about 10 o'clock. Mr. Henry had to walk as Doc took his saddle. I think Doc has acted badly taking the saddle & keeping Pinck out there so long.

Friday 11th - The movers left this morning. I am glad of it. I think they are another Terry set, great rowders. Mr. Henry about the mills. Fair & thawing some. I am getting very helpless, my back hurts me so much.

Saturday 12th - Still thawing, very little snow now. I have worked some on two little flannels, intend to point one with linnen and embroidry the other with tidy cotton. As we are so poor, I am not able to buy a little crewel to work with. What is to become of us I don't know. I think it will take everything we have to pay the heirs of old Mr. Henry's estate. I wish he had kept it all & not been governed by William Tidwell. No word from Pinck & Doc yet. All are well.

Sunday 13th - Cloudy and warm, some snow on the north side. Eddie is not well, his bowels loose. Cold I reckon.

Monday 14th - Worked some on the little skirts, got one pointed. No news. Some snow on the ground yet. Mr. Henry spends most of his time at the mill. Killed four hogs today, Tena rid the guts. She is more accommodating now than ever.

Tuesday 15th - Tena done up the lard and helped make sausage. I have worked some on the skirt. Cold and clear.

Wednesday 16th - Still cold. Nothing of importance going on. I have worked some on the skirt. No news from Doc and Pinck. I am not teaching the children now but will begin soon again. Eddie is the most mischievous little thing I ever saw, climbs into the cradle bed or any where he wants to. He is a dear affectionate child.

Thursday 17th - Finished the two little skirts, they look very neat. Mr. Henry at the mills all day. Very cold, high wind from the north.

Friday 18th - Made some little things. Very cold but no wind. Jane is making a very good hand.

Saturday 19th - I have done odds and ends as I generally do on Saturday. I had to get dinner as Jane is sick. I had just got things cleaned up and George Peak and Mr. Sumner came so I had to get their supper. I don't think I was ever so tired as I am tonight. Zona helped me all she could. Mr. Henry washed the children.

Sunday 20th - Snowed some last night & all day today. This evening 'tis about ten inches deep. Mr. Peak & Sumner here all day. Old Daniel, a negro Pa used to own, came here today moving. He wants to stay here but Mr. Henry is not going to employ him.

Monday 21st - Cloudy but no snow fell today. We have enough for one winter I hope. Mr. Peak and Sumner left today. Old Daniel is going to hunt him a home in a few days.

Tuesday 22nd - Snow melted some, not much though. John Hendrix began to work here yesterday. Pinck & Doc got home last Sunday night, very well pleased with his trip. He has a beggar or memory string full of buttons. The other children had to have one too so I hunted up buttons, all sizes & colors, & strung them up. They will soon lose them. I imagine. Eddie has his. Zona fixed it up with old keys & things generally.

Wednesday 23rd January 1867 - I began an apron. Snow melting slowly, the earth beginning to peep out on the south sides. Mr. Henry at the mill all day. Daniel has not got a place yet. Snow has been off the ground entirely for seven weeks. We have had some very cold weather and a heap of it.

Thursday 24th - Began a little gown, intend to embroid it. I want to get it done this week for I don't know how long I will be able to work. Jane is not so good a hand as Lizzie Bently was.

Friday 25th - Worked on the little gown, got it nearly done. Snow still melting some. Daniel not got a home yet, he seems to be greatly disappointed by not getting in here.

Saturday 26th - Finished the gown, it looks very neat. Emily (Daniel's wife) washed some today for me. She seems very willing to work at anything & seems to be very nice about her work. I would like to keep her a while.

Sunday 27th - Clear and cold, wind from the North. Doc went for Matt yesterday, they will be here soon I expect. I would be glad Matt would marry, she is so dissatisfied here. Pinck, Zona and Willie have gone to spend the day with Mrs. Ballew's children. Gussie and Eddie are playing in the back piazza. Mr. Henry in the room all day with me. He is very kind to stay with me when I can't get out. Mr. Henry went after the children this evening, fearing they would stay till it got too cold. Matt and Doc came this evening.

Monday 28th - I got an old dress from Matt to make Eddie & I some aprons. Made mine today. Matt made Eddie one. Doc went to town today. No news of importance going on.

Tuesday 29th - Made Eddie an apron & done some other things. Mr. Henry went to Sandy Bottom since dinner. Warmer than it has been, snow melting gradually. Still a good deal on the ground.

Wednesday 30th - Crocheted some on some little stockings, they look very nice. I heard this evening Mrs. Morris has a fine son, born Monday night. She and the babe are doing well.

Thursday 31st - I am still crocheting on the stockings, it is very tiresome. I will be glad when I get done. Mr. Henry went to town and got the children some school books. They will start to Sand Hill School next week. Pinck is delighted with the idea of going, Zona don't like it much.

345

February 1867

Friday Feb 1st 1867 - Emily scoured the house down stairs. I am crocheting some little socks for Till. Done one pair, they look very neat. Warm, still thawing, snow nearly all gone. The yard is very muddy, the house will not stay clean long. Mr. Henry tending the mill as Rollins has gone to town.

Saturday 2nd - Very warm, some rain last night and the first thunder of this year. It seems like Spring today. Mr. Henry about the mill. I feel very unwell today, took cold last night and I expect 'tis something else too. I will be so glad when 'tis all over with. Rachel Jones has just left here, came to get a broom. I sell them at twenty five cts. a broom.

Sunday 3rd - Mr. Henry went over to see Till, she is doing finely. Mary Rollins & her children spent the day here, she is a great bore to me. Warm and pleasant.

Monday 4th - I have been mending most of the day. Warm & spring like, it seems we ought to be gardening. Mr. Henry about the mills after dinner. He went to Jacob Starnes' before dinner to get him to look at a little place on his nose. Starnes thinks 'tis a cancer. He is working on it. Mr. Henry is not to speak for two nights after going to bed nor speak before he gets his clothes on. I hope 'tis not a cancer.

Tuesday 5th - I wanted to talk so much last night after going to bed. It seemed just because I should not talk that I could scarcely keep my tongue. Mr. Henry said it was so with him too. Doc started home this morning. I have worked a frill today & made some collars for myself.

Wednesday 6th - Began Mr. Henry some shirt bosoms & made some collars. Don't know how long I will be up. Still pleasant. Mr. Henry about the mills. Pinck & Zona have not started to school yet as Pinck shoes are so bad.

Thursday 7th - Daniel and family started for Tenn this morning. Fair and bright. Betsey Jamison came here yesterday evening, she is to stay with me awhile. Jane Jones went home this evening, her mother is sick & sent for her. I finished the shirt bosoms and cut some quilt squares. Betsy and Matt will have plenty to do now. Mrs. Long was here a short time today. Betsy is ironing, Matt cooking.

Friday 8th - I have crocheted a pair infant stockings, they are very nice. Mr. George Peak stays here tonight. I think we will have some rain soon as 'tis so warm. Mr. Henry has been to Sandy Bottom, did not get home till supper. I trimmed Eddie's hair for the first time. He sit very still, he seems so proud of it.

Saturday 9th - Raining this morning. Mr. Henry and Mr. Peak gone to town. They will be gone till night I expect. I have trimmed all the children's hair and have knit some. I expect to knit this evening. Betsy is spinning, Matt cooking.

Sunday 10th - Fair and very cold. Mr. Peak started this morning. Mr. Henry went to Capt. Moore's. Came home to dinner. The wind blew very hard last night but calm this morning.

Saturday night Feb. 16th - Nothing of interest has happened. Mr. A. B. Jones got his house burned last Wednesday morning about 5 o'clock. Mr. Henry saw the light when he got up. They lost a good many things, supposed to have been an accident. Mr. Henry has tended court every day this week in town. He got up a subscription for Mr. Jones and got nearly all they need now. I have done several things this week. I don't think I can stay up another week. Mr. Henry has gone to bed and all the children. Very warm, frogs singing last night & night before but none to-night as 'tis some cooler. I must go to bed. Don't know when I will write again, maybe never but hope I may write many a book yet for my dear children to read when I am called home to Heaven above.

Sunday 17th - Unwell all day. Mr. Henry sent for the Dr. H. this evening. He is here tonight also Mrs. Ballew. I cannot stay up much longer. Mr. Henry & I went down to Mrs. Knight's this morning. Warm and pleasant, grass beginning to show a little in spots now. Mr. Henry want to start to Tenn tomorrow. I hope I may do well so he can go.

March 1867

March 11th Monday 1867 - I am about well again. I put on my clothes yester-day for the first time. Our baby (a boy)[55] was born Feb. 18th twenty minutes after four in the morning (Monday). I suffered a great deal from 1 o'clock till after four. I did not sleep any all night. Mr. Henry left for Tenn the same day, wanted a R R contract. Came back on Saturday following. I was very glad to see him. My babe has been a good deal of trouble at night and is yet. Betsy has gone to keep the toll gate, went last Thursday a week. She is very well satisfied. Mrs. Morris has spent a week with me. She has gone home this evening. I hope she will come back soon. Mr. Henry went with her. I fear it will tire her to carry her baby so far. My babe rests very well in day time. My eyes are not strong so I will stop this time & lay down and rest a while.

March 12th Tuesday - Mr. Henry brought me the first peach blooms I have seen today. He is ever mindful of me, brings the first flowers of Spring to me every year. Mr. Henry & Kate made some crout today. Very pleasant weather.

Saturday 16th - I have done nothing all week but knit. I am afraid of straining my eyes to sew yet. No news of importance. Mr. Henry stays at the mill most of the time as Ruff Miller is sawing for Mr. Jones' house. They move in the kitchen part today.

Sunday 17th - Mr. Henry, Pinck & Zona went to church at the Academy today. Warm & pleasant. Osborn (a young man Mr. Henry hired about a week ago) is very unwell with a cold I think. He is very thinly clad.

Monday 18th - My babe is a month old today, it still has me up some nights with it. I hope it will soon get over that. Mr. Henry is so kind to get up with it when I am tired & sleepy. It kept us up till near 12 o'clock last night. He would nurse it some & I some. Jane Jones went home yesterday evening. Kate is staying till I can get some one. Jane will be gone two weeks if she comes back then, which I doubt.

Tuesday 19th - Matt & Pinck went to town. She got a big bill of goods for these hard times. Money is nothing to her. Cloudy & cold this evening.

---

[55] Sidney Polk (Siddie) Henry

Wednesday 20th March 1867 - Osborn has been sick all the week, not confined to the bed but not able to do anything. Old Charlie Pendland is here tonight. Mrs. Eliza Knight is staying here now, came yesterday morning before breakfast. I want to keep her till Jane returns, if she ever does. I have sewed a little this week on a quilt. My back is still very weak and gives me a good deal of pain. Rained all day yesterday.

Thursday 21st - This is Zona's birthday. She is eight years old today. She is a great deal of help to me nursing the baby &c. Rained till dinner today, still cloudy this evening. Eliza is not very nice about her work but seems to try to please me.

Friday 22nd - I have a sore finger, the fore one on my right hand. It bothers me some in writing. I can't sew today any good. I don't know what is the matter, it first come a crack nearly two months ago. It hope it may prove nothing serious. I have knit most of the day. Eliza washed. Matt got dinner. This has been a beautiful day. Mr. Henry about the mill all day. Telitha Jones married Else Wilson last Tuesday. Poor girl, I pity her as he is a drunkard.

Saturday 23rd - I have knit some. Eliza ironed & got dinner. I washed the children this evening. Some cooler today. Henry Jones stays here tonight. He is flying around Matt. I don't think they will ever marry, she is too full of notions. Mr. Henry went to Sandy Bottom, got back before night.

Sunday 24th - This has been a beautiful day till late in the evening, it rained some then. Jim Henry was here this evening. He is a radical I think. His baby died about a month ago, that is two sons they have lost. Mollie takes it very hard.

I am tired out of staying in the house. Days, weeks, months & years glide by & I have to stay here a prisoner with my children & no recreation. I try not to repine at my lot, there are a great many in this world in a worse fix than I. "Lord bless us with content."

Monday 25th - Fair with cool wind from the North. Kate making soap and washing. Eliza gone to Riche's today. Matt got dinner. I have mended some & knit some, my finger gets no better. My babe is fretful every evening. Hives I think. It is no trouble now at night, only will not sleep out of my arms which bothers me a little.

Tuesday 26th March 1867 - Raining this morning. Kate has come to finish the soap. Mr. Henry about the mill. I will knit some. I must go now and get out dinner. The little spotted heifer had a calf today, a small heifer calf. Mr. Henry about the mill today.

Wednesday 27th - I have knit some. Kate still at work at the soap, she is very slow. A Mr. Whitmire from Henderson Co. took dinner here today. While he was here, some one stole his pistol out of his waggon at the mill. I think it was negro George as he greased his waggon. He is a dreadful rogue.

Thursday 28th & Friday 29th - I had headache very bad all day yesterday but 'tis entirely well today. Mr. Jack Shipman staid here last night. He went to Ledford's today concerning that mule so Bill Ledford brought the mule home this evening. Those boys are very unprincipled. I re-read "Rose Clark" yesterday & today. 'Tis very interesting.

Saturday 30th - Mended some. Eliza went home this evening. I have been very busy since dinner tending both children as all the other children went with Mr. Henry to pile rocks. They were delighted and wanted to go again. I began to milk but it hurt my sore finger so bad I got negro Jane to finish Muly. Jane came while I was milking. She is to milk till Eliza comes back.

Sunday 31st - Mr. Kirkendoll & wife spent the day here. After dinner we went to see a coon Mr. Penland had in a steel trap above the old dam. The children were highly pleased with the walk but did not like to see it killed. It rained some on us before we got back. Matt took care of Eddie & the baby.

April 1867

Monday April 1st - I have mended some. Went with Mr. Henry over to where they are chopping saw logs. Jim Cannon is hauling. Pinck & I came back together, Mr. Henry staid there. Eliza came home yesterday evening. Her mother and sister came with her, the latter left this morning. Fair and wind from north. Rather cool. Peach trees not in bloom yet but showing the bloom a good deal.

Tuesday 2nd - Mr. Henry made an April fool of me last night by telling me Berry Hogan had come. We were eating supper. I did not think of it at first. We had a good time afterwards. I must fool him tomorrow or soon. I helped him take some sheep to the Joe Green field, enjoyed the walk very much. My babe is very good now, no trouble at night.

Sunday 7th April 1867 - Nothing of importance has happened since I last wrote. Mr. Henry and I spent the day at Mr. Jones'. Till leaves next Wednesday for Ga. I am sorry to see her go, she has been a good friend to me in my troubles. I think more of her than any one in the neighborhood. Her babe is very large to its age. I have made a shirt for Mr. Henry which was nearly all I done. Zona is very good to tend the baby, murmers sometimes. Eddie is not looking well, has worms I think.

Monday 8th - Cloudy all day with a little rain tonight. Rather cool. I fear the peaches will be killed as they are in full bloom. Sewed some on Mr. Henry's shirt. The baby has fretted a heap today. Not well I think. Little Savannah Night died last Wednesday morning of croup.

Tuesday 9th - Still at work on Mr. Henry's shirt, nearly finished it today. The baby has rested very well. Some rain today.

Wednesday 10th - Finished the shirt and began a sack for the baby out of Zona's old waisted dress. She tore it nearly all to pieces Sunday when I was gone. Katy Night & Bud were here, so the children had a gay time.

Friday 12th - I suffered a great deal with headache yesterday and today till after dinner. It is easy this evening. Fair and windy yesterday. Rain today. Old Walker (a Tenn.) came here today, claims Mr. Henry's stallion. I don't think he ever saw the horse before. He is here tonight. I think he is a mean man.

Saturday 13th - I have done several things. Washed the children's heads, cleaned the Spring and did some mending. The old man Walker is still in the neighborhood. He intends stealing the horse I think. Mr. Henry went to Sandy Bottom today, did not get home till night.

349

Sunday 14th - This has been a beautiful day. Matt and Eliza went to the Academy to church, Mr. Henry also. My head ached till after dinner then easy. Old Walker stays here tonight. Kirkendol & Miller sleep at the stable tonight. Some one cut Henry Jones' clothes up badly last Saturday as he came on from town. He did not know the man. I think it some one that is a friend to old Walker.

Monday 15th - Cloudy and cool this morning. I did not rest well last night as I was uneasy about Walker being here. Mr. Henry slept very well. Matt slept in here as Eliza went to Wiley Knight's. I am going to make some snuff & fix some old dresses for myself.

Tuesday 16th April 1867 - I fixed an old dress yesterday, turned it up side down. It is too long. I will have to take it off the waist again. Mr. Henry and Kerkendol sleep at the stable. The old man came last night and demanded the horse, he did not get it. I hope he may never get it. I don't think he ever saw the horse till he came here.

Wednesday 17th - Scoured and scalded the whole house. Old Mrs. Snider helped Eliza. She seems to be a very good hand. Poor old creature, I reckon she is very needy. Matt got dinner. This has been a lovely day. Mr. Henry at the mill and out on the farm all the time. Some men came here last night hunting Caine (a negro). He has been doing some mischief on Mills river, broke in a store. It frightened me a good deal. I thought it was Old Tenn after Mr. Henry, he was sleeping in the stables.

Thursday 18th - Mrs. Snider washed for me, she is a nice washer. I have been doing odds and ends, mending &c. Old Tenn is still in the country.

Friday & Saturday 19th & 20th - I have knit nearly all day. I cleaned the yards and smoke house and scoured the privy, the children & I. Mr. Henry had some beans planted this evening for the first. The children tried to dye them some eggs but did not succeed very well. Tomorrow is Easter. Pinck went home with Mr. Gaston's children yesterday evening & came home today.

Sunday 21st - Mr. Henry and I went over to Mrs. A. B. Jones' who is sick. Mag Morris came back with us but only staid a short time. Willie got hooked by a cow this evening (Nan) in the mouth. It was a very bad looking place at first. I thought he was ruined. Mr. Henry sewed it up, he bore it very patiently. Dr. Hilliard came late at night and put a sticking plaster on it. He cried some when the Dr. sewed it. I think it was getting sore. Mrs. Kirkendoll is here tonight, also Eliza's Mother & Papa.

Monday 22nd - Eddie two years old today. He is very fretful, more trouble than the baby. Willie seems to be doing very well. He has been up most of the day. Eliza went home yesterday, will not be back in several days. Jane Jones had been here today. I have done but little. I feel so distressed about Willie's lip. Mr. Henry went to town today. He slept in the house since Saturday night as Kirkendol had the horse up on bent creek Saturday night & last night. Old Cochran slept up there with Kirkendoll.

Tuesday 23rd - I helped some about dinner. We had our first lettuce today. Willie is doing finely, has a good appetite, lives on soup & mush & milk. He goes about the house & out in the yard a little. I helped Tena make some harness since dinner.

Wednesday 24th - Some rogue went in our smoke house last night and took some of our meat. They dug under. I think it was Caine. Two men staid here last night on hunt of Caine. I hope they may find him. They found some of the goods he had stole at Ike Hawkins'. They took him & his wife to town today. Mr. Henry has gone up on Bent Creek or Sandy Bottom today. Some rain this evening and rather cool. We had some hail last Monday evening.

May 1867

Wednesday 8th May - Two weeks has passed since I last wrote but nothing of interest has transpired. I had the headache very badly last Sunday and Monday. Old Dub died last night. Negroes die when ever they get sick. Jennie came here yesterday evening, she is looking very badly. Eliza Night came back yesterday. Mary Muse has been staying with us a few days since last Thursday. We are picking wool now, have a good deal to pick. Old Mrs. Snider is helping. She has sheared some and washed the wool. I had my loom brought home today. I want to put in a piece of cloth this week for Zona and Eddie some dresses. Bark dye, I am not able to buy indigo. I want to get some indigo to colour some wool. Mrs. Peter Luther came to see Mr. Henry last week to get a job of jeans making. I want a nice piece made for Mr. Henry's clothes. I don't want Jennie to stay here, she is of no use to me.

Thursday 9th - I have been sick all morning with headache but some better this evening. Mrs. Cook & Ella Lawson were here today. Ella is to stay with us a while at 75 cts. seventy five cts. a week. Mr. Henry, the children and Matt went to Dub's burial today. Mrs. Cook kept the baby for me.

Friday 10th - I have mended some. I want to get the children some clothes wove as soon as possible as I have to patch every week. Eliza & Matt put in the cloth today. No news. Old Tenn is still in the country.

Saturday 11th - This has been a busy day, generally mending &c. Eliza wove some & went home after dinner, is to be back on Monday. Fair & warm, things growing beautifully the woods getting green.

Sunday 12th May 1867 - Mr. Henry in the house all day. Evening, he did not get home from the turnpike meeting till after dinner, went up on French Broad last Friday morning. I took a long walk this morning. Had to whip Pinck & Willie. I sent them after one of the cows (white muly). They went catching fish in the race. The water was let off yesterday evening from some cause. I dislike so much to punish my little children. Pinck is a good boy but very thoughtless. Willie's mouth is nearly well but will make an ugly scar, I fear. Pinck offered me all his fish if I would not whip him. It hurt me so, worse than it did them but I had to do what I thought was my duty.

Monday 13th - Mr. Henry & Louis Jones started to Marshall this morning. Got as far Asheville & heard Maj. Rollins had gone to Hendersonville. The Jones boys owe Mr. Henry for the grey mare. They were both in Kirk's command. I fear he will never get anything from them.

Tuesday 14th - I cut Gussie some bodies & sewed some on one today. Fair and warm. No news of importance.

Wednesday 15th - I finished the body, it fits very neatly. Eliza and her mother came here today. Mr. Henry gone up the creek to buy some oxen. Frank's brought home our cows (they have had) last night. Mrs. Snider washing wool.

Thursday 16th - I have wove some, this is my first day's weaving. I wove a little over half a yard. The children bother me so I can't work half the time. Zona attends the baby. Pinck, Willie & Gussie mind the cows over the creek. They are delighted with it.

Friday 17th - I have been weaving some, not much & mending some. Mrs. Snider is done the wool and trying to dye some black. Ella is doing very well. Nothing of importance going on. I had a letter from Sister Matt last Monday, they were all well. Pa has moved up to the place where Berry lives. He is not satisfied so Matt says. I reckon no place seems like home since the house was burnt. Poor old man. His troubles are great. We all have our troubles "every heart knoweth its own bitterness."

Saturday 18th - My baby is three months old today. It can laugh & try to talk and pinch the breast I have, to feed it some. It is a very good babe. Eddie is a dear affectionate child, can say nearly anything. He had the old cripple hen in the churn, churning her today. He is full of mischief. Gussie is tall enough to reach the latch of the middle door.

Sunday 19th - Fair and warm. Matt and the children went to the Academy to church, no preacher came. The negroes have Sunday School at the Academy. I have not been to preaching in nearly two years at the Academy. I went once last summer to Sand Hill. Betsy, Laura Glenn & Lou Shipman came down today for dinner, they stay here tonight. Mr. Henry at home all day. Mr. Henry & I went out walking, took the baby and Eddie. The other children went down to Mrs. Knight's. Pinck went with us up to Mary Rollins.

Monday 20th - Some rain this morning after Betsey & Co. started but fair now. Mrs. Snider still trying to dye black & picking wool. I have done nothing of note today. I want to write to Matt this evening if I can find an envelope. Matt is weaving some today. Mary Knight has just left, says she will come up tomorrow and weave for me. I wrote to Matt this evening. Rather cool, a fire feels comfortable.

Tuesday 21st - Mr. A. B. Jones spent the day here. I filled quills for Mrs. Knight and sewed some on Gussie's body. Mr. Henry about the farm all day. Pinck, Willie and Gus mind the milk cows on the other side of the creek. Zona stays with me, she is a great help to tend the baby and Eddie when I have to be out. Mr. Willis fixed new steps to the back piazza today, it is much better to go in and out than it was. It was really dangerous.

Wednesday 22nd - I finished Gussie's body. Mrs. Knight wove two yds. & a half yesterday. Mrs. Snider not here today, don't know the reason. She washed some yesterday when she was dying. Rather cool all day.

Thursday 23rd - Mr. Henry and Pinck went to town, took old Nan. Mr. Henry wants to sell her. She is so bad to throw down fences. I have done some mending today.

Friday 24th - Nothing of importance going on in the country. Jim Henry has not returned yet. Mollie is very ill. I have fixed Zona's gowns yesterday & today.

Saturday 25th - Mr. Henry had the tombstone taken up to the grave yard today. I went along. Our little baby's grave looks very neat. I worked some in the yard after I came back.

Sunday 26th - This has been a beautiful day. Mr. Henry went to preaching at the Academy. Evans preached. He has gone off to walk since dinner.

Monday 27th - Tena weaving for me. I have filled quills & picked some wool. We had a very hard rain this evening. Mr. Henry & I put out some cabbage plants. Tena's mother has been here today picking wool.

Tuesday 28th - Mr. Henry & I went fishing this morning for a jack fish. Just below the dam, Pinck caught two little fish. All the children were along but the baby.

Wednesday 29th - I have been busy all day fixing for the examination at Sand Hill, it comes off tomorrow. Mr. Henry went to town this morning, came home to dinner. He received a letter from Lou today. Some rain this evening.

Friday 31st - I went to the examination at Sand Hill yesterday. Came home & went to bed before supper, sick with headache. Betsy stays here tonight. The young people went to the entertainment last night at Sand Hill. Pinck and Zona went also. Mr. Henry staid with me. Old Granna staid last night. Pinck broke Zona's vase last night hunting a taper to light the candle after they came home. I am sorry for it. Zona thought so much of her vases.

June 1867

Saturday June 1st - I have ironed and mended some. The children went to hunt strawberries this morning, found some very nice ones.

Sunday 2nd - Matt went to Glenn's with Betsy last Friday to spend several days. This has been a lovely day. Mr. Henry about the house all day.

Monday 3rd - I have picked some wool. Mrs. Ballow spent the day here. She is going to teach a school at Sand Hill. Mr. Henry signed for. I shall miss the children a good deal, they are such a help tending to the baby and doing little jobs generally.

Tuesday 4th - I cleaned up things in the house & kitchen as Ella is washing to-day. Picked some wool after dinner. Granna still picking wool. I will give her some wool and syrup this evening & let her go for I would not feed her for her work.

Friday 7th - I have had headache for two days but did not have to go to bed all the time. It pained me a while this evening. I took a nap and it helped me a great deal. Pinck attended to the baby. He is a better nurse than Zona, she is cross to the baby.

Saturday 8th - I ironed some before dinner. After dinner Mr. Henry, Pinck, Zona and I went to hunt strawberries in Mrs. Jones' fields, found a nice chance, had a pleasant walk. Ella tended the baby. Mrs. Long called here this evening.

Sunday 9th June 1867 - Warm, needing rain. Mr. Henry, Zona and I went to preaching at the Academy (Miller a baptist preacher) a large congregation. A negro girl was burried up there after preaching. The negroes are dying off rapidly. Mag Morris came home with us and took dinner. We had some very nice strawberries and cream. Mag has gone home. Ella is going to milk. I must get out supper while Sidney is asleep. The children start to school tomorrow. I shall miss them a great deal. Matt has not come home yet. Mr. Henry has some little pigs in the yard, he feeds them. They are growing very fast. I have two hogs in the pen that I claim. They are growing very well.

Monday 10th - This has been a long, lonely day to me. The children all gone but Gus, Eddie & the baby. It has been very quiet all day. I miss them a great deal. I have picked some wool. Sidney loves to be nursed so I find little time for work.

Tuesday 11th - Matt came home today. Lou Glenn with her. Lou seems to be a very pleasant girl. Mr. Henry has gone to town today, went yesterday also as 'tis court week. Gussie went to school today.

Wednesday 12th - I made Gussie a pair pants. Rained some this evening, we are needing rain badly. Gus likes to go to school very well. Mr. Henry gone to town.

Thursday 13th - Mr. Henry walks to town every day. He fell on the mill dam and hurt his side last week. He complains of it paining him a good deal now. It is very sore. I sewed some on Willie's pants. Mage Morris & Jennie Presley spent the evening here. We went to the mill to be weighed. Sidney weighs eighteen. I, 122.

Friday 14th - I finished Willie's pants & did some little jobs. Mr. Henry went to town again. We have company nearly every night, someone attending court.

Saturday 15th - I ironed all morning and did several things in the evening. Mr. Henry off to town again. He got Ella a hat and set of hoops. She is doing the best she can. I think she has a very bad temper, does not try to control it at all.

Sunday 16th - Mr. Henry, Zona & I and the baby spent the day at Sandy Bottom. We got very wet coming home, the baby and all. We needed the rain badly, especially in the garden. Henry Jones has been here all day, he and Matt are flying around considerable but I have no idea they will ever marry. She is only doing it for past time I think.

Monday 17th - I cut the children some clothes, sewed some on Zona's dress. I get along very slow. The baby is some hinderence and so is Eddie. Mr. Henry gone to town, court will adjourn tomorrow. Maj. Fulton is here tonight. No news of importance. Sallie Johnston died of consumption this morning in Asheville. Lou died the 9th May. Jennie had a premature birth last Thursday, seven months. I am glad I got rid of her before it happened. Lou Glenn went home last Saturday.

Tuesday 18th - Sidney is four months old today. He is growing very fast and a tollerable good child. Mr. Henry has gone to town. I sewed some on Zona's dress. Rained a little this morning.

Wednesday 19th - Mr. Henry went to Cochram's this morning to get some waggon timber. I have finished Zona's dress. Ella is washing today. I must stop as Sidney is crying. Matt helped Ella wash, she is a very poor washer, sloven at anything.

Thursday 20th - I sewed some on Pinck's pants yesterday evening and finished them today. Mr. Henry went to Cockram's yesterday and up in the Starnes settlement today. We had our first peas today.

Friday 21st - I ironed till dinner & then did some mending. Mr. Henry went to town this morning, came home to dinner. The children came home early from school. Mr. Jones run Lizzie right off from Pinck Ballew's yesterday morning for some bad conduct. She has lost a good home.

Saturday 22nd - I have several things. Mr. Henry & I went up to see Tena just before dinner, got some very nice strawberries and mulberries. I did some mending after dinner. We have some beans, enough for a mess I think.

Sunday 23rd - Rained all day. No one here but the children and I. Matt and Ella gone to Mary Night's, Mr. Henry off somewhere and Pinck and Willie gone after the cows. I must take the baby to the kitchen and warm it.

Monday 24th - Rained some today. I sewed some on Willie's pants and cut Hanes and Lonzo a coat. I want to make them this week.

Saturday 29th - I have been unwell for several days, had colic for two days and then headache. Doc Tidwell came here last Wednesday night, will only stay a few days. He speaks of going to Texas. I have made Hanes' coat and sewed some on Lonzo's. Mr. Henry is very busy on the farm. Grass grows fast such weather as this.

Sunday June 30 1867 - This has been a very warm day. Young Riley, a beau of Matt's, spent the day here. Mag Morris and Betsy came from church (at Sardis) to dinner. Peter Presley's baby was burried at Sardis today. Doc went but none of the rest of the family. Mr. Henry gathered us some cherries this evening. June apples are beginning to fall some.

July 1867

Monday July 1st - Very warm, we had a good rain this evening. I finished Lonzo's coat and sewed some of Gussie's pants. The children came home from school before dinner. Mrs. Ballew sick. Pinck and Willie went to the field since dinner. I imagine they will get very tired before night.

Tuesday 2nd - I spent the day at Mrs. Jones. Mrs. Ballew is quite sick with fever they think. We had a very heavy cloud and high wind, blew down several apple trees on the place. Had a very hard rain here. More than at Mr. Jones'. I had all the children with me but Pinck and Willie. Mr. Henry and Pinck came after us in the evening. Pinck brought Eddie & Gus. Willard came home with them & staid all night.

Wednesday 3rd - I feel very unwell this morning, have toothache and cold generally. I have been milking in the morning this week, I think is the cause of it. It is thundering about today. I think we will have more rain. Sidney is very fretful today. The children enjoyed themselves finely yesterday romping over Mr. Jones' new house.

Thursday 4th - I have finished Gussie's pants and sewed some on Pinck's. Mr. Henry went to town. Mrs. Ballew is no better. The children went to school to Ellen Hawkin's today. She is teaching at the Miller Meeting House. The negroes have a celebration in town today.

Friday 5th - Mr. Henry went to town this morning. I finished Pinck's pants yesterday and sewed some on Zona's dress. I finished it today. No news of importance.

Saturday 6th - I have done up odds and ends all day. Mr. Henry about generally. He did not come home tonight till supper. Capt. Howell stays here tonight.

Sunday 7th - This has been a very warm day. We had our first apple dumplings for dinner. The June apples are very nice now. Mont Stradly & Jack Humphries eat dinner here. They left soon after dinner. Mr. Henry in the house all day.

Monday 8th - Ella washed her clothes this evening. She is going to town tomorrow to get her a home. I hope she may do well. I have done some mending. Sidney fretful, wants to be nursed. 'Tis so every Monday.

Tuesday 9th July 1867 - I have mended some, fixing some skirts for Eddie. Mr. Henry about the farm and sawmill. Pinck is at home today, hoeing some and nursing the baby some. Zona cried when she found Pinck was not going to school. I was so sorry for her. Willie and Gus went with her.

Wednesday 10th - I am still fixing old clothes. Kate has washed today. The children all gone to school. Ella left yesterday. Matt and I are doing the work. Dave Luther and his wife were here to hire today. Mr. Henry thinks of hiring them. They are to come back tomorrow. Tena is milking for me this week, began last Sunday evening. Mrs. Ballew is improving.

Thursday 11th - My head aches badly this evening. Luther and wife set in to work today. She seems to be a neat but very ignorant woman. Mr. Henry about the farm. The children all at school.

Friday 12th - I have been in bed nearly all day with headache. It is some better this evening. We had a very good rain this evening which was needed. Pinck went to Sandy Bottom and did not get back till near sun down. The other children all at home as Zona had to tend the baby.

Saturday 13th - I am very tired tonight as I have helped scour and scald. Kate and Mrs. Luther did most of the hard work. Pinck went to town and got some sugar, salt and coffee. Mr. Henry about the house all day as his back is giving him some pain.

Sunday 14th - Mrs. Ballew is worse. I want to go and see her this evening if it does not rain. Mont Stradly is here now. Matt is not very well. Mrs. Luther is making a very good and neat hand.

Monday 15th - I have been fixing a skirt for my self. I have read some, a novel "Wild Jack" and other stories by Mrs. Hentz. She is a very chaste writer.

Tuesday 16th - Nothing of importance going on in the country. The "Red Strings"[56] still hold their meetings at Tom Candler's. They have negroes and horse thieves generally. Oh! that God would give our enemies better hearts.

Wednesday 17th - Very warm, needing rain. People generally done cutting wheat, it is very good this year. Mr. Henry went to Charlie Pendland's to get some

---

[56] Also known as The Hero's of America, The Red Strings were identified by a red string worn on the lapel, and were organized to protect Union sympathizers and their families, to furnish information to the Union and to organize Confederate opposition. Source: "The Heroes of America" by J. G. de Roulhac Hamilton, *Publications of the Southern History Association*, Volume XI, 1907

turnip seed. The children all gone to school. Eddie is very quiet when they are gone.

Thursday 18th - Sidney is not so well, his bowels running off. I think 'tis his teeth. I have mended some and ironed some. I warped my first piece of cloth yesterday, some sheets. Tena is weaving them, they are filled with flax.

Friday 19th July 1867 - I have mended some. It seems like my patching will never be done with. I don't murmur for my kind good husband is not able to buy what we need now. The war dealt badly with us. It may all be for the best but we are short sighted. Mortals can't see it.

Saturday 20th - This is Pinck's birthday, he is eleven years old. What change has come to us since then. We had plenty of everything then and now we are not able to buy our necessaries. That summer, we had a house full of boarders. Times insatiable can still roll hard on us, at least it has brought us hard times.

Sunday 21st - We have had a good deal of company today. Betsy came down and brought Mrs. Johnston, Lou Glenn and Rach Jones. Mr. Tom Cook and wife spent the day here also. I went to see Love Knight this evening. She was confined last Friday, has a son.

Monday 22nd - Cut Pinck and Willie some pants, sewed some on Willie's. Sidney is fretful, his bowels are still loose. I am not so well, have a cold. The days are very warm and the nights cool. Mr. Henry about the farm, his back has got well. He has had a very bad boil on his left temple, it is running now and not so painful.

Tuesday 23rd - I have finished Willie's pants and picked some wool. I want to send it to the carding machine this week. My head aches a little from the cold I have. I must stop now and write Pinck some copies.

Wednesday 24th - I have picked wool all day. Matt helped some. Sidney is fretful today. Mr. Henry gone up towards Pettit's to get some waggon timber.

Thursday 25th - I am still picking wool. No news of importance. Ellen came home with the children this evening. June apples are nearly gone.

Friday 26th - Mrs. Plott came here this morning on her way home to Haywood. She has been in town a day or two. Mary Johnston was brought home a corpse last night. That is the third grown daughter that has died in the last three months. They have been sadly afflicted.

Saturday 27th - Pinck went home with Mrs. Plott. He is to come back tomorrow. Mr. Henry about the farm. I have done odds and ends all day. We are needing rain badly.

Sunday 28th - Very warm this morning but no prospects of rain. Mr. Henry speaks of going to Miller Meeting House to hear Gen. Martin preach this evening. He is an Episcopal.

August 1867

August 18th Sunday night - Nothing of note has transpired since last I wrote. I finished picking my wool. Olsie Sutten is with me now. Mrs. Luther only staid four weeks. William Tidwell & wife came here last Friday, they are going to Eliza's tomorrow. Sallie Johnston & her brother came with them. William has a sweet babe. Jennie Presley died last Sunday night. I went on Monday and helped make her shrouding. She looked very badly. Charlie takes her death very hard. I am sorry for him. Mr. A. B. Jones has been sorely afflicted in his family. They are all improving now. Newt Taylor came this evening. We went out to preaching at Miller Meeting House, did not get there till preaching was over. The children have not been going to school for more than a week as they have been helping to dry fruit. I want them to go this week as I have a good deal of fruit dried and my wool picked. The children are all asleep but Eddie, he is here playing around me. 'Tis bed time so I must stop.

September 1867

Monday Sept. 2nd - Nothing of interest has transpired since I last wrote. I have been so busy I have neglected my journal. William & Co. left for home last Monday morning. Matt spent last week at Glenn's. The children are at home today. Pinck has gone down on New Found with one of the Reves boys to take a cow. Mr. Boyd came this morning to fix the sawmill. Mease is tending it now. Mr. Henry about the mill today. Olsie has been here four weeks tomorrow. I want to make Pinck a pair pants today. Henry Jones got cut on the eye brow badly last week by a rock thrown at him by Jess Summer. We have had some very cool days, it feels like Autumn is near us. That is the time of year that I have the blues. I want to die in fall when all around looks dreare. I had a very severe headache nearly three weeks ago. I expect I shall die in some of them. If it is my Heavenly Father's will, I will try to be resigned. I would be very sorry to leave my kind husband and dear little children but "He doeth all things well." Help me Oh! Lord to be willing to go at Thy call.

Sunday night Sept. 22nd 1867 - I have again neglected my journal. I would leave it off entirely if it were not for Mr. Henry & the children. He is anxious that I should keep it up. It will be a great source of pleasure to my children in coming years. Nothing of note has transpired. We have a boarder, an old man Mr. Malloy. He is very pleasant. Olsie left today, is not coming back again. I am sorry of it as it makes it very hard on me. The children are very good to help, Zona minds the baby. Pinck often says "Mother you shant work when I get to be a man. I will buy a buggy and take you about every day." He is a noble hearted boy. Willie & Gus carry chips & go the Spring house with me. Zona gets tired of nursing at times but is generally very kind to Sidney. She is trying to read tonight in Rose Clark but Jeff keeps waking Sidney. The other children are all abed. Mr. Henry has Eddie in the piazza talking to Mr. Malloy. I suppose Eddie is asleep. Matt went up to Glenn's today, will spend the week. Kate has milked one week last Friday since I paid her. I owe her for four days washing. Zona wants me to read some in my journal to her. She will not prize it now as she will when she is grown. I pray God to spare my life to my dear children and my loving husband.

Monday 23rd - I sewed some, Sidney's apron, did not finish it. It really seems I get nothing done. I kept Zona at home to mind the baby for me. Mr. Henry hired Mary Hoback today, she came in time to get dinner. The other children went to school.

Tuesday 24th - I had the wool washed. Mr. Henry did not have all the sheep sheared as it is getting late to clip. Mrs. Snider sheared three days. I finished Sidney's apron & darned Mr. Henry's coat. He is about the farm every day.

Wednesday 25th - Cool mornings and nights. Mr. Henry is rather inclined to asthma, had a touch of it last night. It has been about a year since he first felt it. I do pray he may not have consumption. Oh! life would be so cheerless without his bright loving face to me. He is all the world to me. I hope he may live to help me raise our dear children. We have a very interesting little family.

Tuesday 26th - Mary is making a very good hand, does things neatly. I have sewed some on a dress for the baby. He is fretful so I get along slowly. Mr. Henry and Mr. Malloy have gone to Spring Creek. Mr. Henry went to a turnpike meeting and Mr. Malloy went to see the country. They are to return Saturday. Doc Tidwell came last night. He is going to take some sheep home with him.

Friday 27th - This is the last day of Mrs. Ballew's school. Zona is sorry as she is very fond of her. She is too indulgent to the children I think.

Saturday 28th - Mr. Henry and Mr. Malloy came home this evening. Mr. Malloy is very tired. I don't think his trip paid him for the fatigue. I have done odds and ends all day.

Sunday 29th - Mary went home last night. Mr. Henry hired another girl today. Some people that are packing about through the country. I hope she may be contented to stay Sunday as well as any other day. Mr. Malloy leaves tomorrow. We had an application for board yesterday but I thought we could not take him well. Mr. Henry, Zona & Gussie went to preaching at the Academy. Rev. Miller preached old Mr. Muse's funeral. Pinck and Willie have gone to Sandy Bottom for Matt.

Monday 30th - Mr. Malloy left for home this evening. I have sewed some on Sidney's dress and wrote a letter for Matt. I have several letters of my own to answer but I put if off every week till I have more time, till it seems I will never get through being busy. A woman with six little ones has but little time for writing. Mr. Henry about the farm all day.

October 1867

Tuesday Oct. 1st - Cool mornings. I fear we will have frost soon. Doc is still here. Ann is doing very well, tries to please. The children are not at school this week, they start next week to George Penley. Doc went with me to Peter Luther's to carry some thread and indigo. We came home before night, found Dr. Hardy here. Mr. Henry sent for him this morning to see the baby, his bowels are very loose. Teething I think. Mr. Henry thinks a great deal of his children.

Wednesday 2nd - I sewed some on Siddie's dress. Gussie went to town with Doc and got him a pair of shoes. He is delighted with the trip. Mrs. Sutton finished picking wool by dinner today.

Thursday 3rd - Nothing of importance going on. Cool morning but no frost yet. Mr. Henry about the farm. I finished Siddie's dress. Col. Coleman came here this evening, he has been drinking and is sick from it.

Friday 4th - Col. Coleman is some better today. I sewed some on Sidnie's apron or finished it rather. His bowels are improving. Zona is a very good nurse, gets tired occasionally as any child would. I will miss her next week when they go to school.

Saturday 5th - This has been a day of odds and ends as usual. I made some loaf bread, not very nice. We are out of lard and it is better than tough bread. We get new corn meal at the mill now.

Sunday 6th - Mr. Henry and I spent the day at Sandy Bottom, took Eddie and Siddie. Eddie enjoyed it finely. Mr. Henry took Eddie and I over the river in a canoe. He seemed to enjoy it very much. We came home before night. Cool this evening. Zona and Pinck went to a Sunday School celebration at Sardis yesterday. They were anxious that I should go. I imagine they would have enjoyed it more. The children, Pinck, Zona and Willie will start to school this week. I will not send Gussie for awhile as he is not learning much and is most too small. The baby is nearly well.

Oct. 22nd Tuesday - Nothing of note has transpired. The children went to a Circus in Asheville, they were delighted with the riding. I went over with them and kept Eddie at Mollie's. They will remember the show a long time. Mr. Henry took them. He got home from Clay Co. last Saturday, was gone some ten days. We were very glad to have him at home again. He is so kind to the children and they repay all his love in kindness. I pray I may never raise an ungrateful child. I do my duty to them I think, and trust them to my Father in Heaven. Newt Taylor and Doc left for Clay this morning. We will make molasses this week, the children have been cutting cane today. They go to school at Sand Hill to Mr. G. Penley, have been going two weeks. They do not like him much, he is too strict they say. Ann is still with me, makes a very good hand.

Wednesday 23rd - I have been putting an old quilt together. Mr. Henry about the molasses furnace. No news of importance. Very cool this evening. We had the first ice this morning. The children are not going to school this week. We are having beautiful weather, warm and pleasant through the day but cool at night. I generally have the blues this time of year when all nature goes through such a change. I sigh to think all things must decay.

Thursday 24th - I have read and knit most of the day "Rose Lee," a novel I borrowed of Mollie. 'Tis the most natural work of fiction I ever read. Mr. Henry objects to my reading such but does not scold me much.

Friday 25th - Cousin James Robert Love spent the night with us last Wednesday night. He is not so haughty as he once was. I have had headache all day. I sewed some on a quilt. Mr. Henry attending the molasses making.

Sunday 27th - We have had two days of rain, it was badly needed by farmers. I suffered all day yesterday with my head, in bed most of the day. Zona attended the baby very carefully. Mr. Henry insists on me writing to Sister Frank tonight so I must stop as it is near nine now. He has been napping today or he would be in bed.

Monday 28th - Mr. Henry making molasses, made some very nice today, the cane soured some. Some rain this morning.

Tuesday 29th - Mr. Henry at the cane mill all day. I have put a quilt together. The children at home. Pinck helping with the cane. Zona tends Sidney. I expect he will be fretful when she goes to school again.

Wednesday 30th - Mr. Henry up till near ten o'clock with the molasses. I am still quilt making.

Thursday 31st - Mr. Henry started to Pa's this morning to try to get some money. I hope he may be successful as he needs it badly. He will return next week. How I wish I could go with him. I hope to go soon.

November 1867

Friday Nov. 1st - Tom and John Hendrix are at work here yesterday and today. Tom has put up the apples, we some very nice ones. I have been mending yesterday and today. Matt is helping me.

Nove 2nd Saturday 1867 - Sidney's jaw is swollen some this morning. He did not rest well last night. Ann has gone home this evening. Mary Night stays with us tonight. Tom and Hendrix have left.

Sunday 3rd - Sidie rested very badly last night. I did not sleep any till three o'clock, his ear looks red. I fear it will beal. Mary Rollins spent the day with us. Mrs. Luther stays here tonight.

Monday 4th - I fixed up some fruit and flour and sent it to Asheville by Doc Muse. He is going to Weaver's after our rolls. We got our cane done last Saturday. Uncle Sam is making his now. I took them their dinner, they seemed very proud of it.

Tuesday 5th - I finished fixing Eddie's red flannel dress and cut Gussie two shirts. Matt is helping. I got some sugar and coffee, some shirting and linen and some drilling for the stuff. I sent to Asheville.

Wednesday 6th - I finished one of Gussie's shirts & sewed some on the other one. Mrs. Ellerson is here spinning today, began last night. We have our hands full feeding now. Mr. Henry is gone. Uncle Sam put the hogs up Monday morning.

Thursday 7th - I began a shirt for Mr. Henry. Matt and I got dinner as Ann is washing. Mrs. Ellerson spinning. The children have been at school all the week. Siddie is fretful, wants me to nurse him all the time. His jaw has got well. He has a sore thumb, I think the nail will come off. It is some better now. I have a sore arm. I burnt it last Monday morning. Ann did not come back till we had breakfast all on. She is not very truthful I think.

Friday 8th - I went to meet Mr. Henry yesterday evening. Waited at the mill dam till the moon began to cast shadows and then had to return alone and sadly disappointed. I do hope he is well.

Saturday 9th - I went yesterday evening again to meet my dear husband and was again disappointed but he came after eight and Mr. Glenn Peake with him. Ann fixed some supper for them. They were all well at home. Mr. Henry did not get any money. I can't see how we are to get along. I hope for the best. The darkest hour is just before day. May it be so with us.

Sunday 10th - Some rain this morning. Mr. Henry and Mr. Peake went to church at Sand Hill but preaching was at Sardis so they came on back. Matt and I got most of the dinner. Ann went home yesterday after dinner. Her mother came in her place today. Pinck and Gus gone to Sandy Bottom. Some rain today.

Monday 11th Nove 1867 - Cold and windy. Mr. Henry and Mr. Peake went to town as it is court week. We generally have company every night at court. I have sewed some on a shirt for Mr. Henry. No news of importance going on. Siddie is not so fretful as he was last week. He has none yet. He can get about over the floor but does not crawl.

Tuesday 12th - Mr. Henry and Mr. Peake went to town and came home about three o'clock. More pleasant today than yesterday. The children go to school, they like Mr. Penly very well. Sidney is a little fretful today. I have sewed some on Mr. Henry's shirt. I get on slowly at work when I attend the baby.

Wednesday 13th - Mr. Peake left for home this morning. Mr. Henry off to town again. Mag Morris spent the evening here. Willie at home today. I won't send him any more till I can make him some pants.

Thursday 14th - Mrs. Ellerson washed today. Matt did the cooking. Ann came back before dinner. Mrs. Ellerson left this evening. Mr. Miller & brother stay here tonight. I finished the shirt and spun some.

Friday 15th - I have spun all day. Ann's little sister tended the baby. I am very tired tonight and did not spin much over three cuts. It would be a poor living I could make spinning.

Saturday 16th - I made Gus a pair drawers and moulded some candles. Pinck went to the Bottom before dinner and went to meet Mr. Henry after dinner as he walked to town this morning.

Sunday 17th - Ten years ago my little Cora was born. If she had lived, her and Zona would have been a great deal of company to each other. Zona asks me often to buy her a little sister. I would have been so glad if she had lived. I know Zona will feel lonely when she grows up. She has a play house she plays in when little girls come to see her. Mr. Henry went to preaching at Sand Hill today. Says he heard a good exortation (Universalist) from Mr. G. Penly. He is a methodist. I tried to milk this evening as Ann had not come. She took Harriet home this evening. The cows kicked so I could not do anything with them. Red muley had a calf last Friday. We will soon get milk in abundance. We get but little now. Mr. Henry lanced Sidney's gums this evening. I hope he will get well now. He has been feverish all day.

Monday 18th 1867 Nov - I have been spinning all day, get on slowly. Harriet, Ann's sister, is staying here now. She tends Eddie. Willie has not been going to school in some time. Tom Muse began to work here today at fifty cts. per day.

Tuesday 19th - Tom Quin is working here also. I have spun some today. Muse and George killed one of the hogs in the pen by the kitchen. It is a nice hog. I have fed them a good deal. The children call them my hogs.

Wednesday 20th - Mr. Henry has been to Asheville every day this week, till today. The negroes vote yesterday and today, convention or no convention. I am still spinning, get on very slowly. Siddie has his two first teeth.

Harper's Weekly 1867 illustration of
newly freed slaves registering to vote in Asheville, NC
(North Carolina Collection, Pack Memorial Public Library, Asheville, NC)

Thursday 21st - Ann made the sausage meat yesterday and rendered out the lard. It is beautiful. Mr. Henry wants to send it to town. He has gone to the election today.

Friday 22nd - I am fixing some gowns short for Siddie. Mr. Henry took the lard to town today got 25 cts. per lb.

Saturday 23rd - This as usual has been a busy day. Mr. Henry and I went to see Mrs. A. B. Jones this morning. She is very sick with ulcer of the liver. We brought home our calves that Mr. Jones had taken to the mountains for us.

Sunday 24th - Mr. Henry about home all day. Ann went home after dinner, came back to milk and do the other night work.

Monday 25th - Tena brought the thread home this morning. I will warp it tomorrow. Mr. Henry has hands gathering the corn. Ruff Miller is helping.

Tuesday 26th - I am still fixing up gowns for Siddie. Mr. Henry about the farm. George is tending the sawmill. I warped the cloth before dinner today, beamed it and Matt put it through the harness in flats. Mr. Neilson, Billie & Capt. Wilkes stay here tonight. Billie looks badly. Mr. Neilson wants to move back to Tenn., if Sister Jane is willing.

Wednesday 27th - We are having beautiful weather, so warm and pleasant. I got the cloth started by dinner. Mrs. Muse (Tom's wife) is weaving. She does not understand weaving. I do the quilling. I do so many little things when night comes I can't see what I have done.

Thursday 28th Nov 1867 - Nothing of interest going on. Old Mr. Night is very sick at Willey's. I am still fixing drawers for Eddie. Some rain yesterday. Rene Ellerson is spinning, began last Wednesday.

Friday 29th - Rained all day. Nannie Jones came home with the children last night. They enjoyed them selves finely playing blind fold.

Saturday 30th - Mr. Henry went to town. Got his coat cut and did some trading. Very cold wind from the North. Betsy came this evening. I have done several things and nothing much either.

December 1867

Sunday Dec 1st - Christmas will soon be here. I want to make the children a Christmas tree. They will enjoy it I think. I try to give them all the pleasure I can. Yes, let them enjoy life while they are young, cares come with age. Very cold today, the first ice in the room.

Monday 2nd - Mary Muse came this morning to spin. Her and Rene are spinning tonight, Matt went home with Betsy this morning. More pleasant today. Mr. Henry about the farm all day. I am quilting him a coat lining.

Tuesday 3rd - Mrs. Muse got out the cloth this morning. Miller and Quin killed my other hog this evening. Mr. Henry think it has fallen off a good deal since it's mate was killed. I finished the coat lining this evening.

Wednesday 4th - Sewed on the coat all day. It will be a very warm one I think, when I get it done. He needs it badly.

Thursday 5th - I have not sewed much today. Mr. Henry and I reeled some after dinner, he held the breach. He helps me at anything he can, winds all my knitting balls.

Friday 6th - Finished Mr. Henry's coat this evening. He wants to go to town tomorrow. We have had pleasant weather all week.

Saturday 7th - Mr. Henry went to town. Matt came home this evening. Laura Glenn came home with her. Cool today. I have been cleaning in the kitchen, Rene helping. Mary went home yesterday evening. Ann spinning.

Sunday 8th - Mag Morris and Sallie Jones spent the day here. Cold all day. Nothing of importance. Rev. Byrd and Sophia Jones married a short time ago. Some other old maid will step off soon.

Monday Dec. 9th 1867 - Cold and fair. I cut the children some pants, sewed some on Mr. Henry's pants. Matt helped me some.

Tuesday 10th - Very pleasant today. Mr. Henry went to town this morning. Pinck and Zona go to school every day. Willie will go no more this winter.

Wednesday 11th - Laura Glenn still here. She is anxious to go home. Mary Rollins and Mrs. Miller spent the evening here helping make the children's pants. I finished Mr. Henry's.

Thursday 12th - Pinck went to Sandy Bottom. Laura went home with him. Rained some after dinner, turned very cold. Dying some thread. Mary Rollins been here sewing on my dress. I cut it this morning.

Friday 13th - I finished the children's pants. Some snow last night. Mr. Henry moved the eating table in my room as it is very cold in the dining room for the children. The children did not go to school this morning as it was so cold.

Saturday 14th - I have done odds and ends all day. We have only eat twice a day yesterday and today. The children seem to like it very well. Siddie wants to try to walk. He likes to pull up by anything. Harriet is still here. Siddie does not like for her to nurse him.

Sunday 15th - Very cold today. Some snow last night three inches deep. My head aches a good deal tonight. Mr. Henry is playing with Siddie. I must go to bed. Siddie has another tooth, Mr. Henry just found one below.

Monday 16th - Still cold, a bad time on stock as we have neither cow nor sheep house. Mr. Henry is going to have shelters made for them soon. Mrs. Sutton and Ann spooling. I have been sewing on my dress. Pinck and Zona at school today. We only eat twice a day now.

Tuesday 17th - They finished spooling this evening and I finished my dress. It fits neatly. Matt is getting ready to marry the sixteenth of next month. Mr. Henry about the farm and mill. George is employed there again. It is a great trial for me, knowing how he has treated us. I never can forget it but I can't help myself.

Wednesday 18th - Mary Rollins warped my cloth for me today. I tended the spools and knit some. More pleasant today. I am glad of it as it is so cold for the children to go to school. Mr. Henry and Mr. Miller went bird netting this morning but caught none.

Thursday 19th - I have been helping Mary Rollins put in the cloth nearly all day. They killed three hogs. Ann got vexed today, wanted to quit but did not. I have been vexed all day about George being at the mill. The children have a holiday till after Christmas.

Friday 20th - I have sewed some on Pinck's coat but did not get it done. We have beautiful weather now.

Saturday 21st - Nothing new going on. All are well. Mr. Henry about the mill all day. Mrs. Sutton is weaving.

Sunday 22nd - Mr. Henry went to church at the Academy. Matt and I doing the work today as Ann went home yesterday evening. She came back this evening.

Monday 23rd - Ann scoured the house below stairs, I helped some. Pinck gone to Sandy Bottom today. Mrs. Ellerson and Rene washing today.

Tuesday 24th - Mr. Henry and Matt went to town. Matt to get some wedding things. I took all the children to Capt. Moore's to get their photographs. I had mine and Siddie's taken in a nice case for Christmas gift for Papa. I think he will appreciate it. I have fixed the children a Christmas tree and decorated them a table. Pinck, Zona, Willie and Bettie Moore went to see the Christmas tree at Miller's Meeting House. They came back well pleased. The school boys came serenading tonight, made a great noise but little music. Pinck went off with them. The children are well pleased with their Christmas tree. Mr. Henry has seen his present and is well pleased with it. Gus has some glass marbles, so has Willie and Eddie. I try to have little things for my children to please them. Christmas comes but once a year. They will remember their tree a long time. They will soon be grown. I will not have many more years to please their childhood in.

Wednesday 25th - Willie, Gussie and Eddie are delighted with their glass marbles. Matt and I sit up till near 11 o'clock last Monday night, fixing for the children. They will appreciate it some day. I had to whip my dear little daughter today for a trifle. I hate it so much. She is a good child when she tries. Pinck staid at Capt. Moore's last night after the serenade. I have been at work all day cooking. Being gone yesterday, Ann and Rene did not prepare enough. I gave most of it to the serenaders. Mary Rollins and Mrs. Sutton helped some. Rene here today. Ann went home this morning, to be back tomorrow. Betsy, Laura Glenn and Matt went to Capt. Moore's to have their photographs taken. Betsy & Laura staid here last night, they have gone to Ham Cannon's tonight. This has been a very pleasant day, Spring like. I don't think I ever saw it so pleasant at this season in Buncombe. Goodbye Christmas of 1867. You are numbered among the things that are past.

Thursday 26th - Very pleasant. I have had no fire all day. Siddie has crawled out on the piazza several times. He has been crawling a month. He is a very good babe. Pinck and Zona went home with Bettie Moore. She has spent Christmas with Zona.

Friday 27th - I began a linsey dress for Zona, want to finish it tomorrow. Mr. Henry about the mill today. Still very pleasant. I have hired Rene at 50 cts. per week (fifty-cents) and Ann the same.

Saturday 28th - A traveler stays here tonight. I finished Zona's dress tonight. We get on very well on two meals a day. I give the children a lunch about one o'clock.

Sunday 29th - Mr. Henry and I took a long walk to salt some cattle. Came back by Mary Night's. Her baby is very sick but some better today. Cool and cloudy today. Mr. Henry has Siddie. He is so fretful. I will go to bed with him.

Monday 30th - The old year will soon be numbered among the things that were. Mr. Henry about the mill. We have had very pleasant weather for the time of year, till now. I wove some this morning on mine and Zona's balmorals. Matt is going to weave them while I make her wedding chimise. Snowing nearly all day.

Tuesday 31st - I cut Pinck and Willie some shirts, sewed some on Pinck's. Siddie can pull up by a chair. The children did not go to school on account of the snow. Willie has not been going in some time as I thought Mr. Penley too harsh with him.

1868

"...If it were not for hope, how gloomy this world would be..."

January 1868

Wednesday January 1st 1868 - Farewell to the old year, you are forever gone. What may the new year bring us? Health and contentment I hope. I think I am grateful for the blessing of health. I try to be.

Thursday 2nd 1868 - I have been at work for Matt all day. She finished my weaving this evening. The children at home on account of bad weather.

Friday 3rd - Nothing of interest going on. All are well. Very cold and disagreable.

Saturday 4th - Pinck went to the Bottom. Betsey is not making much now.

Tuesday 7th - I had the headache very bad Sunday and yesterday. I feel feeble today but wove a yd. and half and cut the cloth out. The children went to school this morning. They like to go.

Wednesday 8th – I cut some bodies for Eddie and Gussie. I am going to put pants on Eddie's. May Rollins sewed for me today, she is a neat hand.

Thursday 9th - Matt, Kate and Ann washing. Matt washing up things generally. Mr. Henry took the children to have their ambrotypes taken. Turned very cold this evening. Rene washed up my room. I have been sewing on Eddie's body. I asked Mr. Henry to have his type taken for me. He did with Eddie in his lap but told the children not to tell me. We are devotedly attached to each other.

Friday 10th - The clothes all frozen. The children went to school. Got Mr. Henry's type, it is very good one of Eddie also. I am so proud of them.

Saturday 11th - Pinck went to the Bottom. Very cold. Matt drying the clothes by the fire as she is expecting company next week. I finished mine and Zona's skirts & Eddie's pants. My skirt feels very comfortable. Zona is very much pleased with hers. Tom Quin has left us, lice and all. I am glad of it.

Monday 13th - I was sick with headache yesterday. I have wove all day. Got two yds. of Zona's dress done. I like to weave very well, 'tis good exercise.

Tuesday 14th - Rene tends the baby, Ann does the quilling. I have wove two yds. Mr. Ruff Miller accidently killed a little pig, I had it cleaned. It is very nice to bake.

Wednesday 15th - Matt got very angry with me about the children wasting her chalk, packed up her things to leave right away. If she don't mind, she will be sitting up in the cool like Mag Morris. I have been weaving. The children weary me a good deal about my weaving. Eddie has no pants, he looks so small.

Thursday 16th - Matt was to have been a bride today but the man has failed to come. I suppose he did not get the letter. Very cold tonight. Kirkendoll and Jess Case stay here tonight. I have wove all day. Ten years ago I did not think I would weave cloth for my children. Things have changed somewhat with us the last twelve years.

Friday 17th - Willie and Gussie's types are very natural, so is Pinck and his grand Pa whose picture he has in his hands. Matt has not spoken to me yet. I may let her pout it out.

Saturday 18th - I finished what weaving I am going to do. Mrs. Muse will finish the piece. I have done some mending tonight.

Sunday 19th - More pleasant today than for several days. Thursday the coldest night of the season. It was all we could do to keep warm in bed. I sleep with Siddie in my arms every cold night and Mr. Henry takes Eddie in his. Siddie has four teeth, can push a chair across the room and walk after it. Kate and Bud Night are here. The children are enjoying the night finely in the kitchen. Ann is nursing Siddie who is asleep. I will stop and try to put him down. Mr. Henry is sitting by me reading. I won't hear to my giving up my journal. He is so kind to me and the children. I thank my Creator for such a loving husband.

Monday 20th - I have spent the day in mending. Siddie is very fretful. Willie tries to amuse him. He can push a chair across the room. No news of importance going on.

Tuesday 21st - Mary Rollins here today helping me sew for some wool. We are making Willie and Pinck some shirts. Siddie is very fretful, has fever every night. The children are very fond of going to school. Zona has gone home with Nannie Jones tonight, late when Pinck came home. Mr. Henry about the mill every day. George pays up his rent very well, is some behind in wheat.

Wednesday 22nd - Siddie has yellow thrash. That accounts for his being so cross. He has an ugly sore on his gums. I get but little done, he is so fretful. Ann washing some. The weather has been so bad I have not had washing done in two weeks. Some snow on the ground yet.

Thursday 23rd Jan 1868 – Siddie's mouth is getting better. Mr. Henry about the mill. He has rented the sawmill and part of the work shop to Cannon and Knight. I hope his mills may profit him a good deal this year. He is renting his land for standing rent altogether this year.

Friday 24th - The children came home early from school. They ride when it is muddy. They enjoy it finely. Zona has a great notion of riding by herself. She is growing very fast now. Willie is very sensitive, thinks he is ugly. It wounds his pride. He is very passionate. I hope to cure him of it when he gets older. Pinck and Gus have dispositions something alike. Eddie threw his shoe in the fire yesterday morning, burned it so he can't wear it. He has on an old one of Gussie's. He is very bad to throw things in the fire.

Monday 27th - I took the headache Saturday after dinner. Mr. Henry and I concluded yesterday to do without coffee and the consequence was that he was very sick Saturday night with headache. His good resolves all. Fell when he took sick so he started Pinck to town about two o'clock after some. He had got better before I got it ready so when he got up I went to bed with headache. I suffered all day yesterday and it has only gotten well since dinner today. We only eat twice a day. Some rain today.

Tuesday 28th - Warm and pleasant but very muddy. Mr. Henry about the mills all day. Siddie has got nearly well. I am so glad, I hate to see my little children suffer.

Wednesday 29th - I have sewed some on Pinck's pants. I tend Siddie so I can't get much done. We had a heavy fall of snow last night, the trees all laden with it. All the mountains have on their bridal robes, it is a beautiful scene. The children rode to school. They came back very cold. The bushes were so bent over the road. It has turned very cold since morning.

Thursday 30th - Very cold all day. A man stays here tonight, he has been walking all day in the snow. The children did not go to school this morning as it is so cold. Ice on the mill dam four inches thick, a hard matter to get the mill started on account of the ice.

Friday 31st- I sewed some on Zona's dress. Her and Pinck are at home, too cold to go to school. Last night the coldest this winter. More ice in the room on the water.

February 1868

Saturday Feb. 1st - Snow melting, some cold nights and bright days. Mr. Henry hired a negro named Joe last week. George Muse has been staying here some two weeks. He is a good conditioned child I think.

Sunday 2nd - Snow melting on the south sides slowly, still cold nights. Mr. Henry about the house all day. We have some few lambs, Buck killed one last week, he is a bad horse. I saw him running with Pinck today, it frightened me. I must stop now and take Siddie as Pinck is tired of him, I know. Mr. Henry and the children have gone to bed.

Monday 3rd - I sewed some on Gussie's body. Matt made Ann's skirt. Mr. Henry about the mill. He is very well pleased with the rent George pays. Snow melting slowly, still cold. We have had very bad weather for a month now. I will be so glad to hear the frogs for then I will think Spring is coming.

Tuesday 4th - I finished Gussie's body and sewed some on his pants. I get on with my sewing slowly, Siddie needs a heap of attention. I have headache this evening.

Wednesday 5th & Thursday 6th - I was quite sick all day yesterday with headache. Mr. Cook came here last Monday to mend shoes. He has mended a pair of Pinck's old boots for Gus. He is as proud of them as if they were new. Cook left yesterday. Mr. Henry comes to the house at one o'clock every day for something to eat. I generally keep pies or sweet bread for him and the children. I sewed some on Eddie's pants.

Friday 7th - I finished Eddie's pants and cut my saque. Mrs. Ellerson washed here, the clothes froze as she put them out. I fear that old woman will suffer for bread, she does not love to work. The children late getting home from school. I was getting anxious about them. Pinck had to cut wood for Monday. We are having bad luck with our lambs, have lost fourteen and have eleven living. We have the sheep down here, they are staying in the dry house. Mr. Henry has fixed a shed in front of it. Ham Rollins is working with Mr. Henry, makes a very good hand.

Saturday 8th Feb. 1868 - I finished my saque and did some mending. Mr. Henry sent Rollins to town. Got some sugar, coffee, tallow and nails. Still cold. A good deal of snow on the ground yet. It is very muddy. The children help me a good deal on Saturday. Zona tends the baby. She gets tired soon. I had her to feed Sidney at supper for telling a story. She told Pinck I said take the baby. It mortified her a great deal, they take it by turns feeding Sidney. Pinck and Zona have two lambs, they pay a great deal of attention to them. They feed them from a suck bottle.

Sunday 9th - Some rain last night, warm and very muddy. Elick came here last Friday night (one of Pa's slaves) going to Tenn. to Mr. Neilson. He moved back to Tenn. about a month ago. They did not come by to see us. I think they treated us badly. Elick says they are all well at home. Nothing of importance going on. Mr. Henry is getting sleepy so I must soon stop. The children are very attentive to their lambs. Siddie is afraid of them but Eddie and Gussie are delighted. Willie does not care much about them, he is more like an old man. Gus still holds on to the boots. Rained all day. Pinck has just got through washing. I will be glad when the itch gets out the country. As long as the children go to school they have it.

Monday 10th - I sewed some on Eddie's body. Baked some cakes before dinner for Mr. Henry to take with him as a lunch to court in Asheville. Zona's little lamb died today. Snow melting slowly.

Tuesday 11th - I did not finish Eddie's body. Siddie has been fretful today. Two men staid here last night from court. We generally have company at night Court week. The children ride to school every day when it is muddy. Nancy Hawkins came home with Zona last night and Mary Jones tonight. The children have a gay time when they have company. Mr. Henry went to town this morning, did not get home till night. He got some bleached domestic yesterday. Twenty five yds.

Friday 14th - I had the worst spell of headache last Wednesday I ever had. I thought I would die I was so sick. Mr. Henry was in town. Mary Rollins was sewing for me, it took her and Matt most of their time to hold my head. It is nearly well today. I am very thankful my life was spared.

Saturday 15th Feb. 1868 - Mr. Henry did not go to town yesterday nor today. He was greatly distressed when I told him how sick I was last Wednesday. I do hope my life may be spared to raise my children. It would be a sad, sad time they would have and Mr. Henry would miss me a great deal. He is so kind and affectionate. The Frank's cow had a calf today and Droop cow one last Sunday, the latter is not doing well.

Sunday 16th - Mag Morris and Sallie Jones came here yesterday evening and left since dinner. I got most of the dinner. Aunt Tena helped some. Ann went to see her mother today. Mr. Henry was sick last night with headache and is not well today. Zona burnt Eddie's privates last Thursday, it is a very ugly sore. I can't think it was intentional. He did rest well last night with it. Pinck had his first fight this evening with George Muse. I am sorry of it. I want to raise my boys up right if I can. I try to do my duty to them. Zona has the baby. I know she is tired so I must take him. Mr. Henry is better tonight, is reading. The other children have gone to bed some time.

Sunday 23rd - Nothing of importance has transpired for the last week. I have had a day of headache. Mr. Henry about the farm as we are having pleasant weather.

March 1868

Sunday March 1st - Ann Ellerson left last Monday. I hired Tempa the same day. The children's examination came off last Friday. I did not go in the day but went at night and enjoyed it finely. The children acted some tableaus very well. Tempa does not seem to want to stay here. Jennie has told her she could not stand the work. Matt and I have done the most of it this week. I do the milking and she the most of the cooking after breakfast. Tempa moved her things here Friday, she is not very stout. She has a boy Joe with her, he is some help. My head ached a good deal yesterday evening but easy today.

Monday 2nd - I finished Mr. Henry's vest I began Friday. Pinck went to writing school at Sand Hill, Mr. Waters teaching. Matt started but came back. Pleasant after the morning.

Tuesday 3rd - Matt went to her Mother's, not to return soon. Some snow on the ground, fell last night. Tempa sick all day. I have had everything to do. I am sorry Matt has gone. I know she will not be contented down there, she got in a fit. Poor girl, she has a very unhappy temper. Zona went to writing school with Pinck. Joe tended Siddie.

Wednesday 4th - Tempa able to do part of the things, I help some. I help get breakfast. Mr. Henry went to town yesterday, something concerning the rail road. He is about the farm today. Tena making soap for me today.

Thursday 5th - Tempa sick all day. I did all the things. Tena helped me milk this evening. I am real tired tonight. Mr. Henry went to town this morning.

Friday 6th - The children did not go to school as Mr. Waters went to Mag Morris' infare. She was married to Bill Hayes last night. Zona is a good deal of help about Siddie. He crawled up the steps last Monday, his first effort. He can take a step or two alone.

Saturday 7th - Mr. Henry and Pinck went to town. Mr. Henry has had headache tonight. Charley Penland and Mr. Smith are here tonight. I am very tired, I have been busy all day. Tempa had a slight chill this morning. Kate has come to milk for me a day or so till Tempa gets better.

Sunday 8th - Gussie is five years old today, this morning at twenty minutes after eight. The children all have bows and arrows today, they enjoy it finely. Mr. Henry has been gone all day to Tom Cook's. Very pleasant today, frogs hollering last night. Jeff has been sick several days. I think he is some better today. Pinck is tending Siddie. I know he is tired so I will take him.

Sunday 15th - Tempa left last Tuesday, gone to Tenn. I have been without a cook since. Willie tends Siddie and helps me a great deal. He and Gussie carry water and chips. Kate helps me milk in the evening and Mr. Miller in the morning. I get on very well. The children are done with their writing school. They start to Mr.

Barnes' tomorrow. I want to send Willie some. He is not fond of school like Pinck and Zona. I hope Mr. Barnes will be kind to him, he is very sensitive. Mr. Henry about the farm all the week. Charlie took Matt her trunk yesterday. Eliza sent us some cabbage and parsnips, they were very acceptable as we have none.

Monday 16th March 1868 - I have done little else but cook. Zona and Pinck like Mr. Barnes very well as a teacher. Mr. Henry about the farm all day. Doc Tidwell came here last Thursday on business for Taylor.

Tuesday 17th - Mr. Henry gone all day hunting a cook. He does not like for me to do so much drudgery. Willie went to school. I missed him a great deal about Siddie. Gussie and Eddie plays with him, they do their best they can. Mr. Henry did not get home till supper was over. I was uneasy about him. He brought Lizzie Cochran with him. I hope she may be satisfied.

Wednesday 18th - Lizzie has done very well today. I am very well pleased with her but she is so dissatisfied, wants to go home tomorrow. I have hemmed some frilling for mine and Zona's chemise. Mr. Henry about the farm all day.

Thursday 19th - The eleventh of this month was Willie's birthday, he was seven years old. He likes to go to school only tollerable. Lizzie left this morning and Mary Muse came in her place. Mr. Henry about the farm all day.

Friday 20th - We have had a day or so of right cold weather, some snow. Soon melted off, wind from the North. Willie did not go to school today, complained of being sick. Mary is doing very well, makes a tollerable neat hand. Mr. Henry about the farm all day.

Saturday 21st - This is Zona's birthday, she is nine years old this morning. She is a great deal of help to me. If my little Cora could have lived, they would have been a great deal of company for each other. Zona often tells me to buy her a little sister. Mr. Henry went to a mass meeting in Asheville. I very much fear the Radicals will beat us on negro equality. The people seem excited about it. I hope we will not have another war in my time. Lord have mercy on us and deliver us from wars in our midst. Very cold and high winds all day.

Sunday 22nd - Cool this morning but pleasant through the day. Mr. Henry about the house most of the day. The sows he got of Vance have pigs, two of them. He got the sows (3) last Monday I believe. I got dinner. Mary spent the day with her Mother. I have not been well for a week. Weakness in the back. Siddie has not been well for a day or two. He is very fretful.

April 1868

April 5th Sunday 1868 - Two weeks have glided by since I opened my journal to write. I have nothing of importance to write. The country seems to be in a great crisis. I hope for the white man's party but fear it will be voted down by the negroes and their equals. Mr. Henry seems some what excited about it. I have a cough that is giving me some anxiety, it has troubled me for a month. I would hate to have consumption. To think of leaving my little children is very sad to me. I want to live to raise them the best I can. I pray God to spare my life. They can never have another mother. Gussie is sick, worms I think. He has threw up four today. Pinck has gone to the Sandy Bottom since dinner. Siddie tries to walk, can walk half across the room and not fall. He is a good baby when well. The children don't like their teacher much, he keeps them in after school to learn their lessons. I am doing my household work myself now. Mary and Ann ran away last Thursday night. Ann had been back about a week. Till Ashley is to be here next Tuesday evening to do things generally. She seems to be a nice girl. Mr. Henry, Pinck, Zona and Willie went to picnic on Mount Yeadon yesterday. They enjoy it finely. I was at home all day with the three little children. Gussie is a heap of help to tend Siddie, bring chips &c. We have heavy frost every morning. I fear it will injure the fruit. High winds last night and today. I have headache this evening. Mr. Henry is lying on the trundle bed with Gussie and has Siddie. Zona is writing a letter, her first one. I wrote one for Pinck to Eugenia since dinner. Also a composition for him. He is to copy them. Willie and Eddie are out at play. I will go and see where they are.

Monday 6th - Mr. Henry and I were married thirteen years ago yesterday, things have changed since then. I have not regretted my choice and try to act so thay he may never regret his. He is a great deal kinder than my fond heart ever anticipated. We are both growing old, the bloom of life is fading with us like summer roses but not so with our love, it will ever be fresh and green.

Tuesday 7th April 1868 - Till Ashley came today after dinner. Rather cool. Mr. Henry got some sweet potatoes to plant yesterday. We had a few for dinner. They were very nice.

Wednesday 8th - Till washed, I have been fixing a dress. Mr. Henry is not at all well. Has headache for several days. The children have got to learning their lessons at night to keep from staying in. I like the teachers mode very much.

Thursday 9th - This day thirteen years ago, I bade a last adieu to the home of my childhood. Put my happiness in my dear husband's keeping. He has faithfully discharged his trust as far as it lay in his power. I am happier now than I was as a bride for I know him now to be a high toned gentleman. Then I did not. He was almost a stranger to me. When I think of it now I see how much we both risked.

Friday 10th - Siddie can walk. I am very proud of it. He only has five teeth. He is a dear good baby. Gussie has got well. He and Eddie play with Siddie for me. We have a boarder, Mr. Brock, he is going to school. Willie is learning very fast, also Pinck and Zona.

Saturday 11th - The children are a great help on Saturday. I have them out sweeping the yards. Pinck gets tired and says "Mother I see no use in it, they will get dirty again." It generally falls on Zona to mind Siddie. She does very well.

Sunday 12th - Rained nearly all day. Mr. Henry went up to the grave yard. He goes there often to see his friend's and baby's grave. We will all have to lay down in the cold grave some day. What a gloomy place it seems. I want to be burried near the house if I should die before Mr. Henry. He could see my grave often then and would not quite forget me. The children would plant flowers around me, I know.

Monday 13th - I have made a pair of candle mats and made two collars. Rained all day. The children did not go to school. Mr. Brock came this evening. Till is taking on about him wonderfully.

Tuesday 14th - The children went to school. Fair and pleasant. I made a pair candle mats and made a shirt bosom for Mr. Henry. The children got home from school sooner now than they did as Mrs. Barnes assists.

Wednesday 15th April 1868 - I sewed some on Mr. Henry's shirt. Rained again today, the children at home. Mr. Henry took some cattle to the mountains yesterday, did not get home till night. The children learn at home and I hear lessons when it is bad weather.

Thursday 16th - I finished Mr. Henry's shirt. The children at home again. Rained this morning but fair this evening. Betsey Jamison spent the day here. Mr. Henry about the mill most of the day.

Friday 17th - I made Zona two draw bodies. The children went to school. The earth must be very wet as it has rained a good deal. Mr. Henry and Miller floated some logs down for Stevens. They got home for dinner.

Saturday 18th - Pinck and I worked in the yard till dinner fixing up plank along the walk. I finished after dinner. Pinck and Willie went hunting. Pinck shot a rabbit, his first. He is very proud of it. Mr. Henry about the farm. Mrs. Linsey was here for dinner today.

Sunday 19th - I am very sore from my day's work yesterday. Tillda went home this morning to see her mother. I got dinner with the children's help. Cloudy and looks like rain. Mr. Henry has taken a nap since dinner, he has headache. My head aches some this evening. I must take Siddie now as Mr. Henry is not well. Zona reading "The Commandment With a Promise." Pinck learning his Quackenbo's. Willie with him in the kitchen, Eddie asleep and Gussie is here by the fire.

Monday 20th and Tuesday 21st - I was sick all day yesterday with headache. It did not get entirely well till today after dinner. I had to keep Zona at home today. It rained yesterday so the children could not go.

Wednesday 22nd - Eddie is three years old today. My own dear mother died this day nineteen years ago. I did not think what I had lost then, I can appreciate it now. We cannot appreciate our blessings till they past and gone and then we begin to think of them.

Thursday 23rd - I have finished fixing my dress today. I will have to wear it every day as we are not able to get any now. The children came home from school this morning about eleven as Mrs. Barnes is too ill for Mr. Barnes to leave her. I am really sorry for them, they are comparative strangers here. Mr. Henry about the farm all day. This has been rather an exciting time as the state has voted to see if the negroe's constitution is to be ratified.

Friday 24th April 1868 - Mr. Henry went to town today. He is afraid the radicals have beat us. I don't think they would give us justice if the conservatives were to gain the day. I have been busy cleaning the yard and cellar till dinner. After dinner I cut a pair pants for Mr. Henry.

Saturday 25th - I scoured some today and baked some after dinner. Cloudy since dinner with some rain. Mr. Henry about the farm. Nothing of importance. Mrs. Barnes is no better.

Sunday 26th - Mr. Henry and I spent the day at Capt. Moore's. Mrs. Barnes is still very sick. I feel very sorry for her little children. Mr. Barnes tried so hard to get her to take some medicine but she refuses. I thought her very obstinate. Some rain this evening. The children are having a gay time playing. Kate Night is here.

May 1868

Monday May 11th - Two weeks has past since I last wrote, nothing of interest has transpired. Mr. Henry was on the road all last week working it out. The children have not been at school for two weeks. Mrs. Barnes is improving now slowly. School begins next week. Till Ashely left last Sunday, had been sick since Wednesday before. Mary Muse is staying here now. Mrs. Muse dyed some blue and copperas last week. Aunt Tena died the 2nd of May, only sick a few days. I am really sorry for the family. Mrs. Snider shearing sheep today. Clipped some last week one day & a half. Siddie fretful today. Our garden looks well, we have had plenty of rain so far. I must stop now and get some lettuce for dinner.

Tuesday 19th - Nothing of interest has transpired since I last wrote. Till Asheley came back last Saturday, she staid home two weeks. The children going to school again. Mrs. Barnes is still very feeble. Till is picking wool. Maria and Mrs. Quin washed wool yesterday. I fear Mrs. Quin will suffer for bread this summer. She does not manage to try to get along. It seems to me I could do better.

Wednesday 20th - Till washed today. She is so bigoted, she does not suit me much. I like Mary Muse the best, Mary is very quiet. I have been sewing some on Zona a pink calico dress today. Siddie wants to be in the yard all the time. Gussie and Eddie play with him. Till worked three weeks and went home. Came back Saturday 16th May, lost 3 1/2 days since.

Thursday 21st May 1868 - I put in some thread through the harness today, my first. Mrs. Night put in part of it. Till is to weave it. She is a great brag. The children learning very well at school. I have hoped and prayed never to have any more children but I fear I will. I think very few children pay for the care and anxiety of their parents. O! Lord may I not be so unfortunate as to raise one ungrateful child.

Friday 22nd - Mrs. Ballew and Mrs. P. Rich staid with us last night. They had been to the examination at Asheville (the college). They were highly pleased. I used to go every examination but things are sadly changed with us now. I still hope for better days. If it were not for hope, how gloomy this world would be.

Saturday and Sunday 23rd & 24th & Monday 25th - I have nothing of importance to write for three days. I am very sore today as Mr. Henry and I went down to see Eliza yesterday. We took Eddie and Siddie. I got very tired coming back. We found them all well. Eliza has broken a good deal since I last saw her. Her life has been a blank one nearly. Matt said she never expected to come back again. We came home and found the children all well. They did not go to school as they had no dinner to take. George only allows us a half bu. a day to be divided between us, Ham Rollins and Mrs. Muse's family. It really seems Mr. Henry don't care anything about my likes or dislikes but when I think of how George treated us when the yankees came here and how he treated Mr. Henry when he came back, my indignation is so great I can't help but feeling wounded at Mr. Henry's goodness. Yes, to the negro and not to his family. George has stole so much from the customers, all the good ones have quit the mill. It is no use fretting about things I can't help so I have to submit. To think me and my children must want for bread, that a mean negro may get it.

Tuesday 26th - I sewed some on a coat for Mr. Henry today. Till gets on slowly with weaving. Never wove much, at least she does not understand it. Mary picking wool. We have cool mornings and nights. I have not taken off my feather bed yet. The children sleep on matresses. Mary Muse here May 4th Monday, four weeks next Monday.

Wednesday 27th May 1868 - Been sewing all day on the coat. It tires me to sew steady, gives me a pain in my right side. Till gets only two yds. a day, very slow weaving.

Thursday 28th - Till went home after dinner. She is great to gad about. Mr. Henry went to the Bottom since dinner. He has to pay a U. S. postage debt this week. That is why he had to sell the three best cows. I hated to see them go but the debt had to be paid.

Friday 29th - Mr. Henry went to town, did not get home till evening. No news of importance. We are needing rain, the garden is very hard. My poultry is doing very well. I have twenty-one beautiful young ducks. Mr. Henry and the children have dug earth worms for them, they are growing finely. My chickens grow very well. I have only about thirty young ones. I have wove some today. Cut out the cloth and put it in another sley, my first. I only missed one split.

Saturday 30th - Willie went fishing in the branch this evening, caught a mud turtle. He was very proud of it. Pinck has been to the mill twice today fixing his cross bow. Gus split one yesterday and Eddie one today so it seems he has a time to get one. I am afraid he will shoot some of the children's eyes out but he is a child and wants something to play with. Mr. Henry and Cousin R. Love went to town this morning. Cousin Robert staid here last night.

Sunday 31st - Mr. Henry and the children have gone to hunt strawberries so I am alone this evening. Eddie and Siddie asleep. This has been a warm day but no rain yet. I hope Mr. Henry & the children may find some berries and soon come back as I feel lonely. The children have returned, found some berries. Mr. Henry fixed me a saucer of cream and strawberries. He and I went after the cows.

June 1868

Monday June 1st - Some of Mr. Henry's relations spent the day here. Mr. and two Mrs. Orr. The children at school. We had a very heavy rain and some hail. I made a collar for Betsy this evening.

Tuesday 2nd June 1868 - I have wove today. Till quilled for me, she came back late Sunday evening. I only got two and a half yds. Mary is picking wool. The children came home about three o'clock. Mr. Barnes has toothache.

Wednesday 3rd - I am very tired this evening. I have wove three and half yds. Till quilled. Mr. Henry out with the hands. No news of importance going on.

Thursday 4th - I have only wove two yds. today. I took sick this evening, over worked myself. Till can finish the cloth tomorrow. She is very indolent. Mary is better for work than her.

Friday 5th - I have done some mending. Ellen Hawkins and her sister Adda spent the day here. Mr. Henry has some hands at work in the new ground over the creek. He stays with them.

Saturday 6th - I have been doubling thread. Till twisted it. She got the cloth cut yesterday. Mr. Henry out with the hands. I seen an account of Mr. Henry's with Rankin & Co. I am astonished at it. There has not been twenty dollars spent in the family. The bill is $332.50 cts. I have almost lost hope of ever getting out of debt. I get out of heart. I try to get along on a mere nothing. I spend nothing, only for snuff and sugar and coffee though I need clothes very badly. Mr. Henry puts me from time to time. I have not been to church in nearly a year for want of suitable apparrel.

Sunday 7th - Pinck and Willie went to Sunday school at Miller's Meeting House. They came home to dinner. Till is visiting somewhere today, she is great to gad about. Zona, Willie and Gussie have gone to church at the Academy. Mr. Henry also I suppose. We had some new potatoes today, our first. Zona helped me with dinner. Pinck is reading a Sunday School book. Eddie and Siddie playing. I must stop now and write Ellen Hawkins some copies.

Monday 8th - I cut Mr. Henry a sack coat and pair pants. I sewed some on the coat. Anna Jones came home with the children. She brought some paper for me to set her some copies.

Tuesday 9th - I finished Mr. Henry's coat and went with Mr. Henry to get some strawberries. I enjoyed them finely. We got enough for some pies, they are nice. Till left yesterday with a sore finger.

Wednesday 10th - Mrs. Night warped Zona's dress. Mary Rollins minded the spools while I cut a coat for Mr. Rollins. Gen. Vance and little son took dinner here. Mrs. Night is to weave my cloth for wool. Very warm today. I have done but little to Mr. Henry's pants. I helped about putting in the cloth and baked some nice rolls and loaf bread.

Thursday 11th - I sewed some on Mr. Henry's pants. Mr. Henry, Mrs. Night and I went to get some strawberries. They were scattering but still we got enough to fill our buckets. Mrs. Night gets on very well weaving. I have the headache to-night. Gussie has been unwell all day. Worms I think.

Friday 12th - I have a slight headache all day. I finished Mr. Henry's pants before dinner. Took a nap after dinner and then cut the children some pants and coats. We are needing rain, the garden is very dry.

Sunday 14th - I was in bed nearly all day yesterday with headache. It pained till after breakfast this morning. Betsey came down yesterday evening with Pinck and Gussie. She had headache yesterday evening. Mr. Henry went to Mrs. Alford's today. We had some potatoes for dinner. Pinck and Willie went to Sunday School.

Monday 15th - Mr. Henry went to town this morning as this is court week. Betsey still here. We had our first beans for dinner. We have had a nice shower since dinner. Mary Rollins and Bud are here. Mary is very scary about thunder and wind. I must stop and finish Gussie's pants. I have wrote Anna Jones some copies before dinner.

Tuesday 16th - I finished a coat for Willie today, it does not fit neatly. Betsey staid at Wiley Night's last night. She does not like to stay at Mrs. Glenn's this summer as the fare is not very good. Mr. Henry off to town again today. He got me four nice calico dresses and a muslin one, also some shoes for Pinck and I and a calico dress for Zona. I needed the dresses badly.

Wednesday 17th - I made Willie a pair pants. Gus is very proud of his first gallis breeches. Siddie is very little trouble, scarcely ever wants to suck. I am weaning him. Mr. Henry gone to town again.

Thursday 18th - Mr. Henry went to town. Till Ashley came back today and is a poor hand to work. Henry Jones took dinner here. My teeth are sore this evening from washing my feet in cold water last night. I finished Pinck's coats and began Willie's other one. No news of importance going on. Mrs. Night got the cloth cut today. Maria washed.

Friday 19th June 1868 - My teeth are very sore, a gum bile I think. It is swollen down in my throat as I can scarcely swallow. I finished Willie's last coat. Mr. Henry did not go to town today. The children came home soon after four this evening. It was dark last night as Pinck wanted to stay to hear the debate.

Saturday 20th - My teeth are very sore. I did not rest well last night. Suse Muse came after Mary in the night. Her sister was having fits and thought she would die. I hear she is better this evening. I made Eddie a pair pants and took a long nap. I put some dog fennel and vinager on my jaw and throat, it helped me a great deal. Mr. Henry took dinner at Mr. A. B. Jones. My throat was so sore I could not eat any dinner scarcely.

Sunday 21st - This one of the longest days of the year, is very pleasant. We have had fire in my room every morning and nearly every night this spring. Pinck and Willie gone to Sunday School. Zona does not want to go. Mr. Henry and the other children asleep. I must go now and make some custard and coffee for dinner. The custard is for Zona. Mr. Henry has headache so the coffee is for him.

Monday 22nd - I have made Pinck a pair pants and sewed some on Gussie's. The children gone to school. Mr. Henry about the farm. George is acting badly about the mill, allowances us to 1/2 bu a day. It worries me no little and no way to help myself.

Tuesday 23rd - Finished Willie's and Gussie's pants. Till picking wool. Mary does the cooking. Nothing of importance going on. I am very hoarse, cold settles on my lungs of late. I fear that pin injured them.

Thursday 25th - I was in bed yesterday all day with my head. It is some better today. I have finished Eddie's pants and sewed some on Zona's dress. Mary Rollins and Mag Presley spent the evening here. Till and Mary finished picking the wool. I put some wool to dye this evening, cold dye.

Friday 26th - Maria and Till scoured and scalded today, I helped some. My jaw and neck is very sore where I blistered it with dog fennel. Zona has not been to school for three days, has a sore foot now.

Saturday 27th - I finished Zona's dress and did other little jobs. Till and Mary scoured the spring house and kitchen, it looks very neat. We had our first beets today. Mr. Henry about the farm. We got some cabbage plants from Eliza's yesterday. Tom Muse has gone for some more today.

Sunday 28th June 1868 - Mr. Henry and I went up in the mountains to see Mrs. Alford. She is indeed an object of charity. It is some seven miles. I am very tired and sore tonight and have the headache. We got dinner at Mr. Neal's. I enjoyed it finely. We had the heaviest rain I ever saw last Friday, the branch was nearly all over the meadow. We lost part of our milk. It swept the fences generally. Some hail. It split the corn a good deal. Till and Mary both gone. Till will not come back to stay any more, she is not a good hand.

Monday 29th - Till staid here last night and got breakfast. I have had headache all day but got dinner. Till has gone to hire at Capt. Moore's. Mary has left me also so now I have no one. Zona has been at home today. Maria's children have been here so they helped some. Mr. Henry went to town before dinner. Siddie is not well, cold I think.

Tuesday 30th - My head is nearly well, now four o'clock. I was so sick this morning I could not finish breakfast. Mr. Henry and Pinck did the rest. Maria cleaned up and got dinner. Mary Rollins spent the evening here. Till did not get in at Capt. Moore's. I don't know where she is today.

July 1868

Wednesday July 1st - I have finished Eddie's body and sewed some on Zona's dress. Mary Muse came back yesterday evening. Till staid here last night, she has gone to hire at Peter Miller's. I don't think she wants to do any good. She is very lazy. Zona went to school today. She does not have a good chance at school as the others as she has to tend to Siddie when I am sick.

Thursday 2nd - Till has set in to work with us again. She hoed in the garden before dinner. Maria washing today. I made two fire screens yesterday. One for upstairs the other for the front room. They are very nice. I sewed some on Zona's dress. Mr. Henry up with Tom Muse, he is cutting clover. Very warm and dry.

Friday 3rd - Very warm. I finished Zona's dress and made her some collars and cuffs. I have baked some this evening for the children to take to the celebrations tomorrow at the Miller Meeting House.

Saturday 4th - The children went to the celebration. They were well pleased. Gen. Vance spoke. Till went home after dinner. Mr. Henry loaned her Buck, I was really vexed about it. I know the horse will not get anything to eat till he gets home. Very warm, needing rain badly. Jacob Starnes' wife was killed yesterday evening by a horse. She was found dead by a tree. 'Tis a sad affair.

Sunday 5th - Mr. Henry went to Mrs. Starnes' burial. I got dinner. Pinck and Willie went to Sandy Bottom before dinner. Mary and Till are to come back this evening. I want to go and see Uncle Sam this evening, he got his feet scalded badly a week ago. Very warm. Some thunder about this evening. I hope it may rain. I will call Mr. Henry to go with me if he has his nap out. He has been asleep sometime.

We went to see Sam, his feet are improving some. Some rain about this evening but we did not get any.

Monday 6th - I made Eddie a body and sewed some on his pants. Mr. Henry about the farm. Nothing of interest going on.

Tuesday 7th - Finished Edd's pants. Till has been sick all day. I don't think there is much the matter, only big lazy. I sewed some on Mr. Henry's pants.

Wednesday 8th - The children at school. Zona had rather stay at home. Pinck and Willie never say anything about it. Pinck did not go yesterday or Monday, he was not well. Mrs. Barnes assists Mr. Barnes now. I finished Mr. Henry's pants and helped Mrs. Knight warp her cloth.

Thursday 9th - This is the first dog day. Some rain, not a season though. I sewed some on my dress. Till helping making fence. Her and Mary rather work out than in.

Friday 10th - I finished my dress. It does not fit very well. I have lost my patterns. Mr. Henry about the farm all day.

Saturday 11th - I worked some in the garden this morning. It gave me headache so I have done nothing more all day.

Sunday 12th - Very warm. I have had headache all day. It is some better this evening. Mr. Henry gone out to walk. Ham Rollins has been sick all week, asthma.

Monday 13th - I finished Pinck's shirt and began Zona a short sack of my brilliant saque, it looks very neat. Pinck and Zona want to go to an examination up Homeny Wednesday. Pinck went to school this morning but came back about 9 o'clock with colic. He is very subject to it of late.

Tuesday 14th - I finished Zona's saque. Her and Willie came home about four o'clock this evening. Some of Mr. Barnes scholars are going to the examination. Pinck did not go to school this morning.

Wednesday 15th - Pinck and Zona rode the colt, they were dressed very neat. Zona wore white. I made her two skirts today, some of my old dresses. Willie tended Siddie.

Thursday 16th - Some thrashers, thrashing Taylor's and Doc Muse's wheat. Till had to have Mag Presley to help her get dinner. I thought it very unnecessary. They are very easily excited, weak in the head I imagine. The children came home about 11. Zona has headache. They enjoyed the trip finely. We try to give them all the pleasure we can. I finished Zona a swiss waist this evening to wear with a skirt. Very warm. I have suffered more this summer from warm weather than I have since I have been in Buncombe.

Friday 17th - I fixed Zona a waisted skirt of my pointed one. She is very proud of her skirt. Mr. Henry went to town, came home to dinner. Capt. Saunders, who died last Saturday, is supposed to be poisoned by his wife. They have taken up the body and were examining some witnesses today. Mr. Henry says the evidence so far is strongly against her. I sent Pinck and Willie to the Bottom this morning, they got 5$. Pinck and Gussie went to town after dinner, got some sugar, coffee, salt &c. They got very wet. We had a light shower, it will do some good. We are needing rain. Very warm, oppressively so.

Saturday 18th - Mr. Henry spent the day in Asheville. They are still trying Mrs. Saunders. I finished Zona an under waist and did some other jobs. Made some molasses bread this evening. Till's sister Matt came before dinner. She is more intelligent than Till. Very warm and dry. We will soon have roasting years. We have a good garden.

Sunday 19th - Very warm. Mrs. Glenn spent the day here. I had a letter from Sister Frank this morning. Her health is not very good. Lena has been unwell but better. The others all well. Frank is not coming up this summer, has no one to come with her. I am sorry. I did hope to see some of my kindred up this summer.

Monday 20th - Till left us this morning so I will have a good deal to do till I get another. No news of importance. Mr. Henry about the farm. Zona did not go to school this morning. Dollie is helping me today. She is a great deal of help. We had some rain yesterday evening and wind that blew fences generally.

Tuesday 21st - I have mended some. Dollie does most of the work, gets beans &c. Siddie is very fretful, not well. Zona is at home today. The Saunders case is still going on. I fear she did poison him from what I hear. She must be a bad woman.

Wednesday 22nd - Zona has gone to school. She did not want to go much. Gussie went Monday and yesterday, he was well pleased. I cut me a dress, sewed some on it. Mr. Henry went to town today, came home for dinner.

Thursday 23rd - Maria washed today. We had a very heavy rain and several peals of heavy thunder. Mary Rollins and Mag Presley were here. They were sadly frightened. I have sewed some on my dress.

Friday 24th - Mr. Henry went to town. Mr. Rollins took a load of lumber. Gussie went with him. We had rain this evening. Mr. Henry and Gussie late getting home, they both came wet. Mr. Glenn is here tonight. Maria is dying some wool for me today. The Saunders case is still going on.

Saturday 25th - Began to rain about 9 o'clock, has been a steady day's rain. Mr. Henry and Mr. Glenn went to Esq. Thrash's this morning, returned to dinner wet. I finished my dress and ironed some. (Apple) Jimmie Smith took dinner here, he has nearly lost his mind. We had our first roasting years this morning for breakfast. Mr. Henry got me two, one morning this week. He is so kind to me, helps me with the cooking. O! that I was a better wife to him. He is too kind to me. He deserved a better woman. The children are a heap of help. They all seem willing to do what they can to help mother.

Sunday 26th July 1868 - Another rainy day. It has slacked some now, 5 o'clock. A friend of Mr. Henry's called to see him today. Dr. Rogers. He and Mr. Henry studied medicine together twenty years ago, that seems a good while. Mr. Kerkendol is here also. I am very tired of wet weather. I hope it will fair off soon. It is unpleasant cooking as well as anything else in bad weather. I must soon go about supper and then to bed.

Monday 27th - Rain again today. I fear it will injure wheat badly. Dr. Rogers left this morning. The children did not go to school. They started and it began to rain so we called them back. I have sewed some on my apron and ironed some. Faired off this evening.

Tuesday 28th - Spent the day at Capt. Moore's. Mrs. Barnes' baby died yesterday evening, teething. They did not seem to grieve much. It is better off. Maria got dinner for me. She is going to cook for me awhile at seventy five cts. per week. I will get the supper. Mr. Henry does not like for me to cook, wants to get some one else. The children help a great deal.

Wednesday 29th - Pinck and Guss went to the Bottom. Betsey came home with them. Mr. Henry went to the burial at Sardis. I finished my other apron and began to refill a counterpane. It will take me all the week to frill the two. Maria does very well as a cook, tries to please.

Thursday 30th - I have been at work on the frills. Took a nap before dinner. I don't feel well today. Betsey and I went to see Ham Rollins this evening. He is not well, asthma. Mr. Henry went to town after dinner to get some sugar and coffee. Got a curry comb and lost it on the way.

Friday 31st - We have roasting years twice a day. Plenty now. Mr. Henry went to town this morning, came home soon after dinner. Got Betsey and I a coarse comb each, himself some shoes and some cheese of the Polk factory, it is very rich. I finished the counterpane this evening. Mr. Henry and Ruff Miller robbed a bee gum this evening, got a nice lot of honey. Heavy rain about the view this evening, the branch up smartly but little here. The children did not get wet as they were at the sawmill (Mr. Jones'). Our June apples are about out. We did not have many pears this year.

August 1868

August 1st Saturday 1868 - Betsey and I finished ironing before dinner. I got dinner as Maria is washing for herself today. Mr. Henry went to Sand Hill before dinner. The neighbors want to build a new Academy there. I hope they may succeed. Mr. Henry about the mill after dinner.

Sunday 2nd - Cloudy and looks like rain. Betsey left this morning. Pinck and Willie went to bring the horses back, the other children went home with Maria so I am alone. I expect them soon. Mr. Henry spoke of going Sardis, as the funerals of Mrs. Caroline Jones' parents are to preached there today. I don't know whether he has gone or not. My guinnies hatched yesterday, set just four weeks. Mr. Henry and I went to Mary Rollins, had a damp walk. We set a turkey on the way.

Monday 3rd - I cut and sewed some on Zona a calico dress. Very warm today. No news of note. Mr. Henry about the farm. A great deal of wheat has spoiled by wet weather. Mr. Henry's oats has suffered some.

Tuesday 4th - I finished Zona's dress. It looks very neat. Maria does very well as a cook, tries to please. I prefer negro to white labor.

Wednesday 5th - I cut and made Zona an apron, new style. It does not fit neatly. Mr. Henry has several hands hired about the oats and hay and fixing turnip patches. I hope we may raise some as we have had none in two years.

Thursday 6th - Siddie is not at all well, teething I think. He has fallen off some. Mr. Henry went to town, came home for dinner. No news of importance. I cut and sewed some on a calico dress for myself.

Friday 7th - Mr. Henry went to town. I sewed some on my dress. Very warm today. The katydids began to hollow last Wednesday night.

Saturday 8th - Mr. Henry went to Sand Hill, the neighbors speak of building a new Academy there. We had a very hard washing rain, took fences generally. The third rain that has swept fences this summer. I finished my dress this evening. It fits neatly. Siddie is not at all well. Elick sowed some turnips today.

Sunday 9th - Mr. Henry, Pinck and Zona went to Bethel to an Association. A great many people out. Siddie's bowels in a bad condition. I have nursed him nearly all day. I am uneasy about him. Laura Cannon spent the day with me. It has been a long one to me, we had supper before dark. I had a letter from Dora yesterday, all well. The children are asleep. I must read some in my Bible and then to bed too.

Sunday August 23rd 1868 - Two weeks have past since I wrote. Nothing of interest has happened. Siddie has not been well, very fretful but better now. We have had a good deal of rain, our turnips have come up nicely. The mill is not running now, needs some work on it. They will get it started Tuesday or Wednesday. Nothing new. A negro (Whaley) died at Jim Moore's yesterday. A good many have died this summer of typhoid fever. They have no one to care for them now in sickness. My head aches a good deal today. Mr. Henry got Zona and I some nice hats last week. Zona's is beautiful, also a cheap breast pin for Zona. I have been fixing for their examination, it comes off next week. Rained all night last night. Mr. Henry wants to go to Sandy Bottom after dinner. I would like to go but my head feels too badly. I made me a nice pair of Chamois skin gloves last week, they fit very neatly.

Monday 24th - Nothing of note going on. Siddie is better than he has been. I have been fixing Zona's clothes for the examination, it comes off next week. The children anticipate much pleasure there. Let them enjoy life while they are young and free from care. Trouble will come soon enough.

Tuesday 25th - I sewed some on a dress for myself. Very warm with cool mornings. Rene Muse picking some coloured wool for me.

Wednesday 26th - I sewed some on my dress. Mr. Henry has gone to work on the road. Left this evening, will not be back before Saturday.

Thursday 27th - I felt lonely last night without Mr. Henry. Laura Cannon staid with me but no is company to me like he is. I finished my dress, it fits neatly. Zona spent last night with Mary Jones. I missed her a great deal.

Friday 28th - I have made some collars and cuffs for Katy Night and Lena Cannon. Rene is carding me some bats for a quilt. I must make some this fall.

Saturday 29th - I have ironed some and had to give Pinck a whipping for staying at the mill so long. I hate to whip him. He is a good child but thoughtless. Zona has a hasty temper. I fear it will render her very unhappy in future years. Mr. Henry came tonight after supper. We were very glad to see him. Home is not home without him. Some rain today.

Sunday 30th August 1868 - Very warm today. We had our first cabbage for dinner, they were very nice. we have had tomatoes for more than a week. The children all at play but Siddie who is asleep, also Mr. Henry. I want to go to negro John's after some peaches this evening and I promised to write Pinck a composition this evening. Mr. Henry and I started after the peaches. Got to the bridge, it began to rain. We took shelter under a tree but got wet before we got back to the mill.

Monday 31st - I cut some clothes for Uncle Sam's family. Zona did not go to school today as they only decorate the stage. Mr. Henry went to Asheville this morning, came home to dinner, got Pinck and Willie a hat. I trimmed my hat, it looks very neat.

September 1868

Tuesday Sept. 1st - Pinck and Willie are highly pleased with their hats. I have been baking all evening for the children. Pinck and Willie staid after school to rehearse their speeches. Mr. Henry about the farm. George is not paying up the toll well at all, a good deal behind.

Wednesday 2nd - Some rain this evening. Zona got damp coming from school. I have been doing odds and ends all day. Mr. Henry on the road all day. Came home tonight and went with the children to the examination tonight. I was anxious to go but it rained.

Thursday 3rd - They got home about ten o'clock well pleased. I sit up for them. I have sewed some on Lonzo's pants. I intended going to the examination but it rained. Mr. Henry on the road again today. I want to go tonight if it does not rain.

Friday 4th - I went to Sand Hill last night, enjoyed it finely. Mr. Henry wanted me to ride but I rather walk. I soon found I had made a mistake as it was so muddy. Maria staid with the children. Willie did finely, won the prize, a very pretty little book. Pinck done finely, also Zona.

Saturday 5th - I finished Hanes' and Lonzo's pants. Pinck went to town after some soda. Mr. Henry on the road yesterday and today. There seems to be a good deal of excitement among the negroes. It is reported the negroes have taken Charleston and it is feared will burn it. Oh! the yankees have caused us a heap of trouble and I fear it has only begun.

Sunday 6th - Mr. Henry and Ruff Miller were out last night to see what they could see and hear. There was a big meeting of negroes at George's, something unusual going on among them. Mr. Henry and I took the two least children and spent the day at Sandy Bottom.

Monday 7th - Mr. Henry gone on the road, he will be back tonight. I want to write some letters today and cut Mr. Henry a shirt. The children will be at home for three weeks now. I wrote to Dora a long letter. She will be glad to get it I imagine. I cut the shirt but did but little.

Tuesday 8th - Tom Neal's daughter and son came today. He is going to put in some wheat. His daughter is to help do the cooking. They furnish their own provision. I sewed some on Mr. Henry's shirt, sent Pinck with his dinner.

Wednesday 9th - I finished one shirt. Mr. Henry still on the road, will get done that part today. He comes home every night. I am glad of that as I feel lonely without him though Mr. Neal's and son and daughter are here. Celia, Neal and I got dinner as Maria is washing her clothes today.

Thursday 10th - Maria and Kate washing so Celia and Zona got dinner. I sewed some on a shirt of Mr. Henry. He is at home today, will go on the road tomorrow.

Friday 11th - Mr. Henry started soon this morning on the road, took three hands from here. Pinck was to take their dinner but went off with Tom Quinn after the cane mill, did not get back till near four o'clock.

Saturday 12th - Mr. Henry sent me some nice peaches by John Hendrix. He said they got their dinner at Mrs. Creasman's. Maria at home today. Celia & Zona got most of the dinner. Mr. Neal went home this morning. He hurt his back Thursday evening. His sons and Celia left this evening. I finished Mr. Henry's shirt and did some ironing. Till Morris came last Tuesday. I want to go to see her tomorrow.

Sunday 13th - Mr. Henry came after supper. He was very tired. He and I and Eddie have spent the day at Mr. Jones'. Miss Till looks very well. Her baby is sick. Mr. Henry started to the road soon after we got home. We had a nice watermelon and musk mellon after we came home. Some rain this evening, it is rather muddy walking. Mrs. Jones wanted to send me home but I rather walk. Zona has gone after Laura Cannon to stay with me tonight. I will feel lonely if she can not come as I have never staid with the children alone.

Monday 14th - Maria pulling pen fodder so I have the cooking to do. Zona and Pinck help a great deal, they wash dishes &c. I put in a quilt and got it laid off in diamonds. Pinck and Zona both helped some. They done very well for beginners. Laura staid with us last night.

Tuesday 15th - Maria did not get breakfast this morning so it was late as I expected her to get it. I think she is getting tired and wants to quit. Mr. Henry will be at home tomorrow I hope. Pinck went to town yesterday, got me some tobacco and sugar. I have been making my snuff for a month. I do not like it much. We had a very heavy rain yesterday. Pinck and Willie were in town at the time.

Wednesday 16th - I am getting on finely with my quilt. Pinck and Zona help. They make long stitches and crooked lines. It will learn them and keep them out of mischief. Siddie has got well, does not cry so much as he did. Chinquapins are opening some. Willie, Gussie and Eddie go every day for some, they get but few.

Thursday 17th - Mr. Henry came home last night after supper. We were very glad to see him. He is done for awhile. He was not here for dinner, went to measure some of the road. It has rained every day this week.

Friday 18th - I did not quilt any as Mr. and Mrs. Barnes spent the day here. She seems to be very pleasant. Kate helped me get dinner and washed some. We had a nice mellon after dinner. Mr. Henry about the farm and house.

Saturday 19th - I got my quilt out this morning and baked some after dinner. Pinck helped. Mr. Henry went to Easterly's shop this morning, did not get home till near sundown. Some frost yesterday morning. I have not seen anything nipped by it.

Sunday 20th - Cool but pleasant in the middle of the day. Maria has neuralgia in the face, I was up to see her this evening. She is getting better. Some rain this evening. Mr. Henry is waiting on me so I must go to bed.

Monday 21st - The children and I scoured part of the house before dinner. Mr. Neal came back today, brought Nancy instead of Celia. She seems to be very pleasant. I got most of the dinner. I spent the evening in arranging the house. Mr. Henry about the home all day. Glenn Peak came here this evening. No news from So. Ca. All are well except Pa. He has nearly lost the sight of one eye. I am very sorry to hear it.

Tuesday 22nd - Miss Tilda spent the day here. Glenn left after dinner. I am out of snuff and I feel right foolish without. I wish I had never tasted it. Zona went home with Till. Mr. Henry went up the river after a girl to cook since dinner.

Wednesday 23rd - The girl came very young. Nancy seems to be willing to help. Maria washed some today. Mr. Henry about the farm. Hosea and Doc making molasses. I finished binding my quilt and put another one in. Nancy helped. Till Carland carded bats.

Thursday 24th - I quilted some. Our Pide cow lost her calf and died today. I am very sorry. I think the hogs did the mischief. She was a very good cow. We need the milk now and will all winter.

Friday 25th - I have been doing up the tallow of the cow and helped get dinner. Till is not at all satisfied. I think she will leave when Nancy does. She ironed today. Mr. Henry went to Henderson since dinner to a R. R. meeting tomorrow. Newt Taylor came here yesterday evening. He speaks of moving back here. I am no great fancier of Mary's.

Saturday 26th - Mr. Neal's people left this morning. Pinck went for hunting this morning, they caught a live fox. Wiley Night has it. Camp meeting began yesterday, some few tended. Till Carland left this morning, she was but little help and very dirty so I have been busy all day fixing up the tallow. Elick is doing up the soap grease.

Sunday 27th - Mr. Henry did not come home. I felt lonely, only the children but slept very well. I expect him this evening. The children have gathered a quantity of chinquapins and are playing "hull gull." Siddie tries to talk, makes a poor out. I want to write some letters this evening.

Sep 28th 1868 Monday - Mr. Neal and Nannie came about dinner. I have been fixing some odds and ends. No news. Maria is cooking, she is getting tired I think.

Tuesday 29th - I quilted some. Elick killed two pigs for the barbacue tomorrow, will be a busy day with me cooking for the dinner.

Wednesday 30th - I am very tired tonight as I have been on my feet all day cooking. Maria, Nannie and I have been busy all day. Till Ashley & sister are here tonight. Taylor still here, speaks of going home soon.

October 1868

Thurs 1st - I went to the barbacue yesterday. A large crowd of people, men, women and children. All the children except Siddie went. He staid with Maria. Some thought there were eight thousand people out. We had a very good speech from Gen. Clingman, also one from Col. Cook and another from Wade of Geo. I did not hear the latter as I was off with Eddie. The colt sceered and threw me backwards. I was worse scared than hurt. They had a torch light procession. Mr. Henry did not stay to see it. He went to town this morning, did not return till supper.

Saturday 3rd - Dr. Candler staid here last night. He takes Matt rent wheat to Asheville today. Mr. Henry about the mill. Rained all day. Pinck went to the Bottom before dinner and to Asheville after dinner. He did not get home till dark. I was uneasy about him.

Sunday 4th - Rained nearly all day. Tena's funeral was preached at the Academy today. We did not go. Press & Till spent the evening here. Star has a young calf.

Monday 5th October 1868 - I took two comforts apart. I am going to make quilts of them. I pieced one today. The children go to school every day. Pinck began Lattin this morning. Mr. Henry about the farm.

Tuesday 6th - Nothing of interest going on. Mr. Henry went to town today to get some papers. A great deal of excitement about the president's election. I hope for the best but still fear. I made two tops of quilts today. Pinck does not like lattin much. He is a noble boy.

Wednesday 7th - I whipped Pinck this evening, it hurt me so bad. He caught me round the neck and said "Mother, you don't love me but I love you." It hurt me so. It was for dissobedience but he is thoughtless. It was not done intentionally. I hope I may never have to punish him again. He is a very dear child to me.

Thursday 8th - I did not rest well last night thinking of the whipping I had given my dear first born. I love him so much. Frost this morning, nipped nearly everything. Siddie not at all well, fever all day. His gut comes out every time he has a passage. It has been so since last Sunday. Nannie Neal and I put in a quilt since dinner. Kate making soap. Old Nancy washing.

Friday 9th - I have quilted today. Siddie some better but it comes out every operation. Celia ironed this evening. Maria gone home to wash.

Saturday 10th - I have scoured some. Pinck and George Muse did most of the work. Baked some after dinner. I am very tired tonight. Maria at home all day. Nannie went home after dinner. They are getting on well with making molasses. They are tollerable nice. An old man named Pinner is here tonight. Two men, Shuford and Heath were here last night.

Sunday 11th - Some rain last night and some this morning. Pinck gone to the Bottom. We had our first pumpkin custards for dinner. Siddie not well, very fretful. Mr. Henry starts to Morganton in the morning to a R. R. meeting. I hope we may prosper and yet have plenty.

Monday 12th - Mr. Henry left this morning. I was sorry to see him go. Home is not home without him to me. I quilted some, will get it out tomorrow. The children at school. Tom Stradley got his horse's leg broke at the bridge below the dam, fell off the bridge. I am sorry for it as I fear Mr. Henry will have to pay for it. The bridge is too narrow.

Tuesday 13th - I finished my quilt and hemmed it this evening. Siddie is some better, not so cross every time he has an operation. His gut protrudes, comes out some. I fear he will not get over it soon.

Wednesday 14th - Mr. Neal and Nannie left this evening. They are done here now. Maria went home this evening sick so I will have a hard time of it. The children are very good to help. Pinck helps me. Zona minds Siddie and gets the others ready for breakfast.

Thursday 15th - We staid by ourselves last night. I was not afraid. John Hendrix and negro Earl are making molasses just back of the garden so if I get frightened, I can call to them. Kate washed for me today. I have put in a quilt.

Friday 16th - I am very tired having been on my feet nearly all day ironing. The children will do most of the work tomorrow. Siddie's bowels not loose.

Saturday 17th - Mr. Henry came home this evening. We were all glad to see him. Eddie and Siddie almost danced they were so rejoiced. Eddie is very affectionate. Comes up in our bed every night. He sleeps with Zona on the trundle bed. Pinck, Willie and Gussie sleep in the side room. Hendrix & Co. got done their molasses last night. The children and I baked some pies, custards and molasses bread. They are a heap of help and then they are so willing to help Mother. I hope they may make as good men as they have children.

Sunday 18th - Mr. Henry has gone to Mr. Cook's to get him to come and make the children's shoes. He is going to the Bottom before he returns. The children have been gone since twelve hunting chestnuts. It is now three, they have not had their dinner. Siddie and I eat some time ago. We had a killing frost this morning for the first heavy one. I will call the children now as I feel lonely. Siddie is playing with a doll I fixed for him while I write.

I will have to hunt another blank book when I write again. It seems like a piece of foolishness but Mr. Henry is very anxious that I should keep it up so I write to gratify him and then perhaps it may be some pleasure to my children in coming years.

December 1932 – Note from Vance Henry[57]

1932 Dec 16 - I write this 64 years after my mother wrote the above. She died on April 3, 1917, 4:30 AM, 81 years. My father died April 8, 4:30 AM, 1900, 77 years. Of the children she had when she wrote this all are dead except Zona and Edmund. She had five other children, Kate, James, Arthur, Wade, and the writer Vance Henry. I will be 56 years old on Feb. 16, 1933. Wade was youngest. Wade and Arthur dead. I hope the space below will be filled out 64 years from now by our Henry Boy who may be living at that far distant day.

I have two children William 19 and Marrion 17.

---

[57] This last entry for Dec. 16, 1932 was made by Walter Vance Henry, son of William Lewis and Cornelia Catherine Henry

Henry Family Tree

First Generation[58]

1. Robert HENRY was born January 9, 1767 in Mecklenburg Co., North Carolina. He died January 6, 1863 in Clay Co., North Carolina. Robert HENRY and Dorcas Bell LOVE were married May 31, 1814. Dorcas Bell LOVE (daughter of Col. Robert LOVE and Mary Ann DILLARD) was born February 9, 1797. She died February 5, 1857. Robert HENRY and Dorcas Bell LOVE had the following children:

    2   i.William Lewis HENRY, born in 1823; died in 1900.
    3   ii.Mary Louise HENRY, in 1815; died in 1844.
    4   iii.Robert Marcellus HENRY, born in 1821; died in 1885.
    5   iv.Elizabeth Isabella HENRY, born in 1822; died in 1915.
    6   v.Martha Ann HENRY, born in 1825; died in 1896.
    7   vi.James Love HENRY, born in 1835; died in 1884.

Second Generation

2. William Lewis HENRY was born November 24, 1823. He died April 8, 1900 and was buried in Henry Family Cemetery, Buncombe Co., North Carolina. William Lewis HENRY and Cornelia Catherine SMITH were married April 5, 1855. Cornelia Catherine SMITH (daughter of William SMITH Sr. and Mary HOLLINGSWORTH) was born August 19, 1836 in Spartanburg Co., SC. She died April 3, 1917 and was buried in Acton United Methodist Cemetery. William Lewis HENRY and Cornelia Catherine SMITH had the following children:

    i.Robert Pinckney HENRY, born July 20, 1856; married Virginia Alice (Minnie) TROGDON May 1, 1888; died on July 13, 1911, Winston Salem, Forsyth Co., North Carolina.
    ii.Cora Aletha HENRY was born November 17, 1857. She died September 10, 1858 and was buried in Henry Family Cemetery, Buncombe Co., North Carolina.
    iii.Mary Arizona HENRY, born March 21, 1859; married John B. HYATT, on October 16, 1881; died on May 14, 1941, Aberdeen, Grays Harbor, Washington.
    iv.William Smith HENRY was born March 11, 1861. He died January 19, 1888 in Asheville, Buncombe Co., North Carolina.
    v.Gustavus Adolphus HENRY, born on March 8, 1863; married Elizabeth SUBER, on September 6, 1891; died on February 2, 1931, Miami, Florida.
    vi.Edmond Lee HENRY, born April 22, 1865; married Mamie E. POWELL, in August 1894; died on April 25, 1934.

---

[58] Henry Family tree for research purposes only, as it may include inaccuracies

vii.Sidney Polk HENRY was born February 18, 1867. He died September 26, 1891. He was buried in Henry Family Cemetery, Buncombe Co., North Carolina.

viii.Kate Cornelia Love HENRY, born on January 22, 1869; married E. J. BOYLES, on October 8, 1910; died on October 14, 1946.

ix.James Thomas HENRY, born on March 24, 1872; married Maggie Annie HAMS, on December 23, 1902; died on June 6, 1947.

x.Arthur Lewis HENRY, born April 5, 1874; married Maggie DAVIS May 23, 1897; married Mantie MILLER, in April 1910; died on August 15, 1919, Asheville, Buncombe Co., NC.

xiWalter Vance HENRY, born February 16, 1877; married Helen Marion ORPIN, November 6, 1912; died on February 18, 1945.

xii.Wade Hampton HENRY, born February 21, 1879; married Fannie HOLBROOK, Sept. 19, 1917; died December 6, 1924.

3. Mary Louise HENRY was born September 3, 1815. She died April 6, 1844. She was buried in Henry Family Cemetery, Buncombe Co., NC. Mary Louise HENRY and Reuben DEAVER were married April 27, 1830 in Asheville, Buncombe Co., North Carolina. Reuben DEAVER was born May 28, 1807 in Haywood Co., NC. He died on May 23, 1852 in Buncombe Co., North Carolina. He was buried in Henry Family Cemetery, Buncombe Co., North Carolina. Mary Louise HENRY and Reuben DEAVER had the following four children:

i.William Harrison "Harrie" DEAVER was born June 9, 1834. Died July 14, 1864. Buried in Henry Family Cemetery, Buncombe Co., North Carolina.

ii.Eugenia Eliza DEAVER was born on November 23, 1836.

iii and iv.Frances Louiza DEAVER was born in 1838, and Pink

4. Robert Marcellus HENRY was born in 1821. He died in 1885 and was buried in Waynesville, Haywood Co., North Carolina.

5. Elizabeth Isabella HENRY was born in 1822. She died in 1915. She was buried in Cedar Hill Baptist Church Cemetery. Elizabeth Isabella HENRY and William B. TIDWELL married and had the following five children. (also married a Moore and then Dr. Charles Candler after William Tidwell's death.)

i.Martha A. TIDWELL.

ii.Mary Belle TIDWELL, born in 1841; died in 1922.

iii three other children William, Robert, and Thomas

6. Martha Ann HENRY was born in 1825. She died in 1896. Martha Ann HENRY and Edgar John ARTHUR married and had the following four children:

i. Edward L., William, John and Belle

7. James Love HENRY was born in 1835. He died of appendicitis in 1884. James Love HENRY and Mary (Mollie) ALEXANDER had the following children:

i Three children who lived were Belle, Mattie and Paul

Obituaries

William Lewis Henry

WM. L. HENRY DIES AT THE AGE OF 77

HE WAS A SON OF ROBERT HENRY, A SOLDIER
OF THE REVOLUTIONARY WAR

Capt. William L. Henry, one of Buncombe's best known citizens, died at his home near Acton yesterday morning. The burial will take place Tuesday afternoon at 4 o'clock at the Sulphur Springs cemetery. Friends of the deceased are invited to attend, especially ex-Confederate soldiers.

Captain Henry was in the 77th year of his age. He was captain of Company B of the Fourteenth N. C. battalion, which was later organized into the Sixty-ninth regiment.

His father, Robert Henry, was a soldier of the Revolution, and was in the battle of King's Mountain.

Captain Henry is survived by a wife and seven sons and two daughters.

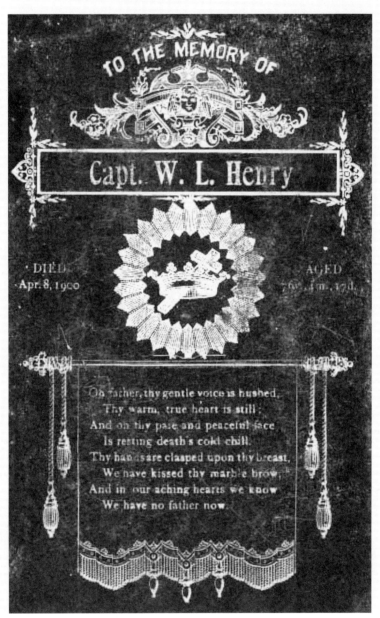

TO THE MEMORY OF

Capt. W. L. Henry

DIED
Apr. 8, 1900

AGED
76y., 1 m., 17 d.

Oh father, thy gentle voice is hushed,
Thy warm, true heart is still;
And oh thy pale and peaceful face
Is resting death's cold chill.
Thy hands are clasped upon thy breast,
We have kissed thy marble brow,
And in our aching hearts we know
We have no father now.

Courtesy Elizabeth Henry Laisy

392

Cornelia Catherine Smith Henry

MRS. C. C. HENRY DIES AT HER ACTON HOME

Mrs. C. C. Henry, eighty-one years old, died at her home at Acton Tuesday morning at 7 o'clock. Although Mrs. Henry had been in failing health for some time, her death was unexpected. Her daughter, Mrs. E. G. Boyles, and her youngest son, Wade Henry, were at her bedside when the end came.

Mrs. Henry is survived by six sons, G. A. Henry, of Miami, Fla.; J. T. Henry, of Senoia, Ga.; E. L. Henry, Arthur Henry, W. V. Henry and Wade Henry, of Asheville; and two daughters, Mrs. M. A. Hyatt, of Aberdeen, Wash., and Mrs. E. J. Boyles, of West Asheville.

Funeral services will be held this afternoon at Acton Methodist church and will be conducted by Rev. A. T. Groce, the pastor. Interment will follow.

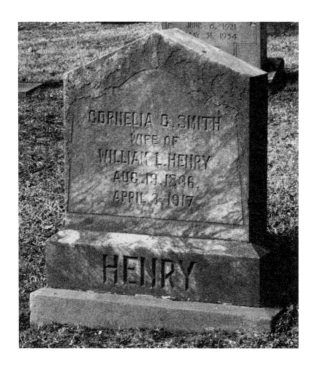

Slave Summary

Slaves Owned by or
Associated with the Henry Family[59]

- Ben - A "simple boy," sold by Reuben Deaver for $300 in 1831.
- Cate - Born approximately 1848. Wife of Charley (son of Tena). Appears on the 1870 Buncombe County census.
- Clois - Probably owned by William Smith, father of Cornelia Henry.
  - Rose - Sent to Cornelia Henry in May 1863 by William Smith. Daughter of Clois, went to Kentucky with Celia in May 1866.
- Cila (Celia) - Bought at a Patton sale for Polly (Henry) Deaver by Reuben Deaver. Sold by Reuben Deaver in 1848 at age 25 to James R Love. Went to Kentucky with Rose in May 1866.
- Dub (Dublin) - "Old man" age 25-30 in 1831. "A lame man but in the prime of life." Owned by Mrs. Henry and given to James L Henry per 1856 will of Dorcas B. Henry. Under the control of Reuben Deaver November 1833 to June 1836. In 1836 went with Mrs. Henry to Haywood for about a year and a half, then found way back to Henry's in Buncombe until 1846. In 1858 a Daublin Thos. Hinry married Dorcas Joice.
- Elaina - Sold by Reuben Deaver in 1848 at age 27 to James R Love, with children Harriet, Mary and an infant
- Elick - Slave belonging to William Smith, father of Cornelia Henry.
- Fannie - married Old Andie March 20, 1860.
- George - Willed to Robert Henry in 1837 from heirs of John Henry. Age 50 per 1870 Buncombe County census. Given to Wm. Henry per 1863 will of Robert Henry.
- Harriet - A Mulatto purchased from Dillard Love in 1832. Sold to Dillard Love in 1835 at age 12, along with James for $400 ($1100 total.) Given back to Robert Henry from Dillard Love when Dillard did not pay.
- Jack - Age 15-20 in 1831, (another account states age 13-14). Had child Catherine with Lin. A "yellow boy," "learnt him to be a carpenter," went to Cherokee with Robert Henry in 1841. Sold in 1843 for $750 by Robert Henry. Under the control of Reuben Deaver November 1833 to spring 1844.
- Jinnie (Jennie) - "Old Jennie" was Tena's sister. Had granddaughter named Harriet. Possibly purchased by Robert M. Henry for $500.

---

[59] This information should only be used as a guide. Care was taken to be as accurate as possible, but errors may exist and some inconsistencies are present due to conflicting records

- Julia - Mother of Lin, age 50 or 60 in 1831. Taken to Cherokee by Robert Henry with her grandchildren Ham and Sarah in 1837. Under the control of Reuben Deaver November 1833 to spring 1844.
  - o Malinda (Lin) - A grown woman in 1831 (age 17), sent to Tidwell in SC in 1836, at Reuben Deaver's 1836 to 1847. Given to Eliza Henry Tidwell on her marriage. Possibly sold in 1852 for $400 by Robert Henry.
    - Sarah - Taken to Cherokee in 1837 with Old Julia by Robert Henry. Given to Mary Taylor per 1863 will of Robert Henry.
    - John -10-11 in 1831. Remained until 1837 then taken to Cherokee by Robert Henry. "Learnt him to be a meat cook." Under the control of Reuben Deaver November 1833 to January 1844. Son of Malinda (wife Mary), willed with wife to Wm. B. Tidwell per 1863 will of Robert Henry.
    - Jane (Tobi) - Given to Martha A. Tidwell per 1863 will of Robert Henry.
    - Catherine - Born of Lin and Jack February 21, 1829. Sold in 1848 for $500 by Robert Henry to John Parks. Had a twin who died. Under the control of Reuben Deaver November 1845 to November 1847.
    - Tusquette - Given to Thomas P. Tidwell per 1863 will of Robert Henry.
    - Eliza - Given to Thomas P. Tidwell per 1863 will of Robert Henry.
    - Sam - Given to Thomas P. Tidwell per 1863 will of Robert Henry.
    - Hamilton (Ham) - Taken to Cherokee in 1837 with Old Julia by Robert Henry. Given to Thomas P. Tidwell per 1863 will of Robert Henry.
    - Child, died of burns.
  - o John - Born February 6, 1823
- Lucinda - Given to James L Henry with child per 1856 will of Dorcas B. Henry.
- Martha - Age 11, given to Eliza Eugenia Deaver, per 1856 will of Dorcas B. Henry.
- Olly (Elly) - Brought by Mrs. Henry 1837, 9 years old in 1831, given to Mrs. Arthur 1847. Given to Martha A. Arthur per 1863 will of Robert Henry.
- Ruth - Given to James L. Henry with Sarah and Amelia per 1856 will of Dorcas B. Henry.
- Sal - Received with her children by Robert Henry in 1814 on his marriage to Dorcas B. Henry as a gift from her father, Robert Love. Robert Henry sold her to Dillard Love in 1820, and sold her sons Jim and Andy to him

in 1827. Dillard Love did not pay, so Dillard gave her, along with Jim, Andy and Hannah (Sal's children), back to Robert Henry around 1831 to 1833 .

- o Jim - 14-15 in 1831, "In digging the mill race was able to throw clay out of the bottom of the race when it was eighteen feet deep with a shovel." James was owned by Mrs. Henry, under the control of Reuben Deaver November 1833 to 1835. Sold with Harriet for $700 (total $1100) in 1835.
- o Andy (Old Andy, Uncle Andy) - Age 12-14 in 1831, "a stouter boy than Jim.." Under the control of Reuben Deaver November 1833 to 1836 then to Haywood County with Mrs. Henry. Willed to Robert Henry 1837 from heirs of John Henry. Under the control of Reuben Deaver 1838 to August 1847. Given to Eliza Eugenia Deaver, per 1856 will of Dorcas B. Henry.
- o Hannah - Age 9-10 in 1831. Understood as the "waiting girl on Mrs. (Dorcas) Henry." Under the control of Reuben Deaver November 1833 to spring 1844 (1836 went with Mrs. Henry by another account). Given to Martha A. Arthur with sons John and Montrabell, per 1856 will of Dorcas B. Henry.
- Sam - (Old Sam, Uncle Sam) - "a stout boy (1832)," Samuel age 51 on 1870 Buncombe County census. Under the control of Reuben Deaver November 1833 to November 1847. Given to Wm. Henry per 1863 will of Robert Henry. Husband of Tena.
- Tena (Aunt Tena) - Wife of Sam. Died March 2, 1868. Purchased from Stacy Webb by Reuben Deaver 9/16/1841. Sold to James R. Love by Reuben Deaver in 1848 at age 43, with children Atheline age 3 and Charley age 1. Given to Wm. L. Henry per 1863 will of Robert Henry. Died 5/2/1868. Had sister Old Jennie.
  - o Betsy - Purchased by Reuben Deaver in 1841, per Bill of Sale Stacy Webb to Reuben Deaver 9/16/1841. Sold to James R. Love at age 11 by Reuben Deaver in 1848. Given to James L. Henry with Wm and Lewis per 1856 will of Dorcas B. Henry. Died June 1864 per journal.
  - o Stacy Lezina - Purchased by Reuben Deaver in 1841, per Bill of Sale Stacy Webb to Reuben Deaver 9/16/1841. Sold to James R. Love age 13 by Reuben Deaver in 1848
  - o Simon - Purchased by Reuben Deaver in 1841, per Bill of Sale Stacy Webb to Reuben Deaver 9/16/1841. Sold to James R. Love age 7 by Reuben Deaver in 1848. A slave named Simon married a woman named Matilda in 1863.
  - o John - Purchased by Reuben Deaver in 1841 (age 9), per Bill of Sale Stacy Webb to Reuben Deaver 9/16/1841.
  - o Alonzo - Born 1854 per 1870 Buncombe County census. Age 16 per 1870 census.
  - o Atheline - Born December 21, 1844. Married Jim on January 4, 1862. Died July 17, 1864 at age 19.

- Baby - died September 9, 1864
  - Caroline - Purchased by Reuben Deaver in 1841, per Bill of Sale Stacy Webb to Reuben Deaver 9/16/1841. Sold to James R. Love age 15 by Reuben Deaver in 1848
  - Charley - Born 1847 per 1870 census. Married Cate per 1870 census. Age 18 in 1865, per journal. Appears on the 1870 Buncombe County census.
  - Elvira - Purchased by Reuben Deaver in 1841. Sold to James R. Love in 1848 at age 17 by Reuben Deaver.
  - Haynes - Born 1854 per 1880 Buncombe County census.

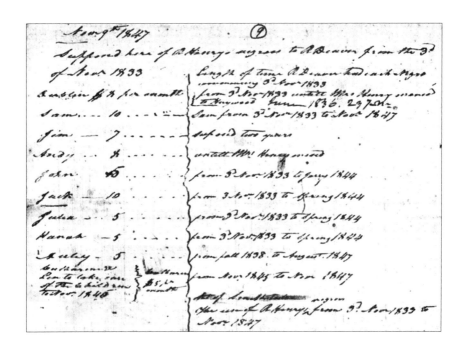

Entry from court case of Reuben Deaver vs. Robert and
Dorcas B. Henry, documenting monthly charges for the use of slaves
(Courtesy North Carolina Division of Archives and History)

Family Photos

Family photos courtesy Elizabeth Henry Laisy

Early photograph of Cornelia Catherine Smith Henry

William Lewis Henry and Cornelia Catherine Smith Henry,
probably on their wedding day, April 5, 1855

The Henry family circa 1911, left to right:
Edmond Lee, Arthur Lewis, Kate Cornelia Love, Walter Vance,
Cornelia, Wade Hampton, Gustavus Adolphus, and James Thomas

Cornelia Catherine Henry

Wade Hampton Henry, Cornelia Catherine Henry
and Robert Pinckney (Pinck) Henry

Top: Robert Pinckney (Pinck) Henry and Tom Clayton
Bottom: William (Will) Smith Henry and Brad Rollins

John and Matt (Sister Matt) Elkins

Top: Margaret Frances Smith (Sister Frank) Hogan
Bottom: Elmira Ann Smith (Sister Ell) Fowler

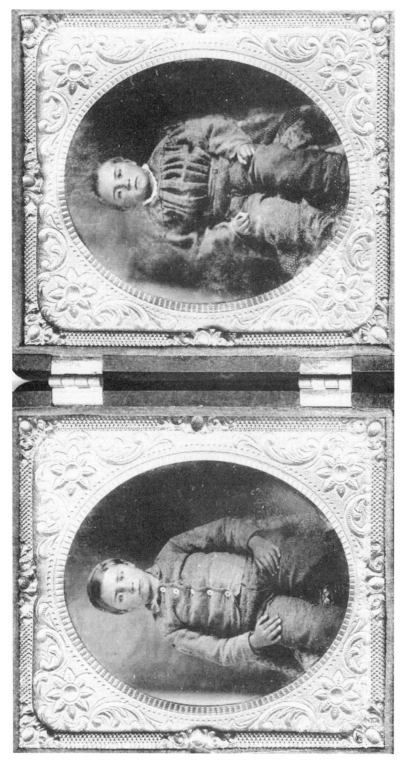

William Smith (Willie) Henry and Gustavus Adolphus (Gus) Henry

Top: Walter Vance and Wade Hampton Henry
Bottom: James Thomas (Jim) Henry, age 26

Top: Arizona Henry (Zona) Hyatt and daughter Sidney
Bottom: Edmond L. Henry and wife Mamie Powell

Top: Pinckney Henry and family:
Pinckney, Patric, Bessie Neel, Minnie, Donna, Minnie Lee (hidden)
Bottom: Possibly Sidney P. Henry, as photo was taken in
Lynchburg, VA, where Sidney was employed.

Valentine's Day envelope addressed to Cornelia C. Smith.
(North Carolina Collection, Pack Memorial Public Library, Asheville, NC)

Front cover of 1854 Valentine to Cornelia C. Smith
(North Carolina Collection, Pack Memorial Public Library, Asheville, NC)

Device I've none, my tenderness to prove,
Without Device, in sober truth, I _love_!
In short, though much I wish I were thine,
I cannot wish to be your Valentine:
To _love_ & be _beloved_ for one short day!
I will be yours forever! — if I may! —

Written by a friend, one who imagines
he was once beloved by you, who still
thinks of you, & of whom he still enter-
tains bright hopes for the future. Of
whom he solicits a few lines before long,
having heard nothing from you since you
left our place.

Asking a thousand pardons for all,
past offences, which I hope will be granted,
I remain yours &c.

St. Valentine. —

P.S. If you know from whom this comes
please write to me soon, & believe me
forever yours
Valentine!

Handwritten Valentine from William L Henry?
(North Carolina Collection, Pack Memorial Public Library, Asheville, NC)

413

Appendix A

Will of Robert Henry
State of North Carolina
Buncombe County

To all whom these presents may come, I the Subscriber Robert Henry, being old but enjoying as good bodily health and soundness of mind as is usual for persons of my extended age to enjoy, but according to the common course of things I must shortly undergo a bodily dissolution. I therefore consider it to be necessary for me to make my last will and testament or final disposal of my property to take effect at my death which is as follows.

To wit, it is to be observed that my wife Dorcas B. Henry in persuance and by virtue of a Decree which she obtained in Haywood Superior Court, divorcing her from the subscriber and giving her a right to hold her property separate and distinct from his and a right to dispose of it by will or otherwise, reference may be made to the records of Haywood Superior Court for further particulars respecting said Dorcas. I therefore do not interfere with her disposal of her property in this my will. But it has some influence on me in the disposal of my property as she made a disposal of her intero property to certain branches of our common family in utter exclusion of others, especially William L. and Eliza, to whom she did not bequeath to them or either of them one cent, and give nothing to either of them previous to making her will, though Eliza attended upon her more for several years of her extreme bad health than any of her children. This has an influence on me in the disposal of my property.

It may be proper for me here to state the reasons why I now make my present will having heretofore made two wills. The first will was stolen or fetched out of my possession before I made the second, and now the second one is also stolen out of my chest, which is the reason for making this will as my circumstances as to property have altered on the situation of my family and circumstances have altered materially since the making of my second will, hence it has become necessary to make my present will.

The following are some of the changes that have taken place in the affairs of my family since the making of my second will. My daughter Eliza made her elopement to the west with Doctor C. N. Candler and remained absent about six months and returned home after her return. The subscriber believing that she had been cured of her vengeance enquired of her if she was satisfied with the provisions made for her in my second will. She replied that she did not want me to will her anything but to divide it among her children, that she would live with them. Since that time she has again eloped with the same Doctor C. N. Candler and I expect she will never return. I need not state the character of Doctor Candler. It is known in Buncombe and Asheville.

In persuance of the request of my daughter and my own will, I bequeath the following Negroes to her family as I consider that they are entitled to them for I

414

offered to my daughter Polly on her marriage to Reuben Deaver a negro woman called Malinda. She refused to take her alleging that she was of no account, that she would take money in her place. I then gave Malinda to my daughter Eliza. The negro woman had the following children, to wit: Catherine, Hamilton, Sarah, Tusquette, Sam, John sometimes called Tobi and Eliza. My daughter Eliza raised these children. William L. Henry sold Catherine to John Park and my daughter Eliza was not benefitted by the sale. I therefore placed Negro John in her room, being nearly of the same age and I sold Malinda and Eliza was not benefitted by that sale. I therefore put negro Mary, John's wife, in her place. In the different marriages of my daughter Eliza I retained the right of these negroes knowing and believing that her different husbands are spendthrifts being part of their faults. After giving the foregoing historical account of these negroes I bequeath them as follows:

Item 1. I will and bequeath to William B. Tidwell negro John & his wife Mary & her increase during the life of the said William B. Tidwell, and that the said Negroes decreed to his heirs. I will no negroes to Robert J. Tidwell as his part will be made up in land.

Item 2. I will and bequeath to my Gran Daughter Mary Taylor negroe Sarah and her children during the life of the said Mary Taylor, then that the said negroes and their increase decreed to her lawful heirs. I also will her one bed and furniture and two cows. I do this because she married a man that I consider a spend thrift, for I do not wish my hand carried property to go to the support of such persons.

Item 3. I will and bequeath to Martha A. Tidwell negroe Jane, sometimes called Tobe and her increase during the life of the said Martha A. and the said negro and her increase, if any to go to the lawful heirs of the said Martha A.

Item 4. I will and bequeath to Thomas P Tidwell negroes Hamilton, Tusquette, Sam and negroe Eliza, with her increase to be his during his life, and at his death the said negros is to go to his lawful heirs.

The reason I have given the historical history of these negros is this. I give to my daughter Martha Arthur upon her marriage a negro woman then considered to be worth much more than the afore mentioned negro Malinda without reserving the title in myself, as I did with my daughter Eliza. Now the woman I give to my daughter Martha has not been as prolific as Malinda and now and putting John in the place of Catharine and his wife in the place of Malinda and their increase to the children of my daughter Eliza it might be thought was too partial in favor of Eliza's children.

I will and bequeath the following tracts of land to the children of my daughter Eliza. To wit, I will and bequeath to William B. Tidwell a tract of land in Macon County of one hundred and five acres on Nantahala at the mouth of Marble Creek in the 12th surveyor district and my undivided half of a tract of land in Cherokee County purchased in the Cherokee Lands in the names of Robert Henry and L. N. Quinn.

I will and bequeath to Robert A. Tidwell a tract of land in the Western District of the State of Tennessee on the waters of the Middle Fork of Forked Deer in Henderson County known by the name of the pond tract.

415

I will and bequeath to Martha A. Tidwell two tracts of land on Tusquette & Compass Creek in the 2nd Surveyors District that I purchased off Benjamin S. Medlock & fifty acres of land on the head of Turkey Creek in the 2nd Surveyors Section during her life & then to her lawful heirs.

I will and bequeath to Thomas P. Tidwell several tracts of land on Tusquette, Turkey Creek & (Sarsilulie?) Branch amounting in the whole to a little over seven hundred acres that I purchased of Peter Mosteller though the conveyance from Mosteller to me is not yet made. Also my share or undivided share, or third part of a tract of land in Macon County on Nantahala known by the name of the Big Grade.

As to Robert M. Henry I bequeath him nothing for the following reasons, to wit: I have had to pay on his account about three thousand dollars - $3000 – and he is a large recipient of his mother's property and his manner of life is well known.

As to James L. Henry he is the largest begatee of his mother's estate. I therefore bequeath him nothing.

I will to my daughter Martha A. Arthur two thousand dollars in the Bonds of the Union & Spartanburg Rail Road Company. I hereby notify and confirm the gift of the negro woman named Elly heretofore given to her by me. I also confirm and notify the gift of a small tract near to the Sulphur Springs in Buncombe County heretofore given to her.

I give and bequeath to the children of my daughter Polly Deaver to wit: To W. H. Deaver, Eugenia Deaver and Louisa Deaver. To W. H. Deaver fifteen hundred dollars out of the note I hold on him for twenty five hundred dollars, & compile and oblige him to pay his two sisters Eugenia and Louisa five hundred dollars each which will be in exchange for his said note of twenty five hundred dollars and I further will and bequeath to my said two grown daughters, To wit Eugenia and Louisa five hundred dollars each in the Buncombe Macon & Spartanburg Rail Road Company.

I will and bequeath to my son Wm. L. Henry the following property; negroes to wit, negro George, Sam and Tena & her family and their increase forever.

Appendix B

Tonight We Are Only Eight[60]

A favored family we have been,
All healthy, robust and strong.
But we've shook hands with grim disease,
Often, through life, as he came along.
We have always said, "we are nine,"
But things have changed of late,
For Providence has frowned on us,
And tonight we are only eight.

We were all at home some days before,
But father and one of the boys.
Still ten were their home comforts to share,
And mingle in our fireside joys.
We knew not that we would be allied,
Ere seven suns should sink
To cross Jordan's chilly stream,
And death's cold waters drink.

A missive came to Sid one night,
(The boy from home away,)
He, smiling opened it, and said, "from home,"
But the smile faded away.
"A terrible scourge is in our land,"
Thus it read I think.
"And our family has not escaped,"
Wrote the oldest brother, Pinck.

---

[60] Sidney P. Henry mourns the death of his brother, William Smith Henry, who died January 19, 1888

"Willie indeed is very low,
Myself and Mother dear
Are at his side most all the time,
And Gus and Eddie are near.
Dear Sidney you need not come,
Perhaps you would be too late.
For in this missive you receive,
We may only number eight."

Our Father we wrote for, in the South
He started, but he could not save,
And as he reached his mountain home,
His boy was in the grave.
Father of his boys was always proud,
For of them thus oft he spoke,
"I've nine boys to battle with the world,"
But tonight there is only eight.

The girls, two, at home there was,
Zona, married, and little Kate.
And boys, nine, for years had been,
But tonight they are only eight.

Truly &c.,
Sidney P. Henry

Alton, SC, Jany 25 1888
W. L. Henry,
My Dear Friend

Condolence of friends do not heal the wounded hearts of parents. But I feel it my duty to express my sympathy to you and your bereaved family in your great loss and to send to you from Spirit-land a message rec'd from your son this morning. I would be doing you an injustice in not giving you a report and let you judge for yourself.

Last night my wife was writing for a lady from Charleston and the spirit refused to sign his name and made a star and a cresent, and said Miss May would know who was writing, and after she found out he seemed delighted and sent long messages.

This morning the same spirit caused writing for my wife to the young lady that had just left and sent a message. Grace then took the pencil and concurred to try and he, the spirit, refused to write for her and my wife asked why he said you would not write last night. She then took the pen and your son wrote his name and sent messages that I will give you when my wife comes in as near as possible.

Dora Hancock was present and asked questions and he told her plainly he would not answer them. Why? "I am now sending messages to my family." I think you saw enough to have been convinced when you was down in your friends giving you through my wife as medium your family tree for 3 or 4 generations when she could not have repeated the names in your own family, and if you asked any questions they were asked mentally and no one knew of them, only you. And they communed with you through my wife as medium and now today your son sends messages to you and your wife that should sooth your torn heart. No one but those that have lost children can sympathize with you. We have lost 3 and we never can be reconciled as there is a void never to be filled. Love knows no bounds.

"Message as rec'd today"

William Henry. Tell my Father I am in Heaven and am "Happy." Tell him I don't want him to grieve after me. Mother you must not grieve for me. I am happier than I was on Earth. Grace asked him do you know who is writing? He answered yes, Miss Grace Elkin. Mother you must believe in this. You must be good and you will see me in Heaven.

Question by my wife "How does Heaven look?" He answered it is beautiful.

Q "Where did you suffer most in your sickness?" In my back and limbs.

Q "Did you suffer much in passing from life?" He said No.

Q "Would you come back to this world if you could?" he said No.

He refused to talk to Dora untill he got through talking to his people. Told her to be a good girl and meet him in heaven.

Maps

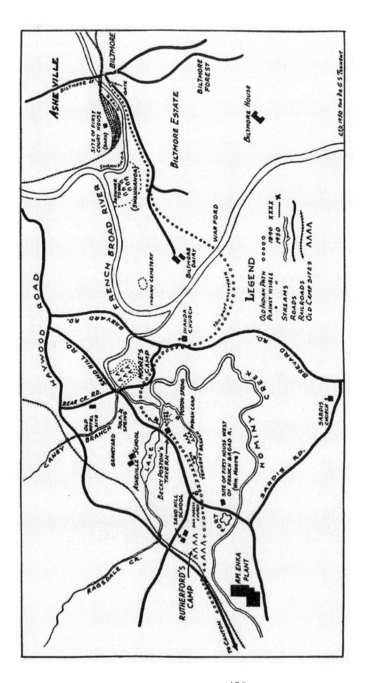

The Indian Path in Buncombe County. Note locations of Sand Hill School, Sulphur Springs, the Graveyard and the Old Hotel Site.
(Courtesy D. H. Ramsey Library, Special Collections, UNCA)

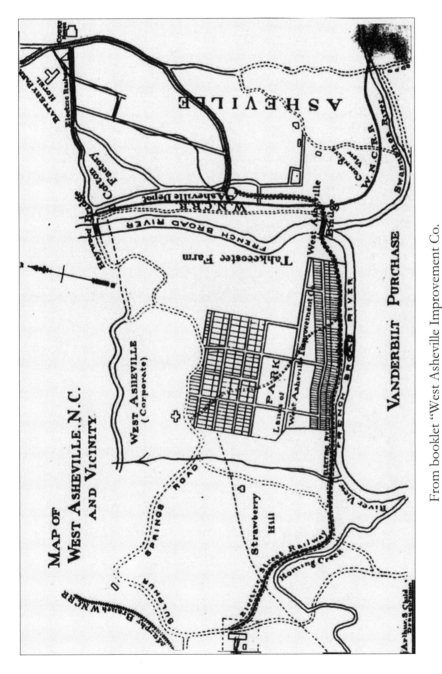

From booklet "West Asheville Improvement Co.
(North Carolina Collection, Pack Memorial Public Library, Asheville, NC)

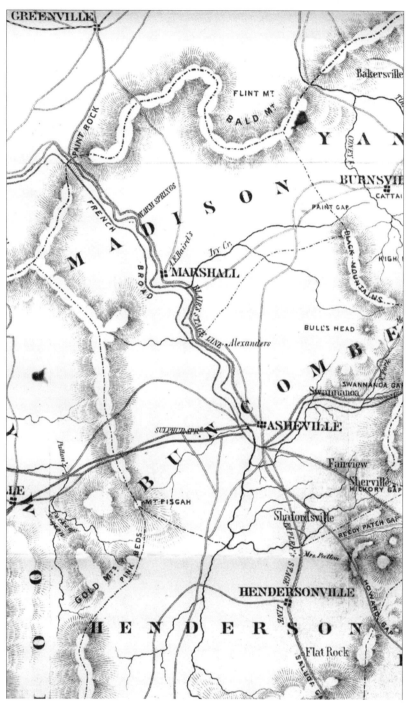

Portion of early western North Carolina map
from "Mountain Scenery," by Henry Colton, 1859
(North Carolina Collection, Pack Memorial Public Library, Asheville, NC)

Sources

- Asheville Times microfilm, Pack Memorial Public Library
- "A Civil War Treasury of Tales, Legends and Folklore," edited by B. A. Botkin
- Bill of Sale, heirs of John Henry to Robert Henry, 11/28/1837
- Bill of Sale, Reuben Deaver to James R. Love, Buncombe County, NC, 3/15/1848
- Bill of Sale, Stacy Webb to Reuben Deaver, Buncombe County, NC, 9/13/1841
- Buncombe County, NC Slave Schedule 1860
- D. H. Ramsey Library, Special Collections, University of North Carolina at Asheville, Asheville, NC
- Dry Ridge Museum, Weaverville, NC
- Early Buncombe Co., N. C. African-American Marriage Records, compiled by Pat Dockery
- "Four Years in Secessia," Junius Henri Browne, 1865, O. D. Case and Company
- Henry Family Collection, Pack Memorial Library, Buncombe County Public Libraries, Asheville, NC
- "History of the McDowells and Connections," John Hugh McDowell, 1918, C. B. Johnston and Co.
- Journals of Cornelia C. Henry, North Carolina Collection, Pack memorial Public Library, Asheville, N. C.
- "Kirk's Raiders: A Notorious Band of Scoundrels and Thieves," Matthew C. Bumgarner, 2001, Tarheel Press
- Laisy, Elizabeth Henry, great-granddaughter of William L. Henry
- "Mountain Myth, Unionism in Western North Carolina" Terrill T. Garren, 2006, The Reprint Company, Spartanburg, SC
- "Mountain Scenery," by Henry E. Colton, 1859, W. P. Pomeroy publisher
- North Carolina Collection Photographic Archives, University of North Carolina, Chapel Hill, NC
- North Carolina Collection, Pack Memorial Library, Buncombe County Public Libraries, Asheville, NC

Sources (continued)

- North Carolina Department of Cultural Resources, Office of Archives and History, Raleigh, NC
- North Carolina Supreme Court Case Reuben Deaver vs. Robert Henry, North Carolina Department of Cultural Resources, Office of Archives and History, Raleigh, NC
- North Carolina Supreme Court Case Robert M. Henry vs. William L. Henry, North Carolina Department of Cultural Resources, Office of Archives and History, Raleigh, NC
- Old Buncombe County Genealogical Society, Asheville, NC
- "Richard Pinckney Allen, Private," manuscript by Jim Holbrook, Asheville, NC
- "Robert Henry and His Clan," Charles Haller, A Lot of Buncombe, Old Buncombe County Genealogical Society, Volume 28, No. 2, May 2007 pp 7-15
- "State Troops and Volunteers, Volume One," Greg Mast, 1995, North Carolina Department of Cultural Resources, Division of Archives and History
- "The Heart of Confederate Appalachia, Western North Carolina in the Civil War," John C. Inscoe and Gordon B. McKinney, 2000, University of North Carolina Press
- "The Heroes of America," J. G. DE Roulhac Hamilton, Publications of the Southern History Association, 1907
- "The Indian Path in Buncombe County," Gail (Gaillard) Tennett, The Stephen Press, Asheville, NC. Special Collections at D. H. Ramsey Library, UNCA, Asheville, NC
- The Western North Carolina Historical Association and Smith-McDowell House Museum, Asheville, NC
- West Asheville Library, Buncombe County Public Libraries, Asheville, NC
- "Western North Carolina, A History (From 1730 to 1913)," John Preston Arthur, 1914, The Overmountain Press, Johnson City, TN
- Will of Dorcas B. Henry, Buncombe County, NC, December 1856
- Will of Robert Henry, Buncombe County, NC, December, 1858
- United States Federal Census, Buncombe County, NC, 1860 and 1870

Index

Burgin, Winslow, 233
Burnsides, 118, 159
Burnsville, North Carolina, 159, 235
bushwhackers, 184, 185, 242, 265, 283
Byrd, 30, 81
Byrd, Mr., 8, 38
Byrd, Mrs., 7
Byrd, Rev., 237, 364

C

Cagle, 147
Cagle, Mr., 137, 139, 142
Cagle, Old Man, 142
Cagle, Old Mr., 135, 138
Cain, Dr., 154
Camp Vance, raid on, 228
Candler, C. N., 414
Candler, Capt. Tom, 208
Candler, Charlie, 94
Candler, Dr., 283, 306, 320, 328, 334, 386
Candler, Dr. Charles, 390
Candler, G. W., 12, 94, 111
Candler, Lou, 6, 31
Candler, R. W., 37
Candler, Tom, 283, 356
Candler, William, 151
Cannon, H., 90, 193
Cannon, Ham, 6, 17, 38, 46, 48, 89, 125, 128, 129, 130, 134, 156, 192, 193, 200, 243, 294, 366
Cannon, J., 103
Cannon, Jim, 133, 349
Cannon, Laura, 383, 385
Cannon, Matt, 294
Cannon, Mr., 196
Cannon, Mrs., 135
Cannon, Nena, 383
Cannon, Watson, 17, 88, 89, 90
Capt. Harris' Cavalry, 168
Carland, Till, 386
Carrier, Edwin, ix
Carrier's Springs, ix
Case, I., 10
Case, Jess, 316, 368
Case, Jim, 35
Case, L., 4, 73
Case, Lac, 240
Case, Old Jim, 137
Case, Sarah J., 10

Case, Stimp, 209, 210
Cataloochee Mountains, 181, 185
Cathey, 38, 75
Cathey, Capt. Jim, 235
Cathey, Col., 329
Cathey, Sallie, 329
Cathey's Mill, 38
Cathy's Store, 119
Causby Creek, 187
Cavalry, 25, 26, 33, 37, 129, 168, 184, 187, 201, 212
Cedar Creek, 173
Cedar Mountain, 333
Celia. See Negroes and/or Slaves
Chandlersville, 140
Chapman, Dr., 41
Chapman, Mr., 14
Charleston, S. C., 8, 9, 49, 68, 85, 130, 131, 136, 150, 152, 155, 156, 159, 260, 384, 419
Charlie. See Negroes and/or Slaves
Charlotte R. R, 267
Chatanooga, TN, 156, 159, 161
Cherokee, N. C., 5, 11, 25, 26, 31, 32, 33, 35, 37, 61, 86, 102, 109, 173, 180, 202, 216, 237, 260, 297, 415
Chester, S. C., 261
chinkapins, 36, 104, 241, 302, 333, 385, 386
chinquapin root, 129
Christmas, 7, 8, 50, 52, 122, 123, 176, 182, 183, 184, 251, 312, 313, 339, 340, 341, 364, 365, 366
Chuns bridge, 99
Cincinnati Commercial, 272
Clark, Mrs., 98
Clay County, 50, 202, 327, 334, 340, 360
Clayton, Mr., 338
Clingman, Col., 34
Clingman, General, 386
Clois. See Negroes and/or Slaves
Cochrum, 354
Cochrum, Lizzie, 372
Cockrum, 258
Coffle, Chris, 66
Cold Mountain, 1
Cole, Edom, 231
Cole, Mrs., 277, 284
Coleman, 180

Ivy, 212, 295, 337

J

Jackson County, 105, 198
Jackson, Mississippi, 150
Jackson, Gen., 139, 140
Jackson, hotel proprietor, 22
Jackson, Mississippi, 151
Jackson, Stonewall, 93, 97, 216
Jacobs, Mr., 306, 308, 309, 310, 311
James Island, 85
Jamison, Betsey, 11, 119, 145, 147, 152, 153, 198, 217, 237, 245, 335, 346, 374
Jamison, Elie, 164
Jamison, Mrs., 14, 108, 111, 113, 116, 117, 118, 119, 122, 125, 126, 127, 128, 129, 130, 131, 132, 133, 150, 154, 156, 159, 192, 193, 195
Jamison, Patsy, 16, 18, 30, 64, 103, 106, 154, 243, 272
Jarrett, Bob, 303, 314, 315
Jarrett, Col., 257, 338
Jarrett, Jessie, 9, 18, 65
Jarrett, Jim, 176
Jarrett, Miss Emeline, 262
Jarrett, Sarah, 48, 238
Jarvis, Capt., 40
Jarvis, Mrs., 40, 41
Jeff Davis Guards, 26
Jengle, Polly, 59
Jenkins, General, 216
Jennie, Old, 327
Jenning, Jane, 24
Jeter, Billie, 235
Jeter, Capt., 235
Jeter's Battery, 238
Jeter's Artillery, 240
Jim. *See* Negroes and/or Slaves
Jimison, Mrs., 17
Jimison, Wilburn, 18
Jinnie (Jennie). *See* Negroes and/or Slaves
Johnathan's Creek, 257
Johnston, 51, 84, 167, 194, 195, 282
Johnston, Andy, 43, 226
Johnston, Bill, 235
Johnston, Capt., 263
Johnston, Foster, 129
Johnston, Hugh, 79, 219

Johnston, Mary, 235, 357
Johnston, Mollie, 235
Johnston, Mrs., 357
Johnston, Rachel, 297
Johnston, Sallie, 354, 357
Johnston, William, 1
Johnston's farm, 196
Johnston's firm, 194
Johnston's Island, 282
Jones boys, 351
Jones Gap, 1
Jones Gap Turnpike Company, 1
Jones, A. B., 17, 26, 32, 42, 52, 66, 73, 76, 84, 92, 98, 112, 132, 147, 156, 172, 215, 218, 219, 224, 231, 235, 242, 260, 279, 281, 282, 288, 304, 305, 312, 323, 334, 337, 340, 341, 346, 350, 352, 358, 363, 378
Jones, Andy, 217, 287, 291, 337
Jones, Anna, 377
Jones, Anon, 226, 227, 229, 230, 232, 234, 235, 236, 254
Jones, Caladonia, 83
Jones, Capt., 233
Jones, Caroline, 248, 337, 382
Jones, Col., 4
Jones, Col. Bill, 35
Jones, Doc, 160
Jones, Dovey, 81
Jones, Ellen, 206, 225, 249
Jones, Fayette, 175, 192, 200, 209, 210, 254, 283
Jones, G. W., 13
Jones, George, 1, 5, 79, 88, 163, 291
Jones, Henry, 225, 248, 291, 316, 323, 341, 348, 350, 354, 358, 378
Jones, Jane, 343, 346, 347, 350
Jones, Josh, 291
Jones, Josiah, 34
Jones, Kate, 337
Jones, Lafayette, 303
Jones, Laura, 230, 271, 272
Jones, Mary, 337, 370, 383
Jones, Millard, 312, 327
Jones, Millie, 201
Jones, Miss Nelly, 96
Jones, Mr., 94, 210, 217, 219, 224, 261, 262, 264, 265, 279, 282, 284, 287, 291, 336, 347, 349, 355, 363, 382, 385

432

Leesburg, 42
Lewis, Miss, 293
Licks Creek, 134, 150
Lincoln, Abraham, 17, 31, 43, 53, 261
Lincolnites, 22
Lindsay, a Scotchman, 7
Linsey, Hosea, 135, 192
Linsey, Mr., 136
Linsey, Old Mr., 31, 216, 220
Locust Knob, 32, 297, 298, 299, 306,
  333, 334, 336, 338
Logan, Dr., 224, 226, 228
Lonergan, W. A., 142
Long, Mr., 265, 296
Long, Mrs., 263, 275, 276, 278, 291,
  293, 296, 298, 299, 346, 353
Longstreet, 182, 190, 191, 194, 196,
  198, 216
Longstreet, Gen., 182
Lopez, Mr., 141
Love Sr., James, 8
Love, Bob, 49, 226
Love, Col. Robert, 389
Love, Dillard, 32, 33, 79, 131, 178, 395,
  396
Love, Dorcas Bell, vii, 389
Love, Harrie, 44
Love, J. R., 55
Love, James R., 395, 397
Love, James Robert, 322, 360
Love, John, 32, 33, 178, 253
Love, R., 376
Love, Robert, vii, 330, 396
Love, Sam, 112, 260
Love's Company, 49
Love's Regiment, 120
Lowry, D., 39
Lowry, David, 38
Lowry, Gen., 39
Lowry, Lurana, 39
Lowry, Old David, 39
Lundy, Old Mr., 164
Lusk, 282
Lusk, Mary J., 32
Lusk, Mrs. J. J., 197
Luther, Bob, 253, 286
Luther, Dave, 356
Luther, Miss, 248
Luther, Peter, 351, 359
Luther, Sol, 299

M

Macon County, 26, 193, 260, 415, 416
Madison County, N. C., 75, 126, 127,
  161, 167, 308, 337
Mahoney's brigade, 216
Malloy, Mr., 358, 359
Manassas, 46, 100, 101, 109
Manassas Junction, 32
Maria, Old, 325
Marietta, Georgia, 228, 229
Marion, S. C., 267
Marshall, 332
Marshall, Miss, 329, 330, 331, 332, 333,
  334, 335, 340
Marshall, Mr., 329, 330, 331, 332
Marshall, N. C., 128, 129, 160, 165,
  168, 177, 205, 208, 209, 212, 320,
  351
Martin, Gen., 357
Martin, General, 198
Martin's cavalry, 198
Maryland, 20
Mason & Slidell, 53, 56
Mathews, Jim, 244
Mathews, Old, 261
McAfee, 298
McAfee, Mrs., 330
McBee, 198
McBee, Mallie, 33
McClelland, 109, 118
McClure, 320
McClure, Ann, 238
McDaniel, Sim, 240
McDowell, Bill, 185
McDowell, Capt., 20
McDowell, Col., 135
McDowell, Mrs., 105
McDowell, W., 85
McDowell, William, 14
McDowell's Battalion, 89
McGrill, Mr., 331
McGruder, 150
McKinnish, Betsy, 44, 45, 47, 50, 52,
  58, 59, 81, 82, 83, 90, 102, 112, 120,
  171, 197, 200, 203, 211, 212, 213,
  215, 220, 231, 234, 280, 286
McKinnish, Bob, 111
McKinnish, Louise, 63, 64, 66, 74, 75,
  92, 97, 211, 218, 220, 249
McKinnish, M., 79

McKinnish, Wiley, 79
McMahan, Mr., 39
McMahan, Old Mr., 38
McParker, 120, 299, 331, 333
McRea, woman named, 224
measles, 38, 39, 42, 43, 44, 235, 247,
    248, 249, 250, 251, 252, 253, 254
Mecklenburg Declaration of
    Independence, vii
Meclenburg Cavalry, 26
Merimac, 70, 80
Merriman's, 133
militia, 74, 126, 127, 128, 129, 146, 147,
    149, 150, 158, 159, 160, 162, 166,
    178, 179, 193, 233, 235, 236, 241,
    327
mill dam, 4, 17, 37, 40, 42, 44, 65, 69,
    72, 78, 82, 107, 116, 260, 309, 354,
    361, 369
Miller, Andy, 294, 313
Miller, Bill, 143, 230, 276
Miller, Mantie, 390
Miller, Mr., 143, 362, 365, 371
Miller, Mrs., 17, 46, 364
Miller, Mrs. Rufe, 312
Miller, Peter, 379
Miller, Rachel, 36, 148, 211
Miller, Rev., 359
Miller, Ruff, 347, 363, 367, 382, 384
Miller, Tom, 325
Miller, W. D., 17
Miller, Wm., 323
Miller's Meeting House, 154, 248, 355,
    357, 358, 365, 377, 379
Mills River, 117, 159, 272, 297, 350
Mississippi, 9, 10
Moffet, Mr., 241
Moody, Mr., 32
Moon, David, 88
Moore, Bettie, 365, 366
Moore, C., 13
Moore, Capt., 30, 57, 83, 86, 132, 142,
    158, 192, 195, 199, 240, 259, 279,
    282, 302, 309, 320, 321, 346, 365,
    366, 374, 379, 381
Moore, Charles, 14
Moore, Col., 6, 30, 31, 86, 293, 328
Moore, Daniel, 74, 195
Moore, Ham, 72, 251, 283
Moore, Jim, 82, 340, 383

Moore, Mary, 30, 39, 41, 62, 64, 106,
    209, 241
Moore, Mr., 90, 137
Moore, Mrs., 156
Moore, Mrs. Bob, 139
Moore, Mrs. Charlie, 98
Moore, Old Mrs. Capt., 48
Moore, Walter, 326
Moore's tan yard, 63
Morgan, General, 239
Morgan, Jesse, 131
Morgan, Mr., 12, 14, 104
Morgan, Silas, 204
Morgan, William, 14
Morgan's Cavalry, 158
Morgan's men, 96, 201
Morganton, N. C., 228, 261, 387
Morris Island, 9, 152, 159
Morris, Arch, 296
Morris, Julia, 7
Morris, Mag, 133, 192, 254, 262, 287,
    326, 350, 353, 354, 355, 362, 364,
    367, 370, 371
Morris, Matilda, 46, 48, 84, 156
Morris, Mr., 295, 302, 308, 335, 336
Morris, Mrs., 128, 308, 345, 347
Morris, T. L., 292, 297, 312, 335
Morris, Thomas, 13
Morris, Tilda, 32, 33, 42, 55, 215, 235
Morris, Till, 69, 85, 92, 121, 122, 128,
    129, 134, 146, 153, 200, 225, 227,
    228, 230, 232, 234, 241, 245, 248,
    252, 254, 262, 271, 299, 385
Morris, Tom, 32, 33, 121, 130, 134,
    200, 219, 270, 282, 305, 310, 334
Morris, young man, 295
Mose, negro man, 222
Mount Pisgah, viii
Mount Yeadon, 44, 145, 373
Mouth of Ivy, 208, 209, 212, 214
mulatto, 1
Mull, 114, 212, 213
Mull, Lee, 283
Mull, Old, 281, 298
Murdock, Dr., 256
Murfreesboro, TN, 125, 126
Murphy, N. C., 180, 181
Murray place, 33, 86, 91, 200, 220, 223,
    227, 228, 230, 234, 236, 274, 275
Murray, Em, 69

Murray, Emaline, 52
Murray, Sam, 130, 131
Murray, Tomas, 9
Murrey lands, 6
Murry place, 34
Murry, R., 7, 280
Murry, Rachel, 7
Muse, 7
Muse boys, 245, 264, 280, 281, 284, 287, 289, 291
Muse, Doc, 361, 380
Muse, George, 369, 370, *387*
Muse, Lin, 290
Muse, Love, 325
Muse, Mary, 351, 364, 372, 375, 376, 379
Muse, Mrs., 299, 363, 364, 368, 375
Muse, Ole Mr., 359
Muse, Rene, 383
Muse, Suse, 378
Muse, Tom, 272, 280, 287, 288, 289, 290, 362, 379

N

Nantahala, 32, 415, 416
Nashville, TN, 68, 70, 118
Neal, Mr., 379, 384, 386
Neal, Nannie, 387
Neal, Tom, 384
Negro John, 383
Negroes: Alston's, 133; as refugees, 158; at Christmas, 52; Atheline, death of, 231; Atheline, marriage of, 55; Betsey, death of, 224; branding of, 338; burial of, 335, 353; Capt. Collins', 158; Capt. Collins', 260; celebration, 355; change in, 293; Christmas Frolic, 122, 123, 251; constitution, 374; corn husking, 45; death of, 351, 353, 383; Dillard Love's, 131; Dub, death of, 351; Elvira, 200; escaping, 264, 272; Fannie, marriage of, 6; fight at mill, 16; freedom of, 278, 307; hanging of, 62, 338; hired, 8, 14, 15, 151, 168; Jim Henry's, 282; Jim, marriage of, 55; Pa's, 344; punishment, 159, 219; Regiment of, 277; stealing, 263, 310, 321, 348; Stephen Jones', 255;

Tena, death of, 375; thrashing of, 47; voting, 362; with measles, 43
Neilson, Billie, 236, 363
Neilson, Charlie, 46, 196
Neilson, Dr., 35, 39, 78, 79, 107, 196
Neilson, Eliza, 101, 192, 237, 242, 243, 265, 293, 311
Neilson, Georgie, 310
Neilson, Mr., 34, 84, 158, 181, 183, 186, 198, 199, 238, 244, 253, 262, 281, 288, 292, 294, 305, 309, 363, 370
Neilson, Mrs., 35
Neilson, W. B., 46
Neilson, Wm., 221
Nelson, Dr., 19
Nelson, Harriet, 81
Nelson, Mr., 33
New Found, 21, 71, 72, 358
New Orleans, 77, 81, 150
New Port, 185
Newbern, N. C., 70, 71
Newport, TN, 46, 177
Nichols, 133, 219, 225, 265
Nichols, Jim, 16, 229, 321
Night. *See* Knight
Night, Bud, 368
Night, Dick, 72, 73
Night, E., 71
Night, E. P., 62, 79, 81, 84, 111
Night, Elijah, 65
Night, Eliza, 351
Night, George, 38
Night, Jim, 33, 42, 47, 72, 120, 126, 127, 132
Night, Kate, 368, 375
Night, Katy, 349, 383
Night, Lige, 38, 238
Night, Mary, 355, 361, 366
Night, Mrs., 50, 51, 99, 126, 375, 377, 378
Night, Old Jim, 62, 118
Night, Old Mr., 364
Night, Old Nancy, 76
Night, Old W., 92
Night, Savannah, 349
Night, Tom, 30, 92
Night, Wiley, 110, 146, 378, 386
Night's shop, 18, 31
Norfolk, 80

Pisgah, 1, 331
Pisgah Guards, 32
Plemmons, David, 39
Plemons, Mrs., 30
Plott, Mrs., 357
Plott, Pingree, 127, 233
Plymouth, 215, 219
Pocataligo, S. C., 108
Polk factory, 382
Polk, Lt. Gen., 228
Portsmouth, 80
Posey, Lt., 211, 215
Potomac, 55, 107, 109
Powell, Capt. J. M., 211
Powell, Mamie E., 389
Powell, Mr., 262, 285
Prather, R. B., 14
Presley, 119, 337
Presley, Charley, 211
Presley, Jennie, 354, 357
Presley, Mag, 378, 380, 381
Presley, Mrs. Peter, 164
Presley, Old Mr., 176
Presley, Old Mrs., 196
Presley, Peter, 355
Presly, Jim, 323
Presly, Mr., 290
Presly, Old, 189
prisoners, 22, 65, 70, 75, 107, 125, 128,
    129, 150, 160, 166, 170, 188, 189,
    190, 256, 261, 264, 269, 270, 282,
    292
Proffit, minister, 6
protection paper, 272, 283

Q

Quackenbo, 374
Queen, 344
Quinn, 1, 33, 34, 36, 37, 42, 43, 58, 76,
    91, 111, 208, 219, 226, 254, 297,
    362, 364, 367, 375, 384
Quinn, L. N., 415
Quinn, Old Mr., 136

R

Radicals, 348, 372, 374
Raleigh, N. C., 21, 23, 242, 259
Raleigh, N. C., 40
Randolph, Capt., 109

Rankin, 165
Rankin & Co, 377
Rankin, Mrs., 113
Rankin's tan yard, 178, 198, 269
Ransom, Gen., 172
Ratliffe's, 91
Ray, Col., 200
Ray, Matt, 151
Red Strings, 356
Reems Creek, 162, 180, 336
Reems Creek Campground, 167
Reeves, Larkin, 243
Renolds, Mr., 22, 23, 30, 33, 40
Renolds, Rev. John, 8
Reves boys, 358
Reynolds, Dr., 39
Reynolds, Mr., 21, 55, 72, 78, 83, 104,
    130, 133, 134, 142, 149, 152, 198,
    203, 223, 224, 229, 235, 238, 240,
    245, 248, 291, 332
Reynolds, Mrs. G., 86
Reynolds, Mrs. W., 171
Reynolds, Old Mr., 17
Reynolds, Revnd., 12
Reynolds, Wm., 335
Rich, J., 17
Rich, Jerry, 275
Rich, Mrs. P., 375
Rich, Peter, 248
Rich, Press, 280
Richmond, VA, 20, 26, 83, 86, 87, 88,
    90, 91, 94, 96, 98, 99, 100, 107, 109,
    156, 208, 215, 216, 217, 219, 223,
    244, 258, 270, 271
Right, Lizzie, 295
Riley, Young, 355
Roanoke Island, 65
Roberts, Capt., 26, 166
Roberts, Capt. Good, 233
Roberts, Joshua, 174
Roberts, Major, 242
Roberts, P., 88
Robertson, Capt., 41
Robertson, Mrs., 40, 41
Rogers, Dr., 381
Rogers, woman, 208
Rogersville, East Ten, 172
Rollins, Ham, 35, 43, 88, 313, 315, 370,
    375, 380, 382
Rollins, John, 324, 337, 339

Rollins, Major, 351
Rollins, Mary, 35, 37, 42, 88, 301, 313,
    320, 324, 328, 346, 352, 361, 364,
    365, 366, 368, 370, 377, 378, 379,
    381, 382
Roy, Lt. Col., 163
Rozencrantz, 161
Rumbeau family, 212
Runbow, 166
Russell, Capt., 179, 180, 226, 250
Russell, J, 15
Russell, Joe, 16, 106, 111, 179, 231,
    256, 323, 331, 333
Rutherford County, North Carolina,
    212
Rutherford, Mr., 146
Rutherford, Mrs., 145, 146, 147, 171

S

salt works, 46, 47, 58, 112, 122
Sam. *See* Negroes and/or Slaves
Sand Hill, 172, 262, 292, 306, 315, 325,
    330, 334, 337, 345, 352, 353, 360,
    361, 362, 371, 382, 384
Sand Hill Academy, 329
Sanderson, 237
Sanderson, Joe, 238
Sandy Bottom, 4, 7, 8, 9, 10, 12, 14, 15,
    30, 78, 180, 313, 320, 345, 346, 348,
    349, 351, 354, 356, 359, 360, 362,
    364, 365, 372, 379, 383, 384
Sardis, 7, 30, 83, 145, 193, 194, 218,
    238, 247, 261, 271, 278, 291, 294,
    297, 322, 355, 360, 361, 382
Saunders, 98, 381
Saunders, Capt., 380
Saunders, Mrs., 380
Savannah, Georgia, 74
Scaife, Charnes, 237
Scaife, Jack, 91
Secession, 9, 11
Serratt, dead man, 78
Sevier, Mr., 278
Sevierville,TN, 190, 191
Sharpsburg, 111
Shelton, 261
Shelton Laurel, ix
Sherman, General, 237, 246, 250, 259,
    260, 261, 264, 265, 267, 311
Sherman's army, 260

Shields, W., 149
Shipman, Jack, 348
Shipman, Lou, 352
Shipman, man named, 132
Shuford, 387
Shuford, Lou, 215, 235
Siler, Capt., 26
Simsville, S. C., 101, 148
Singleton, Mrs., 5
Singleton, widow, 19
Singleton,Old Sack, 17
Skipper, man from Columbia, 102
Skipper, Mr., 103, 104
Slaughter, I. J., 109
Slaves. *See* Negroes; Alonzo, 397;
    Amelia, 396; Andy, 397; Atheline,
    397; Ben, 395; Betsy, 397; Carolina,
    398; Cate, 395; Catherine, 395, 396;
    Charley, 395, 398; Cila (Celia), 395;
    Clois, 395; Dub (Dublin), 395;
    Elaina, 395; Elick, 395; Eliza, 396;
    Elvira, 398; Fannie, *395*; George,
    395; Hamilton (Ham), 396; Hannah,
    397; Harriett, 395; Haynes (Hanes),
    398; Jack, 395; Jane (Tobi), 396; Jim,
    397; Jinnie (Jennie), 395; John, 396,
    397; Joice, Dorcas, 395; Julia, 396;
    Lucinda, 396; Malinda (Lin), 396;
    Martha, 396; Montrabell, 397; Old
    Andie, 395; Olly (Elly), 396; Rose,
    395; Ruth, 396; Sal, 396; Sam, 396,
    397; Simon, 397; Stacy Lezina, 397;
    Tena (Aunt Tena), 397; Tusquette,
    396
Sluder, 166
Sluder, F., 14
Sluder, Mr., 14
small pox, 121
Smith, 212
Smith, circuit preacher, 44, 52
Smith, Dan, 224
Smith, Gen. Kirby, 290
Smith, James, 12
Smith, Jane, marriage of, 19
Smith, Jesse, 86, 220
Smith, Jimmie, 381
Smith, John, 18, 48
Smith, Maggie, 310
Smith, Matt, 116
Smith, Mr., 186, 204, 371

439

Smith, Mrs., 194
Smith, Mrs. Jessie, 191, 235, 240, 310
Smith, Mrs. Winslow, 117
Smith, Old, 57, 63, 118, 177, 178
Smith, Old Tanner, 72, 92, 107
Smith, Tanner, 78, 80
Smith, W., 114
Smith, William, 389, 395
Smith, Winslow, 84, 173
Smith, Winston, 47
Snelson, Bill, 284
Snelson, J., 11, 18, 89
Snelson, John, 17
Snelson, Mrs., 205
Snelson, W., 7
Snider, Mrs., 350, 352, 359, 375
Snider, Mrs. Old, 351
soldiers, 31, 34, 49, 90, 104, 107, 108,
    112, 114, 119, 120, 125, 131, 132,
    139, 140, 146, 155, 159, 160, 170,
    174, 177, 178, 179, 180, 181, 184,
    188, 192, 194, 195, 196, 197, 198,
    201, 202, 203, 205, 212, 223, 224,
    225, 236, 238, 239, 240, 241, 243,
    244, 248, 254, 256, 259, 262, 265,
    266, 269, 271, 272, 278, 282
South Carolina, 5, 8, 9, 10, 19, 25, 32,
    145, 154, 221, 304, 311, 321, 325,
    385
Spartanburg & Union R.R, 261
Spartanburg, S. C., 16, 17, 18, 113, 114,
    116, 130, 303, 309, 310, 311, 322
Spring Creek, 105, 167, 169, 210, 245,
    331, 332, 333, 359
Starnes, 56, 217, 218, 236, 243, 244,
    256, 346
Starnes settlement, 217, 218, 354
Starnes, Burt, 45
Starnes, F. M., 142
Starnes, France, 114
Starnes, Francis, 56
Starnes, Jacob, 346, 379
Starnes, Jake, 217, 265
Starnes, John, 305
Starnes, Mrs., 379
Starnes, Mrs. F. M., 156
Starnes, Tim, 52
stealing, 73, 112, 151, 159, 176, 187,
    198, 202, 215, 217, 218, 220, 307,
    323, 338, 349

Step, Mr., 215, 217
Stephens, 151, 152, 153
Stepp, Mr., 214, 218, 219, 223
Stevens, Mr., 153, 155, 176, 247
Stevens, Mrs., 277, 285
Stevens, S. N., 285, 340
Stockton & Co., 200
Stoneman, 272
Stradley place, 6, 7, 137, 150
Stradley, Mont, 17, 86, 156, 290, 303,
    327, 356
Stradley, Tom, 299, 387
Suffolk, 45
Sulphur Springs, ix, 1, 20, 32, 35, 65,
    101, 134, 138, 185, 200, 203, 221,
    416
Sulphur Springs Academy, 12, 330
Summer, Jess, 358
Summers, George, 2
Summey, Dr., 293
Sumner, Miss, 69
Sumner, Mr., 344
Sutten, man named, 94
Sutten, Olsie, 357
Sutton, Bill, 6, 100, 154
Sutton, Jim, 103
Sutton, Mrs., 359, 365, 366
Sutton, Sue, 2, 43, 49, 63
Swannanoa, 14, 272

T

Taylor, Gen., 150
Taylor, Mary, 5, 47, 48, 49, 50, 52, 71,
    75, 76, 396, 415
Taylor, N., 63, 64, 90
Taylor, Newton, 35, 37, 44, 46, 90, 98,
    178, 297, 332, 358, 360, 386
Taylor, Pinck, 47
Taylor, T., 201
Taylor, Thomas, 32
Taylor, Walter, 47
Teague, 283
Tena. See Negroes and/or Slaves
Tenant, Mrs., 285
Tennessee, 22, 33, 43, 98, 109, 138,
    144, 156, 158, 159, 160, 161, 167,
    178, 180, 183, 187, 188, 190, 191,
    221, 240, 258, 271, 282, 283, 328,
    346, 347, 349, 363, 370, 371, 415
Terry, 4, 7, 11, 14, 15, 16, 17, 18, 344

Also from Reminiscing Books...

My Dear Father and Mother

The Personal Letters of Livingston N. Clinard
Compiled by Karen L. Clinard and Richard Russell

My Dear Father and Mother is a collection of over 250 vintage letters written by the family, friends and business associates of Livingston N. Clinard of Salem, North Carolina. The letters provide eyewitness accounts of living in the post-Civil War era. They also describe early business practices in a small town; entertainment options such as concerts, balls, temperance meetings, and local fairs; and the relationships of a close-knit family.

"... Utterly absorbing in its vivid portrayal of the past ..."

"... I have gotten completely wrapped up in the letters
and the story they reveal ..."

"... one often wonders about the lifestyles of these people; how they conducted their affairs, how they balanced work, family life, and recreation, and how they dealt with various challenges. Clinard's letters contribute greatly to a better understanding of their daily lives in the context of a late-1800s community ..."

"... belongs in the collection of anyone with a curiosity for life ...
during and following the period of reconstruction ..."

To purchase *My Dear Father and Mother* contact:
Reminiscing Books, 1070-1 Tunnel Rd., Suite 10 #326,
Asheville, NC 28805, or e-mail info@reminiscingbooks.com
Also available at your local bookstore, at on-line bookstores,
and from John F. Blair, Publisher, 1406 Plaza Dr.,
Winston-Salem, NC 27103, blairpub.com, 1-800-222-9796

REMINISCING
BOOKS

443

Reminiscing With Pearl Playford

Columns from The Watervliet Record
1959-1966

Compiled by Richard Russell

Pearl Playford settled in Watervliet, Michigan in 1888 at the age of nine, becoming an eyewitness to the growth of this young and prosperous community and the surrounding Paw Paw Lake resort area. In her newspaper columns she told of living in the small village, the pioneering people and the customs of the times.

"I have seen Watervliet grow from a mere hamlet to the city it now is. I can recall the early days when there were no cement sidewalks, no electricity, no city water, no street lights, and but a few houses..."

In the early 1900's Miss Playford embarked on a newspaper career that would continue for over fifty years. When nearly 80 years of age she was asked to write a weekly column for the local newspaper, The Watervliet Record. Thus began "Reminiscing With Pearl Playford."

"When I first began work for The Record conditions were far different from now. The office didn't have a typewriter and all copy was written long hand, and I do not remember that there was a telephone. We went every morning to get a pail of water at the town pump..."

Pearl wrote not only of local history and civic issues, but on a wide variety of topics, including national politics, world history, women's rights, prohibition, holidays, church affairs and even the weather, quoting old records and other sources extensively, especially newspaper and magazine articles she had clipped and saved in scrapbooks over the decades.

"Back in the 'good old days' everything was slow. There were none of the conveniences of the present day, and farmers and housewives worked from daylight to dark, but they had time to be neighborly and were always ready with a helping hand to assist someone in need."

"a treasure trove of local history and down-home observations"
-Karl Bayer, Editor and Publisher of The Tri-City Record

"... a gem, a slice of history that evokes an earlier time and place"
-Dennis Allen, The Historical Society of Michigan

To purchase *Reminiscing With Pearl Playford* for $19.95
visit ReminiscingBooks.com or contact:
Reminiscing Books, 1070-1 Tunnel Rd., Suite 10 #326,
Asheville, NC 28805, or e-mail info@reminiscingbooks.com